LIVING
GRACE

LIVING GRACE

An Outline of United
Methodist Theology

WALTER KLAIBER &
MANFRED MARQUARDT

TRANSLATED AND ADAPTED BY
J. STEVEN O'MALLEY AND ULRIKE R. M. GUTHRIE

Abingdon Press / Nashville

LIVING GRACE:
AN OUTLINE OF UNITED METHODIST THEOLOGY

Original title: *Gelebte Gnade. Grundriß einer Theologie der Evangelisch-methodistischen Kirche.*
Copyright 1993 by Christliches Verlagshaus GmbH Stuttgart
Translation copyright © 2001 by Abingdon Press

This book is printed on recycled, acid-free, elemental-chlorine–free paper.

Library of Congress Cataloging-in-Publication Data

Klaiber, Walter.
  [Gelebte Gnade. English]
  Living grace : an outline of United Methodist Theology / Walter Klaiber & Manfred Marquardt ;
  translated and adapted by J. Steven O'Malley and Ulrike R.M. Guthrie.
    p. cm.
  Includes bibliographical references and index.
  ISBN 0-687-05452-4 (alk. paper)
  1. Methodist Church—Doctrines. 2. United Methodist Church (U.S.)—Doctrines. I.
  Marquardt, Manfred, 1940- II. Title.

  BX8331.3 .K57 2001
  230'.76—dc21

                                                                          2001027919

02 03 04 05 06 07 08 09 10—10 9 8 7 6 5 4 3 2

MANUFACTURED IN THE UNITED STATES OF AMERICA

Contents

Foreword

The United Methodist Church owes itself and those church bodies with which it is engaged in ecumenical discussion a clearer exposition of its theological stance." Statements such as this have increasingly been heard in recent years. Yet this concern is admittedly not heard with any great frequency, since United Methodists are more commonly regarded as specialists in evangelization, church organization, social engagement, or in ecumenical openness than as advocates of a well-defined theology. They have actually contributed to this perception since they frequently assert, "What is distinctive for us is that we have nothing that is distinctive." And the fact that United Methodists are increasing their active participation in ecumenical activities only intensifies the question of whether this is not the time to articulate a theology of The United Methodist Church.

Today United Methodists are frequently at the forefront of facilitating interchurch cooperation in worship and social outreach within many local communities, as well as at the general church level. A clearer exposition of our common understanding of the gospel could provide a foundation upon which the vital "Wesleyan emphasis" could better undergird and direct the Christian witness we are offering in communities across this nation and the world. Our response to this challenge requires our thoughtful attempt to find a solid theological basis for our identity as a church, which will not only accent our distinction as a people of faith but will also assist other faith communities to articulate their profiles of faith. This is certainly not a new or unaccustomed task for a theology that is to be aligned with Methodism, for it has been one of its distinguishing traits since the days of Wesley. It was not originally intended that this *An*

Foreword

Outline of United Methodist Theology would appear over thirty years after
the union of the Methodist Church and the Evangelical United Brethren
Church to form The United Methodist Church. This delay has been the
result of a variety of external circumstances. Nevertheless, the date of its
appearance is not wholly incidental. After a few years in which the united
church was occupied with matters of organization and the charting of a
new beginning, an intensive consideration of its common theological tradition has arisen during the last fifteen to twenty years. This process has
not yet reached its culmination, and the question of its true identity has
repeatedly been raised—sometimes with a skeptical resignation, and
sometimes with a hopeful, forward-oriented undertone. It is our hope that
this *An Outline of United Methodist Theology* will represent an important
step in the direction of a common response to this question on the level of
serious theological reflection.

We are indebted to a recently deceased pastor of The United Methodist
Church in Germany, and to his widow, for providing the initiative for the
undertaking of this project. Their names are to remain anonymous at their
request. They approached Bishop Hermann Sticher in 1982 offering to
institute a prize for the completion of a theology of The United Methodist
Church, since they regarded such a work as a pressing need for our
church. After considerable deliberation, it was determined that the donors
would make available the predetermined sum of money as a subsidy for
the publication of such a work and that the coauthors should be entrusted
with the task of preparing the text. The donors set a period of ten years for
the completion of the manuscript.

In conversation with the donors, Bishop Sticher established a commission for the supervision and review of the project. It consisted of several
pastors and laypersons from the German-language annual conferences.
Since Bishop Sticher retired in 1989, and one of the authors was elected
to be his successor, Bishop Rüdiger Minor of the Central Conference of
the former German Democratic Republic was transferred at the request of
Bishop Sticher to the position of chair of the Review Commission.

In June 1992, the completed manuscript was presented to the commission in a timely manner. It unanimously decided that the work was in harmony with the theology of The United Methodist Church, in accordance
with the requirements specified by the bequest, and they consented to its
publication. The members of the Commission then proposed several revisions for the publication of the work, which the authors could take into
consideration and incorporate into the revised text.

The procedures that were followed in planning this work are also indicative of the character of the book. The subtitle, *An Outline of United Methodist Theology,* has been selected in order to show that this work is concerned with offering more than a presentation of the personal theological convictions of two United Methodist theologians. In accordance with the will of the donors, the Commission was to evaluate the work not only with regard to its quality but also with regard to its capacity to express with consensus the theology of The United Methodist Church. The measure of agreement that was attained is indicated by the fact that the donors' preference was accepted, whereby the original subtitle "A Sketch of the Theology of The United Methodist Church" was replaced by "An Outline of United Methodist Theology."

This work was intended to achieve a twofold purpose. On the one hand, it was to set forth as clearly as possible the biblical basis for United Methodist theology in order to place it in dialogue with the ecumenical heritage of the church. Our intention is to explicate the theological work of the Wesley brothers in a systematic manner, particularly as it is contained within those documents that the church regards as landmarks of our faith. This theological tradition is also to be interpreted in light of the more recent declarations of the General Conference, which assist us in taking theological responsibility in the present day for our Methodist tradition. On the other hand, this work was to represent the effort of a responsible synthesis and reformulation of this tradition for persons in North America as well as continental Europe at the end of the second millennium after Christ. It is an effort to assist theologically reflective persons in and outside The United Methodist Church in formulating and constructing their own theological positions with reference to this "model outline" of a theology of The United Methodist Church.

We have thus already described something of the circle of persons to whom the book is directed. We are conceiving of that audience as broadly as possible. This work seeks to provide information for all those seeking to become theologically informed about the preaching and teaching of The United Methodist Church. Of course, it also seeks to make known to members and friends of the Church the origin and nature of the "form of teaching" that has been transmitted to us (see Romans 6:17). We also intend to provide basic information regarding the distinctive aspects of Methodist doctrine for scholars within the academic domain of theology.

It is our hope that this work will not only enhance ecumenical dialogue but will also give new impulse to the thematic treatment of controversial theological problems. For scholarly reading, endnote citations are provided. Both authors have composed their portions of the text individually, and then they have collaborated to produce a unified text.

When it comes to developing a theology that is representative of United Methodism, there is always more to be concerned about than merely setting in motion an academic conversation. Our greater concern is to articulate the basic Christian experience in a way that is consistent with careful theological reflection. For that reason, the title *Living Grace* has been selected. This conveys the twofold meaning of grace, that it is experienced and personally appropriated and also that it is lived with and for others. We are hopeful that the dynamic of proclaiming grace and the life which flows from grace with which we are entrusted will herein find their expression in a theologically reflective form.

We have much for which to be thankful. The members of the Review Commission have contributed to the improvement of the work with a number of constructive proposals. In particular, Ulrich Jahreiss and Karl Heinz Voigt have helped greatly with their numerous comments. Professor Wilfried Härle of Marburg reviewed the entire work and made a series of helpful suggestions for improvement. A German theological student, Christoph Klaiber, completed a redactional reading of the text and prepared the index. Jonas M. Klaiber read a portion of the proof copy. Barbara Schieker entered nearly all of the manuscript, in its various drafts, into a computer and prepared it for the publisher. Director Walter Siering and his associates at the Christliches Verlagshaus have promoted the production of the work in many respects. They all deserve our heartfelt gratitude.

Since we had to produce this work without a study leave from our regular academic and episcopal duties, this project required that our wives and family members forgo a large part of our family time. They have attended our labors with a great measure of understanding and interest, and thus significantly enabled us to bring our work to completion in a timely fashion. They have our heartfelt thanks.

Although this does not belong to the genre of a foreword, we should certainly not fail to thank God, who has granted us the strength and health for the completion of this work and—we at least hope—who has inspired our reflections through the operation of his Holy Spirit.

Walter Klaiber
Manfred Marquardt

Translator's Preface: This translation is based upon the original German work, entitled *Gelebte Gnade,* and has been adapted for North American United Methodists.

J. Steven O'Malley wishes to thank the authors, for their assistance in editing and proofreading the manuscript, as well as Ulrike Guthrie of Abingdon Press and the members of my Theological German class at Asbury Theological Seminary, especially Timothy Salo, Ronald Matar, Sheryl Alexander, Brian Bernius, John Weston, Martin Epting, and Takahito Iwagami for their assistance in the final editing and proofreading of the manuscript.

Ulrike R. M. Guthrie wishes to thank Abingdon Press for the enjoyable challenge of serving as one of the translators for this work, and her mother, Ingeborg Hellen, a veteran translator, for persisting with German in our home in an inhospitable climate in England even in the 1960s.

1. Responsible Proclamation, or Fundamentals for a Theology of The United Methodist Church

Always be ready to make your defense to anyone who demands from you an accounting for the hope that is in you.
—1 Peter 3:15

W hat can I know? What should I do? For what may I hope?" According to Immanuel Kant, these are the basic questions about human existence and they require philosophical answers.[1] There are still many people in our day who are concerned with these same questions. They scarcely expect to find the answers to them in philosophy. They are searching for that court of opinion which can provide them with adequate answers. Although people today do not always pose their questions in this fashion, Kant's formulation of them undoubtedly indicates three basic dimensions of these existential questions. This becomes more apparent when we understand that the first question, "What can I know?" is not a superficial intellectual inquiry into the possible extent of accessible information. Instead, it is asking, "Of what can I be certain? To what can I really abandon myself? What can I trust? What can I believe?" Kant's critical assessment also reflects these concerns.

It is in this sense that people today are asking these questions concerning the Christian Church and its message. This is usually done covertly, not overtly, with suspicion of some Christians' tendency to put on an air of religiosity with old creedal formulations, but many people are also suspicious when the church temporizes and accommodates itself to faddish trends. Although some questions to the church seem to be superficial and many charges appear to be unqualified, yet: when I engage in deeper conversation with people, they repeatedly ask these basic questions: Upon what can I truly build my life? What ought to be the norm for my behavior? For what am I to hope, both for myself and for this world?

Christian proclamation and theology thereby are placed under a dual responsibility. It is a responsibility to their charge and to the Giver of that charge, and to Jesus Christ, whose word and mission provide the foundation and content of their message. It is important that the church repeatedly ascertains whether its preaching is still identical with its original charge. This is particularly crucial to those persons who do not expect the church to be mechanically repeating what everyone else is saying. Instead, they are expecting that the church will be faithful in offering an uncompromising message.

However, this responsibility is not fulfilled merely by ascertaining that its witness is aligned with and corroborates what is considered to be right belief and orthodoxy. This responsibility entails a willingness to "be ready to make your defense to anyone who demands from you an accounting for the hope that is in you" (1 Peter 3:15). It also assumes a willingness to make clear to every person that this message is the answer to the fundamental questions of their lives.

The "identity" and "relevance" of faith[2] are desired objectives, and the decisive responsibility of Christian theology may well be to provide an undergirding for the preaching of the church as it moves toward this goal.

What is theology, and what is its duty with regard to our convictions within the realm of Christian preaching and church activity?

Perhaps at this point it is helpful if we do not try to offer our own definition or to appeal to a standard work of theology. It would be preferable at this point to refer to a general reference work that speaks of the task of theology, such as Meyer's *Großes Taschenlexikon,* which defines theology as "a systematic, reflective development of religious expressions of faith." In distinction to the science of religion, which "describes all religions as in principal, equally valid articulations of human religiosity, theology proceeds from the truth of its respective tradition: it reflects the phenomenon of religion from a predetermined conviction ('faith')." Christian theology is therefore understood as a "methodical, exact reflection and exposition of faith in God that is founded upon Jesus. Thus, the truth of the Christian substance is expressed in faith (as revealed), and it is also to be accounted for in juxtaposition to the state of knowledge at a given time and in relation to others (apologetics)."[3]

If we accept this description of Christian theology, we are led to the following conclusions:

(a.) Theology is not a science without presuppositions, assuming that anything like that even exists. It does not achieve its scholarly status by taking upon itself alien premises. On the contrary, it clearly sets forth its premises. It proceeds from the fundamental assertions of Christian proclamation and Christian faith and thinks in a methodical, thorough, and reflective manner. For practical reasons, this eventuates in a group of specific disciplines. *Biblical theology* investigates the biblical witness of God's speaking and acting in the history of Israel, in Jesus of Nazareth, and in the early community of faith, and *historical theology* traces the course of the gospel within the history of the church. *Systematic theology* probes the basic expressions of the biblical message and its consequences for faith and action today in conversation with the Christian tradition and with the thought of our time. *Practical theology* reflects ecclesial praxis, in that it examines and develops the methods for preaching, pastoral discourse, and congregational structure, and it confronts theological reflection with the results of an analysis of humanity and society through the disciplines of psychology and sociology.

Yet this division of labor is not intended to put a mere semblance of reality in the place of the fundamental task of theology, which is to attend thoughtfully to preaching and faith and to examine the inner consequences and the agreement of this task with its fundamental principles.

(b.) Theology has a responsibility to "itself and others." The theologian will seek to enlarge this secular expression by the overarching conviction that he or she discharges his or her work in responsibility to God. Yet it is absolutely vital to emphasize the conviction that this responsibility to God also represents a responsibility "to others," especially to those who are distant from the Christian faith.

A central task for theology is to examine and confirm the agreement of contemporary preaching with the basic expressions of the Bible and the church and their original concerns. Theological reflection is always to remain a living expression of the missionary focus of the church. Hence, it proceeds to interpret that focus on the level of reflective thought. The key word *apologetics,* which the dictionary uses with reference to this concern, is based upon the Greek word *apologia* ("defense," or "responsibility") in 1 Peter 3:15*b,* and it portrays this aspect of theological activity as a special discipline of study. In this regard, Emil Brunner has spoken of the "other duty of theology."[4] It was this that provoked his ensuing disagreement with Karl Barth. By so doing Brunner possibly brought his justified concern into a false light, in that he so emphasized the "other" duty of theology that it seemed as if the missionary task might be seen as something secondary or supplemental, and in method quite different from what is treated in theology itself. Instead, the mission task of the church is to be regarded as an indispensable component of the *actual* duty of theology. It is fitting to say that "every theological utterance always needs to be a fresh attempt to formulate in a normative and understandable way the Christian understanding of God and humanity that is anchored in the Bible, in a way that is appropriate for a particular time."[5] A theology that is bound to the Methodist heritage will see this as an especially central task.

(c.) Theology recognizes its responsibility to bring a *critical* perspective upon the church and its preaching. Its purpose is not—as is often insinuated—to offer a critique of the basic principles of the Christian faith. Those principles certainly belong to the presuppositions and to the axioms from which the work of theology is to proceed. However, the examination of church proclamation, in relation to its conformity with the substance of the gospel, requires critical reflection on what is the proper development of its message. The question needs to be asked how those traditions that have been handed down to us, as well as the present praxis of preaching and the forms of church activity, are to be viewed in their relevance and proximity to the gospel. Of course, this also includes the willingness for self-criticism and the openness to allow one's views to be subjected to critical examination from the perspective of the theologian. There can be a vital ferment leading to the development of mutual holiness in the community of faith wherever critical theological thinking is guided by the question of how God's will for persons in our day is to be discerned. Anyone undertaking to write the theology of a particular church must give special attention to this moment of self-criticism!

Thus, theology and preaching belong inextricably together. As in its origin, so also in its purpose, every theological work is finally to be seen as the proclamation in which God himself addresses persons. Yet, theology itself is not proclamation, for whenever it can awaken and foster faith, it can also raise questions and promote uncertainty. It should be seeking much more to facilitate proclamation in sermons and instruction as well as in confession and in Christian action. Preaching, for which theology offers preparation, should serve precisely that purpose—to set aside false "vexations" and to lead to the most unambiguous encounter possible with the gospel. The gospel needs to be protected against misinterpretations and misunderstandings, and theology should contribute to a clear and understandable transmission of the gospel. Theology is not a proclamation of the gospel (although it can on occasion become that), but through its help we take responsibility for preaching, so that the gospel can be given a hearing in our day. It remains a *theologia viatorum*—that is, a theology for the pilgrim, who is directed from beginning to end by the fact that God himself allows what he has commissioned to be brought to fruition.

Thus, theology is to be understood as *one* possible way to respond to God's address. Alongside other responses to God's gift, such as confession and prayer, it is called to offer praise to God and discipleship to Jesus. It intends to serve as guide and thereby to make possible an awareness of the fundamental principles of our existence as Christians and a clarification of the central content of the Christian faith. Christians are thereby made conscious of living as Christians and of becoming alert to answer the inquiries of others.

Within the framework of this description of reality, a theology of The United Methodist Church has a double responsibility:

It shares the basic theological task of every Christian theology in ascertaining that which lies at the basis of our faith as well as determining what is to constitute the preaching and activity of the church.

At the same time, it is obligated to ascertain and set forth how the preaching and praxis of the gospel are accentuated through the doctrinal heritage and order of The United Methodist Church. The points of departure for our presentation are the convictions that are advocated by The United Methodist Church, beginning in Central Europe and extending to the Anglo-American world. These are treated within the framework of the fundamental theological principles that have been formulated by the entire constituency of The United Methodist Church, which also takes into consideration the ongoing theological discussion that is occuring in Methodism and also the background and history of the Methodist movement.

The United Methodist Church is a child of the Great Awakening, which began in eighteenth-century England and was developed most extensively in North America. Among the great evangelists of that age, it was John Wesley who aroused people through his preaching to a decisive encounter with the message of the gospel. In addition, through indefatigable efforts and great organizational skills, he also succeeded in gathering the awakened into societies and thereby prevented the rapid disintegration of the movement. As a consequence, the Methodist Episcopal Church sprang up after 1784. Its work also provoked the rise of other church bodies, such as the Evangelical Association and the United Brethren in Christ, who began laboring among the German population in the Middle States. In 1968 these churches came together to form The United Methodist Church.[6]

Early in their history, these church bodies became extensively involved in overseas mission activity. Special attention should be given to the mission that emerged in continental Europe, since the authors of this study represent that part of United Methodism. The European mission resulted from returning German immigrants who had encountered the message and the new forms of Christian community in England or in America. House meetings were instituted in the German homeland among these persons.[7] The mission work in the German-language areas of Europe, as in America, received significant influence from the heritage of the Protestant Reformation and especially from German Pietism, although that influence had also been operative upon the originators of the movement, Charles and John Wesley.

Whereas American Methodism became increasingly influenced by Protestant liberalism from the beginning of the twentieth century, continental European Methodism has displayed a moderate Reformed and Pietistic imprint. These influences are exemplified in the work of Adolf Schlatter and Karl Heim. Since 1950, the European churches have reflected the influence of the kerygmatic theology of the disciples of Barth and Bultmann, and the historical-critical school of Gerhard von Rad. Since church union in 1968, there has been a marked interest in reappropriating the distinctives of the Wesleyan theological heritage, and this effort continues to the present day.[8]

This brief overview points to the twofold task that lies before us in the preparation of a theology of The United Methodist Church. The theology and preaching of the Methodist movement is deeply grounded in the native soil of the Bible and the apostolic creeds. Wesley had appropriated those norms with his Anglican heritage, and they are most closely joined to the new discovery of the gospel that is implicit in the witness of the Protestant Reformation and its successors. Like other Reformers, John Wesley was convinced that he was not advocating a "new religion." Instead, "Methodism so-called," said Wesley at the laying of the cornerstone for the New Chapel in London in 1777, is "the old religion, the religion of the Bible, the religion of the primitive church, the religion of the Church of England." And this "old religion," Wesley continued, "is no other than love: the love of God and of all mankind."[9]

However, even this description indicates the new emphasis and shows why the Methodist movement led to the first great post-Reformation ecclesial structure.

Hence, if we are to probe the fundamental principles for a theology of

The United Methodist Church, this effort cannot be viewed as anything other than an effort to identify the fundamental principles of all Christian theology. At the same time, we have already indicated that we are defining and shaping this theology through the medium of the history, doctrine, and praxis of The United Methodist Church.

1.1 God's Self-Revelation as an Expression of God's Love

Theology speaks of God and of God's actions toward the world and toward humanity. Anyone wishing to gain an overview of the decisive doctrinal affirmations of The United Methodist Church and its understanding of the gospel could find them summed up in the following confession:

We believe that God loves humanity and the creation entrusted to it, and that God has opened for them the way for salvation, so that they might find and go use it. This salvation is for all humanity. Each and every one should grasp this by faith and become wholly renewed by it, so that God might lead his creation, which is alienated from God and damaged through the sin of humanity, to its full renewal.

But how do we know this gospel, which points toward and opens the way to salvation? For many in our day, it is even questionable whether God exists, or in fact whether we can know anything at all about God. From whence do we know God and perceive anything about God's speaking and actions?

The answers to these questions appear to be near at hand for Christian theologians: from the Bible, of course! Immanuel Kant put it concisely by saying, "Christian theologians demonstrate God's existence by the fact that God has spoken in the Bible."[10]

What, then, do we understand by the term *revelation*?

We speak in everyday language of "revelation" whenever something that was hidden is unveiled. This can take place intentionally: anyone who reveals himself or herself confides in another human being with regard to something that is important, until that which is hidden is disclosed ("an oath of disclosure"). A work of art can also be perceived as a "revelation"—this takes place whenever anyone procures for others a point of access into a reality that formerly had been closed to them. Sometimes that which is hidden is disclosed unintentionally: by means of its concealment or its appearance it is disclosed, and its formerly hidden nature is made known. "To reveal" thereby means to create an openness toward that which is hidden, or to disclose that which is concealed (wholly or partly, directly or indirectly).

The fact that God reveals Godself to humanity is reported in the Bible, in many diverse ways. What is understood by the concept of revelation in present-day theological discourse can in no way be confined to the Hebrew or Greek terminology, rendered as "to reveal" in English.[11] The Old Testament uses a large number of verbs for God's self-disclosure: to make visible, to disclose, to recognize, to give, to speak, and to show. There is no all-encompassing term for these diverse modes of expression. The emphasis is always on the event, which can be presented as a vision, the hearing of a voice, a dream, or an ecstasy. The common meaning is that God steps forth out of God's hiddenness.

Nevertheless, God discloses Godself not only through inward occurrences within persons but also in external events: in thunderstorms and in the rustling of trees (2 Samuel 5:24), and in the gentle blowing (1 Kings 19:12); God can appear as an angel and as a pilgrim (Genesis 16:7; 18:1-2); God can lead God's people in the pillar of cloud and the pillar of fire (Exodus 14:24); God can be perceived as enthroned in the ark of the covenant in the holy of holies (Exodus 25:22) or in the temple (1 Kings 8:12-13; 2 Chronicles 6:41; etc.), from where he encounters people (Isaiah 6).

All of these events are intended to communicate the being and the will of God to the elect nation of Israel and—indirectly—also to the peoples of the earth. Thus, the essential content lies in the Word-event, in the announcement of God's name, commands, call, election, judgment, and forgiveness.

God's self-revelation is encapsulated in the "formula of self-presentation" in the words of introduction to the Ten Commandments. "I am the LORD, your God, who brought you out of the land of Egypt, out of the house of slavery" (Exodus 20:2; Deuteronomy 5:6). God opens up to us his proclamation of the enduring actuality of his saving acts (compare Leviticus 22:31-33).

The prophets above all are the mediators for the ever new self-disclosures of God. Their word communicates an encounter with God for judgment and salvation. They stand under the influence of an unmediated encounter with God ("Now the Word of the LORD came to me," Jeremiah 1:4) and they speak authoritatively in the Name of God ("Thus says the

LORD," Amos 1:3). They receive their message by means of visions or auditory communications, but also by ordinary events, which convey God's communication to them (Jeremiah 1:11ff.; 18 etc.). However, in the unmediated "commands" of God to his people, God discloses that he is precisely God in his essence, in his God-Being, which is revealed in his love that exceeds every human measure (Hosea 11:9!).[12]

Likewise, the New Testament contains no unified concept or doctrine of revelation. Revelation is carried out in story or proclamation as God's self-communication. Jesus sees the operation of God's reign made present in his liberating action with the demoniac (Luke 11:20). His parabolic speech is supposed to open his hearers to the essence of the reign of God, and his entire conduct is "revelation" for those who are "infants"—that is, for those persons who are not able to grasp God's being with their own wisdom (Matthew 11:25; compare 1 Corinthians 1:18–2:16). For Paul, the righteousness of God is revealed in the fact that Jesus died for all, which is revealed in the proclamation of the gospel of Jesus Christ to all who believe (Romans 1:16f. and 3:21-22). Christ himself is the secret of God's universal will to save, which was formerly hidden but is now revealed in the proclamation of the apostle (Colossians 1:25-26, Ephesians 3:3-6, and Romans 16:25-26).

The New Testament also makes reference to the Greek concept of "epiphany," or an "appearance," with reference to the person of Jesus Christ. According to the understanding of the Hellenistic world, this is the central concept of revelation and its technical meaning signifies "the hidden Godhead that is becoming visible, or that is personally appearing or offering information concerning its existence through some kind of symbol of power."[13] The reality of God appears in the person of Jesus under earthly conditions. God's glory becomes visible (compare 2 Corinthians 4:6). However, it also points toward the final appearance of this reality at the end of history. In the New Testament there is a continual awareness that this event is still to come (compare 1 John 3:2). Hence, it is not an accident that the book that looks toward this event in the most focused manner and also unveils its very center as being the unmistakable figure of Jesus Christ, is known by its complete title, "the Revelation of Jesus Christ" (Revelation 1:1). However, according to the earthly witness, which is set forth through a series of visions, the book is known as the "Revelation to John."

Our brief overview indicates that God reveals Godself in quite diverse ways according to the biblical witness. However, one can discern a common denominator that describes what takes place wherever God is revealed in this world. A part, an aspect, or a sign of God's reality in the world becomes recognized by means of an historical occurrence, a human encounter, a parable, or an inward experience. This reality, which is not of itself accessible to us and which we do not perceive as we do the things of this world, is opened to our understanding. Thus, that which is earthbound becomes the bearer of the divine self-revelation. God's self-disclosure takes place through means which basically make possible human access to God. However, these means are only recognized for their character as channels of revelation when they are viewed as signs and manifestations of the reality of God. God's transcendental reality—that is, a reality that exceeds the borders of our transitory world—now becomes available to us as that which is capable of being heard, seen, hoped for, and perceived.[14] God steps out of his hiddenness and meets humanity under the conditions of their power of perception. For the New Testament message, this has occurred in a basic way in the stature and destiny of Jesus of Nazareth.

Thus, God is recognizable only to the extent that God has offered himself to be apprehended. This means that our theology does not concern itself with "God in himself" but with God in his revelation. The question that preoccupies theological inquiry is not "Is there a God?" but rather, "Who is the God who reveals Godself to us?" The living God can never be the object of our investigation, definition, and decision; rather, the true and living God will always be the subject of the encounter that God provides for human beings through his self-revelation.

According to the biblical understanding, revelation is therefore never simply a disclosure of a divine reality that would not otherwise be accessible to us. Rather, it is an event that anticipates a response, an act of communication, that establishes a new relationship between God and humanity. It is the relationship of faith. Revelation awaits a response.[15]

Revelation and *faith* are terms that we are employing here in a twofold sense. On the one hand, they indicate an event or an accomplishment; on the other hand, they indicate the content of that which is communicated, or accepted, in this event. Revelation and faith are thus related to one another in a twofold manner.

They correspond to one another as events, since revelation intends to awaken faith, and faith emerges as true faith only through revelation. They also correspond to one another in their content. Those who believe understand themselves and the world in their state of relationship to God, as this has been disclosed in revelation. The content of faith can therefore only be that which is the content of revelation.

Faith, as the activity of God's revelation, also includes the "yes" to God, the Creator, and thus to our own creatureliness, as well as trust in our Preserver and Father. A new relationship to God is laid open to us through him, into which we willingly enter.[16] This is a reciprocal, personal event between God, the Revealer, and humans, the recipients of that revelation. In faith, we recognize the reality of God as the source and foundation of our lives, and we order our entire existence from the standpoint of this reality. The obedience that recognizes and does God's will is not added to faith as a supplemental task. It is part and parcel of faith, and is that aspect which concerns human actions.[17]

With this initial overview, we have set forth only a part of the basic structure of the biblical understanding of revelation. Important questions remain open with regard to its content. It is clear that the biblical text does not impose a closed system of revelation. Instead, it seeks to provide witness to the dynamic history of revelation. For Christian faith, this revelation points toward God's self-disclosure in Jesus Christ. However, how should the revelation of Christ stand in relation to the history of revelation as a whole? What is the relationship between the acts and discourse of divine revelation to their written deposit in the books of the Bible? And what is to be said about the possibility of God's revelation in creation or in the inward nature of humans independent of the witness to revelation that is found within the Bible?

These questions are to be pursued in the remaining sections of this chapter.

1.1.1 *God's Revelation in Jesus Christ*

Hebrews 1:1-2 summarizes unsurpassingly clearly the meaning of the person and the history of Jesus for the Christian understanding of revelation. "Long ago God spoke to our ancestors in many and various ways by the prophets, but in these last days he has spoken to us by a Son."

God speaks in the Son, and, according to the understanding of this epistle, it is not only the words of Jesus that qualify as the discourse of God. God reveals himself in Jesus' Person, his life and actions, and his death and resurrection. Through his work in its totality, Jesus Christ is "The reflection of God's glory and the exact imprint of God's very being" (verse 3).

In this sense, Jesus Christ is both the center and the totality of the revealing activity of God for the Christian community, and thereby also the measure and the criterion for everything that lays claim to being divine revelation.

The New Testament texts illustrate this principle in a variety of ways.

The Gospels, especially the first three, firmly hold to the distinctiveness of the Man from Nazareth, in that they delineate his earthly life and work, noting both his human limitedness and the transparency of his being and actions in manifesting the reality of the reign of God and of his righteousness.

Thus, the detailed portrayal of his painful and patient suffering on the cross is no less a testimony to God's revelation in him (Mark 15:39) than are the reports of the appearances of the Resurrected Lord, which bestow renewed faith upon his disciples, who had succumbed to fear and resignation.

The New Testament epistles, especially those of Paul, describe the death and resurrection of Jesus as the focal points for the revealing activity of God, who discloses his righteousness and love to a humanity in bondage to the power of sin and death (compare Romans 1:16f., 3:21f., 8:31-39). With a yet stronger emphasis upon the Person of Jesus, it is declared in Colossians 2:9, "In him the whole fullness of deity dwells bodily."

The special concern of the Gospel of John is to expound the ramifications of this declaration. Its prologue, which delineates the way the divine Word comes to humankind, and thereby serves to present something like a concise outline of the history of revelation, is directed toward the statement, "And the Word became flesh and lived among us, and we have seen his glory, the glory as of a Father's only son, full of grace and truth."

The divine reality and the reality of "grace and truth" is experienced in the humanity of Jesus of Nazareth (John 1:14, 17). An Old Testament attribute for God is referenced with these concepts, which characterize God in his kindness, goodness, and grace, and in his abiding faithfulness and truth (compare Exodus 34:6-7). The basic Hebraic expression for this divine quality can only be inadequately rendered in our vernacular. In particular, the Hebraic and Greek equivalents for our word grace describe this personal aspect much more strongly than does the English term, which is oriented to the concept of "pardon" or "the grace that surpasses righteousness."[18] If Moses gave the law that testifies to God's grace and truth, then this divine reality has now become human in form through Jesus Christ (John 1:17).[19] He is the grace and truth of God, God's inexhaustible goodness and faithfulness, that lived among and for us humans! As the One who has loved his own to the end through the laying down of his life, Jesus reveals that God is love (John 13:1; 1 John 4:10, 16). Thus, Jesus can declare concerning himself, "Whoever has seen me has seen the Father" (John 14:9).

To say that the only begotten Son is the only One who knows God and can proclaim him (John 1:18) does not mean that he offers reports on this or that about the Father. Instead, it means that he effects the encounter with God. He does not only attest to the truth (John 18:37) or speak about the way to God. According to John 14:6, Jesus says concerning himself, "I am the way, and the truth, and the life." He summons humankind on his mission, opens to them the truth of God and gives them eternal, that is, true, life. In the encounter with Jesus, God reveals himself to us as the living God.

It is this above all that characterizes revelation: "According to its biblical witness, the manifestation of God is a history which God enters into with humanity, whereby He comes into proximity with them.... Revelation is the opening of fellowship: God comes to humanity. It is not left to its own resources, nor is it permitted to remain alone with itself and the world."[20]

The christological concentration of the content of revelation makes it inescapably clear: revelation is not a product of the human endeavor to perceive. God himself, as the God who turns toward humanity, and thereby the God who is love, is the source and content of his revelation.

The revelation of God "in the Son" is not limited by the witness of the New Testament to the brief tenure of his earthly reality. Through him God has created the world (Hebrews 1:2; 1 Corinthians 8:6); he is the firstborn of all creation (Colossians 1:15-16), and therefore he is himself the Word who has become flesh, the same Word through whom God created all things at the beginning (John 1:1f., Genesis 1:1). Jesus Christ is "the eternal Word made flesh,"[21] and his being with the Father "in the beginning," means that from the very beginning self-revelation was part of the essence of God. We will probe these relationships more extensively in the discussion that follows.

The revelation of God in Jesus Christ has not yet attained its goal: the Christian congregation is also still waiting full of hope for the glorious appearance of our great God and Savior, Jesus Christ (Titus 2:13). However, this One who is coming is none other than he "who gave himself for us" (verse 14). To know him gives certainty to those who hope.

Similarly, in the Revelation to John, what is decisive in view of the future of this world is the realization that "the Lamb that was slaughtered" was found worthy to lead God's cause to its victory (Revelation 5). For the Apocalypse, it is also the case that "revelation," in the last analysis, is not information about the endtime events. Instead, it is a summons to encounter him who says: "Listen! I am standing at the door, knocking; if you hear my voice and open the door, I will come in to you and eat with you, and you with me" (Revelation 3:20).

It once again becomes clear that the christological focus of the biblical understanding of revelation maintains that at its core and essence, God's revelation is not the communication of random facts but the opening of the way of salvation, which God walks with humanity and with the world. In this salvation, "everlasting life is offered to mankind by Christ."[22]

1.1.2 *God's Revelation in the Word*

God wants to find an opportunity to speak—that is the basic conviction which sustains our attempts to speak of God and which is delineated by the biblical witness to the utterances of God. As we have seen, it is repeatedly asserted that God is *speaking* or that his *Word* is going forth, wherever historical events have the character of revelation or where the prophets receive a message through visions. It is completely foreign to Hebraic thought to make a conceptual distinction between the Word that is declared and the thing that it signifies.[23] Without doubt, the position of the Word is so connected to the event of revelation that it is particularly appropriate for us to describe revelation as an encounter. It is not enough for there to be a straightforward historical event or the demonstration of a powerful epiphany. In his revealing actions God addresses humans and he awaits their response.[24]

The revealing Word of God is referred to in the Bible in manifold fashion.

As we have seen above, the saying regarding Jesus Christ as the Word become flesh is central. Not only is the biblical concept of the Word of God that is done, taken up and personalized by this event; through the use of the Greek concept of "logos," the philosophical question concerning the final ground of being and the recognizableness of God is furthermore being addressed.[25]

An additional circle of discourse concerning the "Word" is made known where Paul places the gift of the "message of reconciliation"

(2 Corinthians 5:18ff.), or the empowerment of the word of the cross (1 Corinthians 1:18ff.), alongside the event of God's act of reconciliation in the crucifixion of Jesus Christ. It is inseparably bound to and yet clearly distinct from it. The gospel, the message of reconciliation, is the instrument whereby God's saving activity continues to operate. God's righteousness, which is made efficacious for our salvation, has become manifest once for all in the death of Christ (Romans 3:21-24), and it reveals itself to be new each day in the message of the gospel, leading persons to saving faith (Romans 1:16f.).[26]

God himself addresses humanity in the message of the apostle Paul (2 Corinthians 5:20) and in the Word of those who carry forth this message. From the start, God's revealing activity is thereby open to all future hearers of the Word!

Conversely—that is, looking back on God's words in the Old Testament—it is valid to say, according to 2 Corinthians 1:20, that the "Yes" is spoken to all of God's promises in Jesus Christ. The fact that God has spoken in the last days through his Son certainly does not annul what he "spoke to our ancestors in many and various ways by the prophets" (Hebrews 1:1). On the contrary, God's revelation through the Son confirms and fulfills the validity of those words. No matter how this was implemented in particular exegesis, what the Psalmist declared in principle remains valid for the Christian community, also in view of the words of the Old Testament: "The Word of the LORD is upright, and all his work is done in faithfulness" (Psalm 33:4).

It should certainly be noted that, with the formulation of this declaration for the Old Testament worshiper the "Word of the Lord," was as yet no formally defined entity, standardized by chapter and verse, so to speak. In that time, neither the Hebrew nor the Christian Bible existed in its present form. Its confession of the trustworthiness of the Word of God was founded on its content and referred to the variegated tradition of God's discourse to his people in the community of the old covenant, the affirmation of his faithfulness, and his demand for obedience.

But we also need to be clear that we have the "Word of the Lord" at our disposal—whether in its Old or New Testament form—only in the form of the Bible and through the witness of its texts. We are dependent on this Word whenever we make inquiry into God's word.

Karl Barth has provided a quite helpful formulation regarding this complex phenomenon of the "Word of God" by delineating its "threefold" nature.[27] He distinguished between

31

—the *proclaimed* Word of God, in which God speaks to persons through the preaching and sacrament of the church,

—the *written* Word of God, the Holy Scripture, as the remembrance of the revelation that has occurred, and

—the *revealed* Word of God, the event of revelation itself, that is expressed most fundamentally in the statement "The Word became flesh."

God speaks to us in this threefold structure of his Word, and it is important to comprehend the inner unity and the interdependence of the three forms of the Word of God. We know the revealed Word only through the Scripture, and the written word is opened to us in the actual event of proclamation. Conversely, the proclaimed Word is derived from the Bible, and the written word has its authority from God's revelation, to which it attests.[28]

The declaration that is given in the "Fundamentals of the Doctrine and Theological Task of the United Methodist Church" on the subject of "The Word of God and the Bible," comes quite close to what is contained in Barth's formulation.

> Through the Scripture, the living Christ meets us in the experience of redeeming grace. We are convinced that Jesus Christ is the living Word of God in our midst, whom we trust in life and in death. The biblical authors, illumined by the Holy Spirit, bear witness that in Christ the world is reconciled to God. The Bible bears authentic testimony to God's self-disclosure in the life, death, and resurrection of Jesus Christ, as well as in God's work of creation, in the pilgrimage of Israel, and in the Holy Spirit's ongoing activity in human history. As we open our minds and hearts to the Word of God, through the words of human beings, inspired by the Holy Spirit, faith is born and nourished, our understanding is deepened, and the possibilities for the transformation of the world become apparent to us.[29]

Some illustrative comments need to be added to these basic observations.

(a.) In the final and actual sense, God's Word in his eternal, incarnate Word, which has addressed us in Jesus Christ and in which God has opened himself to us from the depth of his Being, is his unsurpassable love. This Word is the basis and cause for every human witness to God's discourse, from which it proceeds and by which it is empowered.

(b.) We know of God's revealed Word only through the Word that is attested to by the Bible: the word of the Old Testament, whether hidden or manifest, points with bold anticipation, yet also with historical distance, to the revelation of God in Jesus Christ. The words of the New Testament apostles and teachers report to us God's actions in the deeds and destiny of Jesus and proclaim him to be the Christ of God.

Because of the central importance of the Bible as the foundation for Methodist theology, a separate section will be devoted to the questions of its origin and exposition (1.2).

At this point, we will already formulate several basic statements concerning the relationship of revelation and the Bible.

Alongside other Christian communions, we affirm that "the holy Bible, Old and New Testaments, reveals the Word of God so far as it is necessary for our salvation. It is to be received through the Holy Spirit as the true rule and guide for faith and practice."[30]

The following criteria will guide us in identifying what is the proper relationship between God's revelation and the Bible:

(1.) God's revelation is primary to the holy Scripture. The Bible is the witness to enacted revelation.[31] This enacted revelation is reported, attested to, preserved, and transmitted in the Bible—it intends to become revelation anew.

(2.) The character of revelation is to be the revelation of salvation— thus it is not a communication concerning unknown things that could be experienced by means of other channels (geography, history, culture, etc.) but are easier to discover from here. To be sure, the Bible can be used in that way, and this approach has repeatedly been followed. It is also at times apparent that it "is right" on such matters. However, when its character is read as a witness conforming to God's revelation, then the Bible can be regarded as leading us to the knowledge of God and of ourselves, as well as seeking to bring the entire world into obedient relationship with God.

(3.) Revelation and the Bible are not identical, yet neither are they separable from one another. Whoever seeks to express true assertions about God without measuring them against the witness of the holy Scripture runs the risk of succumbing to a deception. Whoever wants to understand the Bible must be open to the expectation of perceiving God's discourse within it.

Being a document of enacted revelation, the Bible bears witness to God's acts, and above all to God's final revelation that is available in Jesus Christ. Thus, both the Bible and revelation must always remain interrelated.

In this mutual relationship they are the source and the basic norm for the theology, doctrine, and preaching of the church. Scripture without the prior provision of revelation is a dead letter (2 Corinthians 3:6). Revelation without the Bible is perhaps a devious self-deception. However, in their juxtaposition they become "canon," or the norm for our theological and pastoral work.

Also, God's self-revelation through the words of the Bible means that these words are intended to be received in faith. First, the words of past ages become the actual and sufficient words for readers and hearers living in the present day. "The Christian witness, even when grounded in Scripture and mediated by tradition, is ineffectual unless understood and appropriated by the individual."[32]

(c.) The Word that is proclaimed by Christian witnesses of our day is also God's Word, through which God himself addresses humanity and produces faith within them. Our witness confronts persons in their most inward being, and by means of weak human speech they are enabled to encounter the saving and life-giving God. The misuse of the Word of God promoted with the homiletical authority of the pulpit in the past has today led to the situation where many proclaimers think too little of its power, and not infrequently they deal with their responsibility for it in a casual manner. The fact that God wants to come to verbal expression through human beings is a high calling, which authorizes and at the same time challenges us to a greater carefulness and faithfulness in the delivery of the message.

The "proclaimed Word of God" thereby occurs not only in the sermon but also in the sacrament and in liturgy, in Christian instruction and in personal witnessing.

The word that we proclaim gains its authority as the Word of God through its grounding in the written word, the witness of the Bible, and through the working of the Holy Spirit. The Spirit makes the message of the biblical witness—fixed in writing and related to the past—the present, awakening, justifying, and life-endowing Word of God for us today.

This relationship of the Word and the Spirit describes an important problem that has been resolved in a variety of ways.

The Reformers, especially Luther in his struggle against the so-called "enthusiasts" ("Schwärmer"), laid great value upon the close connection between the "outer" Word of the sermon and the witness of the Spirit.[33]

In the Methodist movement, stronger attention was given to the work of the Spirit in the heart of human beings, through which the message was actually brought near to its hearers and could be existentially grasped by them. The strong connecting of the operation of the Spirit to the message of the cross was particularly constitutive. That which the Spirit "reveals" is nothing other than the existential certainty that God's love in Christ is personally valid for me, and the operation of his blood suffices to save my life and to constitute it as wholly new.[34]

Methodist theology thereby distinguishes itself very clearly from the viewpoints that are founded on the promise of the Spirit from John 14:16 and that have repeatedly emerged in Christendom since the second century. These maintain that the Holy Spirit has opened for the Christian congregation a new horizon of revelation, which in its content can lead beyond the revelation of Christ.

In John 14:26; 16:13-15, the "christological linking" of the operation of the Spirit is expressed with great clarity, which certainly would represent Jesus' words and work in a new manner, but would not bring forth a new, Christ-transcending message.[35]

This christological connection of the work of the Spirit endures in the praxis of the Christian community, through the connecting of the proclaimed Word to its substantial grounding in the written word of the Bible. Although from 2 Corinthians 3:3-6 the thesis could be deduced that in the "New Covenant" there should be no more "Scripture" but only the "ministry of the Spirit," the early church learned soon that it should hold firmly to the written witness concerning him, in order to maintain its commitment to Christ. It is precisely that "on the written nature of the word hangs His autonomy and independence, and consequently His free power over against the Church."

However, in order that the Bible as critical measure of the Church remains transparent for the actual point of reference of the church—that is, Jesus Christ, as the incarnate Word of God—"sola Scriptura" (the Bible alone) may not be understood in a purely formal way, in which the message of the Bible is diluted into simply providing information about a closed system of revelation and becomes a dead letter. It is more correct to say that "sola scriptura" is to lead to an ever new grounding of contemporary proclamation in the message of Christ, from which it gains its empowerment to address contemporary people in the Name of God. In doing so the preached Word of God attains the highest meaning for the event of revelation: a personal encounter takes place between God and human beings in the present day, and with this activity God's revelation attains its first goal.

1.1.3 *God's Revelation in God's Creation*

The assumption that there was and is a preliminary knowledge of God outside the fullness of the Kingdom and apart from the source of the biblical message has almost always been accepted in the Methodist tradition.[36] In the next three sections we intend to probe the questions concerning the content that this kind of knowledge has and can have, and how it takes place. In the fourth section of this chapter, we want to consider what can or must be acknowledged by this "general" knowledge of God, from the viewpoint of a Christian theology.

(a.) In his *Compendium of Natural Philosophy,* Wesley declares with plainness and simplicity of style that "the world around us is the mighty volume wherein God hath declared himself. . . . The book of nature is written in an universal character, which every man may read in his own language." The perfection and greatness, the power and wisdom of the Creator, his goodness, but also his wrath can be deduced *from nature.* That means "every part of nature directs us to nature's God."[37] The most recent publication in Europe on the doctrine of The United Methodist Church, the book on faith entitled *Underway with Christ,* describes natural philosophy in a way that is quite similar to Wesley's outlook: "As the creation of God, the world bears witness to the Creator."[38] It may be an indication of God's unending and inexhaustible vivacity, his constancy and faithfulness, his glory, goodness and wisdom, but also of his inscrutability. For, in addition to the evidence of God in creation, there "is likewise to be found within nature that which is veiled; beside the similitude of His essence, there is also that which is incomparable, and beside that which is consoling, there is that which is contradictory."

The Bible in many respects bears witness to the fact that humans can discern something of the reality of God from nature, and, indeed, to the fact that they can repeatedly will to displace this knowledge that extends from creation to humanity. The declaration in the twelfth chapter of the book of Job is especially significant and startling: "But ask the animals, and they will teach you; the birds of the air, and they will tell you; ask the plants of the earth, and they will teach you; and the fish of the sea will declare to you. Who among all these does not know that the hand of the LORD has done this? In his hand is the life of every living thing and the breath of every human being" (Job 12:7-10). Many of the psalms invite us to express astonishment for the wonderful order in nature, in praise of its Creator (Psalms 8:4; 29:2-4; 104).

The New Testament gives different, nuanced details in this matter. In Acts 17:22-31, Luke reports a speech of Paul on the Areopagus in Athens, in which it is pointed out how God, through his ordering of creation, has granted to humanity the possibility of discerning him, and by citing a Greek author, it is demonstrated how humans have been brought quite near to this place of discernment. This glimpse of God has certainly been darkened by the idolizing of vividly depicted gods. Yet, its presence is still sufficiently potent that it can be correlated with Paul's proclamation of Christ to the Greeks and thus it can help lead them to the goal.

In Romans 1:19-23 and 1 Corinthians 1:21 Paul expresses himself quite critically on this subject. To be sure, human beings are able and need to recognize the Creator in his creative actions in nature. However, they have despoiled this knowledge of God because they set the creation in the place of the Creator in their veneration of gods that are fashioned in human and animal form. The fact that this knowledge had been possible is the ground for the complaint against humanity, which turned away from God, but for Paul, there was obviously no positive point of contact here for his proclamation of the gospel. Humans certainly inquire about God in view of the wonder of the creation; however, they miss the true God, because they fashion for themselves their own gods.

Since the advent of modern natural science, the question concerning the possibility of knowing God from nature and creation had appeared to be settled. If the Christian natural scientist, such as John Kepler or Isaac Newton, had admired the wisdom and magnitude of the Creator in the harmony of the natural laws, since the beginning of the nineteenth century it also seemed fitting to consider the concept of God as being superfluous as a necessary "working hypothesis" for explaining the origin of the world. Darwin's theory of evolution appeared to be better able to explain the origin of the species than did the belief in a Creator-God.

Strange to say, the question concerning the recognition of God in nature and the need for the concept of God to explain the origin of creation has in recent years been raised with vigor against the background of the theory of evolution and of modern theories of the rise of the universe, as in reference to the so-called big bang theory. Emphasis is once more being given to the question of the recognizableness of God in nature, and the necessity of the concept of God for the explanation of creation. This tendency is also to be found among scientists who have maintained a critical distance from the Christian faith.[39] These investigators have certainly demonstrated clearly that the image of God that results from such considerations is not identical with the God whom the Bible proclaims.[40]

The question of God readily emerges not only with regard to the beauty and magnitude of the creation. The Bible also knows that it is precisely negative experiences in and with nature which cause people to raise questions about God: the transitoriness of human life, as is the case with the life of all creatures, the pains and privations as well as the threats concerning the meaninglessness and uselessness of all toil, cause people to inquire concerning the meaning of these experiences, and of their existence.[41] They proceed from these kinds of questions to the position that there is Someone who is able to provide an answer to that which is beyond human limitations—and not only that, but who can also possibly effect a transformation of the human situation. For these are certainly not scientific questions that arose from curiosity or purely theoretical cognitive efforts. Much more, people are here asking questions in deep existential perplexity, which makes it impossible simply to push aside such considerations and notions.

(b.) There is also this intermingling of astonishment and horror, of wonder and fear, of exaltation and prostration that is implicit in the questions that people ask concerning God and which lead them to seek him. However, there are further areas of experience within the created world which can direct us toward God. Many persons have accepted as true such evidence of a transcendent reality *in the voice of their conscience*, which they are unable to silence. "We feel observed, recognized, and to the core of our being, seen through and judged. But by whom if not an omnipresent and omniscient God, in whose dominion we exist?"[42] Even if the psychoanalytic research of our century has brought us new understanding of the origin and function of our conscience, the ancient perception of the divine in conscience lingers, which implicitly provides us with a scrutinizing court of justice that we finally are unable to avoid. Indeed, the words of our conscience can only be ignored at the price of endangering our existence as human beings.[43]

We certainly are not able to assert that the voice of conscience within us is to be equated with the voice of God. We obviously realize that the conscience is not infallible but is very much prone to error. The question of a binding norm for our behavior is thereby not yet answered. However, what the phenomenon of the conscience makes unavoidably clear is this: our existence as humans as such stands under an unconditional requirement that certainly can take different forms, but which is unchanging in its character. Given the nature of the requirements of conscience, humans have throughout recorded history always joined the question of conscience to an ulterior court of justice to which we must render an account in accordance with our conduct. For Wesley, conscience was a sign that God's prevenient grace was operating within human beings.[44] Paul significantly describes this activity of God in the hearts of human beings in his epistle to the Romans, where he writes, "All who have sinned apart from the law will also perish apart from the law, and all who have sinned under the law will be judged by the law. For it is not the hearers of the law who are righteous in God's sight, but the doers of the law who will be justified. When Gentiles, who do not possess the law, do instinctively what the law requires, these, though not having the law, are a law to themselves. They show that what the law requires is written on their hearts, to which their own conscience also bears witness" (Romans 2:12-15*a*). Even if the heathen—like Jews and Christians—do not involve the will of God in their actions, but rather resist it and put themselves in its place, this changes nothing concerning the truth that they have at least been able to partially recognize the will of God. It is thereby also significant that the reality of God himself makes God noticeable in our world of experience.

(c.) Some brief reference may yet be made to two further fields of experience, without our discussing them in detail. Even *within the field of human history* there has been the repeated attempt to recognize some traces of the activity of God. Here we are not speaking of the history of salvation ("Heilsgeschichte"), which cannot be conceived without God being recognized as its author. Rather, we are speaking in this connection of the general history of humanity and of peoples. Events are perchance accepted in the experience of history as a judgment or as traces of the activity of God. "Do not be deceived; God is not mocked" (Galatians 6:7). This connection, whereby offenses are repaid, whereby injustice does not remain unrecompensed, and whereby that which humans perpetrate upon one another comes back to them, has often been understood as an act of God. It is apropos to say that "God's wheels grind slow, but exceeding fine," wherever an evil deed experiences a delayed recompense.

However, when good deeds or an upright and honorable life lead to the experience of a positive response within a person's biography, and thus a reward, this is interpreted as a blessing of God. As in the previous examples there is an underlying conviction here that history does not simply elapse, with the assistance of the principle of cause and effect and by human deeds. Instead, there is One who "sits in authority," who will finally bring righteousness to pass.[45] Wherever this answer is not recognizable, where evil deeds remain unrecompensed, or wherever diligent, upright persons are having to suffer a difficult fate, many would question the righteousness of God, which appears to be totally absent from their observations.

These contradictory experiences with history, from which it seems one is unable to deduce a unified description of God, brings the matter of the general knowledge of God into the twilight of more important hypotheses. Hence, Theophil Spörri speaks with good reason of the "impenetrable darkness of history."[46]

(d.) Finally, there are also the *far-reaching disruptions* in individual lives or in the lives of other persons that have repeatedly led them to ask about the possibility of an ultimate sustaining Power. Here we are referring to experiences of a nameless, purposeless longing or an existential "angst" that cannot be overcome, which is searching for ultimate fulfillment and security. (There are believers, who see their lives in this perspective when experiences of deep suffering or threatening absurdity happen to them.) In addition, other persons, who had not formerly considered the existence of God, but who have long since refused God or have not come to know him at all, come to such a place in their lives where they are asking beyond this visible reality. Such far-reaching disruptions are probably consistent with the experiences of which we have already spoken. Nevertheless, they describe a new dimension of observation and recognition that can scarcely be ignored. At this point there is not yet a clear recognition of who God is to the extent that God takes form as one to whom a person could turn with complaints, scorn, and bitterness. Only the question of God remains, but not as a question addressed to other persons or to earthly courts of appeal, which are unable to offer anyone help to ascend from the abyss and the personal misery that threatens individual life, but rather as a question seeking God.

1.1.3.2   THE KNOWLEDGE OF GOD IN DIFFERENT RELIGIONS

Scientific research in religion has long sought in vain for a convincing theory for the origin of religions. What has been determined—with tolerable certainty—is this: from the first traces of human life on this earth, there has also been evidence of the presence of religion. It can no longer be ascertained exactly what experiences and observations in particular have led to the veneration of superhuman powers and deities. Perhaps we may be permitted to accept the fact that these questions and experiences were not so very different from those which people in all times have lifted up over the boundaries of their experience of this world. These include their sense of self-elevation in relation to extraordinary experiences of fortune and the attending questions of the origin of those experiences, complaints about suffering and the deficiencies of life, and the emerging question of how to overcome them. An awe in the face of that which appears to be superterrestrial, which appears at the same time fascinating and threatening, has found expression in the various developmental steps in the religious veneration of deities.[47] We may distinguish between dynamic and animistic religions, natural religions and religions of revelation, "primitive" religions and high religions—they all stand here beside one another as a sign indicating that religion is to be viewed as an "original expression of human life."[48]

Even the biblical authors proceed from this basis and uphold the viewpoint that they live with their faith in the one true God in an environment in which other deities are being honored. It is now understood that not only negative influences—including a vigorous rejection of the biblical authors, the prophets and the apostles—have proceeded from those alien religions. A series of biblical texts also indicates significant influences which have been positively received. Basic research has established that the biblical reports of creation in the first two chapters of Genesis bear the influence of motifs that derive from older accounts of creation. The wisdom literature of the Bible assimilates insights from the ancient Egyptians, and in the New Testament there are certainly the so-called "household tablets" (Colossians 3:18–4:1; Ephesians 5:22–6:9). Rules for living from Stoic philosophy were received, and, to be sure, they were in a form that had already been newly imprinted by its use in Judaism. Of course, foreign structures of thought are never simply taken over without being examined. The story of creation itself shows that stories are never connected to the motifs from other religions without modification or contradiction.

For this reason, the prophets of Israel and the proclaimers of the gospel have been able to ridicule in a powerful way the expressions of belief in the gods. Perhaps the sharpest rebuke of this type is heard in the irony from the words that we find in the fortieth and forty-first chapters of the prophet Isaiah. "To whom then will you liken God, or what likeness compare with him? An idol?—A workman casts it, and a goldsmith overlays it with gold, and casts for it silver chains. As a gift one chooses mulberry wood—wood that will not rot—then seeks out a skilled artisan to set up an image that will not topple.... Each one helps the other, saying to one another, 'Take courage!' The artisan encourages the goldsmith, and the one who smooths with the hammer encourages the one who strikes the anvil, saying of the soldering, 'It is good'; and they fasten it with nails so that it cannot be moved" (Isaiah 40:18-20; 41:6-7). In contrast to this trust in such fabricated gods stands the faith of Israel in its God, who speaks to the people: "Do not fear, for I am with you; do not be afraid, for I am your God. I will strengthen you, I will help you, I will uphold you with my victorious right hand" (Isaiah 41:10).[49]

The gods of other peoples are "idols," images of human fashioning and therefore impotent. This polemic is also taken up and developed further in early Judaism and then also in the New Testament. Paul lifts this discussion to a new level when in Romans 1:19-23 he sees the basic sin of the "heathen" in the fact that they undertake to revere the creation instead of the Creator, and thus they seek to deify their own power and beauty.

New questions are certainly being asked in our day. People have learned to listen to the self-analysis of other religions, which in some instances leads into a remarkable depth of religious understanding. Hence, in Islam one encounters a post-biblical, monotheistic religion that in some respects has a stronger hold on the first and second commandments than does Judaism or Christianity. Do not people who adhere to other religions still believe in the same God—even if they present God quite differently in some respects? Biblically expressed, this is the question: Is God only the God of the Jews and the Christians? Is he not also the God of the Moslems, the Hindus, the Sikhs, and all other people, who seek to recognize him in some particular way?

It is undoubtedly valid to assert that God is also a God of the "heathen," that is, the God of all humanity, not only for the adherents of specific religions, but also for the atheists. Hence, this assertion stands apart from the question of whether people are regarded as being religious or not. Thus, this statement should not be hastily cited for the evaluation of non-biblical reverence for God.[50]

However, is all that people do in their religion, whether concerning faith or prayer, totally without meaning for their relationship to the real God?

It is noteworthy that a positive point of contact to the religiosity of the Greeks is made by Paul in his famous words spoken on the Areopagus (Acts 17:22-31). It is made in the context of his critique of the practice of venerating idols. The outward point of contact is the altar that contained the inscription "To the unknown God." For Paul, this inscription points more deeply to an awareness of the true God, to whom all people belong. It is a notion that has remained alive under the polytheistic facade of Greek religion. In this context, Luke has Paul citing a Stoic poet and philosopher, who announces in a hymn to Zeus, "We too are his offspring."[51] The positive acceptance of this citation does not indicate that Paul is identifying the God of the Bible with Zeus. However, he is indicating that there is present a notion of the true and actual God in the distinct form of the meditation on God and his works that exists among the Greeks. This does not lead to a simple confirmation of the religiosity of the Greeks. The critique of their outward forms of expression remains sharp. However great the element of falsehood that is being exhibited in this autocratic type of human religiosity, it is still to be observed that there remains here a decisive reference to the existence of God. And however inadequate the human answer to the question of God may be in many cases, the question as such is a proper and relevant one, and the answer of the gospel is tied to it.

Any comparative study of religions leads one to the effort to discover those marks which they have in common, and that effort certainly results in such signs being found. Perhaps all religions share the common assumption that a transcendent reality has entered into our world, that this encounter brings to persons who are affected by it either blessing or curse, and either awareness or insensibility. Religions also assume that that which is earthly, whether it concerns places or objects (like trees, stones, or cultic objects) or humans, is viewed as a bearer of the divine revelation. In addition, it is assumed that an irreversible relationship persists in which the Godhead represents the deliberating, forgiving, or punishing court of justice, upon which humans are dependent. In all religions, the disclosure of divine reality is not viewed or received as neutral information, but as a living, actual event. The reception of revelation and transformation of life are viewed as being inseparable. The next question to be asked on the basis of this observation and evaluation concerns the validity of this revelation. This matter needs to be addressed in a later discussion.

In any case, the majority of theologians within and without The United Methodist Church are agreed that such a discussion proves to be meaningful, although a few decades ago—at least in Europe—each kind of human religious activity, whenever it was not carried out on the basis of the Christian faith, was viewed as errant and completely sinful. To that end, dialectical theology had entered into an unlikely alliance with the critique of religion of the nineteenth and early twentieth centuries. In the present day, any blanket rejection of non-Christian religions has been superseded by a more candid view of religion as a state of being moved by the unconditional and the absolute (Paul Tillich), or as a way of mediating a sense of personal identity and meaning in a world that has become incomprehensible.[52] Before we attempt to discuss this evaluation more precisely, there is a third way of speaking about the knowledge of God, a way that is not nourished by the well of the Judeo-Christian tradition.

1.1.3.3 THE KNOWLEDGE OF GOD FROM THE STANDPOINT OF THOUGHT

The phenomenon of being affected by a transcendent reality is found not only in the manifold forms of religious veneration, but from antiquity it has also occupied the thinking of human beings. Whether reason, which is not primarily limited to the task of the orientation of the material world, but seeks to comprehend, understand, and order the entire field of authorization and conceptualization, whether this reason is also capable of truly recognizing the reality of God can justly be doubted. However, it is without doubt that reason has posed the question of God and has proceeded along the way from earthly reality to a reality that transcends it, with commanding and decisive steps. Christians can possibly enter more easily upon such a way if they realize that the question concerning the reality of God is not only a question of human thought, but must be attributed to a self-disclosure of God, to some sort of encounter with the reality of his being, without which such a question could not be posed. It is obvious that we cannot question that for which we have no intuition or perception. The reflection of human reason concerning such a reality thus already presupposes its reality.

In the classical antiquity of European philosophy (Plato, Aristotle, and others) and already much earlier in the Asiatic high cultures, there is an increasing conviction of a unified divine reality, despite its appearance in a largely polytheistic religious environment. We have already noted that the apostle Paul is quite aware of such possibilities of knowing God. In Christian theology, at least since the Middle Ages, several ways have been pursued whereby thinking that is derived from observations and the analysis of earthly reality attempts to draw conclusions about a divine reality. These modes of thought, which are generally referred to as proofs for God, were and are understandably considered to be controversial. Not only does the contention over them separate natural scientists from one another, but this debate has also taken place among theologians.[53] In the most significant instance, the Roman Catholic Church expressed itself on this matter in the First Vatican Council (1870), which formulated the following declaration of dogma: "If anyone shall say that the one true God, our Creator and Lord, cannot be certainly known by the natural light of human reason through created things, *anathema sit*."[54]

We already know from Augustine that he was convinced that humanity is so fashioned by God that it seeks for God with inward restlessness until it has found its rest in God.[55] Also, the most significant theologian of the Middle Ages, Thomas Aquinas (1225–1274), proceeds from the conviction that "a more or less undetermined concept of the reality of the God of nature must already be inborn within humanity, because humans, like all creatures, struggle toward fulfillment, although their true fulfillment as human creatures can only be found in the full knowledge of God."[56] Thus, humans can only struggle toward this goal from the beginning because they have such a notion of God, however provisional this notion may be. Thomas Aquinas has described the different ways in which humans can proceed toward a recognition of the reality of God, through pure observation and reflection based upon the sensible experience of the world. These appear in his well-known "Five Ways."[57] They certainly have not all been personally formulated by him, although his description and summation have been the most influential in history. Each of these ways begins in experience and proceeds from there to designate a final cause, which alone can adequately explain the occurrences and circumstances that are observed in this world. Whenever this final cause is found, it is called "God." Thomas reasons from the movement or the change that occurs in everything that is earthly to that which causes this movement, which is, in return, the operation of another movement. Since it is not possible to trace this causal progression backward to the point of an infinite regression, it must be, according to Thomas, that there is an unmoved Mover, who is not moved by any other reality. This first Mover is called God. The second way that Thomas describes proceeds from the standpoint that we find an order in our world of contingent causes, within which no one cause can be the cause of itself. This series of operating causes can certainly not be traced back indefinitely; therefore, it is necessary to posit a first operating cause that, once again, is called God. The third way proceeds from possibility to necessity. Since nothing within the world exists necessarily of itself, it is necessary to conclude that there is Something that exists necessarily, and that is again called God. The fourth demonstration proceeds from the steps that we find in the totality of that which may be said to exist, and thus it concerns the relative priority of one thing over another, until at last we arrive at the final and highest step that, again, is called God. The fifth way proceeds from the purposeful orientation of the totality of nature and concludes that this order could not have come into existence by chance, but only from a purpose. Further, such an order could only have been brought about by an intelligent Being, who has ordered all of nature by his purpose, and thus this One is called God. All of these forms of thought have in common the fact that they attempt to demonstrate the relationships whereby reason, by reflection on the field which it is investigating, is ever pressing toward God as its presupposition and origin. Thomas himself has not understood this way of thinking as a demonstration in the strictest sense; rather, the overall efforts to think of a rational approach to knowing God were conceived more as an outer court for faith.

With a similar inner attitude that finds its outward expression in the form of a prayer, Anselm of Canterbury (1033/34–1109), perhaps the most famous of the Catholic schoolmen, formulated the argument for God's existence that remains to this day the one most discussed in philosophy and theology. It is the so-called ontological argument for God, which clearly he did not intend as a demonstration of the existence of God in the strict sense.[58] Anselm's manner of reasoning can be succinctly described here. God is the Being greater than which none other can be thought. If I possess this idea of God in my mind, then God is understood not only in the imagination, because otherwise there would be something greater than this that could be thought; namely, one that exists in actuality as well as in the understanding. Consequently, God must be that reality who is surpassed by no other being, not only according to what the mind can conceive, but also as actual existent reality. Although this argument for God has been frequently criticized both within Anselm's lifetime and in the later course of the history of thought, his argument nevertheless continues to have several defenders and it has again received positive acceptance in recent times.[59]

In the theology of the Protestant Reformation, the possibility of a general knowledge of God retreated further into the background without being contested. According to Luther's understanding, humanity has received from its Creator an awareness of the existence of God, with regard to his omnipotence and goodness, as well as his commands.[60]

Despite his conviction that the image of God in humanity has been destroyed by sin, John Wesley continued to maintain that persons, as soon as they are able to use their understanding, can recognize something of God.

In his sermon on original sin,[61] Wesley indicated that the meaning of reason for faith and the life of the Christian is to be so highly regarded[62] that we may infer from visible things "the existence of an eternal, powerful being that is not seen" and thereby we may recognize God's existence. However, God is not really known by that means.[63] Although God in his essence, as we know that essence from the biblical revelation, is not also recognized through thought, nevertheless it is to be maintained that the question concerning God, as the source, the ground, and the goal of our existence, was also raised and will and can be openly raised along this path of human reason. The so-called arguments for God's existence indicate "that it is not in the least irrational and unintelligent to believe in one God, from whom and to whom all things exist,"[64] so that true knowledge of God is certainly superrational, although not antirational.

Within the context of American Christianity, the argument for the knowledge of God was significantly reshaped by the theology of Jonathan Edwards (1703–1758), for whom the *sensus divinitatis* was explained in terms of the affective apprehension of God. In his words, "the things of religion (e.g., the knowledge of God through the witness of creation, or through the law and its demands and the gospel and its promises) are true only insofar as they affect us."[65] That is, a genuine awareness of God consists not in a mere cognitive awareness or assent, but in an alteration of one's personal behavior that comes when one's will is induced by the attractiveness (or "excellence") of God—which requires an exercise of judgment—to desire and to choose him as one's "most apparent good." Hence, the "reasons" for belief in God consist not in *a priori* cognitive proof, but rather in an appeal to the ordinary use of reason, as the reason why anyone does the things he/she chooses to do. Further, this means that the terms of theological discourse have been radically relocated to the empirical realm of ordinary human discourse (or "common sense"), which made possible a renewal of Christian apologetics within the increasingly secular milieu of the eighteenth century. It was Edwards's hope that a person's discovery of the moral "excellence" of the "things of God" would result in God—rather than one's private, self-serving interests—becoming the chief motivation for daily living.[66] Edwards's work thereby represented a far-reaching integration of "head" and "heart," of the cognitive and the affective, that also pointed toward a new interest in the uses and role of language in communicating truth.

His disciple, Horace Bushnell (1802–1876), probed further the latter concern in his "Dissertation on Language," in which he argued that "we can never come into a settled consent in the truth, until we better understand the nature, capacities, and incapacities of language, as a vehicle of truth."[67] Truth, which transcends linguistic form, is best understood as paradox, and life is to be viewed as organic; hence, the life of a text is not found in its grammatical structure but in the organic whole of an author's creation.[68] For Bushnell, the Scriptures are viewed not as "a magazine of propositions and dialectic entities," but as "poetic forms of life . . . requiring divine inbreathings and exhalations in us, that we may ascend into their meaning."[69]

This appeal to broaden the terms of theological discussion to account for the possibility of organic thinking was carried further in the pioneer psychological work of William James (1842–1910), who argued that the "vast proofs for the existence of God drawn from the order of nature" are little noted in modern times because "our generation has ceased to believe in the kind of God it argued for"; he argued that, in the sphere of religious thought, "articulate reasons are cogent for us only when our inarticulate feelings of reality have already been impressed in favor of the same conclusion."[70] This American emphasis upon an experiential, organic understanding of religion advances a similar argument that had been raised from a different point of view by John Wesley; namely, in the words of James, "If religion be a function by which either God's cause or man's cause is to be really advanced, then he who lives the life of it, however narrowly, is a better servant than he who merely knows about it, however much."[71]

Yet, these are only preliminary considerations concerning the problem as a whole. The basic question remains. What can we expect from a natural knowledge of God, what can it accomplish, what can it not, and where do these boundaries lie?

1.1.3.4 THE CONTENT OF TRUTH AND ITS MEANING FOR THE NATURAL KNOWLEDGE OF GOD

As an indication of human existence, the question of God is an expression of the ontological connection between the Creator and human beings who are created in God's image.[72] The being of creation refers through itself to the Being of the Creator. In honoring God and in prayer, in piety and in the question of God, this ontological union finds a scarcely comprehensible, many-sided expression. The condition for the possibility of religious existence is the universal presence of God in his creation, which he does not leave in the lurch at any moment.

It is precisely in its often complicated diversity that the world of religions is an expression of the deep question residing in humanity about God, about the object of human life, and about the meaning and basis that underlies human existence. This notion is also found in a nonreligious form, wherever people reflect on the tentativeness of their existence and about the source and order of nature and the cosmos.

What theological consequences are to be drawn from this statement?

(a.) Faith in God, which has its origin in the actions of God and attains its form in the living, actual response of humanity, is indebted to God's self-disclosure. A person knows that even the faintest notion of God, whenever it is more than an empty projection of one's unfulfilled wishes and dreams, would not be possible if it were not God himself who had given himself to humanity in their hearts. Thus, faith will always be ready for the task—not that of deciding between religions that are true and those that are false, but of distinguishing between the real and the unreal. This distinction moves through all religions, including the Christian faith. In their historical form, the Christian churches have also not avoided the influence of sin, which distorts the knowledge of God and impairs the life of the Christian to accomplish the will of God.

Thus, the question of truth cannot be simply dismissed for the benefit of a religious pluralism, so long as there are contradictory and mutually exclusive concepts of the reality of God.[73] Contradictions must also be considered significant in the realm of faith. They are to be excluded because mutually contradictory expressions cannot simultaneously be true in the same way. However, how are we to come to a basic judgment in this matter? This question is not only being raised because there are in general diverse religions and concepts of God, but also because we live in an increasingly multireligious and secular society, in which Christians are needing not only to bear witness to their faith but also to offer data to support that witness.

If our previous reflections are correct, we cannot and should not assume an absolute confrontation between the Christian faith, on the one hand, and other kinds of knowledge of God, on the other. Rather, we need to accept the fact that wherever true knowledge of God exists, it has only come to pass through God's self-manifestation in creation or within humanity itself. The revelation of God is always an event that proceeds from God himself, one that can certainly be received by humanity but which never stands at their disposal. We cannot and do not intend to preclude that God has shown himself in other places and at other times and toward other persons, as we know from the Judeo-Christian tradition; it is not only the above-mentioned reflections which support this view, but also the fact that outside of and independent of Christianity manifestations of God and the world can be found that nonetheless coincide with Christian doctrine.[74]

(b.) Thus, there are parallels in form and content between a philosophical and a religious knowledge of God on the one hand, and our Christian understanding of God on the other, that should not be overlooked. It is precisely those Christians who are living or have lived as a minority in an overwhelmingly Islamic, Hindu, or Buddhist nation who could open the eyes of us Westerners who still have a strong Christian tradition to other religions' moments of truth. Conversely, it is hard to dispute that conceptions of God can be found in Christian churches and groups in some places and times that cannot or can only with difficulty be reconciled with the God who encounters us in the gospel. By whatever norm we measure the other we must measure ourselves.

On the basis of the biblical revelation of God, there can be only one norm: Jesus Christ. All religious expressions, attitudes, and practices that claim truth and value are to be measured against his message of God's saving majesty, into which all persons are unconditionally invited because all without distinction are called to fellowship with God. On the one hand, this norm is clear and plain, but on the other hand, it cannot always be easily applied in practice. It requires a certain capacity to listen closely and differentiate carefully so that cultural, social, confessional, or other peculiarities are not made to appear as being of one piece with the gospel.

This is true for the Christian message, which takes concrete form wherever it is proclaimed—which is to say, it takes that form that makes it understandable and clear to each particular group of recipients. Different groups of persons who hear the gospel do not hear it the same way; rather they hear it in a way suitable to their particular modes of understanding. This "inculturation" of the Christian faith must be taken into consideration wherever we ask about the veracity of various expressions of Christendom or about the delineation of distorted interpretations through doctrine, cultic activity, or praxis.

This task is similar, though incomparably more difficult, with regard to assertions that are made about God from outside of the Christian tradition. To begin with we will be able to exclude all assertions that have nothing to do with our relationship to God. Judgments concerning the world as such, its history, its legitimacy, or similar matters, may be true or false— we do not make judgments concerning them with the gospel as our standard. The line will be drawn at the point where the content of religious assertions is incompatible with the self-revelation of God in Jesus Christ, in short, where God is not being presented, believed, and honored as the One whom we have come to know through proclamation of the life, suffering, death, and resurrection of Jesus Christ.

As we have seen, that does not mean that outside of Christianity there are no true assertions concerning God and no proper honoring of God. It likewise also does not mean that we can only make true assertions about the reality of God as Christians, or that we are to render judgments about the eternal destiny of other human beings. However, it does mean that we cannot deem true and valid that which contradicts the truth that is revealed in Jesus Christ. Hence, mission and dialogue are not only not to be excluded; they are also urgently needed. Mission brings human beings into the encounter with the saving gospel, and dialogue helps structure the common life of humanity with distinctive religious convictions upon this earth that is entrusted to us by God.[75]

(c.) Yet there is still another aspect of the problem to be considered. The actual working out of religion is always being endangered and formed by sin. Within the being of humanity radical evil is at work, perverting its knowledge of God into pride, greed, and unbelief. The Bible depicts this from the beginning (Genesis 3ff.), and it is confirmed by the experience of the history of the church and of religions. "Natural religions" and unchristian religions are not excluded per se from the knowledge of God and of the good, but they often go astray in their thought and practice and they misuse what is given them.

To recognize this fact is also a warning to be aware of the danger that as Christians we can also err and run the risk of confusing the claims and reality of the Christian faith. In Romans 1:18-32, Paul submitted the heathen religiosity and morals of his age to a sharp critique. However, in Romans 2, he turns immediately and harshly to the representatives of "biblical religion," warning them about passing judgment upon others using a different standard than the one by which they are living. From that vantage point, he warns them about their effort to assume a position of superiority just because they are cognizant of God and God's will. The fact that Paul is chiefly addressing the Jews does not permit us to disregard the fact that his warning has validity with reference to Christianity. It can all too easily elevate itself to a triumphalistic pretense of absolute certainty instead of being aware of the fact that we all live by God's grace and owe everything to it.[76]

For Wesley, the assertions in Romans 2:14f. were a clear warning against claiming for oneself a final judgment regarding the acceptance of adherents of other religions by God. It was equally plain to Wesley that our mandate is and remains to proclaim God in Christ as Lord and Savior.[77]

In order that the errors which arise from the limitations of our knowledge, and the sin which leads us astray into arrogance and misuse of the possibilities granted us, do not destroy our faith nor hinder our obedience to Jesus in the concrete achievements of life, we need the fellowship of believers, through which we can help one another remain in Christ. However, to fulfill this task, this fellowship also needs the clarity and power of the Holy Spirit, who leads us into truth. This kind of fellowship, in which the Spirit of Jesus Christ rules, is not characterized by anxious self-defense and nervous dismissal of unfamiliar beliefs. Rather, this fellowship is characterized by inner freedom and composure, care for others, and an openness to their concerns and attitudes. Every *yes* and every *no* that we may speak in this situation signifies not a rejection of persons but rather a rejection of those attitudes, judgments, and behaviors that are not in conformity with the gospel. At the same time, the actions of the community of faith are also to be directed toward inviting others to faith in Christ and to acceptance of the salvation that is granted in him. Religious fanaticism is not commensurate with genuine Christian faith.

In addition, even if God reveals himself to us, the mystery of his reality remains a mystery that we are unable to fathom. The mystery of the reality of God is not a riddle that can be solved and then is resolved for all time. Whenever God discloses himself to us and allows us to recognize his being, the incomprehensible does not thereby become more comprehensible—namely that the Eternal One loves us and accepts us into his fellowship. It is only in this encounter with God, in which faith arises as an unreserved abandonment to God, that the uncertainty about the knowledge of God disappears from one's experience of the world, that the twilight of that notion of God which is perhaps disclosed by the course of history is overcome through the light of the gospel, and that, finally, the groping search for meaning receives a clear sense of direction. Whatever people know about God, the saving and redeeming fellowship with God can only be received from God and only through trust in God. This is what the Word of God declares, as we hear it in Christ.

(d.) Finally, let us also raise the question as to what extent religious and ideological concepts that were derived from extrabiblical sources can serve as a point of contact with the Christian proclamation. A controversy raged over this problem during the 1930s, whose fierceness can only be understood against the background of the ideological threat to Christian faith that prevailed at that time in history.[78] In the context of missions, the search for such a point of contact has always been a factor in the effort to reach persons to whom the Christian message might be introduced. That search was as true in the apostolic era, during the initial spread of Christianity, as it is in the present day, with the translation of the Bible into different languages and thereby into the cultural world of people. It is also evident in the philosophical and theological discussion with the modes of thinking and worldviews of various historical eras. If persons are to be reached with the proclamation of the gospel, it must happen not in our own, familiar language, but its advocates must speak in their vernacular of the hearers in order for the gospel message to become intelligible to them. Further, no spoken language can be separated from the ideological world in which those persons are at home.

Yet it seems to us that it is not so much a matter of propounding specific conceptions of God and of the relationship of humanity and the world to God for the principle purpose of critiquing and then correcting them. Rather, it is more important to ask what expectations and hopes, what experiences and longings can be recognized in such conceptions, so that an answer can then be sought in the gospel. Christians are not to be the religious schoolmasters of humanity, but rather messengers of Christ, who are to point people to the way toward a new life, the way to Christ, in which they themselves have already found eternal life.

(e.) An initial partial answer to our underlying question concerning the meaning of a natural theology has undoubtedly been provided by our observations to this point. Even if we cannot concur on all matters that move persons who are outside of or apart from the biblical tradition regarding God, these considerations are still to be taken seriously and ought not to be disregarded in toto and without close examination.

However, this still does not leave us with a judgment about a "natural theology" as a freestanding part of a Christian doctrine of faith, in which there is posited an "original revelation" which is independent of the biblical revelation and is accessible to all persons and which can serve as the basis and presupposition for the proclamation of the message of salvation and grace. "Grace does not supersede nature; it perfects it," asserts Thomas Aquinas concerning the meaning of "natural theology" for Roman Catholic dogmatics. This position has remained authoritative to the present day.[79]

As biblical theologians, Luther and Calvin have clearly excluded any such possibility of a general concept of revelation, whereas post-Reformation theology since Melanchthon has cautiously endorsed it. The early Karl Barth fought emphatically against natural theology while the reflections of theologians such as Paul Althaus or Emil Brunner sought to introduce the possibility of a point of contact in the general human awareness of God.[80]

This tension is also reflected in the remarks of John Wesley.[81] As we have seen, he speaks about how we may draw conclusions through reason about God's existence, but he insists that we do not thereby really recognize who God is.[82] He assumes that even heathens know of God's existence and being, and can recognize the difference between good and evil, yet at another place he emphasizes how minusculely paltry a knowledge of God is. He establishes that reason alone cannot prove God's existence and that true religion can be based only on biblical assertions,[83] and, in connection with Ephesians 2:12, he quite pointedly formulates his position: "We are all nature 'atheists in the world.' "[84]

The Methodist systematic theologians of the nineteenth century remain true to Wesley's point of view. They did not fully reject the possibility of knowledge of God by study of the world's religions and observation of nature or philosophical reflection. Human beings have never entirely lost the hunch that they are created in the image of God. However, these theologians emphatically refer to the inadequacy and corruption of this knowledge, which makes it impossible to derive Christian faith directly from it.[85]

Our exegetical results and our observations concerning the various aspects of this problem force us to assent to this judgment. At the same time, the question underlying so-called "natural theology" is to be taken seriously. God's action may not be restricted to the area that we would identify as the domain of biblical preaching. God's presence in this world is valid for all human beings, and we will continue to discover evidence which makes this plain.[86]

However, no Christian theology can be constructed upon natural theology, and no part of theology—least of all its foundation—can be permitted to be misdirected by a revelation that is defined as general. As preachers and theologians we continue to rely on the witness of God's self-disclosure in the holy Bible.[87]

1.1.4 *The Triune God and the Missionary Dimension of Revelation*

According to the biblical witness, the essence of God is plainly self-revelation. We do not encounter a closed system of a supernatural world or of divine essence that we learn about subsequently. That which we experience concerning God is inseparably joined to God's will to encounter the world and humanity.

He is God, the Creator, who does not remain merely by and for himself, but rather in creating the world, and particularly humanity, fashions something with which to interact. He is the Father who wants to have a relationship with his children and is ever seeking them anew, and this is also the God who encircles and accompanies them with maternal care.

He is God, the Redeemer, who takes up his residence in the world of humanity, takes upon himself and bears their burdens and needs, their trespasses and abandonment of God. And, as the Firstborn of many brothers and sisters, he opens the way to true human existence before God. If it is repeatedly and explicitly said concerning the Son that God created the world through him and that in the beginning he was with God, indeed, that he was God himself, then this underscores the fact that there is no essential difference between Creator and Redeemer. Rather, it was part of God's essence from the beginning to step outside of himself and to express himself through his creative and redemptive Word.

He is God, who renews and fulfills and is present through the Holy Spirit in the life of human beings. As Spirit, God creates and structures the redemptive fellowship and leads them into full fellowship with God.

If we thus summarize the biblical witness concerning the essence of divine revelation, we will find that witness necessarily leading us toward a Trinitarian structure. The doctrine of the Trinity as such is not yet to be found within the witness of the Bible. Yet, the discourse concerning the triune God is fundamental to the Christian witness of revelation, because it describes the inescapable consequence of the basic definition of the essence of God in the assertion "God is love."[88]

The assertion "God is love" in 1 John 4:8 and 4:16 does not simply name an important attribute of God. Rather, it is the basic definition of God's essence, whose dynamic is disclosed in the movement of the triune

God. He is love, a love that surrenders itself for the beloved; he is love, a love that does not remain merely "in and for itself" but creates its objects; the love that creates the fellowship of love, a fellowship that points toward a complete oneness and yet which does not dissolve the I-Thou relationship. The God who is love is the "mystery of this world" in creation, in redemption, and in perfection.

Thus, the trinitarian understanding of God is also an expression of the "Missio Dei," the mission of God, or the movement in which the triune God is to be found within the world and among human beings. Therefore, the "Missio Dei" is the motivation and the power behind every human mission.[89]

God's revelation crosses boundaries: it brings the eternal to expression within the realm of that which is terrestrial. It lives divine grace in human form. Hence, the nature of Christian mission and proclamation is to cross boundaries.

God's revelation aims for dialogue, that is, for the response of human beings who appropriate the events of the revealing activity of God. Similarly, mission and proclamation seek humans' response.

Perhaps more than any other tradition of Christian proclamation and teaching, Wesleyan theology places central emphasis upon the basic assertion that God is love and, hence, love is made to be descriptive of the content of the Christian "religion." This emphasis also has a bearing upon the understanding of revelation in Methodism.[90]

Overall, the doctrine of the Trinity in Methodism plays a subordinate role. Of course, its articles of faith make reference to the basic assertions concerning the doctrine of the Trinity, and John Wesley dedicated a sermon to that theme, which frankly has more the character of an exercise of duty.[91] Wesley affirms that he is in full agreement with all the basic assertions of the doctrine of the Trinity as formulated by the early church, but he does not wish to indulge in the subtle attempts to describe and cognitively substantiate the Trinity and the nature of Christ. Charles Wesley published a small volume of hymns to the Trinity.[92] In these and other hymns it becomes quite evident what the importance of the Trinity is for the understanding of God's self-revelation.

Charles Wesley's point of entry for appropriating the doctrine of the Triune God is the work of the Holy Spirit. He is the One who reveals "things of God" and makes the Godhead known. Through the Spirit we learn to know "God through God Himself," and we become capable of recognizing "the depths of divine love." That is, "God alone knows the love of God," and thus this must be revealed to us through the activity of the Holy Spirit.[93] The task of the Holy Spirit is to bear witness to and make real the love of God through the death of Christ. The "things of God," or the content of what the Spirit reveals, is God's love demonstrated on the cross. Through the witness of the Spirit and through the blood of Jesus Christ we become convinced and assured that there is no other God than the One who is revealed in Jesus Christ.[94] The hidden God, for whom humans inquire and seek so longingly, becomes the revealed God, who loves us in Christ and reassures us of this love through the Spirit.[95]

For the Wesleys, revelation is not the answer to the more or less appropriated question about the existence of God. Instead, it is the assuring response of God to the question about the meaning of "God for us." Thus, revelation is always treated in a Trinitarian and soteriological manner, that is, directed toward our redemption and toward the salvation of the world. Revelation is never an epiphany of God for its own sake, but is revelation for humanity. This outlook is emphatically expressed in the hymns of Charles Wesley. They also describe with passion the fact that evangelistic proclamation is nothing other than the narrating and actualizing appropriation of the event of salvation, in which God reveals himself as love.[96] This is important for an intimate acquaintance with the Bible as the source of and witness to revelation!

In a certain sense, Paul's word of blessing as found at the end of 2 Corinthians embraces this concept of God's revelation in a succinct form:

The grace of our Lord Jesus Christ—
God's salvific gift, that Christ has loved us and guarded us,
  and the love of God the Father—
God's creative Yes to the world, that he has spoken in creation and in redemption,
  and the fellowship of the Holy Spirit—
which participates in the love of God, confers the Spirit, and establishes community with one another,
  be with us all and with all humanity.

1.2   The Holy Scripture as the Foundation for Theology

All Christian discourse about God, whether it be in proclamation or in theological reflection, basically has its foundation in the self-revelation of

God. This revelation is reliably witnessed to us in the Bible. Thus, the Bible is de facto the basis of every Christian theology. However, there is controversy within Christendom concerning the appropriate way to understand and exposit the Bible. In giving an account of the basis for a theology of The United Methodist Church, our exposition needs to provide information regarding the basic assertions of the relation of revelation to the Bible. It is important to gather this information in conjunction with what we know about the origin of the Bible and the definition of the biblical canon.

1.2.1 *The Origin of the Bible*[97]

For Christian faith, the books of the Bible are the written documents of the self-disclosure of God through his actions in the history of Israel and in the life of Jesus of Nazareth. This document was admittedly not taken into safekeeping like a valuable historical document that is locked in a vault. The Bible is to be read day by day, it is to be expounded Sunday by Sunday, and it is to be lived out within the Christian congregation through the centuries. Its message has shown itself to be salvific, helpful, and trustworthy. It has triggered revolutions and has given human beings the foundation for their lives. The Bible and its books have been transcribed repeatedly since its inception and it has been printed innumerable times. We possess no original autograph of a biblical book, but we can reconstruct the broad and early tradition of the original text of the Bible with more certainty than is the case with any other ancient text.

This dynamic history of the Bible corresponds to its content and its formation. No theological system is revealed within its texts, but we discover instead the history of the discourse and the acts of God. Even the texts themselves have their own history. The Bible does not assert that it was sent from heaven in its entirety or that its content was dictated in one unbroken session. Still, it is possible for us to gain insight into its formation, so that it becomes possible for the attentive observer to reconstruct its history.

1.2.1.1 THE FORMATION OF THE OLD TESTAMENT

The first section of the Bible comprises the books of the "old covenant" (= Old Testament), which have value for Christians as well as for Jews.[98] The origin of the first canonical collections of these scriptures reaches back into the time after the exile (six centuries before Christ). The decisive point signified by the destruction of the temple, the loss of national independence, and the abduction of a great portion of the leading class of the Hebrew population led to the fact that the operation of institutions and of earthly tradition was no longer self-evident. Consequently, people began to organize to a greater whole those varied collections of the law and the texts of sayings concerning the origin of the people that had earlier been committed to literary form. A five-volume work came into existence that the Jews call the "Torah" (wisdom or law), and that we know today by the name of the "Pentateuch" or the "Five Books of Moses." We do not know whether it existed in its present form prior to the reading of the law through Ezra (Nehemiah 8, about 450 years before Christ). Yet, the latest possible dating for it would seem to be the fourth century before Christ, when the Samaritans, who separated themselves from the Jerusalem cultic community toward the end of that century, took it over in the same form.

The words of the prophets had been partially collected and edited at the time of their active ministry (see Isaiah 8:16, Jeremiah 36). Since the time of the exile, when their message of judgment seemed to be fulfilled, their words gained significant authority and were gathered together and—where needful—their message was put into action. In addition, the history of the people up until the exile was now described in relation to the older reports and descriptions and it was made intelligible in its theological meaning as a history of the fall and judgment, and also the history of their return and of the divine rescue. Because of this theological connection, the historical books (Joshua, Judges, and the books of Samuel and Kings) and the prophetic writings (Isaiah, Jeremiah, Ezekiel, and the twelve "minor prophets") were included under the major heading of "prophets." Both of these parts of the Old Testament were already fixed components of the holy Scriptures of the Jewish community at the time of Jesus and the apostles, as the numerous references in the New Testament to the "law and the prophets" indicate (see, for instance, Matthew 7:12).

The remaining books of the Old Testament, gathered together under the title of the "writings," were already held in high regard, especially the Psalms and Job, but also Daniel. Nevertheless, the exact extent of this portion of the Bible was still an open question, as was verified by the discovery at Qumran. This has led to the fact that even today there is no firm agreement as to the parameters of the Old Testament. The early Christian congregations, which almost exclusively used the Greek translation of the Old Testament, the so-called Septuagint, subscribed to the selection of texts that is found in that edition, containing the book of Jesus Sirach, the books of the Maccabees, the books of Judith and Tobias, as well as the books of Esther and Daniel, though the precise contents were not yet strictly established.

After the destruction of Jerusalem, the Aramaic-speaking Jews of Palestine limited their canon to the books that were transmitted in Hebrew, and they rejected the remaining writings of the Septuagint, as well as other highly valued apocalyptic books. Nevertheless, they did choose to accept the still disputed Song of Songs and Esther. While the Greek Orthodox and the Roman Catholic Churches approved the broader canon of the Greek and Latin traditions, respectively, Luther placed those additional writings, known as the "apocrypha," between the Old and the New Testaments.

When he undertook to revise the Thirty-nine Articles of the Anglican Church for the Methodists in America, John Wesley chose to delete the enumeration of these writings that had been found in the Anglican articles, located between the listing of the books of the Old and the New Testaments. However, there has been no polemic against these books in Methodist theology.[99]

1.2.1.2 THE DEVELOPMENT OF THE NEW TESTAMENT

Whenever Jesus and the early Christian community referred to the holy Scriptures, they meant the writings of the Old Testament. They comprised the Bible of early Christianity. Within their message was found the prophecy of the mission of Jesus and of his significance. Here was also found wisdom for daily living. Through these texts, it became a matter of certainty that the Spirit of Jesus would show his community of believers the right way to follow.

As witnesses to the Resurrection and with their basic task of proclaiming the gospel, the apostles were supposed to be concerned for preserving continuity and agreement with the gospel of Jesus Christ. Yet, differences of interpretation were not absent, and Paul had to provide clarity through his letters, which were intended to some extent to act in place of his apostolic presence. There was no thought at the outset that these letters would become a part of a holy scripture of the new covenant. A written scripture did not appear to be necessary or highly significant (note 2 Corinthians 3:3-6).

This outlook would change after the death of the apostles and their students. What was supposed to be the foundation and norm for the Christian proclamation, beside the writings of the Old Testament? The canon of the

New Testament arose in response to this question, a process that lasted a good two and one-half centuries. This process occurred in three clearly recognizable stages:

(1.) Until the middle of the second century after Christ, the "words of the Lord" had the highest authority besides the Old Testament (see Paul's account in 1 Corinthians 7:10, 25). These are sayings found in the Gospels but still cited freely and not according to the wording of a definite text of the Gospel. Besides these, apostolic authority of the apostle became a new factor, which *de facto* was formulated only using the words of Paul. His letters had probably already been collected and read at an earlier date (see 2 Peter 3:15-16) and now emerged as the quintessence of apostolic authority.

(2.) This situation changed fundamentally toward the end of the second century, possibly under the pressure of the Marcionite movement, which rejected the Old Testament and had replaced it with a Christian "scripture." The writings of the Old Testament were upheld, but now the four Gospels, the fourteen letters of Paul (including the epistle to the Hebrews), the Acts of the Apostles, and both of the first epistles of Peter and John, were placed alongside them and became the second part of the Christian Bible. Thus, the core of the New Testament canon emerged, and it emerged without an external, ecclesiastical decision—and served as the basis for the Christian debate with the increasingly threatening ascendancy of Gnosticism. The apostolic status of other writings produced by the early Christian community is still a matter of discussion.

(3.) This theological discussion determined the next one and a half centuries. There are some writings, such as the epistle of Barnabas, the Didache, or the "Shepherd of Hermas," that were highly valued by many and that are even to be found to some extent in the old manuscripts of the Bible. However, in the last analysis, they were rejected—not because God's Word could not be heard in them, but because they were not counted among the original and foundational apostolic message to be read in the worship services. They were recommended for private reading. Of the present New Testament writings, the greatest debate in the Eastern sector of the Roman Empire concerned the acceptance of the Revelation to John, especially with regard to its authorship and its apocalyptic message. In the West, there were problems with the Epistle to the Hebrews, not so much because of its authorship as because of its rejection of the possibility of a second repentance (Hebrews 6:4-6).

The determination of the canon was brought about by a somewhat insignificant occasion: in A.D. 367 the bishop of Alexandria, Athanasius, who was highly regarded in the entire church, established the extent of the biblical canon in his thirty-ninth episcopal Easter letter to the Egyptian congregations. He enumerated twenty-seven books in the New Testament, including the epistle to the Hebrews and Revelation, and thus gave the canon its present generally accepted shape. Apparently the time was ripe for such a decision, for the entire imperial church complied with Athanasius' position on the canon without awaiting any special conciliar action. Only in the border areas like Syria or Ethiopia were deviating definitions of the canon adopted.

1.2.2 *The Significance of the Biblical Canon*

The significance of the collection of biblical books for the Christian church and its adherents can hardly be overestimated. In the biblical canon, the church received a foundation and norm for its proclamation and action. It is not by accident that the Greek term *canon,* meaning "standard," has become the technical term to describe the Bible as a whole. Since this fact has historically been valued in different ways, three aspects of this development are to be illumined.

1.2.2.1   WHO CREATED THE CANON OF THE BIBLE?[100]

The collection of biblical writings emerged in the context of the Jewish or Christian community, yet it would be incorrect to state that the church created the canon. In its essential components, the canon grew together with the church. It developed out of the remembrance of and self-reflection on the earlier discourse of God, which was acknowledged as being foundational for one's own existence before God. No preliminary definition of the canon was determined whereby the church could prove what was supposed to be canonical. It was exactly the opposite. First of all, what had transpired as the decisive witness for the life of the church was simply recognized. In so doing, criteria were attained with which one could make a decision about those few remaining questions of doubt concerning the proper extent of the canon. According to the verdict of faith, this process, whose human aspects are certainly recognizable and describable, ratified the working of the Holy Spirit, through whom God gave the church a foundation and standard for all future proclamation and doctrine.

In allowing this process to occur and in taking it to its conclusion, the church underwent an important act of self-denial and self-restriction. It recognized—either consciously or unconsciously—that it needed an entity by which it must orient itself and by which it could also be measured. Of course, Jesus Christ as its ascended Lord is the decisive entity for the Christian church. However, how does this Lord find expression in the life of the church, and where is his will for today to be heard?

With the creation of the canon and the recognition of its authority, it was basically being established (even if it was not initially recognized fully at the outset), that neither the authority of the episcopal teaching office alone nor the voice of contemporary prophecy alone nor even the ongoing development of a living tradition is sufficient to bring the word of the Lord into valid expression in the church. Above all, the clearly delineated words of the Old Testament promise and of the original witness of Jesus Christ are needed in order to ensure this.

1.2.2.2   THE STANDARDS CONCERNING THE DEFINITION OF THE CANON

In gathering the biblical writings, two tasks came before the church. Negatively, this entailed excluding from ecclesial use writings that were shaped by erroneous teaching, for example, the later gnostic Gospels. Positively, this entailed deciding which books should belong to the basic core of writings that are decisive for the church—practically speaking, in other words, which books should be and may be permitted to be read in the congregational service of worship. In addition to these, there was still a greater number of favorite writings which were considered to be useful for private edification but not suitable for use in the corporate worship service.[101] In establishing the canon, there was therefore not a strong separation of the words of God and of humans. The early church certainly knew that God spoke in the Bible through human beings, and that God's Word came to expression also in the words of the later teachers of the church. It was a case of establishing the limits of the original, church-based proclamation of early Christianity. For the New Testament, this led to the criterion of the apostolicity (i.e., the apostolic origin and authority) of a text. This did not signify that one only recognized books that were personally authored by an apostle. Even the texts of Mark or of Luke had early on been accepted in the context of their use within the congregation. Even the epistle to the Hebrews, whose Pauline authorship always remained in question, was regarded as apostolic in the sense that it represented an important aspect of the original proclamation concerning Christ. This also indicates that it was not primarily the trustworthiness of the historical assertions concerning a biblical text that was decisive regarding its relationship to the canon, but it was its authenticity, or the originality and the immediacy of its witness to Christ.

1.2.2.3 THE ADHERENCE TO THE OLD TESTAMENT

We have observed that a significant impetus for determining the extent of the Christian Bible in the second century came from a Christian named Marcion, who rejected the Old Testament because he thought that he had discovered within its text another God, different from the one he encountered in the Father of our Lord Jesus Christ. After hard inner turmoil, the church finally came through to retain the Old Testament. This position continues to be criticized today. For indeed, much about the depiction of God in the Old Testament seems alien to us.

Yet it was important for the church to make this decision. Keeping the Old Testament meant continuing to affirm God as Creator, and meant that humanity would not become estranged from the world, but that they would seek to live responsibly within the world, acknowledged as God's creation. The church further was seeking to relate humanity to the God of history, who was not to be regarded as some sort of other-worldly idea but as a God whose acts could be observed within the course of history. Thus, God's works in Israel were to be clearly affirmed, as well as God's special relationship to the Jewish people. Further, in adhering to the Old Testament, certain features of the New Testament message, such as the theme of judgment were preserved from being denied or cut out by a one-sided interpretation.

However, it will always be a precarious task of Christian exposition of the Bible to clarify properly what is "old" in the Old Testament, and thereby suspended through Jesus Christ, and what is fulfilled through Jesus Christ and thereby remains valid for faith.

1.2.3 *The Meaning of the Bible in the History of the Church*

Since the formation of the biblical canon, the Bible and its exposition have had a long historical development. Anyone who intends to determine our present relationship to this book also needs to know something about this history. Anyone who pursues the course of that history will discover that the Bible has always enjoyed great respect in the life of the church. The Bible was never forgotten. However, its message was always in danger of being taken over and overrun by the prevailing ecclesial teachings.

It is precisely at this point that the Bible exerts its critical function. From it proceeded the impulses for reform and for summoning the church to a reexamination of its foundation in Jesus Christ.

1.2.3.1 TO THE TIME OF THE REFORMATION

The early church lived by the Bible and with the Bible. Certainly the dogmas of the Trinity and Christology were developed in close relationship to the wording found within the appropriate biblical affirmations of God. These dogmas were intended to explicate the reality of God from the standpoint of the conceptual tools of the Greek and Latin world of thought. The exposition of the biblical books in sermons and scholarly commentaries was therefore an important sign of church life and church teachings. This basically also held true of the Middle Ages, which were not as in the dark about everything as is reported. During this period, the Bible was transcribed, disseminated, and eagerly used. However, there were still some problematic developments that increasingly hindered the furtherance of the biblical message.

First, the strong interest in philosophy, especially that of Aristotle, permitted the statements of Scripture to become the material for constructing theological systems which were built around completely different models of construction than those outlined by the Bible. The continually strengthening institutionalizing of the Papacy led to the Bible being used to offer justification for ecclesial predominance and not for self-examination. The prevailing method of allegorical exposition of the Bible made it easy to expound the literal sense of biblical statements in any direction whatsoever.

Since the masses of the population no longer understood Greek or Latin and education was the privilege of fewer and fewer people, the biblical knowledge of the populace declined. Translations of the Bible into the vernacular might have been necessary, but such efforts, though begun, were hindered and even occasionally forbidden by the church, rather than being promoted. Practically all of the pre-Reformation reform movements—especially those that emanated from the laity—made reference to the Bible. We may simply think of Francis of Assisi, the Waldensians, John Wycliff, or Jan Hus.

1.2.3.2 THE REFORMATION UNDERSTANDING OF SCRIPTURE

For the Reformers, the preeminence of the Bible above every other spiritual authority became one of the essential foundations of their new theological understanding. Yet, theirs was not a "legal" biblicism, as in the case of some movements before and alongside them, that demanded all forms of Christian and church life to be constituted in ways that out-wardly conformed to the model of biblical rules or customs. It was above all Martin Luther who focused on the very center of the biblical message, namely, the gospel of justification by faith alone. The "formal principle" of Reformation theology, "Scripture alone" *(sola Scriptura)* was expressed through the essential principle of "Christ alone" *(solus Christus)*. Only that which is grounded in Scripture is to be believed. Yet, within the diverse witness of the Bible, one was to listen for "that which promotes Christ."

In his preface to the first German edition of the New Testament (1522), Luther could thus cast powerful doubt on the apostolicity of some New Testament writings (especially Hebrews, the letters of James and Jude, and the Revelation to John, which he intentionally set at the end of the canon). This judgment was made more on theological than on historical grounds. It was certainly not Luther's intention to dislodge the authority of these writings. Luther simply wanted to see appropriate emphasis to be made within the Bible.

1.2.3.3 THE DEVELOPMENT OF THE POST-REFORMATION ERA

Whereas Luther was most interested in substantiating the authority of Scripture with regard to its content, namely through the message that it proclaimed, the theologians who represented Lutheran and Reformed Orthodoxy attempted to secure this position in a formal manner. Through their doctrine of the verbal inspiration of the Bible, they wanted to estab-lish that every word, indeed every letter in the biblical books, was inspired by the Spirit of God. As a consequence of this conception, one went so far as to designate the Hebraic vowel points as being inspired, although these had first been appended to the text in the ninth and tenth centuries after Christ—in short, long after the completion of the canon.

But this assumption was shown to be unusable in ways beyond conse-quences such as these that overshot their mark. The richness of meaning inherent within the various biblical assertions was demolished through a doctrine of inspiration that was oriented toward an analysis of individual words, and thus the dynamic of the biblical message, which Luther had discovered, was lost. The Bible became a collection of separate truths of faith that one incorporated into a doctrinal system, through which the normative faith of the church was supposed to be delineated. As praise-worthy as the intellectual worth inherent to this system might be, it undermined the character of the biblical message as a living discourse, one that addresses the hearer from a particular historical situation.

Here is where the critique of Pietism enters in. It shares with Orthodoxy a confidence in the trustworthiness and truth of the Bible. However, it does not look to the Bible for proof *(dicta probanti)* for its own theological system. Instead, the living word of God, which speaks to human hearts, renders faith certain and serves to guide believers in their personal lives. Thus, the Pietists' devotional meetings were above all to be hours of corporate study of the Bible, in which persons who have come to depend on and be moved by the message of the Bible help one another to understand its message.

1.2.3.4 THE BIBLE IN THE HANDS OF WESLEY AND THE EARLY METHODISTS

John Wesley's understanding of the Bible closely approximates that of the Pietists. Full confidence in the trustworthiness of the Bible stands in service to the question of salvation. This is never more evident than in the frequently cited quote from the preface to the collection of his "Standard Sermons."

> To candid, reasonable men I am not afraid to lay open what have been the inmost thoughts of my heart. I have thought, I am a creature of a day, passing through life as an arrow through the air. I am a spirit come from God and returning to God; just hovering over the great gulf, till a few moments hence I am no more seen—I drop into an unchangeable eternity! I want to know one thing, the way to heaven—how to land safe on that happy shore. God himself has condescended to teach the way: For this very end he came from heaven. He hath written it down in a book. O give me that book! At any price give me the book of God! I have it. Here is knowledge enough for me. Let me be *homo unius libri*. Here then I am, far from the busy ways of men. I sit down alone: only God is here. In his presence I open, I read his Book; for this end, to find the way to heaven.[102]

This refining of the understanding of the Bible as a witness for the message of salvation is characteristic of John Wesley's use of Scripture. He lived in the Bible. His sermons and his writings are thoroughly imbued with innumerable citations and allusions to biblical texts. In the Bible he found the "true religion" of the early church, namely, the religion of the heart, and through that channel he understood the meaning of "scriptural holiness."

Otherwise Wesley's doctrine of the Bible possessed little originality. In his Articles of Religion he adopted almost without alteration the corresponding section of the Anglican articles (Articles XI and XII of the Articles of Religion of the Methodist Church). He thereby affirmed the position on the canon that had been set forth by the Protestant Reformers, and he opposed accepting extrabiblical sources of revelation. He does not formulate a specific confession of the Bible as the Word of God; instead, the Old Testament is explicitly elevated as an equivalent witness to the message of salvation through Jesus Christ (Article VI).

Wesley was convinced of the infallibility of the Bible: "If there be any mistakes in the Bible, there may as well be a thousand. If there is one falsehood in that book, it did not come from the God of truth."[103] In the preface to his *Explanatory Notes on the New Testament,* he describes the entire Bible as the inspired Word of God and he summarizes its meaning as follows: "The Scripture therefore of the Old and New Testament, is a most solid and precious system of Divine truth. Every part thereof is worthy of God; and all together are one entire body, wherein is no defect, no excess." (Incidentally, this did not prevent history from working with the best philological means of his time at the tasks of reading and translating the New Testament.)

The Methodist systematicians of the nineteenth century continued to adhere to this conviction, and they represented the Wesleyan doctrine of inspiration over against the beginning of the historical-critical exposition of the Bible. Nevertheless, fundamentalism, in the narrower sense of that term, has never developed in Methodism. Various factors were responsible for this.[104]

Above all, the authority of the Bible was pondered and set forth in the light of its message of salvation (see Article V): "The Holy Scripture containeth all things necessary to salvation...". For this reason, an application of the Bible for the knowledge of natural science does not lie in the interests of Methodism.

Wesley was also able to demonstrate that the different parts of the Bible are of different levels of importance for faith. Since he considered the statements of some Psalms to be "highly unsuitable for the lips of a Christian congregation," he left them out of the Methodist service of worship.[105] In America, it was especially the German American Wilhelm Nast[106] who represented a functional, textually based doctrine of inspiration, which protected the basic authority of the Bible without inflicting violence on the text in its historical embeddedness.[107]

It is into this context that an openness to the concerns of historical-critical exposition of the Bible was reached in Methodism at the beginning of the twentieth century. However, unlike the situation in the Lutheran and Reformed Churches, it did not lead to far-reaching discussions or even divisions concerning the question of the Bible at the official church level, even though this different understanding of the Bible played a significant and often burdensome role in theological discussions about particular themes, and at the congregational level.[108]

1.2.3.5 THE CHALLENGE OF HISTORICAL-CRITICAL EXEGESIS OF THE BIBLE[109]

Understanding a historical-critical exposition of the Bible is a product of the modern age or, more precisely, of the Enlightenment. Its basic assessment was initially thoroughly positive. It intended to free the original message of the biblical writings from the dogmatic overlay of later doctrinal systems and to bring that message once again to the light of day. Its criticism was not directed against the Bible as such but against the doctrinal structure of orthodoxy that tended to stifle the true meaning of the Bible. Early on in its development, however, the instrument of historical research was directed to a critique of biblical testimonies and thus to a weapon for a comprehensive critique of the Christian faith. This tendency is evident in the case of Hermann S. Reimarus or David Friedrich Strauss. The basic expressions of the creed, such as the resurrection of Jesus, were placed in doubt in the name of historical reason, or they were explained "reasonably," with strange, rationalistic constructions of thought.

On the other hand, many scholars who worked with the historical-critical method carried out extraordinarily fruitful works in explaining the biblical books, since they investigated the texts very precisely, without preconceptions, and with great linguistic and technical competence. We have them to thank for a wealth of important insights concerning the Bible and its environment.

To be sure, they were often in danger of setting aside the concrete, time-bound form of the biblical texts as being insignificant for faith, and of searching within these texts to find a timeless core of rational, eternal truths. The decisive turn away from this approach was signaled by so-called kerygmatic theology, whose chief representatives were Gerhard von Rad in Old Testament studies and Rudolf Bultmann in New Testament studies. They and their students recognized that the biblical narratives were above all to be understood as testimonies of faith, and thus they are to be exegeted within their historical limitations and particularities. In spite of their quite deeply grounded historical skepticism, this led to these theologians being able to hear God's call in the words of the Bible. It was certainly a significant reason why, with their help, the historical-critical method of biblical exposition superseded the traditional liberal theology, and why it gained widespread acceptance in the thought of church leaders, such as in Methodism in Europe and in America.

This method of reflection has of course moved on. Nowadays two prevalent forms of historical-critical exegesis can be somewhat simply expressed as follows:[110]

(1.) The historical-critical method, narrowly defined, worked with the three categories which the theologian and philosopher Ernst Troeltsch established as normative for historical study:

(a.) Criticism as methodical doubt: Was it really the way the reports describe it?

(b.) Correlation as a basic condition of historical events: every event stands in a natural relationship of cause and effect.

(c.) Analogy as the ultimate measure for evaluating historical occurrences: through historical discernment and explanation, judgments of probability concerning past events are made on the basis of their analogy to general human experiences.

It is not difficult to see that a closed picture of the world is being presupposed here, in which there is no place for an intervention of God nor for events which have no analogy, such as the resurrection of Jesus. Yet for the scholar who works with this method it is certainly not to be excluded that God may be at work in verifiable, temporal, and causal relationships, and in accounts that cannot be accepted as historic, but where the ancient forms of expression can be appreciated as enduring, valid expressions of faith.

(2.) The historical-critical method in its broader dimensions works in the same way with a wealth of specific philological and historical methodologies (such as textual criticism, form and literary history, among similar ones), yet without bundling these all together as one closed system capable of capturing and evaluating bygone events. As with contemporary accounts of profane history, this method tends to proceed from a basic trust in the reliability of ancient texts.[111] Its critical moment emerges in the distinction between the various biblical narratives and sayings, and it stands in the service of their theological meaning. Critical inquiries into the underlying event do not proceed from the question "Is that possible?"

but from a comparison of corresponding reports (for example, the awakening of the daughter of Jairus in Mark 5:21-43 and Matthew 9:18-26). It is asserted that events without analogy, like the resurrection of Jesus, cannot be historically proved; however, it is also recognized that one cannot say conclusively that God did nothing on Easter morning.

In general, it is increasingly being recognized in our day that the historical questioning of the exegesis of the Bible is certainly indispensable since it deals with historical events, but also that every historical method runs the risk of distancing the texts from the contemporary hearers, since those texts are after all to be interpreted in their original context. Thus, biblical exegesis needs to be complemented by means of ways that promote the personal relationship between the biblical Word and present-day hearers of that Word. Methods of meditation are helpful in this regard, as are methods of exposition that promote the personal identification of the reader with the event and the persons and, above all, that promote an in-depth dialogue with others concerning the meaning of the texts.[112]

Corporate Bible study in pastoral care groups and congregations was always an important aid to the appropriation of its message and to correcting an all too individualistic exposition of the Bible that is always in danger of accommodating the Word to one's own desires and needs.

It is true of all methods meant to assist the "appropriation" of the biblical texts that they not be allowed to hide or eliminate the critical distance between us and them nor the silent assumptions of our exposition of them. This distance remains necessary so that the Bible can declare its own message.

1.2.3.6 Models of the Contemporary Understanding of the Bible

The attentive observer of the current discussion of how to interpret the Bible will note three basic models that lie in tension with one another.

(a.) The "conservative evangelical" understanding of the Bible. In the American theological context, this position can be further subdivided into the Reformed doctrine of plenary biblical inspiration (the Princetonian school), and the Wesleyan-holiness, the dispensational, and the twentieth-century Fundamentalist positions.[113] The first option proceeds from the basic conviction that "The Bible is God's Word," and to this conviction it links a clear conception of the full, plenary verbal inspiration of the entire Bible and its complete infallibility in all matters that it explicitly addresses. The Princeton theologian Charles Hodge (1797–1878), the leading exponent of this position, linked biblical inerrancy to strict Presbyterian confessionalism. His position, which became normative in conservative evangelical circles, affirmed that "everything revealed in nature, and in the constitution of man, concerning God and our relation to Him, is contained and authenticated in Scripture."[114] In this matter it can rightfully appeal to the wide-ranging agreement of Christian doctrine that continues to the present day. However, if the biblical assertions, which after all generally agree with the ancient overall view of the world, are brought into explicit competition with the insights of contemporary natural science, which have been gained from quite different sources, this understanding of the Bible gains a completely new weighting and emphasis. In its approach to the Bible, Fundamentalism begins not with its concrete texts in the context of their history but from a basic conviction of how God's Word must be constituted in accordance with God's essence. In its practical handling of the Bible, it appeals to the nonliteral meaning of texts more frequently than does the historical-critical approach, in order to avoid inconsistencies in the text. However, the approach taken by the historical orientation to the Bible helps the reader to give order and priority to the different theological statements of Scripture, and thus to promote the necessary "critical" work of deciphering the text with historical and theological accuracy. Princetonian orthodoxy would like to fulfill the will of God with great earnestness, as that purpose is attested to by Scripture, but it is not immune from handling the text with a certain arbitrariness. It desires for its adherents the courage of faith that will stand against doubt and that will function by strictly adhering to the outward verification of the objective truth of the Bible as God's Word.

By contrast with the objective emphasis of the Princetonian school, the nineteenth-century Wesleyan-holiness position on biblical inspiration has been identified by Donald Dayton, a leading contemporary historian of that tradition, as being more clearly rooted in the Pietist emphasis upon narrative over didactic texts in Scripture, and upon an insistence that the drama of salvation, as narrated in the Bible, is to be subjectively re-enacted within the heart and life of each believer and within a society transformed by the message of regeneration.[115] As a case in point, the doctrine of sanctification, which was interpreted in subjective-impartational language rather than in the Princetonian objective-imputational categories, came to be defined in personal and social terms. Consequently, Wesleyan holiness evangelists, including Charles Finney, Orange Scott, and others, strongly joined the teaching of Christian perfection to the abolition of slavery in the antebellum era, as the consequence of their biblical hermeneutic. By contrast, the Princetonians tended to take conservative, anti-abolitionist positions, as a consequence of their objective-imputational and nontransformist attitude toward Scripture.

A quite different hermeneutical and sociohistorical outlook was manifested by the premillennial dispensationalist school that was represented by the publicized prophecy conference of J. N. Darby (1800–1882) and by the Correspondence Bible School and the popular Scofield Reference Bible produced by C. I. Scofield (1843–1921). They taught that Christ would rescue all true Christians before the tribulation soon to befall the earth, and they denied what other conservative evangelicals and all liberals believed—that the kingdom of God would come as a part of the historical process.[116]

The Fundamentalist position, the last to be developed among these conservative evangelical options, received its name from a series of twelve booklets entitled *The Fundamentals,* which appeared between 1910 and 1913 under the editorship of a distinguished group of conservative Protestant theologians from Great Britain, Canada, and the United States. Emphasis was placed upon the verbal, plenary inspiration of Scripture, as well as the virgin birth, substitutionary atonement, physical resurrection, and the imminent, premillennial return of Christ.[117] Scofield soon became identified with this group, and by 1925 a Fundamentalist controversy had erupted in the mainline Protestant churches, including Methodism. This was partly a consequence of the debate over evolution that was dramatized by the trial in Dayton, Tennessee, of John Scopes, a high school science teacher who was under indictment for teaching evolution contrary to the laws of the state. Unlike the previous three options, Fundamentalism resulted in divisions in mainline denominations and the forming of new Fundamentalist denominations.

While there is a common thread of emphasis upon the full inerrancy of the Bible in three of these four types of conservative evangelicalism (with the possible exception of the Wesleyan-holiness camp, whose origin and development is not traced to this position), there are also clear points of contradiction and divergence among them that need to be recognized.

Fundamentalism aims to seriously do the will of God, as it is witnessed to in the Bible. And yet, because of its strong identification with the modern American social situation it is not immune to being choosy about which biblical commands to follow. Thus the biblical commands about social and sexual matters are often treated with considerable variation. Fundamentalism offers its adherents a high degree of security, but is in danger of turning the gospel into a law.

(b.) The "liberal" understanding of Scripture.[118] It proceeds from a conviction that the Bible—like every other religious document—contains statements of humans about God and God's actions. Insofar as they are bound to historical assertions, they need to be examined critically, by a strict adherence to the historical-critical methodology. Despite this skeptical approach, an adherent to this model can generally arrive at the position that of all human religious writings, the Bible reveals the essence of God most impressively and helpfully. The liberal can also accept the love command as a basic norm for human conduct, and will attribute the decisive role for individual responsible action to critical understanding.

As in the case of Fundamentalism, the liberal model also is marked by its tenacious adherence to a preferred conceptual framework. For its adherents, there is a considerable degree of personal freedom of decision, but it tends to give little credence to the basic claim of the Bible.

Within the American context, Sidney Ahlstrom has distinguished the following major types of liberalism: the moralists in the tradition of Schleiermacher and his concern for the religious consciousness and of Rauschenbusch and the Social Gospel, who insisted that "ethical conduct is the supreme and sufficient religious act";[119] those who were more interested in metaphysics and the philosophy of religion, such as the idealist philosopher of religion Josiah Royce and the Personalist G. P. Browne; and also those liberals who parted ways over the authority of Scripture, the church, and formal creeds. The latter group included the "Evangelical Liberals," who sought to maintain the continuity of Christian doctrinal and ecclesial tradition, "except insofar as modern circumstances required adjustment or change";[120] and "Modernistic Liberalism," which designates a smaller group of more radical theologians who "took the scientific method, scholarly discipline, empirical fact, and prevailing forms of contemporary philosophy as their point of departure."[121] Methodists were represented in more than one of these groups, including the "Social Gospel" (I. L. Kephart and W. M. Bell of the United Brethren in Christ), Personalism (B. P. Bowne at Boston University), and the "Evangelical Liberals" (H. F. Rall of Garrett).[122]

(c.) The "kerygmatic" understanding of Scripture.[123] It proceeds from the basic conviction that God has spoken through the biblical witnesses and that God also wants to speak through them today, and it identifies its chief task as the exposition of the message *(kerygma)*. Within that context, attention is given to foundational statements from the Protestant Reformers, especially Luther. In this form of understanding the Scripture takes seriously the historical form of the Bible and works with the historical-critical method, especially in its more open, less narrow form. What is essential is not the accuracy of particular natural, scientific, or historical facts but the inner power of the message of God, who has created the world and redeemed humanity through Jesus Christ. The basic norm for Christian action is the love commandment, from which the particular biblical commandments can attain significance as concretizations of love, without treating those commands as law in a restrictive sense. From this point—a departure analogous to Luther's precedent—factual criticism of particular biblical texts is possible, but it never leads to a basic stance of questioning the veracity of those texts.

One problem posed by this model, is that the relationship of the truth of the biblical message to the reliability of the historical statements, in which that message is embedded, is not totally clear. Thus this model demands of its adherents the courage of faith, the ability to trust the truth of the Word even in the face of doubt, and the lack of external proof.

We hope it has become evident by these three models that we have considered only a quite simplified selection from the multiplicity of expressions that concern the question of how the Bible is to be understood. There is a plethora of nuanced explanations. The biblicism of Pietism and of early Methodism stands between the first and the third patterns.[124] Karl Barth was a transitional thinker regarding both of these patterns, even as Bultmann was a mediator between the kerygmatic and the liberal patterns.[125]

A sense of orientation is needed as we search these patterns of biblical interpretation. To that end, the following criteria measure an understanding of Scripture that is "true to the Bible."

(a.) The claim of the biblical texts to report God's activity and words for the salvation of his people and of the entire creation ought to be taken seriously and should become the guideline of our exposition.

(b.) The human view of the canon and its writings and the time-bounded nature of its assertions need to be taken into consideration.

(c.) The meaning of the text is not exhausted in its message to its original hearers; this message can and should also be considered relevant for the situation of humanity in our present day.

Without doubt, a "kerygmatic" exposition of the Bible comes closest to an understanding of the text that is faithful to the Bible, and therefore it should be the basis for the explanations that follow. However, this does not signify a fundamental rejection of other models. Even if the "fundamentalist" approach is in danger of placing the gospel in the chains of a formal legalism, and the "liberal" option threatens to reduce the message of the Scripture to the status of a noncanonical ancient religious document, the expositors who work with these approaches can still hear and proclaim the message of the gospel. That message is stronger than our particular modes of comprehension.

1.2.4 *The Bible—God's Word in Human Words*

On the basis of these considerations, we are seeking to depict an understanding of the Bible that is true to its own witness and its form of expression, one that embodies the impulses of our Reformation and Methodist heritage and also keeps in view the situation which is to be addressed by the text today.[126]

1.2.4.1 THE TRANSPARENCY OF THE BIBLICAL MESSAGE

In order to grasp the meaning and power of the biblical message, an attentive reading and hearing of its text is required, one that is open to being addressed by the words of the biblical witness. However, we don't need as some kind of preliminary work to adopt one particular understanding of the Bible. The conviction that God is speaking to us in the words of the Bible is not a handicap but the gift of God. It arises through the power of the event that encounters us in the words of the Bible, the event of the saving and judging actions of God toward God's people and God's saving and redeeming work in the life, death, and resurrection of Jesus of Nazareth. This conviction is bestowed on us through the gift of the Holy Spirit, through which God moves the readers and hearers of the biblical Word in their inmost being and allows them to recognize that this Word is also relevant for them today. Thus Article IV of the Articles of Faith of the Evangelische Gemeinschaft—the European branch of our former Evangelical United Brethren Church: "We believe that the Holy Bible, Old and New Testaments, reveals the Word of God so far as it is necessary for our salvation. It is to be received through the Holy Spirit as the true rule and guide for faith and practice."[127]

1.2.4.2 GOD'S VOICE IN THE WORDS OF THE BIBLE

The one whose ears and heart the Spirit of God has opened to God's Word, the one who has been moved by the inner power of the figure of Jesus and his message, such a one recognizes God's voice in the words of the biblical witness. In the first instance, this establishes a very personal relationship between the biblical texts and a person, independent of any theory concerning the relation between divine and human speech in the texts of the Bible. However, such a personal relationship pushes one to the basic conclusion that the origin of such a relationship lies not in the reader's capacity for empathy but in the nature of the text which anchors God's Word.

It is certainly evident that the task of summarizing the relationship of divine and human words in the biblical texts in a pithy formula is not an easy one.

For example, the phrase that "the Bible is God's Word" aptly describes the fact that the entire Bible is meant to witness to God's discourse and actions. Yet it conceals the fact that this discourse occurs in quite diverse ways, and that this witness quite consciously also includes human statements—statements that reflect the response of faith as well as the "no" of unbelief, the voices of complaint and despair as well as the song of thanksgiving and praise.

Conversely, a statement such as "The Bible contains God's Word" will mislead us to suppose that God's Word can be separated out from human words in the biblical sayings, through critical procedures or simply by recognizing certain distinguishing marks of the actual discourse of God. Such notions are too static for the dynamism of God's discourse. In addition, what is communicated to us as the actual speech of God is conveyed to us through the mouths of human beings. On the other hand, the Bible can also use the positive and negative responses of humans to communicate something to us.

The question of how the biblical writers were led to write down what God wanted to say through them was often explained in the history of the church through a doctrine of the divine inspiration of the authors or of the texts. In order to grasp this process as precisely as possible, different theories have been developed, and depending on circumstances reference is made to literal, verbal, or real inspiration. For example, we have previously noted that the doctrine of inspiration in contemporary fundamentalism has found very convinced advocates, among them Protestant Orthodoxy and John Wesley. Yet, it has repeatedly been shown that such relatively mechanical presentations of the multiplicity of biblical discourse about God and to God are not adequate. They do not touch the heart of the biblical concept of inspiration, as it is attested to above all in 2 Timothy 3:16. There it is stated that "all Scripture is inspired by God and is useful for teaching, for reproof, for correction, and for training in righteousness."

In the first instance, "all Scripture" means the writings of the Old Testament. It is assumed of them that they are marked and filled by God's Spirit, without this necessitating an exact definition of the relationship between the work of the Spirit and the activity of the biblical writers. This definition of their nature was later related to the New Testament writings, often without, however, paying attention to what the actual goal of the explanation in 2 Timothy 3:16 is. The inspiration of the biblical writings is shown not by their particular attributes but in relation to the function of these texts: they serve to teach people about the will of God, to correct their conduct, and to promote and guide their life with God. On this point, John Wesley has quite aptly pointed out in his *Notes on the NT* that God's Spirit has not only inspired those persons who penned the biblical texts but also continually inspires those who read them with an attitude of earnest prayer.[128]

Only such a functional concept of inspiration will do justice to the evidence that the Bible does not constitute a collection of individual sayings of God but rather is a witness to God's history with humanity. This history has a particular direction and leads to a central point. Its arc spans the narrative of primeval history, which at the same time initially describes a history of human beings' existence before God, over the history of God with the Jewish people, which is an exemplary demonstration of God's fight for human beings as God's companions. The narrative arc culminates in Jesus, in whose life and death the presence of God's love finds its goal in the midst of human need and guilt. Yet it also points to the final fulfillment of fellowship between God and humanity.

This arc is indicated in the biblical texts with a variety of lines. Some aspects are repeatedly underscored, such as the foundational meaning for the OT, the people of the God of Israel being led out from bondage in Egypt, or the meaning of the raising of Jesus for the New Testament gospel. Some aspects are illuminated in a variety of ways, such as the life and preaching of Jesus as portrayed in the various Gospels. A fullness of detail concerning human conduct and destiny has been woven into this great arc. Accordingly, divine inspiration can't be identified in all the details but it is always understood in relation to the whole, to the central matter, to the gracious turn of God to humanity, as it has come to decisive expression in Jesus of Nazareth.

Let us clarify this with an example. The discourse of Job's friends, which, after all, individually contained many heartfelt and valuable declarations, as a whole doubtless serves the function in the book to show how horrible "right" theology is at the wrong place. While Job's friends are presented to us as negative examples, God's Spirit works through them "for teaching, for reproof, for correction, and for training in righteousness" (2 Timothy 3:16), so that we do not need to occupy ourselves with the idle question of whether they are inspired verbatim.

1.2.4.3 THE HUMAN SIDE OF THE BIBLICAL MESSAGE

Over the years of theological reflection, one has been unable to express the relationship of divine and human nature in the person of Jesus other than by the paradox: "true God and true man." To a certain extent, this is true of the Bible. It is wholly the words of humans, to the extent that all that it contains was either said or recorded by humans. This human discourse about God and to God—yes, even the discourse against God!—becomes the "echo" for the speech of God to humanity.

Thus, this human side of the Bible is no "embarrassing residue of this earth" (Goethe) from which we would above all want to free God's Word. Analogous to the incarnation of the Word, it is an expression of God's condescension, and of God's will to come quite close to humanity and to talk in their language and their world. This desire for proximity is certainly not to be understood only in the sense of an outward accommodation, as when during Colonialism the white conquerors used to communicate with the indigenous populations through translators, without allowing themselves to have a genuine encounter with the worldview of those indigenous peoples. Rather it is to be understood in the sense of an actual immersion of divine speech in the experience and suffering of humanity.

No one has described this greatness and lowliness, this beauty and complexity of the Word of God with more clarity and forcefulness than Martin Luther:

> For these are the Scriptures, which make fools of all the wise and clever and are open only to the small and the simple, as Christ says in Matthew 11:25. Therefore dismiss your own opinions and feelings, and think of the Scriptures as the loftiest and noblest of holy things, as the richest of all

treasure troves which will never be able to be sufficiently explained, in order that you may find that divine wisdom which God here lays before you so simply and so unpretentiously as to quench all pride. Here you will find the swaddling cloths and the manger in which Christ lies, and to which the angel also points the shepherds (Luke 2:12). Simple and lowly are these swaddling cloths, but dear is the treasure, Christ, who lies in them.[129]

Thus, we search "in the Scripture"—in the Old and the New Testaments—because they attest to God's actions for the salvation of the world; that is, because we find the witness of Christ within them. It is in this way that the witness to God's original revelation has come to us. The authors and redactors of the biblical texts, as well as its translators and expositors, have been used by God, so that today we can read, hear, and understand God's Word. For this to continue in the future, there must continue to be translators and expositors who pass on the living Word with their limited and imperfect methods, Yet nevertheless guided by God's mandate and the leading of God's Spirit. We simply "have" the Word of God in no other way than by its being reported to us by others who have likewise heard or read it.

1.3   Methodist Doctrine as a Theology for Praxis

Wesley and the early Methodists were of the conviction that they were to proclaim nothing other than the simple truth, as it is attested to by the Bible and the early church. However, this conviction did not remain uncontested. For example, the group that was associated with George Whitefield certainly came to wholly different conclusions from the brothers Wesley on the question of predestination, although they began with the same assumptions. Even within their own ranks, differences of opinion soon emerged, such as on the meaning of the law for the life of the Christian.

The Methodist movement had to have the same experiences as other churches of the Reformation: that *sola Scriptura* (the Bible alone) is an important principle in marking the division with the principle of tradition espoused by the Roman Catholic Church. However, some questions need to be clarified if its particular doctrine is to be set forth positively and in relation to the challenges of the day:

—How is the Bible to be exposited?

—Who exercises the authority for teaching and adjudicates wherever disagreement of interpretation occurs?

—What documents serve to preserve for the future the truth once it has been recognized?

In the following three sections, the responses which United Methodist theology offers to these questions will be set forth.

1.3.1 *Principles of United Methodist Exposition of the Bible*

Wesley set forth the method of his biblical exposition in a condensed form in the preface to his "standard sermons." Following the previously cited confession of the Bible and its validity, he wrote: "Is there a doubt concerning the meaning of what I read? Does anything appear dark or intricate? I lift up my heart to the Father of lights:—'Lord, is it not thy word, "If any man lack wisdom, let him ask of God"? Thou "givest liberally and upbraidest not." Thou hast said, "If any be willing to do thy will, he shall know." I am willing to do, let me know, thy will.'"[130]

Whenever the statements of Scripture remain opaque, the first step of exposition is to request discernment and to trust the leading of the Spirit.[131] However, it is highly typical of Wesley's thought that this is not followed by the advice that one should wait for enlightenment as passively as possible. Instead, concrete steps of practical exposition are described. Prayer, spiritual leading, and diligent exegesis are thereby not excluded for Wesley. He writes: "I then search after and consider parallel passages of Scripture, 'comparing spiritual things with spiritual.' I meditate thereon with all the attention and earnestness of which my mind is capable. If any doubt still remains, I consult those who are experienced in the things of God, and then the writings whereby, being dead, they yet speak. And what I thus learn, that I teach."

Wesley is here summarizing the four principles of his hermeneutic concisely and with precision. They constantly reemerge in a variety of constellations in his sermons and exegetical discourses, and they are described in Methodist theology by the key words of *Scripture, Tradition, Reason,* and *Experience* as his hermeneutical "Quadrilateral."[132] Thus it is important to conceive clearly what is meant by these key words:

1. *The Bible* itself is the best aid to its own exposition.[133] The Scripture should be explained by the Scripture. That is to say, passages that are difficult to understand should be read in the light of those that can be understood, and this "according to the measure to faith";[134] that is, it should be done with regard to the clearly recognizable and underlying faith proclamation of the Bible.

2. The *exposition of the early church* is a further aid for understanding Scripture. For the church of the first three centuries, before the change that occurred with the conversion of the Emperor Constantine (which Wesley judged quite critically), was still quite close to the original understanding of the Bible and its witness should be paid attention to. Wesley can also place beside them later church fathers, the Reformers, and documents of the Church of England, from whom he draws support in his exposition of the Bible. But he uses these sources much more cautiously and never draws them together into a comprehensive witness of church tradition.[135]

It was the document from European Methodism entitled "The Principles of Doctrine and the Theological Mandate of The United Methodist Church" (1972) that first introduced the concept of *tradition,* in so doing including the entire development and unfolding of the Christian witness through the centuries, even where it presents not simply the exposition of the Bible but rather a new contemporary formulation of its message. What is kept hold of—and the reformulation of this document in 1988 has made this even more obvious—is that the witness of tradition can only possess an authority that is derived from the Scripture, or can have authority that points to Scripture.

3. Wesley perceives in the human capacity to think, namely human *reason,* a divine gift through which the Spirit of God assists the exposition of the Bible. What is meant by this is not reason that makes itself the judge over God's Word. Instead, what is meant is that human ability to relate statements to one another and to recognize relationships, and thus to understand the meaning of biblical sayings and make them understandable to other persons. Similarly, in response to the question of how biblical commands are to be fulfilled in our day, considerable importance is placed on there being a sensible consideration of the requirements of the situation at hand and of the possibilities of action.

4. Wesley often cites *experience* as an instrument of biblical exposition and does so in a twofold sense. On the one hand he asks whether particular interpretations can be confirmed through analogous experiences and is convinced that God gives such signs in order that we attain the right understanding. The certainty of justification by faith alone was so deeply rooted in him because alongside the witness of Scripture there was also the experience of persons who reported to him that they had experienced justifying grace. This is further confirmed by the testimony of his own "conversion" on the twenty-fourth of May, 1738, and then time and again as the fruit of his preaching in the lives of other persons. On the other

hand, when it's a matter of practically realizing biblical directives and getting a response to the question of "What does God want of me today?" Wesley values highly the role of experience as an aid in making proper decisions. The biblical injunction offers the basis for my actions. The rational factual reflection and evaluation of experience help with particular concrete goals.[136]

These four terms therefore do not describe unrelated sources of revelation that are simply juxtaposed to one another as being of equal importance. Rather, they portray the dynamic process of a life-giving exposition of the Bible in which the Holy Spirit operates through human instruments. The fact that these aspects have been named and consciously incorporated into the United Methodists' exposition of Scripture lends their exegesis a particular closeness to life and praxis. They also mark out a domain in which newer methods of biblical exposition are viewed critically but can also be accepted and integrated positively.

1.3.2 *The Steps to a Vital Development of Doctrine*

Even where the principles of interpretation are clarified, in the work of a missionary movement and church, questions remain that cannot be answered by an attentive study of Scripture alone but about which decisions must be made. Who is authorized to make these decisions within the United Methodist churches?

Since the year 1744, and thus only five years after the beginning of his evangelistic mission, Wesley gathered about him at annual conferences his most important co-laborers, to whom he posed the following questions:

1. What to teach;
2. How to teach; and
3. What to do; that is, how to regulate our doctrine, discipline, and practice?[137]

The concern was thus about the content of preaching, about its practical methodology, and about the habits of daily life of the movement: that the form and content of the preaching and the diaconal acts of the Society might agree with one another. For a movement which was so oriented toward evangelistic proclamation and which allegedly had little theological emphasis, it is remarkable that the question of "doctrine" is placed at the center of its thematic emphasis. The praxis of its mission is the subject of theological reflection, and this reflection in turn is entwined with the experience and challenge of the praxis of mission—namely in its evangelistic, diaconal, and community-building dimensions. Herein lies a basic principle of United Methodist pedagogy and theology.

The results of these deliberations in the conferences were recorded and published and formed the doctrinal basis of the movement to which one referred. From a historical standpoint, the importance of the "conciliar" element in this process should not be overestimated, for, of course, it is true that Wesley mostly provided the answers. But in the institution of the "annual conference," he fashioned an instrument for United Methodism that enabled the church, even after Wesley's death, to give a united response to the challenges posed by each respective period of history.[138] Even where Methodism gave itself an episcopal constitution, as for example in the United States, the conference remained the body in which the preachers (and later the laity as well) exercised their doctrinal authority in common. To this day the "conference" remains the chief organizational characteristic of Methodism.[139]

The living context ("Sitz im Leben") for early Methodist theology lay not in theological seminaries or faculties, whose founding came relatively late in Methodism, but in the annual conference of the "traveling preachers," who were expressing the mission of the church. It was at the annual conferences that the church constituted itself as a mission and formulated its theology in response to the necessities and challenges that emerged from the praxis of mission and in the controversy with its critics.[140] Theology that comes from praxis and that leads to praxis, and at the same time does not renounce the aspect of critical reflection, is designated by the phrase "practical divinity," which describes the essence of United Methodist doctrine.[141]

As the record of their history indicates, the annual conferences have certainly often not been equal to this task. They have perceived their task to be far more in the sphere of decision making with regard to organizational questions, and they have left the theological work to the academy. Late toward the close of the nineteenth century, Methodist theology in the Anglo-Saxon sphere became aligned with the academic concerns of the prevailing Protestant theology. There were particular theologians who made contributions in the realm of scholarship as well as working significantly within the context of their own church. But in so doing, their theology often noticeably lost any distinctively Methodist aspect. As a result, even in those places where Methodism is a major ecclesial presence, its theological voice is rarely heard.[142] Hence, it is not surprising that after church union in 1968, the attempt was undertaken to address this task anew, with the establishing of a commission to probe the question of "the basis for doctrine and the theological task" for the united church. If the document that was formulated by the General Conference of 1972 in response to this question still strongly emphasized theological pluralism, which was to prevail within the context that was marked by such programmatic terms as *quadrilateral* and *landmark documents*, then the revised version of 1988 placed greater emphasis upon the normative character of those documents for the life of the church.[143] However, the intent of United Methodist doctrine will certainly not be realized merely by identifying and setting aside correct formulations of belief; rather, it will happen only when those responsible through mutual deliberation think through church praxis theologically, and only if out of these deliberations grows a theology for a missionary praxis.

1.3.3 *The Landmark Documents*

Wesley repeatedly emphasized that it does not make sense to dispute over the interpretation of doctrine. Essential agreement in the existential, basic convictions of Christians is what is important ("Is your heart as my heart is?"—that is the decisive question after sermon thirty-nine on the "Catholic Spirit."). To that end, the ecumenical motto is formulated as to "think and let think."[144] The ecumenical breadth of the Wesleys emerges from this conviction, a breadth that even includes Roman Catholic Christians, even if he regards the doctrinal position of the church as problematic. Wesley speaks only occasionally about the decisive doctrinal convictions—which he prefers to call "essentials" rather than "fundamentals." In a letter to the clergy of the Church of England in which he is trying to promote living peaceably with one another, he names three essentials: one, the sinful condition of humanity from the beginning; two, justification by faith; three, holiness of heart and life.[145]

All of this does not mean that Wesley was not seeking to urge his preachers and societies toward clarity and unity in doctrine. Just as he would find himself being of one heart with a George Whitefield, despite their difference with regard to the doctrine of predestination, in like manner his own people were to proclaim God's free grace to everyone, for he believes only this could be recognized as being biblical and meaningful. Hence, in the course of his life he published a great number of doctrinal sermons, which were intended to provide basic guidance to the preachers and the societies.[146] As early as 1784 in a "Model Deed" that was intended to regulate the use of the Methodist meeting houses, he determined that the administrators of these rooms (laity!) should only permit such persons to preach who were in agreement with the doctrine contained in his published sermons and his *Explanatory Notes on the New Testament*.[147] Wesley considered his teachings neither as being the only way to holiness nor as infallible. But he saw in it the gift that God had entrusted to the people called Methodists and that he had blessed and confirmed through the great Revival. To be faithful to these teachings was an ongoing task.

When the Methodist movement was constituted as an autonomous church body at the Baltimore Christmas Conference of 1784, Wesley gave to it a concise summation of Christian doctrinal statements, in the form of the twenty-five Articles of Religion.[148] These articles contain no specific Methodist doctrinal content. Rather, they present a shortened version of the Thirty-nine Articles of the Church of England, which in turn had inherited these tenets from the Protestant Reformation.[149] The Evangelical Association also accepted these doctrines[150] in its German translation of the Methodist articles with minimal changes, but has subsequently repeatedly reformulated them over the course of the years (most recently in 1962), whereas the Episcopal Methodist Church decided as early as 1808 that the General Conference could not change an Article of Faith nor decide to adopt any new doctrine that contradicts the present ones.[151]

The most distinctive feature of the Evangelical Association articles was an extended doctrinal essay on "Entire Sanctification and Christian Perfection," which was appended to the nineteen Evangelical Articles of Faith (1809), and which expresses an essentially Wesleyan understanding of holiness within a conceptual framework that reflects the motifs of German Pietism. This Anglo-Wesleyan doctrinal heritage is counterbalanced by characteristic themes from German Reformed Pietism and Anabaptism in the Confession of Faith of the United Brethren in Christ (1815). The text of this document has been traced back to an earlier credo prepared by Philip William Otterbein for use in his Baltimore (Md.) Reformed parish in 1789. In 1962, these two doctrinal streams were consolidated in the church union that brought into existence The Evangelical United Brethren Church, resulting in the Confession of Faith that remains in the *Discipline* (1996) alongside the Methodist Articles of Religion. It contains articles, such as those on regeneration and Christian perfection, that are not found in the twenty-five Articles of Religion.

In actual practice, both Methodism and the EUB Church manifested numerous shifts in the theological orientation of their principal spokespersons in the course of the two centuries after their founding.[152]

This describes the normative character of present-day United Methodism, which has three signposts to guide and undergird its preaching and action:

1. A standard for preaching is contained in the 53 "Standard Sermons."

2. A standard for exposition is found in the *Explanatory Notes on the New Testament.*

3. A standard for unity with fraternal church bodies that share the heritage of the Protestant Reformation is found in the Articles of Religion and in the confession of faith.[153]

These documents do not have the same function as do the confessional documents of those churches that emanate from the Reformation of the sixteenth century, in that the United Methodist documents have never served as a test of dogma whereby Methodists would be separated from other church bodies.[154] Furthermore, they do not serve as confessional statements to which United Methodist ministers become bound on the occasion of their ordination. Their significance lies far more in the fact that they indicate and show a direction—they designate the direction which leads from the Bible as the witness of the revelation of God's love to its proclamation and embodiment through responsible Christian action in our day.[155]

This outlook also applies to the "General Rules," which Wesley gave to his societies in 1743 and which have been included in the *Methodist Book of Discipline* since 1784.[156] They are primarily to be regarded as ethical signposts to guide members of United Methodist societies. They offer an example for a sturdy and straightforward pedagogy of faith for use by congregations, and they indicate what is for United Methodists the close relationship between the witness to faith and the moral dimension of daily living. Since 1908 this connection has been taken up by the development of the Social Principles.[157]

These foundational theological documents did not have as their goal nor were they promulgated for the purpose of forcing The United Methodist Church into "a bare doctrinal system or of binding responsible intellectual freedom." It was much more a matter of "creating a broad and flexible foundation for doctrine, that was supposed to define the boundaries for the handling of controversial questions within the society of believers. These norms for doctrine have provided United Methodists with a certain protection from doctrinal extremism, and they have also assigned a new role to the laity of deciding on doctrinal standards. This method of orienting all members in questions of doctrine was unique in all Christendom. It bound Methodists to biblical revelation as foundational, without giving them a word for word summary of this revelation. It anchored United Methodist theology in a firm core, but also gave the church freedom of movement in the face of unfolding history."[158]

Other writings with much broader and thorough influence have appeared in the subsequent history of United Methodism, especially the catechisms of Wilhelm Nast and Theophil Spörri for German Methodists, and that of J. J. Esther for the Evangelical Association, [159] as well as the catechisms of the Evangelical United Brethren Church. Although contemporary United Methodists may regard these resources as being overly didactic, they enabled easily remembered formulations of basic Christian issues and concepts to be made available to several generations of United Methodist Christians, for whom the Christian faith cane to have meanings not only in a cognitive but also in an existential sense.

Even if this "Theology of The United Methodist Church" cannot proceed in the same way as its predecessors, it still has set itself the goal of providing information in understandable form about the essentials of our faith and our doctrine, and thus enabling persons in The United Methodist Church and beyond it to be better able to render an account of their faith.

1.3.4 *The Basic Contours of a United Methodist Theology*

We will now summarize our reflections on a theology of The United Methodist Church and attempt to highlight the basic contours that will determine how it will be presented in the following chapters.

The "Doctrinal Standards" of 1988 were formulated as follows: "United Methodists share a common heritage with Christians of every age and nation. This heritage is grounded in the apostolic witness to Jesus Christ as Savior and Lord, which is the source and measure of all valid Christian teaching."[160] When we speak in the following pages of a "United Methodist theology," we do not mean so much a compilation of statements that distinguish us from other Christian churches. Instead, we are describing common Christian doctrine from our perspective. The United Methodist Church is not a church that stands over against some ecclesial adversary. Yet that does not preclude that sometimes—directly or indirectly—it is important to state our beliefs over against particular viewpoints that we view as being inconsistent with the gospel in its basic form. However, we do not judge the persons who represent those views. Each of us stands under the judgment of God, and our theology can also fall into error and require forgiveness, because it is a human theology that has a limited capability of perceiving and judging, and because our language is insufficient to be able to articulate fully that which so far exceeds our understanding. The one who wants to speak about God and our world in its relation to God must therefore remain aware that we always accomplish this only inadequately. With this reservation, we are attempting to describe those theological convictions that are appropriate for our church in North America as well as in Europe.[161] This requires our reliance upon the leading of the Holy Spirit, and it is to be expressed as simply as possible and by necessarily concentrating upon that which is most essential for faith.

Our Outline of United Methodist Church Theology is at the same time a text of our time. On the one hand, it stands within the long tradition of the unfolding biblical message and is inconceivable apart from it. However, it intends to exhibit this message in a way that corresponds to the context of our present-day experiences and perceptions. The multiplicity of these voices, in which the richness of the gospel resounds, finds its consonance in the development of the basic melody, which intones God's voice for us. Thus, tensions and disharmonies are probably unavoidable, and they should not be ignored because they compel us to be silent and to heed anew the voice of the Good Shepherd before we once again raise our own voices. Thus, what we hold in common as well as what is given special emphasis in our tradition will come to expression.

From its beginning, the Methodist movement has highly esteemed in its teaching and preaching those beliefs that we hold in common with Christians from other churches. One of the most impressive examples of this is the "Christian Library," a series of books published by John Wesley, which in fifty volumes made accessible to a wide readership many important texts of Christian authors of different churches and centuries, in abbreviated form. Wesley's intention was to bring about the harmony of a polyphonic choir of witnesses. The books were meant to serve to bring together a variety of styles of piety. Schmidt notes that Wesley's concern was for the unity of the church, meaning unity that was inward and personal faith that was the unspoken intent, and that "he appropriated to himself from every part of the Christian tradition what he considered to be good, adapting it to the purposes of the Methodist movement by abridgement, revision, and clarification."[162] In the document called "Doctrinal Standards," what Christians may hold in common is described in the following way:

> **We hold in common with all Christians a faith in the mystery of salvation in and through Jesus Christ.** At the heart of the gospel of salvation is God's incarnation in Jesus of Nazareth. Scripture witnesses to the redeeming love of God in Jesus' life and teachings, his atoning death, his resurrection, his sovereign presence in history, his triumph over the powers of evil and death, and his promised return. Because God truly loves us in spite of our willful sin, God judges us, summons us to repentance, pardons us, receives us by that grace given to us in Jesus Christ, and gives us hope of life eternal.[163]

Special emphases of our theology, like those which can be traced back directly to John Wesley and to the Pietist heritage that underlay the Evangelical United Brethren Confession, are the emphases on God's grace in its operation as prevenient, justifying, and sanctifying grace; justification and regeneration; the assurance of faith that operates through divine love; holiness as the renewal of the image of God; and growth in love and in the duties of mission and service to all humanity.[164]

These emphases of faith also provide United Methodist theology with a structure:

1. The biblical message of creation and redemption is borne by the universal love of God. The fact that God has created the world and humanity is the expression and action of God's gift and love. Humanity had disrupted its original fellowship with God through sin. Yet, God's intention to have fellowship with humanity has not been broken by that sin. God's love in Jesus Christ has overcome the power of sin and reconciled humanity.

God's unconditional gift is applicable to God's entire creation. God's salvation is offered to all humanity, and in Christ the entire world has become reconciled to God.

This universal aspect of the biblical message is presented in the following chapter, entitled "Universal Salvation, or God's Love for His World."

2. But this world-embracing action of God is valid at the same time for every individual human being. It does not depersonalize them; they are not being infused with God's salvation. Instead, it opens up a new reality.

It sets a person free to make his or her own response. It wants to be grasped and accepted by a person trusting in God's love. This occurs through faith, and thus faith is not a human achievement but the acceptance of the gift and the activity of God that is for our well-being and at the same time the unwavering confidence that God confers. In faith, persons experience that God accepts and justifies their lives; in faith it happens that God shapes and makes holy their lives; and in faith they hope that God is leading their lives toward fulfillment and fills their lives with perfect love. Holiness and happiness in the fellowship that is bestowed through Christ are marks of the new life with God and signs of living grace.

This theme is addressed in the third chapter; "Personal Faith, or the Personal Experience of Salvation."

3. If love is the sign and content of the being of the Christian, then there emerges from that love fellowship and responsibility: fellowship with persons who have been grasped and filled by the same love, and responsibility for one's neighbors, who need the message of the gospel and practical assistance, as well as responsibility for a society that calls itself Christian but has not even come close to obeying the will of God. Finally, there is also responsibility for the world, which remains God's beloved creation, even in those places where sin and suffering deform it. Christians' actions in these areas of responsibility are done in the knowledge that God is leading not only individual Christians but also the entire world to the goal that God has appointed for it.

This latter issue will be the subject of the last chapter of our work: "Christian Existence in Its Wholeness, or the Reality of Love."

In so doing, it is extremely important to take note of the indissoluble connection of the statements in the last two chapters. Being Christian, to which the gospel invites us, is not an existence that is limited to the private sphere of the individual. Rather, it joins what is deeply personal and inward with what is corporate and global. This connection, which is indissoluble in Christian faith, is a primary concern of any United Methodist theology. "Solitary religion is not to be found" in the gospel of Christ, asserted Wesley. "The gospel of Christ knows of no religion, but social; no holiness but social holiness. 'Faith working by love' is the length and breadth and depth and height of Christian perfection."[165] Entirely personal and yet social, entirely focused on those who believe and yet ready to serve others, rooted in the innermost region of the heart and yet with an eye on the breadth of any creation—this fruitful tension provides the internal impetus for the mission impulse of Methodism, which from its inception has sought to extend God's invitation to salvation through preaching and pastoral care, through diaconal and social praxis, and through the gathering and sending of believers into the world.

Thus, these three emphases of the Methodist proclamation of faith determine the organization and content of this theology of The United Methodist Church.

To be sure, there are areas of Christian doctrine, like the doctrine of God or Christology, that do not experience any significantly new content in the Methodist proclamation, but where the development of the biblical affirmations that occurred in the apostolic era is essentially taken over. They are included at the appropriate places within the plan of this work, in order to make clear that they are essential components of doctrine. However, it will become clear that even these vital doctrinal themes are not unrelated to the basic stream of the United Methodist theology of grace.

2. Universal Salvation, or God's Love for God's World

[God] desires everyone to be saved and to come to the knowledge of the truth.

—1 Timothy 2:4

From his fullness we have all received, grace upon grace" (John 1:16). "If God vouchsafe still to pour fresh blessings upon us, yea, the greatest of all blessings, salvation; what can we say to these things, but, 'Thanks be unto God for his unspeakable gift!' And thus it is. Herein 'God commendeth his love toward us, in that, while we were yet sinners, Christ died' to save us." Wesley begins his collection of doctrinal sermons with the programmatic sermon on "Salvation by Faith," from which these sentences are quoted.[1] "God's presence in the world is grace; grace is what God is and always is: love acting."[2] Wesley's understanding of salvation unites the complete dependence of humanity upon God's grace with their responsibility to respond to God's Word as persons who have been addressed by God.

God's *prevenient* grace "prompts our first wish to please God, our first glimmer of understanding concerning God's will," and it "also awakens in us an earnest longing for deliverance from sin and death and moves us toward repentance and faith." With his *justifying grace* "God reaches out to the repentant believer . . . with accepting and pardoning love." God's *sanctifying grace* "continues to nurture our growth . . . in the knowledge and love of God and in love for our neighbor." God's grace alone "calls forth human response and discipline."[3]

The following sections seek to describe these all-embracing actions of God's grace. How God demonstrates Godself as the lover in the creation and protection of the creation, and in the reconciliation and renewal of humanity and the world, is the central subject of United Methodist theology and the foundation for the experience of salvation of individual human beings. The experience of this love of God also establishes the basis for all acts of love on the part of those who allow themselves to be gifted by that grace.

2.1   God's Loving Care in God's Creative Activity

The Sermon on the Mount expresses in its unsurpassable way what is to be discussed in this chapter. In the context of the appeal not to be concerned about either eating or drinking, or about life or apparel, Jesus said, "Look at the birds of the air; they neither sow nor reap nor gather into barns, and yet your heavenly Father feeds them. Are you not of more value than they?" and "Consider the lilies of the field, how they grow; they neither toil nor spin, yet I tell you, even Solomon in all his glory was not clothed like one of these. . . . Therefore do not worry, saying, 'What will we eat?' or 'What will we drink?' or 'What will we wear?' . . . your heavenly Father knows that you need all these things" (Matthew 6:26-32).

What appears to be the portrayal of an idyll is at heart nothing other than the proclamation of the love of God, from which the world had its origin as the living arena of God's creatures. More precisely, God's "Let there be!" is to be understood as a loving act with which God created an object for God's love. The Creator, together with Christ (John 1:3, Colossians 1:16) and the divine Spirit (Genesis 1:2)—the triune God—creates a world which God intends to draw into the movement of his divine love. The world is not God, but of God, and God is in God's world. Thus, much as they might arise from a longing for God, the veneration of old or new deities conceals the reality of the one God more than pointing to God; for everything which is belongs to the one God, who—in Old Testament language—has created "heaven and earth," in short, the entire universe. "The earth is the LORD's, and all that is in it, the world, and those who live in it" (Psalm 24:1). God's creatures do not have their worth through the purposes that they either do or do not fulfill for us; dignity accrues to them simply as God's creation.[4]

The confession of God as Creator was not present at the beginning of faith in the God of Israel. Prior to this was the experience of the release of the people from slavery and oppression and their being given a new place to live. This God, who kept his covenant with Noah, with Abraham, and with Moses, the God of love and faithfulness, was also the Creator of the world in which we live, its sustainer. The people of the new covenant, Christianity, have also adopted this confession, and they have found within it an important element of their common faith. "Christians of all denominations confess the triune God as the Creator, Sustainer, and Redeemer of the world. . . . We Christians believe that the entire creation continues to be upheld by the love of God, which is revealed in Jesus Christ."[5]

Although this theme of theology is not a matter of contention among the churches, there are nevertheless reasons not to treat it too briefly: the renewed discussion about belief in creation and natural science (2.1.1); the question of humanity and our place "between" God and the rest of creation (2.1.2); as well as the task of protecting the created order given its worldwide destruction by humanity (2.1.3).

2.1.1 *God's Loving Care in the Creation of the World*

A theology of creation[6] cannot be developed without taking into account the results of natural science. Likewise it cannot be adequately formulated without taking into consideration the results of biblical exegesis, which mediates the witness of creation faith in the intellectual context of our times and at the same time seeks to free our understanding from errors of interpretation. In reflecting upon the creation of the world, we will therefore need to bring both of these aspects together in order to be fair to both the claims of faith and scientific knowledge of the reality in which we live. In so doing, we seek to avoid errors that have been made in times past, both from the ecclesial side and also from the side of an ideological theory of evolution. The error that occurred in the thinking of the church was to raise to a declaration of faith those explanations of the creation of the universe that came from the era of the biblical authors, which continued to be regarded as true even when clear, scientific knowledge led to changes in the theory of natural history. The error of some explanations of world history that came from natural science lay above all in their conceptualization as worldviews in which not only the question of God was methodically bracketed but the very existence of God was denied.[7] The most serious derailment of this outlook was proposed by National Socialism and its theory that might is right. Subsequently, the struggle for existence was understood to be an ethical principle, which permitted not only the conquest of foreign lands but also the extermination of the Jews. In what follows, we do not want to discuss further the different concepts of the origin of the world, rather we want to acknowledge them insofar as they have established themselves, and inquire about their validity.

In the Old Testament, from which we take the most important texts concerning creation, "diversity is the hallmark of discourse about the Creator and the creation; the event of the creation is not set down in final form; in fact, it cannot be nailed down in this way. Rather each age can describe it in whatever way it can grasp. Therefore, there is not one account of creation in the Old Testament, but many."[8] The two most important accounts of creation in Genesis 1 and 2 have a history of oral tradition behind them and parallels outside the Bible. The subjects of prehistory reported in Genesis 1–11 do not first appear in the high culture of the Mediterranean area, but are also present in still older traditions that reach back to primitive cultures—for example, the formation of humans from earth and their animation through breath, the flood, the first fall, the fratricidal murder, or the construction of a tower. The biblical accounts of creation thus stand in a much wider cultural and historical context; it might therefore be more correctly said "that in the stories of the primeval time, something that was common to humanity as a whole was exhibited . . . an understanding of the world and humanity . . . whose chief features were held in common among the race, the peoples, and the human groups upon the entire earth during an early epoch."[9] One may certainly respond with skepticism or disagreement to this latter statement of Westermann's.[10] Yet what is clear and important is what the creation texts of the Old Testament are about.[11] They are concerned to offer a description of the world created by God, which remains in the hand of its Creator and is at the same time entrusted to humans for its preservation and formation.

The New Testament, above all the preaching of Jesus, but also the letters of Paul, presuppose the Old Testament belief in creation, even though they give greater weight to the reality of sin and eschatological anticipation. Joy in creation and hope for its renewal in the resurrection are the foundational elements. The redemptive activity of God in Christ is applicable to all living creatures. As children of God, Christians are certainly not from but in the world, and as children of their Father in heaven they are concerned about the well-being of everything that is created.[12]

What is the relationship between such statements in the holy Scripture and discoveries of modern natural science? In his explanation of the first article of faith, Martin Luther wrote, "I should believe that I am God's creature, that he has given to me body, soul, good eyes, reason, a good wife, children, fields, meadows, pigs, and cows."[13] This confession is not false because I know how a person comes to be and how I myself came to be. Rather, it is describing the same process (the coming into being of a person) from a different perspective, which takes into account more and different things than simply the scientific without this thereby becoming false.

By noting that the methods of natural science could neither recognize nor assert anything at all about God's existence, the conclusion ought not to be drawn either that God does not exist or that God's existence can be questioned from the standpoint of natural science. The "methodological atheism" of the natural sciences—meaning the attempt to explain the world, including its manifestations and relationships, without the "God factor," did not begin with Darwin. The discoveries of Copernicus (1473–1543), Galileo (1564–1642) and Bruno (1548–1600)[14] had already changed the age-old picture of the world without consideration of theological teachings. In the succeeding centuries, explanation of the movement of the planets and the processes of nature increasingly neglected to appeal to the acts of God. Nowadays we draw on these insights that were partly corrected and developed, as a matter of course. At the same time, something quite different and consequential occurred in relation to these discoveries and their gradual acceptance into human consciousness. Friedrich Nietzsche (1844–1900), the often maligned fanatic of candor, expressed this occurrence as follows: "Since Copernicus, human being has rolled out of the center and into nothingness." Those are the "nihilistic consequences of present-day natural science."[15] The sense of stability and meaning were lost, nihilism appeared to be unavoidable, as human beings, under the influence of the theory of evolution, seemed to have lost their special place in relation to all other life forms and had simply become the final link in a long chain of evolution. While people were still reeling from the offense that was occasioned by Copernicus, there appeared the even more far-reaching offense resulting from Darwin's theory of biological descent.[16]

The result of these far-reaching shifts in worldview was a struggle between the different positions that became increasingly intense. Times of change led to uncertainty; uncertainty engendered aggressive reactions. Some held firmly to that which had been handed down ("The Bible is still right"), while others laid aside the biblical accounts of creation as fairy tales. An altercation erupted, under the watchword that humanity descended from the apes (or, did not descend), in which there was less interest in attaining any real insight and more concern for victory over one's adversaries. Between the fronts stood Christians who held firmly to the belief in creation but did not want to simply dismiss the results of scientific research. They were often ridiculed by non-Christians and were suspected of disbelief by fellow Christians. New understandings of reality were gradually attained that would facilitate a self-critical reflection upon the position to which they had been committed. The natural scientists became critical of the results of their science. It became clear to them that not only did many questions remain unanswered but rather that each answer was giving rise to new questions. Often it was the most important ones that could not be answered by natural science. Christians learned to read the accounts of creation in a new way, not as scientific reports about how the world began but as confessions of faith in the God who has created this world and through whose creative will continues to exist. We must protest any recent attempts to reassert that the Christian faith in God the Creator and the findings of natural science fundamentally cannot be reconciled. The alternative of "science or faith" can neither be reconciled with good natural science nor with good theology.

To be sure, there are natural scientists for whom the accounts of creation mean nothing. It is secondary whether or not their position is grounded upon their scientific insights, for there are many reasons for unfaith or skepticism. Carl Friedrich von Weizsäcker has clearly stated the problem inherent in seeking a unified view of religion and science: "Present day natural scientists can at best merely set forth their private opinions, quite supplemental to their professional work, which reflect their own thinking under the rubric of the religious meaning of the law of nature, and it does not reflect any logical connection with the idea of natural law itself. No amount of good will and no religious zeal can render this development null and void."[17] In order to believe in the Creator, an approach to truth other than the scientific approach is needed. Such an approach is not the result of scientific research. The biologist and Christian Joachim Illies confirms that the theory of evolution itself can "no longer be excluded from modern biology," for it has "stood the test a thousandfold."[18] Natural sciences and Christian theology have to withstand each other as partners in dialogue.

What is the inherent danger of poor natural science? Darwin explained the evolution of plants and animals with the factors of mutation and selection. Later "Darwinists" (E. Haeckel, J. Huxley, J. Monod) asserted that chance was the final reason for evolution. However, what does that mean except that our natural science is not in a position to give a scientific explanation? "Chance" is no explanation. If it is to be given the status of a causal principle, it is no longer a scientific assertion but a personal confession of nihilism. We can agree with Dietrich von Oppen that "the rise of planet earth with its surface conditions occurred against every statistical probability; the same can be said about the beginning of life and about the fact that humanity, with all its defects, has survived to the present day."[19]

On the other hand, theology would make its task too simple if it sought to prohibit or to "refute" scientific insights by recourse to biblical citations simply because those insights no longer correspond to the worldview that they have inherited. This opposition that holds that either the Bible or modern science is correct misses the mark. This can be demonstrated once again by the example of the creation of humanity. The theory of genetics and biochemistry, as well as the fields of medicine and human biology, have brought together much information on the origin of the human race. However, what am I as a human being? Am I the product of the biological development of a genetic program that is biologically specific and that may be seen as being determined by the joining of a twofold series of genealogical data—or am I the creation of God—or both?

A similar question can also be raised in relation to the origin of the species of humanity: is humankind a new step of development with an altered genetic makeup and improved accommodation to the environment—or is humankind a new creation of God made in God's image? The alternative that either the Bible with its perspective or natural science if right does not fit the actual circumstances concerning the matter. In this regard, we may once again cite Joachim Illies: "The fact that all life on earth evolved to increasingly higher forms of life over long periods of time, developing from simple to multiple cell organisms, from amoebas to worms, and from them vertebrates—fish, reptiles, mammals and finally human beings—this is a scientific description of the 'how' question of the history of living things, out of which the question of 'why?' emerges with a sense of urgency." Illies finally comes to a conclusion that is perhaps now no longer surprising: "The path to faith in a Creator is therefore smoothed, rather than barricaded, by the modern insights of evolution." Even if Illies doesn't find only agreement and not all others want to go as far as he does in embracing the insights of natural science, it must at least be said that the insights of natural science hinder no one from being Christian, and that faith in God the Creator does not restrict our freedom to explore the wonder of God's creation but in fact comes with an increased responsibility for the preservation of creation. What the Christian and the natural scientist are doing in this regard is precisely what the authors of the biblical accounts of creation were doing: they have combined their faith in God the Creator with the knowledge and descriptions of their age concerning the formation of the world.[20]

The creation accounts are not the oldest texts in the Bible, even though they come at its beginning. Israel first encountered God as the One who led them out of the land of slavery into the promised land, where God blessed them as God's people. Their confession of the Creator first arose within the promised land. An unnamed author composed the older text that is found in the second chapter of the book of Genesis (Genesis 2:4*b*-25). He probably lived at the time of Solomon and describes how God formed the first persons from the earth and breathed life into them. He describes how God let the man fall into a deep sleep so that a rib could be taken from him and the woman could be formed from it. He also recounts how God planted and watered a garden for the first man, and entrusted its preservation and cultivation to him. We not only find in the old accounts that man was formed from a clump of earth and was brought to life by the breath of God; these older accounts also include numerous observations: a human being disintegrates into earth after death, his lower ribs are shorter, and man and woman are more closely bound to one another than are other persons, even than those who are blood relatives. And all of this was created by God, we owe our lives to God, and God has entrusted to us the created space so that we might use, enjoy, and protect God's gift. Whenever we do not use this freedom in a responsible manner, it is to our shame: God's good gifts can be misused, but in our so doing the Creator is disregarded, humanity has failed, and freedom is lost. These declarations about the second creation account are valid to the present day, and no natural science can shake them.

Something different and yet essentially similar is narrated in the first and later creation account. God no longer is described as creating with God's hands like a sculptor at work, or like a gardener or a surgeon. God creates through God's word: God speaks, and it happens. God's creative work is unconditional; God alone has life in himself (John 5:26) and calls that which is not into existence (Romans 4:17).[21] The text is artfully composed (Genesis 1:1-2, 4*a*), and many insights from the science of that time are inserted—insights that are even confirmed by present-day natural science. However, what we have here is not in essence a description of how the world began but an account of the relationship of the world to God and of the relationship of God to humanity. The world is deprived of divinity (the heavenly bodies are now lamps). There is only One who is God and there is no God beside him (compare the first commandment). The entire world belongs to God, and no one can flee from God's presence (Psalm 139). Humans are created in God's own image (Genesis 1:27). Worth and work, freedom and responsibility are given to them.

What we now have to do is summarize the essentials of the various biblical creation texts—what they say about our relationship to God and God's relationship to us and to this world. It's a matter of linking this witness with the insights that are available to us in the present day and not constructing false alternatives out of anxiety, uncertainty, or unwillingness to be taught. Of course, we also need to be critical of science and to take care that it does not overstep its bounds—and this not only in the interests of faith, but also in the interest of the sciences. Science too must and should remain critical of its findings. For example, the theory of relativity and the quantum theory have either corrected or have demonstrated as erroneous many of the tenets of classical physics. As a result, less is spoken today of the alleged objectivity of science. Much more attention is given to the role of the observer and his or her perspective as being integral parts of the theories concerning the origin and the law of the universe. The theory of natural science is "one that is attained through reason and experience, rather than through limited and preliminary assertions about a phenomenon of nature."[22] The modern scientific disciplines cannot uncover those great secrets that lie on the other side of human cognitive capabilities and that therefore may be the final cause and meaning of the world. The Australian astrophysicist Robert Hanwury-Brown has spoken to this point as follows: "The secret of the creation is untouched; even brought forward almost 20 billion years, yet it remains—as ever—as it was at the beginning. Science can assert nothing at all about the meaning of the world."[23] The scientific mode of observing the world is therefore only one perspective from which we may observe reality, and by no means the only one. Thus, it is important to take other perspectives seriously and to recognize that each of them can only lay hold of one limited aspect of reality. The whole of reality is more than what the insights of either natural science or theology can show us. The Christian doctrine of creation does not disavow the value of the insights of natural science. Rather, it understands all natural occurrences "as being grounded in and defined by the creative acts of God."[24]

The biblical witness of creation shows us the One who is transcendent in the midst of this world and who gives it being and life as its Creator. For this reason it involves good sense that there is a witness to this Creator at the beginning of the Bible, a Creator who seeks fellowship with human beings and with the creation that he has called into being. In our encounter with the creation we recognize the Creator. We must give credit to the natural sciences when we say that God is not to be found among the causes of this world, not even as the first cause. Understood this way, the concept of God would not only be viewed as obsolete and speculative; it would also be superfluous. God is much more the One from whom everything that has being is derived, who is therefore superior to all, who is to be distinguished from all and yet is bound with all in being through love. Everything that is has being only thanks to the power of the creative will of God.

In order to make this clear, the natural scientist and philosopher Charles Birch has reflected in a conference on "Faith, Science and the Future" upon what kind of response God would make to a modern interrogator in the manner of Job 38–42. And he has formulated the following as a possible answer:

"Who is it who observes the plans of the world with His mechanistic models of the universe, that that there is no longer any room for soul, conscience, and purposiveness? Gird up your loins like a hero, for now I am the one asking, and you give the answer. Where were you during that original big bang? How could you come forth in a universe out of pure hydrogen? . . . How can that which is spirit arise from that which is not spirit? How can life emerge from that which is not life? . . . And if you analyzed life down to its molecular DNA-building stones, why then do you believe that you have hit upon the secret of life, although you have not yet discovered the source of love and of all sensitivity? And why then do you want to make out of me either an all-powerful engineer or a powerless nothing, although I am neither?" In response to all of this, we can only answer as did Job: "I spoke without insight, for the ways of God were too wondrous for me, and I lacked knowledge. Before I knew about You only from rumors, but now I have seen You with my eyes. And so I despise myself and repent with sackcloth and ashes."[25]

The belief in creation provides an answer to the questions that remain unanswered for natural science: the questions concerning the whence, the whereto and the why of the world, of humanity, and of my own life. No matter how well we are able to investigate it, a glance at this toy box world with all its building blocks still does not manifest the meaning nor grant the freedom that we need. Chance is blind. From this perspective, the world is not embedded in a larger framework of meaning; thus, humans must themselves confer such meaning upon the world, and this becomes the measure and purpose of all things. And yet, it is also correct that humans are not lords in their own house, and their conduct is not guided merely by reason and proper goals. For here the reality of sin comes into the picture. Screening it out would signify ignoring reality. Freedom and the deeper meaning of life cannot be discovered if we as humans distance ourselves from our Creator and live in alienation from him. The created order, which was declared to be good, is the sphere within which we live, in which there is good and evil, success and failure, happiness and despair, life and death. Even Christians are sinners, beset by doubt and fear, but they know that God has turned toward us, and we are permitted to question this God, and God responds to us.[26]

2.1.2 *God's Loving Care in the Creation of God's Image*

To speak of humans as being the image of God is a concept that is foundational in Christian theology. It has become largely alien to contemporary people. Can any meaningful use still be made of this concept, and is God's gift that is expressed by it made clear in any enlightening way by this concept? In order to probe these questions, we now intend to give consideration to aspects of contemporary reflection on humanity and on our knowledge of human nature.

2.1.2.1 THE HUMAN BEING AS QUESTION

Never has humanity known so much about itself as in the present day. The scientific investigations of humanity in this century have not only revealed numerous aspects, the psychic, physical, and social horizons of human existence; they have also uncovered previously unsuspected, unknown dimensions of existence (such as, for example, the "unconscious" or the "super ego"), with the intent of undertaking research in this realm and advancing it mightily. At the same time, such incomprehensible things have happened through humanity in our century as previous ages never encountered. We need only recall the extermination of millions of Jews in concentration camps like Auschwitz, the destruction of incalculable numbers of human, animal, and plant life-forms through the atomic bombs that were dropped on Hiroshima and Nagasaki, or the death of hundreds of thousands in third-world countries.

People have attained achievements that surely would have appeared impossible at the time of our grandparents (such as the flight to the moon or the discovery of the genetic structure of all living things). At the same time, people have also brought about the circumstances that are endangering the basis for all life on this earth, and have set out on a path at

whose end lies, perhaps unavoidably, the destruction of this very environment. At least in our modern industrial societies, humans have "emanci-
pated" themselves completely from faith in God and from a life lived in
accordance to God's will, instead putting themselves in the place of the
One who measures and tests and decides everything. At the same time,
this brings to light the fact that they have destructively overextended
themselves and are now seeking ways out of the consequences of their
overestimation of themselves.

This questioning did not begin with the realization of the destructive
consequences of human actions; rather it is part of human nature itself, as
far back as there are accounts. This question about one's self is what distinguishes humans from other finite living beings: we make ourselves
conscious of who we are. We don't take our existence fragmentally. In
encountering other persons—either directly as contemporaries or indirectly through history, literature, and art—we see ourselves as the same or
as similar or as different when we compare appearance and behavior. By
their difference, others place us in question, and we try to discover who
we really are, what we are doing, and what we want. This process of
inquiry comes to completion in the sciences of human nature in accordance with methodical, systematic points of view. From ancient days to
the present, philosophy has inquired into the nature of human existence as
such, into its nature and its relation to other forms of being.

As humans, we are therefore the source and plumb line of all statements
about humanity. Whatever is true of all must also be true for us. The converse of this statement is not valid to the same extent; out of the knowledge of individuals we cannot draw conclusions about the totality of life,
reasoning from a knowledge of ourselves to that of human existence in
general, or from our singular experiences to experiences as such. Any particular knowledge is to be tested on its capability of being universalized.
This is also true of our experiences with God. What is true for all must
also be true for us. Negatively formulated, this means that whatever we
recognize as untrue for ourselves cannot be true for all. Vice versa: What
we recognize to be true for ourselves must be referable to that which is
human, without saying that it is actually true for humanity as such. It
might be an individual experience or an individual observation that is true
only for one, or for some, or possibly for the majority of persons. For
example, a person who has always lived among white persons will look
upon a light complexion as a sign of human existence in general, until that
person meets other examples of humanity who are of other colors. A per-

son who has heard no other language except that of his or her mother tongue will universalize that language for humanity in general and will be surprised when another language is heard.

This self-reflection can be understood as an attempt to provide an answer to the question "Who am I?" as an attempt to decode the enigma of human existence. Theophil Spörri (1887–1955) began his *Christian Doctrine of Faith* with a discussion of "Human Existence and Its Enigma." The meaning of our existence is not self-evident. The events of the world as a whole allow the question to remain open as to whether our existence has meaning and purpose or not. Our world of experience is a "world of paradox," in which humans appear as "the enigma of all enigmas." "The contradiction does not merely lie in the destiny of human beings but also in human existence itself, in the disunity of its very being." An answer that gives freedom and meaning with regard to questions about humanity, our inquiry about ourselves, must therefore come from "beyond us."[27]

We can direct this question concerning ourselves and humanity as a whole toward ourselves or toward others. Perhaps we can turn to the experts in the area of the human sciences, who know more than others about the meaning of humanity. Or we can turn to people who know us well—maybe better than we know ourselves. And yet our question may still lead to a greater sense of puzzlement instead of clarity, if we are not able to reconcile contradictory observations and experiences with one another. In his poem "Who Am I?" Dietrich Bonhoeffer pointedly describes the difference between observations of ourselves and of others, between apparently more certain self-awareness and deep self-doubt. And yet he concludes:

> Who am I? They mock me, these lonely questions of mine.
> Whoever I am, thou knowest, O God, I am thine.[28]

What is idiosyncratic of such questions about one's self is that they are never conclusively or completely answered and that any answers are uncertain. Human beings "certainly experience their capacity to inquire into the meaning of who and what they are as what is distinctive about their existence. However, even their initial attempts to resolve this problem force them to the admission that they are overwhelmed by this question above all others. Thus, humans remain in the suspense of an incomparable tension that stems from the necessity to inquire into their nature, and their inability to respond in any way satisfactory."[29]

One will therefore need to probe a bit further if one wants to more closely determine humanity's question about itself and affirm with Paul Tillich
that "the question, asked by man, is man himself. He asks it, whether or not
he is vocal about it. He cannot avoid asking it, because his very being is
the question of his existence."[30] Persons experience themselves as finite
and as anxious in their finite freedom.[31] They do not live in an unconscious harmony with themselves. Instead, they experience themselves as
subject to temptation and guilty, as responsible and as inadequate, and as
being pulled to and fro between ability and obligations, between exerting
themselves and being overextended, between successes and frustrations.

In view of this unclarity of identity and this sense of the transience of
life,[32] it is the task of theology to remain alert to the questions concerning
the meaning and the final outcome of human life and to attain answers to
these questions from the message of the Bible. While the sciences of
humanity investigate the being of humanity in the context of perceivable
causal relations, theology proceeds from the unconditional acceptance of
humanity through God.[33] This acceptance is also valid for persons today
who no longer know that they are in God's hands nor how that can be true.
A view of humanity that is based on the gospel brings to the fore their
God-relatedness, and it brings back into view their existence as ones who
are beloved by God.

We have seen that is basic to their nature for human beings not to simply abandon themselves to the flow of life, but rather to continue to ask
questions about themselves and about humanity as it is actually lived out
or commanded to be lived out. The unresolved and fundamentally unre-
solvable questions concerning themselves are true to the true nature of
humanity. These questions about themselves, about their existence, can,
however, also lead them into profound crises, in which persons no longer
see the value of their lives. They may even conclude that they are merely
products of chance or of failed family planning. After all, we were never
asked whether we wanted to be born and to live. Are we compelled to
exist? Is it not preferable to give back our unwanted and unloved lives?
The Swiss poet Kurt Marti[34] has taken up this question and pursued it in
a poem that concludes that no one was asked except God, "and He said
yes."

2.1.2.2   THE HUMAN BEING AS THE IMAGE OF GOD

Human life—and every individual person as well as humanity in general—begins with and stands under the "Yes" of God. While this fact is

also true for all other creatures whom God has created (Genesis 1:31), human beings are distinguished with a particular dignity and responsibility. The metaphor of the image of God brings this to the fore. In the Old Testament, as well as in a few places in the New Testament,[35] this concept signifies human beings in their particular relationship to God and the relationship of God to the world and to themselves that is established by it. Being the image of God, they are assigned their special place and mandate within the whole of creation. They exist as a part of the created order, and yet at the same time, they stand over against it. God makes human beings his partners. God determined them for fellowship with himself and commissioned them with the shaping and the preservation of the earth.[36]

God speaks to humans. They are able to hear and to respond to God. God shares with humans in his creative and conserving actions, and they are freely permitted to assume responsibility. Humans belong on the side of the creation, because they, like all forms of life, are creatures of God. Humans belong on the side of God, because as his image "they are little lower than God" and they are God's representatives within the order of creation. "Image of God" is to be understood in the context of ancient oriental thinking. It does not mean that humans are to take the place of God; rather, they are supposed to defer to God. Like God, they are to care for his creation in a tender and loving manner, and they are to live in fellowship with God and with God's creation. Being the image of God is a gift given to all humanity and it is also their destiny.

Two things follow from this: (1) All persons are images of God; they are not so as independent beings, but only in fellowship with God and with God's creation. Their dignity cannot be lost, even if it is vulnerable. Whoever damages the dignity of human beings simultaneously also affects their Creator. (2) The concept of the image of God also gives rise to the fact that only through the awareness of having a relationship to God and to their fellow creatures do humans take up the place assigned to them in creation and history. The misuse of this gift is open at any time. Human beings enter into opposition to their Creator and become alienated from God—a distance they cannot remedy on their own— through any attitude that does not conform to the status conferred on them by God and hence to their relationship with the rest of creation, including themselves.

John Wesley described his concept of the image of God in humanity most clearly in his thematic sermon on the New Birth.[37] The new birth is necessary, he says there, precisely because persons who are created in God's own image have lost their original love, justice, mercy, truth, and purity through a willful act of rebellion which in its pride and self-will is more akin to the devil and in its lust and avarice is more akin to animals.[38] Because of this rebellion, humans have become profane and unhappy.

God created humanity according to God's image (the "natural image"), and as spiritual beings God equipped them with understanding, freedom of the will, and affections. God also bestowed on them the "political image," whereby God appointed them to be the governors of the created "lower" world, and as bearers of the "moral image," God created them full of love, justice, purity, and holiness.

However, humanity was not unchangeable. They fell from their exalted position due to a willful act of disobedience, and they lost their life from God. In place of the love of God, there entered fear. Humanity became unholy and unhappy, it sank into pride and self-will ("the image of the devil") and into conscious lust and avarice ("the image of the beasts"). As the result of this rebellion, all the descendants of Adam enter into this world spiritually dead. They also come to bear the image of the devil and of animals. That is the "natural condition" of humanity. They have eyes and see not, ears and hear not. They have neither an awareness of God nor union with God. They are certainly alive as mortals, but as Christians they are dead.

The eyes of their understanding are only opened through the new birth. Then they can hear the inner voice of God and can sense the working of the Holy Spirit, and feel joy in God and love toward God. At this point a human can rightly be said to be alive. Whoever is born anew in Christ in such a manner also has the image of God renewed within them. Love for the world is transformed into love for God, pride becomes humility, vehemence becomes meekness, hatred, envy, and evil become earnest, tender, and unselfish love for all persons. The image of God, which is the entire disposition of Christ, is imprinted upon their hearts. Now holiness can emerge.[39]

In this sermon, the image of God within humans is described as wholly lost. No residue of it remains that might recall the original grandeur of the one who was a partner with God in the creation. In another place,[40] Wesley freely asserts that those who have not been born again are also able to live in a blameless fashion, that uprightness and righteousness can also be found among the "heathen." There are no persons which God's prevenient grace leaves bereft, and therefore everyone has the capacity to do good. Of course, Wesley always maintained that no true knowledge of God and of ourselves is possible without the renewing grace of God. And yet, the harsh portrayal of the perversity of humanity "after the fall into sin" stands in significant tension with the doctrine of the prevenient grace of God, which Wesley expressly and repeatedly advocated. One would think it would not be difficult to find evidence within the realm of experience for both such apparently contradictory judgments. However, it is hardly possible to mediate these two insights from a systematic theological perspective.

Recent investigation of the biblical texts, as well as reflection based upon the entire context of theological anthropology, has led to the conclusion that the basic formulation of this interpretation of the doctrine of the image of God in humanity cannot be upheld even if many individual observations prove to be correct.

The description of a loss of the image of God in humanity finds no support in the biblical texts and is rarely to be found in recent Protestant thought. In the New Testament, it can be said of humanity that in spite of their being sinners, they are nonetheless the image of God (James 3:9; 1 Corinthians 11:7). Neither in the Old nor in the New Testament and also not in Paul, is it ever said that the image of God has been destroyed through or as a result of sin.[41] The majority of theologians in the twentieth century have answered in the negative the question whether God's image in humanity is to be regarded as destroyed through sin.

The concept, rooted in early Judaism, "that with the loss of the image of God one becomes an animal, that is, that one simultaneously loses knowledge of God and ethical awareness,"[42] has been variously expressed by Christians[43] in the course of church history. Their assertions about it occasioned vehement controversy during the age of the Protestant Reformation and during the era of the Enlightenment. So both the expressions which occur in the first creation account—"image" (Latin: *imago*) and "likeness" (Latin: *similitudo*) in Genesis 1:26 were seen as two different components of the image of God. The human spirit or soul which remains in effect through the fall into sin was understood by the term *"imago."* Reason, will, and upright behavior are part and parcel of the image of God, even of sinful humanity. *"Similitudo"* or likeness, by contrast, among whose characteristics are numbered above all holiness and justice, may be lost through the fall. Thus, only a residue of the original image of God remains in humans. Both a more exact exposition of the biblical citations and a dogmatic interpretation of the *imago Dei* doctrine that made sense in itself have led to the separation from this theory that had been handed down. After even the reformers of the sixteenth century had turned against this division, on the basis of more precise exegesis, "the image of God" has come to be regarded in our present century as basically referring to a specific relationship of humans to God.

Human beings did not create the *imago Dei* and thus cannot destroy it against the will of their Creator, who remains true to himself and to his creation. That does not in any way mean to neutralize or to play down the older concept of the loss of the *imago Dei*. By contrast, it is precisely because humans, even in their opposition to God, retain their specific relationship to God that humans can remain limitlessly accountable to the God who draws them to accountability (Genesis 3:9, 4:9). The saving acts of the Creator begin in the fact that "the imago Dei and thereby the personality of humans that comes from God is held and kept in safety even against the opposition of human beings."[44] In light of the gospel of Jesus Christ, humans recognize themselves as sinners on the basis of their experiences with themselves, yet on the basis of the divine promises as made in the image of God. Human alienation from God is overcome through God's turning to humanity; trusting in the validity of divine judgment humans can believe what was promised them: that humans are declared free from their guilt and are accepted as "children of God" (Galatians 4:1-7; Romans 8:14-23). The *imago Dei* is therefore "in no way an expression of a human being's own glory," but is rather an expression of their calling to "participate in the glory of God."[45] The relationship to God that is renewed in this fashion and becomes active in faith (justification) at the same time signifies the onset of a new existence (being born again, or the new birth), in which humans are able to become that for which they were created. Even after a faithful turning of human beings to God, their thinking and their willing do not correspond overnight to the image of God, the close relationship to God such as should give our entire existence more direction and meaning.[46] Humans once again resemble the *imago Dei,* its dignity and responsibility, whenever they act in love, as partners of God from whom they come, toward other humans, to whom they belong, and toward creation, of which they are a part, just as God acts toward us and others in love. In Christ, the original and authentic *imago Dei,* this love has taken form in a historical person; his Spirit is the power which transforms from within those persons whom God has created to be his partners and who embrace God's transforming love.[47]

2.1.2.3 THE HUMAN BEING AS A PERSON

The *imago Dei* in humanity finds its analogy in a central structural element of human existence: the human personality. Personality distinguishes humanity from all other life forms through the specific quality of its relationship to itself, to other humans, to the rest of the created order, and to God. It can be more accurately described as the ability to recognize or come up with alternative courses of action in advance, and to make an informed decision among them. How to evaluate the intentionally made choice—whether it was carefully thought through, whether appropriate ethical criteria underlie it, and whether the choice was successfully carried through—then still remains to be determined. Kant asserted that "the knowledge of what every man ought to do, and hence also [what he ought] to know is within the reach of every man, even the commonest."[48] The relationship to the contemporary world, to the self, and to God certainly includes the possibility of error, deception, failure, or blame. The capacity to choose one's conduct, to make meaningful decisions, is not contested by this but rather assumed. Human beings' "openness to the world," their ways of acting that are barely controlled by instincts, and their ability to make informed choices are the basis for the responsibility humans have: their responsibility to God, to their fellow human beings, to their fellow creatures, and to themselves.

This structure is therefore a sign of human existence as such and in this respect also conforms to the character of the image of God. Just as with the image of God, personality is to be thought of as being-in-relation. Wesley refers to humanity in this fashion, thematizing and describing their capability for relationships, their dependence on others, as well as their actual and possible relations to others.[49] The personality of humans is lived in conformity to the will and the experience of the love of God whenever humans lovingly turn toward other humans. This solicitous concern is a basic sign of a renewed being; it comes from God's turning to humanity and humanity's turning to God. In this way, renewed human beings (once again) conform to their original creaturely destiny.[50] In truth, the being of humanity cannot be grasped if this literally foundation-laying relationship of persons to God is not recognized as the reality which has predisposed them, carried them, and enabled them to live out their being as humans in the first place.

The human personality's highest worth comes from its having been fashioned with the capacity to be addressed, not only by the words of other humans, but also by the Word of God. "By reason of his creaturely being, [Man] is capable of meeting God, of being a person for and in relation to Him, and of being one as God is one."[51] In fulfillment of their self-knowledge and their personal accountability humans always stand before their Creator. And God has not remained mute to them but has deemed them worthy of his words of address and fellowship and has drawn them, who were created out of love, into the movement of his love.

The personal structure of human being as being-in-relation is most supremely expressed in the conscience. The conscience differentiates itself as an anthropological constant, as the ability given to each human to judge his or her relationships by ethical standards, and as the concrete capacity to know in a normative sense what to do, which is different among individual humans, groups of humans, cultures, and religions. Ethics and holiness are concerned with this second aspect.[52] The first aspect is our concern here, in our reflection upon God's devotion in God's creative acts.

The conscience is often experienced as a sort of place of struggle. If a person acts against what the conscience recognizes as being acceptable, then the conscience is "pricked." Our guilt overwhelms us and we can only evade the voice of our conscience by silencing it and thereby damaging the core of our personality. However, the conscience also convicts before the disapproved-of deed is done, for it warns us of what we have not yet done, in order that we might not do it. The three faculties thus combine to constitute our personal being: the inner anticipation of possible actions, the ethical evaluation of them, and the decision as to whether to undertake or refrain from the action.

However, the term *conscience* (Greek: *syneidesis,* Latin *conscientia*) is not nearly as old as the thing it describes—this phenomenon of the personality. Still, early Greek philosophy already had long known it as a designation for the consciousness that is cognizant of itself. Soon the term was concentrated upon its ethical content and as the tool of God that causes the conversion of humans (Philo), or as the observer of humans (Stoicism). The apostle Paul introduced this concept into the language of Christian theology; according to him, the conscience judges our behavior in view of an ethical demand, but it cannot simply be identified with the voice of God. The demand can come from the Torah, but it can also be inscribed upon the hearts of persons (Romans 2:14-15). Conscience not only has the function of an inquiring, adjudicating presence within human beings; it can also function in relation to behavior yet to be actualized, to evaluate it in terms of its knowledge of what is good and evil. With regard to scriptural demands, it can be in error—as in the case of the Corinthians who thought that Christians should eat no meat that had been sacrificed to idols; however, even the conscience that objectively is in error is subjectively binding, and its decision is therefore also to be respected by others. For good reason, the protection afforded by conscience is among human rights. The binding conscience is always the individual conscience; its judgment, which either acquits or condemns, is valid for the individual ego, which bears responsibility for an individual's behavior. No one can set free the person who is bound by conscience; the judgment of another does not affect the one whose conscience is absolved (1 Corinthians 4:3; 10:29).

John Wesley dedicated a sermon to the theme of conscience, because he considered the use of the term to be particularly unclear in his day.[53] According to his understanding, conscience is "a tribunal in the breast of men," that "faculty whereby we are at once conscious of our own thoughts, words, and actions, and of their merit or demerit, of their being good or bad."[54] In this capacity, conscience serves as a witness and judge and executor of judgment, in that it effects a sense of well-being (in response to good actions) and malaise (in response to evil actions). More precisely, "natural conscience" is a gift of God, whose care God has entrusted to us. Through disobedience to God's will, which is recognized by one's conscience with the help of God's grace, defective types of conscience can arise: the hypersensitive, scrupulous conscience and the hardened conscience that takes notice of increasingly fewer events. No one can have a good conscience without the help of the Holy Spirit. However, the conscience as such—thanks to the prevenient grace of God—is also operative within the "natural," unbelieving person. No one is without a conscience, without the capacity for perceiving both good and evil, or without a certain measure of moral norms and virtues. Thus, all humans are responsible and accountable to ethical standards; their behavior can be imputed to them.

In the course of recent history, the theme of conscience has undergone several changes,[55] in the work of Immanuel Kant and Sigmund Freud, among others. According to Kant, conscience is seen as an inward court within humans, which judges whether practical reason has undertaken the examination of behavior that befits it in light of its ethical quality. In other words, conscience has a formal mandate to fulfill, since practical reason supplies criteria with regard to content of the moral law. Sigmund Freud described conscience above all as a function of the superego, a function that is gained during the socializing process of early childhood. It functions largely unconsciously and, as an internalized alter ego, it is the cause of the sense of guilt in humans.

According to the preceding considerations, a theological definition of conscience could be as follows: We distinguish between the fact of conscience as an anthropological constant and the obligations of the conscience. The conscience as an anthropological constant is part of the structure of the human person. It designates the capacity to recognize as such an ethical demand that is directed toward doing and/or being. The capacity to make moral judgments that is inherent in conscience is derived—apart from a minimal amount—from the process of socialization.[56] This capacity of internalized norms remains basic, yet cannot be varied at will. Over the course of a life the conscience can take on board new impressions as well as change old ones, and even obliterate them. To this extent, on the one hand, the person's ego is obligated to his/her conscience and its demands. On the other hand, the person's conscience also bears responsibility for the existence of norms stored in the conscience. Connecting both aspects of the conscience we could therefore say that conscience is the self-awareness of a person with regard to the agreement or nonagreement of their being and conduct to their ethical conviction.[57]

The confrontation of a person's conscience with the biblical commands, especially with the command to love, has a twofold function:

1. On the one hand, it discloses the alienation of humanity from God and God's will. This alienation appears inescapable; for it is exactly those who seek to become upright before the will of God in their being and action who find themselves at odds with themselves (compare Romans 7:14-25*a*). I am not I.[58] The experience of alienation from God manifests itself in their self-alienation and in their inability to extricate themselves from this dilemma by their own strength.

2. On the other hand, the liberating of conscience is meant to lead to maturing of the self. According to the biblical conviction, such maturing of the self is only possible through experiencing an unconditional, absolute sense of being accepted. Only then will the conscience actually be set free, "comforted" (Luther) and unburdened from its self-accusations, without being mortified and without denying one's personal capacity for guilt. The conscience itself is also changed through the awareness of an identity that has been given gifts and has developed. Increasingly, it ceases to be a function of the superego, and to the same extent becomes a part of the ego, a personal conscience. To be sure, a greater or lesser

residue of a superego conscience remains as long as we live; it is to be endured and can be endured because the good conscience is capable of withstanding charges against it since it reflects the operation of justification through faith.[59]

In this context, the duty of Christian preaching, doctrine, and education consists above all in offering forgiveness and release, in the pledge that God gives my self to me and thereby releases me for loving life in community with others. This advances the resolution of false feelings of guilt and the capacity for clearing up actual guilt, as well as the operation of the personal, theonomous conscience in the examination of ethical alternatives and in instruction in good works. The stronger such a conscience is developed to be, the more a person becomes true to himself or herself and capable of responsible awareness of the lasting freedom in love.

2.1.3   *God's Loving Care in the Providential Oversight of Creation*

God's creation has not yet reached its end. God accompanies God's creation and God's creative activity continues. Even the guilty conduct of human beings and the destructive power of evil have not suspended God's faithfulness to the created order, in which God creatively upholds the basis for life (Genesis 8:22).

2.1.3.1   GOD'S CREATIVE POWER

There are a few psalms in the Bible that bring this to emphatic expression:

> The eyes of all look to you,
>   and you give them their food in due season.
> You open your hand,
>   satisfying the desire of every living thing. (Psalm 145:15-16).

Psalm 104, whose first section describes the beginning of creation, then continues:

> From your lofty abode you water the mountains;
>   the earth is satisfied with the fruit of your work.
>
> You cause the grass to grow for the cattle,
>   and plants for people to use,

> to bring forth food from the earth,
>> and wine to gladden the human heart,
> oil to make the face shine,
>> and bread to strengthen the human heart. (Psalm 104:13-15)

God's actions in the creation finally lead the one who prays to praise their Creator: "I will sing to the LORD as long as I live; / I will sing praise to my God while I have being" (104:33).

Praise of God's creation, perceived as wonderful, does not lack the awareness of transience and suffering. The same psalm thus declares, "When you hide your face, they are dismayed; / when you take away their breath, they die / and return to their dust" (104:29). Many are well acquainted with these verses from Psalm 90:

> You turn us back to dust,
>> and say, "Turn back, you mortals."
>
> You sweep them away; they are like a dream,
>> like grass that is renewed in the morning.
>
> The days of our life are seventy years,
>> or perhaps eighty, if we are strong;
> even then their span is only toil and trouble;
>> they are soon gone, and we fly away. (Psalm 90:3, 5, 10)

Yet, even here, the description of this experience, which after all has the form of a prayer, is embedded in a turning to God and in the confident request for God's attention; this is also characteristic of the faith insight that recognizes God's action in ongoing creation and in God's care of creation. God's covenantal faithfulness[60] demonstrates itself in the fact that God keeps his promise: "As long as the earth endures, seedtime and harvest, cold and heat, summer and winter, day and night, shall not cease" (Genesis 8:22). God remains faithful to the creation and God's creatures, although humans repeatedly endanger the work of God and their own continued existence through sinful conduct. No area of the world in which we live lies outside of the creative power of God. This creative power endows all things that have life with their existence and also does not allow the transient world to fall out of God's hands. We can therefore affirm that our reality is founded and entirely supported by the reality of God, by God's creative goodness and power. God's faithfulness demonstrates itself in the fact that he stands by his world. God preserves it in spite of the sin of humanity, and he has destined that world for redemption and perfection. No part of our larger experience falls outside of this encompassing reality, not even that which is wholly deformed through sin and directed against God. Even the greatest distance from God is not a distance which exceeds God's reach. Even the smallest and weakest creature is included in God's care. However, only persons of faith know this and they know it not only for themselves, but also for the whole of creation.

2.1.3.2 GOD'S PROVIDENCE

The conviction that God cares for his creation and upholds it arose not from a theoretical necessity but from the experience of the protecting and self-giving nearness of God in the face of fear and sorrow. As we have already noted in considering the verses from the Psalms, what comes to expression here is not so much an interest that is directed toward a general perception as the confidence in the God who does not leave his creation in the lurch. Similarly, there are numerous instances in the New Testament where God's concern is expressed in connection with these declarations: "Do not be afraid" (Luke 12:7) or "Therefore . . . do not worry about your life" (Matthew 6:25).

The doctrine of divine providence has arisen in the course of church history as a result of reflection upon this relationship.[61] It is not surprising that this doctrine is among John Wesley's favorite themes. For example, he preached on the text of Luke 12:7, "Even the hairs of your head are all counted," no less than forty-five times! Sermon 67, "On Divine Providence," contains a kind of summary of his opinions of this doctrine.[62] He declares in the beginning of this sermon that nothing is so small or insignificant that it could not be the subject of God's concern and providential care. Nothing is too trivial for God if it touches upon the welfare of any of his creatures. Just as God, the all-wise and all-gracious One, created all things, so he also preserves them. God is omnipresent and looks upon the entire creation; he is all-knowing and knows all, and he disdains none of his creatures. "We are his children," Wesley can say of human beings.[63] Hence, God does not forget them. His concern is for all his creatures, not only, but above all, for humans.

Wesley does not conceal that the evil and the misery in this world make such a conviction appear problematic. Could not and must not God destroy sin and its evil nature, as well as its consequences? Must God banish suffering from the world? Wesley's response is first of all an admission of his lack of understanding. He holds firmly to the conviction that

God's wisdom and goodness and power go hand in hand. "And we cannot doubt that He has used His entire power to preserve and guide everything that He has created."

And yet, Wesley would not be Wesley if he did not attempt to give an explanation for the continuation of evil and destruction in spite of the protective and creative power of God. His carefully proposed interpretation looks like this: God could not deny himself. He could not reverse the creation nor extinguish the image of God within humankind in order to eradicate sin from the world. Otherwise God would contradict himself. God has destined humans for freedom, and though without this freedom there would be no evil, there would also be no virtue. Thus, the providence of God reveals itself in the fact that God guides the reason, will, and freedom of human beings, instead of destroying them, to attain the goal of their lives and to strive in freedom for their salvation (Sermon 67, 15).

However, this doctrine of *general providence* is only a part of the doctrine. The other part refers to the personal concern of God for humans as individuals *(particular providence)*. In Wesley's sermon, the stronger emphasis lies upon the latter. The doctrine of general providence seems to a significant extent to form the theological background of Wesley's expositions concerning God's devotion to individual persons. In this regard, Wesley defends the biblical faith in God's intervention in creation, in God's miracles, which can even transcend the laws of nature. While God as Creator has concern for all human beings, and not only for Christians or for truly believing Christians, his special concern is still for those persons who trust him completely and to whom God has given a charge. The Bible asserts at one point that, whenever God wants to protect one of his servants, then the stone will not fall, the fire will not consume, the floods will not overtake her or that God's angels will bear her up on their hands and carry her through all dangers.[64]

Wesley shares the view of most of his contemporaries that God regulates the world through the laws of nature, which he created. However, God has held in reserve the option of rescinding them in exceptional cases. Wesley adheres firmly to the biblical promise that God hears and grants prayer requests and he defends this conviction against all the incursions of the Enlightenment, which only recognize a general view of providence and the unbreakable authority of natural law (for example, David Hume and Alexander Pope). Wesley's interest in holding fast to this conviction lies not only in his adherence to the biblical tradition; above all, it is based in seeing the smallest and weakest and poorest as being included within the care of God. These human categories are quite insignificant in the eyes of God. God cares about each human being, as though he were concerned only for that one alone, and he cares about all, as if they were only one.[65] Thus, the sermon presses to the conclusion that all persons should put their entire trust in God, to thank him for his protection and care, as well as to lead their lives humbly and close to God. Sad is the situation of those who do not trust in God; but happy is the person who puts his confidence in him.[66]

Many persons of our day will find it difficult to follow Wesley's theoretical reflections entirely. Don't we in the meantime know too much about the structure of the world to draw upon God's providence as an explanation for the world as we know it, thus once again assigning to God the role of a "working hypothesis" (as suggested by Laplace, 1749–1827)? Is God one factor alongside others that influence the events of the world, or is he perhaps an absolute monarch, who regards the world as his province? Is it not impossible to think in these terms in the context of the recognized rational view of the world of today, and does not every attempt of that kind come across as either defenseless or comical?[67]

The representations of the miraculous by the biblical writers certainly must not be allowed to be fit into an antiquated, causal-mechanistic worldview from which they don't arise. The idea of the miraculous reaches much further than this, for it has less to do with isolated occurrences and their ideological classification and more with the "experience of an undeserved and unexpected possibility which has been realized contrary to expectations."[68] It is a personal occurrence that nevertheless is not to be attributed only to personal experience. Instead, it certainly involves an objective unforeseeable event. Some accounts of miracles are certainly to be attributed to the ancient world or to the incomplete understanding of that day; yet innumerable experiences of a wonderful healing or a rescue from imminent death are after all a strong argument for the reality of scientifically incomprehensible occurrences, which those who experience them—often as unexpected answers to prayer—understand in terms of God's helping intervention. It is therefore more appropriate to state that we do not believe in miracles but in the God who often cares in miraculous ways for his people and for his creation. This is also true where experiences of suffering are not removed and the destiny of death has not been circumvented, and where the transience and finitude of the creation are only all too painfully being experienced. Faith in God and trust in God's goodness also helps us to accept such experiences, without thereby permitting our trust in God to be destroyed. For the believer can rely on the fact that neither a blind destiny nor a cold nothing stands behind the events of the world or one's individual experiences of life, no matter how terrible these may be in particular instances. Instead, it is the Creator, who loves the world and holds it in his hands, even when we fall into apparent bottomlessness, who undergirds all creation. Our lives are not a string of more or less isolated events but the realm of activity and experience which God grants to us in his creation. God has created, enabled, and equipped us, so that we might be shaped according to that activity.

2.1.3.3 GOD'S GOODNESS AND THE EXPERIENCE OF SUFFERING

Do these reflections not seem too superficial and too easily thrown out there when we consider the actual and immeasurable suffering of this world, the inconceivable evil, the unbearable unrighteousness or the totally incomprehensible suffering of human beings, who to our knowledge are much less guilty than many others for whom things are going well? Does God not disappear behind such experiences, and must we not therefore come to terms with living in a world without God? The Seventy-third Psalm is the prayer of a person who has believed in God but who has nevertheless been cast into profound doubt through experiences of this kind. He declares, "All in vain I have kept my heart clean / and washed my hands in innocence" (verse 13). And he continues, "All day long I have been plagued, / and am punished every morning," while all is going well for the boasters and the godless. There is no suffering for them. They are healthy and free of the toils and tribulations that plague other persons.

The Psalmist is directing his question to God in this prayer; however, these questions are often directed against God. Faith in God was being questioned and contested and then those people who continue to speak of God and God's care for the world have to justify themselves. Or, must even God be justified in the end?[69]

In the context of the acceptance of such an all-bountiful and also almighty God, the question arises, "How can faith in this God be represented, in view of the suffering of the innocent in the world?"[70] This question reaches more deeply than does the question about the hiddenness of God, from which God can of course emerge once again. It complains not only of the silence of God, which causes people to become mute, but it asks the question whether it may be possible to talk about God at all in this biblical sense, or whether God hasn't resigned and isn't long since dead, if he in fact ever existed at all.

The atheistic attempt to solve the problem of suffering in the world, which in no way appears to be reconcilable with the talk of an all-good and all-powerful God, looks like this: because God does not exist and because therefore he also does not reign, this problem doesn't exist.[71] Suffering is the "rock of atheism" (Büchner), on which faith in a good and omnipotent God is shattered. The counterpart to this atheistic attempt to explain the problem of evil lies in the assumption that everything must lead back to God and God's actions, even the suffering and the evil in the world. Of course, a two-headed God arises this way. We do not know whether this God intends to cause us evil or good. Such a conviction is not without some support in the biblical text, as the word of Amos shows, "Does disaster befall a city, / unless the LORD has done it?" (Amos 3:6*b*).

Between both of these two concepts is the dualistic attempt to solve the problem: there is one God and one Antigod; the one is good and the other is evil. The early Christian theologian Marcion (second century) distinguished thus between the Creator God and the Father of our Lord Jesus Christ. In other portrayals, the Antigod becomes the same as the devil. If God and the Antigod are regarded as being on the same plane, then God is no longer really God, since he must share his power with another.

Finally, one can also fend off the whole thing and ask, with Paul "But who indeed are you, a human being, to argue with God?" (Romans 9:20). Some regard the question as being inadmissible, because we must refrain from speaking of unrighteous suffering before the cross of Christ.[72]

In view of these different outlooks, the temptation is great to take the last approach toward resolving the issue; yet we do not want to make lighter of the problem than absolutely necessary, and therefore on the basis of our faith and life experience, we pursue the tension that grows out of such suffering. It is not least our pastoral interest that gives us this task. In these considerations, we intend to leave aside two aspects which would certainly be valuable to discuss, but which mainly provide a background for the questions at issue here rather than constituting the heart of the matter. On the one hand, we could reflect on whether we as humans have a claim upon luck. On the other, it is of course not at all certain what is good or bad for us; could a life without pain and without suffering be a desirable life? We will return to this second point at another time.

The causes of human suffering can be distinguished in three ways: one lies in the finitude of our existence and its subjection to the decay of death; the second lies in the evil actions of human beings; and the third lies in physical causes over which we have no influence. The fact that we are mortal and our earthly life has an end does in fact make our earthly existence questionable, because we ourselves and everything that we do are subjected to this transience. The fact that humans act unjustly toward other humans leads into what is possibly the most severe form of suffering, and there are millions of persons in our day who have to suffer the consequences of sinful behavior. Wesley has already provided an answer to this dilemma in his sermon: it is the freedom of human beings, with which God has equipped us, which also permits an evil and perverse use of human possibilities. But the most incisive and deepest-reaching questioning of the goodness and omnipotence of God arises out of the experience of physical evil—the bodily suffering of some humans who are not more guilty than are others. Occurrences such as the death of a young man by cancer or the indiscriminate loss of life through natural catastrophes repeatedly convulses or shocks us to agonize about God's righteousness. How can we respond to such questions from the resources of our faith?

First of all, we know Christians take evil seriously. They do not argue about its existence, as in the case of the religions of the Far East, for example. They also hold fast to the belief that God is gracious, all-powerful, and all-knowing, for this is how they encounter him in the witness of the Bible. However, they then ask, if we love a person or are inclined toward that person, we do not unnecessarily inflict suffering upon that person; why then, does God inflict suffering or, if God does not do it, why does God allow it?

Before we seek for an answer from the Christian faith, we want to reflect a little on the meaning of suffering for human life in general. A person who wishes suffering upon himself or herself is apparently physically ill or spiritually presumptuous. Yet, humans know suffering as a means to attain a higher goal. We willingly submit to a painful procedure whenever the restoration of our health demands it. We undergo exertion to reach a desired goal. We stay with a person in order to be near to that one, even if it entails doing without something and suffering. And we can often come to the realization that times of suffering are needful for our development and maturation. Important processes of change within our lives seldom happen without suffering. The English author Aldous Huxley has offered a test case for the correctness of this assumption through his novel *Brave New World*. A world without suffering leads to the dehumanization of humanity.

However, does this justify suffering? Is there not also suffering which utterly shatters persons and their life energy? Can we generalize from a partial truth, that some suffering serves for our good, to say that suffering in any case must be beneficial? Even if a life without suffering, even given the present constitution of the world and of humanity, is not desirable, it can nonetheless not be said that all sufferings are meaningful, and the question concerning the vindication of our faith in a gracious and all-powerful God remains open, in view of the suffering that is experienced in this world. It is advisable at this point to propose a distinction that seems insignificant at first glance, namely a distinction between God as all-powerful and God as the sole powerful agent in creation. The omnipotence of the Creator includes the fact that God causes everything. However, in the creation, God has limited himself, since God created humans with a realm of free agency and the freedom for personal action.

Thus, at least when it comes to historical events, we are probably able to speak of the all-powerful working of God, but not of God as the sole agent in effecting these events. Insofar as physical evils are caused by humans, they are an indirect cause of God's freely chosen limitation of his power. This conviction narrows our inquiry, but it does not yet respond to the remaining questions.

Perhaps we can come closer to an answer by asking what experiences of suffering mean for persons who are believers. As a follow-up to the biblical passages that were previously cited, a detailed exposition of the book of Job would be meaningful here. Though we are not able to do that now, what must be said is that the question about the meaning of suffering and the vindication of God in light of suffering cannot be answered from the safe distance of theoretical speculation. How great and understandable is the temptation to set forth a resplendent Christian worldview, one "that excuses God in a human manner," and "to trust in something other than the hidden Father, whose will is unveiled by the man of uffering, the Crucified One, with whom the evil forces of the world particularly sported."[73] The friends of Job, with all their attempts to explain the meaning of his trials, skirt right over the problem, for it is only for those who are affected by suffering—either that of themselves or of others who are near to them—that a door is opened that gives us access to the possibility of an appropriate answer to that problem. This answer is always linked to a personal encounter with God, and apart from this our view of senseless suffering possesses no meaning. In the encounter with God, Job experiences not only that God has not at all turned himself away from him, but that God has also—indirectly but also distinctly—taken heed to his complaints against his suffering and that God is attentive to his question about the righteousness of God. At the same time, God takes him into his all-embracing reality, in which even the suffering of Job has its place. And Job, who at first was struck dumb by the super power of God, is now led into a new experience of the goodness of God and the freedom to be found in praising God. This praise of God was not granted him so long as he sat in ashes. For those who ask for God's presence in the midst of their suffering, his fate can be a sign that God's goodness is not spent, but that it is available to us even when we do not experience it.

There is another Christian experienced in suffering who can give us a further indication of how we might be able to hold fast to our faith in the creative power and goodness of God in the face of suffering in this world. We refer to Martin Luther and to his statements about the "hidden God."[74] Luther's achievement lies first of all in the fact that this ambiguity was to be taken seriously in the face of the doctrine that was being disseminated in his day concerning the general revelation of God. God's will is often unrecognizable and impenetrable. It seems that God wills the death of a sinner, although his Word does oppose that. The *deus absconditus,* the hidden God, is an important delimiting concept for the reality of God to the extent that God is unrecognizable to us. No assertions can be made concerning the will of God to the extent that God remains hidden to us. We do not know all things about God and therefore as Christians we cannot suppose that we can explain all incomprehensible suffering. Luther himself attempted to say more about this than he was able to say, given his own premises. He made substantial statements about the hidden God,[75] who thereby was given a Janus-like appearance.

A further, decisive point of view, which should be included here, is the following: Christian theology is essentially a theology of the cross. God allows Jesus, the Innocent One, to suffer and God himself suffers in him. Through the suffering and death of Jesus, God reveals his innermost essence as love. The greatest love is that which gives one's life for one's friends and enemies, as Jesus himself has done. On the whole, there is no love without suffering. What Christians can say about the question of suffering in the world invariably has to do with the theology of the cross. With this conviction the apostle Paul could say, "For I am convinced that neither death nor life . . . will be able to separate us from the love of God in Christ Jesus our Lord" (Romans 8:38-39). Because God is for us and has given his own Son for us, this love that is real in Christ binds us with our Creator also in the face of suffering. Thus, every kind of prettification of evil and suffering is repulsed; they are only too often horrifying and incomprehensible, and every pedagogical[76] or strategic[77] "explanation" skirts the seriousness of this problem. In Jesus' participation in the suffering of humanity, we find not a theoretical explanation but a point of entry into understanding suffering in the world: it is nearness to those who suffer and the proximity of God in suffering that can bring our questioning to a place of resolution.[78]

We must concede that thereby the problem of the suffering of the innocent in the world and the question of the vindication of God is not in the least solved theoretically. However, it is the best that can be clearly affirmed by Christians: it is the turning to God in suffering and the experience of the nearness of God in suffering that allow us to continue to bear witness to a loving and all-powerful God and trust in him. Such a witness can be believed and it can be maintained in one's own experience, but it cannot yet be proved. In the end, what maintains this belief is hope in God's coming day of consummation, when all tears will be wiped away and all evil and all trouble will be overcome. Even though there is therefore no resolution of this problem, there is nevertheless a well-founded hope for a solution, and this must suffice for us under the conditions of our earthly existence. Without this eschatological perspective, there would be no hope and without hope there would be no trust in God's future actions to overcome pain and evil.[79] However, this hope has repeatedly proved itself trustworthy. "The contradiction of [God's] goodness and [humans'] suffering is not resolved like a riddle. God takes it upon Himself."[80] The question remains, but it can be raised in the confidence of the God who is revealed in Jesus Christ. Also, the person praying the Seventy-third Psalm, which was cited at the beginning of this section, only experiences the answer to his question in the encounter with God.

So that no misunderstanding arises, it should be added here that the acceptance of such suffering does not in any way signify that we are not to seek to remove its causes, so far as it is possible, in order to mitigate unwarranted suffering that is brought about by humans. We are to remain near to a suffering humanity in the midst of its need, and we are always to give aid and do everything to ameliorate the effects of such suffering. Faith in the God of grace, who also bears his creation through suffering, does not lead to fatalism that accepts whatever happens in our world as if it were God's will and without entering into resolute conflict against it.

For that reason preaching and pastoral care are not about offering explanations and the theoretical answers but about drawing near to persons who suffer, about bringing their laments before God, and with them—or, in case that is not possible, without them and for them—petitioning God on their behalf, that he may meet those who suffer in the depths of their need.[81] Part of doing that can involve being silent with those who suffer, suffering their laments and our poverty of response, perhaps learning a new language for lament with the biblical psalms of lament, and allowing God to speak to us. Instead of forcing ourselves upon humans in need, or avoiding them, we should be accessible to them, and make space for them where they can meet God. Then, they can continue onward, comforted and encouraged for their life journey.

God accompanies God's creation. God's work of preservation begins with his Creation, which cannot endure without God, and it flows into his finished new creation, which will usher in a new world. Heaven and earth shall pass away, because this created order is temporal and thus finite. With its disappearance, God will also suspend his own limitation upon himself, which he imposed at the creation of humanity, and the powers of destruction and death will have to give way to him through whom God reconciles all things with himself, namely, Jesus Christ (Colossians 1:20). However, the consummation of the world will not occur in such a way that its past is extinguished, rather the consummation will bring to fulfillment that for which the creation was destined from the beginning—a place of fellowship with God (Revelation 21:1-4).

2.2   God's Loving Care in His Reconciling Acts

The shared starting point of the biblical message and the Christian proclamation is a common basic principle: the trustful and salvific companionship of God and humanity that was God's intent in the creation has been profoundly disturbed by humans. Humans no longer live in their original reliance upon God. Thus, their relationship to themselves, to their fellow humans, and to the entire creation has been disturbed at its root. God's renewing actions are required to repair this breach. The history of the Bible is the history of these actions of God.

2.2.1   *Sin and Its Consequences*

The Bible refers to the cause for the destruction of the relationship between God and humans as *sin*. The terminology used—especially in the

Old Testament—is varied. The so-called story of the fall in Genesis 3 describes the circumstances without even using the term *sin*.

Two basic explanations for understanding sin can easily be distinguished in the biblical message:

(a.) Sin is a deed of humans which destroys their relationship with God.

(b.) Sin is the power and the misfortune which reigns over and destroys the life of humanity.[82]

In contrast with this biblical viewpoint, the word *sin* is pushed to the margin in present-day nontheological use, and it is used in a rather insipid fashion. One speaks of traffic sins and even the days when it could be ironically asked, "Can love be sin?" are long gone.

And yet people nowadays do indeed experience something of the inner breakdown and the loss of roots and loss of direction of human existence. However, their "estrangement" from God is often so far advanced that they can scarcely recognize the One from whose fellowship they have fallen. At best, the broken relationship of contemporary people with God continues to be articulated whenever one hears their accusations against God for all the suffering in this world. Yet, a biblically oriented theology needs to speak of sin and its consequences. It does so precisely for the sake of those human beings, whose situation before God must be diagnosed as honestly as possible, so that we may proclaim God's gracious turning toward the world as powerfully and aptly as needed.

2.2.1.1   THE UNIVERSALITY OF SIN FROM THE BEGINNING

What is referred to in Christian theology as "original sin"[83] was strongly emphasized by John Wesley. He consistently includes this among the "essentials" of the Christian faith. He devoted some of his most comprehensive theological discussions to this theme and he summarized its consequences in one of his doctrinal sermons.[84] In the doctrine of original sin he sees the "grand, fundamental difference between Christianity . . . and the most refined heathenism" and he declares that "all who deny this— call it original sin or by any other title—are but heathens still."[85] In so doing they are denying the basic need for redemption that exists within humanity.

Barely one hundred years later, the Danish philosopher of religion Søren Kierkegaard proposed that "the idea which qualitatively distinguishes Christianity from paganism is precisely the doctrine of sin; and therefore Christianity quite consistently pursues the notion that neither paganism nor the natural man knows what sin is." "In paganism of course this sin did not exist. . . . Yet Christianity has secured itself from the very beginning. It begins with the doctrine of sin." He pointed out that it must be accepted as a revelation from God for it to be made evident what sin is. This also means that it is not the doctrine of reconciliation that is the qualitative difference between paganism and Christianity. "No, one has to begin at a far deeper level, with sin, with the doctrine of sin, as happens in Christianity."[86]

The greatness and the universality of the biblical message of the grace of God is only experienced where the reality of the separation of humans from God is grasped in all its depth and radicalness.

After Paul, Augustine was the first who saw this in all its clarity and gave it a new formulation. It is true that the way in which he defined "original sin" above all as (sexual) desire and ascribed its "transmission" to the act of procreation does not conform to the biblical witness. However, in his teaching on sin Augustine firmly upheld the belief that the human ability to do good has been marred down to its very root.[87] Reformation theology rediscovered this biblical truth and emphasized it anew, and Wesley also, who otherwise gladly defended Pelagius, Augustine's theological opponent, clearly shows that at this point he thought neither as a "Pelagian" nor as a "Semi-Pelagian."[88]

Within the context of American Christianity, the doctrine of original sin underwent significant alteration from the time of the early Puritans, who upheld the doctrine as a corollary to their conviction that human salvation is *sola gratia,* as the consequence of God's foreordaining will in establishing a covenant of grace with his elect, who were typologically identified as "God's New Israel."[89] The New England colonies of Massachusetts and Connecticut were established by the Puritans as covenant communities. Significant alterations occurred in the Puritan doctrine of original sin by the time of the early nineteenth century, under the impact of the moralistic and pseudo-"Arminian" emphases that came into prominence under the impact of the Second Great Awakening. As a result, God was viewed as a Moral Governor, who does not impute sin to humanity by virtue of their solidarity with Adam but who permits actual sin and who punishes it not as an expression of wrath but as a means of establishing the authority of moral law.[90] This popular erosion of the doctrine of original sin signified a shift from theological to moralistic concerns that coincided with the building of the nation. Revisionist Methodist theologians in the nineteenth century tended to reflect this trend away from the doctrine of original sin, as Robert Chiles has documented.[91]

The biblical basis for the doctrine of original sin is to be found in Romans 5:12-21. Paul says in verse 12, "Sin came into the world through one man, and death came through sin, and so death spread to all because all have sinned."

This statement contains a double assertion: both sin and its consequences are a peril, in that through the transgression of *one person,* namely Adam, it has come upon the entirety of humanity (compare also vv. 15-19). However, the sin of the one has such deadly effect within because *all* human beings have sinned and continue to sin. Paul apparently wants to assert a double truth: each person is found to be a sinner because the power of sin has taken hold of all humanity. However, no one is merely a victim of his or her fate since all have power to sin through their own sinfulness. John 8:34 formulates this with classical brevity: "Everyone who commits sin is a slave to sin."

Thus, for Paul too, sin is not simply an individual deed. (This is mostly described by him by the term *transgression* of the law).[92] Sin is a power that has prevailed in humanity from the beginning of the human race. Paul describes the origin and essence of sin as "disobedience" (Romans 5:19) or, even more sharply, as persons being "enemies of God" (Romans 5:10, cf. 8:7).

The Pauline observations concerning original sin are based upon the description of the sin of the first humans in Genesis 3. The history of the so-called "fall of sin" actually contains no doctrine of sin. However, it impressively describes how a breach in the fellowship between God and humanity occurred, and thereby makes clear the essence of sin. Adam and Eve appear on the one hand as individual persons who were to manifest "what is exemplary in the human attitude toward God."[93] They are the corepresentatives of humanity, in whose destiny human history is portrayed.[94] These persons are depicted as those who have everything that they need for fellowship with God. They experience their limitation as creatures through the prohibition not to eat of the tree of knowledge. However, the prohibition awakens the temptation within them to transgress its command, which is personified in the form of the serpent.[95] The serpent's doubting rejoinder, "Did God really say that?" leads to the declaration of taboo ("We are never to touch that!") and to the contrary description of the voice of temptation that is larded with half-truths. Their center is the assertion that promises human beings that they will be like God through the eating of the forbidden fruit and will know what is good and evil.[96]

The outward step of transgressing the prohibition of God and eating the forbidden fruit represents a very deep-going inner event, namely the attempt of humans to step over the boundary of their creatureliness and to emancipate themselves from their relationship to God. By transgressing this boundary that had been affixed to them, the human wanted to "transcend himself," that is, he wanted to elevate the meaning of his own existence into the realm of the superhuman.[97] The "original sin," as it is described in the account of Genesis 3, is therefore disobedience against God's command, but it is also unbelief, which mistrusts God's promise and displaces God as the decisive orientation and foundation for their own lives. According to Genesis 3, the fundamental human error was "the effort to free themselves from Yahweh and to determine their own lives autonomously."[98] It is therefore not surprising that Genesis 3 was viewed by many interpreters in the Christian tradition not as a "fall into sin," but rather as the actual step toward "becoming human."[99]

However, the biblical account defines the consequences of this event in other terms. That which the serpent had predicted actually occurs: the eyes of the humans are opened—but the first thing they recognize is that they are naked! They are unmasked before one another. They can no longer endure their sexual differences and have to protect themselves from each other's sight. Likewise, the breach with God is documented in the need to hide themselves from God. Shame and fear because of what they have done, the need to justify themselves, and as a consequence the attempt to blame someone else now characterizes the situation of humanity, which has entangled itself in sin.[100] The break in the relationship with God also leads to the disruption of human community, as well as the disruption of the relationship of humans to themselves. God's "curse," whereby he charged human beings with their deed (Genesis 3:15-19), is intended to restrain them with regard to the finitude of their existence. The brokenness of human existence is painfully experienced and suffered ever anew in the joy and pain of childbearing, in the lust and misery of sexual relationships and dependency, in the success and drudgery of human struggles for daily bread within a nature that has become "two-faced," and above all in the inevitability of their own death. The subsequent accounts of the primeval history of humanity, especially the story of the first murder (Genesis 4), the condemnation of the generation of Noah (Genesis 6), and the building of the tower of Babel (Genesis 11), indicate further effects of sin within the life of humanity, including its universality and the mortal threat that it represents for humanity.

Wesley summarized these effects of sin with the phrase "the loss of the image of God."[101] What is critical for Wesley is that sin has resulted in the loss of the love of God, through which humans fall out of fellowship with God and forfeit the righteousness and holiness that had been bestowed on them by God. That was the *doxa*, the brilliance of God's essence, which according to Romans 3:23 all humans lose, because they join forces with sin. By their relationship with God, they have in the final analysis lost God himself in their lives. Humans in sin are *atheoi en to kosmo*—without God in this world (Ephesians 2:12), a statement that, for Wesley, refers not to a theoretical atheism that denies God but to the existential condition of human beings, who are "alienated from the life of God" and who therefore can no longer have any actual and effective knowledge of God. They neither experience the happiness of God's love that provides a harbor against the anxieties of life, nor are they able to live in the holiness of life that is marked by the voluntary love of God.[102]

This practical "atheism" certainly does not keep people from paying allegiance to the service of idols. On the contrary, because "the alienated person . . . no longer seeks the destiny and fulfillment of their life in their Creator but in themselves and in the created world," such persons fabricate their own gods, on which their hearts depend and into whose strength and power they fall.[103] Paul has described this process in Romans 1:20ff., where he draws from Oriental and Hellenistic religions above all for his examples. In his description of service to idols, Wesley reproves the idols of his day, which are made not of stone or wood but out of the love of self and the world, which is shown in pride, egoism, or avarice just as much as in the absolutizing of aesthetic values or human achievements.[104]

The kernel and mainspring of sin is always anxiety for oneself, which results from the broken relationship of human beings to their Creator and leads to a fatal self-love. Paul often describes this by the term *flesh*—creatureliness of humanity that has been seduced from anxiety to greed. The biblical concept "flesh" in the first instance shows complete neutrality with reference to that which is earthly, human, and bodily, characteristic of which are precisely human transitoriness and frailty (see Isaiah 40:6-7). However, exactly because humans reject this side of their natures, "flesh" becomes the operational basis and the fertile ground for sin, which resists God. Augustine identifies the core of sin in the self-love that is derived from anxiety for one's own life, which wants to justify and safeguard one's own existence, and, as a last consequence, implies hatred toward God.[105] On this basis, Luther has designated fallen, sinful humanity, characterized by self-love, as those who are "in themselves crooked persons," who are *"homines incurvati in se ipse."*[106] By resisting each demand that comes to challenge this egoism, the "atheism" of sin consequently becomes enmity against God.[107]

This actuality of sin is the reality of unredeemed humanity, in which each particular person finds herself or himself and which each one repeatedly makes the reality of his or her existence by his or her own sinfulness. Psalm 51:5 speaks of this fallenness of humanity when it affirms, "Indeed, I was born guilty, / a sinner when my mother conceived me." It is not procreation nor conception nor birth that are presented as sinful acts and as means of conveying original sin. Instead, sin is exposed as the essential condition of human existence.[108]

But to what extent are humans in a position to recognize this situation without the help of God? To what extent can this condition be made evident to us? Is the revelation of the "wrath of God," that is, God's uncompromising "No" spoken against "all ungodliness and wickedness of those who by their wickedness suppress the truth" (Romans 1:18), also evident for persons who (intend to) know nothing about the revelation of the righteousness of God in the gospel of Jesus Christ?

The answer provided by the biblical witnesses and the Christian tradition appears to be ambiguous. Paul himself declares in Romans 3:20*b*, "Through the law comes the knowledge of sin." That was one of the reasons why John Wesley held the preaching of the law as an indispensable condition of the Christian proclamation.[109] Yet, Paul himself had also acknowledged that the law can hinder a person from recognizing one's real situation before God. For it is not only through the outward, visible transgression of the law that humans demonstrate that they are sinners. Those who, measured by the requirements of the law, can regard themselves as "blameless"—so long as they seek their own righteousness by this—also live far from God and in opposition to God.

Thus, it is very strongly emphasized in recent theological discussion, especially in its systematic consideration of the relevant portions of the biblical witness, that the actual knowledge of sin emerges first from the encounter with God's grace in the gospel. How dark the darkness in which we live really is can first be measured by persons only when God sends God's light into their lives. Wesley emphasized this too when he stated that "So long as a man born blind continues so, he is scarce sensible of his want. Much less, could we suppose a place where all were born without sight, would they be sensible of the want of it. In like manner, so long as men remain in their natural blindness of understanding they are not sensible of their spiritual wants, and of this in particular. But as soon as God opens the eyes of their understanding they see the state they were in before."[110]

However, W. Pannenberg has claimed that "what Christians say about human beings as sinners is true to life only if it relates to something that characterizes the whole phenomenon of human life and that may be known even without the premise of God's revelation, even if this revelation is necessary to bring its true significance to light."[111] In this context, Wesley has referred to the way in which "our daily experience confirms" that the meditations and observations of the human heart are evil and certainly only evil and that forever and ever. For Wesley, this is certainly to be accompanied by the restriction that the "natural man" is unable to perceive this.[112]

In actuality, the brokenness of human existence is incalculable. It is not by accident that the biblical concept of "alienation" has been evident with different nuances through a long history of spirituality.[113] Even in secular usage, for example, in Marxism, the term *alienation* betrays some degree of the knowledge that humans are estranged from their original destiny, and thus they are prevented from attaining a fulfilled life.

A motif that has garnered considerable attention in contemporary thought is the phenomenon which the Greeks called *hybris,* or that false pride of humanity which is one of the essential causes of their internal and external suffering. In his influential study *All Mighty: A Study of the God Complex in Western Man,* the psychotherapist Horst Eberhard Richter has investigated the causes for this development.[114] The "God complex" refers to the human effort to seek to be as God, which has stood behind the modern efforts to emancipate humanity that have developed, either consciously or unconsciously, since the end of the Middle Ages. The therapeutic proposals of Richter are not identical with the use of the biblical message. However, his diagnosis agrees in several important respects with the biblical analysis of humanity and of the essence of sin. Research in depth psychology has exposed anxiety as being precisely the conscious or unconscious motive of human actions.[115] Out of this anxiety, humans want to secure or rescue their lives, and if they fail to do so, they will in many instances even destroy their own lives or those of others. It is the fear that something important is being withheld from us that provokes us to disregard the wholesome and protecting boundaries that are set by God for our lives.

The "lostness" of humanity without God is therefore a phenomenon of human existence whose symptoms even weigh heavy on those who know little or nothing about God and the message of the gospel. Its deepest cause, the broken relationship of humanity toward God, is, however, not recognizable or understandable for them. And yet is part of the "grip on life" that is part and parcel of any biblically-oriented proclamation of the gospel to challenge the hearer of the gospel about this broken relationship. Without doubt, this has always been a distinguishing mark of Methodist preaching. Only one thing must be kept clear here: it is impossible to demonstrate the necessity of the saving activity of God in Christ and its meaning for personal living if one begins with a person's own experience of deficiency. At this point, the gospel needs to speak for itself.

2.2.1.2 SIN AS A DEED

At the beginning of the last section we identified two basic thrusts of the biblical understanding of sin: sin as a deed and sin as a power. When original sin is denoted, the second aspect naturally stands in the foreground. That was also the case with Wesley. He speaks quite emphatically at this point of sin as a "fatal disease,"[116] that has taken hold of and corrupted the entire being of humankind. This sickness manifests itself in such concrete symptoms as pride, self-love, love of the world, lust, or false ambition. In contrast, God's saving activity in Christ is nothing other than a *therapeia psychês,* "God's method of *healing a soul* which is *thus diseased.*"[117] The love of God, which appeared in Christ and is given through the Spirit to human hearts, is the effective means of salvation for all manifestations of this sickness, because it is able to heal the source of that evil of egocentric self-love and love of the world that issues from it.

However, for Wesley, this includes the fact that he consistently views sin as a voluntary act of a human being. This was already true of the transgression of the first humans, which Wesley characterizes as a "wilful act of disobedience," but it is also fundamentally applicable to sin in general, which Wesley defines as a "voluntary transgression of a known law."[118] This idea of sin, with its strong orientation toward voluntary action, caused Wesley a certain degree of difficulty with regard to the character of involuntary transgression. However, it was not chosen casually. It stands in the service of the argument to prove that a Christian could be free of sinful acts. This concept of Wesley's will continue to occupy us below. For now it will suffice for us to state here that Wesley emphasized much more the understanding of sin as a deed than did other theologians who reflect the heritage of the Protestant Reformation.

Hence, he stands without doubt in the biblical tradition. In particular, it is in the Old Testament that the word *sin* becomes "conceived almost exclusively as a deed which expresses itself in errant behavior, considered in light of God's commands."[119] The authors of the Old Testament have a diverse vocabulary at their disposal to portray the different aspects of such errant behavior.[120] Even in the New Testament mainly concrete, particular sins are meant, where *hamartia* (sin) is spoken of in the plural. Paul fairly consistently uses the term *transgression* for this aspect of sin.[121] Naturally, the concrete character of the transgression of sin is recognized with particular clarity.

Thus, it is again the Old Testament that highlights two important assumptions of Christian discourse concerning sin and guilt.

(a.) There is no basic distinction between guilt toward humans and guilt toward God. Wherever I err in doing God's will, I will be guilty not only before God but also toward my fellow human beings. Conversely, every injury of the human rights of another is guilt against God, who protects their lives by his commandment. For those who confess their sin before God, this aspect can emerge quite clearly into the foreground without thereby excluding their guilt against their fellow humans.[122]

It is often difficult to speak of these relationships in our present situation, in which norms that protect individuals or society are strongly relativized and are no longer identified with God's command. The reality of guilt, which consists in the fact that I destroy or defraud the environment, the rights, and the means of living for other people, is not therefore in any way less grievous, and we are not to relinquish the duty to tell people that this guilt will destroy their relationship to God, the ground of all being and all orders of life.

In the New Testament, the fifth petition of the Lord's Prayer explicitly sets forth the relationship between forgiveness through God and forgiveness between human beings. It also indirectly underscores the inner relationship of guilt and punishment. Through the Greek word for "debt" or "debtor," which is used in Matthew's Gospel, an aspect of sin and guilt is drawn out that is not grasped by the terms *transgression* or *failure*. Guilt arises from the fact that we are in debt to others in some way![123]

(b.) A further important observation that is based upon the linguistic usage of the Old Testament has to do with the deep, inner relationship between guilt and punishment. In the biblical sense, *punishment*—which is often denoted by the same word as the word for guilt—is not a sanction independent of the guilty deed. In the biblical sense, "punishment" is that potential for condemnation that lies within the sinful deed itself and points back to those who are guilty if God does not turn away the effects of sin from the sinner through his gracious intervention. In the Old Testament, this consequence of guilt is not only interpreted individualistically and personally; for it also affects the community in which an offense occurs. If it is not punished or atoned for, the destructive potential that stems from the offense reverts back to the community and disturbs its life. This especially applies to the case in which murder has been committed.[124]

If at first glance these notions appear strange to us, they nevertheless carry a deep truth within them, whose effects we are able to discern wherever offenses are no longer prosecuted or suspected within a society—that is, where a system rules that perverts the right, or where the ruling authority has become too weak either from outward or inward causes.

In the New Testament, the intertwining of sin and punishment are most clearly recognizable in Romans 1:20-32. The failures that Paul enumerates in verses 24 to 31 are already the consequences of human godlessness and lawlessness, to which God "gave them up," and to that extent, are at the same time guilt and punishment.[125] Here and in other places in his letters, Paul binds the two aspects of sin together. Their concrete effects for the common life of humanity and their relationship to God are described, clearly in the so-called catalog of vices, but also in the depth dimension of human sin, which is made evident in the destroyed relationship with God and with the reliance upon the "flesh," or the egocentric concern for one's own existence.[126]

The strong emphasis upon the meaning of sin as a deed in Wesleyan theology and preaching was a strength but also a hazard for Methodist preaching. One can call it a strength in that it became possible to address quite concrete problems of human life, and persons were given the possibility of confessing plainly those failures which burdened them, that they might be forgiven and attain a transformed praxis for living through patterns of therapeutic, pastoral care within the Methodist classes.[127]

What this matter of speaking about sin risks is apparent. Wherever one is oriented toward the naming of concrete, particular sins, there is the peril of stereotyping based on a fixed moral code, the peril of preaching judgment, and above all, of losing the insight about how deep sin actually penetrates human existence. With reference to Wesley, it can at least be noted that when he concretized the New Testament "catalog of vices," he placed less emphasis upon sexual lapses and more upon the transgressions of social behavior. This contrasts with the pattern found in the larger tradition of evangelistic preaching. Because of this emphasis, at times Wesley had to defend himself against attacks.[128]

That does not mean that he excluded from his sermons the realm of sexual covetousness with its consequences. Jesus' exposition of the seventh commandment in Matthew 5:28 is cited in his sermon on original sin as an important measure for evaluating the human situation. However, the consequences which Wesley drew from Jesus' words are most noteworthy: "So that one knows not about which to wonder at most, the ignorance or the insolence of those men who speak with such disdain of them that are overcome by desires which every man has felt in his own breast! The desire of every pleasure of sense, innocent or not, being natural to every child of man."[129]

Language about sin that is biblically grounded and oriented toward the Methodist tradition must therefore both speak very concretely about guilty behavior and must speak publicly and in pastoral care situations about the reality of becoming guilty. However, it will have to do this with sensitivity and not by prejudging the behavior of others based upon inappropriate, stereotyped standards. At times persons are guilty in completely different ways than they appear at first blush! At the same time, a complete relativizing of norms of conduct in terms of a one-sided situational ethic is certainly not appropriate for United Methodist theology.[130]

When it comes to putting guilt in concrete terms, a peculiar kind of double-mindedness reigns in contemporary Protestantism. There are circles which refer to sin only in a completely privatistic sense, limited to a moralistic interpretation of the Ten Commandments. Every hint of the possibility of a structural cause for sin is rejected. However, others limit the realm of sin completely to social injustice and they bracket the question of personal failure because of their fear of succumbing to a moralistic ethic.

Once again, the Old Testament may provide us with a model here, a model in which the shared responsibility for right and wrong in society is as deeply etched as the question of personal guilt remains of elementary significance. Wesley consistently maintained an ethic that held together both the personal and the social dimensions: the responsibility for a society in which people do not find the environment for life that they need, and which is therefore even structurally marked by sin, coupled with an awareness of individual sin in response to which comes, in typically Wesleyan pragmatic style, a call to transformation.[131]

It should be of particular significance to contemporary people in their encounter with the phenomena of sin and guilt that both sides of this dynamic are made conscious to them; their entanglement in the web of guilt, from which they are unable to extricate themselves, and which they can also not deny or trivialize, and their personal responsibility, upon whose claims they repeatedly founder.

2.2.1.3 SIN AND THE LAW

Especially in Pauline theology, the significance and efficacy of sin and the law are inseparably and multifariously bound together.[132] In Galatians 3:19 Paul says, the law "was added because of transgressions." At first that sounds as if the law is being considered as a temporary effort to stop the flow of the consequences of sin. This idea is reiterated a few verses later (3:23), where a kind of "protective custody" is mentioned in which we were kept "imprisoned and guarded under the law." A comparison with parallel statements from the Epistle to the Romans indicates that Paul did not ascribe any positive educative function to the law.[133] Romans 4:15 and 5:13-14 maintain that sin has exerted a destructive force in humanity since Adam. However, this first becomes recognizable and susceptible to judgment when humans are provoked to commit concrete acts of transgression through the existence of the law. Paul describes this process in Romans 7:7-12, using as an example the command "Thou shalt not covet," which first activates in persons the greed and the hidden sin of coveting that already existed within them.

On the one hand, then, sin misuses the God-given good law so that the command that was supposed to give life causes death instead, since sin sets in motion its judging power. Through the law, sin now becomes even more powerful in its death dealing power (Romans 5:20). The actual operation of the law is therefore negative: it condemns sinners.

On the other hand, it is precisely like this that the law does its real work: it makes hidden sins known and it becomes an unerring indicator of how things really stand for a person. The only positive effect of the law is that it shows up humans' guilt.

If humans first come to know sin in its true character through the law (Romans 7:7), can one then say that the law has also subjectively led them to the "knowledge of sin" (Romans 3:20) and to the awareness of their need for redemption?

Wesley was firmly convinced of this. In his sermon on "The Original, Nature, Properties, and Use of the Law" he said, "To slay the sinner is then the first use of the law; to destroy the life and strength wherein he trusts, and convince him that he is dead while he liveth; not only under sentence of death, but actually dead unto God, void of all spiritual life, 'dead in trespasses and sins.'" He continues, "The second use of it is to bring him unto life, unto Christ, that he may live."[134] With these two functions, the law accepts "the part of a severe schoolmaster," according to Galatians 3:24. Wesley draws from this practical consequences for preaching. Conviction of the sinner comes not through preaching the gospel, but through the law. "One in a thousand may have been awakened by the gospel. But this is no general rule. The ordinary method of God is to convict sinners by the law, and that only."[135]

In this discussion, Wesley remains close to the exposition that Martin Luther had given. By using the concept of the *usus theologicus* or *elenchticus* (for the theological or the converting use) he emphasizes the converting and condemning power of the law. Yet, he would most energetically contend that the law in itself is able to lead us from itself to Christ; taken in itself, the law leads one into doubt, into the impenitence or the self-satisfied arrogance of those who think that they have done everything that was expected of them.[136] In conformity to this outlook, Paul also records in his own biographic comments how the law became for him the motive for his effort to attain his own righteousness, which he judged to be unblemished according to the measure of the law (Philippians 3:6; see also Romans 9:30–10:4). It was his encounter with the resurrected Christ that first of all showed Paul where he actually stood before God.

The encounter with the law can apparently release quite different subjective reactions within people, and one wonders what inferences can be drawn from it concerning the reality of sin and the human awareness of it. We therefore need to consider carefully whether that which is asserted by the term *law* is only relevant for the biblical Torah or also for other forms of "law."[137]

The conflict between sinful humanity and the law plays itself out at different levels.

(a.) The conflict can be an open dispute. By establishing limits through the law—especially in the form of prohibitions—sin finds a concrete foothold in humans. The prohibition lures one toward transgression, the command induces resistance, then the inward rebellion of people manifests itself against God, and they fall into judgment. The term used to characterize this is *antinomian* conflict.[138] This conflict unmasks resistance to God. Of course, this conflict surfaces not only with reference to the Mosaic law. Even the heathen, who have the law inscribed on their hearts (Romans 2:15), stand in this conflict and experience in their consciences the struggle between accusing and excusing thoughts.

In view of this situation, it certainly remains an open question to what extent a person who has transgressed appropriate norms of behavior (and thereby incurred injury) is able to become aware of her or his guilt or come to an awareness of a culpable separation from God. A wealth of strategies for excuses and denials is evident.

(b.) The conflict can be repressed. Sin wraps people in the illusion that if they could fulfill the law they would find true life, and thus they are enticed to construct their own rules and norms based upon their own achievements of the demands of the law. There is no intimation of rebellion here, but a vindication of their own lives against God by using God's will as a tool to vindicate their lives before God. The command becomes the tool of their own justification of themselves. On the one hand, the consequence of this outlook is fear of not attaining this goal. On the other hand, there is the self-justification which achieves its standards through a comparison with the attainments of others. A prototype of this attitude is the Pharisee in Jesus' parable in Luke 18:9-14, and also Paul's analysis of himself in Philippians 3.

This is called the *nomian* conflict. Although obedience and the fulfillment of the law are on the agenda here, the conflict has shifted to the unconscious level. The pressure to seek to justify oneself has taken the place of a confident reliance upon God. This is also the effect of the basic sin of humanity, which is its separation from God. It hides itself under the mantle of external righteousness and piety and is thus no less dangerous than are other expressions of sin. The mark of this kind of conflict with the will of God is that the fulfilling of the law is oriented to formal, external precepts, so that the effort to stand pure and without blame often leads in situations of conflict to wronging other people in a deeper sense, in that they are misused by being made an object of comparison with our glossy description of ourselves, which then becomes a base for building a monument to ourselves. Self-justification becomes stifling for others and for oneself. In his interpretation of the commands in the Sermon on the Mount, Jesus intensified the depth dimensions of guilt. In particular, the summary of the law in the love command opposes our effort to suppose we can formally conform to the will of God by our deeds.[139]

Moreover, this form of the conflict is not confined to a direct altercation with the biblical law. Paul observed the tendency of people to "boast of themselves," that is, to cite their own achievements or wisdom, rather than God and his grace, as the foundation upon which they would build their lives and as what one considers the content and goal of life. He proceeds to expound this as a general human dilemma.[140] Paul has uncovered the superstitious anxiety that is produced in the religious realm, efforts to please God through the precise fulfillment of cultic commands. He found this tendency within Judaism, but also in the various forms of pagan religiosity (Galatians 4:8-10). It is evident that self-justification, as well as anxiety based on denial, emerges in a completely secular guise in the form of modern religion of success. It is unfortunately no less true that many expressions of the Christian faith can be misrepresented in a "legal" manner. In the abstract, helpful forms of spiritual discipline, like prayer or regular Bible study, can become means for measuring one's religious achievements (or lack of them).[141]

(c.) A final form of conflict is the denial of conflict. In place of rebellion and self-justification, resignation or self-surrender enters the picture. The best biblical example of this tendency is the parable of the talents (Luke 19:12-27). This might be called the *a-nomian* conflict. People feel that the law demands too much of them, and they refuse to even begin to accept its demands or arguments. They are scarcely guilty of transgressions, and they are also not inclined to justify themselves by their achievements. However, they remain guilty before themselves and God. Such a condition often conceals deep wounds and spiritual hindrances that were inflicted in childhood. However, the deep "absence of God" is reflected in this phenomenon too, an absence from which people suffer. This form of the experience of sin is only hinted at in the biblical witness. In particular it is often women in our day who show that not only the "active" form of sin in the sense of a transgression or presumption, but also the "passive" kind of sin that exists in the form of undervaluation or sabotaging of a person's own possibilities.[142]

Our analysis points to a twofold result:

1. Even persons who are no longer under the influence of the Mosaic law discover through the natural and social circumstances of their lives

that their lives are both limited and "challenged." They react to this in a manner similar to that which the Bible describes as a reaction to God's law, namely, with rebellion, self-justification, or resignation. So, in the reality in which people live there is apparently a basic structure that corresponds to that of the law in a quite general sense and which signifies for people something of the greatness of the task that is set before them as well as the impotence of their existence as mere "pip-squeaks." With regard to its content, what becomes apparent as a demand or a boundary is not equated with the biblical law, even if at points it may have similarities. In particular, the phenomenon of sin can only be truly apprehended in situations where being true to God (as in the first commandment) is held as the basic issue of human life.

2. We will see below to what extent the Mosaic law, summarized in the Decalogue or the love commandment, is in the final analysis identical with a general moral law, as Wesley assumed.[143] In this context we must ask the question of whether knowledge of sin is possible through the proclamation of the law alone—in other words, apart from the gospel. We have noted how the law makes clear to different extents people's enmity with God and their need of God. However, it should also not be overlooked that sin misuses the law precisely to encourage the tendency of humans to denial and suppression. So, one is forced to establish that although humans "get to know" sin as a concrete reality through the law (Romans 7:7),[144] they do not have the power to recognize its significance as a radical questioning of their lives. It is also questionable whether Paul wanted to speak in Romans 3:20 about a knowledge of sin through the law before or apart from Christ. The section on "the wrath of God revealed from heaven," which concludes with Romans 3:20, is inserted into the declaration of the revelation of the righteousness of God in the gospel (Romans 1:16-17; Romans 3:25ff.). The reference to the gospel is thus a hint allowing people to recognize how things really stand with them.[145]

From what has been said, the following consequences may be drawn for United Methodist doctrine and preaching:

1. The fact that humans cannot fulfill God's will by themselves and that they therefore also fail in their lives is a reality that must not be suppressed in Christian preaching. If it was long the danger of Methodist preaching to speak of God's law in an overly frightening manner and to force people into a heightened feeling of guilt, today the danger is without doubt seen in the neglect or even denial of the dimension of guilt, and

thus the preaching of "cheap grace."[146] People always stand under the law, and God's judgment for their unrighteousness and godlessness is revealed to them, whether they realize it or not. Let us not pound it into them with rhetorical means. Instead, let us repeatedly attempt to make them conscious of the situation in which they find themselves and also confront them with the reality that their lives belong to God and that they are responsible to God. They are also to know that if they fail in this responsibility they are lost before God. The symptoms of this failure are concrete guilt, and also discontentment, the "uncreative revolt"[147] against God and the basic conditions of one's life, or the deep resignation to which a person surrenders himself or herself. However, people do not experience this failure only in their refusal of God; it also needs to be made clear to them how they have missed the purpose for their lives in their presumed strengths, their successes and achievements.[148] This is true not only of individuals; social relationships and modes of conduct are also marked by the effects of sin.

2. A knowledge of sin in its full depth is only possible where it is also recognized that God, who challenges and circumscribes our lives through the law, is none other than the One who receives and fulfills our lives in his love. Only where we are held by love can we look into the depths of despair, that cavernous hole which is gaping because of our sin. Only where the greatness of God's love is grasped will the attitude of indifference, resistance, or rejection of subservience to God or of pretensions against God be recognized for what it really is: enmity against God. The love command becomes, so to speak, the point of intersection between the law and the gospel. It shows us the greatness of the demand which God rightly makes of us and it contains the announcement that we live by God's love and thus are ourselves able to love.[149]

2.2.1.4 SIN AND SUFFERING

According to the conviction of the Bible, human sin destroys not only people's relationship with God but also their relationship to one another and to the surrounding creation. It seems to be the purpose of the Yahwistic creation story, and especially of Genesis 3, to show "that all sorrow comes from sin."[150] Illustrative of this is the discussion in Genesis 4 of the far-reaching destruction of social relationships. Already in the second generation of humanity, envy leads to murder, and the vicious cycle of force and counterforce escalates ever further in the history of humanity.

Paul also sees the consequences of sin primarily in the social realm, in the corporate life of humanity. God's judgment on sin consists not in some sort of supplemental or despotic sanction. According to Romans 1:24ff., God simply abandons people to the results of their wrong decisions, decisions which replace the worship of the Creator with a false love of the creature, which have resulted in the idolatrous worship of themselves. The surrender of human beings to idolatrous self-love leads to the contamination and the destruction of their interhuman relationships in all areas of their lives (1:30-31).[151] This then also shows that persons who live under the sway of sin are not only its propagators but also its victims. For it is always others who suffer the results of sins, like lack of mercy, avarice, malice, envy, strife, or murder. In their polemic against the rich and the powerful, the prophets in the Old Testament made clear that these consequences of sin were not only due to individual transgressions but are also often attributable to "class-specific" attitudes. Thus, already in the biblical message there is the observation that "structural unrighteousness" is also a consequence of sin.[152]

Alongside the destruction of ordinary human relationships, the biblical tradition also indicates that sickness has its cause in sin.[153] This connection is easily made since death is seen as a consequence of sin (see Romans 6:23), and in biblical times (more than in the present day), illnesses are viewed as harbingers of death.[154] In fact, there are no places in the Bible that speak directly of this relationship between sin and sickness. However, such a relationship seems to be assumed where the forgiveness of sins and healing of illness are spoken of together as in Psalm 103:3; Mark 2:10-11; and James 5:15-16.

But there is a misunderstanding that needs to be excluded from our consideration, one that has already been tackled in the biblical writings themselves, namely, the assumption that individual and particularly severe illnesses can always be traced back to especially grave sinful acts. There are psalms of lament, in which the psalmist confesses that his eyes were opened to his sin through an illness (see Psalm 32:1-5; 38:2-9; 41:5, etc.). However, there are also other psalms that protest passionately against the insinuation of such a correlation between sin and sickness (see Psalms 35 and 102) or at least do not even consider the topic. Within the context of the entire biblical witness, it is the book of Job that once for all prohibits any general conclusions to be drawn about the link between the sickness of individuals and a particular offense that was committed. Of course, this does not exclude the possibility that an affected person may recognize and confess their belief in a connection between sickness and guilt.

In the New Testament, the possibility of a fundamental connection between sickness and a particular sin is expressly rejected in John 9:2—which would raise certain problems for a person born blind. For Jesus, his healing the sick and his exorcism of the demons are signs of the approaching reign of God, which indicate that God's Lordship is stronger than those powers of evil which bring disease. However, Jesus never mentions a particular connection between sickness and sin in the case of specific persons, and, in Luke 13:1-5, indirectly excludes such a connection.[155] It is precisely the possessed, whom Jesus helped, who are examples of the fact that humans have become victims and suffer under the power of evil; nowhere is it even hinted at that they are guilty as individuals for their condition.

For Paul, it is an important component of the community of faith to acknowledge that Christians no longer stand under the power of sin (Romans 6). The consequences that Paul draws from this, however, concern the ethical sphere exclusively, and particularly the behavior of Christians among one another and toward other persons. Paul never says that Christians are supposed to be set free from the burden of sickness and from bodily weaknesses. Of course, he reckons with the healing power of God, but he perceives that the vulnerability of the human body is an unavoidable sign of the fact that Christians still wait full of hope for the conclusive and complete deliverance of their bodies (Romans 8:18ff.).[156]

Wesley essentially follows Paul's lead at this point. As we will see, one of his central theological concerns is that the victory over sin is a reality that is really experienced in the life of the Christian. Wesley also understands the existential realm, in which this reality is lived and experienced, to be the area of one's relationship with God and with one's fellow human beings—in short, the dimension of love.[157] Love overcomes the most horrible suffering that sin causes, which is the social results of sin. However, bodily and spiritual weaknesses are for Wesley regarded as conditions that humans are required to bear until their deaths. That does not exclude the fact that Wesley, as a medical practitioner, is also aware of the healing effects that a new inner attitude toward life has upon the health of humans, nor that he quite consciously reports on miraculous healings that were occurring in his day.[158] However, there is no basic linkage between the forgiveness of sins and the healing of illnesses.[159]

Before we consider the consequences of our discussion for a contemporary theology of The United Methodist Church a third aspect of the destructive power of sin and its implications for life on this earth must be mentioned. In Romans 8:20, Paul emphasizes that the entire creation has been subjected to decay because of human sin, and that it is waiting with anxious longing for the salvation of the children of God, through which it will also be transformed into its imperishable reality.[160] Wesley adopted this point of view and from it developed the conviction that not only humans but all forms of life were originally created in a condition of imperishability,[161] inviolability, and immortality. We will need to return to this question at a later point when we address the relationship between sin and death.

Hermeneutically, such considerations draw contemporary expositors into a peculiar situation. On the one hand, it will be difficult for them to share these concepts in light of the knowledge of natural science in our day. Sickness, as well as the phenomenon of the food cycle, in which some life forms kill and consume other forms of life, should be regarded as a very ancient phenomenon in nature that cannot properly be attributed to the results of primeval human history.[162] On the other hand, there is a wealth of signs today that indicate that people have endangered the existence of creation through their hubris. What is fascinating and also shocking about this is that the cause of this danger can with precision and certainty be traced back to a human attitude that the Bible refers to as original sin. Humans want to be like God and they fail to fulfill their destiny as those created in the image of God to represent God's creative and protective concern for this world. The tragedy of this phenomenon lies in the fact that this attitude had its beginning precisely within the Christian culture, which has certainly followed in a secular form the command to "take dominion" over the earth.[163] Both of these observations would suggest that the relation of sin and suffering is to be anchored less in the conditions of natural law, and that it is rather to be described as a consequence of the basic disorder that is seen within human existence.

Thus, the relationship of sin and suffering has distinct dimensions. The fact that suffering or illness turn out to be a consequence of concrete guilt and sin in the case of one person cannot be excluded, and yet it does not permit us to make a general rule to that effect. More frequently, guilt and sin work themselves out in the suffering that we inflict upon others. And frequently a direct connection between the guilty conduct of some and the suffering of others cannot be proved at all. The sovereignty of sin also manifests itself within the structures of unrighteousness, which become anonymous causes of want, suffering, and illness. Voluntary acts by persons of goodwill can accomplish little in circumventing these causes. Since they can see through these structures and do not readily participate in such patterns of behavior, it is often the ones who live in conscious fellowship with God who have to suffer under the opposition and rejection by others.[164] One of the important traits of a United Methodist theology is the fact that it critiques the destruction of the depth dimension of human fellowship and of those persons' relationship to God in such a way that one cannot speak of the one apart from the other. The disruption of relationship with God invariably has tragic implications for the common life of humanity as well as the relation of humanity to creation as a whole.

2.2.1.5 SIN AND DEATH

The destructive power of sin is most radically revealed in the fact that through its rule even death has attained its power over humanity. Paul presupposes this relationship in Romans 5:12: "Therefore, just as sin came into the world through one man, and death came through sin, and so death spread to all because all have sinned. . . ." In Romans 6:23 this notion is strengthened by saying, "The wages of sin is death," and then the contrast is stated, "but the free gift of God is eternal life in Christ Jesus our Lord" (compare also 1 Corinthians 15:56). Paul obviously interprets Genesis 2 and 3 to mean that it was through sin that death first entered into the world of creatures.[165]

It is questionable whether this corresponds to the original intention of Genesis 2 and 3. The account of paradise and the fall into sin certainly leaves open this question. According to Genesis 2:9 and 3:22, 24, the tree of life was withheld from humanity, and Genesis 3:22 precludes that in those primeval conditions humanity was represented as being immortal.[166] The finitude of life is part of the creatureliness of humanity;[167] it would have been fatal for humanity and the creation to break through this boundary; therefore, the first human beings were hindered from stepping over this threshold.[168]

However, a second difficult problem of interpreting Genesis 2 and 3 is connected to this. Was the threat of death expressed in 2:17 fulfilled, or was the serpent who had denied this from the beginning to be regarded as correct? The old account leaves this question open and thus permits different possibilities of interpretation.[169]

For Wesley, the answer to both of these questions was clear. All life lost its original immortality through the sin of humanity, and God's threat of punishment became true in that the first humans did perish in "spiritual death," as a result of their sinfulness, in the sense that they fell out of fellowship with God.[170] However, for their part, contemporary expositors would not be able to ignore the fact that, according to our knowledge, death and dying are unavoidable marks of multicellular life. Therefore, we will need to interpret the biblical statements concerning the relationship between sin and death not as biological statements, but rather in terms of their anthropological and theological dimensions. Among the most important marks of human existence is the fact that humans know about their impending death. Martin Heidegger has correctly characterized human existence as "being unto death."[171] A person experiences this "being unto death" with anxiety, and as an occasion for concern or also for either resistance or denial. For the death of a human being is not simply the "perishing" of an organism; it is my own life that unmistakably and irreplaceably comes to its end. "Fear of death pierces deep into life. On the one hand it motivates us to unrestricted self-affirmation, regardless of our own finitude; on the other hand, it robs us of the power to accept life. Either way we see a close link between sin and death. The link is rooted in sin to the extent that only the nonacceptance of our own finitude makes the inescapable end of finite existence a manifestation of the power of death that threatens us with nothingness."[172] Simply stated, because I cannot accept the limitation that is placed upon my life, the biological end of my life becomes an all-threatening death. However, I cannot accept this limitation, because my fellowship with the Creator, who has created my life and who also encloses it within his boundaries, is destroyed. That which is "deathly" in the death of a human being is therefore the fact that one dies the death of a sinner; that is, the death of the one who is distant from God and thereby distant from life. Death is therefore "an essential consequence of sin" rather than a "punishment that God has arbitrarily set and imposed." [173] Death makes final and irrevocable that which occurred within life. "The moment of death ends the possibility of a new decision and makes final everything that has taken place."[174]

Conversely, it ought to be such that where God's saving and justifying grace has led a person out of sin's absence of God and into the life that bestows fellowship with God, then death and dying begin to appear within a new light. The border that is set for our lives remains. However, it lies in the hands of God. Even death cannot separate us from his love (Romans 8:38-39). Whoever believes in Jesus Christ will live, even if that one dies (John 11:25). In its emphasis upon "holy dying," early Methodism perceived a particularly important aspect of holiness, that is, the intensive fellowship with God, the victory over sin, and the joyful testifying to that reality as Christians entered into rest or went home "triumphantly."[175]

In our day, we have come to stand against such standards of judgment since we know that the manner in which a person suffers her or his death is particularly dependent upon somatic processes. The struggle of death is first of all a struggle of the body against death. For that reason, it always remains as a sign of the "brokenness" of our human existence. And yet, the certainty that God's hand securely holds those who belong to him, even in death, remains valid apart from the external manner of our death. It is a sign that the power of grace and the love of God are stronger than the power of sin and death, whenever we are able to experience in the company of the dying the way this certainly provides them with inward support and comfort.

2.2.1.6 SIN AND THE POWER OF EVIL

According to biblical understanding, people bear full responsibility for their sinful actions. However, persons find themselves at once in a vicious circle of the actions undertaken through their own responsibility and the fact that these actions are ruined by the power of sin. Thus, in particular situations the power of sin and of evil can be cited as a cause for human sinning. The power of evil is personified in the form of Satan or the devil. Instead of living under the wholesome rule of God, persons who sin give themselves over to the destructive power of evil. "Everyone who commits sin is a child of the devil; for the devil has been sinning from the beginning" (1 John 3:8; see also John 8:44). This assertion is also related to another: "The Son of God was revealed for this purpose, to destroy the works of the devil." Whether a person is descended from God or from the devil does not imply that her or his fate has been predetermined. Rather, that is decided in the encounter with the freeing word of Jesus.[176]

In the history of Christian faith and spirituality the first part of 1 John 3:8 has unfortunately received the primary emphasis, so that the second sentence ("The Son of God was revealed for this purpose, to destroy the works of the devil") has been largely robbed of its meaning and effect. The realistic analysis of the "structures of evil," which reach much more deeply and are more effective than is the evil will and deed of an individual person, degenerates into merely a belief in the demonic. Yet the history of demonic beliefs is in many respects a piece of the history of calamity! There are therefore not a few Christian theologians who are of the view that it would be a service to Christian preaching and theology if the language of the devil were to be abandoned.[177] In the face of a world in which the diabolical is rather on the rise than in decline, one would first need to very carefully investigate the actual function of the biblical language concerning the power of evil.

(a.) In the Old Testament, the figure of Satan plays only the role of a marginal figure. Above all, Satan is not his proper name, but it signifies the adversary, the enemy, and the accuser.[178] The function of the accuser also signifies that figure in the heavenly world that confronts us in Zechariah 3:1 and in Job 1. In the history of Job, the role of Satan almost appears to be tantamount to that of a "heavenly public attorney." The fact that the motives of the godly are questioned and tested is an admissible, and indeed almost a necessary concern. And yet, the mistrust does not proceed from God, even if God allows the testing. Nor is it a question of whether calamity comes from God or the devil. Job struggles alone with God about why he was suffering, and this conforms to the line of thought found throughout the entirety of the Old Testament.[179]

The serpent in Genesis 3 is not yet identified with the devil in the Old Testament.[180] Yet, it is also the personification of a temptation which assumes power over humans through the skill of its questioning, without this thereby excusing them. The cause of sin is not the serpent or the devil, but rather the sinful deed itself.

Meanwhile, 1 Chronicles 21:1 names the figure of Satan as the author of David's temptation, while the older account in 1 Samuel 24:1 says that God suggested these thoughts to David in his anger. This renders significant the struggle concerning the question of whether temptation to sin can proceed from God. This tension also permeates the New Testament expressions that deal with this theme.[181]

(b.) In the intertestamental period, the concept of the devil developed in early Judaism beyond these Old Testament beginnings, to the idea of the devil as a power standing over against God.[182] Even as the angels exist to serve God, so Satan rules with the help of his demons. These powers contend for the heart of humanity. Those who surrender themselves to the power of evil are the children of darkness, and those who belong to God are the children of light.

The New Testament shares this view of a flawed world, but it also takes over the presupposition that at last even the kingdom of evil will be subjected to the Lordship of God and will be overcome by it. However, this takes place precisely through the work accomplished by Jesus.

The devil appears as a spiritually articulate tempter, and he is sent away by Jesus (Matthew 4:1-11). Through Jesus' power, being able to drive out demons, Jesus breaks into the kingdom of Satan, and he establishes the rule of God (Matthew 12:24-29). The figure of Satan and the demons also make clear that the suffering and self-destructive behavior of certain people is due not simply to their individual sins; they are victims of the powers that gain their strength from connections that transcend individuals and that follow from the openness of humanity to the power of evil.

Thus, in the New Testament, the figure of the devil becomes the epitome of the suprahuman, God-opposing potential for danger and destruction that lies within this world. It explains why people close themselves off to the gospel (2 Corinthians 4:4; Matthew 13:37-39; John 8:44). It characterizes the destruction that threatens those who fall out of fellowship with God (1 Corinthians 5:5), as well as the danger to which Christians are still always exposed (2 Corinthians 11:14; Ephesians 6:11-12). Apocalyptic traditions expect a final, decisive clash between God and his Christ and the devil and his minions (see 2 Thessalonians 2:3-12; Revelation 13;19). However, these powers already realize that before God the power of Satan is already broken (Revelation 12:7-12).

Thus, a "soteriological functionality of the declarations concerning Satan" predominates widely in the New Testament[183]—that is, these statements are not for the sake of understanding Satan himself; they are made with reference to the events of salvation that the gospel is announcing.

(c.) If we attempt to systematize the biblical message, two possible consequences for the relationship of God and Satan transpire.

(1.) The figure of Satan is a form that speaks of the dark side of God, of the hidden God, who appears as an enemy. What actually has no place in our conception of God, namely that God tempts and accuses, that he destroys and kills, becomes evident here, and this speaks of a tension "which exists within the circumstances of God Himself."[184] Luther expressly asserted that God appears in the guise of the devil.[185] This aspect is alien to Methodist theology.

(2.) There is no longer a division in the image of God: Jesus sees Satan as lightning that has fallen from heaven (Luke 10:18), and the Revelation to John reports the expulsion of Satan from the heavenly realm

151

(Revelation 12:7-12). The voice of the accuser has become silent before God, no matter how much he may yet rage on earth. For Wesley and early Methodist theology, the fact that the power of evil is broken is the pivotal point for speaking of the devil.[186]

The devil, who is subdued by Christ, is certainly not as yet annihilated. Thus, further data about the devil is given in the witness of the New Testament: "That the one who is subdued by means of this faith is still active due to the eschatological reservation, should be emphasized in light of the ever-present danger of a Satanic resurgence. The assertion that evil is Satanic therefore represents the negative corollary to the assertion that salvation is the activity of God."[187]

In view of all that which is "infernal and Satanic" in this present world, the dimension of evil as a power needs to be taken seriously still today and ought not be reduced either to "nothingness" or merely to moral aberration.[188] The power of sin has attained a life of its own in this world, that goes far beyond the effects of evil deeds and the evil will of individuals.

References to personal evil, that is, to the devil, in this context can emphasize that this power confronts us in its operation and its consequences in many situations, through a *modus operandi* that works itself out resolutely and often with diabolical intelligence. Yet, it is certain that to speak of this reality with personified attributes must always remain a figurative language at its deepest level, since that dimension which denotes a personal relationship at its deepest level (the "I-Thou" relationship) fails to be addressed by that language.

As helpful as it is to note that in the seventh petition of the Lord's Prayer and in the question that is asked candidates for church membership in The United Methodist Church ("Do you renounce evil and do you trust solely in the grace of God?") the question remains open as to whether evil or the evil one is intended,[189] it is equally important that this question does not at the same time restrict the realistic assessment of the power of evil. The act of turning to Christ is more than an activation of goodwill; it has to do with a change of power so that the liberation through Jesus Christ is concretely carried out through the renunciation of the powers that had enslaved us and through the constant petition on behalf of our deliverance by Christ.

In view of the negative experience with demonic belief, some definition of "rules of discourse" are to be commended:

—To speak of the diabolical, the satanic, or the infernal places several possibilities of linguistic expression at our disposal with which to characterize that which is inhuman in this world, with its evil and animosity toward the sacred. However, this ought not to lead us to demonize human beings or groups of humans. Even the person who appears to be a tool of the devil remains God's beloved creation in Jesus Christ.

—If we perceive the demonic as an "overwhelming power to whom people are delivered and who so completely robs them of their personhood that they can no longer resist that power which, as it were, simultaneously devours them,"[190] we will be able to recognize the proper limits of bondage and not confuse victims with wrongdoers. However, at the same time, this knowledge is undertaken with the certainty that in Christ the power of the demonic is overcome and we need give up no single person. Thus, the ritual act of exorcism, which is inevitably endangered by misuse, is not as needed as is the patient accomplishment of care and resistance through the power of Jesus Christ. In the encounter with Christ, people are even set free to see through false excuses by rebuking the devil, and to become capable of becoming genuinely responsible in their actions.

—"The devil is not an object of faith. However, as a confession to God, every Christian confession of faith is in reality a repudiation of the devil and the scheme of this perverted world."[191] Therefore, we can always only refer to Satan in terms of negation, in the sense that those enemies have already been overcome by Christ. This reality has not often been acknowledged within those circles in which the role of Satan has been a matter of emphasis. Their peril lies not only in the fact that they actually tend to limit the power of evil to the realm of the occult, and thus do not do justice to the real scope of its activity. It lies primarily in the fact that in their constant concern about the devil and his intrigues, they actually strengthen the authority of the demonic, and in their opposition to the occult and demonic possession they become prisoners of their own anxiety. If the Son of God has come to destroy the works of the devil, then he also frees us from constant preoccupation with this theme.

2.2.1.7   SIN AND GRACE

Why did God not prevent Adam and hence his descendants from falling into sin? Why has God given them the freedom to make decisions that are contrary to God and to God's commands? Wesley asks this question in different contexts. And alongside the answer that this freedom conforms to the essence of humanity, since God wanted to create humans as those who stand over against God,[192] a quite amazing answer comes to light that

Wesley acquires by his exposition of Romans 5:15-21. That is to say, if Adam had not sinned, and if Christ had not died, then we would not have come to know the fullness and the depth of the love of God. Thus, love for God and one's neighbor actually first becomes a possibility through God's redemptive work and, by inference, through the means of Adam's fall! "And herein appeared not only the justice but the unspeakable goodness of God! For how much good does he continually bring out of this evil! How much holiness and happiness out of pain!"[193]

Wesley in no way derives an "excuse" for sinful humanity from this affirmation. At the same time, human sin cannot finally stand in absolute opposition to God's redemptive intentions. Instead, sin needs to be of "service" to humanity in a particularly dialectical and unanticipated manner. Insofar as Wesley accepted the profundity of Pauline thought in Romans 5:15-21, to that extent he also made the angry outcry of Romans 6:1-2 his own, the outcry with which Paul repulses all misunderstandings of this line of thought. To speak of sin and grace not only means to speak of the surpassing of the effect of sin by the effect of grace; it also means preaching the overcoming of sin itself through the liberating grace of God. This should become the center of Wesleyan soteriology and its doctrine of grace.

2.2.2   *God's Covenant Faithfulness*

In the midst of the Christian proclamation is the fact that God has responded to the inability of humans to help themselves through the sending of Jesus. However, that does not mean that the time before this event had simply been "void of salvation." God's gift to his fallen world in the "Son" is a sign of the nature of the living God and is not limited to the coming of the Incarnate Word in Jesus of Nazareth. Thus, John 1:1-13 sketches the "history of the logos," whereby God encounters humans from the time of the creation—albeit without them accepting him![194]

2.2.2.1   GOD'S FAITHFULNESS TO CREATION AND TO HUMANITY

The biblical account of primeval history is already infused with the witness that God has not simply abandoned humanity to its fate after the fall.[195] The guilt of humanity is exposed without indulgence, but God's concern for his creation does not cease because of this. Genesis 3 movingly explains how God makes clothes for the naked humans to cover them. Even Cain, the murderer of his brother, receives from God the "mark of Cain," which was not primarily a stigma that would brand him as a murderer but a sign to protect him from willful assassination.[196]

This juxtaposition of human guilt and divine faithfulness is set forth most impressively in Genesis 8:21-22. The same statement that leads to the decision of God to destroy the creation, as reported in Genesis 6:5-7, becomes the basis for God's decision in 8:21-22 to renounce further judgments of punishment in the future. "I will never again curse the ground because of humankind, for the inclination of the human heart is evil from youth."[197] The parallel priestly account in Genesis 9 speaks of the covenant which God established with Noah, his descendants, and with everything which resided upon this earth. God's "covenant" with his creation is therefore not an alliance between equal partners concluded by means of fulfilling predetermined conditions. Instead, it is God's one-sided pledge of unceasing faithfulness and trustworthiness, and it also includes the obligation of humans to have reverence for life.[198]

In particular, it is the Psalms that describe in the tradition of the Old Testament how it is God's faithfulness to his creation (most English Bible translations have "righteousness") that enables and preserves the lives of humans and animals (Psalms 36:6-10, 65:6-9, 89:11-15, 93, 96, 104). God's faithfulness restrains the powers of chaos, which repeatedly threaten creation, and it provides for the wholesome ordering which makes salutary life possible.[199]

Though some of these psalms appear at first glance to depict life in a highly idyllic manner (for example, Psalm 104), nonetheless they do not obscure the fact that the creation is marked by death and destruction after the fall and the flood. Hence, the process of devouring and being devoured belongs to the reality of nature, and the forces of nature which bring ruin repeatedly threaten the existence of the globe. However, God's faithfulness and goodness prevent the powers of destruction from gaining ascendancy.

In view of these statements, a Christian theology stands before a twofold responsibility. It has to demonstrate the fact that the world which was marked by sin, that is, by the need for God and enmity toward God, is, according to the biblical witness, not a godforsaken and godless world, but a world that continues to live by God's faithfulness—though admittedly in the form of a "broken" existence, which includes the sign of preservation, but also the experience of threat and destruction. With regard to God's pledge of faithfulness, it has to consider what kind of promise humanity's common responsibility can and must perceive, *and* what overall boundary is established for human effort, and for God's pledge to preserve the present condition of humanity by the announcement of the radical eschatological renewal of heaven and earth that is to occur through the crisis of death and rebirth.

In a series of sermons, Wesley characterized the ambivalence that exists within the condition of humanity and creation in general between the fall and redemption.[200] Although he certainly regarded as determinative the biblical statements that speak of the basic corruption of all humanity before God, he was not able to speak about a total perversion of all human capabilities. Humanity retains freedom of decision and responsibility precisely because God holds them secure in the face of their false decisions against God. God does not simply remove sin from the being of humanity. God's providence is also extended to the whole of creation, even if his concern for his children remains central. In addition to the gratitude for God's wondrous rule within nature, there is also the humble acknowledgment of how little humans can recognize of God's wisdom and providence.

2.2.2.2 God's Faithfulness to Israel

At this point in our discussion, a biblically oriented theology needs to address the theme of God's covenant with Israel. It is our contention that the Hebrew word for "covenant," which is *berit,* as well as its Greek equivalent, *diatheke,* does not in any way intend to designate an "alliance" between two equally yoked partners. In the Old Testament, *berit*//*covenant* is "an expression of the *personal commitment of Yahweh* to faithfulness toward God's people."[201] The Deuteronomic theology, in which covenant thought is central, quite emphatically emphasizes this thought through the concept of the "election of Israel."[202] The central affirmation of this concept is found in Deuteronomy 7:6-8:

> For you are a people holy to the LORD your God; the LORD your God has chosen you out of all the peoples on earth to be his people, his treasured possession. It was not because you were more numerous than any other people that the LORD set his heart on you and chose you—for you were the fewest of all peoples. It was because the LORD loved you and kept the oath that he swore to your ancestors, that the LORD has brought you out with a mighty hand, and redeemed you from the house of slavery, from the hand of Pharaoh king of Egypt.

For the reader of the Pentateuch in its final form, this election unfolds in a long series of covenants: in the call of Abraham and God's promise to him that he was to become a great people and to possess the promised land,[203] in the renewal of this promise to Jacob (Genesis 28:13-15) and the preservation of his family in Egypt, and in the deliverance of the people from Egypt and the (renewed) covenant commitment at Sinai.[204]

Wesley strongly relativized the meaning of this history of election in that he contrasted the new "covenant of grace" in Jesus Christ with a "covenant of works," which began not with Moses but rather with Adam.[205] In making this distinction, he was following the tradition of Puritan and Reformed Pietistic theology. When Wesley refers to God's history with Israel, he usually treats it as "the history of evil" of the "old church of God." According to 1 Corinthians 10:1-13, the new people of God were to guard themselves against such disdaining of God's gracious presence.[206] Hence, the description of the rejection of God by the people of the Old Testament becomes a mirror for the rejection of God by the "visible church of God" in England. In making such claims, Wesley did not shy away from very concrete attacks on the administration of justice in his day.[207] Following this call to repentance issued to the church of his day, Wesley appealed with great empathy to the Independents (Presbyterians), Baptists, Quakers, Catholics, and also the Jews. To these, he said that he did not doubt that all of Israel would be saved—whenever all the heathen attain the salvation appointed for them (Romans 11:25-27). However, he continued, in the interim is there not reason to call out to God with the words of Daniel 9:7-10, 18-19?[208] For now, Wesley's reference to Romans 11:25-27 appears to be more of a biblicistic marginal note, which in Methodism has not led to a deepened preoccupation with the question of the ongoing election of Israel.[209]

If the position of Wesley in this matter had been examined precisely, Methodism would have prepared the way for an earnest Christian-Jewish dialogue early on. The question of the Messiah is placed in the background, without being fundamentally disregarded, but the conversation with Israel is for now conducted primarily on the level of the Old Testament! The seriousness with which Wesley took Romans 11 is indicated by his note on Romans 11:12, where Paul speaks of the "fullness" of the number of the Jews:

> So many prophecies refer to this grand event, that it is surprising any Christian can doubt of it. And these are greatly confirmed by the wonderful preservation of the Jews as a distinct people to this day. When it is accomplished, it will be so strong a demonstration, both of the Old and New Testament revelation, as will doubtless convince many thousand

Deists,[210] in countries nominally Christian; of whom there will, of course, be increasing multitudes among merely nominal Christians. And this will be a means of swiftly propagating the gospel among Mahometans and Pagans; who would probably have received it long ago, had they conversed only with real Christians.[211]

Thus, for Wesley the Jewish people are not only a cautionary example because of their denial, but through their existence are equally a prominent sign for God's faithfulness and a bearer of hope for the fulfillment of God's ways with the whole of humanity.

2.2.2.3   THE COVENANT OF LAW AND THE COVENANT OF GRACE

Based upon the biblical tradition, one would expect that the discourse about the law must inevitably be in relationship to the "covenant of Sinai." However, with Wesley, the "law" has a much more universal meaning. In its theological meaning, "law" is neither the ceremonial law nor the entire Mosaic law (or Roman law at the time of the New Testament), but solely the "moral law."[212] This moral law is essentially contained in the form of the Ten Commandments exposited by Jesus in the Sermon on the Mount. The moral law is summarized in the twofold command of love for God and neighbor.[213]

For Wesley, however, the essential meaning of the law, as *one* side of God's act of revelation, led far beyond this description of content. In its essence, the law preexisted and already before the foundation of the world it was made known to the angels as "first-born children." Subsequently it was "engraven . . . by the finger of God" upon the hearts of the first humans, "free, intelligent creature[s]."[214] The essence of the law is therefore not to be comprehended merely by the recitation of the Ten Commandments. "The law is a copy of the eternal mind, a transcript of the divine nature; yea, it is the fairest offspring of the everlasting Father, the brightest efflux of his essential wisdom, the visible beauty of the Most High. It is the delight and wonder of cherubim and seraphim and all the company of heaven, and the glory and joy of every wise believer, every well instructed child of God upon earth."[215]

The inner knowledge of this law was lost to humanity in the fall. Certainly, the "true light which enlightens every man that cometh into the world" continues to direct people toward that which is good and is required of them by God. However, their hearts remained in darkness until God "chose out of mankind a peculiar people, to whom he gave a more perfect knowledge of his law."[216] However, the pithy sayings that were inscribed on tablets of stone remained only an expedient measure until that time in which God began anew to give his law to humanity according to his promise and to inscribe it within their understanding (Jeremiah 31:33).

Consequently, for Wesley, the "covenant of works" was concluded not at Sinai but with Adam before the fall. Here Wesley follows the model of the Reformed "federal theology."[217] However, he strongly transformed its meaning. "The first covenant supposes him to whom it is given to be already holy and happy, created in the image of God; and prescribes the condition whereon he may continue therein, in love and joy, life and immortality."[218]

Against this, Wesley posited the covenant of grace. It "supposes him to whom it is given to be now unholy and unhappy; fallen short of the glorious image of God, having the wrath of God abiding on him, and hastening through sin, whereby his soul is dead, to bodily death and death everlasting. And to man in this state it prescribes the condition whereon he may regain the pearl he has lost; may recover the favour and the image of God, may retrieve the life of God in his soul, and be restored to the knowledge and the love of God, which is the beginning of life eternal." In sum, "The covenant of works, in order to man's *continuance* in the favor of God, in his knowledge and love, in holiness and happiness, required of perfect man a *perfect* and uninterrupted *obedience* to every point of the law of God; whereas the covenant of grace, in order to man's *recovery* of the favour and life of God, requires only *faith*—living faith in him who through God justifies him that *obeyed not.*"[219]

It cannot be doubted that with this understanding Wesley distanced himself on exegetical grounds from Paul, and he had to inflict violence on his texts at some points.[220] Wesley would not agree that the law is "added because of transgressions" (Galatians 3:19ff.; Romans 5:20). This may be true of the "Mosaic dispensation," which Christ nailed to his cross (Colossians 2:14).[221] However, with regard to the true law of God, it means that it existed from the foundation of the world and its true meaning is only through faith.[222]

However, Wesley's understanding of the law is not unbiblical. It accepts important elements of the Old Testament theology of law and wisdom, which are found again in the New Testament in Matthew and James.[223] As much as Wesley devalues the Jewish perspective on the law, on the one hand, whenever he sharply distinguishes between the "Mosaic dispensation" and the law of God as the "moral law," he also, on the other hand, restores to the law much of its theological content, in that he assumes several key elements of the spirituality of the law, such as the concept of the preexistence of the law or joy over the law.[224]

However, what is the function of the law in an age that no longer resonates with the "covenant of works" as an expression of soteriology but rather stands solidly within the concept of the "covenant of grace"? Like the Protestant Reformers, Wesley too distinguishes a threefold use of the law.[225]

The first function of the law is "to convince the world of sin," and "to slay the sinner, . . . to destroy the life and strength wherein he trusts, and convince him that he is dead while he liveth; not only under sentence of death, but actually dead unto God, void of all spiritual life, 'dead in trespasses and sins.' "

The second function of the law is "to bring him unto life, unto Christ, that he may live." In both functions the law assumes the role of a "severe schoolmaster," of the "disciplinarian" of Galatians 3:24. And although it urges on with force, rather than drawing by love, yet "love is the spring of all. It is the spirit of love which, by this painful means, tears away our confidence in the flesh, which leaves us no broken reed whereon to trust."[226]

The third use of the law "is to keep us alive." Through the working of the Spirit, the law becomes a means of grace that is "the grand means whereby the blessed Spirit prepares the believer for larger communications of the life of God."[227] Even if the law has run its course as a means of justification, according to Romans 10:4, in another sense it is not yet done: "It is still of unspeakable use, first, in convincing us of the sin that yet remains both in our hearts and lives, and thereby keeping us close to Christ, that his blood may cleanse us every moment; secondly, in deriving strength from our Head into his living members, whereby he empowers them to do what his law commands; and thirdly, in confirming our hope of whatsoever it commands and we have not yet attained, of receiving grace upon grace, till we are in actual possession of the fullness of his promises."[228] For this reason, the Christian can as little dispense with the law as she/he can dispense with Christ. "Indeed each is continually sending me to the other—the law to Christ, and Christ to the law. On the one hand, the height and depth of the law constrain me to fly to the love of God in Christ; on the other, the love of God in Christ endears the law to me 'above gold or precious stones'; seeing I know every part of it is a gracious promise, which my Lord will fulfill in its season." [229]

Wesley's theological valuation of the law is not without its problems. The concept of the law itself is not fully clear. Can the "moral law" also clearly convey the meaning of law with reference to its content? How can it have a relationship to the Mosaic law and to that which humans experience as "law" within their lives independent of the biblical commands? We have already taken up this question in regard to the problem of whether through the law the recognition of sin is really brought about—which is also an inquiry into Wesley's concept of the law.[230] On the psychological level, the danger of falling into a "neurotic circle" through the constant referral to the law by Christ and by the law to Christ cannot be ignored.[231]

Yet, these legitimate questions should not conceal the actual theological concerns of Wesley, which are also to be taken seriously in contemporary theology. In the final analysis, the unity of divine revelation is at stake for Wesley. Even the demanding side of God's revelation—and that means "law" at the core of its theological meaning—is the valid self-disclosure of God, and it is the turning toward the creature, who is marked by God's love and goodness. God is love—and therefore both the gospel *and* the law are expressions of that love. The law is summarized in the twofold love command. This basic assertion of the New Testament finds its systematic explanation in Wesley.[232] It is here that Wesley believes that the "full agreement of the law and the gospel" lies.

> From all this we may learn that there is no contrariety at all between the law and the gospel; that there is no need for the law to pass away in order to the establishing of the gospel. Indeed neither of them supersedes the other, but they agree perfectly well together. Yea, the very same words, considered in different respects, are parts both of the law and of the gospel. If they are considered as commandments, they are parts of the law: if as promises, of the gospel. Thus, "Thou shalt love the Lord thy God with all thy heart," when considered as a commandment, is a branch of the law; when regarded as a promise, is an essential part of the gospel—the gospel being no other than the commands of the law proposed by way of promises.[233]

In his work "Gospel and Law," Karl Barth comes to a similar conclusion, though using quite different presuppositions, when he explains that "the law is nothing other than the necessary *form of the gospel,* whose content is grace."[234] It is for this reason that the law can and will not be the "law of sin and death" forever. "If the gospel triumphs, then it does not position itself only as overflowing grace, overflowing directly upon its enemies—no, then the law as well, the form of the gospel, is *restored* from its literal form to the totality of its words, its own concrete words; from the command, 'Thou shalt!' to the promise, 'Thou wilt be!' and from the claim upon our accomplishments to the claim upon our trust."[235]

Wesley's concern is no different when in reference to Romans 3:31 he speaks of the "law which is established by faith," and expects from the proclamation of faith that persons will become enabled to live a life of love and holiness.[236] Wesley did not polemicize against "cheap grace," as did Bonhoeffer, but in the same sense he spoke of the grace that is operating through faith and lived in love, expressed in Pauline terms, by faith, which is active in love.[237]

Thus, the phrase "the two words of God" can never be expressed in a United Methodist theology, as the Lutheran W. Elert did provocatively.[238] It is the *one* Word of God that reveals God's eternal reality to us. The phenomenon that assertions are often made for Christ in the New Testament that in the Jewish tradition are true of the Torah[239] causes Wesley to come to the opposite conclusion that assertions about the Son also apply to the law. Such a conclusion is seldom found within the realm of Christian theology. "It [the law] is 'the streaming forth' or out-beaming 'of his glory, the express image of his person' " (see Hebrews 1:3), and "it is the heart of God disclosed to man."[240] The revelation of God in the law and in the Son are therefore not alternatives, but rather they are congruent with one another.[241] This can of course only be stated and explained with theological coherence if the law is understood entirely from the standpoint of the love commandment. If this is so, then it is an important reason to understand God's revelation as being of one piece. And it would be thoroughly congruent with a biblical-Judaic theology of law, as accepted by Wesley, if, with respect to this unity, we would incorporate the fact that we in the created world discover there an order that aims at life and enables life to occur. This does not suspend the distinction between love that is commanded and love that is promised; a person does not through faith become an "automaton" of the love of God. Law and gospel remain distinguishable in their function, but in their content they are expressions of the *one* Word of God.

At the same time, it is necessary to explain what the relationship is between the "law" in its basic theological meaning and what is known as "law" in the biblical, ecclesial, and secular tradition. The love commandment is obviously in need of concretization. Limits need to be laid out whose transgression would contradict the love commandment. Perimeters must be drawn. Adherence to these is for the sake of transforming the love commandment into daily praxis. The Ten Commandments, whose relationship to the love commandment is disclosed by Jesus in the Sermon on the Mount, are to be understood in this way. The entire Mosaic law is basically to be understood in this way even if the inner relationships with the love commandment are not evident in all places.[242] However, the warnings and commands that are explained in detail are precisely those that mislead sinful human beings toward committing transgressions or engaging in self-justification. These connections have already been examined in our previous discussion. In the case of Christian ethics we will conversely need to explain how the Christian can accept the concrete prohibition and commandments as an exposition of the love commandment, and thus can facilitate the concrete expressions of love, which do not once again become jumping-off points for resistance, self-justification, or resignation. At that point, we shall further establish that, in light of new challenges, the need to actualize or to formulate afresh those ethical norms that are derived from the love commandment is constant. Wesley exemplified that process in his response to the problem of slavery.[243] Taking the "General Rules" as an example we will have to examine whether the "law" in the form of rules for living can be a "means of grace" for those who seek salvation be it as a "means of grace of piety" or of "mercy."[244]

2.2.2.4 COVENANT AND COVENANT RATIFICATION IN THE UNITED METHODIST TRADITION

In the United Methodist traditions, covenantal thought has "had great significance from the beginning."[245] In its proclamation as well as in its ordering of congregational life, John Wesley, influenced by Puritan and Reformed Pietistic theology, allowed a significant place for covenantal thought. From a historical theological perspective, it is in addition significant that Wesley was influenced not only by Reformed thought by the Puritans but also by "Federal Theology" that emerged in early German and Dutch Reformed Pietism, which came to fruition in the work of Johannes Cocceius (Koch, 1603–1669) and which found its way into English theology and influenced Wesley.[246]

It is stated in chapter 7 of the Reformed Westminster Confession of the Presbyterians of 1647 that "the distance between God and creation is so great that rational creatures have been unable to partake in God's blessing and reward, except as it pleases God, through the voluntary humbling on the side of God, which it has pleased God to bring to expression through the means of the covenant."[247] Based on similar grounds, covenant theologians (Zwingli, Bullinger, and especially Olevianus) had already previously described the acts of God in sovereign love and therefore justified the baptism of infants. The baptismal liturgy of the earlier Methodist Episcopal Church mirrors this outlook, and agrees with Wesley's perspective in saying: "In his great mercy God enters with us humans into a covenant relationship, in whose grace and benefits children are also included."[248]

The covenant theme also played a seminal role in the theological tradition that influenced Philip William Otterbein (1726–1813) and the early Confession of Faith of the United Brethren in Christ (1814).[249] Otterbein was educated at the German Herborn Academy, a center of the federal (covenantal) school of Reformed Pietism in the eighteenth century. Derived from Cocceius, and transmitted to Otterbein through F. A. Lampe's *Mystery of the Covenant of Grace (Geheimnis des Gnadenbundes),* the covenant theme became the organizing principle for theology, in contrast to the deductive, Aristotelian pedagogy which had prevailed in Protestant orthodoxy. History, not confessional articles, was viewed as the vehicle for understanding revelation, and Scripture was read as a complex of historical types or symbols that were to be interpreted in terms of prophetic fulfillment. Creeds were to be read in the light of Scripture, not the converse, and especially in light of Scripture's ongoing, symbolic-prophetic significance. This federal theology was guided by a hermeneutic of growth and fulfillment,[250] and it also sought to fuse the themes of covenant and the kingdom of God, which meant that the more the covenant of grace became generally manifested upon earth, the more the eschatological reign of Christ's holy kingdom would be realized as well. Hence, Otterbein interpreted his revival preaching among the German Reformed colonists and the emerging United Brethren in America as an anticipation of a "more glorious state of the church on earth than has ever been known."[251]

This theological outlook also reflected the normative teaching of the Heidelberg Catechism (1563), which bypassed the "high" Calvinist doctrines of double predestination and supralapsarianism as it presented doctrine in the personal, covenantal language of the "comfort" that comes from knowing that "I belong to my faithful Savior Jesus Christ" and is to be appropriated in terms of a recognition of one's sin, grace, and gratitude expressed in a life of good works. In the hands of the Reformed Pietists, these steps were to be appropriated in a progressive fashion by each earnest believer-pilgrim, under the spiritual guidance of each one's pastor. Among the numerous traces of this *ordo salutis* that can be found within the early United Brethren Confession of Faith—which is the forerunner of the Confession of Faith found in the current *United Methodist Book of Discipline*[252]—we may note the reference to Article IV, where the authority of Scripture as God's Word is explicated not in terms of a theory of biblical inspiration, but rather in view of the Bible's trustworthiness as the pilgrim's guide, in connection with the "influence of the Spirit of God."[253] The course of this covenant life is depicted in the statement that "no one can be a true Christian without repentance and faith, the forgiveness of sins in Jesus Christ, and following after Jesus Christ *('Nachfolge Christi')*."[254] This covenant-grounded credo poses a question for United Methodists today, namely: do we desire to "give ourselves to God" in response to his gracious self-giving to us, to the end that our resources are continually being placed at his gracious disposal, and so that others may through us be helped to be ever more vitally connected to God in Christ, and not merely to human programs or strategies, however well conceived?[255]

In this tradition, the biblical presentation of covenantal activity of God is adopted to the extent that it concerns the anticipatory or prevenient activity of God, who pledges himself in unconditional love and faithfulness to his people (the covenants at Sinai and with David), or toward his creation (the covenant with Noah). The substantial meaning of the concept of "covenant" only becomes recognizable through its use within the particular biblical context. Yet, the diverse meanings have something decisive in common, which preserves the concept from a simple double meaning: God's covenant actions are always expressions of God's personal commitment to his covenant partners as well as of their obligations to their God. God's faithfulness, which can be variously expressed (life upon earth, land, descendants, and being the God for Israel), establishes a relationship with the recipients of the covenant which first of all blesses them with grace but then also calls them to faithful obedience. With each action of the covenant "a binding relationship of fellowship is established"[256] or renewed. The covenant of God in Jesus Christ is also established by mere grace and "purposes to be the new order of salvation in reconciliation that is sealed by God through the sacrifice of Jesus Christ."[257] Even within this covenant, God's partners are challenged to do the will of God.

It is noteworthy that John Wesley, in taking up the covenant theme, drew out the aspect of God's grace and his loving care toward sinners and sought to impress his hearers and readers with this truth. In his sermon "The Righteousness of Faith,"[258] he unfolds the traditional doctrine of the covenant of works and the covenant of grace, then climaxes: faith first! Do not seek your own righteousness, the righteousness of the law, but seek the grace that is to be found within the covenant of God's unmerited love and mercy. The viewpoint he expresses in this early (1742) and frequently preached sermon obviously lies in its emphasis upon the unconditional love of God in Jesus Christ, without which we fallen humans could not live in fellowship with God or carry out God's will. As we have previously indicated, the differentation between the old and the new covenant is not—as we might presume—undertaken in conformity to the two testaments. The new covenant of grace already existed in early Israel. If the "covenant of works" (concluded with Adam before the fall) demanded perfect obedience, then the "covenant of grace" is received by faith alone, and it finds its fulfillment in God's saving acts through Jesus Christ, the "second Adam," who represents all of humanity in his work on the cross and institutes a covenant that is "established by Christ through the atonement, that God works in all men by prevenient grace to prepare them for faith in Christ."[259]

Wesley has here given fitting expression to the meaning of God's covenantal actions: the recipients of God's covenant always live in grace and by the covenantal faithfulness of the Creator, despite human unfaithfulness, and they are freed and enabled precisely through that, to act according to God's will. In distinction to the "covenant of works," all of God's covenantal stipulations in the course of the history of salvation subsequent to Adam's fall demonstrate God's love which does not repay like with like. "The covenant becomes a model of a partner relationship which is characterized by love, wherein the first partner does not abandon the other although the latter disappoints him."[260] Through God's covenantal actions, a new relationship of fellowship is therefore established that has the character of an agreement that is binding on both sides. The recipients are bound to obedience to the will of the One who instituted the covenant, but the demand of the covenant Instituter is not like a demand for the performance of additional works; instead, it is recognizable as what was from the beginning; it is obedience that is given and enabled by God—obedience based upon insight and discernment.

God's covenantal actions do not remove from his human covenant partners the ability to make decisions. On the contrary, God has enabled them to exercise it through his prevenient grace. They also choose whether they want to serve God or not. This choice is certainly not conferred in any way other than by the prevenient, elective action of God. It is therefore not by accident that, whenever the renewal of the covenant including the demands of the covenant occurs in the celebration of worship, the congregation of the new covenant is addressed as follows: "And now, my beloved, we freely choose to bind ourselves to our God, to the Lord of the covenant, and take upon ourselves the yoke of Christ. Taking his yoke upon us means that we are ready heart and soul to be assigned our place and service by Him and that He alone may be our reward."[261]

John Wesley had established the model of the "Renewal of Covenant" at Christmas in 1747, when he repeatedly and emphatically urged the Methodists of his day to renew their covenantal vows to God.[262] The first service of covenant renewal reported by Wesley took place in Spitalfields in August of 1755.[263] The services were preceded by prayer and fasting; before long, the first Sunday in the new year was designated for this. Their central emphasis was upon the renewed surrender of the members of the congregation to the God of the covenant. Wesley was pleased that the Methodists had again taken up a means of grace that had almost fallen into total disuse, and had received rich blessing from it.[264]

Those who joined in the celebration of this service of worship and also offered the prayer that Wesley had formulated for this occasion fulfilled with words what is expressed in the prayer: "I am no longer my own, but thine. Put me to what thou wilt, rank me with whom thou wilt; put me to doing, put me to suffering; let me be employed for thee or laid aside for thee, exalted for thee or brought low for thee; let me be full, let me be empty; let me have all things, let me have nothing; I freely and heartily yield all things to thy pleasure and disposal. And now, O glorious and blessed God, Father, Son, and Holy Spirit, thou art mine, and I am thine. So be it. And the covenant which I have made on earth, let it be ratified in heaven. Amen."[265] With these words, the worshipers accomplish that for which prayer has been made: the renewed turning toward God and the free surrender of their lives upon the basis of the gift and the covenantal faithfulness of God which they have experienced. God's covenant opens the possibility for a critically necessary turning again of their lives to God.

Turning to God is not the final step. Rather, it leads to a new attitude of community with God and the world. It is precisely in the service of Covenant Renewal that the faithful experience themselves as a part of a covenant congregation that needs this community in order to be able to appropriately carry out the mission tasks that are given by God.[266] The possibility of offering renewed service to God first grows from the actions of God, and in him our acts of Christian service stay grounded and meaningful. In Rüdiger Minor's fine and concise words, "The covenant is a structural element of Christian existence that serves as a bridge to community in faith and in action."[267] Through the experience of fellowship with God under the power of his word, in prayer, and in the celebration of the Lord's Supper and hence in the fellowship of the body of Christ, a community is created which can prove itself as the instrument of action in the world.

2.2.3 *The Reconciliation of the World in Christ*

Without detriment to the high rank that Wesley attributed to the law, one thing remains clear and in complete accord with the Pauline concept of law: the law is not capable of removing the "need for God" in persons who live in sin, and it is not able to free them from their enmity toward God. As "demand," the law always remains "over against" humanity, since it obstructs the way to God instead of opening it.

God himself had to take the decisive step to reconcile his enemies. The phrase in 2 Corinthians 5:19 that "in Christ God was reconciling the world to himself, not counting their trespasses against them" pretty much presents a "Christology in nucleus," in that he makes clear that God himself was at work in the destiny of Jesus Christ and has provided for the salvation of humanity through his redemptive acts.

Methodist theology has been only slightly concerned with Christology in its narrower sense, that is, the question of the place of the Son as the second Person of the Trinity and the relationship of the divine and human natures in the Person of Jesus Christ. Wesley published a sermon on the Trinity in which he emphasized that he resolutely believed in the fact of the incarnation but that he knew nothing about the manner in which these things happened, nor did he regard this as a matter of faith.[268]

Other than the areas of soteriology or the question about the law, Christology was not a point of controversy for the Methodist movement. Central to its proclamation and discussions stood the doctrines of redemption and human salvation, which definitely have christological implications. In his investigation of Wesley's Christology, John Deschner speaks of the "presupposed Christ" and describes his task of formulating a Christology of Wesley as the attempt of "translating the Wesleyan message of salvation into christological terms."[269]

This reconstruction of Wesley's Christology indicates that he is a representative of the classical two-nature doctrine, as it was developed by the Council of Chalcedon in the formula "Truly God and truly man." In Wesley's practical exposition of this doctrine, the divine nature dominates, and the thought of the preexistent Christ stands much more in the background than is the case in the theology and understanding of most Christians in our day.[270]

A strong interweaving of Christology and soteriology leads also to an independent and, for Wesley, a characteristic reciprocity between both of these thematic areas. In his sermon on the purpose of the coming of Christ, Wesley asserts, on the basis of 1 John 3:8, that the goal of the coming of Christ consists not only in the forgiveness of sins and liberation from its power but also in the restoration of humanity to the image of God and the infilling with the fullness of God. It is in this way that the figure of Christ as a whole in its description as the image of the living God has become formative in presenting the salvation that God has brought about in Christ. The consequence of salvation is described not only in terms of the incarnation or the death and resurrection but also as the life and teaching and the being and work of Jesus Christ as a whole, in order to clarify how and for what purpose God redeems humanity in Jesus Christ.

In order to do justice to this breadth of the saving work of Christ in all its dimensions, Wesley gladly works with the motif of the "threefold office" of Christ as his mode of description, which he takes over from Reformed theology. Thus Christ is described according to his functions as prophet, priest, and king.[271]

Since Wesley provided no systematic sketch of his own of this Christology, and in view of the fact that a contemporary United Methodist theology must most especially consider the questions and results of the newer exegesis and systematic theology in this field of study, the following description of the christological aspects of our faith follow an arrangement which is modeled more strongly on the statements of the New Testament. However, the basic structure of the "threefold office" of Christ will also be easily identifiable within this discussion.

2.2.3.1 LIVING OUT OF GOD'S WILL

In the New Testament, the life of Jesus Christ is depicted in a double perspective:

(a.) In the Johannine and Pauline writings, Jesus' life and its meaning is repeatedly described with the formula of "the coming of the Son" or "the sending of the Son."[272] Strangely enough this most often happens where the older tradition is cited, and the work of God in Christ is summarized in catechetical or hymnodic form. For example, Galatians 4:4 describes the sending of the Son to assume the destiny of a human being with the biographical aspects of human life ("born of a woman") and with the dimensions and limitations and demands of human existence ("born under the law"). The purpose of the mission of the Son is "that we might receive adoption" (lit., "sonship"). Hence, the intertwining of Christology and soteriology is therefore also exemplified within the New Testament itself! A similar assertion is found in Romans 8:3-4, Philippians 2:6-11; John 1:1-18; 3:16-17; 1 John 4:9-10.[273]

Common to all of these sayings is the fact that they speak of *the* Son of God and not about *a* Son of God, which is further underscored in the Johannine tradition by the concept of the "only begotten," and the "only" Son (John 1:18; 3:16; 1 John 4:9; also Romans 8:32).[274] A descent of some persons from God, who thereby become half-gods, heroes, or superhuman beings is not intended here, as is the case in Greek mythology and also in other religions. Instead, the statements from John point to the full, unique origin of the Son from God, in which God discloses himself to the world and makes his Word manifest. First John 5:20 summarizes this with great emphasis: he, the Son Jesus Christ, "is the true God and eternal life"![275] All expressions concerning the preexistence of the Son have no other function than that of anchoring the sending of Jesus Christ within God and within his being.[276]

But it is precisely the Son of God of whom we are told that he has taken upon himself the nature of humanity with all of its implications. In addition to Galatians 4:4, this is particularly emphasized in Philippians 2:7-8, where the same insight is expressed in terms of the "self-emptying" of God. Therein lies the foundation for enabling God's work of the redemption through Jesus Christ: because the Son is the same as God the Father, he can withstand the temptation to desire to be as God. He can also take upon himself human nature with its limitations and its challenges, and fulfill the law and so live a truly human existence. Even his way to death is at first nothing more than a willful acceptance of the destiny of humanity, an expression of the "obedience of life," which Christ manifested as the new Adam (besides Philippians 2:8, see also Romans 5:19). His path to death is of course also his acceptance of the curse of death, under which humanity suffers because of their separation from God.

So the New Testament assertions do little to help us in our effort to respond to the questions of classical Christology concerning the relation-ship of the two natures of the Person of Jesus Christ. Yet, the Chalcedonian formula "Truly God and truly man," is precisely the basic assertion of New Testament Christology. It asserts that Jesus Christ, in his life and work, is completely "God for us," and also that, as a man, he lives wholly for God.[277] Hence, he is the Image of God in a double sense (Colossians 1:15): in him humanity encounters God's being, his glory in the labor of his love (see 2 Corinthians 3:18; 4:4-6), and at the same time he so lives the human life as God has meant it when he created human being in his image (compare Genesis 1:27 with Romans 8:29).

As the witness of the Gospel of John and that of Paul indicate, the state-ments about the uniqueness of the divine Sonship of Jesus can be pro-claimed and believed through the Holy Spirit without any reference to the reports of his miraculous conception and birth. The birth stories reported in the Gospels of Matthew and Luke are narrative presentations that emphasize the basic truth that Jesus' life and being are wholly derived from the will of God (Luke 1:35) and that through him, "God is with us" (Matthew 1:23).[278]

(b.) The work of Jesus Christ is depicted from another perspective by the Synoptic Gospels. Mark was probably the first who included the reports of Jesus' words and deeds with the passion narrative and placed them under the heading "The beginning of the good news of Jesus Christ, the Son of God."[279] Matthew and Luke have followed him in this and have above all extended the tradition about Jesus' preaching and teaching. The Gospel of John also basically took over the schema of describing the sig-nificance of Jesus through the history of his deeds between the appearance of John the Baptist and Jesus' Resurrection, although he developed his own direction in terms of form and content.[280]

These narratives are also not objective historical descriptions, but rather are shaped by the witness of faith of the community of the disciples. However, they describe the significance of Jesus not only with basic the-ological concepts but also through the tradition of the words that he spoke during his lifetime, through the account of the deeds which he performed in Galilee and Judea, and through the report of his suffering, death, and resurrection, in which his work came to its fulfillment. Even if this tradi-tion communicates not only naked historical facts but intends to bear wit-ness to the faith in Jesus as the Christ, that witness nonetheless is based upon the trustworthy accounts of the remembrance of Jesus' works that were passed down.[281]

The center of Jesus' message is the call "Repent, for the kingdom of heaven has come near" (Matthew 4:17; Mark 1:15). He thereby links himself to the message and work of John the Baptist, though giving it in a different emphasis. If the message of John concerned the nearness of the reign of God under the perspective of the threatening, inevitable judgment to come, with Jesus there is the beginning of the reign of God that is synonymous with the incursion of the freeing and redeeming activity of God in a world ruled by evil, suffering, and sin.[282] Jesus understands his powerful deeds, especially the healings and exorcisms of the demons, not only as signs of his personal power but above all as the manifestation of the inbreaking rule of God. A key term for the self-understanding of Jesus is found in Luke 11:20 (parallel Matthew 12:28): "But if it is by the finger of God that I cast out demons, then the kingdom of God has come to you." The example of those who are possessed by demons demonstrates most sharply the situation of persons without God; they are at the mercy of the destructive powers of evil, which alienate them from themselves and push them to the point of self-destruction. Conversely, their healing makes clear what the incursion of the rule of God signifies: the freeing for fellowship with God and thereby also for fellowship with themselves and with others.[283]

In spite of the miracles of Jesus, the announcement of the approaching reign of God apparently aroused the question among his hearers of how the reality of this divine reign was to be set in operation in that day and age. Jesus answered this question by means of parables. In particular, there are the so-called parables of contrast that appear to speak to this situation, in which a beginning that promises only a small, unremarkable result is contrasted with an overwhelmingly great yield at the outcome of the event. In response to the question "What is it that is happening now?" Jesus invites his hearers to rely upon the power of the kingdom of God, which is capable of accomplishing what it announces. It is typical of Jesus and his deeds for him to embellish his message with examples from everyday life. Hence, the kingdom is likened to a woman at work who entrusts a little leaven into a colossal amount of meal, or to a Galilean farmer who with confidence hopes for a good harvest, in spite of all the adversities of the soil, or of a single, tiny mustard seed from which there emerges a great bushy plant. In like manner, the hearers of Jesus are encouraged to place confidence in his word and works—even if they seem to be quite insignificant and limited—and in the belief that through them God will bring about the breakthrough of his kingdom.[284]

At two places in the Gospels, Jesus' work is interrelated with the words of Isaiah, that through him "good news is preached to the poor" (see Isaiah 61:1-2; Luke 4:18-19; Matthew 11:5, paralleled in Luke 7:22). This takes place quite concretely in the Beatitudes of Jesus which promises the poor: "Blessed are you who are poor, for yours is the kingdom of God" (Luke 6:20; compare Matthew 5:3).[285] It is said to people in need, people who have nothing and are worth nothing: The kingdom of God belongs to you, you will experience its transforming power for yourselves, therefore you are already blessed today.

Among those persons in need, to whom Jesus particularly turned in his preaching, were apparently also those who were despised because of their circumstances and were excluded from the life of the community, because of their manner of living or their adherence to marginal groups within the society. Jesus' care of them took place not only through words but above all by the fact that he made personal contact with such persons and sat and ate with them. For "sinners and tax collectors," his table fellowship became a sign of their acceptance by God. It was precisely because of this behavior that opposition was kindled against him in the circles of the pious and the righteous, who thought that if Jesus was on the side of God he could not without further ado get involved with those sorts of persons. Here Jesus also sought to make clear through parables that he, being sent from God, had come precisely to reach those persons who need God's nearness and help most desperately. For this reason, Jesus indicates in his most impressive parables how God searches for lost persons and how joyful God is in finding the lost, thereby unmistakably indicating that the meaning of his redemptive deeds represented the very moving of this seeking God toward a lost humanity![286]

The message of the unconditional promise of God's saving presence, which is contained in Jesus' preaching, is to be matched by the undivided surrender of life of those who belong to him. This claim is presented in the context of the summation of the law, and for Jesus this is found in the love commandment. This results in a "radicalization" of the commandments from within, which in turn leads in the so-called antitheses of the Sermon on the Mount at least in one instance to the abolition of an Old Testament precept.[287] In the comparison "You have heard that it was said . . . , but I say to you," Jesus shows himself to be a powerful interpreter of the law. God's will is not confined to committing humans to some clearly defined, minimal demand for the common life of humanity. He intends that people should help one another toward life and should mutually protect and promote one another. He aims at peace in the sense of the Old Testament *shalom,* and thus makes love the measure of human conduct.[288]

If he ever was, John Wesley was a congenial interpreter of the biblical message on this point. In his preaching on the Sermon on the Mount, he summarized his exposition of the "beatitudes" with the "antitheses" and thus demonstrated his understanding of the gospel.[289] For Wesley, it is in this powerful exposition of Scripture that Jesus expresses the "prophetic office" of his mission.

The claim of God upon the life of humanity, which corresponds to the promise of his saving nearness, also finds its expression in the call of Jesus to discipleship. First of all, not all hearers were meant by this call of Jesus. There are some who in an exemplary manner are called out from their former livelihood and from their families and who leave everything in order to follow Jesus in his works. They become examples to others of how God's reign completely lays hold of persons and takes them into his service.[290] Hence, the existence of this circle of disciples becomes the prototype for the community of Jesus, whose members have heard God's call and who place themselves wholly at God's disposal, even if they remain in their existing life context.[291]

The reports of the first three Gospels lead to a twofold question. In view of what Jesus does and to what power he lays claim, the question was asked then and now, who is this One? On the other hand, these Gospels— and particularly Mark, the earliest—clearly report a great reservation on the part of Jesus to declare himself as the Messiah or the Son of God. Based upon that reservation, the question has often been raised in recent New Testament research whether Jesus in fact regarded himself as the Messiah.[292]

The starting point for answering this question cannot be to continue to juxtapose in a critical fashion the different witnesses of the Gospels. For the answer to the question "Who was Jesus of Nazareth?" is not found by a historical inquiry into those texts that address how Jesus referred to himself but rather by observing how he spoke and acted.[293] Jesus himself said, "If it is by the finger of God that I cast out demons, then the kingdom of God has come to you." In his works, the reign of God breaks out, and his Person becomes the decisive focus for that presence of God that brings about salvation. In him the Father seeks his lost sons and daughters, through him God grants people the forgiveness of sins and allows the glad gospel to be proclaimed to the poor. It is because of this that the disciples already had begun to call him the Messiah even within his lifetime on earth, although they possibly joined this to their conceptions about what his future function would be. Those conceptions were first corrected through the events of the cross and the resurrection. Thus, the Gospel of John has properly translated the depth dimension of the being and acts of Jesus when it reports his open declarations of his messianic identity that are translated as the divine "I am." And the Gospel of John intentionally affirms what the other Gospels implicitly testify: that Jesus demonstrates himself to be God's Son precisely in the fact that he wholly and exclusively points to the Father.[294]

The Messianic deeds of Jesus and the reign of God are therefore not in the least demonstrated only in his miracles that show him to be possessed by divine powers. These things are demonstrated far more decisively in the manner in which he lives out his human existence. "As the man whose existence is from God, Jesus makes possible the faith in God's fatherly nearness, the nearness of God as the Father."[295] The fact that Jesus is rightly called the "Son of the Most High" (Luke 1:32) is paradoxically verified by the way in which he takes the suffering of human death upon himself. "If you are the Son of God, come down from the cross" (Matthew 27:40), exclaimed the mockers standing under the cross. However, the tradition of Jesus' death, as found in the forms of narrative and proclamation, affirms that he demonstrated himself to be God's Son precisely by remaining true to God's will, and that "he learned obedience through what he suffered" (Hebrews 5:8). Thus, there is profound meaning in the comment that was made by the Roman official standing under the foot of the cross who, according to Mark's Gospel, was the first human to witness to what heretofore had only been spoken from heaven: "Truly this man was God's Son!" (Mark 15:39; cf. 1:11; 9:7).[296]

2.2.3.2 DYING FOR ONE'S ENEMIES

In a twofold sense, Jesus' death upon the cross is therefore the consequence of a life lived in accordance with God's will.

Jesus' condemnation to death is the result of his conflict with the religious authorities of his time. His inner freedom toward the prevailing interpretation of the law, which above all was shown by his sovereign handling of the Sabbath regulations, his involvement with the fringe members of the society of his day, and the claim which he made about his person—even if it was done in a hidden manner—led the prevailing circle of authorities to hand him over to the Romans under the complaint that he had laid claim to be the lawful king of the Jews.[297] There can be no doubt that Jesus was condemned unlawfully, but this miscarriage of justice is the symptom of a much more deep-lying conflict between the claim of God's love for humanity and human resistance to this demand. What is more, it is the sign for the way that human beings deal with one another and sacrifice others in order to attain their own goals.

However, Jesus' death is also a consequence of his obedience. This obedience is not only oriented toward particular commands; rather, it embraces his entire life, which he lives in actual relationship to God. This "living obedience" of the Son of God includes his "yes" to death. The solidarity of the Son of God with human destiny as an expression of the salvific condescension of God is described especially in Hebrews 4:14–5:10, as well as in Philippians 2:6-8. This also indicates the readiness of the One who comes from God to enter into death, which is lifted up as the goal of this path of life.

The fact that Jesus died the death of a criminal, the fact that this was death at the gallows, carried out through crucifixion, and the fact that this was the most despised manner of execution of that time, was reserved for slaves and insurgents, and was a death that served as a sign of damnation in Judaism (Deuteronomy 21:22-23; cf. Galatians 3:13)—each of these considerations pointedly highlights the double consequence of the death which he suffered. First, there is the consequence of his complete obedience, in which he lived as a man before God. Second, there is also the consequence of a deadly conflict between God and humanity! Because Jesus suffered his death in terms of this double consequence, the Christian message states that he died this death for the salvation of all.[298]

However, this assertion is one of the statements of faith that persons of our day find particularly difficult to understand. Many ask the question whether Jesus did not simply founder or, in a best-case scenario, if he was not simply a martyr who held true to his cause unto death. Apparently this was also the judgment of his disciples at the beginning. It was their encounter with the resurrected Lord that first opened a new perspective for them. Through his resurrection, God has acknowledged himself to Jesus and justified him and his work—as 1 Timothy 3:16 expresses it. However, that also places his death in a new light. Jesus did not simply suffer a deplorable error of justice, which God subsequently rectified. God completed the work of his love precisely in and through Jesus' surrender to the caprice and the deadly calculations of men.

At his last meal with his disciples, Jesus himself had interpreted his forthcoming death as a surrender of his life "for many" (Mark 14:22-24), that is, for humanity as a whole. In doing so, he was making a connection to Isaiah 53:11, and to the biblical-Judaic tradition of the vicarious suffering of the righteous. The post-Easter Christian proclamation has accepted this reference and deepened it by finding ever more clearly within the Old Testament the prescription that indeed Christ must die for our sins, so that we might find forgiveness and redemption.[299]

In order to clarify this, different models of interpreting the meaning of Jesus' death are considered. The two most important are the presentation of Jesus' death as an offering for sin and as a vicarious surrender of life. The first explanatory model has its roots in the cultic realm: the life of one sacrificial animal is offered for the forfeited life of a guilty person, or for an entire people, and the blood is shed upon the altar in place of the life of the guilty ones.[300] The other model is rooted in the realm of the profane. One person's life is inserted for the threatened life of another—it may be that he is offered up in a battle, or that he draws a curse upon himself or takes upon himself the punishment that is meant for another.[301] The literature disputes how clearly these two lines of interpretation are distinguished in the early history of the interpretation of Jesus' death. In each instance, it assists our understanding if the two models are kept distinct, particularly as Paul either the one or the other models stands in the foreground at different places within his letters. However, common to both is the conviction that God gave his Son Jesus Christ unto death in order to set us humans free from guilt and its deadly consequences.

A vehement protest from contemporary observers arises at this point, and it is certainly not only an external protest but one that has emerged from within Christian theology. How can the unlawful death of one atone for the guilt of another? Is this not to paint a picture of a sadistic God, who requires the sacrifice of a human life for the appeasement of his wrath? Can the theory of the necessity of propitiation be reconciled with the preaching of Jesus about the unending love and goodness of God, who forgives all without conditions and reservations? If there is a God who first of all must sufficiently fulfill the requirements of righteousness through the punishment of an innocent person, in order to enable his mercy to have free course, is such a God not a prisoner of his own law?[302]

What almost all of these questions have in common is that they do not grasp the true depth and meaning of the biblical assumptions of the notion of atonement and vicarious sacrifice. At the same time, they are also in danger of thinking too superficially about the reality of human guilt. The following observations are crucial for the correct understanding of the biblical statements and the reality of the human situation, about which they speak:

First of all, guilt and punishment are not two completely different realities in biblical thinking. In the Hebrew *one* word can stand for both of them. Thus, punishment is not primarily the sanction which a judge imposes on a guilty person or remits for pedagogical reasons "Punishment" is the potential for condemnation that lies in every offense.[303] Whoever is guilty before God and humanity destroys the relationships of life or even life itself. The ensuing "damage" threatens to fall back upon the guilty one or also upon the community in which that one lives. Thus, the question for biblical theology is not whether God imposes punishment or in certain cases, whether God refrains from it, but rather how God deals with the disastrous results of an offense. It is a question of whether God allows the offense to revert back to the guilty or whether he stands between the guilty and their guilt, so that it is covered and they are extricated from it and—in contemporary language—they are assisted in overcoming their guilt.[304] However, that is the function of the expiatory offering. It does not serve the purpose of reconciling them to the offended Deity, but is God's gift to the offenders that enables them to ransom their forfeited life.

Behind this conception stands a deeper insight into the reality of human guilt than can be made intelligible by superficial observations. Depth psychology, which seemed initially to give the impression it was only about feelings of guilt, has helped to make known the phenomenon of the suppression and the displacement of guilt, and its unwholesome consequences. It is not by chance that the ritual of the scapegoat in Leviticus 16 became an adage. Whenever people have difficulty recognizing guilt and pondering its meaning, they look for scapegoats on whom they can dump their guilt, or they seek to expiate guilt by means of self-punishment.[305]

The message of Jesus' vicarious death for our sins therefore says one thing above all else: God has made Jesus become the "scapegoat" for us, indeed has become sin itself, in order to break through the vicious circle between the suppression and the displacement of guilt and to show humanity upon whom they can discharge their unbearable guilt.[306]

Paul has indeed unequivocally stated in 2 Corinthians 5:18-19 that it is not that God was reconciled through Christ, but rather God was in Christ reconciling the world to himself! God took all the consequences of human sin upon himself in Christ so that peace might be established. In view of the tradition of Christian piety and proclamation, which speaks so emphatically of how God must be reconciled as the *object* of Christ's reconciling acts, it is quite remarkable to observe how unanimously the New Testament speaks of the truth that it is *God* who has reconciled the world with himself. Thus, God is the logical and actual *subject* of the reconciliation that took place in Christ (see Romans 5:10; 2 Corinthians 5:19; Colossians 1:20)!

A more careful examination of Romans 3:25f. also indicates that Jesus' sacrificial death was not necessary in order to offer proof of the formal righteousness of God and thereby to make room for the exercise of God's mercy, as was indicated in the older tradition of exposition. Such exposition proceeds from a false concept of biblical righteousness. God does not demonstrate his *punitive* righteousness when he "puts forward" Christ for the expiation of sins. Rather, it is God's *creative and saving righteousness,* through which he works out the expiation[307] for the guilt of humanity and liberates them into the way of fully salvific fellowship with him, their God.

With his "satisfaction theory" in the eleventh century, Anselm of Canterbury undertook the grand and also consequential attempt to demonstrate convincingly, within the context of Germanic legal thought, that the incarnation of Jesus and his vicarious death were necessary in order for God to redeem humanity. He insisted it was only possible in this way for God to achieve this redemption if Christ offered a sufficient sacrifice for the wounded honor of God the Father.[308] In retrospect, it is clear that a human is doing too much if he thinks he can prove what God must necessarily do for the salvation of humanity. However, within the context of Anselm's reasoning, there occurs a statement which he asserts against his adversary, which will always retain its validity whenever anyone seeks to render intelligible the truth of Jesus' sacrificial death: "*Nondum consi-derasti quanti ponderis sit peccatum*—you have not yet thought sufficiently just how heavy the load of sin weights!"[309] As little as it can be demonstrated that Jesus' sacrificial death was the only logical possibility for God to follow in redeeming humanity, a biblically oriented theology will always seek to make intelligible how God has taken the sin of humanity upon himself through Jesus' death. Through it, the divine "must" for Jesus' salvific death, as found in the "proofs of Scripture" as recorded in the New Testament, is interpreted in its real depth. It is not only a matter of the formal fulfillment of scriptural prophecies; rather, it is a matter simply of the fulfillment of the salvific intention of the biblical witness as a whole. And the account of Jesus' death thereby loses all "theatrical" qualities that it appears to have from the perspective of some superficial observers. The "must" of the announcement of Jesus' suffering is a testimony to the sovereignty with which God brings to completion his plan of salvation for the liberating of a rebellious humanity, precisely with the help of that rebelliousness.

Only if that is recognized, the concern of the traditional manner of expression can be taken up as it is formulated in a hymn stanza such as "God's Son is born man, and has appeased the Father's wrath."[310] Here it is established that the "need for reconciliation" persists on the human side, and they are the ones who stand in need of Jesus' sacrifice if they are to overcome their guilt and to restore their relationship with God.[311] Jesus' death does not only represent God working through actual sin, it is much more a matter of laying a new foundation for a fellowship that had been destroyed. That is precisely what the message of reconciliation announced: God's reconciling actions reconcile humanity to their God.

All of this is not clear unless the dynamics of these events are taken into consideration:

1. The witness of Jesus' vicarious death is not the report of the execution of an individual through whom the question of guilt is solved once for all and without regard to all inner relationships, and that event is not a transaction comparable to the settlement of guilt in a heavenly bank account. As we have previously noted, Jesus' death is the deepest expression ever of the entering of God into the sphere of human need and misery.[312] As High Priest, the Son is not only sacrificed once for all; he also suffers in the deepest solidarity with humanity. God does not sacrifice another. In the Son, God sacrifices himself—and he does so in order that, in the life and death of the Son, his image as the image of self-giving love may be established. In a manner similar to Lutheran theology, Wesleyan theology in the context of worship can also speak of the crucified God, and it speaks of the joyous insight of the revelation of God's love in the image of Jesus Christ perhaps even more emphatically than does the former.[313]

2. The fact that God has reconciled us to himself through the death of Jesus Christ his Son when we were yet sinners (Romans 5:10) is the deepest expression and the clearest demonstration of his love that is available to humanity, for it does not require any preliminary condition or achievement on the part of human beings. However, this message of unconditional acceptance through God leads people into the deepest kind of crisis of self-understanding. Are those who hear this message ready to recognize

that they need this love in its radicalness and depth, or do they want to base their lives upon their own achievements and self-esteem? Thus, there also lies within the saving power of the word of the cross a critical element that effects decision and separation among persons (see 1 Corinthians 1:18ff.).[314]

3. Jesus' vicarious acts for us need to be understood in an exclusive as well as an inclusive manner. They are exclusive in the sense that Christ died for us when we were yet sinners: through Christ, God the Father has brought about our salvation without our assistance. Christ is made sin for us, so that in him we became the righteousness of God (2 Corinthians 5:21). This also means that our guilt can be laid upon him and he bears it (away). But his taking our place is inclusive in the sense that we are incorporated into the death of Jesus in faith and in baptism. We die with Christ in order to be raised with him.[315] That which took place without us yet for us has through him become reality for us. The correlation of both of these dimensions of representation could be described by means of a modern comparison: as in the process of modern psychoanalytical therapy a patient is permitted at first to transfer to the therapist all of her or his unresolved relationships, with all their desires, aggressions, and unattained possibilities, in order to be able to work through them, so we are permitted to transfer our guilt to Christ in order then to accept it as part of who we are and then to be able to work through it with him.[316]

The purposeful dynamic of Wesleyan soteriology corresponds to this. The heart of what occurred at Golgotha should and can be carried to completion step by step within the life of those who permit God's unending love to operate on and in them—a love which he demonstrated in the death of Jesus for us.

2.2.3.3   RISEN, THAT GOD'S PEACE MIGHT LEAD TO VICTORY

The resurrection and the ascension of Jesus belong together, when viewed systematically and also in light of the fundamental sayings of the New Testament. They designate two different aspects of the same event.[317] Resurrection from the dead indicates the creative inbreaking of God into the world of death, which occurred in the person of Jesus Christ and which places both him and his destiny within the reality of the divine life. The ascension to the right hand of God the Father indicates the introduction of his person and all which he accomplished into the decisive position in relation to God. How God encounters humans in the future is determined and marked by the human life which Jesus has lived.

"God has raised Jesus from the dead" was apparently the first confession of the early Christians.[318] It was based upon the witness of the disciples, whom the resurrected Lord had encountered. Of those appearances, it was the encounter of the resurrected One with Peter that has a particular fundamental importance (cf. 1 Corinthians 15:5 with Luke 24:34 and Matthew 16:18). The reports of the discovery of the empty tomb through the Easter morning visit of the women have a function that is more demonstrative than substantive. In other words, the empty tomb is a question in the first instance before it is a demonstrable argument. Their subsequent encounter with the resurrected Lord is what provides the solid answer to this question.[319] The message of Jesus being raised from the dead was a confession full of joy about Jesus' life and ministry not ending in ruin, and full of hope that the redemptive work which had begun with Jesus' life and death will be fulfilled at last by God. On the basis of biblical thinking, "Resurrection from the dead" certainly signifies not only the elevation of an individual, exemplary human being to divine rank. It signals the beginning of the end-time awakening of the dead and thereby the incursion of God's end-time acts in general. Hence, the early Christian community regarded Jesus' proclamation about the reign of God drawing near as being fulfilled in the raising of Jesus from the dead.

The christological significance of the resurrection of Jesus—that is, what is being asserted concerning his person and work—and its soteriological meaning—that is, what is being promised for the benefit of humanity through God's acts in Jesus Christ—therefore belong closely together. And especially for a Methodist theology, it is the soteriological aspect, the investing of Jesus with his "kingly office," that is, his full empowerment to exercise his salvific rule, that always has been of great importance.

This salvific rule is set up and put through on different levels:

(a.) As we have already shown, God "justified" the work and destiny of Jesus by raising him from the dead. God thereby "ratified" what Jesus had spoken, done, and suffered. The salvific meaning of Jesus' death is disclosed on Easter. The full power of his words and instructions is placed in a new light through his resurrection from the dead. His path as a whole becomes the sphere and mode of life for those who submit themselves to his rule. In Philippians 2:5-11, Paul has most clearly called into awareness the fact that Jesus' ascension to the Lord whose Name is "above all names" means that God does not relegate Jesus' life of humility to an antiquated past, but instead, God makes the course he followed into a decisive and shaping reality for all who belong to him. The Crucified One is the Creator of the cosmos, the Lord of the universe! Only by experiencing is it possible to walk the way of genuine and benevolent humility, as Jesus and Paul required.[320] A "theology of the resurrection" and a "theology of the cross" are therefore in no sense contradictory when cross and resurrection are so intimately related.

(b.) Through the raising of Jesus, the news of God's saving acts through him is brought into currency. This basic assertion is presented in the New Testament in a diverse manner.

Matthew 28:16-20 reports the sending out of the apostles by the resurrected Lord. This so-called Great Commission makes clear that the full empowerment of Jesus and the empowerment of the disciples stand in a causal relationship. Jesus' fullness of power that comprehends the entire world establishes the task of the disciples to call all peoples into obedience to him and make them disciples. They become disciples by becoming participants in God's saving acts through baptism and by being directed into the way of righteousness through the instruction of Jesus' command.[321]

Paul experienced his encounter with the resurrected Christ not only as a demonstration of the truth of the Christian message and the absurdity of his own ways. Rather, through this encounter, he received the task of proclaiming the gospel to the heathen. The relationship of the raising of Jesus and the empowerment of the preaching of the gospel takes on an exceptional meaning in Pauline theology.[322] What God did for humanity on the cross of Jesus becomes living, salvific, and critical in their midst through "the message about the cross" (1 Corinthians 1:18-25).

The message of the cross and of the resurrection of Jesus is therefore never a confrontation with naked facts that in the first instance are required to be believed; it is an encounter with the reality of the living Christ and with that which God has accomplished through him in the cross and in the raising of Christ to life.[323]

(c.) The power with which God raised Jesus from the dead also works in the lives of those who belong to Jesus, changing them now and reshaping them into new persons.

In Romans 6 Paul answers the objections which are fictively or overzealously intended to show a consequence of his theology of grace. "Should we continue in sin in order that grace may abound?" provokes the counter question "How can we who died to sin go on living in it?" However, Paul is not satisfied in answering this question just in terms of the evidence that Christians have been "baptized into Christ" and thereby have died to sin. He carries the discussion further with the declaration "Therefore we have been buried with him by baptism into death, so that, just as Christ was raised from the dead by the glory of the Father, so we too might walk in newness of life" (Romans 6:4). The creative power of God, which raised Jesus from the dead, is now already at work in the life of Christians so that they may receive the power for a new manner of living.[324]

The letters to the Colossians and the Ephesians go yet a step further than this. They speak of how Christians are raised with Christ and have been awakened to a new life (Colossians 2:12-13), indeed how they have been seated with him in heavenly places (Ephesians 2:4-5). That does not mean that Christians already reside in heaven and thus no longer have to contend with earthly reality. On the contrary, in the worldview of Colossians and Ephesians, which see the area between earth and heaven as ruled by the devil and his angels, it means this: whenever Christians have been joined by faith and baptism to the destiny of Christ, they are removed from the realm of the devil and have their spiritual "home base" with God, and they are protected in the world as persons who belong to God. Persons who were dead in sin, because they have been excluded from the fellowship that creates life from God, have come alive as a result of the raising of Jesus, and they now experience in the life of grace what may truly be called life.[325]

This dimension of the reality of the resurrection was of great consequence for Wesley. For it attested to what was really important to him: Jesus' cross and resurrection not only include the possibility of ever new forgiveness for ever newly committed sins. Instead, they establish the basis for a fundamental victory over sin, which even now, though only initially and fragmentarily yet with the promise of fulfillment, begin to find a place within the life of the individual Christian. For Wesley, it is here that the special meaning of the "royal office" of Christ lies.[326] This theme will be more completely developed in the section on holiness; but it is not insignificant that it has already become clear that holiness is anchored not only in the operation of the Holy Spirit but also fundamentally in the event of the raising to life of Jesus.

(d.) The raising of Jesus confirms the hope for the fulfillment of the reign of God.[327]

In his discussion with the congregation at Corinth, Paul makes three things clear about the question of the resurrection of the dead.

1. Christian faith is empty and of no avail if it cannot be based upon the fact that God has intervened in the world of death in a new and creative manner through the raising of Jesus. Whenever faith does not recognize in the resurrection the sure hope in God's transforming and recreating acts for one's personal life, then that faith is empty and useless, for ultimately it remains dependent upon that which is existent and transitory (1 Corinthians 15:12-19, 29-32).

2. The way in which God brings about this event in corporeal terms, that is, how he takes within himself the whole of human existence in the process of recreating life from an eschatological perspective and transforms it into a new mode of existence, should be left to God's sovereign power and should never become a matter of controversy. It is possible that the dimension of God's acts exceed our capabilities of conceiving them (1 Corinthians 15:20-28, 50-57).

3. The purpose of the raising and the empowerment of Jesus Christ is not only for the redemption of a renewed humanity, which belongs to Christ, but also for the restoration of the unlimited rule of God, in which God will become "all in all."

Revelation 21 presents this with a splendid vision and, by the use of an Old Testament motif, it draws a picture which shows God's unlimited rule precisely as his unlimited presence for the universe and for his creation. God's identification with humanity (the *Mitmenschlichkeit* of God), which in the appearance of Immanuel ("God with us") is revealed as the ground and goal of God's salvific actions, finds its fulfillment therein: "See, the home of God is among mortals. He will dwell with them as their God; they will be his peoples, and God himself will be with them; he will wipe every tear from their eyes. Death will be no more; mourning and crying and pain will be no more, for the first things have passed away" (Revelation 21:3-4).

2.2.4 *The Messenger of Reconciliation*

The congregation of Jesus Christ carries out its activities in light of the time when the reign of God is fully realized, but it is not yet at its goal. It lives between the resurrection and the return of Jesus, and this existence "between the times" of the revelation of the life-giving glory of God is the time of mission, of proclamation and of service in the name, in the commission, and with the power of Jesus Christ. What God has done in and through Jesus Christ is not frozen as a fact of the past that can only be retrospectively contemplated through an act of remembrance. Instead, it remains alive in the Word of proclamation, which the message of God's saving acts carries forward.

The fact that God has reconciled the world to himself in Christ is made known to human beings by the word of reconciliation, which God "established" through the authorization of the apostles, that is, which he has instituted with validity and efficacy. Further, Christ himself entreats humanity through the words of the apostles and the Christian proclamation, "Be reconciled to God" (2 Corinthians 5:18-20).[328] The authority of the reign which Christ exercises through his messengers is the authority of the invitation. It is the invitation to let the peace which God has instituted in Christ become effective and operative in one's self. The "representation" of Christ through the Christian community is therefore not conceivable except through the acceptance of his mission and the proclamation of his cross. The claim of the community of Jesus to the authority that is in the name of the Resurrected One finally has efficacy only if it remains the "authority of the interceding Christ."[329]

According to John 20:21, the resurrected Christ says to his disciples: "As the Father has sent me, so send I you." With that, the community of the disciples is received into the *missio Dei,* God's loving care of humanity, which attained human form in the mission of the Son and which is to be carried forward through his community, in its proclamation, its service, and its entire being. The Johannine tradition thus shows itself to be a witness to the close connection between the raising of Jesus and the mission of the community of faith; it also underscores the close relationship between the mission of that community and the way of Jesus. The preaching of the Resurrected Lord knows about the death of Jesus on the cross; it sees in him not failure but rather the splendor of the love of God. However, because of this the way of the post-Easter community remains a way of following the Crucified Lord, and the power which is conferred by God's presence in his Spirit by the preaching of the community of faith does not spare it the suffering that is brought about by faithful engagement, in the footsteps of Christ and in his loving surrender of himself for others.[330]

At one point, however, a basic extension of the mission of the disciples in relation to the mission of Jesus occurs through the Easter event. Jesus had concentrated totally on the realm of the Jewish people, and only in exceptional cases drawn the heathen into his saving work. Nevertheless, within this limitation, he lived with great consistency, offering God's universal love as available for all, including the poor, the rejected, the unclean, the possessed and the branded, and those who had been written off. Yet after the resurrection, the scope of God's saving activity spread beyond all limits.

The radicalness of the revelation of the love of God in the cross of Jesus penetrates beyond the former realms of the saved and the unsaved as those had been defined through the law. The insight that in light of the cross all have shown themselves to have succumbed to evil expands the area of effectiveness of God's salvific action. The unfathomable love of God, which is demonstrated in the cross of Christ, is valid for all persons, and this love now needs to be experienced by all.

It is not by chance that the early Christian theologians, who in their own encounter with the crucified and resurrected Christ experienced the revolutionary meaning of the event of the cross most deeply and radically, were also those who most consistently comprehended and theologically espoused the task of the mission to all humanity. Paul was neither the only one nor the first one who attained this understanding of the gospel (see Acts 11:20), but it apparently required a long and difficult struggle for the early church to come to agree on not only the "that" but also with the "how" of the preaching of the gospel among the heathen.[331]

This discussion of what were to be the consequences of its universal task in mission recurred many times in the church of Jesus Christ, in the course of its proclamation that took place both outwardly and inwardly. The basic limits which were imposed on the gospel, either consciously or unconsciously, were often not noticed or were defended as being imposed by God.

Methodism was a vital part of the awakening movements of the eighteenth and nineteenth centuries, which attempted through their missionary and evangelistic activities to transcend such limits, limits that were imposed both internally and often externally. The gospel with its invitation to reconciliation in Christ was brought to fellow human beings who were formerly excluded as "unreachable," which included the uncharted masses in the great cities, as well the undiscipled peoples of the earth.

However, already within his lifetime, Wesley had to admit that even the Methodists were frequently tempted to be content with merely gathering within their chapels and guarding and cherishing that which had been attained, rather than always breaking up and following the crucified and resurrected Jesus on his way in going into the highways and byways, before the doors of the city or in the marketplace, to the poor and the exiled, those who suffer and need help as well as the forgotten and the excluded.[332]

The missionary conception of the Letter to the Ephesians must be noted in this connection. This letter speaks of the inclusion of the community of Jesus Christ in the raising of Jesus, and of their being set "in heavenly places" with him, but this certainly is not intended to carry the community off into rapture and separate its members from their earthly duties. Instead, it describes the empowerment of the Christian congregation to proclaim and effectively engage the victory of the love of Christ to the powers of this world, through its preaching and its inward nurture in organizational unity. It also permits the body of Christ to grow to its fullness and completion through the missionary penetration of humanity.[333]

Without taking over the "high" and somewhat speculative ecclesiology of the letter to the Ephesians, the rise and growth of early Methodism was also viewed by Wesley with similar eschatological categories. With the effectiveness of its evangelistic preaching that in a new way penetrated the nations, breaking through human restrictions as it went forth, God propelled his work toward its goal![334]

These statements not only need to be subjected to a reasonable critique of the realities of the intervening centuries of church history but also need to be read in light of the theological tension that exists among the quite different statements that are found in the Revelation to John. However, there is a crucial biblical element of United Methodist theology that remains for us. It is the basic declaration that the power that enabled the raising of Jesus to life also enables and empowers the community of faith to fulfill its existence as the leaven in this world, and so to penetrate every corner of this world with the message of the love of Christ.

It is here that the mission-minded community of faith needs to remain conscious of a vital truth. Its task is not to promote the "churching" of the world; rather, it is preaching Jesus Christ. Much as a messenger of reconciliation lives as a reconciled person, and should bring about actual reconciliation among people, to that extent their service, their word, and their existence should always point to what God has done for our reconciliation, and thereby to the person of Jesus Christ and his destiny.

That leads us once more back to the basic meaning of Christology in our proclamation and theology. The question "Who is Jesus and how has God acted through him?" is for the New Testament and for every Christian theology something quite other than an academic question. The salvation of humanity depends upon our answer to this question—not because God has chosen this answer to be the "password" that must be freely chosen to enter through the door to heaven; instead, it is because through this answer people can unlock for their own lives the reality of what God has accomplished for them in Jesus Christ. This is what is to be understood by Paul's Romans 10:9 summarized formula: "If you confess with your lips that Jesus is Lord and believe in your heart that God raised him from the dead, you will be saved." Although it is expressed in the form of a conditional statement, the confession of Jesus and faith in his resurrection are not the achievements of human beings. Through the publicly declared affirmation that "Jesus is Lord," by which a person validly puts himself under the rule of this Lord, the conviction can reach into the inner depths of that person that in Jesus' resurrection, God's creative power has overcome the rule of sin and death. This allows one to experience God's justifying and sanctifying work for herself or himself.[335]

The christological confession of the New Testament and its development in the ecumenical creeds of the church is therefore nothing other than the recognition and description of what God has done for us in Christ. A United Methodist theology lives out of this foundation common to every Christian theology. It also places its own distinctive accent on the christological dogma, in emphasizing that the coming of the Son in its very being signifies the coming of God's love into a world that has become loveless. This love was lived out bodily in the life and death of Jesus, under the conditions of our human existence, and so he is the reality which brings love into effect.

The answer to the basic question of Christology: "Who is Jesus of Nazareth?" turns out to be the christological answer to the question of humanity: "Who is God?" and it reads, "God is love" (1 John 4:16).[336]

2.3 God's Loving Care in God's Renewing Actions

It is characteristic of the being of God, who is love, that he devotes himself to the world and to humanity. This happens from the beginning in his creative deeds and it is demonstrated as well in his reconciling acts toward the humanity that had turned against him. However, neither the creation nor reconciliation ought to be regarded as a merely one-time event; reconciliation aims toward ongoing fellowship, which lives from God constantly renewing that fellowship by his love. The Bible combines this renewing activity of God with the operation of his Spirit. God meets us in his Spirit, creates new life where we only still see death, and creates fellowship where humans can recognize only enmity. Therefore, the work of the Spirit is closely bound up with what Jesus Christ has accomplished through his life and death: the forgiveness of sins, fellowship with the Father, and love for God and one's neighbor, as well as a real hope for final redemption in God's eternal kingdom. The different ways in which God reveals himself to humanity only enter gradually into their reality and consciousness. Yet, they have always been anchored in the being of God. This is why the holy Scripture declares that the Son (or, the "Word") was preexistent with God, although his works first came into full operation and were only properly recognized in the coming of Jesus of Nazareth. However, God's reconciling care has been granted from the beginning in the relationship between God and humanity. It is as much a part of God's being as his creative care.

The same thing is true of the work of the Spirit of God. It is first given in the fullness promised by the prophets to the congregation at Pentecost, after Jesus' resurrection. However, the renewing and community-building work of the Spirit from the beginning belongs to the being of God. It is for this reason that the early church's doctrine of the Trinity, after initial hesitation but then encouraged by particular NT Trinitarian formulations, spoke about God's Spirit as the third Person in the Trinitarian unfolding of God's being.[337] Here we find a series of difficult problems of exposition for a theology of the Trinity. Methodist theology has offered no particular solutions for them. Yet it was important to it that the work of the Spirit be viewed as the personal operation of God in the life of believers and in the church.[338] This outlook is also intended to define the description of the different aspects of God's renewing acts in the discussion that follows. Throughout our discussion, the Trinitarian formulation is basic, but we do not intend that it be employed in a fashion that would force the discussion of the relevant issues into a rigid system.

2.3.1 *The Work of the Spirit in the World*

In accordance with his being, God, who is love, does not intend to be without the world and humanity. Thus, this world can never be void of God, even if human beings separate themselves from God, become God's enemies, or put in God's place more or less subtle forms of "gods," which they have fashioned for themselves. As we have seen, the biblical image of the Creator is not that of a great clockmaker, who fashions the universe like an enormous mechanism and sets it in motion so that he then might abandon it to its predetermined course.[339] The God who has created this world remains near to his creation, and the biblical message perceives in this continuous condition and renewal of creation that God remains at work, acting as the "Father," the source of all things, as well as the Logos, the "Son," who as God's creative Word and wisdom is also the "Mediator" of the creation, and the Spirit as well, through whom God preserves and refashions life. Here there can be no sharp delineation between the "persons" of the Trinity and their work. God is present in this world in his fullness and is interacting with it.[340]

Already in the first verses of the Bible we find evidence that God's creative Spirit, his "breath," the storm of his creative energy, was moving over the waters of chaos to form and breathe life into the chaos.[341] Genesis 2:7 and especially Psalm 104:30 tell us that first of all God's spirit gives creatures their power of life, which they need day by day. Perhaps we could translate this into contemporary language by saying that we experience the working of the Spirit of God in the miracle of the continuing "self-organization" of living things, so that life not only arises but also remains viable and capable of development in spite of opposing circumstances.

God's power is present in history, no less than in nature. At first this is made explicit in only a few instances within the biblical testimony, namely at those places where it is a question of the relationship of world history to the history of the people of God. According to Isaiah 7:18-19, God whistles for Egypt and for Assyria so that, like swarms of destructive insects, they might bring ruin upon faithless Israel. Conversely, God's wrathful breath convulses Assyria to its foundations (Isaiah 30:27-31). In Isaiah 40:15-17 the prophet speaks with incredible sovereignty of how, to Yahweh, "Even the nations are like a drop from a bucket, and are accounted as dust on the scales" and at the same time God makes the rulers of the nations instruments in his handling of Israel (Isaiah 44:24–45:7).[342]

The historical scope in which God's activities are portrayed becomes even more comprehensive in apocalyptic literature. The picture of history represented by the four world kingdoms in Daniel 2 and 7 is much more universal and is presented with less focus upon Israel, but it also allows less of God's direct influence to be recognized on the course of world history prior to its end. According to apocalyptic, the course of world history appears to be predetermined; it would therefore remain devoid of salvation, if the aim of this history were not revealed in terms of God's purpose being realized through it.[343]

It remains noteworthy that where God's power in history is referred to in such general terms, God's Spirit and his works are not mentioned. Where the biblical tradition speaks of the incursion of the Spirit of God, this always has a soteriological significance.[344] Hence, it is God's Spirit who repeatedly awakens savior figures in the time of the judges for the people who had gone astray.[345] God's Spirit will fill the Davidic king of peace and enable him to rule in justice and righteousness and so to be a helper particularly to the poor and the suffering (Isaiah 11:1ff.). In an impressive vision, Ezekiel sees a field of dead bones, which become alive again through God's Spirit and thus become a sign that God can awaken new life within a people who are without hope (Ezekiel 37). If God's Spirit has been poured out upon parched land, then nature and society are revived (Isaiah 32:14ff.; 44:3ff.). The peace which the prophet has announced "is the result of a transformation which gives new form to nature and humanity, the cosmos, and society. However, that is the work of the Spirit."[346]

Where reference is made to the work of God through his Spirit, the element of a completely new creation is included and herefore also the eschatological element—the fact of the inbreaking of God's creative power into the world of death, strife, and unrighteousness, in short, the fact of God's revelation as the author of change. Where God's Spirit is at work, occurrences become unambiguous, because they lead on to the confession that God is at work here. The promise of Zechariah to Zerubbabel, "Not by might, nor by power, but by my spirit, says the LORD of hosts" (Zechariah 4:6), is the sign for this unmistakable activity of the Spirit of God.[347]

These observations stand in a certain opposition to the attempts to see God's will in history as a whole as the working of his Spirit, and to ascribe to his presence everything that is good and that creates freedom, peace, righteousness, or love among humanity, even if the people who effect those virtues know nothing at all about this.[348] Viewed from a biblical perspective, God's Spirit inherently has always the intention to make his works known among humanity so that he will not remain incognito.

Yet, establishing this is initially nothing more than a rule of speech intended to assist one to be theologically understood. It does not exclude seeing God as fundamentally at work in the history of humanity or at least believing that he is at work where we experience developments which are positive either for particular groupings of people or for the wider human community, whether or not those who are responsible for bringing about these changes want to know anything about God or not. But this may be true also where we can recognize only a conglomeration of good and evil, or, in the worst of cases, where everything appears to be turning into suffering or destruction.

To make it clear: it is not God's will that humans enter into war, kill one another, defraud, torment, or deceive one another. People do all these things and they bear the responsibility for it. However, nothing which persons inflict upon one another can disempower God's will for salvation and God's plan to complete it and bring it to pass. Luther addressed this subject when he spoke of the works of the *deus absconditus,* of the "hidden God," who can encounter people even in the mask of suffering or even through evil.[349] Wesley—who had little sympathy for paradox—was convinced of the work of divine providence over all and in all. In spite of the difficulties that exist in believing or in recognizing this divine power given all the evil in the world, he holds firmly to this belief on the basis of the biblical witness. He attempts to explain that if God were to take away humanity's freedom to commit all sorts of destructive acts of evil which they direct toward one another, God would also take away the freedom to do that which is good.[350]

However, theologically Wesley wants to distinguish between the general providence of God, with which he leads and directs the destiny of all, and the working of the *Spirit* based upon the prevenient grace of God, which touches all persons. Wesley ascribes to prevenient grace the fact that among persons who know nothing about the biblical message and its commands, there are signs of love and justice, mutual help and genuine piety. Here Wesley directly opposes the viewpoint ascribed to Augustine, that the virtues of the heathen may be nothing more than "splendid sins."[351] As the example of Cornelius in Acts 10 illustrates, the activity of the Spirit of God can occur in a person even before he or she knows anything about the gospel itself.[352] Wesley is certainly not constructing a general theory of religions on this. He understands this working of the Spirit within the framework of prevenient grace, which is strongly directed toward the message of the gospel.[353]

Hence, Christians also know the Spirit of God in nature, history, and in the religious struggles of human beings, for God's being and work aims at fellowship, because God is love. The work of the Spirit is to create fellowship from and with God. However, the work of the Spirit can only be identified and known where this activity attains its goal. God's Spirit is poured out only in those places where new life buds out of a parched earth (Isaiah 32:15), and he is at work only where justice and peace prevail (Romans 14:17), and only where the most inward familiarity with God springs up, and where God's Spirit is at work in our hearts (Romans 8:14-15).[354] This descriptive determination of the working of the Spirit is what explains the Spirit's impenetrable bond in the revelation of the Son, and therein lies the essential correctness of the occidental addition to the Nicene Creed of the *filoque* clause, the phrase that signifies that the Holy Spirit proceeds from the Father *and the Son*.[355] Yet, this signifies a definition of the nature of the Spirit and it is not intended to impose a limitation on the work of the Spirit to the internal realm of the Christian congregation.[356]

In terms of the United Methodist doctrinal standards, it is the Confession of Faith (EUB) that speaks not only of the Person but also of the work of the Spirit within the world, with its affirmation that the Spirit of God "convinces the world of sin, of righteousness and of judgment. He leads men through faithful response to the gospel into the fellowship of the Church. He comforts, sustains and empowers the faithful and guides them into all truth." The Confession is also distinct in including pneumatological aspects within its discussion of other cardinal doctrines, such as the Bible (Article IV: The Bible "is to be received through the Holy Spirit as the true rule and guide for faith and practice"), the church (Article V: "Under the discipline of the Holy Spirit the Church exists for the maintenance of worship, the edification of believers and the redemption of the world"), regeneration (Article IX: "We believe regeneration is the renewal of man in righteousness through Jesus Christ, by the power of the Holy Spirit"), and the article on sanctification and Christian perfection (Article XI: "We believe sanctification is the work of God's grace through the Word and the Spirit" and believe that through entire sanctification the believer "rules over [the world, the flesh, and the devil] with watchfulness through the power of the Holy Spirit."[357] Several of these aspects are addressed in the discussion that follows.

2.3.2 *The Renewal of Human Beings Through the Spirit of God*

Already within the Old Testament, the conviction which belongs to the basic assertions of the apostolic preaching in the New Testament has been presaged that for an actual renewal of the relationship between God and humanity to take place, it is necessary for there to be a basic renewal of human beings from within. And conversely stated: the actual work of the Holy Spirit, his place in the operation of the Trinitarian God, is the renewal of humanity from within, a renewal which readies humans for fellowship with God and with one another.

The primary sources for this conviction in the Old Testament are found in Ezekiel 11:19-20 and 36:26-27: the renewal of the people to actual obedience takes place through the transformation of the heart, the "center of personhood" of each individual within the people of God. Through the Spirit of God, the "heart of stone," which is dead, callous, and unmoving, becomes a "heart of flesh," one that is ready to hear and to sense what God is doing for the people and what he wants from them.[358] (Jeremiah 31:31-34 articulates the same insights with somewhat different motifs.) In the words of a prayer we find the same conviction in Psalm 51:12-14: God must give the people a new Spirit and create a new heart within them, in order to purify and renew that relationship that has been broken by guilt.

In addition, the promise of Joel 2:28-32 affirms that God will give his Spirit "to all flesh"—that is, to his entire people and beyond them to humanity in general, so that they will be in a position to recognize what stands before them and where salvation is to be found. Thus, in the final day there is to be a company of prophets of all believers, which is already desired in Numbers 11:25-29.[359]

In many of its texts, the New Testament attests to the fact that this promise has been fulfilled on the basis of the work of Jesus with his disciples after his death, resurrection, and ascension, and that his work is therefore now continuing on in a new manner among and through his disciples. The picture that Luke as well as John and Paul give of the post-Easter community of disciples consists of persons who have been transformed by God's Spirit and of a community that is led by his Spirit.[360]

In the succeeding centuries, the church did not make things easy for itself with regard to this experience. The danger of enthusiasm—and certainly the reality but often the fear of it as well—repeatedly led to the fact that the work of the Holy Spirit was held in check and was objectified within the confines of institutional structures. That tendency can already be observed in the period of the early church, where the work of enthusiastic groups of "Montanists" offered overly acute lines of demarcation between those with and those without the Spirit.[361] However, it was also true of the Reformation period, which, in its struggle against the "Schwärmer" (radical enthusiasts), led to a necessary but in many instances overly rigid and uninsightful exclusion of the gifts and work of the Spirit.[362]

The fact that Wesley placed the possibility and necessity of the personal experience of the renewing work of the Holy Spirit at the heart of his message soon led to criticism of "enthusiasm" being leveled against him. And a great part of the discussion that Wesley conducted with the

Anglican divines during the first two decades of his evangelistic ministry also had to do with this matter.[363] Such criticisms were all the more pertinent because in the course of the ministry of the brothers Wesley and their preaching assistants, enthusiastic manifestations did indeed repeatedly occur. However, that was not the heart of what concerned Wesley. What mattered to him was the basic question that he posed in the course of his discussion with one of his most insightful and earnest correspondents, whom we know only by the pseudonym "John Smith"; namely, "Is there perceptible inspiration or is there not?"[364]

In this regard, Wesley was never preoccupied with the external signs of the reception of the Spirit, such as speaking in tongues or prophecy, which for the Pentecostal movement have become indispensable indices of genuine inspiration through the Spirit of God. Whenever he spoke of the experience of the operation of the Spirit, Wesley focused upon the basic question of soteriology, the assurance that one was accepted by God.

Hence, his pneumatology is actually the other side of his soteriology, namely the description of how God acts in the life of people, so that they may enter into holy fellowship with him and may be able to remain and live in that fellowship.[365]

Excursus: Receiving and Being Baptized in the Spirit

The promise of the Spirit that is found in the Old Testament is taken up in a distinctive way in the word of promise of John the Baptist. Concerning him who is to come after him, he says, "I have baptized you with water; but he will baptize you with the Holy Spirit."[366]

When was this promise fulfilled? Jesus himself is apparently not represented as the baptizer in the spirit, but in Acts 1:5, 8 the prophetic words of John the Baptist about the resurrected Jesus are revisited, and the account of Pentecost without doubt intends to describe the fulfillment of this promise. This promise is also remembered on the occasion of the outpouring of the Spirit upon Cornelius and those present in his house (Acts 11:16). However, where it is a question of particular persons or groups receiving the Spirit, the phrase "be baptized by the Holy Spirit" is missing. The concept is not bound up with biographical experiences of individuals but basically denotes what Christ has promised and what has taken place for Christians (see also 1 Corinthians 12:13). The practical experience of the reception of the Spirit is described in a variegated manner.[367]

Over against this diversity, there stands the more monolithic position on the baptism in the Spirit in the older and newer Pentecostal movement, in which it is understood and experienced as the second or third (and in any case, the last) step of becoming filled with the Spirit of God, an experience that is to be accompanied by receiving the gift of the prayer language or speaking in tongues. It is also distinguished from the experience of new birth, or regeneration.[368] Behind this concept stands a particular interpretation of Acts in which the outpouring of the Spirit is frequently made known in the phenomenon of tongue-speaking. However, it also has roots in Wesley's doctrine of the new birth and the witness of the Spirit, which confirms the new birth. It is even more strongly rooted in Wesley's understanding of the gift of entire sanctification, which is accomplished by God and is imparted to persons in a moment. This also raises the question of a "second blessing." John Fletcher, one of Wesley's closest coworkers, proposed introducing the term "baptism in the Spirit" for this experience. It has customarily been held that Wesley was not in agreement with this usage, although this has recently come under reexamination.[369] This line of questioning was extended by the holiness movement of the nineteenth century. At the center of this sharing stood the promulgation of "perfect love," which relates to the Pauline witness concerning the working of the Holy Spirit.

However, the decisive impulse for the newer doctrine of Spirit baptism proceeded from the earlier Pentecostal movement, for which this doctrine is clearly characteristic. When referring to this doctrine, charismatic groups prefer to speak of "renewal of the Spirit" in order to avoid an unbiblical misappropriation of the concept of Spirit baptism.[370] For the New Testament also leaves no doubt that the Pentecostal conception of Spirit baptism is not biblical.

(a.) In the early Christian church, the basic experience of receiving the Spirit was also a basic experience in the sense that it was inseparable from the beginning of one's existence as a Christian, and is connected with faith and the new birth. Galatians 3:2; Romans 8:16; Ephesians 1:13-14 (cf. 4:30); Titus 3:4-7; as well as John 3:3-5 all attest to this.

(b.) First Corinthians 12:13, the sole Pauline source that speaks about baptism in the Holy Spirit, makes clear that *all* are baptized through the Spirit into one body in the congregation, although not all speak in tongues (cf. 12:30)!

Nevertheless, the United Methodist theology sympathizes with the concern which stands behind the phrase "Spirit baptism" and does so not only for historical but also factual reasons.

—United Methodist preaching does not assume that all baptized church members have already had the experience of the new birth and the certainly of faith, which is conferred by God's Spirit. Its goal is that persons open themselves to this basic experience of life with Christ.

—The assertion that every believing and regenerated Christian has received God's Spirit cannot remain only an abstract theological proposition. Based upon our heritage, we need to remain sensitive to the fact that when we confess faith to be the work of God, we are also intending that this become an existential reality in the life of the believer. Thus, it is appropriate for us to remain open to everything that aids the discovery of the work of the Spirit in us and among us, to allow that work to become deepened and hence to permit ourselves to be renewed through the Spirit's activity. This can take place in an ongoing process but also in breakthrough experiences which open to us new dimensions of our existence as Christians.

—The gift of the Holy Spirit is not a static, one-time gift; instead, it places us within a dynamic process which repeatedly opens us to new understanding and certainty and equips us with power for new service and areas of challenge. It also points us toward new ways of living as Christians. This dynamic conception of the work of the Spirit is wholly in accord with the New Testament. It is prayed for by Christians who "were marked with the seal of the promised Holy Spirit" (Ephesians 1:13), so that God might impart to them the "spirit of wisdom and revelation," to know Christ better (1:17), and they are admonished, "Be filled with the Spirit" (5:18).

It is the work of the Spirit to penetrate God's love into the hearts of human beings (Romans 5:5). Everything that purports to be an outpouring of the Spirit must be measured against this, and therefore 1 Corinthians 13 remains the unsurpassed standard for what are the gifts and graces of the Spirit.

It is nonetheless unbiblical to limit the idea of "Spirit baptism" to an individual biographical experience. According to the New Testament linguistic usage, "being baptized with the Holy Spirit" points to the promise that became fulfilled at Pentecost, that God is present in his community of faith and in its members through his Spirit and he gives them new life.

If we examine the New Testament witnesses to the renewal of humanity through the work of the Holy Spirit, we discover different aspects of this work. Some of them were of particular importance for Wesley. There are those that describe how God's Spirit encounters, fills, and transforms human beings in their personal lives. Yet, the other aspects, which emphasize the significance of the Spirit for the fellowship, mission, and hope of Christians, are also not excluded from Wesley's consideration, and they are crucial for a theology of The United Methodist Church in our day. Several of these aspects are also addressed in the pneumatological articles within the Confession of Faith of The United Methodist Church.[371]

We will describe these aspects under the following seven headings.

2.3.2.1 THE FUNDAMENTAL RENEWAL THROUGH GOD

> *"God's love has been poured into our hearts through the Holy Spirit." (Romans 5:5)*

As is well known, Wesley identified this text from Romans 5 to be the only true designation of a Methodist. Of course, he did not mean this in a manner that would be limited to a confessional declaration unique to Methodists, but he wanted to make clear that a Methodist could be distinguished by nothing other than by what is valid for every true Christian.[372]

Nevertheless, with this characteristic mark, of course, an unmistakable accentuation is given, which Wesley—quite distinctly from some others in his day—held to be the heart of Christian existence: their renewal through God from their center. This renewal takes place precisely through the operation of the Holy Spirit, so that the love of God becomes the center of life for our personal living. What a person hears in the message of Jesus Christ, of how God has so demonstrated his love for that person and for the entire world that he gave his only begotten Son for them, is personally grasped in the concreteness of a person's life through the work of the Spirit.[373] The indissoluble connection of the "subjective" certainty of God's love through the work of the Spirit within us to the "objective" confirmation that "God proves his love for us in that while we still were sinners Christ died for us" (Romans 5:8) is characteristic of the Wesleyan proclamation of the work of the Spirit and is basic for the encouragement of all who may doubt God's love for them.[374] God loves me, even me—not because I am so lovable, but because God's love is sufficient to fill the need for love within my life. To be so touched and filled by the love of God in our innermost being creates within human beings the room and the ability for love toward God and toward other persons.[375]

This love is the basis and the standard for the renewed fellowship with one another which Christians experience within the body of Christ. It is the motivation to live no longer for ourselves but in service so that this love of God may become a gift that is shared with others. This love also confers a new way of perceiving humanity and the circumstances in which people live. It can only be lived out imperfectly under the conditions of earthly existence, and so it contains the germ of longing and hope for the completion of that fellowship with our gracious Lord. The statement that God's love is poured out into our hearts through the Holy Spirit therefore includes everything which can be expressed about our new existence as human beings in Christ.

2.3.2.2   THE RENEWAL OF THE RELATIONSHIP WITH GOD

> *"When we cry, 'Abba! Father!' it is that very Spirit bear-*
> *ing witness with our spirit that we are children of God."*
> *(Romans 8:15-16)*

This Pauline declaration is also a central text for John Wesley, because it makes clear that our new relationship with God, which is grounded in God's acts in Jesus Christ, can be personally experienced with reality and certainty within the lives of Christians.[376]

At the same time, no temporal sequence of renewal is to be construed through the outpouring of the love of God in the hearts of human beings and the renewal of their relationship to God, simply on the basis of the succession of these two sections.[377] Both sides of the event belong indissolubly together, so that Paul in Romans 8:14-16 and Galatians 4:6 himself refers to the logical connection of being a child of God and the witness of the Spirit in the opposite order.

The entire section in which this word occurs certainly has special importance for Paul, and it represents both a high point and a goal for the statements made in his letter to the Romans. If justification by faith in chapters 1–4 is grounded and anchored in the events of Christ, then chapters 5–8 describe how it is that through the event of justification the life of the Christian is actually renewed and transformed through the operation of the Spirit.[378] Through Christ's death and resurrection, not only is enmity between God and humans overcome and the results of human guilt borne, but also a new relationship with God is established that is marked by trust and love. The Bible describes this relationship as one that corresponds to the relationship that exists between children and their father. The "basic trust" that human beings need for life, and which is missing in a life without God, is planted within their hearts by God's Spirit. The childlike call "Abba, Father" is an expression of this newfound trust, which leads people not into a slavish dependency but rather into a fellowship which is characterized by real maturity and by genuine, inner freedom.

Wesley also speaks of a prevenient work of the Spirit in the life of a person through the law.[379] For, according to John 16:8, it is precisely the work of the Spirit to open the eyes of the world in regard to "sin and righteousness and judgment." However, Wesley perceives clearly that seen from the entire witness of the New Testament, this is not the actual work of the Spirit, since it leads persons into a situation which is defined by the spirit of bondage and fear.

The Spirit of God that meets us in Jesus Christ is the Spirit of adoption. He drives out the fear of punishment as well as the anxiety that comes from fearing the inadequacy of our own achievements. The Spirit also expels the shame and resignation over the unworthiness of our own lives and the false security that we can and must justify our lives by ourselves. He delivers us from the arrogance to love and honor ourselves above all things. In place of these acts, he establishes within us the certainty of our acceptance by God and our knowledge that we are secure in God, which is the assurance that we are loved and valued by God.[380] True faith, faith which lives from this certainty, is therefore always a gift of the Holy Spirit whereby God comes near to us until that which God in Christ has done for us, without our assistance, becomes living and active in us.[381]

As we shall note, Wesley further distinguishes between justification and the new birth: the doctrine of justification relates to that great work which God accomplishes *for* us, in that he pardons our sins; the doctrine of the new birth relates to that great work which God accomplishes *within* us, in that he renews our fallen nature. The two are closely joined together: "In the moment in which we are justified by the grace of God through the redemption that is in Jesus, we are also 'born of the Spirit.' "[382] However, for a Methodist theology, it has always been particularly important to lift up the aspect of the new birth through the Spirit because it is the Spirit who establishes and announces the transforming power of the grace of God.

In the next chapter we shall consider how this new reality works itself out in human lives. In this context, it is to be emphasized that the renewal through the Holy Spirit is most deeply rooted in the event of Christ. We are "new creatures" in Christ. It is also to be noted that the transforming power of the Spirit is joined to the transformation of our relationship to God. It is not a matter of an isolated transformation of personality based upon the ego of a person. This transforming and renewing Spirit of God is the Spirit of adoption, of trust, and of love.

And a final point is this. It pertains to the essence of the Spirit of God, that he is sovereign in his operation. "The wind blows where it chooses" (John 3:8). However, it is of decisive importance for Wesley that God's working in the Spirit does not become arbitrary. In the so-called means of grace, God has made known to believers that they can open themselves to the operation of the Spirit.[383] The means of grace do not operate automatically or magically. However, they can show those persons who want to open themselves to the working of the Spirit of God where and how they can make themselves ready for this operation.[384]

2.3.2.3   THE RENEWAL OF THE MANNER AND THE MODE OF LIVING

> *"If we live by the Spirit, let us also be guided by the Spirit."*
> *(Galatians 5:25)*

If God's Spirit renews persons from within and places them in a new relationship with God, then it is to be expected that his working also has effects upon the practical lives of Christians, including their manner and mode of living. For Paul, this was particularly important with regard to questions concerning how God's will is to be fulfilled. He had experienced that the doing of the law did not lead persons to salvation, but only faith alone did. However, that led to the question of how God's will, which the law proclaimed rightly with regard to its content, could be expressed in the actual actions of human beings. And here, Paul replaced the "you must" or the "you should not" of the law with the guidance of persons by the Spirit of God. The unwholesome fluctuation between the command that confronts a person from the outside and one's rebellious or slavish egoism is broken through by the work of the Spirit: he fills persons with a new principle of action, namely the principle of love, which replaces the old principle of action that had to do with the fear-laden or self-justifying ego (which is "the flesh," for Paul) and makes people ready to do God's will in freedom.

Among the deepest theological statements of Paul is the assertion that a person finds true freedom precisely in the inner union with God, a union that cannot be regulated anew by religious managers but is intended to be lived in relationship to Christ and to the mutual connection that results from our becoming members of his body.

This work of the Spirit does not take place automatically. The underlying truth that my ego no longer defines myself, but Christ is my life center (Galatians 2:20), is to be lived out daily by faith in him who loved me and gave himself for me. In like manner, the motivating and upbuilding power of the Spirit must repeatedly overcome all other powers which stand against God. This dynamic of the Spirit's operation in the Christian's life also informs the tenor of the apostolic warning, that whatever fundamentally defines our lives must now be allowed to guide each step of our daily activity. Where the Spirit is allowed to work like that, the "catalogues of vices," which indicate what is brought about by human egoism, are replaced—but not by a "balance of achievements," which enumerates many good deeds, but by what Paul characterizes with striking symbolism as "fruit of the spirit": models of conduct which God's Spirit allows to develop within our lives, such as "love, joy, peace, patience, kindness, generosity, faithfulness, gentleness, and self-control" (Galatians 5:22-23).[385]

This aspect of Pauline theology is the common heritage of all Christian churches; but it has a special importance within Methodist preaching, and we will encounter it once again in the doctrine of holiness. Here what we must hold firm to and emphasize is that the new mode of conduct that is created through God's Spirit, as well as the new relationships that develop among persons, are a matter not primarily of human activity but of taking seriously the working of God's grace. Further, the social components in the working of the Holy Spirit are not to be overlooked, because the "fruit of the Spirit" is always concerned with newly shaped relationships.[386] In a day when people have become allergic to every attempt to impose an alien regulation (heteronomy) upon their actions, and also when they have repeatedly foundered in seeking an adequate self-determination (autonomy), the possibility of defining life through God (theonomy)—which is to be clearly distinguished from all forms of heteronomy—should be an important emphasis of the Christian message.[387]

2.3.2.4 RENEWAL FOR TRUE FELLOWSHIP

"For in the one Spirit we were all baptized into one body."
(1 Corinthians 12:13)

The life of humanity is directed toward fellowship. Humans are "social beings." At the same time, they repeatedly experience their failure and the brokenness of their existence in the fact that they are not capable of fellowship. Hence, an essential aspect of the renewing activity of God pertains to the enabling of persons for fellowship. Not only does the particular person as an individual become a new creation, the reality of the new creation begins in the solidarity of humans: where persons by baptism and faith have "put on Christ" as their determining reality, it can truly be stated that "There is no longer Jew or Greek, there is no longer slave or free, there is no longer male and female; for all of you are one in Christ Jesus" (Galatians 3:28). Of course, this does not mean that such distinctions immediately vanish. However, it does mean that religious origins, social position, gender—and we must add, race, ethnic identity, educational differences—all these qualifications whereby people distance themselves from one another have through Christ lost their power to create divisions. By contrast, there emerges a new quality of relationship, a reality given by God that, according to Paul, is conferred by God in the work of the Spirit. "For the kingdom of God is not food and drink" (that is, in context, different opinions of food regulations based on religion, which threaten to destroy fellowship) "but righteousness and peace and joy *in the Holy Spirit*" (Romans 14:17, emphasis added). Or 1 Corinthians 12:13: "For in the one Spirit we were all baptized into one body—Jews or Greeks, slaves or free—and we were all made to drink of one Spirit."

It is noteworthy that Paul developed his most detailed reflections on community and worship in relation to the discussion about spiritual gifts. Arising from people's joy and pride over special capabilities and gifts, apparently in Corinth the danger had arisen that these gifts were being lived out in totally unspiritual ways, namely as marks of individual distinction and as evidence of a personal possession of the Spirit. However, this would mean to pervert the work of the Spirit and to forget that gifts of the spirit are gifts of grace, or charismata from God, and that they are for the congregation as a whole (1 Corinthians 12–14). God's grace is always "grace that is given" (Romans 12:3, 6), and thus an endowment of living grace. The multiplicity and stratification of the particular gifts, which Paul names in his various enumerations of the gifts, shows that he is neither oriented to the standard of the "extraordinary" spiritual gifts nor does he intend to draw up a "charismatic order for the congregation." What matters to him is an organic cooperation of different services, offices, and talents in a congregation for the use of all.[388] All of them, be they deemed significant or insignificant, are expressions of the basic "Yes" that God has spoken to a person.

Everything which the Spirit accomplishes, he accomplishes for the community and for the mutual needs of upbuilding one another. It is not the individual endowment, the inspiration of particular persons, that is the foundation for the community of faith. Instead, it is the reality of the body of Christ, into which the Spirit incorporates, which he continually joins together and which he enlivens and nourishes through the gifts that he gives. Then in all things love will become the decisive standard for measuring the worth of a gift (1 Corinthians 13).[389] We acknowledge that God's Spirit operates in the church in word and sacrament for the appropriation of salvation, thereby constituting the congregation as the body of Christ. At the same time, the Spirit is also creating a renewed human fellowship, which lives as the body of Christ with the diverse spiritual gifts functioning in organic mutuality. The recognition of both of these truths has been more a lived reality in Methodism than an explicitly articulated doctrine. This fact is a function of the ambivalent character of Wesleyan ecclesiology. The article on the church in the Methodist Articles of Religion and in the Evangelical United Brethren Confession of Faith hardly deviate from conforming to the declarations about the church that come from the Protestant Reformation. However, within the life of United Methodist congregations and groups, there developed what is today referred to as "charismatic congregational development": the discovery of gifts that God gives to the congregation through its particular members, the incorporation of these gifts into worship and congregational life, the overcoming of sociological lines of separation and the integration of persons of quite distinct origins into the life of the congregation. This process, however, has not always been adhered to within the history of United Methodist congregations.[390]

The spiritual and charismatic character of Christian fellowship is demonstrated not in the presence of fully defined, conspicuous spiritual gifts but in the power of this fellowship to integrate persons of different origins and peculiarities so that they may go about the task of assimilating conflicting modes of thinking into a mutuality of esteem and assistance. Only then can a Christian congregation make clear in all its actions and positions just what it is that empowers its life—the grace of its Lord Jesus Christ, the love of God, and the fellowship of the Holy Spirit (2 Corinthians 13:13).[391] Hence, the congregation becomes the place where God is worshiped both in Spirit and in truth (John 4:24)!

2.3.2.5 RENEWAL FOR MISSION AND THE COMPETENCY FOR WITNESSING

> *"You will receive power when the Holy Spirit has come upon you; and you will be my witnesses."*
>
> *(Acts 1:8)*

The Acts of the Apostles places a wider aspect of the work of the Spirit into the foreground. God's Spirit empowers the disciples for missional proclamation and qualifies them for effective witness for the gospel. This is announced in Acts 1:8 and is fulfilled in the miracle of Pentecost, which depicts through a deeply symbolic event the equipping of the disciples with the full power of the Spirit for their preaching mission. This is repeatedly confirmed in the further development of Acts. It is God's Spirit who fulfills and guides the apostolic missionaries, leading them, even on unaccustomed paths, and enabling them to overcome even what had been insurmountable barriers.

Acts does not stand alone in this conception. In Mark 13:11 (paralleled in Luke 12:11-12; Matthew 10:19-20; Luke 21:14-15) the disciples are promised that the Holy Spirit will stand by them in the face of persecution in the courts of their interrogators, and he will instruct them about what they should say in that hour. In John 14–16, this promise is further developed in a miniature theology of the Spirit through the doctrine of the Paraclete, concerning the "advocate," who brings to mind the message and the Person of Jesus for the disciples, and so also represents these to the world with freshness and power, thereby enabling them to carry forward Jesus' work. Hence, because God's Spirit fills them, "rivers of living water" (John 7:38) will flow from those who believe in Christ.

The competence to become messengers of the gospel, and, hence, messengers of reconciliation and life, is for Paul also a gift and work of the Spirit. He engaged in a very difficult discussion with persons who on the one hand reproached him for incorrectly expositing the law and, on the other hand, asserted that he failed to exhibit the signs of the fullness of Spirit-imbued missionary power. In response, Paul describes in 2 Corinthians 3:3, 5, 8ff. how the full empowerment through God's Spirit is seen in the fact that God's unbreakable "Yes" encounters their lives in the message of the apostle. According to 1 Corinthians 2:1-5, the actual "demonstration of the Spirit and of power" is seen in the fact that the foolish and shocking proclamation of the crucified Lord as the salvation of the world finds and leads people to salvation.[392]

In the early days of Methodism, this manner of the Spirit's working was experienced in two ways and subsequently became the subject of theological reflection.

One way is the experience of the extraordinary activity which Whitefield's and Wesley's open-air preaching set loose. In response to a need, they had ventured to overstep the existing restrictions upon the preaching of the gospel. They were also permitted to experience that the same message which met with widespread rejection in the churches became the impetus for a life-changing encounter for many completely unchurched persons. In this Wesley saw the operation and confirmation of the Holy Spirit. Strictly speaking, it was only by taking this step beyond itself on April 2, 1739, that Methodism had experienced its hour of birth as a missionary and an awakening movement.

The second way of experiencing the Spirit's working was the discovery and introduction of lay preaching. After initial strong objections, Wesley had to accept the notion that God's Spirit desired to work through men and women(!) who were uneducated but were empowered for the preaching of the gospel. Wesley recognized this and then accepted them into the organization of his movement, in a manner reflecting his pragmatic approach to ministry.[393]

The "prophetic office of all believers" is understood by Wesley and his Methodists less as a literal fulfillment of Joel 2, with its emphasis on dreams and visions, than as an analog to Acts 2 and above all to 1 Corinthians 14. This is to say that Wesley recognized the inherent competency of all—or, stated more carefully, many—Christians to respond to God's mandate to offer an effectual word to others, either in personal conversation or by preaching within the congregation. The old Methodist designation of "exhorter," which was used for those who exercised the simplest form of this service, allows us, despite its often misunderstandable sound, to surmise that this manner of prophetic *paraklesis*, that is, admonition and encouragement, describes the theological basis of the ministry of the lay preachers.

All of these ministries were instituted quite early in the Methodist movement within its developing institutions, so that the classical opposition between Spirit and office were at least relegated to the background. However, like all churches and movements, United Methodist theology and church order must also ask itself this basic question: How are the ordered office of preaching and the free call to be related to one another, related to the task of acquiring exegetical and hermeneutical competence and the authorization through God's Spirit? How does the openness for the leading of the Spirit relate to sound churchmanship or to church life that is characterized by patterns of responsible and achievable structures for decision making? Above all, it was in the "conferences," which were developed as an organizational principle of Methodism, in which the attempt was made to integrate both dimensions. Today we need to prevent

the misunderstanding that such conferences are nothing more than ecclesiastical parliaments. The Spirit of God does not automatically speak
through the decisions of majorities!

Finally, the missionary operation of the Spirit is also demonstrated in
the working of "prevenient grace." As Wesley also indicated, Acts 10
shows quite impressively that God's Spirit is present in some settings
prior to our missionary efforts. This is not to suggest any flat identification of religious phenomena in other religions with the working of the
Spirit, but it does lead us to the thankful acknowledgment that God's
Spirit prepares people to accept the message of the gospel before we
actually proclaim it.

2.3.2.6 THE RENEWAL OF INSIGHT AND REFLECTION

> *"When the Spirit of truth comes, he will guide you into all
> the truth."*
>
> *(John 16:13)*

> *"The Spirit searches everything, even the depths of God."*
> *(1 Corinthians 2:10)*

God can only be recognized through himself. Thus, all aspects of the
knowledge of God are rooted in the fact that we are known by God, and
because we are known through his love, we can recognize him as love (see
1 Corinthians 8:3; Galatians 4:9). Thus, it is God himself who discloses
God's being to us through his Spirit. Paul expounds this same thing in
1 Corinthians 2:6-16 in discussion with a speculative theology of wisdom.
The highest form of wisdom is to acknowledge that which is given to us
by God (1 Corinthians 2:12).[394] In a similar manner, the Johannine Christ
promises in his farewell discourse to the disciples that the gift of the Spirit
will be the way of his presence, which leads all humanity into the whole
truth.

This places us before the task of considering how a Spirit-imbued
knowledge of God and a reflective, responsible theology can be placed in
proper relationship with one another. Do they not exist within an insurmountable tension? The relationship of faith and reason has been an area
of tension since the beginning of Christian theology. Where it was a matter of substantial questions, Wesley was always prepared to place statements from the Bible above those that human reason was capable of
accepting. But he was nonetheless a determined advocate for a use of rea-

son that was guided by the Spirit of God. One of his chief criticisms of Luther was that the latter spoke so dismissively of reason.[395] When it came to the exposition of Scripture and to the task of developing a hermeneutic that reflected his concern for evangelistic preaching and practical service, Wesley emphasizes the work of the Spirit, yet including the careful study of biblical texts, church tradition, and Christian experience, and neither did he exclude logical and critical thinking.[396] It is to be regretted that later Methodists scarcely attempted to develop a theological understanding of knowledge based upon this foundation. From its beginning, Methodist theology has been particularly prone to demonstrating the relationship of knowledge and love (see 1 Corinthians 8:1-3). Yet, this relationship has perhaps been more a matter of the inward condition of the expositor than it has been the content of a theological epistemology.

2.3.2.7 RENEWAL FOR HOPE

> *"We ourselves, who have the first fruits of the Spirit, groan inwardly while we wait for adoption."*
>
> *(Romans 8:23)*

The gift of the Spirit is the pledge, the deposit, and the firstfruit of a future fulfillment. The images that Paul employs in these formulations emphasize the intensive, properly related congruity of beginning and end.[397] When Paul declares that "the kingdom of God is [now already] righteousness and peace and joy in the Holy Spirit" (Romans 14:17), this line of thinking also pertains to the fact that what is conferred by the Spirit is also a "foretaste" of the coming kingdom of God. However, the renewal of hope consists above all in the assurance that hope does not allow us to be put to shame—in spite of affliction and temptation that is set in the believer's path, for the love of God has been shed abroad in our hearts (Romans 5:5). Here a New Testament pneumatology from a Methodist perspective comes full circle: what is the actual, present assurance of God's love in and for us also provides the basis for our certainty of a future consummation. Within our sense of assurance of this grace there is also to be found the wellspring of our earnest desire for its fulfillment. In one of his most moving passages, Paul speaks in Romans 8:19-26 of the ardent waiting of the creatures of this world for their release from their condition of transience, and of the longing desire of the children of God for the redemption of their bodies unto full fellowship with God. He drives forward this line of thinking with the assertion that even the Spirit himself longs for this consummation, and brings before God all of our speechless groanings and mute longing that cannot be articulated with concepts and words and intercedes for us. (See also Revelation 22:17*a*!) God himself shares in the cry for redemption.

2.3.3 *The Consummation of the World*

The renewal which persons experience through the working of the Spirit is therefore only the beginning of the transforming activity of God that aims at the complete renewal of this world. God's Spirit establishes the divine "principle of hope" not only in the hearts of Christians but also, through their witness and their acts, within a world which is so often without hope.

The hope, which the biblical message formulates and which God's Spirit makes certain, has a threefold scope. It is hope for individuals that God is fulfilling their lives in the eternal fellowship with him. It is hope for the congregation of Jesus Christ that he guards them on their way and leads them to their goal in fulfillment of their task in history. It is hope for the world that God is renewing it from the ground up, so that it will be what God intended it to be: his good and perfect creation.[398]

2.3.3.1 PERSONAL HOPE

In Romans 8:11 Paul declares, "If the Spirit of him who raised Jesus from the dead dwells in you, he who raised Christ from the dead will give life to your mortal bodies also through his Spirit that dwells in you." This statement leads us deeply into the entire character of Christian hope. The experience of the creative power of the Spirit, which has taken hold of the lives of Christians, awakens and assures within them the hope that this power is stronger than the mortal fallenness of the human body. This is the reason for the hope of the resurrection of the body, which stands at the center of the New Testament message of the hope of Christians.

This hope already begins to be illumined toward the end of the history of revelation in the Old Testament.[399] It is based not so much in the fact that the concept is derived from other religions, even if it is not to be excluded that impulses for new models of understanding the actions of God were taken from them. However, the actual basis lies within that circle of godly persons in the Old Testament who were concerned with the question of whether their fellowship with God was actually terminated with death, which had been the conviction within ancient Israel.[400]

Those who call upon God in their hour of deep affliction receive the certainty that God will not abandon them even in death.[401] At *one* place in the Old Testament, the hope of the resurrection of the dead is explicitly stated, and at the same time it is bound together with the expectation not only that those who have abided in God will live in eternal fellowship with him, rather also that those who have separated themselves from God by their actions have to experience the pain of being separated from God eternally (Daniel 12:1-2).[402]

This perspective is taken up in early Judaism and also in the New Testament. It is expressed in the message of Jesus and the apostles, not only as a part of its contextual framework, which was taken over from Judaism, but also as the consequence of faith in the God who creates life and who does not abandon in death those who belong to him.[403]

The experience of Jesus' resurrection gives this hope a new basis: in the raising of Jesus the power of God's love has already broken through the power of death at *one* point in history, and has done so totally! This attests to the message of the bodily resurrection of Jesus, and upon this is based the hope of the resurrection of the body, which Paul sets forth as a basic tenet of Christian hope in 1 Corinthians 15, where he defends it in the face of the denial of this message that occurred in the congregation at Corinth.[404]

Being Greeks, the Corinthians had difficulties with the concept of the resurrection of the body, and so they rejected this and preferred the view that (in baptism) the divine spirit of humans was translated into the heavenly world.[405] In opposition to this, Paul confirmed the faith in the bodily resurrection for three reasons:

(1.) It is not an immortal, divine spark within humans which guarantees our continuing fellowship with God and eternal life; it is the creative power of God—who created the world out of nothing, raised Jesus from the dead, and justifies the godless—which gives us new life beyond death.[406]

(2.) God's new creative action grasps the *entire* person and everything that constitutes his or her personhood: spirit, soul, and body.

(3.) Hence, we stand with our entire being and actions in accountability before God, and that includes the bodily dimension of our existence.[407]

Hence, the Christian church quite early accepted the Greek concept of the immortality of the soul into its teaching—not as a substitute for the hope of the resurrection, but as a complement that in the course of many centuries certainly became a theological and existential foundation of the

Christian hope.[408] This development led to some problematic deviations from the basic Christian message:

(a.) God's creative work was no longer based upon the continuity of life with God but upon an immortal "part" of the human person.

(b.) From this arose the danger of either denying or dislodging the painful and threatening reality of death, which is clearly given the greater emphasis in the biblical witness.

On the other hand, the concept of the immortality of the soul to some degree accepts the notion, which we find in some parts of the New Testament, that the fellowship with God and with Christ between death and the resurrection is not removed. Instead, Christians are allowed to have the certainty that death cannot separate them from the love of God and that they will somehow be "with Christ" in an entirely new manner.[409] Still, this hope is not based upon the immortality of the soul but upon the indissoluble union with God.

The biblical witnesses for the hope of the resurrection and eternal life are quite hesitant to unite this hope with overly concrete explanations of this existence. Jesus cautions the Sadducees against assuming that complete fellowship with God is simply a continuation of earthly living (Mark 12:18-27). Paul refers to the manifold possibilities available to God for fashioning an ongoing "corporeal" existence, and in 1 John 3:2 we see the most striking summation of the New Testament statements on this matter in the words "We are God's children now; what we will be has not yet been revealed. What we do know is this: when he is revealed, we will be like him, for we will see him as he is." The heart of the Christian hope lies in the expectation of being accepted into full fellowship with God.[410] It is important to grasp and hold fast to that basic content of this hope, over against all time-bound and time-related marks of Christian hope across the centuries.

2.3.3.2   THE HOPE OF THE CONGREGATION OF JESUS CHRIST

Eternal life as fellowship with God is therefore not simply a continuation of the individual existence of particular persons but the fulfillment of one's relationship with God. Thus, the hope of individual Christians is closely bound up with the hope for the fulfillment of the congregation of Jesus Christ. Paul almost always refers to this eschatological destiny in the plural, with reference to "those who belong to Christ" (1 Corinthians 15:23; 1 Thessalonians 4:16), and the Revelation to John gives to the persecuted and suffering community a preliminary view of the perfection of the church of Jesus Christ (Revelation 7; 14:1-5).[411]

There are three basic lines of thought that are important in reference to this outlook:

(1.) The perfected church is the universal church, the church of Jesus Christ, which comes "from every nation, from all tribes and peoples and languages" (Revelation 7:9). A horizon of hope is thereby given to the church, which wholly conforms to its missionary task.

In a particular way, this expectation is joined to the fact that "the full number of the Gentiles" as well as "all Israel" will attain salvation (Romans 11:25-26). Paul only hints at how this will occur. He apparently expects a meeting of Israel with Christ, which Israel will be granted apart from the mission of the church. However, this encounter is intimately connected with the missionary faithfulness of the church toward the non-Jewish world. To its shame, the church of Jesus has over the centuries forgotten that the universal hope of the consummation of the community of faith also includes the hope for Israel.[412]

(2.) The course that the congregation of Jesus is to take toward this goal is characterized by two opposing descriptions of that course:

(a.) The congregation is called and empowered to erect signs of the coming rule of God through its mission in preaching, active love, and the manner in which it lives out its life as a fellowship. It does not establish the kingdom of God, but in its words and deeds it is focused on God's coming. Amid controversy over right behavior in the congregation, Paul declares, "For the kingdom of God is not food and drink but righteousness and peace and joy in the Holy Spirit" (Romans 14:17). The preaching of the gospel to all peoples serves as a prerequisite to the approaching end time (Mark 13:10),[413] and the growth of the congregation into Christ is set forth in the letter to the Ephesians as the most important dimension of the eschatological event (Ephesians 3:8-10; 4:15-16).

The church thus stands before the task of forming and structuring its life and—as far as possible—that of the society in which it lives in the light of God's kingdom. It was Wesley's deep conviction that the missionary movement of his day with its evangelistic and diaconal activities was a step toward the fulfillment of this task and this promise within the context of the church and the state.[414] Thus, Methodism has been given the task of proclaiming the message of the gospel and working for greater righteousness and peace in this world, always seen in the perspective of the fulfillment of the Christian hope. In some times and places this may have occurred in an imbalanced manner with the expectation that our deeds must create and build the kingdom of God.[415] Nevertheless, this perspective of the path of the congregation will remain significant if we continue to understand that we neither can nor ought do more than by our actions, erect signs that point toward what God will do.

(b.) The congregation of Jesus Christ must know that its path into the coming kingdom of God will traverse temptation, persecution, and mortal threats. There is no unbroken transition from an ever growing church that is increasingly penetrating the larger society to the full reign of God. Rather, the transition is marked by the utmost dangers for the community of faith and its members. A basic feature of the end-time proclamation of the New Testament—from the end-time discourses of Jesus to the visions of the Revelation to John—is the intent to make known the full gravity of this event, but likewise to assure the disciples of Jesus of the faithfulness of their Lord. Wherever the Church of Christ has forgotten this truth it has been reminded of it through painful events. Conversely, the attempt to identify particular results of church history with specific end-time predictions depicted in the New Testament has been shown to be futile. The announcement of end-time seduction and persecution serves as a warning signal that Christians in all times should remain awake and attentive, and it can help them to evaluate the situation faced by the Christian community in terms of these threats, but also to look with confidence to God's protection. It is important not to calculate the "signs of the times" in a chronological fashion, but rather to comprehend and take note of them again and again as warning signs and encouraging testimonies in this regard.

(3.) The congregation of Jesus Christ finds the fulfillment of its task in the unending praise of God (Revelation 7:10). On the one hand, the literal sense of these statements describes what the encounter and the fellowship of the congregation with its God accomplishes. In addition, a dynamic is transcribed through the symbolism of the images that exceeds everything that can be expressed by human words. The renewed existence of those who belong to the people of God is saturated with the revealed presence of the living God. It is carried forward with adoring wonder over God's perfect love and is devoted to its Creator and Redeemer with all its being. It is a new level of life that has discovered itself completely in the midst of true being and deepest peace in the highest rapture of perfected joy. Many times in his hymns, Charles Wesley has taken up these images from Revelation concerning the praise of the redeemed as a description of the perfection of the community of faith. Hence, the Christian hope is described in a manner which has marked the "people called Methodists" to the present day far more than would numerous theological tracts.[416]

2.3.3.3   THE HOPE FOR A NEW HEAVEN AND A NEW EARTH

The widest horizon of hope which the biblical message describes is the hope for a new heaven and a new earth, which God will create.[417] Here is the presentation of a new order of nature, in which all creatures of God can live in peace and harmony and be free from the chains of perishability.[418] At the center of this renewed common life of God's creatures stands a new humanity, which exists in the life-giving presence of God without suffering, pain, and death.[419]

The picture drawn of this new order has a twofold profile: the new humanity comprises the people of God (see Revelation 21:3), which dwells in close fellowship with God in the holy city. However, this image of the end-time community is delineated in so universal and general a manner that in some places it breaks through the framework of ecclesiology and takes the form of hope in a renewed humanity (see also Romans 5:18; 11:32).

Yet, within the entire biblical witness and church tradition it is maintained that there are persons who are excluded from this fellowship with God. The anticipation of the judgment of God, in which God separates those who belong to him from those who have rejected his fellowship, is a basic aspect of Christian eschatology.[420]

2.3.3.4   JUDGMENT AND CONSUMMATION

The description of God as Judge belongs to the basic elements of a biblical proclamation of God.[421] It has its source in the Old Testament and is quite a lot older and more comprehensive than the motif of the end-time judgment upon all humanity. God's judgment includes not only his punitive verdict but also the saving reclamation of his people and the whole of creation.[422]

The difficult task of telling the people that they stood under the inescapable judgment of God fell to the older prophetic writers.[423] This judgment was to be carried through by natural catastrophes, annihilating defeats, and deportations within the events of history. However, the heart of the announcements of judgment is the call for a dreaded confrontation of the people with their Lord: "Prepare to meet your God, O Israel!" (Amos 4:12).[424]

In the prophetic discussion between the demands of God, which arise out of his love and faithfulness, and the faithlessness and contempt on the part of the people, the motif of the "wrath of God" becomes a synonym for the concept of judgment. With its heightened emotion, it says that it is not a question of a mechanical reckoning between God and his people, but rather it is about a personal relationship with their God, who has been deeply injured and effaced through human guilt.[425]

And yet in some places, even amidst the dark threat of judgment, the hope is born that on the other side of judgment there will be a new beginning of God's dealings with his people (Hosea 11:8ff.). This theme is especially prominent within the exilic and postexilic prophetic writings, particularly in sections of Ezekiel and above all in the later chapters of Isaiah (Deutero-Isaiah).

The concept of judgment receives a new character in the Old Testament through Ezekiel 18 and 33. Over against the understanding of a collective liability that includes the entire nation, these sections emphasize the responsibility of the individual, and the significance of her or his turning toward God now is set forth. Through this the concept of individual judgment concerning the life of every individual is presaged, which is then developed further in Daniel 12:2, eventually to be developed into the general judgment of all persons on earth that will occur at the last day. This depiction forms the implicit background for all relevant New Testament statements.

With full prophetic authority, John the Baptizer sets the entire nation of Israel over against the inevitable judgment. Only those persons who take this judgment upon themselves through baptism will escape from it.[426] Jesus announces the redemptive inbreaking of the rule of God, but he also weeps about those who are excluding themselves from fellowship with God by their rejection of his message, and who therefore fall into the judgment.[427] It is precisely in light of this judgment that Jesus' proclamation is run through with a deep tension because of its very nature. There are parables that—like the parable of the workers in the vineyard in Matthew 20:1-15—defend God's manner of giving to people what they need without taking account of their achievements. However, there are also others, such as the parable of the talents (Matthew 25:14-30) and the description of the judgment of the world (Matthew 25:31-46), which inculcate people's responsibility before God.[428] This call to responsibility inquires not about extraordinary achievements but about the self-evident deed that is done for the love of the neighbor. Matthew 25 is only apparently concerned with a judgment of works; it is truly concerned with a horizon of life which is so wide that one's needy fellow human becomes visible and that which is "self-evident" takes place.[429]

When examining Paul's proclamation of the judgment, two basic aspects must be named:

1. The world stands under the wrath of God, his "No" to all unrighteousness and the godlessness of humans (Romans 1:18ff.). The mission of Jesus is God's "Yes" to humanity, through which the severity of guilt and injury is not simply effaced but is settled through Jesus' death (see Galatians 3:13). The judgment that results from the results of human sin is therefore excuted in Jesus. Whenever Paul proclaims Jesus as the crucified Lord, he points also to the fact that humans are destined for judgment and in need of redemption. But precisely this marks the parting of the ways. This is an offensive word, and whoever refuses the life that is held out in Christ chooses death. The judgment is already fulfilled in the gospel—this is a concept which is clearly set forth in John's Gospel (John 3:16, 36). Perhaps this is the reason why Paul barely speaks about the future judgment of non-Christians.

2. Wherever Paul speaks of the last judgment, it is almost always with reference to the judgment of Christians (Romans 14:10; 2 Corinthians 5:10). The fact that this is a judgment concerning the deeds of Christians astonishes and places the question of the relationship of the concept of judgment to justification by faith.[430] Apparently this is not a judgment concerning life and death but a judgment concerning one's responsibility before God, which also is not abolished by the acceptance of life on the basis of faith (see 1 Corinthians 3:12-15).

In the Revelation of John the severity of the tension into which the thought of judgment leads Christian proclamation becomes evident: no one is worthy to carry out judgment over the powers of this world, and so to bring God's glory to its end, except alone the Lamb, who is slain and who has purchased by his blood persons from all tribes and languages and peoples and nations (Revelation 5:9-12). It is precisely this Lamb, this messenger of God, who appears at the Final Judgment with garments soaked with the blood of his victims, and it is he who reaps a dreadful harvest with his two-edged sword among his enemies (Revelation 19:11-21). The most horrible pictures of the conduct of war in antiquity are used to make clear that it really is a matter here of solving the "power question."[431] Judgment is being portrayed as victory over the powers of evil in this world, but also their destruction, as well as the destruction of their allies.

The comprehensive and completed fellowship of God with humanity is depicted with moving words (Revelation 21:1-7), but there is also the announcement of the destruction of all who have rejected God's command—which is largely omitted in the reading of this text in our day.[432]

—In the small judgment scene (20:11-15), two different books are opened.[433] The "book of life," which designates those who belong to God because he has called them to himself (20:12, 15; see 13:8; 17:8), and the books with the records of those to be judged according to their works (20:12*b*, 13). However, only those whose names appear in the book of life will be saved (20:15).

Apparently the message relating to the idea of judgment in the entire biblical witness can be expressed only through "antinomies," or essentially necessary contradictions.

1. On the one side stands God's comprehensive and universal "Yes" to his creation but on the other God's will to take seriously the "No" of humanity in rejecting fellowship with God, even if it brings them to death, and also his "No" against all the powers of destruction, with which they have disastrously entwined their lives. However, behind the statement of judgment there repeatedly stands the hope that God is able to bring about salvation through judgment.

2. The basic assertion that the fate of humans is decided by whether they have opened themselves to the reality of God's grace and life, which was disclosed to them in Jesus Christ, stands alongside the concept that there is no encounter with God which releases anybody from responsibility before him. An abiding statement of importance, which is both comforting and encouraging, is that nothing that we do or do not do, and also nothing that happens to us, is simply passed over by God. Apparently it is a truncation of the biblical concept of God and judgment for "judgment" to be presented only as a decision about death and life, or about more or less reward and punishment, and not also as a rectifying restoration of the whole of life.

3. Even in eschatology, we need to hold tight to the fact that God has established no legitimate reign except the reign of the Crucified One and, hence, the reign of love, which attains its authority from the supplication and the sacrifice of Christ. However, it is simultaneously attested that this love is not condemned to eternal powerlessness, but that its transforming power will decisively conquer the powers of evil, egoism, and death. To use Wesley's terminology, the "kingdom of grace" and the "kingdom of glory" are to be so related to one another that it remains clear that it is a matter of differing modes of appearance of the *one* kingdom of God![434]

All this explains why the idea of judgment is and must remain a constitutive element of Christian theology, one which, even where the end-time statements of the Bible are viewed critically, is not abandoned but is given new meaning.[435] The question about the judgment is the question about righteousness, and it is not accidental that Immanuel Kant, within the context of the discussion of judgment, has allowed the postulate of practical reason, that there is a supreme court of justice over humanity, to be the single form of proof for God.[436]

However, this very expectation places in question the Christian proclamation of judgment, for its text is not the parable of the ring from Lessing's "Nathan the Wise" but the basic assertion that God's judgment of humanity is decided by their position toward Jesus Christ. The longer a relatively uneventful history of missions continues and the more humans live without hearing about Jesus, the more difficult this assertion becomes. How can God judge the world rightly under these assumptions?

Wesley, who could, by the way, occasionally preach quite powerfully about hell,[437] was relatively often concerned with this question. For him, his doctrine of justification, which was oriented toward the fruit of faith, was helpful. In developing this understanding, he occasionally touched on the idea of a twofold justification—by faith in the new birth and a final judgment by works. He took seriously texts such as Matthew 25:31-46, Acts 10:34-35, and Romans 2:5-16—in spite of their ambivalence concerning the message of justification. That enabled him, particularly in his later sermons, to express himself very cautiously as to how far we as Christians may define the extent of God's judgment concerning the heathen. Wherever faith in Christ is made the standard for judgment in the New Testament, it is made so for those to whom the gospel is being preached. "Others it does not concern; and we are not required to determine anything touching their final state. How it will please God, the Judge of all, to deal with *them,* we may leave to God himself. But this we know, that he is not the God of the Christians only, but the God of the heathens also; that he is 'rich in mercy to all that call upon him,' 'according to the light they have'; and that 'in every nation he that feareth God and worketh righteousness is accepted of him.' "[438]

As Paul declares in Romans 2:16, whenever God will judge what is hidden in human beings through Jesus Christ, "according to my gospel," this is not to cite a formal standard that is to be attained by the agreement of certain statements of faith, but it signifies a revealing encounter with God, which is defined in the substance of the gospel of Jesus Christ and is decided according to it, even where it was not known *expressis verbis.*[439]

We are herewith reaching the extent of what can be affirmed on theological grounds, and we remind ourselves that the biblical idea of judgment is theocentric and is oriented toward the implementation of the divine purposes of God. Therefore, it always implies a wholesome, even if painful, setting right of people. The idea of judgment is not an instrument in the hands of humans, and therefore it removes itself from our inner disposal by which we seek to make decisions about others. Hence, the question remains open whether God in his love will take seriously the "No" spoken by humans against him in a way, so that God still continues to act in accordance with his "Yes" to them.[440]

All this being said, we have arrived at establishing a basic state of affairs of eschatological thinking. The reality of consummation only permits itself to be cautiously described, in symbols or in a *via negativa,* in short, through sayings about what it is *not.* Hence, we repeatedly encounter series of statements that appear to exclude one another and yet are all approximations of the same subject, which we cannot comprehend as a whole. For example, this is true of the conception of a new world, which is depicted for us as a world that is healed of all evil, and that also appears as the eschatological *totaliter aliter,* the "Wholly Other," which alone can conform to the transcendent encounter with the reality of God.

3. Personal Faith, or The Personal Experience of Salvation

Jesus said, . . . "Those who believe in me . . . will live."
—John 11:25

God's care is intended for the whole world. This basic statement expresses the basis for the biblical witness of the salvific revelation of God. At the center of the biblical statements about this however, we find again and again God's loving care for humanity. It attains its depth and significance in the fact that it is a personal show of concern. The essence of this care is not action performed on a weak-willed mere object, but is an encounter with a Thou.

"Adam, where are you?" is the question asked of the person in paradise. Abraham is called from his homeland and the New Testament proclamation of the gospel is summarized by Paul in a very personal appeal, "Be reconciled with God!"

This call never means individuals only on their own. They are part of the creation, of humanity, a people, a family, and, as Christians, are also members of one community of faith. For that reason, they are entwined in a fellowship with a common destiny, dependent upon the decisions of others and also having influence upon others with their decisions, but they always remain responsible for their own lives. The balance between a relationship to God that is communicated through being a part of the people of God and one's personal relationship to God has without doubt changed in the course of the history of the biblical witness. Whereas the Old Testament tends to emphasize the former, the latter emerges as dominant in the New Testament. Because the gospel is meant for all, it is also meant for each and every person; there is no longer any collective salvation or damnation.[1]

However, we must also pay attention to the other side: as little as individual persons were fully submerged into the collective in the history of the Old Testament, just as little is the new covenant directed only toward isolated individuals. This new covenant also represents a new fellowship of persons who are renewed in Christ. But this fellowship does not have the character of an "institution of grace," which is interposed between God and individuals. The "immediacy of access to God" is not only a nineteenth-century concept; it is an important legacy of the New Testament message.[2]

In this sense, the personal experience of salvation stands at the center of Methodist preaching and theology. The question of personal holiness, and hence personal salvation, was the motivation of the life of the Oxford Methodists surrounding the brothers Wesley. The experience of justification by faith alone, which gave their lives a whole new direction, was similarly a most deeply personal experience, and so their preaching was directed very personally to the hearts of their hearers, who were deeply touched and aroused by this message of the living gospel.

The central theological concern of the Wesleys was to set forth the way to and nature of a personal experience of salvation in Christ. Many sermons which John published served this purpose, and most of the hymns written by Charles revolved around this theme. The knowledge that Christianity is essentially a "social religion" was thereby not pushed to the periphery, but was rather integrated into this concern: life in Christian fellowship and social responsibility are inseparably linked with the fulfillment of the personal experience of salvation.[3]

This means that chapters 3 and 4 of this book are to be read and understood in a parallel fashion, and many aspects of both sections are to be seen in an inseparable relationship, even if an integrated presentation of both thematic areas has turned out to be impossible for a number of reasons. For Wesley the "path to salvation" *(Heilsweg)* for the individual is always bound up with the life of community. Those who are awakened by the message of the gospel are gathered into societies and small groups, in order to assist one another in pastoral nurture. The gift of justifying faith emerges out of this joint opening of people toward God's actions and has the effect of being an encouraging witness of the assurance of faith that is inviting for others. In its essence, holiness is love, and so it is inconceivable apart from a social dimension.

In another sense, the presentation of a contemporary United Methodist theology which has this theme at its center makes us face both a difficulty and a challenge. We discover ourselves here in the center of what characterized the Methodist movement in its beginning. If our presentation intends to remain true to the Wesleyan heritage, it will have to bear in mind that historical distinctive. To consider this legacy for our present day largely constitutes the justification for undertaking a "United Methodist theology" in the first place.

On the other hand, the inner pressure, emanating from this legacy, to stop with the historical presentation of a theology of Wesley is nowhere so great as it is here. However, this would not be sufficient in itself. For it could be that anyone who today said exactly what Wesley did would not arrive at the same outcome. For example, it could be that the social dynamic which developed the "individualism" of the Wesleyan message in the eighteenth century[4] may lead to a flight from social responsibility at the beginning of the twenty-first century. Added to this, some of Wesley's concerns need to be thought through anew in our day, on exegetical as well as hermeneutical grounds.

The design of this chapter stays relatively close to the precedent of Wesley's soteriological construct. The first section (3.1, "Liberation for Listening and Conversion") describes the basic steps en route to the personal experience of salvation, while the second part, (3.2, "The Renewal to Life in God") describes how salvation and deliverance can be experienced in people's lives through the encounter with Christ and the infilling of the Spirit of God.

3.1   Liberation for Hearing and Conversion

Persons who live in sin without God are no longer capable by themselves of responding to God's caring concern. This is also true where their lives are being played out in the guise of religion, to the extent that they are not filled by God's presence and power from within. A soteriological concept that assumes that God's saving work attains its goal when people respond to God's call and accept his reconciling acts will first have to explain how people become capable of responding positively to God's caring concern.

3.1.1   *The Abiding Love of God—Prevenient Grace*

Our inquiry has clear parameters: God addresses humans. However, they are not capable of really perceiving what God says. By themselves, they are not able to find their way to God and attain salvation. Still, how does it happen that there are persons who do come to faith in Christ? Is there perhaps still a tiny glimmer of "ability" in them? Or is it God who works either belief or unbelief in them?

The riddle of unbelief in view of the message of the gospel is first fully pondered by Paul through the example of Israel (Romans 9–11).[5] Paul goes about this in a very dialectical manner. In a first section of reflections (9:1-29) he emphasizes the absolute priority of the activity of God over against the "Yes" or the "No" of humanity (see also 2 Corinthians 1:19-20f; 1 Corinthians 2:15-16) and the unlimited sovereignty of God, which does not allow a single claim to be voiced against and diverted from God's promise. This emphasis of full freedom and sovereignty for God thus stands in the service of the message of grace: God is bound by no human assumptions and preconditions.

Moreover, the explanation found in 9:30–10:21 indicates that the pious, law-abiding people of Israel are not open to the claim and the action of God, who has incessantly taken great pains on behalf of his people. The unbelief of Israel is therefore not a consequence of an obduracy determined by God in his decree but is a refusal of the message of God's free grace.

The third section (Romans 11) is directed toward the believing "pagan" Christians, and it cautions them against viewing their faith as a more certain possession or as their own achievement. Faith lives solely from the goodness of God; if it abandons this foundation, it will surely become unbelief and come under judgment. However, Paul settles the view concerning the mystery of God's saving activity: he has deferred Israel for a time (this is how "hardening" is apparently to be understood here), to give the heathen an opportunity to turn to God. But this certainly does not nullify the basic election of Israel, "Just as you were once disobedient to God but have now received mercy because of their disobedience, so they have now been disobedient in order that, by the mercy shown to you, they too may now receive mercy" (11:30-31).

Although Romans 9 therefore provides the essential elements for the later doctrine of predestination, at least linguistically and partly in terms of content, such a doctrine cannot properly be deduced from Romans 9–11. For Paul, it is not a question of establishing the eternal, numerically predetermined destiny of individual persons. For him, it is probably rather a question of the preeminence of God's grace above all human decisions. It is a thought which Paul exhibits in terms of salvation history and not in terms of the fate of the individual![6]

Giving absolute preeminence to God's grace above every condition to be fulfilled by humans was also the concern of all the theologians who in the course of church history have developed further the New Testament assertions into the doctrine of predestination. The primary and most normative theologian was Augustine in his debate with Pelagius.[7] Then, in his controversy with Erasmus over free will, Luther drafted a highly distinctive exposition of this doctrine as part of his defense of the unconditional nature of justification. With his logical clarity, Calvin ventured to explicate the concept of a double predestination to salvation and to damnation, and set forth in a systematic fashion a concept which Augustine and Luther did not explicitly teach, but which they accept as the reverse side of the decree of election to grace.

It is precisely this point that remains a subject of wider controversy. The Lutheran Formula of Concord on the one hand clearly states, "The understanding and reason of man in spiritual things are wholly blind, and can understand nothing by their proper powers . . . We believe, teach, and confess, moreover, that the yet unregenerate will of man is not only averse from God, but has become even hostile to God, so that it only wishes and desires those things, and is delighted with them, which are evil and opposite to the divine will."[8] It does not view the basis for damnation of the godless in God's decree of rejection, but "in their actual refusal to be grounded in God's Word."[9]

During his preparation for ordination, Wesley had already critically engaged the doctrine of predestination, since Article XVII of the Articles of Religion of the Church of England teaches "predetermination to life" of those whom God in Christ has chosen out of humanity as a whole.[10] While Wesley's friend George Whitefield had already become convinced to place the doctrine of God's electing grace at the center of his theology through his experience of the assurance of salvation, so that the doctrine of *sola gratia* (salvation by grace alone) might be uplifted, Wesley on the other hand, after his Aldersgate experience, became a more decided opponent of the doctrine of predestination, which he considered in every respect as being dangerous and damaging to evangelistic preaching.[11]

The basis for Wesley's decisive rejection of the doctrine of predestination can be grouped under three headings:

1. If God's election and reprobation alone decide the salvation and damnation of humanity, then every evangelistic proclamation and call to faith becomes meaningless. For come what may, one group of its hearers will be saved, and another group will be lost.

2. The doctrine of double predestination runs the danger of destroying Christians' earnestness to seek holiness and their zeal for good works. For, if God's grace operates irresistibly, then there is no motivation for Christians, or those who consider themselves to be Christians, to continue therein, so that they might not have received the grace of God in vain. Yet the doctrine destroys the comfort of the Christian message, which

allows everyone to be confident in faith of God's love and redemption through Christ.

3. The doctrine of unconditional reprobation, which results necessarily from the teaching of unconditional election (which Wesley could accept), contradicts the biblical image of God and the clear statements of Scripture that God intends that *all* persons are to be saved. Not only does the *sola fide* become meaningless, but the *solus Christus* is also depreciated, for the crucifixion is then no longer God's comprehensive act of reconciliation for all humanity, but only a limited means toward the fulfillment of God's decisive decree concerning the elect. However, for Wesley, the cross of Christ attests to the basic affirmation that "The grace or love of God . . . is free in all, and free for all."[12]

By contrast, Wesley holds that the proper understanding of predestination or foreordination through God asserts that

1. He that believeth shall be saved from the guilt and power of sin.
2. He that endureth to the end shall be saved eternally.
3. They who receive the precious gift of faith, thereby become the sons of God; and, being sons, they shall receive the Spirit of holiness to walk as Christ also walked.[13]

In brief, God's decree of salvation does not include individuals whose reaction to the gospel is known in advance by God yet is not foreordained; rather, God's purpose is to make known the way of salvation.

In contrast, Whitefield's rebuke of Wesley's address reads as follows: whenever Wesley says "free grace," he really means "free will" and thereby once again ascribes to humanity the decisive share in the attainment of salvation.[14]

Wesley's self-understanding was not at all correctly represented by Whitefield's characterization. He would later adopt Article X of the Thirty-nine Articles of the Church of England, which rejects free will, in his abridgment of those articles in the Twenty-five Articles of Religion of the Methodist Episcopal Church (as Article VIII), while deleting the article concerning God's election. In Article X he found evidence for an understanding of "prevening (or preventing) grace," which enables persons to respond to the gospel.[15] In its basic meaning, Wesley is therefore fully in accord with the sense of the above-cited formulation of the Formula of Concord. Yet he is of the opinion that there is virtually no human being in whom God's prevenient grace does not in fact operate as a preparation for the reception of saving grace.[16]

In connection with his conversation with his Calvinistic friends and opponents, Wesley now appeals quite specifically to a Dutch Reformed theologian named Jacob Arminius (1560–1609), from whose name he derived the most important self-identification of his movement.[17]

The degree to which Wesley actually incorporated the thought of Arminius is a matter of discussion. However, two points which are significant for the doctrine of Arminius are also very important for Wesley:

(a.) The meaning of God's grace: "The reality of grace is not irresistible. God allows persons either to accept or reject the possibility of grace." "By nature a person is not free; however, under the leading of the Holy Spirit freedom is restored to a person."[18]

(b.) The meaning of the work of Christ: Jesus Christ is "not only the Executor of the decree of election . . . , but also its foundation. . . . Christ has died for all, and not only for the elect."[19]

With his "Arminian" doctrine of grace, Wesley may intend to represent the *sola gratia* of the Reformers with all its consequences. However, he also maintains that God's grace takes humans seriously as creatures of God who were created for responsibility. The conference protocol from 1745 describes this in a terse and precise manner: "Wherein may we come to the very edge of Calvinism? — A. (1.) In ascribing all good to this free grace of God. (2.) In denying all natural free-will, and all power antecedent to grace. And, (3.) In excluding all merit from man; even what he has or does by the grace of God."[20] The basic theme of the sermon "On Free Grace" reads, "The grace or love of God, whence cometh our salvation, is free in all, and free for all."[21] Whatever a person may do on behalf of his or her salvation is not the cause but the effect of grace. "Whatsoever good is in man, or is done by man, God is the author and doer of it."[22]

However, the operation of grace does not restrict persons; it abides by them and enables them "like Mary to choose the better part."[23] If God's grace appears with irresistible power in particular moments in a person's life, this is still not necessarily the case for all persons. It is in this context that Wesley gladly cites a statement from Augustine, who declared, *Qui fecit nos sine nobis, non salvabit nos sine nobis*: "He that made us without ourselves, will not save us without ourselves." [24]

God's grace precedes all human knowledge and decisions. That is the basis for the Pauline message of grace, as it was discovered anew in its full depth and radicalness, by the Protestant Reformers and as it was represented by Wesley in his own way. However, this does not exclude human knowledge and decisions, rather causes and enables them.

Wesley's basic desire was to hold fast both aspects of this insight and to pass them on to the people of his time.[25] The task of a United Methodist theology is to formulate them anew for our day.

3.1.2 *The Awareness of Human Distance from God—Awakening*

The motif of prevenient grace has a twofold function in Methodist theology. First, there is the basic function that makes clear that God's saving grace precedes all human effort. We have already discussed this function. Second, Wesley speaks of the works of prevenient grace in a special sense whenever he speaks of a first phase of the working of grace within the life of a person.

The working of prevenient grace is a first step in the life of a person en route to salvation and is mainly described by Wesley as referring to the fact that God awakens the voice of conscience within a person. Unlike the majority of philosophers and theologians of his time, Wesley does not regard the ability to hear the voice of conscience as a natural gift of humanity, but rather as a "supernatural" gift of God. This gift is certainly to be found in almost all people and is therefore considered by many to be part of human nature, but in actuality it is God's Spirit who awakens the conscience.[26]

In one of his sermons, Wesley presents a brief description of his understanding of the whole way of salvation. This presentation forms the basis for the structure of chapter 3.1 and should thereby be cited at the outset of this discussion:

Salvation begins with what is usually termed (and very properly) "preventing grace"; including the first wish to please God, the first dawn of light concerning his will, and the first slight, transient conviction of having sinned against him. All these imply some tendency toward life, some degree of salvation, the beginning of a deliverance from a blind, unfeeling heart, quite insensible of God and the things of God. Salvation is carried on by "convincing grace," usually in Scripture termed "repentance," which brings a larger measure of self-knowledge, and a farther deliverance from the heart of stone. Afterwards we experience the proper Christian salvation, whereby "through grace" we "are saved by faith," consisting of those two grand branches, justification and sanctification. By justification we are saved from the guilt of sin, and restored to the favour of God: by sanctification we are saved from the power and root of sin, and restored to the image of God. All experience, as well as Scripture, shows this salvation to be both instantaneous and gradual. It begins the moment we are justified, in the holy, humble, gentle, patient love of God and man. It gradually increases from that moment, as a "grain of mustard seed," which at first is the least of all seeds, but gradually "puts forth large branches," and becomes a great tree; till in another instant the heart is cleansed from all sin, and filled with pure love to God and man. But even that love increases more and more, till we "grow up in all things into him that is our head," "till we attain the measure of the stature of the fullness of Christ."[27]

Here Wesley emphasizes quite heavily what we have designated above as the "active" character of the biblical conception of grace—that is, grace is much more than pardon and remission of sin; it is the loving turning toward those who stand in need of aid.[28]

Out of Wesley's concept of the efficacy of grace, and especially its character as prevenient grace, Albert Outler has developed an insightful description of what is the essence of grace for Methodist theology:

> *Grace is a real action of God in the heart of people;* it is the actual opera-
> tion of the love of God within human existence. In its different dimensions,
> it penetrates and lays hold upon the whole of life. It is prevening, justifying
> and sanctifying, and because it is normally communicated through the cre-
> ated order, it is also sacramental. *Grace is God's love in action:* in Christ,
> in order to reconcile us with Himself, and in the Holy Spirit, in order to
> sanctify us wholly. . . . Because God's love is sovereign, it precedes every
> human action and causes each of them to be a reaction. Because God's love
> is universal, His mercy rests upon *all* His works and the promise of His
> grace is valid for *all* of His children. Because grace possesses a personal
> character, it can be refused; its acceptance must be expressed in responsi-
> ble human actions. Because it makes use of created circumstances and
> means as its outward and visible signs, it is sacramental. Even so, it remains
> *God's* grace and it persists without constraints.[29]

To some extent, these aspects of grace correspond to the Trinitarian revelation of God: prevenient grace corresponds to the work of God as
Creator, justifying grace is related to God's redeeming work in Jesus
Christ, and sanctifying grace corresponds to the work of the Holy Spirit.[30]
The way of grace toward humanity and with humanity is an inward unity,
and therefore the way to salvation and of salvation is nothing other than
lived grace.

We will have to return to Wesley's description of the way of salvation
on other occasions. But first of all, we accept what Wesley said about

prevenient grace and attempt to explore it within the context of present-day experience.

(a.) There are *impulses* that repeatedly occur in humans' lives through which God's grace prompts them to reflect on the circumstances of their lives. Wesley saw such impulses above all in the voice of conscience. He began by saying that almost all persons are guided by their conscience to recognize what is good or evil. However, he certainly recognizes the fact that there are persons "whose conscience is seared as with a hot iron."[31] In our day one may more often have the impression that many persons are void of conscience and can accept no standard outside that of their own judgment. Above all, scarcely anyone can avoid gaining the impression that the standards which are imprinted within the consciences of people are quite diverse and are often hardly comparable.

However, the operation of prevenient grace does not have its beginning only at the point at which a person recognizes clearly that he or she has been guilty before God and humanity. It is already the very general consciousness of bearing responsibility or of foundering—according to whatever standards—that promotes the question of whether our lives can stand before a final court of justice—however vaguely that might be expressed. Persons who have attained their life achievements in full agreement with accepted standards and civil morality, as well as those who have sought their own advantage without regard for others and with no reference to the prevailing social mores, can alike come to the point where they discover that the consequences of their actions have made them lonely and stunted as human beings. At this point, the unsettling question is often raised: What is going to happen now with my life?

There are numerous opportunities out of which such impulses of thoughts about grace emerge: unexpected strokes of fate with regard to health, family, or business success. However, in the same way, there are high points in life in which goals are attained and one can look back gratefully. But it is precisely in the calm of achievement that the questions arise as to what all this effort is in aid of and whether any new perspectives for life will be opened.

External prompts can come from encounters with persons who adhere to a completely different model for living and who have found in their faith the orientation and security for their lives. Again and again a word of the Bible somehow encounters people and inwardly so touches them that they have begun to reflect upon its meaning for their own lives.

(b.) Through such impulses, people discover *symptoms* through which they recognize their distance from God. If they are coming from a secularized milieu, they might certainly express this in nonreligious terms or only refer to God in a vague sort of way. The question that is not satisfactorily resolved concerning the meaning of life, their confrontation with deeply rooted anxiety of life and their lack of a "primeval trust," as well as repeatedly emerging relational problems with other people, and the effects of unmastered guilt—all of these issues can become symptoms by which people painfully notice that their lives are sick at their core and that they are in need of deep-seated healing.

(c.) For Wesley, it was quite important that *helps* for the diagnosis and the healing of these conditions were to be found in the "means of grace," which are provided by God and are also the way to God.[32] Persons who have been "awakened" to inquire about God find in these means of grace signposts which help them continue on their way. It may be a sermon which speaks to the heart; reading the Bible and books that help them understand the Bible; first attempts at personal prayer and the fellowship of persons who teach by example what it means for them to begin to open their own lives in prayer to God; participation in the Lord's Supper—all those are steps which lead persons to the place where they can find their way to God. Thus, the "means of grace" assist us in turning to God, they become *"converting"* means of grace. This is true not simply through their external use, but on the basis of the promise with which God has given them to us as the way and the method of opening ourselves wholly to him.[33]

This conception provides the basis for an evangelistic methodology which includes more than the customary organization of evangelism. Evangelistic efforts need to be part of a comprehensive concept of mission that leads persons in a very personal way into faith, questions the basic orientation of their lives, and begins to suggest that their lives stand in need of a totally new foundation if they are going to be able to prevail. It is for this purpose that persons are invited to participate in missionary cell groups, in which they can concretely experience how life and faith belong together and how persons can entrust everything that concerns them to God in prayer. Included in this is an introduction to understanding the Bible as God's Word that still speaks to us today through preaching and discussion of the Bible. The invitation to participate in the worship life of a congregation is also to be made within this context, a congregation which opens itself in praise and adoration and in word and sacrament to the gifts of God.[34]

Colin Williams has drawn attention to the fact that in this structure of faith developed by Wesley, the traditional methods of demonstrating the existence of God play no role. He is certainly correct if he does not trace this back to the fact that the question of the existence of God was not so contested in the eighteenth century as it is in our day—particularly in Europe. For Wesley, the proofs for God are insignificant on theological grounds, because

> God directly intervenes in the lives of men seeking to start them on the road to salvation. This prevenient grace gives us our first opportunity for responding to or resisting his work. This is why Wesley never bothers to use the traditional arguments for the existence of God. These are quite irrelevant, for God makes himself known directly; first, in a preliminary way (through conscience) by prevenient grace, and then in a direct way (through the gospel) by convincing grace. The task, therefore, of theology and preaching is to explain God's immediate relation to man and to urge man to accept the grace by which God seeks to bring us to himself.[35]

It is not the change of intellectual conviction about a possible existence of God that is the key to our encounter with God but the change of one's entire orientation of life toward God and his love.[36]

3.1.3 *Turning to God—Conversion*

The working of God's grace aims at basic change in the life of a person. It is not a question of the fulfillment of religious needs or the healing of particular defects or the removal of needs in the lives of persons. It is a matter of the far-reaching and comprehensive transformation in one's life orientation: away from such substitute gods as money, power, knowledge, or sexual satisfaction, which can define our lives and are expressions of our being imprisoned by our egoism, because they keep our egos, our actual selves, in bondage. It is about orienting ourselves toward God, in whom we find the true meaning of our lives, and hence—true freedom.

The *convincing* grace of which Wesley speaks therefore has a double aim: to open persons' eyes to the actual condition of their lives without God and at the same time to point them to the One who saves them from this forlornness of this life. This occurs when a person enters into *repentance*. Wesley at times distinguishes between repentance ordained by the law (*legal* repentance), which leads to a deep conviction of the sinfulness of one's life, and repentance occasioned by the gospel (evangelical repentance), which consists in the "change of the heart (and consequently of life) from all sin to all holiness."[37]

What Wesley is describing corresponds to the biblical concept of "turning around," which is frequently rendered in the theological tradition as *repentance* or *conversion*. Before we concern ourselves with the particulars of Wesley's position, we will briefly examine the biblical witness about turning to God and conversion.

3.1.3.1 THE BIBLICAL WITNESS CONCERNING CONVERSION

The biblical concept of turning around or conversion, which is further developed in the concepts of conversion and repentance, has its roots in the prophetic proclamation of the Old Testament.[38] It is used by the prophets within the context of its concrete, everyday meaning. Turning around means turning away from a wrong course and from wrong goals; that is, turning away from false gods, but also from a counterfeit piety, which worships God with festive services of worship and many sacrifices while at the same time snatching away human rights and living space, thereby scorning the will of God. Turning around at the same time means turning around to God, turning to the God who loves Israel, who has created, led, and saved Israel, and it is therefore always a return to the God who has called Israel into life and is the reason for her existence.

The message of the older prophetic writings is certainly defined by the firm conviction that the people have refused this call to turn around. It is only where God opens the way for Israel to turn around that Israel confirms the possibility of a new beginning. Above all, the invitation of God to return to God is spoken of in this new manner by the prophets after the judgment through the destruction of Jerusalem and the temple, and through the wandering of a portion of the people in exile.

In that postexilic era, a greater emphasis began to be placed on the role of the individual in Israel. It is now not the collective guilt of past generations that decides life and death but the personal turning around of every individual to their God (Ezekiel 18 and 33). The imploring question "Why will you die, O house of Israel? For I have no pleasure in the death of anyone" (Ezekiel 18:31*b*-32*a*) is one of the basic motifs of the later revival sermons in the Methodist tradition.[39]

John the Baptist once again takes up the message of the older prophetic writings with utter seriousness: the call to turning around and the announcement of the people's complete fallenness with regard to the law correspond to one another. Only through judgment—symbolized by the submersion in baptism—is there salvation.[40]

The content of Jesus' preaching presents the message of turning around quite differently. Though the gospel writers also summarize his teachings as a call to repentance,[41] in practice what seems to have been particularly offensive is that Jesus does not set sinners on a difficult path to repentance but accepted them into his fellowship, eating and drinking with them, thus sharing with them the nearness of the Kingdom of God.

Jesus defends his conduct in a series of parables, which Luke has placed together in chapter 15 of his Gospel. Wherever persons are found by God's searching love, wherever they open themselves to finding help in the house of their father, and wherever they immediately (without prerequisites of remorse and repentance) find themselves in the open arms of the Father, who hastens to meet them, this is where their conversion occurs, this is where they turn toward the Father's love and away from a life in which they had been lost. Such a change of life has effects and consequences for practical conduct as well as the working through of the past, as the example of Zacchaeus shows (Luke 19:1-10). Hence, Jesus' invitation to the Father awaits an answer, and a series of Jesus' words speak of the painful consequences for those who refuse his call and his work.[42]

According to the witness of Acts, the early Christians' missionary proclamation of the invitation to be devoted wholly to God for the sake of Jesus and to permit his saving work to occur in them was conveyed through different concepts. The apostolic sermon calls one to repentance, conversion, baptism, and faith in the name of the Lord Jesus Christ, and all these concepts, which are used separately or in different combinations, can signify partial aspects as well as the entirety of a conscious surrender to God. Amidst all the urgency placed on the reaction of people, the conviction remains that the decisive work has been done by God. Through the raising of Jesus, God gives the Jews as well as the heathen the opportunity to turn around toward life (Acts 3:26; 5:31; 11:18).

With Paul, the call to turn to God diminishes as an operating concept. In its place, there stands the invitation to faith in Jesus Christ. Paul himself experienced a change of life in his encounter with the risen Christ, in which he recognized that his intended zeal for God and for God's law was in the final analysis a zeal for himself, which led him away from God. In being willing to count as loss all of that which he held as gain in the balance of his life, through Christ, he gained access to fellowship with

God (Philippians 3:4-9). He recognizes God in his love, because he is known by God (Galatians 4:9).

The biblical message concerning God's words and deeds for the salvation of humanity is therefore dependent upon the response and reaction of people. Because the salvation of humanity lies in the fact that God welcomes them into fellowship with God, God's saving acts find their mark wherever persons turn from their self-centered ways, which lead them away from God, and turn toward God and allow themselves to be incorporated into his fellowship. It is consistently clear that obedience to God's call cannot be reckoned as the personal achievement of a person. It is God who grants the reversal from self to himself, and God's call and action are the foundation that enables the turning toward God. Indeed, depending on the situation, biblical examples and accounts can describe this life change as an often plain, undramatic occurrence of turning to God and of finding oneself in the realm of his grace,[43] but they can also inquire very concretely into the practical effects of such a step, meaning into the "fruit of repentance."[44]

3.1.3.2 REPENTANCE AS A STEP ON THE WAY TO SALVATION

Within the history of the Christian church, the biblical message of repentance and turning around has been taken up in quite diverse ways. In the early church, the basic, life-changing, and therefore one-time character of the biblical concept of turning to God was still so alive that the question of whether a "second repentance" was possible in the life of a Christian was actively discussed for a long time. A positive answer to this question certainly conformed to the spirit of the New Testament message.[45] At the same time, however, it was ominous that from this "yes" to the possibility of a renewed conversion in the life of a Christian, the medieval institution of penance developed in the age which followed.[46]

Luther reacted to the worst consequences of this institution, the giving of indulgences, with his Ninety-five Theses, the first of which contained these well-known words, "When our Lord and Master, Jesus Christ, said 'Repent,' he called for the entire life of believers to be one of penitence."[47] This is one of the most important examples in the history of the church for the fact that in certain situations something quite different had to be said than the New Testament pattern in order to actually say the same thing. Luther's words accurately expressed the deep earnestness and the radicalness of Jesus' call for persons to turn to God. However, as further development showed, his formulation of the biblical message harbored the danger that it would become too formal and would be used as an excuse to evade a basically new orientation of life. Thus, it was necessary to repeatedly return to the basic meaning of repentance and turning to God.

Wesley also did not adopt the full breadth of the biblical witness in this matter. With his distinction between "legal repentance" (repentance determined by the law) and "evangelical repentance" (repentance determined by the gospel), Wesley described both sides of the process of turning to God: turning away from sin and turning toward God. However, in his writings, he mostly emphasized only the "negative" side of the process of repentance: repentance is the recognition of the whole depth of lostness before God.[48] The preaching of the law particularly led to this recognition, whenever God's Spirit makes the law a tool of convincing and converting grace.[49]

At the same time, the preaching of the law catapults persons who are addressed by it into a deeper dilemma. The same law that opens to them their need for God and shows the need for their surrender to God cannot in itself point the way which can lead to God. It points to the justification of one's life before God based upon one's own deeds, a task which invariably causes persons to stumble. Wesley relates Romans 7:18-25 to this phase in the life of a Christian. In this passage, Paul depicts a person who wants what is good but is not in the position to do that good.[50] The situation of the "awakened" person, who still remains under the law, is thus far more unfortunate than is that of the "natural" person, who is living in sin without the sting of conscience and in presumed freedom. The faith which this person has is only the faith of a slave and not the faith of a child.

For Wesley, repentance is therefore only the outer court of fellowship with God, as opposed to actual faith, which is the door to that fellowship, and also sanctification, which is the real essence of that fellowship.[51] What is distinctive in the theology and praxis of Wesley is the fact that he does not simply say to a person, "leave the outer court and go as quickly as possible through the door to real faith." For Wesley, saving faith is the work of the Spirit and is not simply up to the will of people as to when God confers it.[52] Hence, Wesley poses the question of how people can be open to the work of the Spirit. Is it correct to avoid every strain of repentance and to "be still" and trust in God's work—as the Moravians had advocated[53]—or is there another Scriptural way to prepare and open oneself for this work?

In his "General Rules of our Society," John Wesley sought to show such a way to persons who were "deeply convinced of sin, and earnestly groaning for redemption." For such people, he instituted his "societies," which are nothing other than "a company of men 'having the form, and seeking the power of godliness,' united in order to pray together, to receive the word of exhortation, and to watch over one another in love, that they may help each other to work out their salvation." The sole condition for entrance into the societies is "a desire to flee from the wrath to come, to be saved from their sins."

Wesley was convinced that "Wherever this [longing] is fixed in the soul, it will be shown by its fruits." That happens when the members of the society take pains to follow three basic rules:

> *First,* by doing no harm, by avoiding evil in every kind. . . .
>
> *Secondly,* By doing good; by being in every kind merciful after their power, as they have opportunity doing good of every possible sort and as far as possible to all men. . . .
>
> *Thirdly,* By attending upon all the ordinances of God. Such are:
> The public worship of God;
> The ministry of the Word, either read or expounded;
> The Supper of the Lord;
> Family and private prayer;
> Searching the Scriptures; and
> Fasting, or abstinence.[54]

During almost the whole of his active life, Wesley grappled with two theological and practical problems that emerged from these concepts.

(a.) To possess only "the form of godliness" and not to seek its power was the position that Wesley came to recognize at the time of his Aldersgate experience as the basic error of his own religious efforts. He referred to this as the condition of the "Almost Christian," and he regarded it as more dangerous than the position of the non-Christian, because it misleads those affected as to their actual condition.[55] Yet, in order to appropriate the power of fellowship with God, he considered it to be indispensable to recommend an adequate structure that would facilitate living with God. This form has no value in itself. But as a vessel that is to be open to receiving God's grace, it is indispensable. The fact that it is not sufficient to remain in the "outer court" does not abrogate the need of crossing through it.

(b.) Wesley had difficulties giving a theologically satisfying answer to the question concerning the relationship of repentance and faith. He was convinced that, according to the witness of the New Testament, as a rule repentance should precede faith,[56] but he likewise saw the problem (or if he didn't see it, others brought it to his attention) that he stood in danger of depreciating *sola fide* (faith alone) by commending a broader condition for salvation and then replacing justification by faith with justification based upon works.

Wesley attempted to circumvent this danger through a twofold suggestion: when Scripture urges us to "bear fruit worthy of repentance" (Matthew 3:8), it does not undermine the fact that faith alone justifies; rather it is inquiring into the earnestness of this faith and of the desire for salvation.[57] The "works of love and mercy" that are done as the fruit of repentance are not supposed to justify but to hold fast a person's orientation on God. The second point he made is that, in the most literal sense of the term, there is only one condition for salvation, which is a trusting faith in Jesus Christ. That is why examples of this can be found within the New Testament, so that the certainty of salvation is given to a person in a single moment or the fruit of repentance first follows their acceptance by Christ.[58] However, as a characteristic of true faith (and not perhaps a supplemental condition), the fact is that persons are to be "active in love," and so it is that they are steeped in worthy repentance and regret with regard to their own failures.[59]

Although Wesley appears to have come close to the Catholic theological position in some instances, which affirms that persons must first of all do that which is possible for them *(facere quod in se est)* in order to be saved,[60] he nevertheless distinguishes his position very clearly from it. It is not those who are "ever striving to attain" who are saved; rather God always justifies the godless,[61] and it is God's grace within those who seek out that salvation which effects the fruit of repentance. Repentance is the end of every false expression of trust in self and the beginning of that learning process which leads to being able to entrust oneself wholly to God. Evangelical repentance begins at the point where pagan morality ends.[62] Wesley's doctrine of repentance is an attempt to describe in practical theological terms the truth that persons are not in a position to create their own salvation. At the same time, they share in the work of God's grace with human resources that are certainly no longer inert and weak-willed. Instead, they are taken up into the service of God's work with all their possibilities.

Thus for Wesley, repentance is also not an event which a Christian is to get behind himself or herself once and for all. Since a believer can repeatedly fall back under the dominion of sin, the "repentance of believers" remains a divine necessity and a human possibility for the one who wants to find his or her way back to fellowship with God.[63]

3.1.3.3 THE CONCRETE FORM OF CONVERSION TODAY

In contemporary United Methodist theology and praxis, besides the doctrine of Christian perfection, it is certainly Wesley's conception of repentance that has undergone the greatest transformation among the themes important to him. The call to repentance and faith was very soon coalesced into an appeal to conversion.[64] In a certain respect, that was appropriate. The event of turning around or conversion from a life in sin and toward surrender to God is one inner entity, and, without doubt, Wesley's clear distinction between these two certainly stood in danger of tearing apart that which properly belongs together. However, it also meant that the meaning of the individual decision of will was often pushed to the foreground, and the emphasis upon the urgency of "decision" became for many a negative characteristic of Methodist preaching.

In contrast, until well into the twentieth century, Wesley's understanding of the necessity of a clear recognition of sin and active repentance was maintained. In the German catechism of the EUB Church, written by J. Schempp, Jr., who was certainly quite open to Lutheran theology, the question was asked, "What is evangelical repentance? Repentance is the divinely wrought change of consciousness, whereby we recognize, confess, and heartily regret our sins, despising them and also, so far as possible, allowing the wrong that we have committed to be put right and turn faithfully toward God."[65]

For some time now, this aspect of repentance has almost completely disappeared from the preaching of The United Methodist Church—an observation that is made in the context of the European church, but which may also be quite applicable in the American context. With Schniewind, we can affirm the joy of repentance,[66] emphasize our unconditional acceptance by God, and avoid trying to awaken in people a heightened consciousness of their own guilt through the preaching of the law. To be candid, we need to question whether this is taking place because of a superior theological insight or because of an insufficient readiness to speak uncomfortable truths to others.

The fact that Wesley's understanding is in need of revision has already been indicated in the course of our discussion.

—His classification of the law and the gospel is too schematic. To say that only the preaching of the law can lead people to personal transformation corresponds neither to the witness of the Bible nor to the experience of Christian community.

—Hence, the division of the event of personal transformation into one act of repentance that is determined by the law and another that is determined by the gospel is problematic in this strict interpretation. The essence and the full import of sins are only recognized in the encounter with God's love.[67] The movement of turning away from evil and toward God are closely bound to one another in the evangelical understanding of repentance. It is not only the painful longing for God that drives people toward God; they also experience in the event of transformation that God comes to meet them and draws them to himself.

—The understanding that repentance is something like a precondition for faith and acceptance by God is not without its hazards, despite the assurances of Wesley. The misunderstanding that persons are required to demonstrate their seriousness about repentance before God can accept them is pretty close to reality and could make Wesley's doctrine more like the Pharisees' conception of repentance than Jesus' preaching on turning to God.

Still, Wesley's concern should not be simply abandoned. Important promptings for contemporary preaching of the gospel can still be derived from it:

—It is important to know and to bear in mind in both preaching and pastoral care that the way to fellowship with God also has a deep dimension of crisis to it. The awareness of actually being "unacceptable" can open up the process for being accepted by God in all its depth and painfulness. The lost son expresses his confession of sin while he is yet in the arms of his father. Our discussion of Wesley's doctrine of repentance should protect us from transforming the wonderful message of God's unconditional assumption of human sin into a superficial theology of "good feelings," which wants to save us and others from dealing with the need and the guilt of our lives, and which would therefore not really assist people in the quest for salvation. The fact that some movements and styles of preaching that appear to be very conservative and rather "legal" have appeal to secularized persons in our day has surely partly to do with the fact that, in their feelings of being lost, such persons—to some extent quite unconsciously—come to know that they are being taken seriously. A critical extension of Wesley's doctrine of repentance could help us to do the same thing in a genuinely evangelical manner, without falling into the danger of legalism.

—Assistance in ordering life with others and before God is part of accompanying persons who are en route to God. Protestant theology here either tends to a strict all-or-nothing position, which is little help to persons who are gropingly seeking the next steps for their lives, or they fall into the other extreme and equate their finding of practical helps for living with a genuine encounter with the gospel. At this point, Wesley opted for a kind of evangelistic-pedagogical "double strategy," which offers persons who are searching for a new relationship with God concrete steps for living with their fellow human beings, and which clearly says, on the other hand, that God himself is the One who comes to people and finds them.

—The course of the way to God therefore has a quite paradoxical form. It can consist in the single point in which God finds and accepts that person into his fellowship, turning that one to himself and embracing him or her in his arms. At the same time, the way to God has the form of a pilgrimage, or an inward process of breaking free of destructive habits and egotistical attitudes amid the exercise of a new, gracious, attentive, and open mode of conduct, which is nevertheless not centered on the success or failure of one's own action but rather on an ever-deepening relationship with God. As an interpersonal love relationship develops, small acts of care, gifts, and consideration toward one another are not the real thing; if the relationship stayed at this stage, it would harden into an empty form. Yet, these things could be important and helpful in facilitating the growth and development of love between two persons. In the same way, the practice of living with God and of finding assistance in daily accepting his love can be of great significance for persons who are inquiring and seeking to experience a decisive encounter with God. In our days people who have a first encounter with Christians or with a Christian congregation often have no idea of genuine Christian faith, and so it is important that they find a fellowship of believers and seekers, which draws them into their pilgrimage of faith and encourages them to yearn for God and to open their lives to encountering his presence. The advice to "be still" and wait upon God's actions can be a dangerous half-truth. At the same time, it needs to become apparent in all of these efforts that being a Christian is not tantamount to accepting certain Christian modes of conduct. Instead, it finds its true source in the deep encounter with God through personal faith in Jesus Christ.[68]

3.1.4 *Coming Home to God—Faith*

Thus, everything points toward faith as the key to the experience of salvation by God. For Wesley, this conviction leads to a twofold mode of knowing. After foundering in his effort to receive the certainty of justification and acceptance by God, he was referred by conversation partners influenced by the Reformation to the Pauline doctrine of justification by faith alone and became convinced of its theological correctness. However, it also became clear to him that this would only become an assured truth for him if he could also experience its power in his own life. This happened in that famous experience on May 2, 1738, on Aldersgate Street in London. During the reading of Luther's preface to the epistle to the Romans, Wesley was granted the assurance that he could now trust in Christ alone for his salvation and that Christ had taken away his sins.

What is repeatedly designated quite imprecisely as Wesley's conversion was thus not the decision of his surrender to God, which had long since occurred, but rather the gift of faith and the certainty of personal salvation.[69] It was the homecoming to God of a person who had finally surrendered the attempt to make preparation by his own holiness as the basis for accommodating the gracious presence of God. Wesley experienced how a person can be opened to saving fellowship with God by faith, without meeting any preconditions, and how this fellowship became for him the environment of grace and love and of peace and trust. This theological and existential knowledge became a matter of personal assurance for Wesley, confirmed by actual experience. However, its truth was based upon the biblical understanding of the relationship of faith and salvation, and it came alive for him through the rediscovery of the Pauline doctrine of "through faith alone," which had been rediscovered in the Protestant Reformation.

3.1.4.1 THE BIBLICAL UNDERSTANDING OF FAITH

The statements about faith as the appropriate means of accepting God's saving deeds are encountered in the texts of the Bible in various degrees of concentration.[70]

In the Old Testament, there are few places that address this understanding of faith, but these are places which are highly significant because of the intensity of their expression. Genesis 15:6 sounds like a summation of the history of the Hebrew fathers: the fact that Abraham relied on the promise of God against all appearances is the only appropriate human response to God's promise that would be suitable for fellowship with God. Likewise, Isaiah and Habakkuk also describe reliance upon God's promises as the only certain foundation for the existence of the people (Isaiah 7:9; 28:16; Habakkuk 2:4).[71] The experience of God's saving activity, which produces faith, is already present in the Old Testament (compare Exodus 14:31; Psalm 106:12); and the surrender of the heathen to God can also be described through the motif of faith (Jonah 3:5; Judith 14:10).

In the Jesus tradition, faith is primarily referred to in relationship with signs and wonders. Here faith describes the constant anticipation that is propelled by the imperturbable confidence of persons who stand in great need. It is an anticipation that does not cease even in the face of hindrances. By Jesus' hand, such faith receives miraculous help from God.[72] Jesus' words concerning faith, which gives believers a share in God's omnipotence, indicate that faith is not a power given to humans to work miracles, but rather it is "reliance upon the unlimited goodness of God."[73]

Under the impact of the raising of Jesus, the message of Jesus attains a wholly new dimension. That which God has wrought through Jesus' life and death, as well as the way God has revealed Godself in Jesus' Person, becomes the content of the disciples' preaching and thereby also the basis and the object of the faith to which they appeal. Faith in God, in Jesus Christ, including the faith that God has raised Jesus from the dead, almost becomes a synonym for the missionary preaching of the early church, because their message speaks of the saving acts of a God who has revealed and designed Godself in Jesus' life, death, and resurrection as "God for us." Faith that God has raised Jesus from the dead therefore means much more than the agreement with the historical truth of this message; it means the acceptance of the power of God's love in Jesus Christ, which has overcome both sin and death.

These statements are given theological depth in two areas of the New Testament. In the new formulation of Jesus' message in the Gospel of John, faith in the reality that Jesus is God's Son, who has entered into this world, in itself becomes the content of faith.[74] It is the belief that God is revealed in Jesus and thereby has revealed Godself "as the power of love."[75] Such faith is not a condition for salvation: it is salvation itself. Whoever believes has eternal life, because in faith that person has opened him or herself to God's saving presence and thereby has passed from death into life and from darkness into light (John 5:24).

Paul also stands in the tradition of the early Christian mission, but deepens it at decisive points in making faith the fundamental description of Christian existence before God. For Paul the missionary, this first of all signifies a colossal universalization of the message of Jesus Christ. If God's salvation is valid for every person who believes, then this means that the gospel breaks through the religious, social, national, or educational lines of separation that exist among humans and human groups, and it can reach all who hear the message.[76]

The anthropological-soteriological deepening of the concept of faith also stands in the service of this universal horizon in which the gospel is proclaimed. As an antithesis to regarding the demand that circumcision and the adherence to the law be considered necessary for salvation, in addition to countering the demand that required religious wisdom and ecstatic experience for salvation, Paul maintains that faith alone is descriptive of that existential position which is suitable and congruous in relation to God's saving acts.[77] Those who live by faith are children of Abraham, heirs of his promise, and they are placed over against those who live by the works of the law and who bring death upon themselves by their trust in their own achievements (Galatians 3:6-14).

The contrast between faith and works, which Paul affirms, also excludes the view that faith is to become a kind of substitutionary achievement that is demanded of a person. Paul makes this clear in Romans 4 with the example of Abraham. The "faith reckoned as righteousness" is not the recognition of an achievement of Abraham, but rather the gracious acceptance of those who anticipate everything from God and nothing from themselves. The justification of the one who believes is the justification of the one who relies upon the fact that God justifies the godless. The person who believes does not become preoccupied with calculating achievements, but trusts the God who has created her or him from nothing, who brings the dead to life, and who has raised Jesus from the dead.[78]

Here we encounter a second important definition of Paul: faith is always faith in Jesus Christ, a trustful acceptance of that which God has done through Christ and which faith first makes possible. So it is not their own faith, but God's promise and saving acts that are the foundation of trust and hope. Faith comes from hearing (Romans 10:17), that is, it arises not from the decision of the one who believes but from the Word that presses from outside upon the ear and into the heart.

Faith as a posture of receptivity and total trust and faith as acceptance of the message of salvation therefore belong intimately together, and they explain each other. Without the support of God's saving work, the posture of faith would become only a heroic or empty gesture. And without the disclosure of the existential realm of trust, the message of faith would become a demand for a *sacrificium intellectus,* that is, a meritorious sacrifice of their own way of thinking. Thus, as a posture, faith is nothing other than a firm reliance upon that which God has done, and the content of the message of faith first and foremost has reference to the grounding of trust in the saving acts of God.

Where Paul must raise the question of how responsible conduct can be established apart from the demand of the works of the law, he refers to the fact that those who believe subordinate themselves to the rule of Jesus Christ and are led to love by God's Spirit. The freedom in which faith places one becomes the realm of action for a faith that is active in love. The early Christian triad of faith, hope, and love therefore describes not supplemental values to be added to faith but dimensions of fellowship with God, a fellowship that begins and is grounded in the fact that persons in faith entrust themselves and open themselves to the justifying acts of God.

All this is of highest significance for Wesley's understanding of faith.

3.1.4.2 The Reformation Rediscovery of "By Faith Alone"

Despite the clarity of the biblical evidence, Wesley's discovery of the meaning of faith would be hard to imagine without the rediscovery of the Pauline doctrine of *sola fide* ("by faith alone") through the Reformers. He came into contact with this doctrine through the Moravians, especially Peter Boehler. He encountered the doctrine in the course of his study of the homilies of the Church of England, and finally it was the passage from Luther's commentary on Romans, where the renewing and transforming power of faith is described, that led Wesley to the experience of the assurance of faith.

Intrinsic to Luther's concept of faith is the correlation of *sola fide* with the *fides Christi,* or faith in Christ.[79] Luther derives this formulation from Paul in Romans 4 and emphatically underscores that everything that is said about faith is only valid if it is declared from the stance of faith in Christ. Conversely, Christian assertions concerning faith in Christ are meaningful only if they are expressed in terms of justification by faith. "The Augustinian distinction between the content of faith and the accomplishments of faith is rejected." "Where until that point the formulated content of faith was to be reflected in the existential actualizing of faith, and where the verbal confession of faith was to be seen in the active witness to the faith . . . , Luther kept only the contrast between a dead and a living faith; the 'faith of demons,' being faith without works, is generally no faith at all, according to James 2:18ff."[80]

For Luther, even "the possibility of speaking of faith without love" is excluded. In connection with Galatians 5:6, faith that is active through love is also a "sign or criterion for true faith." All these are emphases which will reappear with Wesley. The same thing applies to the definition of faith as the work of God, who however includes people and their deeds in his work.

What is missing in Wesley is that element of ultimate radicalness in the concept of faith which is repeatedly found in Luther:

> Faith is the substance of the new reality of humanity that is created through the activity of God. Therefore, the being of a human and the being of God flow into one another through faith and in faith. We repeatedly encounter in Luther those peculiarly pointed usages in which it is stated that Faith makes God, and He makes the person. For as a person is, so also is his God.
> . . . That is the familiar definition for the exposition of the first commandment, ". . . that the trust and faith of the heart alone bring to pass both God and that which is a false God (an idol). If faith and trust are just, then also is your God just, and conversely, where trust is false and not just, then the just God is also not to be found. For the two belong together, faith and God. Whatever you hang your heart upon and trust (say I), that is actually your God" (BSLK 560, 15ff.). Faith is the creator of the Godhead, because that which concerns God in Himself only becomes a reality in me and for me through faith.

The Reformers who followed Luther then once again undertook to systematize the faith and its activity yet more strongly. Melanchthon and Calvin distinguished once again between *assensus* (agreement with the content of faith) and *fiducia* (personal trust in God for Christ's sake).[81] As emphasis was placed upon taking into consideration the requirements of a differentiated, systematic exposition of doctrine as well as the psychological evaluation of religion, there also arose the danger that the original, Pauline concept of faith, fragmented into its component parts, would no longer have the power of its total meaning.

3.1.4.3   FAITH IN THE THOUGHT OF JOHN WESLEY

Where Wesley offers a description of justifying faith, which he had first sought and later found, he gladly accepts a formulation contained in the Anglican homily "Concerning Salvation," in which it becomes clear that the true, living, Christian faith is more than only a matter of cognitive assent. Instead, it is to be the inward attitude, "which God has wrought in the heart of the believer, a sure trust and confidence in God, that, through the merits of Christ, my sins are forgiven, and I reconciled to the favour of God."[82] In this, Wesley expressly rejected a definition of Thomas Aquinas, which insisted that faith is an "assent to divine truth, upon the testimony of God" or "upon the evidence of miracles."[83] This would be no more than the faith of the demons, according to James 2:19, and thus no more than a "dead faith."

Wesley gladly lays hold of the definition in Hebrews 11:1 to describe faith, and he circumvents the meaning of the difficult-to-translate Greek term *elenchos* (literally, "evidence"; Luther: "not doubting") with "godly conviction and inward certainty." "Justifying faith implies, not only a divine evidence or conviction that 'God was in Christ, reconciling the world unto himself'; but a sure trust and confidence that Christ died for *my* sins, that he saved *me*, and gave himself for *me*. And at what time soever a sinner thus believes, be it in early childhood, in the strength of his years, or when he is old and hoary-haired, God justifieth that ungodly one."[84]

This personal certainty distinguishes saving faith, which alone justifies and sanctifies. It is the "faith of a son," who is now freed from the anxiety and the convulsive achievement efforts of a servile relationship with God, and fills a person's heart with peace.[85] The one to whom this faith is given no longer doubts the love of God; this love fills her or his heart and brings about love for God and for one's fellow humans.[86] The assertion that faith is active in love therefore does not cite any supplemental conditions for the proper relationship to God, rather it describes how faith works itself out. Thus, through Wesley's discovery of *sola fide* as key to salvation, it has become clear to him that persons are not only justified but also sanctified on the basis of faith in God—even what Wesley calls "entire sanctification" and considers as the goal of the life of a Christian with God is given to the believer by God.[87]

Some of Wesley's statements are also to be understood in this sense— those in which he somewhat ambiguously designated faith as the door to the reality of being a Christian, whereas in fact this reality consists of "loving God with all our heart, and our neighbour as ourselves."[88] However, this does not mean that for Wesley faith is merely a stepping stone to becoming a Christian. Where Wesley writes about the meaning of the triad faith, hope, and love, he repeatedly emphasizes that faith is not only the first of these three marks of a reborn Christian but is also the foundation for all the others.[89]

Hence, faith remains the unrelinquishable foundation for the life of a Christian. Through it we feel the power of Christ every moment resting upon us, whereby alone we are enabled to continue in spiritual life, and without which, notwithstanding all our present holiness, we should be devils the next moment. But as long as we retain our faith in him we "draw water out of the wells of salvation." Leaning on our Beloved, even Christ in us the hope of glory, who dwelleth in our hearts by faith, who likewise is ever interceding for us at the right hand of God, we receive help from him to think and speak and act what is acceptable in his sight.[90]

Precisely because faith does not proceed from our own efforts, it is appropriate to recognize that the "deep conviction of our utter *helplessness*—of our total inability to retain anything we have received, much more to deliver ourselves from the world of iniquity remaining both in our hearts and lives—teaches us truly to live upon Christ by faith, not only as our Priest, but as our King."[91]

Wesley is also aware of this where he says that faith is the condition—and in fact the only truly valid condition—for justification.[92] Wesley held firmly to this position because it conforms to the witness of the Bible and also because it nowhere affirms that faith is to be a condition attained by humans that God then rewards with justification, which is the objection raised by superficial critics. Hence, Wesley states most clearly, "In strictness, therefore, neither our faith nor our works justify us, i.e., deserve the remission of our sins. But God himself justifies us, of his own mercy, through the merits of his Son only. Nevertheless, because by faith we embrace the promise of God's mercy and of the remission of our sins, therefore the Scripture says that *faith does justify yea, faith without works*."[93] As such, faith

is the gift of God. No man is able to work it in himself. It is a work of omnipotence. It requires no less power thus to quicken a dead soul than to raise a body that lies in the grave. It is a new creation. . . . It is the *free gift* of God, which he bestows not on those who are worthy of his favour, not on such as are previously holy, and so *fit* to be crowned with all the blessings of his goodness, but on the ungodly and unholy, on those who till that hour were fit only for everlasting destruction, those in whom was no good thing, and whose only plea was, "God be merciful to me a sinner." No merit, no goodness in man, precedes the forgiving love of God. His pardoning mercy supposes nothing in us but a sense of mere sin and misery; and to all who see, and feel, and own their wants, and their utter inability to remove them, God freely gives faith, for the sake of him "in whom he is always well pleased."[94]

Hence, faith for Wesley is first of all a complete receptivity, complete acceptance of that which God has done and is doing still:

Faith, according to the scriptural account, is the eye of the new-born soul. Hereby every true believer in God "seeth him who is invisible." Hereby (in a more particular manner since life and immortality have been brought to light by the gospel) he seeth "the light of the glory of God in the face of Jesus Christ"; and "beholdeth what manner of love it is which the Father hath bestowed upon us, that we" (who are born of the Spirit) "should be called the sons of God." It is the ear of the soul, whereby a sinner "hears the voice of the Son of God and lives"; even that voice which alone wakes the dead, saying, "Son, thy sins are forgiven thee."

It is (if I may be allowed the expression) the palate of the soul. For hereby a believer "tastes the good word, and the powers of the world to come"; and hereby he both "tastes and sees that God is gracious," yea, and "merciful to him a sinner."[95]

However, because Wesley proceeds from the position that God gives the hearers of the message faith, he very emphatically calls them to faith, and he does so with an emphasis and a directness which can dispel our concern that we should be too worried about what Wesley in other places says about appropriate preparations for faith:

Whosoever therefore thou art who desirest to be forgiven and reconciled to the favor of God, do not say in thy heart, "I must *first do this*; I must *first* conquer every sin, break off every evil word and work, and do all good to all men; or I must *first* go to Church, receive the Lord's Supper, hear more sermons, and say more prayers." Alas, my brother, thou art clean gone out of the way. Thou art still "ignorant of the righteousness of God," and art "seeking to establish thy own righteousness" as the ground of thy reconciliation. Knowest thou not that thou canst do nothing but sin till thou art reconciled to God? Wherefore then dost thou say, I must do this and this first, and then I shall believe? Nay, but *first* believe. Believe in the Lord Jesus Christ, the propitiation for thy sins. Let this good foundation *first* be laid, and then thou shalt do all things well.

Neither say in thy heart, "I can't be accepted yet because I am not *good enough*." . . .

Do not say, "But I am not *contrite enough:* I am not sensible enough of my sins." I know it. I would to God thou wert more sensible of them, more contrite a thousandfold than thou art. But do not stay for this. It may be God will make thee so, not before thou believest, but by believing. . . .

Nor yet do thou say, "I must do something more before I come to Christ" . . .

Whosoever thou art, O man, who hast the sentence of death in thyself, who feelest thyself a condemned sinner, and hast the wrath of God abiding on thee: unto thee said the Lord, not "Do this; perfectly obey all my commands and live": but, "Believe in the Lord Jesus Christ, and thou shalt be saved." "The word of faith is nigh unto thee." Now, at this instant, in the present moment, and in thy present state, sinner as thou art, just as thou art, believe the gospel, and "I will be merciful unto thy unrighteousness, and thy iniquities will I remember no more."[96]

3.1.4.4 BASIC GUIDELINES FOR PROCLAIMING THE FAITH IN OUR DAY

The contemporary concern to find a suitable form for understanding and proclaiming the faith can best be described as a struggle about the relationship between the two Reformation formulas of *sola gratia* ("by grace alone") and *sola fide* (by faith alone). What for Paul belongs together most essentially when he writes that the promise of salvation "depends on faith," and therefore "rests on grace" (Romans 4:16) and whose integral relationship was also freshly reappropriated by the Reformers and by John Wesley as a liberating truth, threatens to break apart in the contemporary world. Among other things this is brought about by the fact that many substantive statements of Christian faith are difficult for many contemporary persons to understand, or they even appear unbelievable to them. To require that they believe this in its entirety appears to some to be an unusually difficult condition to impose upon one as a basis for being taken up into fellowship with God. This perception is heightened by the fact that not a few conservative circles that are primarily concerned with upholding the basic truths of the faith arouse the impression that faith is first of all a call to sacrifice all rational reservations against all biblical assertions. However, this would mean that faith itself would become a "work," and the Pauline antithesis of faith and works is undermined.[97] Thus, it becomes understandable that in recent Protestant studies it has quite clearly been established that "every form of *legalism* which makes faith into a requirement and intends to elevate it to be a condition for justification, contradicts the all-sufficiency of God's grace in justification and would make faith into a work."[98]

To be sure, the opposite danger of sacrificing the validity of *sola fide* in favor of *sola gratia* obviously exists as a countertendency.

The efforts of theologians to overcome this dilemma take two directions.

(a.) Faith is first and last an act of God. This has preeminently been posited and articulated by Karl Barth in his *Church Dogmatics*. In saying this, Barth does not exclude the tenet that faith is a human act, and he expressly states that we are to speak "of a free act of man based in God's act, and an act of the human heart, but *not* an act of God Himself and as such." However, the implication remains clear: "Faith is the human activity which is present and future, which is there, in the presence of the living Jesus Christ and of what has taken place in Him, with a profound spontaneity and a native freedom, but also with an inevitability in the face of His actuality."[99] Or, in connection with John 8:36, "The Son makes a man free to believe in Him. Therefore faith in Him is the act of a right freedom, not although but just because it is the work of the Son."[100] "For this reason, unbelief has become an objective, real and ontological impossibility and faith an objective, real and ontological necessity for all men and for every man. In the justification of the sinner which has taken place in Jesus Christ these have both become an event which comprehends all men."[101] "But the action of faith is the doing of the self-evident—just because it takes place in the free choice beside which man has no other choice, so that it is his genuinely free choice."[102]

This position has recently been reformulated with renewed poignancy by W. Vorländer, as an antithesis to all attempts to describe faith as a self-generated experience: "Faith is always God's act in the Holy Spirit. Lack of faith is always a human act that is contrary to the Holy Spirit. Faith means letting oneself be placed by God in the wrong, and just by this receiving God's righteousness. Lack of faith means placing oneself as right before God, and just by this forfeiting God's righteousness. Faith is an act of passive reception, lack of faith is actively forfeiting grace."[103] With regard to this conception, if it is necessary to describe human participation in the actualizing of faith, then it can be said that "faith means to be affected and to consent! As such, faith is the 'yes' of humans to the act of God. Hence, faith actualizes nothing that has not already been accomplished in God's redemptive work."[104]

This position has recently been given support by some exegetes. Proceeding from such texts as Galatians 3:23, where there is mention of the "coming of faith" as a saving reality within history, F. Neugebauer has already stated that "faith is *primarily* the gift of God."[105] G. Friedrich has taken up this definition and has referred to the fact that, in the " 'work of faith,' a person allows everything to be relinquished which he could assert in the face of God, and he allows God alone to work."[106] Hence, for the appropriation of faith, it is fitting to say that "One cannot give a gift to oneself. However, one can reject a gift. It is not possible to believe by one-self, but it is possible not to follow the call of the gospel and remain dis-obedient (Romans 10:16). The person who lacks the capability to earn salvation for herself or himself nevertheless does have the possibility of negation."[107]

However, exegetical considerations need to be raised over against this conception. In the New Testament, the call to faith is apparently more than simply the demand to offer no resistance to the work of God. It is the invi-tation for one to open one's heart to God's gift and actively to join one's own "yes" to the "Yes" of God.[108]

(b.) The second possibility of circumventing the dilemma that has been described is to provide a new definition of what is meant by "faith." For the most part, the question of the content of faith *(fides quae creditur)* is either placed in the background or it is bracketed altogether over against the achievement of faith in the sense of an unconditional trust *(fides qua creditur)*. It was Paul Tillich who developed this option most significant-ly. He took up the Reformers' tendency to equate the justification of the believer with the justification of the sinner (or, in Paul's terms, the justifi-cation of the ungodly), and he maintained that in light of the contemporary experience of reality, this should lead to the thesis of new justification of the doubter.[109] Only when the consequences of this position are followed can "Protestantism break out of its negativity and into univer-salism."[110] For Tillich, faith is "being grasped by that which concerns us unconditionally, the ground of our being and awareness. The courage to be is an expression of faith. And what faith is must be understood from understanding the courage to be. . . . Faith is the experience of the power of being itself, which gives to that which is becoming the power to be." Thus, in the terminology of Tillich, the justification of the believer means "the state of being accepted in spite of being unacceptable."[111]

Tillich carries this line of thought yet further, in that he speaks of an "absolute" faith, which is the other side of that which usually appears as faith or doubt in certain truths and which withstands the anxiety of doubt and foolishness. This is a faith "which has been deprived by doubt of any concrete content, which nevertheless is faith and the source of the most paradoxical manifestation of the courage to be."[112]

Rudolf Bultmann proceeds in the same basic direction, although he is more strongly oriented toward the statements of the New Testament. In his program of radical demythologization, he aims at "the parallel to the

Pauline/Lutheran doctrine of justification by faith alone apart from the works of the law. Or again, his concern is for its consequential realization within the realm of knowledge."[113] The creedal statements in the Bible are therefore "not to be examined in terms of their conceptual content, but in terms of the understanding of existence that is expressed in these concepts. The question to be asked concerns their truth, and their truth gives consent to faith, which is not permitted to be bound by the conceptual world of the New Testament."[114] However, as a decision for a new self-understanding, faith is also the act of the person, "an act in the supreme sense. As such it is the opposite of every work or achievement, since the act of faith consists in the negation of all the work which establishes man's existence."[115] For Bultmann, faith is therefore certainly a question of the will,[116] and he points very strongly to the fact that nowhere in the New Testament is faith explicitly described as a work of the Holy Spirit.[117]

In his way, E. Drewermann advocates a similar program, except that he emphasizes the depth-psychological interpretation of the Bible in place of existential analysis. The message of the Bible is rightly proclaimed where its images and symbols awaken the potential for trust, which slumbers within the soul of every person. The specifically Christian content of faith has to recede or be eliminated in exchange for the general truth of the human soul. Only that which persons discover within themselves to be the truth can be the content and object of faith—if such a formulation seems to be appropriate at all.[118]

Thus, what is at stake is intimated whenever the content of the proclamation of faith is replaced or even eliminated in favor of the act of faith. The content of the proclamation of faith is the guarantor of the *extra nos* of our salvation, that is, of the fact that God has occasioned our salvation apart from us. Here persons are told that they neither can nor must redeem themselves, but that they are redeemed and reconciled through what God has accomplished in Christ. Anyone who wants to avoid the offense of proclaiming those historical events of God's saving acts as the point of origin for faith has also eliminated the "archimedial point"[119] of our redemption, which has taken place *extra nos* and apart from our help.

If one hopes to resolve the contemporary dilemma posed by *sola fide,* without surrendering the basic affirmations of the biblical proclamation of the faith, one will need to try to accept the concerns of both of these attempts to resolve the dilemma that we have sketched, but also to reformulate them in such a way that they remain consistent with the biblical witness, and thereby also with themselves.

253

1. The decisive key for resolving this question is found in the priority of the gospel, that message which awakens faith and therefore inquires of faith before the act of faith. "Faith comes from preaching," Luther had translated Romans 10:17, pointedly but fittingly. Faith does not arise from itself but arises from the message of faith (Galatians 3:2, 5), and so it is the gift of God not, however, in the actual sense of an "act" of God but as an act of the person who has been freed and enabled for faith.[120]

H. Weder has characterized this interlacing of proclamation and faith with some very striking images. "Faith is . . . no subjective human possibility, no spiritual activity whereby I could soar. Faith rises where that which is saving appears. Faith is something that must be served to me, as laughter is served to me through wit, or dancing through music. Certainly, faith is completely my own action, and yet is wholly other than my own work. Jesus elicited faith from persons, in that He healed them of madness and lameness. With His use of parables, Jesus elicited faith from persons in that He made room for God in their world."[121]

This applies not only to the preaching of Jesus. The message of the raising of Jesus is likewise not a message that first of all demands faith; it may be and should be preached with the conviction that it creates faith and thereby also repeatedly finds faith.

2. The second consideration follows from the first. The inseparable correlation of the content of faith with its appropriation of *fides quae* and *fides qua creditur* is the decisive foundation for a proclamation of the faith in the sense of *sola gratia*. In New Testament usage, trust is always trust in God and upon what God has accomplished in Jesus Christ, and, conversely, the "saving facts" are proclaimed not as isolated, historical facts that are to be believed but as fixed points of the redemptive God's encounter with the need of humanity in history. It is an encounter which becomes efficacious for me quite personally in the preaching of the salvific actions of God. The fateful division of the process of faith into *assensus* (consent) and *fiducia* (trust) is to be overcome, but not in such a way that the content of faith—what faith depends on and in what it trusts—is thereby dissolved into an act of "self-determination." Rather, it is to be overcome through a proclamation that makes clear that "consent" to that which God has done for us occurs precisely in entrusting oneself completely to God on the basis of this message. Conversely, this "yes" of trust in the God who is for me in Jesus Christ is repeatedly articulated in the sometimes tentative and sometimes very confident "yes" to the message of God's historical acts with God's people and in Jesus Christ.[122]

3. A further consideration is to be added. After his experience of 1738 it was clear to Wesley that justifying faith is always a faith that is conscious and certain of its salvation. Toward the end of his ministry, however, his pastoral sensitivities led him to place considerable emphasis upon the conviction that God's acceptance of a person is not dependent upon that person's subjective feeling of the assurance of salvation.[123] However, he did not retract his basic conviction that God does impart the certainty of salvation along with faith. When our contemporary ecumenical and inter-Protestant discussions on this theme are considered, it is almost curious to note that one of the most important points of demarcation which the Council of Trent brought forth against the doctrine of the Reformers was its rejection of the possibility of a personal assurance of salvation. Yet, Luther was less interested in the subjective assurance of salvation than in the objective certainty of justification by faith, whereas the Council would maintain that the conclusive result of the process of becoming righteous in the life of a Christian could only be ascertained at the point of death.[124]

However, Wesley wanted also to give the subjective side of the certainty of salvation its legitimate place in preaching and theology, and part of the historical effectiveness of the Methodist movement is without doubt to be ascribed to this dimension of its message. The dangers that threaten such a conception had already been partially recognized by Wesley. The certainty of faith must not be based upon particular feelings of inner peace and joy, and temptation and doubt must not be denounced lock, stock, and barrel as enemies of a living faith, for many who want to believe may find themselves plunged into spiritual distress. If one wishes to make Wesley's concern, which undoubtedly has a biblical basis,[125] fruitful for the present day, then it is to occur above all through preaching that confers that certainty. Such preaching would repeatedly underscore the fact that what God's Word promises to faith is *valid*—and namely not on the basis of some kind of demonstrable qualities of our faith, but on the basis of the promise of God in Christ. Further, it is valid for all who allow it to be applicable to themselves, both for those who experience inner joy and confident certainty and for those suffering temptation and doubt. The prayerful petition, "Lord, I believe; help my unbelief" (Mark 9:24) has its legitimate place here.

3.1.4.5   FREED FOR RESPONSE—AN ATTEMPT TO SUMMARIZE

God's grace precedes all human effort and activity. It is not we humans who seek and find God. What is represented in exemplary fashion by the story of the election of Israel as the people of God in the old covenant takes place for all persons in Jesus Christ. God opens himself in his love and seeks out persons in the midst of their lost condition. God demonstrated his love for us in that Christ died for us when we were yet sinners, and while we were yet his enemies God reconciled us to himself through the death of his Son (Romans 5:8, 10). Thus, grace is in the deepest sense always "prevening," and it is always grace that precedes our response. It is God's Spirit who transforms our hardened hearts into hearts that are truly alive and are opened to God's love and the need of our neighbors (Ezekiel 11:19). It is the warning call of the law and the alluring power of the gospel which moves us to turn about. It is God's creative Word that creates faith out of the nothingness of human unbelief, that causes the light of the knowledge of God's love to shine into the darkness of doubt and resignation and awakens the spiritually dead to a life with God.

It is precisely through this that we humans are freed to make our own response to God's summons. We are incorporated into God's acts as willing and feeling persons and are called forth, invited, and bidden with the deepest earnestness of the saving love of God to turn around, to be reconciled to God, to let our lives be transformed, and to accept in faith everything that God has granted unto us and has brought about on our behalf. Some of the basic marks of United Methodist preaching include holding open this space for the response of faith and discipleship through the witness of God's prevenient grace in word and deed, in preaching, pastoral care, congregational life, and diaconal activity. Thus, persons are encouraged to enter into this space step by step. What takes place here is solely a gift, but at the same time, it is actively lived grace.

3.2 The Renewal to Life in God

The goal of God's actions for and with humanity is their redemption and salvation.[126] That is one of the basic presuppositions of the theology and preaching of John Wesley. He shares with the entire Christian tradition the understanding that this salvation of humanity will find its fulfillment in eternal fellowship with God. However, what is distinctive in the theology of Wesley is that he understands and preaches that God's saving action for humanity is an event that is present, and it is one that also includes the whole person.[127] The goal of the working of God's grace is to enable persons now to enter into a life that is lived in harmony with God and with themselves, or, as Wesley liked to formulate it, it is a life that is lived in "holiness and happiness."[128]

When Wesley sets out to explain what he understands by the redemption and salvation of humanity, he repeatedly points to two basic dimensions: justification and sanctification.[129] Justification "implies what God *does for us* through his Son," and sanctification is "what he *works in us* by his Spirit."[130] Or, in another basic definition, he states that "by justification we are saved from the guilt of sin, and restored to the favour of God; by sanctification we are saved from the power and root of sin, and restored to the image of God."[131]

Both of these affirmations are key motifs of Wesley's work between 1738 and the time of his death in 1791. In "Salvation by Faith," his first sermon after his transforming experience on May 24, 1738, Wesley summarizes the quintessence of the message of redemption in the statement "Through faith that is in him they are saved both from the guilt and from the power of it."[132] And in one of the sermons preached in the last year of his life, he opposes the view that, when he began to preach "By grace you have been saved through faith" (Ephesians 2:8), he had surrendered his former motto of "Pursue peace with everyone, and the holiness without which no one will see the Lord" (Hebrews 12:14). "But it is an entire mistake; these Scriptures well consist with each other; the meaning of the former being plainly this, 'By faith we are saved from sin, made holy.' "[133]

However, Wesley can occasionally also place justification and regeneration beside one another as basic dimensions of redemption. The definition that is then offered is almost identical with the previous one. Justification refers to "that great work which God does *for us,* in forgiving our sins; the latter [the new birth] to the great work which God does *in us,* in renewing our fallen nature."[134]

It is clear that regeneration and sanctification belong together, but they are not identical. Regeneration is "a part of sanctification, not the whole; it is the gate of it, the entrance into it."[135] Conversely, although justification and regeneration occur together in a temporal sense, they are still to be cognitively distinguished from one another. Wesley also sees that justification in the language of the New Testament can be used to comprehend the entire saving activity of God on behalf of humanity, and thus it also includes both regeneration and sanctification,[136] but overall, the two are distinguished in the sense that sanctification is "in some degree the immediate *fruit* of justification, but nevertheless is a distinct gift of God, and of a totally different nature."[137]

In this chapter we will proceed to describe the saving activity of God in the life of persons in a manner that provides a modest systematizing of the order of Wesley's affirmations regarding justification, regeneration, and sanctification. However, we will need to keep in mind that this order can only be viewed as a temporal sequence in a quite hypothetical sense, since it is to be understood much more as an essential ordering of the various dimensions of redemption, viewed in its entirety.[138] The relation of those aspects of redemption which God has done for us *(pro nobis)* and are therefore valid for us and of those which God intends to do to us and in us *(in nobis)*, based upon what he has done for us, seems to be foundational for Wesley.

3.2.1 *The New Relationship to God—Justification*

The significance of the message of justification for the present age has been questioned from several perspectives. What was valid for the churches of the Reformation as the *articulus stantis et cadentis ecclesiae* (that is, the articles of faith, with which the church stands or falls), and which also has occupied a central place in Methodist preaching, appears to no longer speak to persons of our time, and thus seldom appears in preaching or teaching.

Wesley's treatment of this theme was indirectly dependent upon the Protestant Reformers, through the mediation of the Thirty-nine Articles and the homilies of the Church of England, and also directly through his familiarity with the Reformation texts. On the other hand, for Luther the rediscovery of the Pauline doctrine of justification by faith was the decisive impetus for a new conception of Christian proclamation and theology. The situation of the medieval church appears to have actually been a *kairos* moment, in the sense that the message of justification could be heard as *the* pertinent Word, as it seldom had been heard in the history of the church.

In the course of the twentieth century, new insights into the presuppositions and the character of the biblical message of justification have been attained especially in the realm of exegetical study, which not only have contributed important insights to our understanding of this message but also have contributed new impetus for its actual significance. Of course, these insights were not available to the Reformers or to Wesley. They had intuitively understood some nuances of these insights correctly and rendered them in terms of their own conceptual framework. At other points we will have to set new emphases on the basis of the results of this research.

3.2.1.1 THE BIBLICAL FOUNDATIONS

The biblical statements about justification have their roots in the Hebraic legal procedures. For this reason, one often speaks of the judicial or "forensic" dimension of justification. If the innocence of the defendant became evident during an Israelite lawsuit, the decision of the judge (or also of the plaintiff or accuser) was "You are righteous."[139] In contrast to the Latin or Germanic legal thinking more familiar to us, some noteworthy differences transpire:

(a.) The decision is more than the negation of a negation ("You are not guilty"; or, "You are acquitted of the accusation!"); the decision brings forth a positive statement: "You have behaved properly."

(b.) The decision is more than an immediate statement about a past matter ("You are in the right in this matter"). At the same time, it qualifies one's future membership in the fellowship of the righteous. "You are righteous" also means "you are faithful to the community," you have conducted yourself in conformity with the standards of the community and once again you fully belong among us. The decision is therefore not only one of acquittal, which "dismisses" the accused. It is also a statement of justification and explanation of honor, which admits one into community. Hence, justification is not only a decision that establishes a matter of fact, but also a decision that brings about what it declares.[140]

In the Old Testament, the theological significance of this terminology surfaces not in the situation of the judgment of God toward humanity but within the context of God's controversy with his unfaithful people, in which God takes on the position of a defendant. Hence, in Isaiah 43, God demands that a people who have rebelled and complained against him should go to court with him in front of the nations. God declares, "Accuse me, let us go to trial; / set forth your case, so that you may be proved right" (verse 26). The result of such a lawsuit, however, can only be the confession that "no one living is righteous before you" (Psalm 143:2), or, as it is declared in the confession of one individual in Psalm 51:4, "Against you, you alone, have I sinned, / and done what is evil in your sight, / so that you are justified in your sentence / and blameless when you pass judgment." The human who is God's opponent acknowledges defeat and says, "You are right!"

Above all, this is found with respect to the judgment of God on Israel in the destruction of Jerusalem and their being led into exile: "The LORD is in the right, for I have rebelled against his word" (Lamentations 1:18). Or Daniel 9:14, "the LORD our God is right in all that he has done; for we have disobeyed his voice" (similarly, Ezra 9:15; Nehemiah 9:8, 33). However, the hope for aid comes precisely from this recognition of the righteousness of God: "O Lord, in view of all your righteous acts, let your anger and wrath, we pray, turn away from your city Jerusalem, your holy mountain" (Daniel 9:16).

Here a further important observation concerning the biblical terminology is to be made. In biblical terminology, righteousness is apparently not the formal, judicial righteousness, which acquits the innocent and punishes the guilty (the *iustitia distributiva*). Instead, it is the faithfulness of God to God's covenant and to God's people, which does not fail in spite of their faithlessness. Therefore, mercy is never a contrast to the righteousness of God in the Old Testament, but it is frequently a parallel concept (Daniel 9:16 with 9:18; and Psalm 103:17). Hence, in the Old Testament and in early Judaism it can be said that the central hope for the people of God is that God's righteousness may be made known to the people (Psalm 98:2; Isaiah 56:1).[141]

This is the linguistic and theological background against which early Christianity formulated the belief that God demonstrated his "righteousness" (faithfulness to the community) in the death and the raising of Jesus. Through his atoning death, Jesus has removed the guilt of humanity and thereby created the conditions which allow people to be accepted into his fellowship, that is, to become justified.[142]

It is at this point that Paul connects his message of justification. Apparently the fundamental principles of this matter were already clear to him even at the time of his call and his theological processing of it.[143] Paul had persecuted the Christian community as a man who was zealous for the law. It appeared to him to be blasphemous to God that this community asserted that a crucified man—and for Paul that meant a person who had been cursed by the law—was the Messiah of God. Now that crucified One had appeared to him as the One who had been raised by God, and thus One who had been justified by God and who had been confirmed in the fullness of power to be God's Son. Through this, his attempt to establish his own righteousness through flawless obedience to the law was shown to be a failure. God had provided Jesus Christ to be "righteousness and sanctification and redemption" for humanity (1 Corinthians 1:30), and thus had opened the way to fellowship with God through Jesus' Person, his life, and his death. Through this, the wall that was drawn around Israel by the law was now penetrated, and the way was now open to proclaim God's saving acts even among the heathen. The eschatological revelation of the righteousness of God, his faithfulness to salvation, is now brought to its fulfillment for Paul in the gospel of Jesus Christ, but not only for Israel before the eyes of the people, but rather for all those who accept that righteousness in faith (Romans 1:16-17).[144]

It is not certain exactly when Paul formulated this conceptually. He had developed his teaching on justification, which has functioned so significantly in church history, at the latest by the time of his altercation with the false teachers in Galatia. However, it is clear that this describes not only an "anti-Jewish propaganda doctrine."[145] It is also evident that in this situation central insights into the renewal of relationship with God through God's saving acts are grasped and communicated with particular clarity. Hence, Paul's central thesis is that, as Jews, "we have come to believe in Jesus Christ, so that we might be justified by faith in Christ, and not by doing the works of the law, because no one will be justified by the works of the law" (Galatians 2:16; also, Romans 3:28).

If one follows the argument of Paul in the letter to the Galatians carefully, one realizes that the contrary position does not consist simply in the converse statement—that a person may be justified in the final judgment on the basis of the works of the law. Apparently what was stated was that, for the fulfillment of saving fellowship with God, what is needed is one's incorporation into the covenant of God with Israel through circumcision and adherence to the law. Hence, the discussion did not simply concern the question of what the forgiveness of sins accomplishes, but rather it had to do with the basic question of where persons are to find an abiding place before God.[146]

For Paul, the example of Abraham here serves as a basic model of the promised fellowship with God. Abraham believed, and it was reckoned to him as righteousness, and for Paul this fundamentally excludes the principle of achievement and reward in relationship to God.[147] For Paul, faith is the stance of the one who expects all things from God. Abraham believed in the One who justifies the godless, those who can and will possess nothing before God. However, this is precisely the stance that is consistent with proper fellowship with God and that will thus be acknowledged by God as righteousness. This is not a kind of record-keeping on another level, but it establishes a new relationship with God. Being justified means for Paul being accepted as a child of God, and being incorporated into a living Christ-centered fellowship with other persons, a community which is no longer divided by the confinements of race, position, and religious origin. The social dimension of justification is as significant here as the positive description of the new community with God, which is described in Galatians 4 as the condition of children who have "come of age" and who have entered into the position of freedom in confident relationship to the heavenly Father.

Hence, justification is much more than an amnesty for the sake of Christ; it is the foundation for a new fellowship with God. At the same time, the justifying activity of God is the revelation of his righteousness and thus the revelation of the God who remains true to himself in his salvific deeds. According to Romans 3:24, redemption takes place in Jesus Christ, so that God is righteous and justifies the person who lives by faith in Jesus. By revealing his being as righteousness and love, God opens to humanity a new life in his fellowship.

This embracing of the saving activity and the self-revelation of God is particularly emphatic in Romans 4, where the faith of Abraham is described as the faith in the One who justifies the godless, and this affirmation is placed in the context of faith in God, who creates out of nothing, who raises the dead, and who has already raised Jesus from the dead. God's justifying actions are thereby placed in relationship with his sovereign creative acts and with the hope of the raising of the dead. From a soteriological perspective, justification is seen as creation from nothing, and thus it is the end of all despair and self-accusation, but also of all notions of self-competency and of all pious or secular expressions of self-justification.

This creative power of the righteousness of God also fashions the new relationship with God. It establishes a fellowship that is characterized by "peace with God" and that endures amid opposition, affliction, and temptations (Romans 5:1-5; 8:31-39). It enables the service of righteousness, which is lived in the power of the coming resurrection. It makes the activity of righteousness accessible in practical ways within all aspects of human life, and thus leads toward consistent holiness of life, which spills forth in the uninterrupted fellowship with God in eternal life (Romans 6).

Paul can express the same intention in regard to the terminology of justification with the concept of reconciliation.[148] In Romans 5:8-10, Paul describes in two parallel affirmations the operation of the grace of God, which preceded all of our efforts, because Christ died for us when we were yet sinners, and reconciled us when we were yet enemies of God. That gives hope to those who now wait as those who await their final redemption as persons who are justified and reconciled—who are no longer sinners and enemies, but who also have not yet reached their goal![149]

The question of how we can prevail before the judgment seat of God is therefore for Paul only one aspect of the message of justification. The more far-reaching question is "How do persons who have been separated from God and who have become his enemies find entry again into redemptive fellowship with him?" Paul's answer is clear: this fellowship with God has been opened for us by Jesus' surrender of his life, which conveys God's love to a world of people ruled by sin and death and communicates the steadfast gift of God's redemptive grace to humanity. Those who accept this gift as the foundation of their lives and who also live out of that resource are the ones who stand in right relationship with God—as well with themselves. That is the New Testament message of justification.

3.2.1.2 THE UNDERSTANDING OF JUSTIFICATION AMONG THE PROTESTANT REFORMERS

Of all Christian theologians, Luther has undoubtedly taken up Paul's doctrine of justification most intensively and has integrated it most thoroughly into his theology. One can ask whether it is even appropriate to speak of a "doctrine" of justification in Luther, within the context of his theology as a whole, rather than referring to Luther's theology as one which as a whole is shaped by the message of justification. Luther's theology of justification is not systematically developed; rather it is an extraordinarily dynamic, very complex, but nonetheless interrelated and coherent exposition of the event of justification. We can only highlight some of the more important features of his treatment of the doctrine in the context of this discussion.

It is well known how Luther's struggle to attain the proper meaning of the message of justification, particularly in the context of the understanding of the phrase "the righteousness of God," is concentrated in Romans 1:17. In the Preface to his Latin writings (1545), Luther, reflecting upon what his discovery of this message meant for the emerging Protestant Reformation, wrote:

> For I hated that word "righteousness of God," which, according to the use and custom of all the teachers, I had been taught to understand philosophically regarding the former or active righteousness, as they called it, with which God is righteous and punishes the unrighteous sinner. Though I lived as a monk without reproach, I felt that I was a sinner before God with an extremely disturbed conscience. I could not believe that he was placated by my satisfaction. I did not love, yet, I hated the righteous God who punishes

sinners. . . . At last, by the mercy of God, meditating day and night, I gave heed to the context of the words, namely, "In it the righteousness of God is revealed, as it is written, He who through faith is righteous, shall live." There I began to understand that the righteousness of God is that by which the righteous lives by a gift of God, namely by faith. And this is the meaning: the righteousness of God is revealed by the gospel, namely, the passive righteousness with which merciful God justifies us by faith, as it is written, "He who through faith is righteous shall live."[150]

What is foundational for the further development of Luther's theology of justification is the inseparable connection of the righteousness of Christ and the righteousness of faith.[151] The righteousness which God grants to humanity is the righteousness of Christ, which he has lived out for them in both his death and his resurrection. Thus, the reckoning of this righteousness is not the charge of an "objective good" to their account; rather, it is "a literal, active drawing nigh of that which occurred in Christ, the actual acquittal and declaration of the righteousness of the sinner."[152] The word of the gospel that is proclaimed, in which this promise is met, is for Luther "the real preacher of our salvation. *Faith* alone conforms to this Word, in which persons ignoring all results of their own lives abandon themselves as unconditionally to the promise as it is extended to them. Such a faith is not a psychic achievement but the pure willingness to allow that gift to be conferred upon one. Even faith itself is, of course, God's gift, for through the Holy Spirit God brings about faith in His Word within persons."[153]

It also follows that for Luther there can be no separation between the *declaration* of righteousness and the *making* of righteousness. He did not regard the sinner's declaration of righteousness to be a merely empty declaration "as if,"

which leaves the actual empirical condition of persons unaltered. Instead, within God's declaration of righteousness he saw the efficacious Word of the Creator and Redeemer, who also will bring about that which He promises. God will also bring to victory the person to whom He declares His righteousness. Such a person will also overcome the reality of that sin, whose reign has been overcome by God's declaration of righteousness on behalf of humanity. This event commences at the very point that Christ becomes *actively* present through His Spirit within the believer. Though sin remains in that person, it will be completely removed only in death. However, its rule over that person is broken as the Spirit operates to bring about the beginning of new, eternal life within. Thus, faith remains, which with reference to one's own salvation can be only a bare receptivity, but, with reference to serving one's neighbor in the world, it is absolutely not passive. Because faith means coming into the living power of Christ, the works of love proceed from Him spontaneously. Indeed, Luther can say that true faith can in no way exist apart from such works.[154]

The dynamic character of the Lutheran formulation of *simul iustus et peccator* (simultaneously just and sinner) is described in this way. The one who believes is justified with reference to the righteousness of Christ, though in light of her or his own actions, that person remains a sinner, although God's promise to set that person free of sin is now operating in that person's life, until it is fulfilled in death. Up till that point, however, confidence can be in Christ's righteousness alone, and never in one's own righteousness, however much the renewing power of the Word of God may have already done in one's life.[155]

In this connection, a text from Luther should be cited that indicates instructive parallels and differences in view of certain questions that also revolve around Wesley—for example, questions concerning the validity of the law, the relation between faith and love, and the necessity of good works.

> Therefore the law is fulfilled in a twofold manner: through faith and through love. Through faith it is fulfilled in this life, in that God has meanwhile through Christ gratuitously reckoned us as righteous, in fulfillment of the law. This will be fulfilled through love in the coming life, when we shall become perfect as God's new creatures. . . . Then faith itself will cease, as well as God's reckoning and the forgiveness of sins, together with the entire office of the Spirit. . . . However, meanwhile we are protected in God's bosom as a beginning of the new creation, until we are made perfect in the resurrection of the dead. However, this beginning becomes evident whenever He is really there through good works, which make our calling sure. Thus, if one may speak about this in human words, we do not become righteous through deeds *[we accomplish actu perfecto]*, but through the power which draws nigh unto us *[potentia propinqua]*. For Christ is continually being formed in us, and we will continue to be formed according to His image, so long as we live. Hence, as we are justified apart from the law and the works of the law, so we live by faith, but not without works.[156]

To Melanchthon fell the difficult task of systematizing Luther's theology of justification. Through this he became the actual creator of the Lutheran "doctrine" of justification, and he thereby set in motion a series of difficult internal controversies within the Protestant Reformation. Article 4 of the Augsburg Confession had concisely summarized the Pauline declarations, while the Loci Communes of 1535 offered an explicit and comprehensive definition: "Justification signifies the forgiveness of sins and the reconciliation or acceptance of a person into eternal life."[157] According to Melanchthon, the declaration of righteousness, which means being accepted by God, and being renewed through the Spirit, which means holiness, belong closely together. However, for clarity of thought, he chooses to keep these aspects distinct. And yet, this

> conceptual separation of justification and sanctification (*iustificatio* and *sanctificatio*) . . . obscured the inner relationship of both in the event of personal acceptance by Christ. One is *isolated* from the other; the one is justification, understood as a juridicial act of amnesty, and the other is holiness, that becomes something subsequent which must follow, and this "must" can become a problem. Is this inward "must" the spontaneosus fruit of faith? Is this the "must" of an intentionality, an obligation, which now has to be added to the gift of the declaration of righteousness? How could the "result" of holiness be so grounded in this gift that one does not fall into the path of a legal moralism?[158]

A series of questions were thus raised which played a role not only in the development of Lutheran doctrine but also in Wesley's discussion with his Anglican dialogue partners, on the one hand, and with the Moravians, on the other.

Calvin's doctrine of justification draws out this line of questioning further but lays stronger emphasis upon the actual transformation of persons in repentance and regeneration, as well as the correct behavior of Christians in the world. He asserts, "Thus it is clear how true it is that we are justified not without works yet not through works, since in our sharing in Christ, which justifies us, sanctification is just as much included as righteousness."[159] It becomes clear here that it was not without reason that Wesley cited Calvin over against the English "Calvinists," for instance where Calvin emphasizes that works are "better established and confirmed" through justification by faith.

> For we dream neither of a faith devoid of good works nor of a justification that stands without them. This alone is of importance: having admitted that faith and good works must cleave together, we still lodge justification in faith, not in works. We have a ready explanation for doing this, provided we turn to Christ to whom our faith is directed and from whom it receives its full strength.

Why, then, are we justified by faith? Because by faith we grasp Christ's righteousness, by which alone we are reconciled to God. Yet you could not grasp this without at the same time grasping sanctification also. For he "is given unto us for righteousness, wisdom, sanctification, and redemption." Therefore Christ justifies no one whom he does not at the same time sanctify.[160]

This overview should not be concluded without considering the decrees on justification at the Council of Trent. Attention has repeatedly been drawn to the proximity of Wesley to some of the affirmations of this Council (either positively or negatively). An actual comparison is difficult, because the judgment of the content and the intention of the Council's declarations is variable and disputed.[161]

Above all, there are two points where the statements of the Council and the intentions of Wesley appear to coincide:

(a.) There is the conception of prevenient grace, which "awakens in the sinner faith in the truth of the proclamation of salvation . . . joined with an initial impulse of hope and love for God." According to the interpretation of the decrees of the Council, persons must cooperate in free agreement with God's grace. This is certainly not characterized as merit, but it still stands in opposition to the Reformation view of *sola fide*.[162]

(b.) Justification by faith is only the beginning of justification. Faith is therefore the "basis and root of all justification," from which actual righteousness emerges in a lifelong process through the interworking of faith and works, which originates in an initial gift of righteousness.[163] Concepts of this type strike us at first glance as having a structure similar to Wesley's thought. Yet, it is also necessary to heighten our awareness of the differences between their positions. In Trent, the correlation of the three essential marks of Christian existence, faith, hope, and love, are clearly understood as supplemental graces infused into the recipient. Love and hope must be added to faith. By contrast, Wesley's position demonstrated in *sola fide* serves as a guarantee for *sola gratia*—even with all of his emphasis upon holiness and active love. Trent's rejection of the assurance of salvation, which is a basic conviction for Wesley, even where he appears to speak of a double justification, designates the clearest difference between his position and the Council of Trent.[164]

In sum, it is noteworthy that the basic questions of the Reformation and the post-Reformation times were still being asked two hundred years later in the England of Wesley's day. The theological resolution of the question of how faith and works are to be related repeatedly surfaced as a fresh challenge. It was no longer a question of the continuing validity of the Mosaic law, as it had been for Paul. Instead, two basic questions concerning human (or religious) existence were being asked. One had to do with the relationship of grace and one's own works in light of one's relationship to God, and the other concerned the basis for a responsible life in this world.

3.2.1.3   JUSTIFICATION IN THE THOUGHT OF WESLEY[165]

When Wesley explains what he means by *justification,* he is close to the position espoused by Melanchthon. For Wesley, "justification is another word for pardon" and thus it is "the forgiveness of all our sins, and . . . our acceptance with God."[166] Two aspects of this doctrine are raised up that are also important for the biblical concept of justification:

(a.) Justification is the cleaning up of the past, the forgiveness of guilt and absolution from the accusation that the law had raised against us.[167] For Wesley, this aspect stands in the foreground. Justification occurs on the basis of the vicarious death of Jesus, through which the righteousness of God was satisfied, in which the punishment was fulfilled by Christ but through which room was also made for the mercy of God, whereby he justifies each person who believes in Jesus.[168]

(b.) Justification simultaneously constitutes a new relationship with God, which is characterized by the peace that God gives and the joy that rises from the hope for God's glory.[169] This second aspect is also quite important to Wesley. However, since its content overlaps with what Wesley has to say about regeneration and holiness, this aspect often takes a backseat in Wesley's statements about justification.

As our overview at the beginning of this chapter indicated, when Wesley gave emphasis to justification, in contrast to regeneration and sanctification, he was referring to what God has done for us *in Christus* (therefore *extra nos*). The "subjective" character of regeneration and holiness ("in us") is based upon the "objective" character of those saving events that were granted unto us in justification. Conversely, there is only a "relational"[170] change with reference to God that occurs in justification, whereas in regeneration and sanctification there is a "real" change that is actualized. We will need to return to this distinction at a later point.

In his preaching during the first few months and years following his discovery of *sola fide* in 1738, the following declarations stood at the forefront of Wesley's message:[171]

—Justification precedes sanctification and not the reverse, as Wesley had formerly taught and as many of his contemporaries continued to teach.

—Justification is the justification of the ungodly: it is valid for all without any preconditions. The only "condition"—if one may call it that—is to accept it in faith.

—Justification occurs on the basis of faith without the need for preparatory or for undergirding works. The teaching of the Thirty-nine Articles (especially Article XX), and the Anglican homily "On Salvation," which bears the imprint of the Protestant Reformers was so little known in eighteenth-century England that its emphatic proclamation by Whitefield and the Wesleys called forth strong protest and opposition.[172]

The discussion of the following years was soon defined by the altercation within the Methodist movement, or with closely related groups such as the Moravians.[173] Its theme had points in common with those of the post-Reformation controversies. It concerned the issues regarding "faith and works" particularly as regards two different points of contention. First it concerned the relationship of active repentance to justification by faith alone. Our discussion has already dealt with this theme. Second, there is the question of the meaning of works that are done following justification. In contrast with the assertion of the indifference (occasionally also the perniciousness) of good works for faith, Wesley represented what was to him the only possible biblical view, that for justification only faith and in no case good works can be seen as definitive, but also that the genuineness and vivacity of faith would be demonstrated by good works, which grow out of love for God and humanity as the fruit of faith, and so fulfill the command of the law.[174]

In this discussion, Wesley was seeking to make clear that adhering to a correctly understood and lived-out "by faith alone" does not mean that faith remains alone. Instead, it is to become active through love and by bearing fruit. As Wesley once put it, "being 'justified through his grace,' we have 'not received that grace of God in vain.' "[175] Wesley was here using a train of thought which we saw had also been expanded upon by Luther and Calvin, and yet he could occasionally depart from it amid the harshness of the debate and come dangerously close to a form of justification based upon works.[176]

Two additional thematic positions pertain to this discussion. One concerns the relationship of righteousness that is "imputed" to a person and righteousness that is "indwelling" or "implanted." In this matter, which had already been discussed in the time of the Reformation, Wesley was subjected to the sharp attacks of the Moravians and Calvinists, who were convinced that the acceptance of a righteousness that indwells the heart of a person misleads one into relying on one's own righteousness.

In his sermon "The Lord Our Righteousness," Wesley tackles these accusations. The "indwelling righteousness" is not the basis for our acceptance by God but is its fruit. It does not take the place of imputed righteousness but is its consequence. Wesley said, "I believe God *implants* righteousness in every one to whom he has *imputed* it. I believe 'Jesus Christ is made of God unto us sanctification' as well as righteousness; or that God sanctifies, as well as justifies, all them that believe in him. They to whom the righteousness of Christ is imputed are made righteous by the spirit of Christ, are renewed in the image of God 'after the likeness where-in they were created, in righteousness and true holiness.'" Hence, the righteousness of Christ is "the whole and sole *foundation* of all our hope," and even faith does not take its place. "It is by faith that the Holy Ghost enables us to build upon this foundation. God gives this faith. In that moment we are accepted of God; and yet not for the sake of that faith, but of what Christ has done and suffered for us."[177]

It is more difficult to assess Wesley's position with regard to the other thematic position, which concerns the question of the twofold view of jus-tification, one occurring at the beginning and the other at the goal of the life of a Christian. In the year 1739, we find Wesley clearly denying the concept of a twofold justification in whatever form.[178] In contrast, in his exposition of James 2:21, he appeared to be operating from just such a twofold notion: one that would affirm Paul's understanding of justifica-tion, which comes through faith, at the beginning of one's life as a Christian, and another that affirms James's understanding, which is based upon works that flow out of faith. "St. James's justification by works is the fruit of St. Paul's justification by faith."[179]

In one of his last sermons, entitled "On the Wedding Garment," pub-lished in March 1791, shortly following his death—and consciously con-sidered by Wesley as his final testament—he clearly expresses that holi-ness is the "wedding garment," which will be worn on judgment day. Justification by faith alone and the statement from Hebrews 12:14 ("holi-ness without which no one will see the Lord") can be unified, for in Christ, only faith which is working through love is valid.[180] The question to which Wesley is here responding is a difficult one that is lodged deep within the biblical message. It does not only result from the conflict between the statements of Paul and of James. It is also found in the tension that is difficult to resolve in a systematic fashion between justification by faith and the judgment of works in Paul.[181] As much as Paul occasionally emphasized that the final salvation of those who believe is still to be expected, and that they have not yet attained their goal, he did not postulate any notions of a double justification, whereby the one is brought to its fulfillment by grace and faith alone, and the other on the basis of the confirmation of faith through the evidence of its fruit. The statements about a judgment of works must (and can) be integrated within the message of justification by grace, as an aspect of accountability, which is evoked precisely through living in faith and in the Spirit.

Hence, Wesley does not speak in these final statements about a twofold justification. For him, it is a question of the wholeness of God's saving actions for humanity. God's love produces faith in persons, and faith is operative in love through persons. It is not a matter of a supplemental achievement and preservation of those who believe. Instead, it is a matter of finding an adequate conception of God's saving acts for humans and within humans as a whole. In this line of thinking, Wesley strongly emphasizes the continuity of his proclamation of justification by grace in the more than fifty years of his evangelistic activity. He consistently maintained this position, even if he occasionally became unsteady in view of its character as *articulus stantis et cadentis ecclesiae,* the article of religion, by which the church either stands or falls.

If one pursues the debate over this question through the course of the Wesleys' ministry, one may gain the impression that it became more of an academic controversy among theologians than anything else. A citation from Wesley's preaching will illustrate just how lively this message resounded in his preaching:

Thou ungodly one who hearest or readest these words, thou vile, helpless, miserable sinner, I charge thee before God, the judge of all, go straight unto him with all thy ungodliness. Take heed thou destroy not thy own soul by pleading thy righteousness, more or less. Go as altogether ungodly, guilty, lost, destroyed, deserving and dropping into hell, and thou shalt then find favour in his sight, and know that he justifieth the ungodly. As such thou shalt be brought unto the "blood of sprinkling" as an undone, helpless, damned sinner. Thus "look unto Jesus"! There is "the Lamb of God, who taketh away *thy* sins"! Plead thou no works, no righteousness of thine own; no humility, contrition, sincerity! In no wise. That were, in very deed, to deny the Lord that bought thee. No. Plead thou singly the blood of the covenant, the ransom paid for thy proud, stubborn, sinful soul. Who art thou that now seest and feelest both thine inward and outward ungodliness?

Thou art the man! I want thee for my Lord. I challenge *thee* for a child of God by faith. The Lord hath need of thee. Thou who feelest thou art just fit for hell art just fit to advance his glory: the glory of his free grace, justifying the ungodly and him that worketh not. O come quickly. Believe in the Lord Jesus; and *thou*, even *thou*, art reconciled to God.[182]

3.2.1.4 THE MESSAGE OF JUSTIFICATION TODAY

This citation from Wesley has clearly shown us the significantly different theological context of his day and our own. The question of how persons are to stand before God is no longer the greatest concern which troubles persons of our day, whether they have been reared in a secularized environment or whether they have experienced some Christian socialization. Through definite forms of evangelistic discourse, the attempt has been made to enforce this awareness anew, but the results of these methods are more than anything counterproductive for the proclamation of justification by faith.

As an outcome of the fourth plenary discussion of the Lutheran World Alliance, together with the deliberations that preceded it, it was stated that the elementary prerequisites that are needed for proclaiming the doctrine of justification appear to be missing in the consciousness of contemporary humanity. "The person of today no longer asks, how can I have a gracious God? Persons are now asking more radical, elementary questions, that are asking for nothing less than: Where are you God? Persons today are not suffering under the wrath of God, but under an impression of God's absence. Persons are no longer suffering under a sense of their own sinfulness, but under the senselessness of their existence. They are no longer asking about a gracious God, but they are asking whether God is real."[183] This realization has unleashed a heated discussion, into which the results of recent biblical exegesis have also been partially introduced, and which has resulted in focusing new theological emphases for comprehending the message of justification for our time. It is difficult to say whether this has also led to practical consequences for the actual proclamation of the message of justification.

We may now draw our own conclusions to this discussion in three points:

(a.) If we take seriously the analysis that has been sketched in the above citation, then we may say that the doctrine of justification still yields some important emphases for contemporary Christian proclamation. For the "more radical, and also more elementary question" of contemporary persons, which is "whether or not God is real," is certainly not the same question as asking "Is there a God?"—which is how the question is occasionally stated in abbreviated fashion. It is much more a question of whether God has really entered into relationship with us, whether there is a "God for us," or whether such a God is capable of being experienced. However, this is the message of the doctrine of justification in its overall biblical form, and, by the implication of the biblical idea of grace, the reference to a "gracious" God is the message about not only a God who forgives sins but also the God who emerges from his hiddenness and turns himself toward humanity with the power and the beauty of his Being. It is the message of the God who through Jesus' death makes himself available to those who suffer due to the hatred and the absence of God within humanity. It is likewise the answer to the question about the efficacy of God in light of the suffering that obviously passes before him. The message of the revelation of the "righteousness of God" for all whose lives are threatened by the "absence of God" is that Jesus Christ brought the love of God into a world filled with hatred and death, and he stood the test unto death, so that his resurrection established in our midst the Word of God who is for us.[184]

Perhaps the main text for our time should no longer be Romans 3:21-31 but Romans 8:31-39. However, in any case we may clarify that justification not only includes the cleaning up of one's sinful past—it certainly does that—rather it establishes a new relationship, a fellowship, which God grants to us.[185]

(b.) We may add to this a further paradox of our current situation. It is that the question of justification by works appears to have died theologically. No one is seriously advocating it, and at the most it appears in the form of a protest against those Christian groups who appear to place undue emphasis upon their benevolent or sociopolitical agendas. And yet, our entire society is permeated with the conviction that the value and meaning of human life is determined by what a person produces or achieves or has. The *homo faber*, the human whose life is led successfully, has certainly become the model for our society—in spite of the protests which have been made by women in particular against this masculine form of self-valuation. Outwardly, this basic definition of present day existence is manifested in quite secular ways, and also occasionally with religious padding, but almost always it is without any conscious reference to the question of the justification of one's life before God. However, existentially this definition is in fact a deeply religious phenomenon, an ultimate search for justification, meaning, and worth which in its secular form also decisively forms us as Christians. Sensitized persons like the elderly, persons with disabilities or the ill, and not a few women and sometimes also thoughtful children, painfully perceive how the value of their life tends to be measured in terms of achievements and results, and they suffer for this, so that they are set aside in the literal sense of the word.

If our analysis has been correct, that self-justification apart from and in opposition to God is an outcome of the basic sinfulness of humanity, then it can also be said that the day in which we live needs nothing more desperately than the preaching of justification by grace alone. This imperative is underscored by the fact that the consequences of the sin of self-justification in our day are evident not only in the case of those who are languishing because they are unable to keep up the pace, but also with reference to those who intend to justify their lives by their own efforts. What certainly remains necessary is that we spell out what is meant by accepting one's life through God, whether we are among those who have not achieved or those who have, and also whether we are among the self-sufficient or those who are in doubt and despair. It means being set free to see that the worth of life does not reside in the "product" of our activity, nor does it founder in unfulfilled achievements, but it is based instead upon the love of God for us. It is being graced with a reason for life that does not distinguish between the "haves" and the "have-nots" but rather is based on the truth that our lives find their purpose only in God.

(c.) In the biblical perspective, justification is the comprehensive, creative, dynamic, and saving activity of God for humanity. Luther and Wesley have indeed presented this quite emphatically in their own ways. Forgiveness of guilt and dealing with the past is one aspect of this event, which remains foundational to the present day, but which does not include all those aspects of the doctrine that need to be recognized. Overlapping this aspect is the gift of reconciliation with God, which we are permitted to accept in faith. In place of a deep mistrust toward God, which inevitably includes fear about one's own life, and which has become the motive for a life that is lived without and against God, there enters a new, underlying trust in God, which becomes the reliable foundation for our feeling, thinking, and acting. God's presence in Christ becomes the basis for our existence and for an environment in which to live in which the past is overcome and the future is made accessible, and in which reconciliation with ourselves and with our fellow human beings begins to grow.

As liberation from one's self and also for one's self in relationship to God, the event of justification also always contains a social and an ethical dimension, which is grounded in the surrender of one's life to Christ and then unfolds from that basis. It is here that grateful activity and patient inactivity has its place, as well as concern for our fellow human beings and joy in what God bestows upon our individual lives.

3.2.2 *The New Life from God—Regeneration*

The theme of regeneration, or the new birth, has a key position in the theology and preaching of Wesley. And yet it is not an all-controlling theme, although it is a litmus test of any comprehensive theological exposition of God's saving deeds toward humanity. It is closely associated with justification, on the one side, and with sanctification, on the other. Regeneration is the basis and the beginning of really living life anew under grace. That is why it is so central to Wesley's theology. In developing its meaning, Wesley typically lays hold of the declarations of the New Testament. Prior to Wesley, there was no ordered exposition of the doctrine of regeneration to which he could appeal.[186]

3.2.2.1 REGENERATION IN THE NEW TESTAMENT[187]

The witness of the New Testament to regeneration is not very expansive, yet some of the places where regeneration is discussed have a signal character. This is particularly true of the most significant theological reference to regeneration, namely John 3:3 and 3:5.[188] To Nicodemus' assumed but not stated question "What must I do to be able to enter the kingdom of God?" Jesus responds, "Very truly, I tell you, no one can enter the kingdom of God without being born of water and Spirit." In the Greek text, the words meaning "to be born anew" are a play on words with the other possible meaning of "to be begotten from above" (= from God). The condition for the saving encounter with God is a new existence, which only God himself can grant. This takes place "through water and the Spirit," in short through the outward sign of appropriating the destiny of Jesus in baptism and through the receiving of the Holy Spirit, who renews persons from within. According to John 3:9-21, this birth from above, which God produces, demands only faith on the human side.[189]

We repeatedly find this basic conviction in the Johannine writings. Those who accept Jesus Christ as the Word of God are empowered to become the children of God. They are persons who are born of God

(John 1:12-13). According to 1 John 2:29, 3:9, and 4:7, one knows whether one has been born of God and is now his child above all by the presence of love and by the turning away from sin.

The idea of being "reborn" also appears in some places in the letter of 1 Peter. Christians are born again unto a "living hope" (1:3), not from "perishable seed" but by the "living and enduring Word of God" (1:23) and they are called like "newborn infants" to constantly nourish themselves with spiritual food of the gospel and thus grow into salvation (2:2).

The last central place for this discussion is found in Titus 3:5, where the salvation of Christians is spoken of in terms of the bath of regeneration and the renewal in the Holy Spirit (with a pronounced opposition to justification by works). As in John 3:5, baptism and the infilling of the Holy Spirit are seen as means to the full renewal of the person who is being delivered from sin.[190]

The picture of a new birth also undergirds the (occasionally critical) statement that Christians have remained small children (1 Corinthians 3:1-2; Hebrews 5:12-13). In contrast to this, the motif of adoption by God is not always linked with the new birth. Galatians 4:5ff. and Romans 8:15ff. refer back to the image of adoption, in order to describe acceptance as children of God.

In a wider sense, the Pauline statements about the "new creation" (2 Corinthians 5:17 and Galatians 6:15) and being clothed with the "new self" (Ephesians 4:24 and Colossians 3:10) also belong to this context.

The inner connection between the rather meager testimony to the notion of "regeneration" with the total witness of the New Testament is also highlighted with this. It is a matter of the creative reconfiguration of human existence through God in an act of their acceptance through him. Regeneration is the description of that which takes place because of God—and solely through him—on behalf of humanity whenever persons turn to him in faith. The fellowship that is opened by God with humanity establishes a new existence, and this new existence that is created through God's Spirit is the presupposition for living in fellowship with God!

3.2.2.2 WESLEY'S DOCTRINE OF REGENERATION

As we have already seen, Wesley emphasized both aspects: not only the close connection between justification and regeneration, indeed, their temporal interpenetration, but also for the sake of conceptual clarity the necessity of maintaining the essential order of succession between justification and regeneration. For him, justification and regeneration are not "only different expressions denoting the same thing." It is certain that "whoever is justified is also born of God and . . . whoever is born of God is also justified" and that "both these gifts of God are given to every believer in one and the same moment." Although it is true that

> justification and the new birth are in point of time inseparable from each other, yet they are easily distinguished as being not the same, but things of a widely different nature. Justification implies only a relative, the new birth a real, change. God in justifying us does something for us; in begetting us again he does the work *in* us. The former changes our outward relation to God, so that of enemies we become children; by the latter our inmost souls are changed, so that of sinners we become saints. The one restores us to the favour, the other to the image of God. The one is the taking away the guilt, the other the taking away the power, of sin. So that although they are joined together in point of time, yet are they of wholly distinct natures.[191]

Wesley bases the *necessity* of the new birth upon that which he also describes as its *goal*.[192] Since people have fallen from fellowship with God, and thereby have lost their proper destiny to live in the image of God, it is necessary that they be reinstated in that *imago Dei*. Only through this can they begin to live in fellowship with God.

The *essence* of the new birth (regeneration) is described by Wesley in a very impressive comparison with the process of one's natural birth.[193] Although an unborn child lives in the midst of the visible world and although that child also already has ears and eyes, she or he truly knows as good as nothing about this world. The same thing is true for persons before they have experienced the new birth. God has provided them with all the prerequisites for perceiving Him and they are completely surrounded by him in whom everything that has life, "lives, moves, and has being" (Acts 17:28). Yet, such persons do not perceive God. They have no sensitivity and no awareness of his presence and they have "no true knowledge of the things of God." The "eyes" of their hearts are closed so that they see nothing of the Spirit of God.

As in the case of natural birth, this situation changes with the new birth of a person.

> The "eyes of his understanding are opened" (such is the language of the great Apostle). . . . His ears being opened, he is now capable of hearing the inward voice of God, saying, "Be of good cheer, thy sins are forgiven thee": "Go and sin no more." . . . He feels, is inwardly sensible of, the graces which the Spirit of God works in his heart. . . . And now he may be

properly said *to live*: God having quickened him by his Spirit, he is alive to God through Jesus Christ. . . . And by this intercourse between God and man, this fellowship with the Father and the Son, as by a kind of spiritual respiration, the life of God in the soul is sustained: and the child of God grows up, till he comes to "the full measure of the stature of Christ."[194]

Wesley summarizes this essential meaning of the new birth as follows: "It is that great change which God works in the soul when he brings it into life: when he raises it from the death of sin to the life of righteousness. It is the change wrought in the whole soul by the almighty Spirit of God when it is 'created anew in Christ Jesus,' when it is 'renewed after the image of God,' 'in righteousness and true holiness.' "[195]

The "*marks* of the new birth,"[196] which are confirmed in the life of the reborn, are first of all the essential marks of the identity of a Christian in general: faith, hope, and love. It is the event of the new birth that causes the true qualification of these marks to become clear. This faith is a living faith, which leads a person into the most intimate fellowship with God, so that the Christian is now set free from the compulsion to sin (see 1 John 3:9). The hope that fills the reborn Christian is the hope which God's Spirit places within his or her heart, which assures him or her that he or she is indeed a child of God and thereby also partaker in the heritage of eternal glory. And love is the love for God and the neighbor, which no longer needs to be incited by the external commandment but now does what God wills and what serves the neighbor, through the infilling with God's love, which leads to voluntary acts of obedience.

The *goal* of the new birth is defined practically from its necessity. The purpose of the new birth is sanctification, the life that is lived in conformity with God, for "gospel holiness is no less than the image of God stamped upon the heart. It is no other than the whole mind which was in Christ Jesus. . . . But 'without holiness no man shall see the Lord,' shall see the face of God in glory. Of consequence the new birth is absolutely necessary in order to eternal salvation."[197] However, as the goal of the new birth, Wesley placed "happiness in this world" in second place, but as of almost equal importance after holiness.[198] Whenever persons comes clean with God, they also find peace in themselves. This is true happiness and it is given to persons through new birth.

At the close of his sermons on the new birth, Wesley repeatedly makes this point to his hearers with great emphasis: "You must be born again."[199] Because there can be no fellowship with God apart from this basic transformation and renewal of one's existence, this challenge of the gospel cannot be met by a call to baptism or to the doing of works of love and mercy. The demand is clear: you must allow your life to be totally renewed by God; you must be born again. But it is precisely this which a person cannot do alone. What one can do is nothing other than place one's full trust in God and plead for the gift of the new birth. And it is to that gift that Wesley summons his hearers.

In our current United Methodist doctrinal standards, the Confession of Faith (EUB) is distinct in devoting a separate article to regeneration, as the consequence of justification. Here the understanding of Wesley is reflected, in its affirmation that "we believe regeneration is the renewal of man in righteousness through Jesus Christ, by the power of the Holy Spirit, whereby we are made partakers of the divine nature and experience newness of life. By this new birth the believer becomes reconciled to God and is enabled to serve him with the will and the affections."[200]

3.2.2.3 Baptism, the New Birth, and Conversion

To whatever extent Wesley's theological assertions can remain constant and complete in themselves over the decades, when it comes to the question of baptism and the new birth, he shows a peculiar hesitation.[201] In his sermon on "The Marks of the New Birth," which was published in 1748, he speaks about the privileges of the new birth as being "ordinarily annexed to baptism,"[202] and in his father's treatise on baptism, which John published under his own name, the Anglican doctrine of baptismal regeneration is likewise represented, albeit in a mild form.[203] However, already in the sermon on "The Marks of the New Birth," which we have mentioned, Wesley warns his hearers to "lean no more on the staff of that broken reed, that ye *were* born again in baptism."[204]

In a sermon which was first published in 1760, entitled "The New Birth," Wesley then once and for all established "that baptism is not the new birth," and he also maintained that it is not so according to the doctrine of the Church of England, but rather it is only the "outward and visible sign" of the "inward and spiritual grace," namely, the "death unto sin" and the "new birth unto righteousness."[205] In his brief treatment of Article XXVII of the Thirty-nine Articles of the Church of England (Article XVII of the Methodist Articles of Religion), he then writes that baptism "is also a sign of regeneration or the new birth."

From his evangelistic work, it was clear to Wesley that the reference to baptismal regeneration was problematic and dangerous, since the spiritual condition of almost all baptized persons shows nothing of the reality of a regenerated Christian life, and the reference to baptism signified a dangerous inoculation against the promise and the claim of the gospel. However, he hesitated between the position that the grace of regeneration that was received in baptism could be lost and that a new act of regeneration would be required and the position that baptism is only a sign and an emblem of the new birth that is experienced in faith, which can temporally collapse with the event of baptism, although it will not necessarily do so (not even in the case of the baptism of adults!).

Especially within Methodism in continental Europe, which operates within the context of the established Lutheran Church (or *"Volkskirche"*), the rejection of baptismal regeneration became almost a kind of confession that was shared with the adherents of Neo-Pietism.[206] The danger of succumbing to a theological diminution of baptism was certainly at hand in this.

The fact that baptism and the new birth stand in relationship to one another is clearly shown by John 3:5 and Titus 3:5. In so doing, one ought certainly to keep in mind that the New Testament assumes missional baptism, in which conversion and baptism are closely related. However, whenever the New Testament texts mention the outward rite of washing by water, in addition to the renewal that occurs through the Holy Spirit, they also make clear that baptism is not a matter of an inward event of faith, but that it also takes place outwardly for the candidates of baptism.[207] Conversely, the reference to the work of the Holy Spirit in the history of Acts, in which receiving the Holy Spirit and baptism occur apart from one another in time, recalls that the spiritual precedent is not to be identified with the external rite.[208] This applies not only to the baptism of children but also to the baptism of adults, which can (and should) be the baptism of believers, but at the moment of baptism, there can be no guarantee that the inward certainty of being a child of God that pertains to the new birth has occurred. The event of baptism actually functions as an effective sign: baptism confirms to us in quite personal terms the gift of new life in Christ, and it steadfastly guarantees God's pledge. Jesus' death and resurrection have taken place for me. Our conscious life in this reality begins at the point when I place myself before him in faith and allow God's Spirit to work within me.

This account already indicates what are the basic parameters of our answer to the question concerning the relationship of conversion of the new birth. The new birth is wholly God's gift. We must be born anew and we cannot ourselves give birth to our new existence. What can be accomplished by persons who are awakened by the gospel is to turn themselves to God, to open themselves to his working in prayer, to give trusting assent to the gift of faith, and to experience the renewing of their own lives through just such an abandonment of themselves to God.[209]

Strangely enough, the question "Are you born again?" has actually become a rather uncharacteristic and almost indecent question in many United Methodist congregations. There are understandable reasons for this. In the Wesleyan tradition, the new birth has been strongly identified with emotional experiences that are not accessible to all. To be committed to this outlook exerts inappropriate psychical pressure on many persons. The misuse of the slogan "born again" as a status symbol in some segments of Christianity in North America, which assume one has once and for all taken possession of this experience rather than a basic reality of life, has brought this motif into disrepute. Yet, the matter must not be given up. The possibility and the necessity of a basic renewal of life in fellowship with God are part of the basic witness of the New Testament. However, its reality can be recognized not only by the quality of one's initial experience but also by the newly attained aspects of the quality of life with God. In accepting the image of the new birth, it could be said (although it may be doubted in our bureaucratic age) that the best evidence of my birth is not the birth certificate but the fact that I am living. The evidence for my new birth lies in the fact that I know I am God's child. It is God's gift to us that we can consciously experience the onset of our new life with God, in contrast with our physical birth, but it is never an object of spiritual proof nor a measuring instrument.[210]

3.2.2.4 ADOPTION BY GOD, ASSURANCE OF FAITH, AND PRAYER

According to the New Testament and John Wesley, an essential mark of the new life of regenerated persons is that they are now permitted to live in the certainty that they are God's children.

The New Testament references to adoption by God comprise two different pictorial elements.

(a.) One stems from Jesus' preaching in parables, where he uses the example of a child to teach his disciples what it means, to accept the Kingdom of God like a child (Mark 10:15; Luke 18:17; and Matthew 18:3-4). The point of comparison at which Jesus arrives in the parable is contested by biblical scholars, since the parallel Gospel texts differ. The fact that children gladly hold open their empty hands, the fact that they are small and are in need of help—all of that makes them symbolic figures for communicating the meaning of a right relationship with God and with his lordship. It is not by chance that the promise of the kingdom to the children (Mark 10:14) is structurally identical to the word of promise of the beatitude of the poor (Luke 6:20). God's succor is intended for those who are in need of help, the powerless, the least ones, and children.

The command to become like children is therefore the invitation to rely unconditionally upon God. Here can be seen a seamless joining of Jesus' instruction that God is to be addressed in prayer with words that would be used by children,[211] together with the image of the newborn child, which is suggested in the motif of the new birth. To speak of this in contemporary terms, it is an invitation to a "therapeutic regression" to allow oneself to fall into God's love, as a child nestles into the arms of its mother, and thereby to regain that seminal trust which was lost.

(b.) The other structural element is more strongly defined by the father-child relationship, and it is not at all imprinted with the motif of the small child or a suckling infant. By contrast, we even find in Galatians 4:1-7 a sequence of images which describe how a genuine, ripened, father-child relationship can first become a living reality only when mature children find themselves in fellowship with God. It is not only due to the masculine-dominated language of the New Testament that the Greek text uses the word *sons*. From the background of ancient legal standards, they are the children who are characterized as being fully competent, as having full legal capacity (which, of course, is true for all children of God, whether they are sons or daughters). The motif of adoption (Galatians 4:5) underscores the gracious character of this relationship.[212]

A parallel account is the taking up again of the images of the "lost son," the festive garments, and the finger ring, images signifying the father's recognition and empowerment of the son's coming of age.[213] Hence, the motif of adoption by God is not in the least based upon the return to the symbiotic condition of early childhood. A constitutive element of being a child of God includes responsible partnership. It is characterized by the freedom of those who have found a mature relationship with the Father, one that outgrows adolescent rebellion or childish and servile expressions of excessive zeal. These are persons who thereby truly live as mature children of God.

Both of these dimensions of adoption by God are to be distinguished from one another, but they cannot simply be attributed to different steps in one's life development. We continue to live out of both dimensions in our relationship with God: we are able both to be sheltered in God's maternal care and to be accepted by our Father as mature sons and daughters and are thereby fully empowered through his confidence in us to be co-laborers with him. Even mature children can say, "Abba, Father!" This once again sheds important light upon the question of the "assurance of salvation." Seen in light of the New Testament, there is above all the certainty that we are children of God, a certainty granted us by God's Spirit. To this is joined the certain hope of also being an heir, a partaker in the coming glory of God and of his Christ (Romans 8:16-17). Without doubt this statement was also central for Wesley, and he repeatedly cited it and reflected upon it. However, it may prove helpful if we raise some important issues concerning his theology, such as that although this certainty had to do with the status of being a child, in fact this "status" presents nothing other than a "relationship." In this regard, it becomes evident that the sharp distinction between relationship and being, which Wesley posits in view of the new birth, turns out to be problematic. I live out being a child in the relationship to the Father and never anything else.

The tension between "assurance of salvation" in the present and the future is thus resolved, for it never consists in the certainty of a "possession," neither for the present nor the future, but consists in the certainty of a relationship which is founded upon God's faithfulness.[214] In this distinction the tension can be resolved between the necessary warning against a false security of salvation and the consolation of a certain and trustworthy hope, which is also found in Paul.[215]

It is *prayer* called forth by the Spirit in confidence that is the expression of this new relationship to God. This does not mean that only those who have been born again can pray. Wesley views prayer as a means of grace that is at the disposal of all persons who desire to be in fellowship with God, right from the beginning of their faith journey. The promise that God hears prayer also applies to groping efforts to address him and to enter into relationship with him. There is deep symbolism to the fact that the simple and unadorned prayer, such as Jesus taught his disciples and which many still utilize as their first primer in prayer, begins with the same address to the Father as does the Spirit-filled call of those who are reborn as children of God. If Jesus sets this prayer over against a "heaping up empty phrases as the Gentiles do," the intent is not to provide us with a better "technique" for prayer. Instead, it is to be an exercise in a manner of discourse that trusts wholly in God.

Hence, the essence of prayer is speaking to God, and it may begin with simply emptying one's heart before God, which leads into the experience that God hears and responds, and finally it leads to the deep experience of the trustful fellowship of conversation with God.[216] It is unfortunate that, in our day, prayer is often restricted to petitions and requests, together with occasional thanksgiving. However, we will only experience the essence and power of prayer when it becomes an expression of a comprehensive encounter with God, in which our lives are made to belong completely with him and before him. To this is joined grateful wonder about him and about his power in nature and history that is expressed in praise and adoration, amid the many laments about suffering in this world, and amid all the questions and all the planning that we lay out before God and talk through (not just voicing our specialized wishes) and full of thanks for those experiences with God and with other humans that we encounter as his answer to our prayers.

3.2.2.5 IDENTITY AND CHANGE

A final question needs to be thought through in connection with the theme of the new birth. The image of new birth describes a wholly new beginning. Strictly speaking one could say it marks the beginning of the life of a new person.[217] In contrast to this, the basic affirmation of the message of justification is that God accepts persons as they are, so that they can now stop hiding from or denying themselves. This need not be a theological contradiction. Wesley would say that God accepts sinners as they are, and then creates them anew as is needed for fellowship with him. However, from the standpoint of psychology, the question arises concerning the identity between the old and the new person in relation to God. Is there an "I" which remains constant in both, and how is the relationship between the three aspects to be defined? Or is there a complete break between the old and the new? And if so, is there not a danger then that the existence of the old person is denied and therefore that the "redeemed" person finally refers not to him or herself, but keeps on running away from him or herself? Hence, the psychological inquiry also has a theological dimension, as does every genuine question that concerns human existence.[218]

With Luther, this inquiry appears to be resolved in terms of the dialectic of *simul iustus et peccator,* whereas for Wesley it remains open and in fact seems to be addressed more squarely.

The answer to this question lies also in the fact that the new being is a being in a new relationship. Paul has expressed the fruitful tension that arises from it in two central phrases of his letter to the Galatians. First of all, he writes "I have been crucified with Christ; and it is no longer I who live, but it is Christ who lives in me" (Galatians 2:19*b*-20*a*).[219]

The change of identity is here described in a completely abrupt and radical fashion. Paul's "ego" is crucified with Christ, and in its place Christ enters as the center of his being. However, Paul then continues, "The life I now live in the flesh I live by faith in the Son of God, who loved me and gave himself for me" (Galatians 2:20*b*). The "ego" of Christians is therefore not simply extinguished and replaced with Christ, who guides our lives with what seems like a totally new agenda. The fact that Christ lives within me takes place so that I (!) hold myself to faith in him and his love. If one pays careful attention one can see that the same thing applies to the negative side of this duality. The ego has not simply died; it has died unto the law (Galatians 2:19*a*) and sin (Romans 6:11) and now lives for God.

Hence, the new birth does not mean an exchange of personalities but an exchange of lords. The new person, who is born through dying and being raised with Christ, is not another person's dream through which I am always trying to flee my actual self. It is I who am the new person just as God has intended, with my own abilities, my character, my gifts and defects, and I am all of this in relation to God, under the lordship of his Spirit and thus his love, instead of being under the lordship of the "flesh," my egoism trapped within myself.[220]

In the New Testament witness, this condition is described by saying that the new person is newly created "according to the image" of Christ.[221] In the final analysis, only Jesus Christ is the image of the invisible God, because only he reveals God's true unfalsified being. However, God, who has created persons in his image as Creator, also renews his work in allowing persons to share in the image of his Son. By this we mean that God welcomes them into their appointed relationship as sons and daughters so they become free for a new mode of life that is appropriate for their proper destiny with God.

Thus, the "image of God," to which God intends to refashion me, bears twofold characteristics. These are the characteristics of Christ, into whose image we are transformed (2 Corinthians 3:18), for it is his "disposition" in which we represent God's nature or his love in this world. However, this picture keeps a human face as well, which is my face, which God does not take from me but gives to me in Christ.

3.2.3 *Liberation for Love—Sanctification*

In the large collection of the minutes of several conversations between the Rev. Mr. Wesley and others, the third question that is asked is "What may we reasonably believe to be God's design in raising up the Preachers called Methodists?" And the answer is, "Not to form any new sect; but to reform the nation, and particularly the church; and to spread scriptural holiness over the land."[222] It is not only this doctrine of sanctification but also the preaching and the life of sanctification that is for Wesley the justification for the existence of the Methodist movement.

With this we have come to the center of United Methodist theology in so far as it wants to remain true to its original calling. However, for this very reason it is all the more valid to show that it is not sufficient for us to point out how all the lines of Wesley's theology converge at this point. We also face the task of outlining the basis for the biblical witness, as well as developing a theology of holiness that reflects the Wesleyan heritage, which can also function today in our church and beyond as the core of our evangelical preaching, Christian living, and ecumenical doctrine.

The relationship of justification and sanctification will be considered in relation to two aspects within the tradition of Christian theology:[223]

(a.) Justification and sanctification are related to one another as indicative and imperative. That is the classical solution of the Protestant tradition since Melanchthon,[224] as well as of A. Köberle in his book *Justification and Sanctification,* a discussion with the holiness movement, and also of Karl Barth, which brings the relationship to the following formula: " 'I will be your God' is the justification of man. 'Ye shall be my people' is his sanctification."[225]

(b.) Justification and sanctification are related just as are *declaring one righteous and making one righteous.* That is the outlook of Orthodox and Roman Catholic theology, but it is also a basic element of Wesley's theology.[226] It should be recalled that his definition of sanctification is that God "works in us by his Spirit" and we are "restored to the image of God."[227]

Of course, Wesley does not overlook the imperative aspect. However, what is emphasized in the comparison of justification and sanctification is not the relationship of God's work and the work of humanity as its consequence. Instead, it is the description of both of the qualitatively different dimensions of the divine activity for us and in us. Even with sanctification what takes priority is what God does.[228]

However, before we sketch the broader emphases of the Wesleyan doctrine of sanctification, we first of all need to at least present the basic features of its biblical foundations. Wesley's statements will be examined in light of the biblical witness, and upon that basis we will be able to reflect upon the meaning of sanctification for our lives today.

3.2.3.1 HOLINESS AND SANCTIFICATION IN THE BIBLE[229]

The motif of holiness is a basic aspect of religious thought, and it is therefore also a foundational theme within the biblical tradition. Sanctification is only a partial aspect of holiness. The testimony to this concept is therefore rather brief, although the subject of sanctification certainly has much greater significance than that fact would indicate.

The meaning of the term *holy* can basically only be described indirectly. God is holy, and so is everything which belongs to God, everything that is set apart by God and has thereby been made holy. Hence, the Temple and its vessels are holy, as well as the priests and the sacrifices which they bring there. For the most part, holiness is thus a cultic concept, which is intertwined with very "concrete" concepts. There are also areas of holiness that are separated out from everyday life, which are not to be contaminated, and there are areas of the "profane" that lie "pro fano," that is, before the area of the Temple.

God's holiness shows that he is the "wholly other," who eternally surpasses humanity and therefore is unapproachable for them. For God to be seen in his glory and holiness by a human would mean death for that person, unless God has previously removed her or his sin from him or her and thereby made that person holy (Isaiah 6:1-9).

God's holiness is certainly also seen in his faithfulness. The holy God is the God who stands by his people and delivers them, upon whom they are to rely and who therefore expects trust and loyalty from them.[230] However, God's holiness, God's being in contrast to the being of humanity, is evident above all in the boundlessness of God's love (Hosea 11:8-9).

The person who belongs to God is holy. This ought also to apply to the people of God, not only to the cultic regulations for the time when they were abiding in the Temple, but to all areas of their common life. "You shall be holy, for I the LORD your God am holy" (Leviticus 19:2) is the guiding principle of the so-called law of holiness, a collection of laws which is collated in Leviticus 18–26.[231] All areas are claimed through the call of God: the religious-cultic area, the area of sexual taboos, but also the area of inter-human common life within society, which is ordered by a series of noteworthy regulations of social welfare legislation that culminate in the command to love one's neighbor (Leviticus 19:18, 34).

The call to be holy, which means to live by God's will, is directed toward human actions, but it is founded on God's saving and freeing actions, through which God has accepted his people into his fellowship before they could do anything at all about it. "I am the LORD; I sanctify you, I who brought you out of the land of Egypt to be your God" (Leviticus 22:32*b*-33).[232]

For the exposition of the New Testament, it is not unimportant that, at the beginning of early Judaism, in short, somewhat before the time of the New Testament, two explicit holiness movements arose within Judaism, which set themselves apart by the fact that, drawing on Exodus 19:6 ("You shall be for me a priestly kingdom and a holy nation") they applied the Levitical purity commands to those who were not priests. These two movements were the Qumran community and the party of the Pharisees. From the perspective of the New Testament, their endeavors at some points appeared to be very external and legalistic, but those efforts were sustained by the consciousness that God had set apart the entire people as his own possession and had called them to holiness.[233]

From this background, Jesus' remarkable freedom with reference to these regulations and prescriptions is striking. According to Mark 7:15, he said, "There is nothing outside a person that by going in can defile, but the things that come out are what defile." Jesus was rejecting the concept of a concrete distinction between the holy and the profane, the pure and the impure, which characterized the entire ancient world. Paul and his school also followed his path (see Romans 14:14; 1 Timothy 4:4-5; Titus 1:15).[234] There is no rational critique of magical notions underlying this, but rather a new view of the meaning of God's creative acts. Everything belongs to the Creator, and it is for this reason that all things are holy, in that they are perceived to be gifts of God through his Word, and are to be enjoyed with thankful prayer (1 Timothy 4:4-5; 1 Corinthians 8:3-6). Through this, there is a basic liberation from the religious taboos of the Old Testament and of the religions of antiquity, which bequeaths the whole earth to humanity for reasonable use. However, wherever the knowledge that everything belongs to the Creator is lost sight of, the danger of an unlimited exploitation of these resources threatens.

Jesus lived in God's holy Presence in a wholly new way. Wherever he performs his wonders, heals the sick and forgives sins, persons fall down before him, because they sense the presence of God in him (see Luke 5:8; Mark 5:33). That is characteristic of Jesus' sanctifying deeds and of the manner in which he led persons into fellowship with God. He did not suppress their wholesome alarm over their mortal distance from God. Through his words and deeds, he made clear that God's reconciling love was overcoming the cleft between God and humanity.

Jesus lived in this comprehensive love of God without diminution, and he expressed it in what he said and in what he required. He consistently lived out this reality, whether he was with the poor, the sick, the weak and sinners, or with the rich and the healthy, the strong and the godly. However, he came into conflict with those who apparently had erected more formidable reserves based upon their own strength and piety. He is not the one who confirms people's holiness; rather, he is the embodiment of the sanctifying and saving love of God. However, that was not acceptable. He was pushed aside, handed over to the pagan occupying forces, who left him to be put to death "outside the city gate" (Hebrews 13:12), in the most disgraceful fashion, on Golgotha's cross. And it is precisely by this that God's love arrives at its goal—in a peculiar combination of divine will and human resistance against God. The holy God becomes accursed (Galatians 3:13), in order to reach people who stand under the curse of their separation from God with God's saving Presence. God reveals himself as the "wholly Other," as the Holy One, in that he bursts open the stereotypes of the human image of God, in that he goes the way of weakness and folly in the cross, in order to reach persons in their weakness, their error, their sin, and their death. This sanctifying activity probes into the depth of our existence, it penetrates the most hidden roots of our needs, it lifts us out of the realm of enmity toward God and into life-giving fellowship with him. Christ is the new arena of life for us; he alone is our wisdom, righteousness, holiness, and redemption (1 Corinthians 1:30).

That is the basis upon which the New Testament speaks of the holiness of Christians, who are members of the new people of God. They are the temple of God, which is holy (1 Corinthians 3:16; see also 6:19; 2 Corinthians 6:16). The "holy ones," the old title of honor for the eschatological people of God, is the title now given to them because they are sanctified through Jesus Christ (1 Corinthians 1:2).[235] The basis for holiness is therefore the saving act of God in the death of Jesus, through whose blood everything that separates and is unholy, all that is impure and unjust, is washed from persons, and through him humanity has been purchased for God (1 Corinthians 6:19-20).[236]

Therefore, holiness is not only the result or consequence of justification. Justification and sanctification both describe the basic redemptive activity of God on behalf of humanity, whereby he accepts the sinner into his fellowship for Christ's sake. The concept of holiness expresses in cultic language what is otherwise expressed in the language of justification in terms of justice and social relationships. However, on both levels, persons are granted acceptance by God and acceptance into his fellowship.

Living in this fellowship, then, also has consequences for the practical aspects of living. Paul indicates this in Romans 6, in relation to his discussion of the doctrine of justification. Belonging to God means being freed from sin and making oneself available to God as an instrument of his righteousness, with regard to all things that pertain to life. This is precisely how the sanctification of life occurs (Romans 6:19, 22). Sanctification is "lived justification," and it is the "demonstration of the reality of justification."[237] First Thessalonians 4 also shows the interrelationship of God's deeds and human responsibility. "This is the will of God, your sanctification" (verse 3), and "God did not call us to impurity but in holiness" (verse 7).

In this sense, 1 Peter 1:15-16 refers back to Leviticus 19:2: "Be holy, for I the LORD your God am holy."

What God has fundamentally done to humanity by taking them into his fellowship and sanctifying them should become a reality that is lived out day by day in their lives in all of its aspects. In this "process of holiness," God and humanity are joined as one.[238] Therefore, God, who sanctifies persons thoroughly through his Spirit (1 Thessalonians 5:23), is joined with humans, who are wholly placed at God's disposal with all of their members, together with all their concrete possibilities for living (see Romans 6:19, and above all Romans 12:1ff., a small compendium of practical "holiness" without this idea being explicitly stated!).

The special importance of the motif of holiness in the New Testament lies in the fact that this penetration of daily living with God's presence and character, through the actualization of his will, is given special emphasis in this definition. When sanctification is spoken of as the condition for full fellowship with God in eternity (Hebrews 12:14; cf. Romans 6:22), this is not done in the sense of an achievement and a reward. To remain in fellowship with God in this life is the inner condition for the fulfillment of this fellowship in God's eternity.

3.2.3.2 SANCTIFICATION IN WESLEY[239]

Within the context of this volume, it is not possible to present the individual steps of the development of sanctification in the work of Wesley, from his days at Oxford onward. We will need to limit our presentation to some of its basic highlights.

Of central importance to Wesley's doctrine of sanctification, and for its understanding in our day, is the strict equation of sanctification and love. Wesley speaks of how sanctification is to consist of the recovery of the image of God. However, since Wesley equates the image of God with the mind of Christ, and this in turn with love, we see that the circle is thereby once again closed.[240]

The equation of sanctification and love provides Wesley's doctrine of sanctification with its unmistakable characteristics, which can be set forth in a fourfold manner.

1. Sanctification is God's gift, just as love is God's gift. It "has been poured into our hearts through the Holy Spirit" (Romans 5:5), which Wesley repeatedly highlights as the culmination of the new birth and the beginning of sanctification, and which is the particular mark of a "Methodist." For Wesley, the interaction of the indicative and the imperative is based upon holiness. Where God's love becomes so central to our lives, we ourselves are enabled to love God and our neighbors. Wesley never tires of expounding this decisive grounding of the possibility of living in sanctification.[241] For him, this event is to be likened to a "transmission belt," which transmits the power of God's love into the life of a Christian and enables him or her to live a life with God and his or her fellow human beings. Hence, Wesley maintains, with great emphasis, that we are sanctified by faith, for only faith lays hold of the love which God grants to us.[242] That is the message of "scriptural" holiness, which is to be spread abroad by the Methodist movement. It also indicates the characteristic difference from Wesley's doctrine of sanctification before 1738, when he was still convinced that sanctification was to precede justification.

2. Sanctification and holiness receive a positive meaning through love. They are not only defined by the delineation of what is not holy, although this point of view is certainly not overlooked by Wesley. They are primarily delineated in terms of conformity with God's being, as God is revealed to us in Jesus Christ, which is God's love. The "otherness" of their being, an important structural feature of those who are sanctified, is oriented not only toward what a Christian is not to do but above all toward that which defines this being and doing. Hence, Jesus' description of his disciples as being the "salt of the earth" and the "light of the world" is taken up (Matthew 5:13-16). Salt and light are distinguished from their environment; otherwise they could not function in them. However, they are not altogether distinguished by what demarcates them from their surroundings, since this would hinder their operation according to their nature. The "otherness" of their being consists in the power of saltiness and lightness, and likewise the "otherness" of Jesus' disciples is grounded

in the power of love, which does not conform to the nature of this world, although it operates within it.

3. Because sanctification is love, it is also always of necessity social holiness.[243] As much as Wesley sometimes appears to concentrate upon the experience of individuals in the witness to their own sanctification, the arena of the event of sanctification is always the community. The fight for perfect fellowship with God is inseparable from a right relationship to one's fellow human beings.

4. Wesley's emphasis upon holiness as an aspect of redemption is strongly connected with his identification of present salvation and sanctification.[244] Sanctification is the recovery of the fellowship with God that had existed in paradise. It is the recovery of the image of God, and thereby a person becomes not only holy but happy as well.

This idea would smack of enthusiasm, if it did not maintain its solid content through the equation of sanctification and love. That person is happy who loves God and one's neighbor as one's self, and lives in the fellowship with God and is holy. That person is happy who is freed from egotism and contempt through the love of God has gotten things straight with one's self and has become free to love others and is happy. Adapting the words of John, "Whoever believes in the Son has eternal life," Wesley was able to connect this aspect of his doctrine of sanctification with the declaration that whoever *loves* lives life eternal.[245]

John Wesley, and even more, his brother Charles, speaks impressively about the perfection of this love in the heavenly fellowship with God. However, that the first installment of the Spirit is not only a note of security in a legal sense, but rather through the peace which God bestows and the love which he grants is already a portion of the reality of heaven upon earth, belongs to the basic convictions of the Methodist movement.[246] This is the point when Zinzendorf and the Moravians separated. For Zinzendorf, in Christ and through faith Christians are wholly sanctified and perfected in love. But this is only "in Christ," and not in themselves ("in se"), and whether they now in fact do love more or less is of no consequence as regards sanctification. For them, everything depends upon faith.[247]

Wesley shares Zinzendorf's assumptions. Christians are sanctified only by faith through Jesus Christ.[248] However, Wesley remains convinced that the sanctifying power of God's Spirit invades human life and enables persons to have perfect love for God and for their fellow human beings. Grace that is believed and grace that is lived are different, but they are not to be separated from one another or played off against one another. Sanctification in Christ and the sanctification of life form a basic unity, and they also cannot be seen as fully separated in practice, even if they are not fully identical with one another.

The relationship between "holiness in Christ" and "indwelling holiness" conforms to the relationship between justification and the new birth. In the new birth, everything necessary for fellowship with God is given to the believer: love in the Holy Spirit, retrieval of the image of God. Yet new birth is only the beginning of sanctification. For Wesley, new birth is related to sanctification like the newborn child is related to the adult.[249] At birth, a human being has all of the human organs, but nourishment and exercise are necessary for growth, so that all the functions of the body can develop properly. Another picture could also be used, one that did not suggest itself to Wesley, which emphasizes more strongly the relational character of sanctification. If two persons affirm their love for one another before God and their fellow human beings, then everything needed has been said. There is nothing "more" that can be said beyond this foundation. Yet, it remains a lifelong task for love to penetrate all aspects and dimensions of a relationship, and to protect and deepen it amid difficulties. A love that is not lived, and which does not repeatedly press toward fulfillment, dies. Thus also does the holiness in which we are placed by Christ want to be lived out day after day as sanctification.

The difficulty that is raised for Wesley in this connection, and the danger to which Zinzendorf rightly alerted him, is the question of whether Wesley's effort to confirm the reality of this doctrine in real life does not lead him to succumb to the temptation to make something that lies within humans become the basis for trust and hope, and hence the norm by which holiness is to be measured. Then, one comes to depend too much upon external phenomena to confirm the reality of sanctification.

Above all, we will have to clarify this question with reference to Wesley's doctrine of Christian perfection, which he viewed as the heart of his doctrine of sanctification, and which emerged in the holiness movement of the nineteenth century as one of the driving forces of evangelical Christianity. However, there were frequent misunderstandings and divisions because of this doctrine both within and far beyond the scope of the Methodist movement.[250]

These issues are investigated in an addendum at the end of this chapter. In anticipation of that discussion, it may be noted that we will not seek to investigate and represent Wesley's basic concerns for sanctification without adopting his conception of Christian perfection, but our primary concern will be to investigate the consequences of his doctrine of sanctification from the standpoint of the biblical witness.

3.2.3.3 SANCTIFICATION IN THE CONTEMPORARY WORLD[251]

There are pros and cons for the use of the terms *holiness* and *sanctification* for our present day.

We begin with the latter: *holiness* and *sanctification* are terms drawn from the language of the cult and are therefore even less accessible to present-day Europeans and Americans than are those terms that are drawn from the realm of human relations, such as *reconciliation, justification,* or *forgiveness.* On the other hand, these concepts are, even in their unfamiliarity, especially suitable to make clear that what is at stake is our relationship to God as well as the need for us to make room for him and his will in our lives and in this world. The theological aspect of soteriology comes to the surface at this point, and its religious and historical background may signal the concreteness of the claims of God within the temporal realm to our day. "God in the midst of humanity" is what is at stake in sanctification.

The ambivalence of the terms is also particularly indicated by the term *saints.* In the understanding of the Roman Catholic vernacular, which generally prevails within contemporary Western society, this idea certainly designates the difference and probably also the exemplary nature of that kind of human life, but it also points to its distance from the world, and it appears to refer to a special kind of religious achievement. By contrast, a doctrine of sanctification that is oriented toward the New Testament must express the proximity of God's saving activity to our daily lives, by which God embraces all areas of life. It is there that God and his love come into play. At the same time, the basic character of grace of this event needs to be emphasized. The life and death of Jesus demonstrate the affirmation that "Christ is made to be sanctification for us." It is the presence of the love of God among humans![252]

Within this context, Wesley's doctrine of sanctification could facilitate the apprehension of the imminence of God's redemptive work, in which a person does not remain reliant upon him or herself but comes to experience the transcendence of the love of God in everyday life. There are three very much interrelated areas in which the activity of the sanctifying grace of God comes to expression:

(a.) Personal Sanctification

It is difficult to determine whether the sanctification of the individual or of this community of believers should be placed first. Within the New Testament, both aspects of sanctification are inseparably intertwined with one another, and it is difficult to establish a clear order of priority. With Wesley, the aspect of personal sanctification is clearly dominant, and even today it will probably grant the most direct access to the whole issue. For that reason, we will begin our discussion with this aspect, but certainly not without noting at the outset that it can only be seen together with the other aspect, that of the sanctification of the community of faith.[253]

Even within this aspect, there are three levels of relationship, which Wesley explains:

—the relationship to God
—the relationship to the neighbor
—the relationship to oneself

1. *One's relationship to God is essentially renewed through God's grace.* Justification places persons in fellowship with God. As it is expressed in the language of the priestly cult, Christ has granted human beings access to the Holy of Holies. He has opened the heart of God, and now people can experience God's presence within their lives in an unmediated fashion.

This life before and with God not only lives out of the kairos of the actual moment. It also requires certain structures for fellowship with God if this life is to be extended and maintained. Here, *sanctification* signifies finding ways and means by which, out of the immediacy of access to God, God himself will lead us again and again into a new encounter with himself, ways which deepen and sustain that relationship in the midst of difficulties. At this point, the means of grace should be mentioned again. They are instrumental in the promotion of personal holiness, but that means not confusing the "form" of godliness with its true power. Genuine sanctification does not distort the need for finding practical aids in the life of faith through the imposition of legalistic requirements, but it also does not forget that without external form, even the strongest power is dissipated and rendered ineffectual.

2. *Links to our neighbors are forged.* Our fellow human beings are sisters and brothers for whom Christ has died. Hence, our relationships to them have been "sanctified," they have been taken into the loving fellowship of God. This applies not only to persons whom we encounter within

a Christian community but also (and primarily) to our encounter with persons in general.

In the process of sanctification, it is now important that this new disposition is not paralyzed by a great exuberance of all or nothing, but rather that it is lived out in concrete encounters and amid practical deeds, in which the possible and the attainable are distinguished very carefully from the desirable in a sober fashion. At the same time, we should not lose sight of the horizon of God's all-encompassing love.

In principle, the love commandment provides considerable freedom and flexibility of activity. It is certainly the case that neither the New Testament nor Wesley reduces its content to a general directive: Love—and do what you will![254] Even love can be interpreted and is in danger of being manipulated under the pressure of self-interest. Hence, we repeatedly discover within the New Testament enumerations of concrete commands, which to some extent are the signposts on the path of love.

A final comment in the discussion: the way of sanctification, as it brings us into relationship with others, is also not limited to what I do on behalf of others. Even the humility of allowing others to help me can be a way in which we conform to the sanctifying activity of God's love in our conduct.

3. Also, *the new relationship to ourselves is established by God.* God has accepted us into his grace and has thereby also given us a new relationship with himself. This frees us for a sober, yet not loveless, self-esteem, in which we remain aware of our weaknesses but are also thankful for our gifts and our strengths.

The command "You shall love your neighbor as yourself" refers to the standard for the love of neighbor that is based on the sound perception of what we would need and desire for ourselves. There are not a few persons in whom this sensitivity for what they truly need is deformed. They will not be capable of actual love for the neighbor until they find a new, unrigid relationship to themselves. Yet, it is not appropriate to develop a commandment for self-love from that and to speak of a "threefold" love commandment. Love of self does not need a commandment; it needs to be incorporated into God's love so that a relationship to the self can develop which is amiable toward oneself without becoming egotistical.

Within this context, Jesus' call for self-denial has brought numerous Christians into difficulties (Mark 8:34-35 and par.). Totally ignoring oneself and looking only toward God and one's neighbor appears to be the royal way to sanctification, but Jesus' words need to be seen within their context and from the standpoint of their internal epigrammatic meaning. Self-denial is not self-disdain or self-annihilation but the readiness to place oneself at the disposal of God's love and to wholly rely upon him. Within the security of God's love, we are enabled to desist from keeping a tight grasp on our lives and seeking to live for ourselves. By contrast, we are now enabled to let loose of our lives and to surrender them wholly into the hands of God. This leads precisely to Jesus' declaration that those who are prepared to surrender themselves are the ones who receive their real selves back from God as a gift.

Wherever this occurs, there will be space free for a development and a maturing of one's life in fellowship with God, which no longer needs to take place in competition with the life space of others. Self-surrender and the attainment of life, the realization of one's own destiny and being there for others, are no longer opposites. They are now objectives that truly belong together. This process of maturing in holiness thrives on openness to change in the encounter with God's Word, on the richness of life with others, and also on the challenges that come from positions of responsibility in the world in which we live.[255]

To place into God's hands everything that constitutes our lives and to allow everything to be given form by him is part of this process of the sanctification of our personal lives. This applies equally to artistic and scientific gifts as it does to deficiencies, obstacles, or burdens with which we must live. The path to sanctification can consist in the fact that some of our burdens are removed for us by the passage of time, but also by learning to live with many of them, even as Paul reported concerning himself in 2 Corinthians 12:1-10.

It is part and parcel of the New Testament witness to sanctification that the delineation of false conduct or the avoidance of areas of danger is also seen as an important task of sanctification. This was in the foreground of German Pietism as well as in the Methodist tradition for a long time. It has led to the situation in which many preachers and practitioners of pastoral care are rather inclined to reject entirely those kinds of prescriptive codes. This would be a false and a dangerous reaction. It will be an important task for the future to develop practical provisions for assistance in this direction that, on the one hand, are not legalistic, but that also do not simply burden the individual with every decision. Instead, there need to be normative precedents to assist persons in working through their problems. We see modern forms of asceticism emerging, which are appropriate within the context of certain challenges, such as encountering persons who are in danger of addiction, and developing means of intervention that will assist them in overcoming this behavior.

In the biblical tradition, the warnings concerning sexual aberrations assume considerable importance among the prescriptions against false social behavior in general. This concern diminishes greatly in importance for Wesley. Amid the search for responsibly developed lines of demarcation, it would be important to develop a positive response for our day, so that sexuality and sanctification are not viewed as being mutually exclusive. Instead, even this basic area of our lives can be lived gratefully in fellowship with God and can be integrated into the maturation process of our lives.[256]

(b.) The Sanctification of the Community

As we have already indicated at the beginning of the last section, we find in the New Testament a series of parallel statements about the sanctification of the community and the sanctification of individual lives. It is said of both the community of faith and the Christians' body that they are God's temple and are therefore holy. The strongest emphasis regarding the sanctification of the community is in Ephesians 5:25-27. Here the discussion of sanctification applies both to the individual and to the church, who have been cleansed of sin and sanctified by Christ. Here the church almost appears to be a kind of corporate personality in whom God's saving work takes place—detached from God's act on behalf of individual Christians.

Wesley repeatedly emphasized that there is no sanctification other than social sanctification.[257] The common life of human beings constitutively belongs within the realm of fellowship with God. If we follow how Wesley brought this basic assertion to life, we realize that the sum and the coordination of the relationships of individuals with one another are what leads to what he calls social holiness. Yet, in one respect, there is also for Wesley a holiness of the church that transcends persons. This stands in relationship to the catholic tradition, in which the *communio sanctorum* is not seen first of all as the community of *sancti*—that is, of holy persons— but as a community of *sancta*—that is, of the holy sacraments.[258] Aside from the question of whether this is the exposition that is historically correct, it is quite obvious that in the history of theology, it has been proved as not lacking in danger. The claim of the church to administer the real "holy things" within an "institution of salvation" has not been free of hazards, and it can lead to a strange split between an ideal church, identified with the structures of the official church, and the actual congregation of persons who are themselves filled with life.[259] Yet we mustn't overlook that this tradition possesses a kernel of truth by taking up that line of thought from the New Testament that makes clear that the holiness of the Christian congregation consists of more than the sum of what its members have realized. Since the New Testament community is not only a federation of believers but also a body established by Christ, it is also valid to infer that the community as a whole has been sanctified by Christ. This sanctified nature of the community has to be actualized through practical living as a community.

The essence of holiness within the community of the New Testament can perhaps be most succinctly characterized by stating that Christ has made it to be the living environment for grace. How the church lives in this mode will be described in detail in the following chapter. Here we will simply sketch the three principal aspects of this area of concern:

—*The Dimension of the Encounter with God:* This is the realm of the congregation, in which persons can encounter God through fellowship, through their speech and action, their prayers and singing, their preaching, and their common silence before God. United Methodist church structures have no "holy" rooms, although the term *sanctuary* is often used for the worship space. However, they must be conscious within the life of the community of the need for space and time for encountering the presence of God, in which persons can experience that the "place" on which they stand is holy.

—*The Encounter with One Another:* What takes place in the community's space is more than the individual contacts of particular Christians, although togetherness in the community is not conceivable without these living relationships of individuals and groups to one another. However, it is only in the wide mesh of relationships with an entire congregation that the organism of the body of Christ can actually be lived and experienced in all its diversity. At this point, a reciprocal assistance takes place, as well as allowing self-help, where persons are encouraged but also (and this is an essential aspect of communal sanctification) called to task if their behavior gives cause for concern.

—*The Relationship to Persons Outside the Church:* The church is only conceivable as the realm of grace if the dimension of openness to the outside is present. In the New Testament understanding of the concept of sanctification, the church is in need of "places of contact" with the world in which it lives, so that something of the nature of God's love, for which the church is a sign, becomes clear. "Holy places" are signs of the presence of God. The call of the Christian community is nothing other than this.

(c.) Sanctification and Society

Sacred places have the character of signs. They are not reservations for the pious, "residual biotopes" of the religious life, but rather they are supports for the promulgation of life out of God's love in a world which threatens to become a life-destroying wilderness. This is certainly the proper understanding of the idea of holiness and sanctification, as we know it above all in the Old Testament, so that on the one hand it aims for what is extraordinary, what is set apart for God, and which thereby refers to what belongs wholly to God.

It is within this context that the New Testament refers to the relationship of the first three petitions of the Lord's Prayer. This is how Luther formulates it in his exposition contained within his larger catechism: "When we say, 'Hallowed be Thy name,' we are thereby petitioning that His name, which is otherwise holy in heaven, will be and also will remain holy upon earth with us and all the world."[260] It is precisely the relationship with the next two petitions which indicates that the hallowing of the name is not limited to the circle of the disciples, but that it is also true of the holiness of God's name throughout the entire world. The fact that God is given the honor that his will is done and his kingdom comes characterizes three different but closely related aspects of God's deity being effective throughout the entire world for its salvation.[261]

Wesley had this dimension of God's saving acts in view, as well as the discipleship of Christians, whenever he referred to the task of the Methodist movement in terms of spreading scriptural holiness across the land.[262] At that point, he did not explicitly indicate how this spreading of sanctification throughout the land occurred. However, it is clear that he had two particular ways in mind. One is evangelistic preaching, which announces to persons both the need for and the possibility of sanctification, which occurs by faith alone through God's grace. The other is the example of the fellowship of Christians and the witness of their lives of love toward enemies—which urges on the matter of holiness.

Wesley was of the view that, with these means, something of the order of the "sanctification of the world" would be attained. He "was firmly convinced of the fact that the time will come when Christianity will have the upper hand and will cover the entire earth. Then wars will cease, hatred and suspicions that divide us will be overcome, unrighteousness and poverty will be removed, and love and justice will prevail upon the earth. This goal must always lie at the heart of our efforts, and must be the measure for our expectation in view of the gifts which God wants to grant us."[263]

This hope has proved illusory, and hence, Wesley's assessment appears to us today to be too narrow to bring the transforming power of the gospel to bear upon the needs of this world. Yet, we should not allow ourselves to be led astray to undervalue the significance of preaching and of encouraging the personal modeling of the transformed life in Christ. Evangelization is not only the invitation to personal salvation but also always a declaration of the claims of God over the world and over humanity, which indwells it. Whenever this voice is missing, social and political modes of behavior are ambiguous and ineffective. The personal example of engaged Christians who get involved in the needs of the world remains the soul of all social efforts conducted by the church. What is attained through these efforts often appears to be less than a drop that falls upon a hot stone, and yet, without them, political demands or measures are strangely ineffectual because the Spirit of love is missing from them. On the other hand, the example of the inconspicuous and even basically ineffective though devoted work of a Mother Teresa has a value that can hardly be overestimated for the continued effectiveness of the power of sanctifying love in this world.

Yet, we need steps which lead us beyond the limits of the engagement of individual Christians. They are enumerated here only in a brief fashion and will be described more explicitly in the following chapter.

1. *Holiness and society* is an area which must not be lost from our sight. Despite all of his social engagement, Wesley had no perception of the deeper corporate causes of social misery. For the most part, later Methodism developed in a rather conservative way and did not emphasize the vision of the connection between Christian perfection and a new, comprehensive social ethic to which it occasionally aspired.[264] Perhaps beginnings of a responsible theology of liberation can lead onward.[265]

2. *Sanctification and Nature.* As it has previously been indicated, the overcoming of the taboos of antiquity that were bound to nature are not only shown to be beneficial, but they are also seen as extraordinarily dangerous at particular points. The question that emerges is, can we recover the truth of holiness from the earth, water, trees, and so forth without at the same time falling back into magical thinking, which only brings us into a new dependency and slavery? It is worth considering that not only rooms for worship, but also nature reserves can be called a "sanctuary." These areas cannot and may not be for us sanctuaries in the sense that we are to worship God in nature. However, they could probably be places that could instruct us in developing the deep respect for all life which is created by God and thereby assist us to safeguard this life.

301

In this connection, we may note the discussion of the new appreciation for fallow seasons for land, for a Sabbath intended for humanity and its time, and for a year of jubilee for the economic indebtedness under which persons are burdened. Not to be forgotten is the history of these arrangements, which in particular contexts could develop from a blessing to a plague, and yet we need to attempt to understand them as signs of the sanctification of that which God has entrusted unto us. We must urgently discover anew the function of sacred places and times, which clarify for people that this world is not our own, but that it rightly belongs to God, and therefore to all of God's creatures.

It is probably no accident that the New Testament nowhere says that the world is sanctified in Christ, as is said of the community of faith and the Christian. The sanctification of the world is an eschatological event which is accomplished whenever God becomes "all in all." However, this also summons Christians and the Christian churches to the task of being signs of the coming kingdom and the coming holiness in a world which has basically already been redeemed by God.

3.2.4 *Excursus: The Perfection of Love —Christian Perfection*[266]

Wesley ascribed a very high value to the doctrine of Christian perfection for his theology and his preaching. He saw within it the special task that God had entrusted to Methodists within the framework of Christian theology. He viewed rejection of it as being incompatible with the task of working together within the movement.[267] The fact that Wesley made some statements that conceded this position for sanctification is no contradiction. Hence, his doctrine of Christian perfection and the doctrine of sanctification, as he represented them, were for him essentially identical.

This is not the place to even provide a sketch of the history of the development of this doctrine and the controversy surrounding it during the time of Wesley's work and thereafter. Here we can only sketch a basic outline and then attempt to achieve some theological insight concerning its significance.

For Wesley, it was always important to make clear what the doctrine of Christian perfection is *not*.[268] Christian perfection does not mean inerrancy, nor freedom from errors or from weaknesses, and it is never absolute, for only God is perfect in every sense and every respect. When Wesley used the term *perfect* he meant someone having "the mind which was in Christ," and who so "walketh as Christ also walked"; a man "that hath clean hands and a pure heart," or that is "cleansed from all filthiness of flesh and spirit"; one in whom is "no occasion of stumbling," and who, accordingly, "does not commit sin." . . . We understand hereby, one whom God hath "sanctified throughout in body, soul, and spirit"; one who "walketh in the light as He is in the light, in whom is no darkness at all; the blood of Jesus Christ his Son having cleansed him from all sin."

This man can now testify to all mankind, "I am crucified with Christ: Nevertheless I live; yet not I, but Christ liveth in me." . . . He "loveth the Lord his God with all his heart," and serveth him "with all his strength." He "loveth his neighbor," every man, "as himself"; yea, "as Christ loveth us." . . . Indeed his soul is all love, filled with "bowels of mercies, kindness, meekness, gentleness, longsuffering." And his life agreeth thereto, full of "the work of faith, the patience of hope, the labour of love." . . .

Thus it is to be a perfect man, to be "sanctified throughout"; even "to have a heart so all-flaming with the love of God . . . as continually to offer up every thought, word, and work, as a spiritual sacrifice, acceptable to God through Christ."[269]

Why did Wesley say anything at all about Christian perfection? The first answer that he provided in response to such a question was that the Bible bears witness to the doctrine of Christian perfection. This is certainly correct, at least to a degree, especially with reference to 1 John, which Wesley used as a basic source in the development of the doctrine, as well as a basis for its defense. At another point, Wesley was admittedly satisfied with locating passages that made reference to the point "perfect," from which he proceeded to explicate the doctrine.[270]

As a second motive, Wesley cited the norm of experience, which is to say that, in the course of the history of the Methodist movement, he personally encountered a series of persons who could offer explicit testimony that God had gifted them with total perfection. He also located sources from within the wider stream of Christian tradition that bore witness to the doctrine, beginning with the Greek church fathers through to the mystics of the medieval and early modern eras. What presses them to struggle for Christian perfection may be the same thing which is presumed to have been behind Wesley's interest in the theme: the longing for a "realized eschatology," for eternity, which can be experienced now within the life of the Christian upon earth, and which completely fulfills and defines them and their actions. Admittedly, Wesley declined to make a personal profession of this experience. The fact that he acknowledged the doctrine in a sober and honest manner certainly served rather to strengthen the authenticity of his struggle about the doctrine.

In evaluating the doctrine of Christian perfection, the following observations may be important:

(a.) For Wesley, Christian perfection is the gift of God, one that is received in faith. On occasion, Wesley also says quite clearly that in entire sanctification nothing other than the power of God's love is at work, through which the believer is justified, regenerated, and then sanctified.[271] Christian perfection is experienced either through a gradual development, which then culminates in entire sanctification, or as an immediate and instantaneous experience, in which persons receive the certainty that they are completely filled with the love of God, that every sinful tendency has been eradicated from their hearts, and that they are able to praise God full of joy. In the final analysis, it was this immediate experience that Wesley had in view when he spoke of Christian perfection. But it was just this experience that was responsible for the fact that this event began to function independently within the ordo salutis, and by the use of the term *second blessing,* it became the actual fulfillment of the purpose of the Christian life. Although this development is problematic, it demonstrates the conception of an entire sanctification that is directly imparted to human beings, which plainly established the gracious character of Christian perfection for Wesley.

(b.) Christian perfection is to be described positively as "perfect love." As with sanctification, it is also to be noted that the key concept and the basic reality that is operative here is "love." This also permits Wesley to conceive of the dynamic quality of perfection, in which a continuing growth into greater degrees of perfection is envisioned, which also does not exclude the fact that persons may repeatedly require forgiveness and new installments of divine grace, which also became a source of controversy and discussion in the history of the Methodist movement. It is probable that the contention over the term *perfection* made it necessary for Wesley to frequently have to explain how this "imperfect perfection" was to be conceptualized and presented. Present-day advocates of the doctrine of Christian perfection therefore prefer to speak of the "integrity" of one's life with God, who confers his grace upon them.[272]

(c.) The second sign that characterizes Christian perfection is "freedom from sin," to the point of actual sinlessness. According to Wesley, since humans are delivered from the "power and the root of sin" by the new birth and sanctification, it was not illogical to expect that these are persons who no longer sin. Above all, Wesley appealed to Paul's argument in Romans 6–8, where he sets forth that Christ has died for sin and therefore, through him, one is set free from the power of sin. He finds positive support for his affirmation of attainable sinlessness in 1 John 3:9, which provides the central text for Wesley's doctrine: "Those who have been born of God do not sin, because God's seed abides in them; they cannot sin, because they have been born of God."

In order to be able to explain this teaching in a believable manner from a practical and theological point of view, Wesley returns to one aspect of his doctrine of sin, which above all emphasizes the voluntary nature of sin, understood as a voluntary transgression of a known law of God, but which also excludes the "sinful impulses" of one's thoughts and disposition. It should be noted that Wesley, as in the first letter of John, has a twofold argument.

—Inside and outside the movement there were people who taught a perfection in which it was no longer possible to sin at all, or rather to fall back into sin. Added to these were others who totally rejected the notion of sin since the law, which after all first brings sin to light, is no longer valid for Christians. Wesley struggled against all forms of enthusiasm and antinomianism for a realistic conception of perfection that recognized the ongoing possibility of sinning and the frequent occurrence of the experience of relapsing (or "backsliding"). To that end, he published a number of sermons with fitting titles.

—Conversely, Wesley also intentionally struggled against denying the reality of the victory over sin, which has been made possible through Christ. The power of sin has been broken, and Christians no longer have to sin.

Wesley found that the Augustinian *non posse non peccare* (that is, it is impossible not to sin), which Luther took up in his *simul iustus et peccator,* clearly contradicted the witness of Scripture concerning the power of grace in the life of the Christian. However, he also resisted the temptation to isolate the *non posse peccare* (it is impossible to sin) of 1 John 3:9 from its context (see 1 John 1:8ff.); he taught a simple *posse non peccare* (it is possible not to sin)![273]

(d.) Christian perfection does not exclude the knowledge of a perfect dependence upon God, rather this is precisely what it includes. Wesley could not accept the formula *simul iustus et peccator,* which for Luther was the guarantee of one's ongoing dependence upon Christ.[274] Based upon his experience, Wesley advocated a lifelong capacity for being *partim-partim* (partly sinner and partly righteous),[275] as he observed it with reference to the phenomena of the presence of sin within believers and also with their tendency to relapse into sin.

Beyond this, Wesley could, whether perfect or not yet, set forth in very expressive terms how all are dependent on God's help, amid their poverty of Spirit, and are to reach out for God's presence amid the tribulation over the apparent absence of God in this world. They are also ever to remain aware that nothing that they have done or experienced could stand before God apart from his grace. In his sermon upon the "Repentance of Believers," he wrote that "we may observe . . . a deep conviction of our utter *helplessness*—of our total inability to retain anything we have received, much more to deliver ourselves from the world of iniquity remaining both in our hearts and lives—teaches us truly to live upon Christ by faith, not only as our Priest, but as our King."[276] And in his "Plain Account of Christian Perfection," Wesley writes, "The holiest of men still need Christ, as their Prophet, as 'the light of the world.' For he does not give them light, but from moment to moment: The instant he withdraws, all is darkness. They still need Christ as their King; for God does not give them a stock of holiness. But unless they receive a supply every moment, nothing but unholiness would remain. They still need Christ as their Priest, to make atonement for their holy things. Even perfect holiness is acceptable to God only through Jesus Christ."[277]

It is not easy to draw a conclusion. However, despite our description, which is weighted very heavily toward the positive elements of Wesley's doctrine, we should not overlook some basic problems found in his conception of sanctification.

—The intent to objectify, even to document cases in which persons have attained entire sanctification leads to an orientation toward outward signs. The conception of sin, which Wesley can express much more deeply in other places of his writings, as, for example, in the discussion of original sin, is here limited to the phenomenon of the voluntary sinful deeds. The sharpening of Christian conscience through Jesus' exposition of the commandments, which anchors the onset of sinful deeds in the first stirring of the human heart, is rescinded at this point. This may certainly control a hypersensitive scrupulosity in the practical area of pastoral care and also may hinder a complete leveling of the concept of sin,[278] but, from a theological point of view, it is too flimsy to be able to bear the weight of the doctrine of Christian perfection.

—The interest in the ascertainable experience of Christian perfection leads to even more isolation of the individual, and to a very individualistic view of sanctification and perfection, and it makes the renewal of Christians a subject of (self-)observation. However, within the context of the early phases of the American Wesleyan-holiness movement, it should be observed that the concern for personal holiness of life was closely intertwined with great social issues, including the antislavery impulse. The American Antislavery Society was founded and advanced under the leadership of holiness advocates such as Charles Finney, Theodore Weld, and others.[279] However, the danger that sanctification becomes oriented toward and measured by the pious ego is not to be dismissed. Like sanctification in general, so also the discourse concerning Christian perfection, if it is to be used in meaningful ways, should not be primarily oriented toward the condition of individuals, but rather toward the tasks and demands which are to be accomplished in the power of God's grace.

—Despite Wesley's efforts to promote sanctification, which we have noted, there remains a tension between the striving for a clearly established perfection and the abiding awareness of one's dependency upon God, yes, even including the need for ongoing forgiveness and reconciliation, even in the "best" life.

—However, precisely this aspect of Wesley's doctrine of perfection that envisions the possibility of "classifying" particular Christians as perfect is certainly not scriptural. The passages that Wesley cites for this (for example, Philippians 3:15) are viewed by Paul in more of a polemical way and refer to a more dynamic concept of striving for Christian perfection than we find in Wesley.

Without devaluing the corresponding experiences which Wesley reports about particular contemporaries of his—claims which some Christians also make in our present day—one also needs to establish that maintaining a clearly confirmable condition of entire sanctification as the decisive goal of the Christian life is more suited to obscuring the positive features of Wesley's doctrine of sanctification than it is to summarize them positively. Hence, for a theology of The United Methodist Church in the present day, which must also ponder the painful experiences that attended the struggles in the earlier days of the holiness movement, the conception of Christian perfection must be seen in general not as a doctrine but rather as underscoring specific important tendencies of the doctrine of redemption.

Three elements are important here:

(1) The discourse concerning Christian perfection is only meaningful— but then plainly necessary—if it is understood as the evidence of the

perfection of Christ, who has lived the perfect love of God under the conditions of an earthly existence.[280] We enter into the realm of this love in faith, we are filled with God's love and imbued by this in our actions through his Spirit. However, it is *his* love that alone is perfect and remains perfect. F. Hildebrandt has referred to the fact that Charles Wesley corrected his brother at this point and also warned the Methodists against the tendency "to make yourselves your endless theme."[281] Two things belong inseparably together: to rely upon the transforming power of perfect love in Christ, and to abandon the judgment concerning its operation to Christ alone, who "knows your works" (Revelation 2:2).[282]

(2) The discussion of Christian perfection signals our openness to the comprehensive and searching operation of God's grace. Wherever we unburden this discussion from the need to demonstrate that "Christian perfection" is attended by an observable and experimental status, we free it to point to the fullness and the richness of God's grace, which is valid for our lives. Hence, as a curve approaches its asymptote without attaining it in finite terms and yet simultaneously refers to this point of intersection with the infinite, thus can the topos of "Christian perfection" become the signpost for a life lived in grace.[283] Once again, it is Charles Wesley whose highly acclaimed poem "Wrestling Jacob" points to the hope for perfection as an unconditional adherence of the weak and the helpless to that One who is complete love:

> Contented now upon my thigh
>> I halt, till life's short journey end;
> All helplessness, all weakness, I
>> On thee alone for strength depend;
> Nor have I power from thee to move:
> Thy nature, and thy name, is LOVE.

> Lame as I am, I take the prey,
>> Hell, earth, and sin with ease o'ercome;
> I leap for joy, pursue my way,
>> And as a bounding hart fly home,
> Through all eternity to prove,
> Thy nature, and thy name, is LOVE.[284]

(3) The discussion of "Christian perfection" must remain part of a doctrine of sanctification. The superscription which G. Ebeling has given to the third volume of his *Dogmatik des Christlichen Glaubens ("Dogmatics of Christian Faith")* refers to the statements from the third article of the

Apostles' Creed: "Faith in God, the Perfector of the World." In it he treats not only eschatology but also pneumatology, soteriology, and ecclesiology. He includes this theme under the caption "Perfection as the Signature of the Action of God."[285] This highlights a perspective in which emphasis is given not only to the perfection of Christians or of the community of believers but also to the perfection of the fact "that God is the Creator and the Redeemer of the world."[286] To live out of grace is to live toward this goal. It is life in faith that experiences God's perfect love and that through love becomes certain of the hope for God's perfection. Then, through hope, one is freed from concern for oneself and is enabled to love God and one's neighbor from the whole heart, the whole soul, and the whole disposition and with all one's power. "Christian perfection" can be nothing less than this. Once again, let us hear Charles Wesley's words on this:

> Assert thy claim, maintain thy right,
>   Come quickly from above;
> And sink me to perfection's height,
>   The depth of humble love.[287]

4. Christian Existence in Its Wholeness, or the Reality of Love

The only thing that counts is faith working through love.
—Galatians 5:6

This theme leads into the center of theology, above all of United Methodist theology, which has been understood from the outset as being a theology of love. In his sermon delivered on the occasion of the laying of the cornerstone of the City Road Chapel in London, the church and early center of the Methodist movement,[1] Wesley repeated what he had previously written using almost identical words some thirty-four years earlier:[2] In view of the entangled and miserable situation of his fellow creatures, as well as the problem of the largely only former religiosity, the Methodists had as their mission to find and to live the full life of a Christian, which would conform to that grace which is granted by God. What they discovered and apprehended was not a new faith but rather "the old religion, the religion of the Bible, the religion of the primitive church," the religion of love, the love of God and of all mankind. Wesley did not understand the heart of this love to be an emotional experience that overcomes us in a dramatic moment. Rather, it is seen as that love that comes from God, which is "the medicine of life, the never-failing remedy, for all the evils of a disordered world, for all the miseries and vices of men. Wherever this is, there are virtue and happiness, going hand in hand. There is humbleness of mind, gentleness, long-suffering, the whole image of God, and at the same time a 'peace that passeth all understanding,' and 'joy unspeakable and full of glory.' "[3] It is only from this center that theology in the tradition of Wesley is to be understood, developed, and assessed. The concept of a religion of love, which comes from God and intends to penetrate into the coldest and darkest regions of this world, is the constructive principle and the hermeneutical key for every expression of United Methodist theory and praxis. It speaks of the God who is love, and therefore not of a distant, other-worldly Being, but the God who acts in the world, which means within history and the realm of human experiences and actions.

And this theme extends further. It concerns individuals and their entire lives, as well as the congregation and the church of Jesus Christ in the world, and the world as a whole. It concerns both the present and the future, faith and love, as well as the reception of salvation and its realization in history. And in all things in the final analysis it is about the activity of God for the salvation of all humanity and for this world. The entire world is reconciled to God in Christ (2 Corinthians 5:19). Being a Christian is not limited to the private sphere of one's self-confined existence. Instead, it joins together that which is most deep and intimate with that which is social and global. This connection, which is integral to the Christian faith, is also a primordial concern of every United Methodist theology. To express this once more in the language of Wesley, as contained in the sermon that has just been mentioned, "This religion of love, and joy, and peace,[4] has its seat in the inmost soul, but is ever showing itself by its fruits, continually springing up, not only in all innocence—for love worketh no ill to his neighbour—but likewise in every kind of beneficence, spreading virtue and happiness to all around it."[5] The being of the Christian is located in the most inward dimension of the heart, and it also has the whole of creation within its purview. This fruitful tension is the inner momentum of the Methodist mission movement (Galatians 5:6).

4.1   God's Renewing Presence in the World

The faith which becomes effective through love knows that it is dependent upon God's presence within the world and that all the necessary prerequisites for its activity are already bestowed upon it by God. "The best of all is, God is with us!" were Wesley's words at the end of a long and productive life.[6] What we designate by the concepts of creation, covenant, reconciliation, or redemption is an event that points toward its Creator and takes place within the context of earthly reality. The community and the world are places where God is active, and apart from this activity they would cease to be what they are. The promise of the Resurrected Christ, "Remember, I am with you always, to the end of the age" (Matthew 28:20), is the prerequisite for the mission of proclaiming the gospel to the entire earth. And the social action of Christians receives its distinctive characteristics through the fact that Christ himself meets them in the midst of the needy and the weak, to whom their ministry is to be directed. And finally, apart from God's renewing presence within the world, there would really be no content for the hope that there is a future for this world, which is to end not in chaos but in the new creation of heaven and earth (Revelation 21:1)—even if the world must first pass through judgment.

4.1.1 *Love as the Operation and Sign of God's Presence*

Humans have experienced God's Presence in quite distinct ways. Even the sentiments that this experience has occasioned within them were by no means alike. The biblical texts that tell of the experiences of God themselves attest to this: they can release fears and unrest,[7] but also joy and confidence[8] and questions and clear signposts.[9] Despite all the differences in the experiences of the presence of God that persons have had according to their own testimony, there are nonetheless common attributes which distinguish them from other experiences with similar sensations: the genuine experience of God is always bound up with the feeling of dependence and the consciousness of being affected by this Reality, God's greatness and power and sovereignty, which does not permit one to be simply a bystander. This even applies where God appears in the form of a man. If the Roman centurion, who had witnessed innumerable crucifixions, could say of the crucified Christ, "Truly this man was God's Son,"[10] then his words reflect the encounter with surpassing greatness even in death.

These examples have already brought us closer to the different characteristics of the experience of God, as it is attested to in Christian faith: it is the encounter with the God who is love. Even when the behavior or the attitude of persons stands under God's repudiating judgment, God still remains disposed toward them in love.[11]

Hence, those scriptural citations that speak of God's judgment and wrath ought not to be ignored. And yet, their meaning is really seen not in the final judgment of sinners, but rather in the salvation from condemnation and the turning toward a new and authentic life.[12] God's love can thus also be experienced as something of a contradiction—as a painful "No" to our conduct or to our previous way of life, which nevertheless turns out to be a manifestation of love in that it takes humans seriously as those who exist in God's image, those created as God's counterpart.

However, do not such differentiations within the presence of God result in an unsettling insecurity in relation to God's "Yes" to human beings? For those who encounter God and take God's Word seriously, does there not remain a residue of fear before the God of judgment? Let us respond to this as follows:

(1.) God's love for humanity is not dependent upon whether persons are worthy of the One who loves them. What we find written about this matter in Deuteronomy[13] was also briefly but aptly summarized by Luther when he stated that "the love of God does not find its object but rather creates it. Human love starts with the object."[14] If the conception of creation expresses the worth of all humanity,[15] and if God renounces a portion of his sovereignty in order to take seriously humans as God's covenant partner, then God's presence as love becomes still clearer in the christological and Trinitarian exposition of the New Testament declarations.[16]

(2.) The apostle Paul has expressed the union of faith in Christ and the assurance of God's love most clearly when he writes, "For I am convinced that neither death nor life . . . will be able to separate us from the love of God in Christ Jesus our Lord" (Romans 8:38-39). John Wesley experienced the same assurance when he became impressed within his inner soul in a new way; no matter how his life were to be evaluated to that point, God's pardon applied to him and he was now a child of God. When this assurance of salvation fills a person, there is no longer room for anxiety concerning one's recognition by God nor is there room for fear of God's judgment. It is God's perfect, undefeatable love itself which completely overcomes this fear. "It is clear that it is not love as a human activity which can achieve this unbounded assurance of salvation, but rather it is only by living in the love that is experienced as God's gracious gift."[17] The final chapter of our theology of The United Methodist Church is devoted to considering the role of this life that is lived in the experienced love of God and lived out in numerous practical expressions of love.

4.1.2 *Love as the Fruit of the Spirit*

Whenever God's Spirit is at work within a person, what Paul calls the "fruit of the Spirit" (Galatians 5:22) emerges. The primary fruit, from which all others issue, is love. It draws its nourishment from the anchoring of the self in the love of God, from which love for God and for one's fellow humans in turn emerges.

In his sermon entitled "The Witness of the Spirit,"[18] Wesley presents in a series of clear reflections how it is that the love for God and for our fellow humans arises from the operation of the Holy Spirit, how our lives are thoroughly transformed, and how our consciences can affirm the effects of this love.[19] This love that changes lives is received in faith, for faith is also the way for receiving God's love.[20] The love that is received through faith in God and through the encounter with the gracious acts of human beings transforms persons from their inmost being and volition down to the concrete implementation of this love in the service of other persons.

From this point the new mode of existence begins. It is marked by love, or, in the words of Kierkegaard, "God, the Creator, who is love, needs to implant love within every person."[21]

From this reception of love arises the authorization and the obligation to act out of love. Without love, faith loses its power,[22] and with it faith becomes the distinguishing and binding mark of Christians,[23] and those who have become guilty through transgressions and the lack of love can, by trusting in God again, be gifted with faith, which is active in love.[24] Hence, the experience of the love of God makes persons certain of their acceptance, and it frees them from the necessity of having to secure the meaning of their own lives by themselves. It puts them in the position of being able to love without conditions. Without love for the neighbor, love for God is either impossible or it is perverted. Whenever it is affirmed in this fashion, it discredits the Christian faith as well as Christ himself, the One to whom that faith is directed. Wherever Christians' relationship with God does not qualify their relationships with other persons through the mind of Christ—and that means allowing their lives to be characterized by his gracious interaction with others—then Christians lose not only the authenticity of their faith, but even more, the ultimate authenticity of their existence as Christians becomes questionable. A Christianity that purports to act in the name of Jesus but whose countenance is distorted through an egotistical struggle for power wrongly appeals to the One who gave his life in service for others and out of love for humanity.

4.1.3 *Love as the Basic Norm for the Conduct of Life*

In the two preceding sections, we have attempted to make clear that Jesus' love commandment has a prehistory of being the basic norm for the Christian's conduct of life. If we do not pay attention to this prehistory, the love commandment can neither be rightly understood nor can the intention of its author be rightly followed. Every human act of love, which is recognized not only by emotional feeling but also by righteous turning and inclination toward the neighbor, has its roots in the love of God. An ethic which presupposes Christian faith as the impetus for the conduct of life and for living responsibly within the spheres of the personal, the social, and the public domains of life presupposes divine love as what enables and orients. When the love of God is personally experienced, it awakens within us the readiness and the desire for gracious interaction with other persons,[25] and that gift of love becomes the standard that explicitly informs our conduct as well as the disposition that underlies it.[26] The statement "God is love" (1 John 4:8, 16) names not only the central "attribute" of God but also, still linked to it, the basic definition of God's being, whose essence functions as the movement of love. The movement of love that creates its beloved image, which is personally sacrificed on the cross for the beloved, also creates the fellowship of those who live by love. They are those who identify themselves as the beloved and who want to pass this love on to others.[27]

If the ethics of John Wesley and of those Methodist theologians who followed in his train of thought are closely examined, then it can be postulated that their basic principle is the love of neighbor, which is born out of the experience of the love of God and which also becomes the subject of their ethical reflections.[28] According to them, a responsible life is based above all upon God's prevenient actions for the redemption and the liberation of humanity. It proceeds from their basic experience of being affirmed, and it understands the unconditional and the unlimited love of God as the basis of his standards. God's rule of love, of which they are persuaded, transforms persons and also makes possible a world-changing obedience to God. An ethic of change is based upon trust in God's present and future kingdom, and it is pledged to solidarity above all with the suffering, the weak, and the poor. It understands the ethic of Jesus not as an interim ethic for a limited bygone era, but rather as the challenge to humanity to examine the usual standards of behavior and to correct them if the occasion arises. Only one standard is final: the command of love, which includes the love of the enemy.

The love commandment is certainly not sufficient as the only standard for responsible and worthwhile actions, because in every context people need to draw actual consequential results from the love commandment. To use the command in that fashion would be, as a rule, to impose an excessive demand upon the individual as well as upon the community. Therefore, it is worthwhile to allow further norms to come into effect as concretizations of the love commandment. That the door to legalism could be opened at this point can be proved by various observations from within the New Testament[29] as well as from church history. There have therefore been repeated attempts to posit a Christian "agapism" (or a pure love ethic), to counter the tendency toward legalism. The best-known statement of such an ethic is the demand of Augustine, "Love, and then do what you will!"[30] In the twentieth century, ethicists such as Joseph

Fletcher or J. A. T. Robinson have developed such an ethic, one that is often ambiguously characterized as "situation ethics."[31]

It is actually not a pure situational ethic (as perhaps in J. P. Sartre), but rather it recognizes the love commandment as the only valid norm. Other ethical rules are also taken into consideration; however, they "have validity only insofar as they serve to advance the actual prevailing conditions of love."[32]

From this point of view, the responsibility of the persons who are active in the service of love is related to the actual situation as well as to the love commandment. This basic norm is introduced in a confessional manner when Fletcher writes, "The key category of love *(agape)* as the axiomatic value is established by deciding to say, 'Yes' to the faith assertion that 'God is love' and thence by logic's inference to the value assertion that love is the highest good."[33]

The proximity to the Christian love ethic is close at hand if Fletcher's outline is intended to be even a particularly successful variant of such an ethic. And yet, an ethic that leads into concrete actions must go beyond this theory; it must—for reasons of practicability and accuracy—discuss also the purpose and the adequate means of action as well as the problem of conflicting purposes on the same basic obligation[34] at least in an exemplary way.

Above all, in a time in which rapid changes occur within the moral norms of society, there is need for a reorientation of the norms of behavior through an ethical discussion that is directed to the love command and that reflects the situation at hand as well as the traditional rules. The love commandment may not and cannot replace our individual responsibility for our actions, but it should provide people with more assistance in understanding them. One area in which traditional rules appear to be placed in question through the practical modes of persons' behavior, including Christians', and for which a revision, and a new understanding, thus turns out to be needed, is the area of sexual behavior, including the institutions of marriage and the family. Here the social principles, but also the concrete aspects, of pertinent biblical texts have tried to help guide us.[35] If the love commandment remains as the recognized basis for the structuring of ethical norms, then that foundation does not succumb to either a mindless adherence to tradition or to a superficial accommodation to what is customary.

For Wesley, the incorporation of concrete norms for action into ethics is not only nor primarily self-evident on the basis of its practicality. His doctrinal sermons 34-36 focus uncustomary breadth on the single theme of the understanding of the law.[36] In order to counteract[37] the reversal of the message of justification by faith alone and the righteousness that is given to us through Christ by the promulgation of "cheap grace,"[38] Wesley emphasizes the continuing validity of the law, not only in its convicting or political function[39] but also as a binding norm for the conduct of life among believers. Not the cultic law but the moral law of the old covenant, the Sermon on the Mount, and the paraenetic texts of the New Testament (Romans 10:4 notwithstanding) are binding according to the doctrine of justification, because God's authority stands behind them. Its utility lies not only in that it keeps us close to Christ and that it directs strength from him as from the head to the members—thus reminding us of our remaining sin—but that it is also useful "in confirming our hope of whatsoever it commands and we have not yet attained, of receiving grace upon grace, till we are in actual possession of the fullness of his promises."[40] The hope that is thus awakened for transforming persons through grace through the commands of God finds impetus for practical living in sanctification.[41] However, "the end [goal] of all the commandments of God" is love. Hence, Wesley closes the circle of this line of thinking as follows: God's love awakens faith within me, the joy of adoption by God, and above all, love, which finds in God's law guidance for the conduct of life out of love and for obedience based upon insight and free will (that is, a will that has been freed by God's grace!). Nevertheless, the measure and purpose of all laws, as well as the basis and limits in concrete cases,[42] is love. "Love is the end, the sole end, of every dispensation of God, from the beginning of the world to the consummation of all things."[43]

With his preaching and his living, his suffering and death, Jesus expressed what all this means in concrete terms: "Love your enemies, do good to those who hate you, bless those who curse you, pray for those who abuse you" (Luke 6:27-28). This message is not first of all intended as a command or a law. Rather, it is to be experienced as the healing and helping power of love. It is summoning not a movement of individuals but the new community that is being formed in obedience to Jesus.[44] This new community has experienced the power of love and will thereby be so ready to regard and accept others that it is not the criterion of achievement and merit that defines their worth. Just as they know themselves to be loved unconditionally by God, they now understand themselves to be instruments of God's actions toward other persons, through which he likewise intends to let them experience God's liberating and healing love.

Acts that are done based upon love and in the spirit of love cannot have the goal of perfecting the rule of God in a temporal way. However, based upon faith in God's present reign, they can try to bring about results out of the experience of God's nearness and the recognition of God's will, as God is made accessible to them in the preaching of Jesus. Christians who act this way are aware of the provisional and imperfect nature of their deeds. Since they have experienced God's love within this world and time, the motives and criteria for their conduct are not optional for them. And they also know that they are particularly dependent on this power of love when understanding and accepting others becomes difficult and yet is required of them. The maxim "You ought, since you can" does not arise from their own abilities but from those that are given to them by God.

4.2   The Community as the Creation of the Love of God

What finally distinguishes a Christian community from other, similar social entities is neither its structures nor its rites, nor other externally recognizable signs. It is much more its origin in the renewing love of God.

God's healing and saving love has taken on human form in the person of Jesus, in his interaction with men, women, and children, in his words and deeds, and in the surrender of his life, which was completed in the death upon the cross. Jesus' fellowship of love with his disciples became the origin of a new divine community, to which all humans are invited. "Repent, and believe in the good news!"[45] The men and the women who accompanied Jesus during his earthly ministry, and whom he also encountered as the Resurrected Lord, formed the beginning of the church of Jesus Christ. They had received the Holy Spirit, who disclosed to them the truth of the Easter message: the Lord is truly resurrected! (Luke 24:34). God had authorized the surrender of his Son and reconciled the world with himself. Since then, the door to fellowship with God has stood open for all persons.[46]

The community understands itself as the fellowship of co-laborers in God's work, as those who issue the call to turn about and who serve as the vanguard of the coming kingdom of God. Their faith and the recognition and experience that is conferred with that faith oblige them to live a life that reflects the rule of God, and it places responsibility on them according to the measure in which it is entrusted to them. They come from the basic experience of being affirmed through God's love and they understand this unconditional and unlimited love as the basis of their existence, both as individuals and as a community. God's love transforms them and enables them to exercise world-transforming obedience. The community that attempts to live and act according to this ethic of love allows itself to be gifted anew with the promise and the experience of the love of God in worship, in the use of the means of grace, and in fellowship with other Christians. It is also entrusted with the charge to serve God in the dailiness of life.

The community lives as a visible fellowship, with its attending defects and inadequacies, apart from which there is no church. Hence, the community of Jesus Christ is also a hidden community. Its membership cannot be ascertainable with certainty though it consists of visible, living human beings. Not only do Christians make the essence of the church of Christ recognizable through their deeds; their deeds also conceal it.[47] Even if we take care to regulate admission into the church,[48] we only see "the outward appearance" (1 Samuel 16:7). Regarding the activities of the (visible) community and church, it is therefore essentially a matter of truthfulness, on the one hand, but also of spiritual orientation, on the other, for us to distinguish between the essence of the church of Jesus Christ (that is, its identity as church, or that which essentially pertains to it) and its historical manifestations, which conform to its essence either more or less, sometimes wholly or sometimes not at all. As a historical entity, the church is in no way free from distortions of its nature, because the persons who belong to it are sinners. Moreover, as a social entity it is never protected from persons who seek to manipulate and misuse the church from non-Christian motives, according to their own purposes. Therefore it is and remains mandatory for us to describe the church according to its true nature and its historical intricacies, as well as with its limitations.[49]

4.2.1 *The Community as the Body of Christ*

The origin of the Christian church, its beginning and its abiding *raison d'être*, does not reside in the decisions of humans but in the acts of God for the salvation of the world, as this has taken place once for all in Jesus Christ. The fellowship of persons who belong to God no longer consists of only the tribes of Israel. There has appeared a new people, gathered from throughout all the peoples of the earth, as the prophets had announced and the New Testament witnesses had seen happen. Christ, who has been lifted up, has joined together persons from different cultures, races, and nations into a new and distinctive kind of fellowship. Hence, it is correct for us to say that "the church is the body of Christ; the community that bears the message of salvation and incorporates those who are in the way of salvation into its own body."[50]

Already in the New Testament, the church was characterized by means of different concepts, and each one highlights a distinctive aspect of its nature. No single image incorporates all features of the being of the church, and therefore each image needs to be viewed in light of the others if we are to arrive at a truly comprehensive understanding of the church as a whole. The term *ekklesia*[51] emphasizes the aspect of the gathered congregation, *koinonia*[52] emphasizes the fellowship character of the church, which entails mutual sharing and receiving as well as common participation in the salvation which is granted in Christ,[53] and *the people of God*[54] is supposed to highlight both the continuity and the differences between the New Testament community and the chosen people of the old covenant.[55] The concepts that have been cited, which have with good reason been drawn from a greater number of images, will be taken up in the following three sections, without however thematizing them.

The metaphor of the body of Christ (1 Corinthians 12:12-27) is eminently suited to illustrate the uniqueness and the inner as well as the outer structure of the community of faith. It is a living organism, a fellowship of mutuality bound together through Christ and of persons who represent him, who are en route as disciples of Christ. They are a fellowship that is realized in the daily life of individual believers, but also in their common life and activities.

The first congregations understood themselves to be the "body of Christ." They viewed themselves as being with Christ, and they were bound together as closely through him as members of one body and were appointed for a life in fellowship with one another.[56] In spite of the growing number of Christian congregations, and the tensions within Christianity, the church of Christ is one, because its Lord is one. The church is established through his reconciling work. He calls it to life through his Spirit and upholds it through his fellowship. Its unity is already a given through the relationship of all members to Christ, the Head of the church. The oneness of the body of Christ is not produced by us. Rather, it is something to discover and to shape, through believers accepting that they are mutually bound together with Christ.

The unity that is conferred with this connection to Christ must find its analogue in the mutuality of believers, of congregations, and of churches. It does not require uniformity in ministry and dogmas, or in rituals and ordinances. The church can reflect the multiplicity that exists within human life, which is supposed to come to expression in the church of Christ. However, the church is to be held together through the "bond of peace," which helps safeguard the unity in the Spirit. "There is one body and one Spirit, just as you were called to the one hope of your calling, one Lord, one faith, one baptism, one God and Father of all, who is above all and through all and in all" (Ephesians 4:4-6). Care should be taken to identify what it is that leads to separation and thus endangers the fellowship, and what is a development that reflects the diversity of persons reconciled in Christ. This distinction can only be appropriately drawn by attending to the central message of the gospel, which is valid for all churches, and also by entering into dialogue with one another.

In the unity that is conferred upon the church through Christ, which joins the most diverse sorts of persons into one fellowship of love, the gifts of all members can be nurtured, and they can be fitted for service to one another and to those persons who are outside of the church. Tensions within the community that arise from one's own convictions of the truth over against the contradictory conceptions of other Christians can be tolerated because of the experience of a gifted unity. However, upon this foundation of unity in Christ, self-correction and criticism are possible if done with the mind of Christ.[57] Both a flaccid coexistence and also a loveless adversarial existence are to be overcome in the Spirit through a reconciled diversity.

4.2.1.1 THE FELLOWSHIP OF SEEKERS AND BELIEVERS

"God's seeking love is the actual content of the gospel."[58] The Wesley brothers had experienced and understood this. Two movements of inquiry had intersected: God's search for humanity, which he had created and destined for fellowship with himself, and humanity's search in which the longing for liberation and a meaningful life, for recognition and love, had been awakened.[59]

What grace is, as God's merciful turning toward humanity, becomes most emphatically recognizable through this searching of God. This searching is like that of the good shepherd who seeks out his sheep who have lost both their shepherd and themselves,[60] and it awakens within them the longing for God. "This [prevenient] grace prompts our first wish to please God, our first glimmer of understanding concerning God's will, and our 'first slight transient conviction' of having sinned against God. God's grace also awakens in us an earnest longing for deliverance from sin and death and moves us toward repentance and faith."[61] For a number of reasons, Wesley placed great emphasis upon this operation of God's prevenient grace, which first awakens persons to the reality of God at all. Both his evangelistic preaching and his assembling of those who had been awakened to faith, as well as his impressive acts of love and mercy along with their ethical grounding, can all begin to be understood in terms of this theological concept of prevenient grace.[62] The people of his day noticed Wesley's affection for those who were weak in faith, including the doubters, the questioners, and the seekers. After all, he took such persons seriously not least by the fact that he offered them a social context in the groups with spiritual overseers, in which they could introduce themselves, together with their questions, experiences, and their notions, and from their conversation with the Bible and with one another they could proceed from faith to faith, grow spiritually, and mature. Thus the body of Christ could assume a structure that could be experientially known. In the fellowship that was being renewed and enlivened through the Spirit of God, social relationships developed that had the deepest and most intimate interrelationships, in which all members were interconnected, even if their relationship to God was intensively and individually structured. From that context, their quality and latent strength emerged. In love that is experienced, God draws near to humanity, and thus humans can draw near to God.

In light of this tradition, The United Methodist Church seeks to structure its work in concentric circles. Church members receive their baptism, and through their confession of faith they have taken the step into the binding fellowship of congregation and church.[63] Whoever is not yet ready, or is not yet in the position to take these steps, might nevertheless have a share in the work of the church, and can remain a member of the church,[64] or allows his or her name to be entered into the church records under such a category.[65] In addition, the nonmember "constituents" of the church play an important role in the work and the life of the church in almost all congregations. Those who remain so-called friends of the church play an important role in the work and life of the church in most congregations; among them are Christians who remain members of another church yet (also) want to be part of The United Methodist Church. However, the church needs to reach out to such persons, to whom they remain more or less intimately connected and relate to others within their spheres of living. Wesley's stepping beyond the boundaries of the parish structures of the Church of England with the conviction that "the world is my parish"[66] remains for United Methodists a call to step out from the narrowness of their own lives into the larger world in which God's love wants to reach human beings. Hence, in our understanding of the church, a structured "outer courtyard" must always remain as an integral part of the Christian congregation, a place in which persons are able to make themselves intimately acquainted with the congregation without fear of being pushed into membership before they make a decision about their membership in the church.[67]

The gift of the new fellowship with God cannot be received except through the free consent of faith. God's grace frees persons. It coerces no one into faith. Faith and fellowship with God have much more to do with the conviction that the message of Christ is true, and that I am a being that is desired and loved of God, created in his own image. Here there is no coercion, for coercion would also contradict the essence of the meaning of fellowship with God. Without personal faith, however, a person cannot receive the salvation that is granted through Christ. With the response of faith, through which persons respond to God's call, they are also affirming their membership in the fellowship of believers. There is no such thing as a believer in Christ who only lives this faith within a private sphere. One's context for living is now the community of Jesus Christ, which is the entire arena of human existence.

In the history of United Methodism in America, numerous efforts have been made to introduce these features of Christian community. Membership and active participation in class meetings was required of all Methodists until the mid–nineteenth century, when the obligatory class meeting was first replaced by voluntary prayer meetings,[68] which lacked the element of accountability in spiritual growth that had been basic to early Methodism. Evangelicals and African American Methodists retained the class structure with authenticity into the twentieth century.[69] In the nineteenth century, women took leadership in forming mission societies, and Methodists and Evangelicals formed covenant communities of deaconesses, who were commissioned to minister in hospitals, schools, and congregations in a time before the ordination of women was recognized. In the late–twentieth century, new configurations of church life are being formed to respond to the needs of seekers as well as those of age groups within the church.

4.2.1.2   THE OBLIGATORY LIFE OF A CHRISTIAN

This is not an incongruous statement, because there really is no nonobligatory existence at the core of our Christian identity. It is still the case that, for a society that still sees itself largely as Christian, church membership is not infrequently viewed as a Christian identity that is free of obligations. Hence, it is necessary and meaningful for us to speak of the obligations of the Christian life. And just what are those?

It is first and foremost life in fellowship with Christ and membership in the body of Christ. "God has, as it were, extended his hand to the believer, bound himself to that person and does not intend to let go. Obligatory faith has arisen . . . that means, my life is bound in a sense to God, so that I, being filled with his joy, intend and am allowed to be his child."[70] This obligation to the "pioneer and perfecter of our faith" (Hebrews 12:2) and to his community is the lifeblood for Christian existence. It is the means of conveying to Christians the power for their tasks and for their capacity to be sustained amid the deficiencies and the disappointments that are also an inevitable part of this existence.

Whenever the apostle Paul speaks of the way in which believers are in Christ and Christ is in them,[71] he is talking about this close and life-giving relationship without which Christian existence is really not possible. This position of being joined to Christ also has ecclesiological[72] as well as pneumatological[73] significance. Its earthly concretion ultimately becomes evident in the disciples' self-understanding and in their readiness for discipleship. They should remain ready "for waiting in hope, for the service of love, and for the joy of faith" as those who are "occupying" the places where they love with their capabilities and weaknesses. "If each one does this in her or his special place, then solidarity arises, that is, unity among those who are diverse. These, belonging to the same Lord, endure tensions that would otherwise stand between them, and they allow themselves to become collectively fruitful in the midst of the world in which they live. It is like this that we find the lordship of him who creates one body out of many members expressed in the midst of the world."[74]

However, the obligatory life of a Christian also has a second meaning that is connected to the first: persons who belong to Christ and who live out of his life do not remain in the unconnectedness of a mode of living that avoids every commitment or obligation. Instead, they experience that their own wills are increasingly being directed toward the will of God, whenever they live in fellowship with God. This alignment of their lives arises not from the fact that an alien will is superimposed upon them, but rather because their own wills are changed from within. The direction is provided for them by Christ himself, and it thereby becomes clear that every form of coercion would be something alien and contrary to the purposes of Christ for our lives. It is a matter of growth and maturity in loving God with our whole hearts, our whole souls, and with our thinking, as well as our growth in the love of our fellow human beings, to whom we become neighbors (Luke 10:36-37). For the United Methodist understanding of connection, that certainly does not mean that living in connection with Christ remains confined to a purely private sphere, or that it could take place "with no real relation to the culture and the social structures of this fallen world."[75] The obligatory life of a Christian is also a program for an entire human life in all of its personal, congregational, and societal aspects. The early Christian congregations clearly recognized the fact that this did not arise by itself, nor is it conferred upon us at the beginning of our lives as Christians. The controversies in the mother church in Jerusalem, in Corinth, or in the Galatian congregations, as well as the admonitions of the apostle Paul to congregations (composed, after all, of saints), indeed the strife among the apostles themselves and among the leading persons of the early church, show that what was primarily at stake in all of these was not contention over external rules and commands. Instead, the point was above all to allow believers to temper their own thinking, willing, and acting again and again through the love of Christ. Conflicts were not to be denied, nor circumvented, nor repressed, nor eliminated by the exercise of power; rather, believers were trying to resolve them by enabling all sides to become increasingly oriented to the message of the gospel. Thus, "the true members of the church of Christ 'endeavor,' with all possible diligence, with all care and pains, with unwearied patience (and all will be little enough), 'to keep the unity of the Spirit in the bond of peace'; to preserve inviolate the same spirit of lowliness and meekness, of long-suffering, mutual forbearance and love; and all these cemented and knit together by that sacred tie, the peace of God filling the heart. Thus, only can we be and continue living members of that church which is the body of Christ."[76]

As a part of the obligatory life of Christians, which is received in freedom, it is also expected that Christians will allow themselves to become encumbered with this decision of sharing in the tasks and burdens of the congregation and with the commitment that comes with it. A decision which is intended to be serious is also to be taken seriously. Hence, the conduct of its members is not a matter of indifference for the church.

Rather, "All members are to be held accountable for their faithfulness to their covenant and vows with God and the other members of the Church. Should any member be accused of violating the covenant and failing to keep the vows which the member entered into with God and the other members of the local church," and "If a professed member residing in the community is negligent of the vows or is regularly absent from the worship of the church without valid reason, the pastor and the membership secretary shall report that professed member's name to the church council, which shall do all in its power to reenlist the professed member in the active fellowship of the church."[77] The requirements of an obligatory fellowship involve making an inquiry so that recalcitrant members are not simply left to their own resources. No boundaries are to be fixed here for the ingenuity of love. It also certainly requires patience, for we can wait for developments to occur—a patience which the rigors of our holiness tradition sometimes have not recognized. In addition, it should be noted that the person who is being sought and that person's salvation must remain the goal of all these efforts for reclaiming church members for personal participation in the life of the congregation, and not the questionable objective of achieving a "pure and flawless" congregation. Only for this purpose can exclusion from the congregation be justified as a final measure, even if a transfer into another congregation or denomination is no longer a viable possibility. The decision of a congregation which leads to the expulsion of a church member[78] only represents the vote of humans, and God's judgment may be quite different from this human decision. What Paul wrote to the congregation in Rome (Romans 14:4) has application to such human judgments: "Who are you to pass judgment on servants of another? It is before their own lord that they stand or fall. And they will be upheld, for the Lord is able to make them stand." Hence, it becomes clear that, even if the obligatory Christian life is to be expressed in conduct, and if the mode of regulating that conduct is contained within a structure for mutual accountability, such conduct still finds its roots and its vitality in the inward life of the person, in the heart, in the will. What remains decisive is what indwells a person, and what then comes to outward expression.[79]

In this regard also Wesley is a modern man, in that he places special emphasis upon the individual person in his ethics. In his theoretical as well as his practical work, and in the ethical instruction of his coworkers, extremely great value was placed on the fact that in each person the image of God is seen, regardless of one's race or nationality or social position, and each one is provided with an eternal soul and an immortal worth.[80] Along with seeing the unique significance of individual persons, Wesley also never lost sight of the social relationships in which persons must be bound together if they are to live a life that conforms to their destiny to love—that is, if they intend to experience and to order their lives by this norm. The forming of his "classes" and the emphasis upon the covenant of God with humanity are only two important examples of this pervasive motif in his theology. He arrived at an active spirituality which actually changes the way people live as individuals as well as congregations, and from that position it sets out to renew the conditions and structures in which people live. However, for Wesley this always begins with the renewal of individuals, who allow themselves to be conformed to Christ and to let the disposition of Christ define how they carry out their deeds and thoughts.[81] Even if we see the limits of this outlook in our day, it still remains correct to say that, because God has bound himself to persons in freedom and love, they can learn to lay hold of their own worth and, in the same freedom, they can turn to form and care for relationships with others.[82]

The renewal of believers according to the image of Christ essentially happens as the imprinting of the person in the whole of her or his thinking and feeling, including value concepts and basic convictions, so that image first attains a living and perceptible form in the practical conduct of life. The will of persons needs to be recast by a power, which must become personally manifest within them, to wholly transform them from within. "The message of the justifying and living love of God brings us to ourselves, in which we become a part of this very reality."[83] Christ, in whom God's kingdom has become present, becomes the norm of full humanity for the realization of reconciliation, the overcoming of egoism, and the creation of a fellowship of everything that is created through his love. As the love of Christ undergirds the salvation of the faithful, it also becomes the only final criterion for the building of Christian character and for responsible action. Being in Christ is the starting point for a new existence amidst the old. The "old" signifies all that is disfigured by sin, which increasingly passes away, and that which is "new" signifies the emergence and growth of that which is imprinted by God's Spirit.

4.2.1.3 BAPTISM AND ACCEPTANCE INTO CHURCH MEMBERSHIP

The fact that persons find the way to faith within a Christian congregation is an occurrence that takes place through God's grace, which precedes all human actions and creates the possibility of entering into salvation. The salvation that is founded upon the reconciliation through Christ (2 Corinthians 5:19-21) frees from burdens and heals the wounds of sin, which have torn people away from fellowship with God. All persons are offered this gift through the proclamation of the gospel, and they personally receive it in baptism (Matthew 28:19; Acts 2:38). The objective side of God's saving deeds is visibly expressed in baptism, through a person being incorporated into the fellowship of new life with God. Baptism, which the church carries out by the commission of Christ, is supposed to make visible the justification and acceptance of those who have been separated from God. It takes place only as the work of grace. God, who gave us our earthly life, also wants to give us an eternal life, for which our efforts are neither needed nor efficacious. A sinful person is transformed by the crucified and resurrected Christ in baptism, and the new life in the power of Christ and his Spirit is promised to that person. Like the Lord's supper, baptism is the "visible word of God," the authentic sign instituted by Christ for the new fellowship into which Christ admits the baptized.

The "yes" of faith is the response of the baptized person to baptism, in which God's salvation is accepted. Baptism, faith, and the church therefore belong indivisibly together. No one of these three is adequate in the sense of the New Testament tradition, apart from the other two. On the one hand, baptism is the "pledge and the actual sign for that completely personal saving activity of God which applies to the person who is baptized."[84] On the other hand, it is dependent on the believing "yes" of the person who gladly gives access for God to do his saving work. By this, persons affirm the new identity of being children of God, which was or is promised to them in their baptism. The name of the baptized child is given together with the name of the Triune God. In this way it becomes clear that this person belongs to God, who faithfully and with patient love pursues a person and awaits that person's mutual love.

In the United Methodist tradition, the covenant action of God has been located in this event, which has already laid a foundation between God and humanity in the old covenant with Israel, and now has been made available in the new covenant for all peoples. Baptism is the sign of this new covenant of God's grace, a covenant from which children are not to be excluded. Wesley, in his "Treatise on Baptism,"[85] had already designated the "entrance into the covenant of God" as one benefit of this sacrament, and this connection is strengthened[86] in association with the

Covenant Renewal Service.[87] In this sense, worship with the celebration of the Lord's Supper is understood as a confirmation of the grace of baptism and as a new duty to live no longer for oneself but for Christ.

This service of renewal of the covenant with God, as a means of representing God's promise of salvation and the renewal of the baptismal pledge,[88] is intended to meet a deserved need for many Christians who were baptized as infants, a need that cannot be met by having them undergo a second act of baptism.[89] In brief, this service of renewal is the experiential integration of the promise of salvation and personal confession of that salvation within the corporate worship of the congregation. In agreement with the doctrine of our church, that action of integration can be the "renewal of the covenant of baptism," in which youth or adults are baptized and received into the church,[90] or it can occur in the aforementioned service of covenant renewal. This prevents a depreciation of baptism through an impersonal, mechanical administration of the sacrament which frequently generates a felt need for a second baptism. Where baptism and faith and a committed relationship to the church are taken seriously, there can no longer be baptisms that do not require an accountable profession of faith.

Although baptism is a part of being received into the church, we do not regard it as necessary for salvation. The authenticity of the salvation that is promised in it is dependent neither upon the "correct" doctrine of baptism nor upon particular conceptions of faith (which often are linked to an intellectualizing of faith). The decisive foundation of salvation is much more God's unconditional love that is promised to individual persons in baptism, a love to which the believer submits, as he or she does their acceptance as a child of God. On this basis, we can also speak of the practice of the baptism of children and adults as the *one* baptism, for "what God does in baptism, does not first of all become valid and true through subjective faith."[91] Thus, we can agree with what F. Herzog drew to our attention: children do not belong to the church simply because their parents belong to it; yet it may be a "correct intuition of the church" "that the renewal of a person is not dependent upon whether someone possesses a developed intellect or a mature mode of thinking. One does not need to be an adult in order to participate in that which occurs in baptism. What is decisive for the baptism of children is the confidence that even the unspoken word activates the conscience—above all in the context of the Christian congregation."[92]

After numerous conversations about the competing concepts of baptism with reference both to children and to adults, theologians and laity of The United Methodist Church in Europe developed a decisive formulation of this issue:

> Faith is virtually always a response to God's saving acts, but the point in time when faith is operating is different. Those who are baptized as children have given their response in a moment in which the Spirit of God opens their eyes and hearts to that salvation that is already bestowed. However, those who have to be baptized as adults are repeatedly admonished to offer a response of faith that is expressed in obedience. Faith must not first of all create the foundation upon which God could begin to work, because that foundation is laid once for all in Jesus Christ. From this perspective, the baptism of children is also seen to be baptism in a biblical sense. Its efficacy must of course repeatedly be grasped anew in faith.[93]

This connection between the promises of salvation based upon God's redemptive deeds (in the proclamation of the gospel and in the "visible word" of baptism) and the acceptance of salvation (in faith and personal confession by those who are baptized) is a polar and irreversible relationship, as is the connection between a particular attribution and a personal appropriation of salvation. These connections now come to expression in the structure of our church in that one's acceptance into church membership comprises not only baptism but also the confession of faith in Christ. Baptism attests to the visible and sufficient promise of God's love, and confession attests to the audible and personal expression of the human response of faith.[94]

"Baptism," as we say with our churches, "is the indispensable foundation to church membership and it is given once and for all, unrepeated, just as Christ died and rose again once for all."[95] Whoever was baptized a child and has been led to personal faith in Christ is in the position to be accepted into membership in the fellowship of believers. Whoever has found the way to faith and has not been previously baptized will receive holy baptism upon entrance into the church.[96] United Methodism in Europe has clearly affirmed that "Baptism and the acceptance into church membership therefore belong together as one event, even if these are temporally separated from one another in the case of children who receive baptism," and American United Methodists similarly affirm that "once baptized, we have been initiated into Christ's body the Church and are members of Christ's family."[97]

The "yes" of faith finds its visible and experiential expression in the celebration of a person's acceptance into church membership. All who have found God and, in him, themselves, now find in other Christians the fellowship of those who together are pilgrims headed toward the goal of their lives, which is perfect fellowship with God. This institutionalization of the acceptance of Christians into the local congregation, and thereby also into the church, is an essential aspect for the self-understanding of The United Methodist Church.[98] The basis for accepting members is not a test of faith, which is possible for no one, but rather it is the reception of the salvation that is given in Christ, which has become visible in baptism, audible in the confession of believers, and confirmed as worthy of acceptance by the congregation.

Those who are accepted into the membership of the church also pledge themselves to a way of living that is guided by the Spirit of God through participation in the life and service of the church.[99] Members of the congregation are to join with them in renewing their covenant "to faithfully participate" in the ministries of the Church; a more explicit covenantal affirmation is found in the European United Methodist service, where members also pledge to receive those who are newly admitted as their sisters and brothers and to let them "experience Christian love and concern in the context of heartfelt fellowship."[100] In the latter affirmation, each baptized believer "is thereby given the responsibility of confessing throughout their lives the salvation that is reckoned to her or him in baptism, to continue to love God and to keep themselves faithful to Christ and His church."[101]

The conclusion of church education for children, which is celebrated in worship when they attain the age of twelve to fourteen, is commonly also referred to as "confirmation," but it is not to be identified with acceptance into church membership. It is much more a question of two different processes that can both be celebrated. Nevertheless, young persons can be confirmed after the completion of their church instruction and, at the same time, other youth and adults can be received into the full membership of the church in one and the same service of worship.[102] In this service, the fulfillment of the congregation's promise given at the baptism of the children, that they be instructed in the Christian faith, becomes evident.[103] Meanwhile, the congregation prayerfully awaits the personal decision of faith and is ready to provide space for life and growth for the young persons in their midst until they are able to accept the responsibilities of full church membership based upon their own decision.[104] For all United Methodists, it is affirmed that both sides of God's saving acts take into account the unconditional love which reconciles the whole world to God through Christ and which promises salvation to all persons and the liberation and empowerment of believers to be able to make their own, personal affirmation, which activates their love for God and their acceptance as God's sons and daughters.

Baptism is not the new birth; that is true of the baptism of those who are mature as well as the immature. Nevertheless, it is a "sign of regeneration or the new birth."[105] Wesley's understanding of baptism, which remains strongly rooted in the Anglican tradition, has never been developed into a doctrine of baptism with the clarity one would wish for teaching purposes. For this reason, to the present day there is a wide variance in the theological understanding of baptism in Methodism.[106] If we take his statements on baptism as a whole and in their context, it can rightly be said that Wesley has achieved a "creative synthesis of objective and subjective elements,"[107] that is, he has continually joined together the basic objectivity of divine grace, as it comes to significant expression in baptism, and the necessity of the new birth, which is experienced as a special, inward event, through which the Holy Spirit allows faith to arise, which gives the event of salvation its subjective aspect. Baptism is an "external work," and the new birth is an invisible "change wrought by God in the soul."[108] Wesley certainly never gave up the doctrine of baptismal regeneration with reference to the baptism of infants.[109] However, it actually plays no role in the self-understanding of faith, because the operation of regeneration is lost through sin and the baptism of children does not mean that the new birth is unnecessary for persons of mature age—even among those who were baptized as adults.

Thus, it can be maintained that the baptism of children and regeneration essentially belong together. In both cases it is a matter of the different ways in which the grace of God is operating in relation to persons. Both events signify the beginning of one's life as a Christian. Both are directed to personal faith and to a living out of love, although they are almost always (temporally) distinct from one another.[110] Keeping this distinction in mind, it may be concluded that baptism and the new birth belong together as elements of God's saving activity with regard to individual human beings. The operation of both is received in faith, it is publicly announced in the confession of Christ, and it is sealed by one's admittance into the local congregation, which realizes membership in the body of Christ as a dynamic which entails the "renunciation of every form of half-heartedness" (Bishop C. E. Sommer).

4.2.2 *The Congregation as a Fellowship of Life and Service*

The new fellowship of brothers and sisters has arisen from such persons who have experienced the power of the Spirit of God. They know that they have been unconditionally accepted by God and have been freed for a new life in faith, hope, and love. At the same time, they know that the new life in Christ has only just begun with them. For its protection and nurture, they need fellowship with other Christians. Thus, one of the most important duties of a congregation is to accept the young, the wavering, and the weak into its midst and to make room for spiritual and human life to emerge for them. Together they build the new "house of God," for which Christ unites them, the "royal priesthood" of all believers, through whom Christ may continue his ministry in the world (1 Peter 2:5, 9).

In Methodism as well as in early Christianity, it was inevitable that a structured church would soon emerge out of this movement, as the history of all churches and congregations illustrates. On the other hand, implicit within this development are the lurking dangers of rigidity and narrowness. In The United Methodist Church, structures should be so fashioned that the entire multiplicity of gifts and possibilities for members can be ordered so they may share in the ministry of the gospel. This summons is applicable not only to a small group of ordained clergy or those who are delegated with the principal authority for ministry. Instead, the summons applies to all Christians. Christ is the "Head of the congregation," and therefore the decisive authority for the church. He leads and structures the congregation through his Spirit. He allows believers to recognize his will and he also grants to them the freedom and the power to do it.

This leading and structuring of the congregation takes place in a twofold manner. On the one hand, this occurs through the members of the congregation, who understand what Christ wants by hearing God's Word, so they may follow him with discernment. On the other hand, it occurs through the members who are called into a function of leadership (pastors, superintendents, and bishops), who interpret God's Word in each actual situation and spur on the congregation, as well as individuals, to discipleship. Ecclesial life is therefore structured in a twofold manner: through the working of the Holy Spirit in the congregation that is listening to God's Word and through the operation of the Spirit in the appointed commissions or offices of ministry.

(1.) The "general priesthood of all believers"[111] is founded upon the call of all disciples to hear the gospel and bear witness to it through word and deed. This "general call" is the office that is "charged to all Christians," so that they deploy their gifts appropriately. God's grace takes these talents into consideration, so that the rule of God can occur through them.

(2.) The "special" offices are not founded upon a hierarchy but for their part are founded in the fact that the church has need of them to fulfill its tasks. The unrelinquishable task of the Christian church, for whose fulfillment it exists and has its life, is the public proclamation of the gospel through Word and sacrament. To that end, called and authorized women and men are ordained to the office of "elder" (or pastor) in The United Methodist Church. They receive their assignments for ministry (after previous consultation) by the responsible bishop and they form a connectional fellowship of ministry within the church. To that end, they are given life membership in an annual conference.[112] As members of the people of God, they remain within the congregation, in whose midst they carry out their service. As proclaimers of the gospel and those commissioned by Christ, they also stand opposite to the congregation to which they are sent. However, their authority is none other than an authentic execution of the work of the gospel, together with their commission received through the church, that is bound up with that ministry.[113]

Both of the modes of leading a local congregation that have been described are dependent on the working of the Holy Spirit, and therefore they can only be exercised together, not in opposition to each other. They come into expression in The United Methodist Church because there is no hierarchical ordering of church offices; instead, all church members can work together in the conferences at different levels to do God's will. The discussion that is conducted there with mutual attentiveness, openness, and self-control is intended to serve to "increase the union between the preachers (as well as that of the people),"[114] through tasks such as synchronizing the doctrine, order, and the praxis of the church. It is based upon the hopeful expectation that God's Spirit may be active in this conversation. Likewise, this "democratic" procedure makes clear everyone's responsibility for the church, and especially the responsibility of the members of the conference, without thereby guaranteeing that this represents a full agreement with God's will. Every authority in the church must finally be based in the fact that it serves for the building up of the congregation and "is transparent for the working of God's grace."[115] This operation of the grace of God is possible whenever persons remain in constant relationship with God. It is the lifeblood for all believers, apart from which their existence as Christians would be without duration, stability, clarity of direction, and purpose and would have no energy to make progress with Christ. The congregation becomes the living context for the grace of God in the fellowship and life and service with Christ and with one another, in which a texture of relationships with one another allows its existence as the body of Christ to be experienced.

4.2.2.1 THE GATHERING OF THE CONGREGATION: WORSHIP

According to Wesley's conception, worship belongs among the means of grace. Despite this, we will be dealing with it now because it represents the central weekly gathering point for the congregation, and thus it tends to be the gathering point for all groups and for individual members of the congregation.

Each Sunday, in worship Christians celebrate their fellowship with God and the experience of the nearness of his rule in the congregation and in the world. They join in the common praise of our Creator, to whom belong the kingdom and the power and the glory forever. The congregation comes together in the different forms of common celebrating, experiencing, and listening to the Word of God. In hearing the Word of proclamation, in the celebration of the sacraments, and in their common confession of their Lord, they receive what they need in order that they may not lose courage nor despair, but rather move on the way in which God wants to lead them in this world. Through worship they receive new joy, as well as new power to remain with Christ on their way to the kingdom.

On the other hand, the service of worship is also the place to which they turn back from the realization of their tasks among people and their worship in the "daily life of the world," in order that they might share their experiences with one another and might upbuild those who have become tired and overstressed. They also come together to experience rest, to renew their strength, to share with one another the ways in which they have experienced God's love and leading, and to set out anew upon the path of discipleship.

Entering and departing, giving and receiving, remaining still and listening, finding one another and departing from one another, relieving and shouldering burdens—all of this and more can and should occur in a service of worship. In a gathering of soloists, who remain alien to one another and who simply worship "for themselves," all of this can only happen in a very limited manner. However, in its essence, a United Methodist congregation is one that is gathered under God's Word, and it is a fellowship of sisters and brothers who meet one another in the love of Christ. It is the place where persons are baptized and received into the congregation, where they receive the Lord's Supper together and send forth those who are called into ministry. Hence, worship is a presentation not of the pastor[116] but of the congregation. Members and groups from the congregation therefore work with the pastor—from the opening greeting to the organ postlude, and in the planning of church dinners.[117] The heart of worship remains the praise of God—in hearing the Word, in singing and praying with mouth and heart, and also with the service of our hands.[118] The fact that the singing that comes from the heart was once the sign of United Methodist fellowship, along with the active life of a Christian, is being experienced again today and will become more so.[119]

And finally, the service of worship experiences no alienation or desecration whenever it is combined with a congregational meeting in which there is discussion of common tasks, election of leaders of boards, or other decisions. The converse is true: worship can be protected from being misled into purely pragmatic forms of organization wherever the daily concerns with the Sunday service, as well as listening and acting, praise, and living are so closely bound together that they will be experienced as congruous parts of the life of the congregation.

Moreover, nowhere else does a congregation experience what it means to be a congregation of Jesus Christ in any comparable way. Further, the service of worship only functions as the central event of a Christian congregation at that point where it allows itself to be called together, given gifts, and sent out by God's Word.

4.2.2.2   THE SIGNIFICANCE OF THE MEANS OF GRACE

In his doctrine of the means of grace, Wesley distinguished between the "instituted means of grace" and the "prudential means of grace." Both kinds are given to Christians so they may live in continual fellowship with God.[120] Through this fellowship the grace of God desires to flow into us as through vessels. These means of grace connect the congregation like arteries do an organism, linking individual Christians to their Head, Jesus Christ. To be sure, this reception is not a procedure whereby God's grace could be made available to them like some kind of divine substance. By contrast, God himself enters into relationship with those persons who need his grace. God's Spirit makes use of them, leading their recipients into a clearer recognition of the will of God and filling them with heartfelt love.

The public service of worship, Communion, prayer, Bible study, and fasting belongs above all[121] to the means of grace.

(1.) Those who join together in the worship service within the local congregation are seekers and the faithful, the anxious and those who are certain of their salvation, the burdened and the liberated, in order to meet God together with their brothers and sisters. The preaching of the Word of God and fellowship strengthen faith, mediate hope and courage, and allow the path of discipleship to be discerned. The worship of God and the celebration of his blessings are important parts of the worship service on Sundays, the day of Christ's resurrection. On the special days in the church year persons are gratefully reminded of God's work for the salvation of the world. The reality of being bound together through their identity in Christ extends also to the sick, the old, and those brethren and sisters who are absent from the service of worship for other reasons, and they are all united together in the act of listening to God and in prayer.

(2.) The Lord's Supper (Holy Communion or the Eucharist), which was celebrated weekly or daily in the first centuries of Christianity and still is in many churches of our day,[122] is a remembrance of the suffering and the death of Jesus and a representation of the redemption which he has achieved for all persons. In the Lord's Supper, the resurrected Christ gives himself in the bread and the wine, the signs of his life that are given to all who receive them in reliance upon his promise. He offers forgiveness of their sins and liberates them to a new life that is based upon faith.[123] The congregation brings its thanksgiving for the reconciliation of the world with God and its hope for God's future consummation of his saving work. The extremely high value placed upon the Lord's Supper by John and Charles Wesley was never fully shared by the European continent nor by North America. The cause for this cannot lie in the fact that the first small classes were formed only from among laypersons. That was equally if not more so the case for United Methodist churches. As in Pietism, one senses here "a contradiction between the holiness of the Lord's Supper and the unholy lives of the communicants,"[124] so that the need for special preparation[125] and lofty conditions for participation in the Supper were established. To some extent, this also reflected the influence of the state churches, where increasingly the Lord's Supper was separated from the main worship service and the number of celebrations and participants declined steeply.

Within the last three decades, change has occurred both in the understanding of the Lord's Supper and in the manner and frequency of its celebration.[126] The emphasis upon an earnest self-examination has not vanished, but it is directed less to the quality of the persons who are to commune (and of their actions) and more to the earnestness and the sincerity of persons' longings for that which Christ gives in the Supper. The fact that such earnest longing is inherently linked with one's ethical conduct is not to be overlooked.

In the celebration of the Lord's Supper,[127] there are different aspects of the New Testament message that come into play. It signifies the remembrance of Jesus' death and is a representation of his reconciling work, the celebration of fellowship, as well as the eschatological hope of the believing community. As with baptism, the Lord's Supper is a "sign of the new covenant" with God. However, for those who participate in this meal, its meaning becomes something different than in baptism, for participating in the Lord's Supper means that "the salvation made available in Christ" is continually being given anew, and these promises are now being seen and tasted in the signs of the bread and wine. "Here the Holy Spirit makes us . . . certain of our fellowship with the ascended Lord and with the pardon He extends."[128] Finally, the frequency of the celebration of the Lord's Supper has again increased, but it has not yet attained the standard envisioned by Wesley, who advocated the weekly celebration of the Lord's Supper in worship.[129]

God's Spirit can both lead persons into faith through participation in the celebration of the Lord's Supper and strengthen them in its certainty. God can renew them in their consecration to Christ and to their fellow human beings, and also in their consecration to assume responsibility in all areas of their lives. For Wesley, an important consideration was that the Lord's Supper can be received as a means of grace in either its prevenient, justifying, or sanctifying aspects.[130] And because an earnest desire for this working of God's grace appeared to him to be more important than some special kind of preparation, United Methodists continue to celebrate an "open table" in the Lord's Supper. No one is excluded who desires either to experience fellowship with Christ or to be renewed in that relationship. It is not the congregation but Christ who invites persons to his meal. And whoever is invited should have access to his table. Hence, the celebration of the Lord's Supper also has a missionary dimension, since it is open to all "uncertain, unconverted seekers of salvation."[131] Their "worthiness," through which they are authorized to participate in the Lord's Supper, does not lie in any moralistic perfection or sinless conduct of life, but in their need and their desire to be blessed by Christ. Unrepentedness and unloving behavior, however, contradict the meaning of the Lord's Supper and bring under condemnation those who shut themselves off in this way to the work of the Spirit. Those who have lightly valued sisters and brothers, and with them, Christ himself, "without discerning the body" of the Lord, consequently "eat and drink judgment against themselves" (see 1 Corinthians 11:29).

While preaching, baptism, and the Lord's Supper are the central means of grace, which are also cited in the normative theological statements in United Methodism,[132] it is also true that additional "means of grace" are provided by Christ for his congregation: prayer, searching the Scripture, fellowship (class meetings and small groups), and fasting. They too do not find their meaning in themselves, as though their use were intrinsically meritorious.[133] However, they present a possibility of allowing persons to open themselves to the Word and the work of the Spirit of God and thus to receive the clarity and power for pursuing the path of Christian discipleship. Prayer, Bible study, and fasting can be used by individual Christians by themselves but also in fellowship with others—in the family, in groups, or in the congregation.

Through these "means," God's grace wants to work within those who truly desire it. Thus, no limitation is imposed for the operation of grace, as though it could only operate through these "channels." It can also reach and transform persons through numerous other ways. However, everything that may be designated as a means of grace has been entrusted by Christ to his community and is furnished with his promise, so that ignoring them would not only be unfortunate for individual Christians but would also be contrary to God's will. Through their use, God wants to meet all persons as those who are loved and blessed and he intends for fellowship with him to be an inexhaustible source of life for them.

Hence, the denial and the emptying of these forms remain dangers to be avoided. Forms wait to be filled. God's grace needs instruments in order to reach persons.[134]

4.2.2.3 THE CONGREGATION AND MINISTRY GROUPS

The beginnings of the Methodist movement were characterized by a double strategy, whose goal it was to win persons for life with Christ and to lead them upon that path. At about the same time (1739), under pressure from George Whitefield, Wesley began preaching in the open air, and he thereby gave the "classes" that emerged from this labor their distinctive structure. His concern for persons in general did not mean that he would abandon his concern for individual persons, and the concern for small groups did not narrow his sights, which extended to the entire land, including all of humanity. While our discussion of missions and evangelization is reserved for a later point (Section 4.3.3), here we intend to look at the form, the tasks, and the significance of groups in The United Methodist Church.

"The koinonia of the Christian life is experienced in its most typical and intensive form in the smaller groups of Methodism."[135] Whether Wesley's "classes" present a viable model for the structuring and nurture of that kind of fellowship *(koinonia)* is—once again—disputed. Yet, "It is rewarding to study this model for Christian fellowship."[136] What was distinctive about this model, and what could be reclaimed for our day? Every local fellowship was composed of groups of about twelve members, who had a layperson as leader. What was distinctive about these "classes" was the accountability they provided with respect to both participation in the weekly meeting and also the preparedness to speak about the faith and discipleship of the group members and thereby to "watch over one another in love."[137] Bible study and prayer certainly were included in their obligations as class members, as was the collection of contributions for the tasks of the fellowship. Class leaders were carefully selected, and for their preparation they were required to give special attention to writings recommended by Wesley. Moreover, class leaders were required to visit members at least once per week in order to advise, admonish, comfort, and, if it proved necessary, to provide assistance.

In the first decades of the movement, this model functioned extremely well to the extent that it contributed decisively to the extension and strengthening of Methodism. Living fellowship and Christianity that was lived in accountability were promoted through the class system. This was also true of other countries in which Methodist congregations developed. However, with the ecclesial institutionalization of Methodism, "the most intimate forms of fellowship for the most part disappeared." Nevertheless, "the structures for small groups, even if they are looser in form, always need to be emerging anew in Methodism, in light of the constant need for closer contacts in faith and life."[138]

This need is being addressed in differing ways in The United Methodist Church of our day. Both in Europe and in North America, small groups, house meetings, and a growing number of spontaneously formed growth groups within congregations have persisted, alongside the required ministry groups[139] that are charged with carrying out specific tasks on behalf of the congregation. These spontaneous groups meet regularly and they are dedicated either to the spiritual growth of their members, the sharing of spiritual journeys, and corporate praise to God and intercessory prayer, or to specific tasks to which they commit themselves. In European Methodism, it is noteworthy that official congregational groups, which were supposed to take the place and function of the earlier class meetings following church union in 1968, are described in their adapted version of the *Book of Discipline* as follows: "Through the charge conference, there should be established for the church membership and constituency a plan for nurturing fellowship and pastoral care through small groups within each congregation. The members of these groups are also to seek spiritual contact with persons outside their membership, and conduct house visitations, as well as forming home-based Bible study groups and prayer fellowships" (Kirchenordnung, 1992, ¶ 123).

In North America, the local United Methodist congregation is charged with the more open-ended mandate to provide "opportunities for persons to seek strengthening and growth in spiritual formation," which entails "planning and implementing a program of nurture, outreach, and witness for persons and families within and without the congregation" (*UM Book of Discipline*, 1996, ¶ 245). However, only one line appears that allows that "a structure for classes, class leaders, and class meetings may be organized within the local congregation" (¶ 261). The formation of such congregational groups in present-day United Methodism has had partial success. What is needed is a far more pervasive reflection on these needs and a more intensive sharing of experiences in order to convey the following goals with one another, goals that have often been harbingers of tensions: (1) the standard of accountability, which presupposes a relatively high degree of openness and mutual trust, and the need to establish contact with outside persons, who are not easily won over to such intimate accountability with one another; (2) the need for sociable gatherings in which the members can introduce themselves and share the abundance of their gifts, and the necessity of a biblical-ethical orientation for daily living; (3) the respect for free decisions, in view of the measure and the manner in which individuals engage themselves, and the need for integration of the congregation as a whole, apart from which there can be no congregational groups the way their name implies, but only private circles. If it is correct that the koinonia within United Methodism is experienced and lived above all in small groups that function to enhance personal accountability, then a rewarding piece of work is waiting to be carried out by those who hold responsibility in the congregation and the entire church.[140] A church that allows the element of accountability to be missing in its local structures or that reduces it to the obligation of collecting contributions from members is able to expect accountability as the inner condition of its members neither there nor on the level of the larger connection (the annual, jurisdictional, or general conference levels). Things that do not grow in a context that is overseeable will not be able to bear fruit as a larger entity either.

On the other hand, the ministry groups are an essential element of all local churches. Sunday schools, children and youth groups, and congregational choirs often fulfill their tasks with great initiative and enthusiasm on the part of those who are responsible, together with their coworkers. The women's ministry is active even in most of the smallest of congregations. Together with the lay preachers, the ministry groups form the personnel backbone of the work of the church, and, as a rule, pastors and congregations know what they have in them. The fact that a certain number of members or constituents of the congregation oppose these groups, members who either are not ready or are not in a position to cooperate in the ministry of the church, must repeatedly become an occasion for the supervising activities and ministry structure provided by the charge conference.[141] If they are not functioning, for what purpose were they called to life? Are they active but demoralized or do they arouse joy in being colaborers in the gospel? Do they realize their talents, or are they too busily engaged in placing demands upon those in the church who are charged with responding to requests? Wesley's maxim, "all for the work and always for the work," with the two-sided "all/always," is an exorbitant demand and hence not to be understood in a literal sense. The commission which Christ has given to his disciples, that no gifts may simply lie fallow, makes the cooperative and freely and willingly given work of all those who are able an important purpose of building awareness within the church.

4.2.2.4   *Connexio:* The United Methodist Church as a "Connectional" Church

It may be surprising to some that the term *connection* is here referred to as a structure of The United Methodist Church.[142] Thus, we must ask, what does *connexio* mean? What is it, and what is its meaning and purpose for the church?

The meaning of *connexio* for the entire Methodist movement concerns those things that groups are supposed to accomplish on the level of the local fellowship. "Movement" and "connection" have been two significant signs of Methodism from its beginning.[143] A suitable English synonym for this may be *connectedness*[144] which is to be understood in contradistinction to the hierarchical structures that prevail within the Roman Catholic and Eastern Orthodox churches, as well as in contrast with the independence of individual congregations in the congregational type of church polity. Unlike these options, United Methodism seeks to lay hold upon and nurture the mutual, living connection among congregations and charges and conferences. Wesley provided tight leadership for the connection in his lifetime, because he was convinced that he carried an appropriate responsibility for the souls of the persons entrusted to his oversight, who had come to personal faith through his preaching or through that of his lay preachers. Together with his brother Charles and a series of preachers, he made provision in a timely manner for the continuation of that connection after his death[145] and in the "Deed of Declaration" (1784) appointed the annual conference of the preachers to be the chief instrument of leadership. Hence, to the present day, the annual conference is the "basic corporate structure" of the church (Article X of the Constitution of The United Methodist Church), which now consists of a parity of lay and clergy delegates. In this structure, all aspects of this network, which is the connection, come together as these are reflected in the connectedness of the congregations and of the charges. The principle of this connectionalism, which a well-known church historian once characterized as "one of the greatest contributions made by Wesley to ecclesiastical polity,"[146] is supposed to help to mitigate the egoism of the congregation and strengthen the solidarity of congregations with one another and with the church as a whole. As an ellipse has two foci, so does the connectional system have a "helpful, serving centralization on the one hand and an optimal autonomy for congregations on the other—both are, as it were, fitted together."[147] Methodism will always depend on holding together in a dynamic fashion the tension between being a movement and a connection, and between individual congregations and the sense of being a church in a larger context.[148]

The inner meaning of this connection therefore has a threefold dimension. First of all, there is the sense that its members remain in contact with God. This connection is the lifeblood without which Christians would neither endure nor have life. Second, from that basis, Christians come to experience a precious fellowship with one another, in which the unity that has already been given to them in Christ becomes concrete. Every living Christian congregation also allows the mutual love of members one for the other to enable others to observe what is the true content of the gospel. Through them, Christ wants to find visible expression in the world. As Dietrich Bonhoeffer once said, Christ intends to exist as a congregation within the world. Third, Christians thus seek to be connected with other congregations and also with other persons outside the church. They do this not as a supplemental task that does not belong to their being as Christians. Instead, this threefold connection becomes something that essentially belongs together, which signifies a defining characteristic of the church. It must be made recognizable that they are indeed a connectional church, yet not in an exclusive sense but in the sense of Christ's mission to the entire world.

The concept of the covenant, of which we have already spoken repeatedly, may also be recalled in this context. This allows us to think that our fellowship as a realm of experience and as an instrument of God's actions has its source in the promise of God. God has entered into fellowship with us, so that we might have new life, that we might lead our life differently—including in it not only ourselves and those who are like us, but again and again looking at the entire creation from God's perspective.

There is a relationship between these three dimensions of connection: the more firmly persons are connected with Christ and with one another, the further they can go without having to worry about themselves. The looser their connection with Christ and his congregation, the greater becomes the danger of slipping out of that quality of life that is lived in God's will and allowing oneself to be influenced by other principles or ideologies or simply by a false attraction to the spirit of their age ("Zeitgeist"). Freedom and being in connection are therefore not only not mutually exclusive; on the contrary, they presuppose one another.

This fellowship of Christians with one another also safeguards their connectedness in those times in which it is not possible for them to come together for common celebration, listening, and singing. In this regard, we need only recall the example of the fellowship of United Methodism in Europe that persisted for decades despite borders separating East and West. Congregations in Europe will not forget those invaluable experiences made during a time when the authorities in the East and the West erected walls between them: they were walls made of stone or of money, walls made of images of enemies or of physical threats, and walls made of class hatred or of anti-Communism. The walls were not all of the same height, nor were all impenetrable, but they were real and they were dangerous. They destroyed human life and bisected human fellowship.

Despite all of this, the members remained bound together as one body in Christ. Despite all of this, they recognized one another as sisters and brothers whenever the opportunity of meeting together was afforded them. That strengthened their confidence that God's kingdom extends further than do the boundaries of earthly power blocs.

As we have already indicated, the connectional system finds its structural identity in the conferences of the church, which include (1) the annual conference, which consists of all pastors under appointment and an equal number of lay delegates; (2) the jurisdictional conferences (or central conferences, in areas outside North America), in which the annual conferences are grouped together; and (3) the general conference, which is responsible for the worldwide United Methodist Church. The conferences cited under (2) and (3) meet every four years. Specific responsibilities are assigned to these bodies, which are to be fulfilled by the larger church. The jurisdictional and central conferences are responsible for matters pertaining to the evangelistic, educational, missionary, and social efforts and programs, and for the election and assignment of bishops to their episcopal areas.

The general conference is responsible for revising and adopting the *Book of Discipline* (and in the case of the central conferences, the adaptation of that book) for use by the church. The general conference consists of a concise ten thousand delegates, including both clergy and laity, from all areas of the worldwide church,[149] and is responsible for formulating and adopting the international tasks and programs of the church, the protection of the constitution of the church (through the Judicial Council), and it is also responsible for adopting legislation needed for the whole church.

Finally, on the other end of the scale there are also charge conferences for each pastoral charge in the church, which are responsible for the church work of one or more congregations. The foundational and thus most important conference is the annual conference. It is the place in which each year the work of all church activities and programs, and of all boards and commissions, which have responsibility for particular areas of ministry, is reported and deliberated. It elects persons who are given responsibility for this work as well as the delegates to the jurisdictional (or central) and general conferences, and it is responsible for the financial support of the work of the church. Changes in the constitution that have been approved by a two-thirds vote of the general conference require a two-thirds vote of approval by the delegates to the annual conferences.

Although such decisions are only seldom made, the task of theological consensus-building and the execution of their activities according to the content of the Bible and doctrinal norms of our church are among the permanent and ongoing functions of the annual conferences. The conciliar principle of church leadership is used in the theological and organizational activities of the annual conferences and in their working groups, as a common responsibility of its specifically Methodist feature as a "connexio." This responsibility also was established "for the discovery of truth in obedience to Jesus Christ and for the realization of His mandate in worship and witness, service and fellowship."[150] The openness to the work of the Holy Spirit and the use of established (and changeable) structures thus do not need to be seen as being in conflict. Instead, as conference members pay due heed to these connectional duties, they can preserve the church from paralysis as well as from an unspiritual fracturing of its powers.

The United Methodist *Book of Discipline* (1996) has undergone significant changes as a result of legislative action at the 1996 General Conference of the Church. In particular, the office of diaconal ministers, who had been consecrated to a nonordained, nondiaconal service as an extension of the ministry of the Church, has been replaced by the permanent order of deacons, which is a nonitinerating order of ordained ministry that is added to the order of itinerating elders. Deacons are ordained to a ministry of service and of the Word, whereas elders are ordained to the ministry of Word, sacrament, service, and order. It is significant that elders also carry responsibility for service.

A second major change concerns local church structure: there are now fewer "shall be" provisions and more options for organizing the work of a local congregation, under the direction of a local "charge conference" and a "church council" that meets between the annual sessions of that conference. This indicates a shift away from an episcopal in the direction of a more congregational understanding of polity.

There is now more emphasis placed upon general church boards and agencies serving as facilitators of the work of the local congregation, and this may well entail significant restructuring of those boards and agencies at forthcoming general conferences. Annual conferences are increasingly becoming realigned to conform to state boundaries and to reflect regional identity, so that, in the words of Thomas Frank, they are becoming "a peculiar blend of covenant community and regional labor union."[151]

Local pastors, who serve congregations without ordination, are now eligible to apply for ordination after meeting certain educational requirements, and now deacons, elders, and local pastors are all entitled to vote as clergy in conference matters. Increased functions have been given to bishops, including their appointment of deacons to their places of service—whereas formerly diaconal ministers were regulated through the Board of Diaconal Ministry—and bishops also have received responsibility for judicial decisions.

4.3   The Church as the Mission of God

Mission means sending out, in relation to the Christian faith. It means the sending of persons by God, whom Jesus Christ has revealed as the One who loves all persons. Thus, mission is first and foremost God's action, "the action of the God of grace,"[152] but then it is also, in a derived sense, the task of all Christians as their grateful response to what God has done and is doing. Christianity has observed this task in the course of its history in quite different ways. The early church missionized by its mere existence. Through the preaching of the apostles, through the pattern of church fellowship and social service, and through the faithfulness of its church members, it intentionally and increasingly changed its society. After the establishment of Christianity as an imperial church, the work of mission increased both in extent and in structure, but it also began to reflect tendencies that were fraught with peril. Alongside the preaching of monks, who pressed to the North and the East and who also introduced cultural and political changes alongside the Christian message, Christianity was now spread as the religion that helped consolidate imperial unity through such methods of force as wars and enforced baptisms. An especially dark chapter in this history is the conquest of Latin America under the sign of the cross. What should have happened as disseminating the legacy of Christ's love that Christians had received and a call to fellowship with God was repeatedly misused for the benefit of conquering individuals and whole peoples. The missionary history of the Christian church contains some dark chapters, which we cannot unwrite.[153] While the concern for world mission receded into the background in the era of the Protestant Reformation and the subsequent era of Protestant Orthodoxy, the eighteenth and nineteenth centuries—particularly on the basis of Pietism and a theology of awakening—set in motion a strong missionary movement which continues into the present century.

In our understanding of Christian mission it is fully clear: mission can only be a free offer of God's grace, which is not permitted to rob persons of their freedom nor of their cultural identity. This grace should serve to liberate persons within the context of the sociocultural milieu in which they live, which includes their liberation from sin, unrighteousness, and all those forces that tend to destroy life. For the mission of the church arises as the mission of God's saving acts, and through this it receives its substantial and methodical character. God's active presence within the world *is* grace; it is love in action. Thus, true Christian mission always has the character of "giving our lives in sacrificial love."[154]

This theme is reflected in the Social Principles of The United Methodist Church as follows:

> We acknowledge our complete dependence upon God in birth, in life, in death, and in life eternal. Secure in God's love, we affirm the goodness of life and confess our many sins against God's will for us as we find it in Jesus Christ. We have not always been faithful stewards of all that has been committed to us by God the Creator. We have been reluctant followers of Jesus Christ in his mission to bring all persons into a community of love. Though called by the Holy Spirit to become new creatures in Christ, we have resisted the further call to become the people of God in our dealings with each other and the earth on which we live.
>
> Grateful for God's forgiving love, in which we live and by which we are judged, and affirming our belief in the inestimable worth of each individual, we renew our commitment to become faithful witnesses to the gospel, not alone to the ends of earth, but also to the depths of our common life and work.[155]

Accordingly, from its beginnings The United Methodist Church has assigned a special significance to mission.[156] To belong to Christ means to be sent into the world. The world is to experience the same love with which Christ has loved us. The gospel that attests to this love is therefore passed along to others. "As the Father has sent me, so I send you," said the resurrected Christ to his disciples (John 20:21), and he sends them to those persons who are called to adoption as children of God. The personal confession of faith and the loving social acts, witness and service, belong together in this mission. They mutually enlarge and strengthen one another. Love for God thus belongs together with love for the neighbor, "with . . . a passion for justice and renewal in the life of the world."[157]

Passing the gospel on to other persons—persons who do not yet know or have not yet comprehended its central meaning for their lives—is part of the commission of the church in a comprehensive sense. This proclamation of the gospel in one's own country is usually designated as "evangelization"; through it persons are led into fellowship with Christ and faith in him. We are increasingly directing the mission of the church in other lands in ways that harmonize with those Christians and churches which already exist in those places. It includes not only the preaching of the gospel but also the service of love and the gathering of the congregation. Both modes of mission are an essential part of the life of the church.

For Wesley, mission was even the key to understanding the gospel in its original meaning, because it is heard and read differently in the mission context than in a land that has been marked by the presence of Christianity for centuries.[158] Under the influence of Pietism (esp. Philip Jakob Spener and A. H. Francke), the external mission of the church received a new impetus, since Pietism on the one hand tried to perceive the traces of the kingdom of God emerging within history but on the other was also ready to take part in the "work of the kingdom of God." It was no longer the expectation of the coming of the last judgment but the experience of God's saving acts in this world that became the basis for numerous missionary and diaconal activities, which one saw being developed here. The "experience of grace and the love of God, which one traces within one's own conversion and awakening, is placed within the context of a rich missionary and especially a diaconal activity of love," that became manifest in the various Anglo and American revivals as well as in the German awakening movement. The growth of the kingdom of God is accomplished as "a gradual penetration of all natural and historical ordinances with the Christian Spirit."[159] The church bears witness to the world, proclaiming and embodying its witness to the Lordship of Christ. It does not require its hearers finally to be subordinated to the worldwide reign of Jesus Christ. Instead, they are invited to entrust themselves to this Lord through personal faith. The "free invasion of love" (Emilio Castro), which God has initiated in Jesus Christ, is the point of departure for the mission task of the church. In selecting suitable means to achieve this, the church orients itself to the message of the gospel as well as to those persons to whom it would bring the gospel. "Offer them Christ!" was Wesley's charge to his first assistants whom he sent over the Atlantic Ocean to the American colonies. And it is also true here that above all Christ should be brought to those who need him the most. It is particularly the liberation theologians who remind those of us who live in the rich nations that "in Christ, God fully identifies Himself with the oppressed, the suffering, and the persecuted."[160]

Within this wider context, mission is therefore the witness of the church of Jesus Christ, a response to God's presence in the world and a sign of the rule of God. Our fathers and mothers up to the time of the Second World War understood all church activity to be the work of mission in this sense.[161] "The heart of Christian ministry is Christ's ministry of outreaching love. Christian ministry is the expression of the mind and mission of Christ by a community of Christians that demonstrates a common life of gratitude and devotion, witness and service, celebration and discipleship. All Christians are called to this ministry of servanthood in the world to the glory of God and for human fulfillment."[162] Thus, Christians do not have to choose whether they intend to participate in missions or not. They have undertaken this task by virtue of their decision for Christ and for a life with him under the Great Commission of Christ, which is part and parcel of being a Christian congregation. The connectional framework of The United Methodist Church also is authorized to uphold this task, in which persons from the congregational level serve in common with those on the level of the worldwide church, including laity, theologians, and pastors, together with other coworkers.

4.3.1 *The Witness of Individual Christians*

In a pluralistic, overwhelmingly secular society, the work of missions is certainly more necessary and perhaps more difficult than it is in a Christianized society. In any case, it is true that individual Christians, if they intend to live by their calling, are easier to identify in that kind of society. Their life achievements are inevitably a witness for what they believe and for how they understand themselves. That applies in a positive as well as in a negative sense. Either they are a "letter of Christ," as Paul wrote to the Corinthians (2 Corinthians 3:3), or they deform the content of the Christian faith through their conduct and their words or they function as Christians only in an on-again, off-again manner. However, they are seen, and the meaning of Christianity comes to be understood as a mosaic, whose pattern is read according to the perceived conduct of Christians. In this regard, our times resemble those of the early Christian centuries, with the difference that Christianity is no longer a young religion, but rather it carries along with it a two-thousand-year-old history, by which it lives and which burdens it. Added to this is open communication, which is primarily characterized by the electronic media of our day, in whose polyphonic voices the preaching of the gospel can sometimes scarcely be heard. And finally, the picture to which Christians and churches have borne witness in their life with and opposed to one another has often not operated in an inviting manner toward those persons who ought to be won to that confidence in the One who is love.

Hence, from a long-range perspective, missionary efforts are only significant if individual Christians are faithful witnesses for their Lord. The cessation of material benefits or social position allows the question of coming to Christ to be directed to the center of Christian existence and its single content: the new life in Christ. However, if this is not recognizable in the context of the actual lives of Christians, then the verbal proclamation of the gospel is not convincing, and Christians unintentionally become counterarguments to the message that they themselves believe. They have then ceased to be the salt of the earth and the light of the world.

Hence, those who are not church officials or pastors, namely, the so-called laity, are the ones who are the chief bearers of the mission of God. "The layman lives and works in that world, he knows its language and its pressures."[163] They do not bear this responsibility alone, for here is also where the connectional context of United Methodism comes into play. However, without them the significant concepts of mission can be neither developed or actualized. The movement of God's love to humanity—and mission is nothing besides this—needs all who have experienced this love to be its bearers.

4.3.1.1 FAITH AND LIFESTYLE

In the year 1743, John and Charles Wesley published a report on the beginnings of the Methodist societies (the "United Societies"[164]), and of their arrangement into classes, which had already been undertaken soon after the beginning of the movement. In small groups of twelve persons each, persons were to help one another to find and walk the way to Christ. In order that this could take place seriously, after preliminary experiences with negligent members, rules were formulated and membership cards were distributed. In these "General Rules," particular attention was paid to being aware that being a Christian was not to consist of theoretical convictions or external customs but rather to consist of persons being transformed by the message of the gospel both in their inmost beings and in their entire daily conduct. Therefore, it is stated very clearly in the Rules that those who earnestly seek God's salvation and desire to remain in fellowship with one another should manifest their godly intention "by doing good; by being in every kind merciful after their power; as they have opportunity, doing good of every possible sort, and, as far as possible, to all men."[165] The celebration of worship, the personal encounters of believers with one another, and their common departure for service in the world has since then been part of the self-understanding of United Methodists. They should trust in the fact that Christ can use them, to work through them in their sphere of living and beyond. "Therefore, they refuse every inactive form of Christian living, whose misinterpretation of the doctrine of justification by grace alone leads them not to take seriously the task which is given to all Christians. Hence, Christians refuse every form of superficial activism which does not see its beginning and basis in the word of Christ. . . . They also refuse every illusory perfectionism, which no longer takes into consideration the weaknesses and errors, as well as the fallibility of believers."[166]

It all comes down to life together and the correct relationship of "inward" and "outward": a purely inner Christianity, which above all serves to nurture one's own (private) spirituality and which thereby overlooks the importance of good works operating outwardly in one's life, is a spirituality that buries a person's talents (Matthew 25:14-30) and harms the love commandment through egotistical inactivity. The adherence to Christian norms, as these are described in the General Rules, may operate impressively without the depth dimension of faith and love, and bring about much good, but it ignores the One from whom everything good comes and apart from whom no one can do good. Wesley gave explicit warnings of such a flattening of the Christian life. "We do not place the whole of religion (as too many do, God knoweth) either in doing no harm, or in doing good, or in using the ordinances of God. No, nor in all of them together, wherein we know by experience a man may labour many years, and at the end have no true religion at all, no more than he had at the beginning."[167]

The lifestyle of a Christian needs to be genuine; the goodness of one's acts must derive from the goodness of the person, whom the Holy Spirit has transformed and continues to transform. Everything that is contrived and is put on for show does not arise from the actual renewal of a person, but arises for a purpose which seeks to attain secondary goals by the use of such behavior, such as pleasing other persons (or God), getting something back, or similar goals. However, good fruit only grows on a good tree, and the goodness of the tree (or the person) is based upon the action of God. The question of the concrete form that is assumed by the lifestyle of a Christian, as well as of a missionary, must therefore be answered with reference to the Source of all good things. By being connected to that

Source, persons are able to receive a lifestyle that conforms to the gospel, and their attitudes and modes of behavior receive their appropriate character. Since we neither can, nor need to earn God's goodwill, the impulse of love grows out of this connection, which has in its purview the well-being of one's neighbor. The way to the inward life, to personal fellowship with God, will therefore be expressed by itself as a movement from within to acts that are undertaken for the sake of other persons and of the whole creation.

And conversely, the insight is correct that one's fellowship with God is made complete in the service to others.[168] "In this manner, we do not arrive at a state of coexistence but to one of pro-existence with our fellow human beings, whom God loves and who so need the conviction of the love of God in our day."[169] This "pro-existence"[170] as a human mode of existence leads to a diaconal-missionary lifestyle, which enables the gospel to become visible. How important this is immediately becomes apparent when one considers how few persons are reached through what is preached. In such a situation, a loveless manner of acting can destroy even the small possibilities for bearing witness to the faith.[171] In a positive version we hear Jesus saying "Let your light shine before others, so that they may see your good works and give glory to your Father in heaven" in a positive light.[172]

It is inevitable and also significant from the standpoint of missionary activity that such a lifestyle continually stands in contrast with that of other persons. This is not to argue that there is to be a principle of non-conformity, meaning a Christian must always be able to be differentiated from a non-Christian even in matters of outward appearance and conduct. This would tend toward trivializing Christian life and overvaluing things that are external, as we can discover by studying the history of our church.

In early Methodism, there were two substantial criteria for the individual or social form of a Christian lifestyle: love, which grants and does good to others, and the conviction that everything we have is not our own but was entrusted to us by God, to be used in accordance with his will. Simplicity and the willingness to share, impartiality toward money and the duty to use it for good and the aid of others, joy and contentment with what God gives, and the avoidance of luxury and indolence—those were concrete signs of the lifestyle Wesley imagined and himself practiced.[173] The sum of the whole remains: the inner change that was brought about through the Spirit of God, as well as through one's entire conduct of living, which gradually comes to express the reality of that change, is responsibly handled. The preserving effect of salt and the illuminating effect of the light need not be sought, for they appear by themselves.

4.3.1.2 THE PERSONAL WITNESS OF FAITH

In the course of church history, and especially under the influence of the theology of the Reformation, with its high regard for the quality of the sermon, the proclamation of the gospel has increasingly become a task of the professionals. Added to that, in our time there has arisen an increasing inarticulateness regarding the basic content of the Christian faith, as well as a certain timidity to speak with others concerning matters that deal with one's most inward issues. Even among Christians, there are adherents to an attitude that has been disseminated in a pluralistic society that proceeds from the view that, when it comes to questions of religion, each one should live according to one's own private convictions. Taken together, that has greatly raised the threshold for a personal witness of faith.

On the other hand, little is more impressive and convincing today than a witness from "person to person" that is undergirded by careful reflection and personal experience. A pastor's sermon is a function of his office, and the suspicion is not easily dismissed that pastors speak as they do simply because they are obligated by their call to do so. Personal witness does not stand under this suspicion, since it does not appear to be linked to any generally recognized compensation. Therefore, such a witness carries a higher sense of credibility than the professional talk of pastors and other functionaries of the church. Moreover, since all believers are called to bear witness to Christ and to their attitude to him, there are both internal and external reasons to take this ministry more seriously and to train the members of the congregation more carefully in this than has formerly been done. Based upon the reasons cited above, there are certainly linguistic difficulties in making the content of the gospel intelligible to other persons and to make evident its relevance for their lives, particularly when those persons increasingly lack any prior Christian socialization. After undertaking a basic preparation, practicing the personal sharing of faith stories is learned. Both the linguistic capabilities and the courage to witness grow once one has begun.[174] This congregational passing on of the biblical faith to others is not only an important support at the beginning of one's Christian life; it also guards against the proliferation of eccentric, individualistic approaches to witnessing, through which the testimony of the gospel can be falsified. Yet, the vital tenets of Scripture that have been grasped should always become integrally bound together with one's personal witness in these testimonies. They should help to make evident how a principle of faith or of action has been authenticated, what experiences someone has had with prayer, and how God's nearness and guidance have become evident amid difficult life situations, even if the expected and requested divine help was not realized. It is precisely the personal significance that depends on actual experiences that can help make the biblical statements become credible and genuine. The great significance of the personal witness of faith lies in this.

Living Christians, who have allowed themselves to be given the courage for this kind of personal articulation of their faith, and who do not avoid conscious preparation for this service, can help to facilitate the possibility that other persons will be able to come into contact at a quite "normal" level with the claims of the Christian faith, as it is actually being lived out by persons in our day. Most of those who come to faith today have found their way by means of these simple messengers.[175]

4.3.1.3   THE CALL TO THE MINISTRY OF PROCLAMATION

The ministry of proclamation in The United Methodist Church takes place through clergy and laypersons who are called to that office. It is part of the task that has been given to all members of the church: to bear witness to the gospel of Jesus Christ in all the world. Individual members are called by Christ into a special responsibility, just as took place through the earthly ministry of Jesus and as is reported of the church in all ages. The structure of this ministry did not take form, nor does it in our day, by means of a rigid schema, but in a manner that conforms to the need of congregations and the gifts given by God.[176] To this day, the church regards the form of full-time service to be a task which is to be constituted ever anew in responsibility before God and for the sake of those persons whom the gospel is to reach.[177] However, in spite of all the difference within the United Methodist church family, as well as in Protestant Christianity as a whole, the ordained ministry has certain common traits, which can perhaps be named as follows: "In the succession of the apostolic ministry, they (that is, the pastors) receive the task of gathering together and upbuilding the body of Christ through the preaching and instruction of the Word of God, as well as through the sacraments, and to lead the life of the congregation in worship, in its mission and in its pastoral service."[178] Thus, the ordained officeholders serve the congregation. They come from it and are sent to it—not least to equip the members of the congregation for service (Ephesians 4:11). So, in response to the question why in general the ordained office of ministry is required, it may be said, "With this, the church, including all of its members, remains ready for immediate action and it can fulfill its tasks."[179]

Three distinct traditions have flowed together into the present understanding of office in The United Methodist Church. (1) The Pauline tradition of ordering the congregation, in which the office—with the authority that is authorized by Christ—is anchored in the partnership of all co-laborers of the congregation. (2) The tradition of the office of preacher in the Protestant Reformation, in which those who are ordained gather and tend to the congregation through Word and sacrament. (3) The tradition of the Methodist and EUB traveling preachers, who are sent by the annual conference to their fields of labor.

If we take into consideration that, in the English-speaking lands and the United Methodist churches that are strongly shaped by them, the influence of the Anglican understanding of the offices of ministry has resulted in an emphasis upon ordination and the threefold office of deacon, elder, and bishop, which is stronger than the understanding that exists within German-speaking United Methodism, then a fourth element of tradition is added, which reinforces the tensions within the self-understanding of pastors, but which sees their position as a particularly appropriate exercise in bridge-building.[180]

Nevertheless, it is quite possible to describe the office of a pastor in The United Methodist Church very precisely, as a glance at the *Book of Discipline* shows. The way into the full-time office of preaching is clearly regulated there: the home congregation recommends an applicant, whose aptitude and credibility convince one of that person's call to ministry. Then follows a mentoring period, which entails oversight by a supervising pastor, for the purpose of safeguarding and deepening the certainty of their call, as well as displaying their capabilities or talents that correspond to that call.[181] In cases of nonapproval of candidacy, the candidate for representative ministry will receive no recommendation from her or his charge conference, and the passage to the office of preaching will be terminated. On the other hand, later disappointments based upon false expectations or assessments will be avoided. After study in a theological seminary,[182] there follows a further probationary period, after which the men and women who are now theoretically qualified again need the judgment of the mentoring pastors and the charge conference in whose area they learn to transform their knowledge and capabilities into the practical exercise of ministry. Whenever candidates' personal assurance of a call to ministry has been followed by the confirmation of that call by the action of the church, the candidates become "probationary members" and ordained as either deacon or elder and accepted as members of their annual conference, with full connection.[183] Among the duties of deacons are the ministry of the Word and service; those of elders now include preaching the Word of God, the administration of the sacraments, officiating in the services of marriage, funerals, and consecrations of homes, plus other functions, and also providing leadership in the area of church order, which represents the fulfilling of its missionary tasks in the world. They stand at the disposal of the church throughout their active years of ministry and annually receive their appointment by the bishop.

Now as ever, the conviction is fundamental that pastors function as persons who are called by Christ to their ministry and confirmed by the congregation and by the annual conference in the work of the church and of their Lord. As such, they stand over against the congregation, but as members of the people of God they are bound together in the congregation and its common work. Being United Methodist also signifies that pastors assume responsibility for the entire connection by virtue of their ordination;[184] as such, they serve as an important connecting link between the charge and the congregation, on the one side, and the conference and also the entire church, on the other. The centrality of the task of the proclamation of the gospel through Word and sacrament is an inheritance of the Reformation of the sixteenth century, an inheritance that continues to be given prominent emphasis in United Methodism. In our church, ordination brings together the plenary power of proclaiming the Word and the administration of the sacraments with those functions of ordering the life of the congregation, which are exercised in the context of conciliar fellowship within the charge conference, the church council, and their committees, on the one side, and with the authority of church leadership, on the other.

Pastors and authorized laypersons join together in the task of proclamation. From its beginnings, lay preaching has had great significance within Methodism. It enables laypersons to discover their gifts and style of ministry, and not just at those times when pastors are incapacitated, when they serve in the pastor's absence. The goal is to enhance the application rather than the exposition of Scripture (K. H. Voigt), and they can draw illustrations from real-life situations which indicate how decisions can be made upon the basis of the gospel and what models of action can take place from the perspective of faith, within concrete situations of daily living. The different kinds of preaching by pastors and laypersons could lead to mutual stimulation and reflection, as well as to conversation about Christian faith and its practice. This valuation of lay preaching also helps to avoid and to correct the un-Methodist pattern of the occasionally bemoaned "pastor's church," not with the outcome that pastors would withdraw from assuming their corporate responsibility for their charges, but that they, together with all members, each according to their gifts and possibilities might become coworkers under God and so fulfill their tasks within their respective spheres.[185]

Also on the level of the annual conferences, pastors and laypersons bear common responsibility for spreading the gospel through the ministry of the church within its particular area. In doing so, the special task of supervision and making real the connection with the larger church lies in the hands of the superintendents and bishops. It is precisely in the ministry of proclamation, with its diverse forms of expression, that the connection of all members of the church can be upheld and facilitated.

4.3.2 *The Congregation as the Social Form of the Gospel*

The congregation is an instrument of God's action within this world in a twofold sense. It is the social structure of the gospel, which is entrusted to it and which is to define the life of the congregation,[186] and it is to carry the message of the reconciliation of the world through Christ to all persons. The congregation can become a useful instrument of God's actions to the extent that the will of God attains form in the congregation. We believe that Christ creates reconciliation. He has laid the guilt of humanity upon himself and borne it on the cross, so that enmity might be removed and we may be permitted to live. That has the consequence that we ourselves live this life of reconciliation and want to do so. The admission of our own failure and guilt is part of that: "Without an inward work of absolution there is no capacity for reconciliation. Persons who do not critically cultivate a sense of their own guilt always need the fiction of external debtors in order to stabilize their own sense of self-worth."[187] Without this admission, no reconciliation can occur within the life of our congregations and groups, even if we know that Christ has died for all. His reconciliation remains ineffectual in our common life so long as its life-renewing purpose has not been grasped and appropriated. Walls between persons that were erected by faulty behavior cannot be dismantled without admission of one's own share in the construction of those barriers. Wherever areas of tension are taken seriously and problems are not suppressed, but solutions are sought, then "room for trust" arises, in which faith can flourish as a characteristic of the church.[188]

According to the reports of Acts (6:1-7), very early in the history of the congregation at Jerusalem, conflict developed between the Hellenistic and Jewish Christians. The Hellenistic members of the congregation observed neglect of their widows at the distribution of provisions. What did the apostles say? They summoned together the entire congregation and conceded that they could not yet fulfill this additional task. They intend and are required to devote their strength to preaching, to which they were called. The first step toward the solution of the problem is their admission of their own erroneous conduct and inadequacy. The next must follow, for the task must not be allowed to remain untended to if their preaching is not to become unbelievable. Hence, co-laborers are selected to undertake the necessary service. The common responsibility of the congregation is realized in such a way that the limitations do not divide the fellowship but rather lead to a common responsibility in different areas of service.

The measures by which the congregation intends to assess the ethics of human actions are therefore to be applied first to themselves. Are Christians ready to let their own lifestyles be so transformed that they will not be preaching to others while allowing themselves to be disqualified (1 Corinthians 9:27)? Are they ready and do they train themselves in resolving conflicts within the congregation and in the church in the light of the gospel? Are they themselves the kind of fellowship of life in which they can argue with one another in a peaceable manner? Do they live as an alternative community that renounces the personal use of power, in the midst of a society in which the strong and the influential too frequently prevail? Jesus understood the community of the disciples as "a fellowship which constructs its own life space and in which one lives differently and associates with others differently than is the case within the rest of the world. The people of God, whom Jesus intends to gather, could be designated as an alternative society. The power structures of the world should not prevail within this fellowship, but rather reconciliation and brotherly conduct."[189]

The old question of whether new, transformed hearts are the condition for new relationships or whether it is only new relationships that create new persons, cannot be answered with a simple yes or no. It is certainly contrary to an optimistic belief in progress to say that the elimination of unrighteousness within the world and the transformation of society does not yet bring about the kingdom of God. God's actions toward the reconciliation of the world change human hearts *and* relationships. The former occurs through the operation of the Holy Spirit, who makes us become new persons from within; the latter occurs through the medium of transformed persons who are freed to love and are ready for solidarity with other human beings. However, that is not yet the end of the matter, for precisely the experience that changed persons also can effectively change the living standards of others and allows their faith and their testimony to appear genuine, and this in turn invites others to faith. Therefore, whoever subordinates himself or herself to the reign of God is also ready to share in the sufferings of other persons and, where and however that is possible, to share in burdens not one's own and to take on the negative consequences of actions not one's own. This also means strategizing in the alteration of unrighteous structures within politics, economics, and society. Such a readiness repeatedly places us in the position of being under the cross, so that in that place we can experience the all-transforming love of God in the midst of our own weakness and inadequacy. Hence, the church bears witness not only with its preaching but also with its social structure and with its ordering of its life, so that "the church of Christ is and will be what it preaches—or else it denies this witness."[190]

4.3.2.1 THE CONGREGATION AS THE REALM OF THE LOVE OF GOD

The congregation of Jesus Christ is alive whenever the reality of God's love, by which it lives, defines its collegiality. In any case, the witness to God's love can only be a reality when this love can be experienced in the congregation. It cannot be conceded here that this "naturally" is only an ideal description of a congregation, in the sense that "realism" is to be distinguished from "naiveté." This kind of concession hinders the enhancement of commonality among persons, and it prevents them from recognizing and identifying a loveless attitude for what it really is, namely, a violation of the only command which Jesus gave to his disciples (John 15:12-17), and it is therefore a sin.

This love is not to be confused with an only apparently "peaceful" manner of conduct, which ignores unrighteousness, covers over evil, gives way to those who are strong, and ignores the mistakes of others. Veracity belongs to love, but so does humility, which knows that I live solely by the forgiveness of God and of my fellow human beings, and I am not immune from falling into temptation and succumbing to it or from becoming an occasion for others to sin. The apostle clearly warns the unfoundedly and therefore falsely secure when he says, "So if you think you are standing, watch out that you do not fall" (1 Corinthians 10:12). It is not to be disallowed from the outset that Christians strive with one another; and even if it is better to suffer unrighteousness than to commit unrighteous deeds, it is not always a matter of having such a clear alternative. Neither Jesus nor Paul, neither Luther nor Wesley passively submitted to every unrighteous deed that befell them. Yet, the love commandment remains valid in such cases, and it applies not only to friendly neighbors and the stranger (Leviticus 19:18, 34), but also to our enemies (Matthew 5:44). It also applies to our relationship with those who as God's children are sisters and brothers and therefore form the family of God.

What cannot be experienced in the congregation can also not be credibly lived in relation to other persons. Christians are not permitted to be two-faced, even if the friendliness and courtesy may be more difficult to achieve within one's own family than among strangers. Whoever promises something outwardly that is not to be found within the inner realm of the congregation only contributes to the increase of a breach of credibility, which impairs the witness of the church for many.[191]

A series of concrete examples can be added to this basic challenge that the congregation should be a realm of love that can be readily experienced. At least, such an explicit and literal series of examples should be indicated. The acceptance of one another is an important aspect in realizing that realm of experience where Christian love becomes incarnate. This is much more than merely acknowledging the validity of another. It has its pattern in our acceptance through Christ (Romans 15:7), and therefore it is at least a benevolent turning toward those who awaken within us no spontaneous sense of affection.

The appreciation of others also is a part of realizing the realm of the experience of love, including those who appear to be undergifted, as well as those who are offensive and insulting. "If you love those who love you, what credit is that to you?" (Luke 6:32). That also includes admitting the validity of other ways of thinking and other lifestyles which are not our own. How small the spectrum has become into which persons are to be fitted who have found faith in Christ but live differently and who as a rule simply want to remain themselves! Here is where a great deal of the Wesleyan distinction between "essentials" and "nonessentials" (or "opinions") is lost. Congregations should therefore try to take great pains to make more mature judgments and have greater tolerance, not primarily for tactical reasons, but because love commands it.

4.3.2.2 THE CONGREGATION AS A WITNESS TO GOD'S LOVE

The social texture of gracious relations in the sphere of the Christian congregation is the basis for an ethic of love, which is ready to share in the suffering of other persons, to shoulder others' burdens, and to overcome negative consequences of actions. It stands under the cross, where Christians can become witnesses to the overcoming and transforming love of God amid the experience of weakness and powerlessness. By being there for others, by passing on the gospel, and by the service of its members, the church witnesses to God's love, allowing what it has received to be shared with and flow out to others.

Before we speak in depth about the mission of the church in the next section, this source of its existence and its task ought once again to be quite consciously brought to our awareness. In formulating its policy of providing aid for congregations, the official church board in the former German Democratic Republic (East Germany) clarified what is to be the missionary self-understanding of European—and perhaps American—United Methodism, with regard to the immediate situation which they faced: "The congregation has an advantage that exceeds the rest of humanity only in the sense that it has begun to recognize and to appropriate God's love in Jesus Christ . . . and thus has found faith in Him. Therefore, it has first and last no other task than to lead persons to faith in His love." It must therefore "make clear . . . in every way possible that the offer of God's love applies to all persons and to the entire world," and this does not mean that "others . . . become merely objects for mission, or sought-out bases for testing ecclesiastical strategies, or convenient vehicles for testing the validity of our missional and pastoral concepts. Instead, the task of Christian mission sets in motion the love of God and it finds others for their own sake."[192] The task is connected to the reconciliation that has been given to them, which does not shrink from identifying with those who suffer and from accepting the risks of misunderstanding and rejection. These results accompany the preaching and uplifting of the gospel to others, as well as enabling its message to intervene in the daily conflicts of human living. The witness of God's love can become credible and resilient precisely in that it is dependent upon neither transient feelings, a common cultural identity, an attachment to like cultural values, nation, nor race. This witness also allows its voice to be raised whenever persons are singled out through those kinds of criteria and treated and judged accordingly. For everything—simply everything—which Christians, congregations, and churches do, that love which is given and offered by God remains the ultimate criterion, but also the never-failing motivation.

4.3.3 *The Mission of the Church*

We have already reflected upon the church as the mission of God.[193] In the following consideration, we are probing somewhat more deeply into the two basic concepts that undergird missionary activity, which our church knows and for which a wide variety of different activities and programs are coordinated. The first is evangelization, as the transmission of the Christian message to unbelievers or to nominal church members in our own land and to the society that relies upon us. The second is the outer mission, which is the transmission of the gospel into other lands, including places from which witnesses to the gospel have in the meantime also come to us, and in which we attempt to fulfill Jesus' task of mission together with the churches in those locations.

Yet, before we get to that, a typical missionary structure for The United Methodist Church must be made the focus of our awareness: the principle of appointment to ministry. It is a principle which has not been understood by many churches and has only been understood in a very peripheral manner by some pastors, even though it has been a part of the Methodist movement from its inception. This principle assumes that pastors do not seek congregations nor do congregations seek pastors, but rather the field of labor is assigned and the persons in that location are entrusted to the service of the pastor. Corresponding to this, the ordination examination that describes this aspect of pastoral ministry reads as follows: "As an elder in the Church, you are called to share in the ministry of Christ . . . by exercising pastoral supervision of the people committed to your care, ordering the life of the congregation . . . by leading the people of God in obedience to mission in the world, . . . and by being conformed to the life of Christ,. . . you are to be in covenant with the elders in this Annual Conference, and a coworker with the bishop, other elders, [and] deacons . . . to proclaim by word and deed the gospel of Jesus Christ, and to fashion your life in accordance with its precepts."[194] This principle of mission has its origin both in Wesley's practice, which has given to the Methodist churches their great flexibility as well as its strong sense of cohesion, as well as in the practice of Jesus and of the early church, which sent out coworkers to do the work of preaching the gospel.[195] In our day, the laws regulating work and civil servants, the familiar, mutual obligations of living marital partners, the maturity of congregations, and other factors have prevented this principle of ministerial appointment from being exercised without serious restrictions and major modifications.[196] The system of appointment can only function if it is being upheld by more than a minority of the clergy, for all church members will need to give recognition and support to that system. Only then will there be a responsible, personal acceptance of the charge to be sent out in mission, along with a sense of partnership in relation to the charge to the church as a whole, including all of its members. Only then can we hope to overcome the tensions among "leading brethren and sisters" and pastors or between congregations and pastors. And the decisive feature of the church, in the United Methodist understanding, is that the church "allows itself to be sent into the world in order to bear witness through word and deed to the liberating love of Christ, by whom it lives."[197] Is this the reality that is encountered within the church today?

4.3.3.1 EVANGELIZATION

The concept of being sent into ministry, containing both common and variable features, is also applicable to the task of making the gospel known to unbelievers, which we call evangelization. Both aspects are applicable here: the offer of personal salvation and the announcement of God's will for the world as a whole. Evangelization is about individual people and their relationship to God, and also about the message that proclaims the rule of God in society. Only this collegiality of the public proclamation of faith safeguards the message of the gospel from being narrowed simply to the realm of individual salvation. Such a confining view of evangelism tends to screen out the larger needs of humanity as a whole, so that the love commandment is dishonored, and it tends to abandon social, economic, and political issues to the realm of the profane. According to the theoretical and also the practical interpretation given by Wesley, the theme of the "salvation of souls" includes both dimensions: both the renewal of one's relationship to God and also the concern for the whole of humanity in its earthly existence, the renewed grounding of faith in a personal assurance that God grants to the believer and the experience of the benefit and blessing of God within the whole range of life.[198]

The ways of reaching people, ways in which persons may attain the call to Christ and to a life with him, have repeatedly adapted themselves to the actual cultural, social, and political possibilities. Thus, what is needed is a combination of far-reaching measures that seeks to gain the attention of as many as possible[199] and above all intends to safeguard the "witness to

Christ from one person to another." There are certainly always dangers to be avoided in some methods of "conversion," methods in which all kinds of physical or psychic pressures are exerted that do not go well with the proclamation of the gospel. Yet, as there are different gifts, so also there are different modes of passing on the gospel, which need to coexist and be utilized in complementary ways. The important thing is "that Christ is proclaimed in every way, whether out of false motives or true; and in that I rejoice" (Philippians 1:18).

The United Methodist Church is connected with other churches and fellowships in the ministry of proclaiming the gospel to persons who do not have a living faith. The pain of the fragmentation of Christianity was felt most keenly by those Christians who were caught up in movements of awakening. Hence, the Evangelical Alliance was formed in London in 1846 with the hope that, through a common alliance of Christians, the unity of the Church of Jesus Christ might be experienced and promoted by bringing together Christians from different churches and nations in the task of evangelization. They hoped that this would conform better to "Jesus' command to mission in the entire world."[200] The "mission to the heathen" should be pursued not only in the traditional mission fields of Africa or Asia, but also in the homeland, for "every nation may be considered a mission field today."[201] Leading figures of the former Methodist Churches participated in the formation of the Evangelical Alliance, and to the present day, pastors and laypersons from The United Methodist Church in Europe are active participants in its work.[202]

In more recent times in Europe, extra efforts in reaching secular persons have been exerted, including the "mission to new lands"—"church members, congregations, charges, or conferences take aim at new lands, in order to reach persons with the gospel who are at a distance from the faith and the church, and to gather them into congregations."[203] This also entails the upbuilding of mission-minded congregations, which "is concerned with the formation of a congregation that works as a team in formulating and carrying out mission strategies, and where members are committed to witness and service."[204] Moreover, United Methodism is "evangelistic in structure," but with subsequent generations it has, in many respects, lost its readiness to respond to the mandate to evangelize. That development has not only sociological but also theological causes, so that not only the methods but also the theology of evangelization are in need of reflection and new definition. This has now begun to take place with the publication of seminal works and with conferences that have been held at all levels of the church.[205] Perhaps the day is coming when we may reclaim the truth of G. Wainwright's statement that "in the outlook of Methodism, evangelization probably remains as the primary task of its life as a church."[206]

4.3.3.2 THE OUTER MISSION

It is not by chance that the mission document of United Methodism bears the title "Grace upon Grace." It is the boundless benevolence of God that has been our personal experience, from which the service of mission arises. It is the trust in God's presence and the promise of his nearness until the end of the world that repeatedly causes persons to risk taking the step into a specific willingness to respond to this mandate. Whether this ministry takes place in a foreign land or in one's homeland, it is in every case a response to God's love, and an expression of thanksgiving that arises from a benefit that has been personally experienced.

This ministry reaches beyond one's particular church into the entire inhabited earth *(oikoumene)* and into the worldwide tasks of the work of mission. On the other hand, we are also entering increasingly energetically into intentional ministry to quite a variety of persons in our own homelands. Not only are the older Christianized nations increasingly themselves becoming places of mission, now persons from other lands are coming to us, and we are indebted to them for the gospel and the ministry of love.

The context in the area of world mission is also to win persons for Christ. This mission carries out its activities in other nations or places on earth in a partner fellowship with the churches of those places. In addition to the proclamation of faith, their ministry also includes the care of the sick, social and educational work, and partly also aid in the development of other projects. These are all means of bringing salvation in Christ to life in people through the witness to the love of God. In our era of growing dialogue among different Christian churches, as well as with representatives of other world religions, this ministry is only possible on the basis of the conviction that our task as a church lies in offering Christ as the way to salvation.[207]

This sole and unique offer of salvation, which we are obliged to extend to all humanity in the name of God, is not the same as a so-called Christian claim to absoluteness. As Christians, we can undoubtedly learn from others, who honor God in different ways. Anyone who wishes to argue this point must deny at times horrifying errors and crimes that accompanied the history of Christian missions. To the conviction of being empowered for the proclamation of the resurrected Christ is added the humility that comes from love and the modesty that recognizes one's own fallibility and the limitations of all persons. The only viable measure and the motive for all the work of Christian mission is love for those persons whom they want to win over without removing or constricting their freedom of decision. On the contrary, this love desires nothing other than the response made as a free decision—the freest that can be conceived is the decision for faith in Christ. However, what may be worse than the absence of such a decision, or the conscious rejection of this love, would be an enforced decision, which would be no genuine decision at all and would be a slap in the face of the gospel. The first goal of mission, and the one that affects all others, must and can legitimately only be "to give witness in all the world, through word and deed, to the revelation of God in Jesus Christ and to deeds of love, through which He has reconciled humanity with Himself."[208] Thus, the churches who dispatch co-laborers into other lands are not in the least the only givers; on the contrary, through the experiences which they have with the power of the gospel in the midst of foreign cultures and societies, they themselves receive an impression of the independence of the Word of God from the patterns of Christian living and church life that happen to prevail within their own civilization. They themselves hear the gospel from the mouths of messengers from those lands in a fresh and challenging manner.

Since The United Methodist Church is an international, missionary church, missions and ecumenics belong inseparably together. Wherever Christian churches work against one another, their proclamation suffers in its authenticity, since they are outwardly denying the one Lord, to whom they belong and in whose service they are called. On the other hand, in a day in which United Methodist missions are being planted in nations where state churches have a favored legal advantage (as in Russia and Poland), we cannot accept the position that would hold that all persons living within a given land are to be claimed for one state church, since they belong to one national group (or *Volk*). Such nations defame the evangelism and mission work of all other churches as "proselytism." United Methodists regard all nonbelievers as human beings with whom Christians are obligated to share the gospel, and they respect the decision of every person to choose to belong to a different church or to no church at all. The ecumenical fellowship, to which The United Methodist Church is committed by virtue of its constitution,[209] and which has defined its work from the beginning,[210] remains as an unquestionable principle for its evangelistic and missionary work: "Mission is ecumenical as we seek to live in cooperation and communion with the many authentic Christian communities that God in grace calls into existence. We desire to live in communion with all who are in communion with Jesus Christ. We are thankful for all sisters and brothers in Christ and we seek unity amidst our diversity."[211] Hence, United Methodists gladly are those who are "bridge builders for God,"[212] which has repeatedly been actualized.

4.4   The Church in the World

The apparently trivial place designation "in the world," which is used here to refer to the church, also makes necessary a series of more precise definitions, which describe the temporal existence of the church in such a way that it also delineates its relationship to the "world," at least in a foundational way.

"In the world—not of the world" makes clear one difference that the "mixed" reality of the church points to regarding its essential relationship. That is, its realm of living is the world, but its origin is "from God."[213] The church is the representative of God's loving reign in the world. Its being "in the world" is an existence for humanity, for whom God sent his Son into the world. The difference from the world does not permit a chasm to be formed between church and world, nor does it permit retreat from the world. The church is an institution of the Spirit of God, which rules through the Word, apart from earthly power, and which establishes the community of brotherly love. Insofar as the church is defined by this Spirit, it is the representative of the rule of God in the world. Its ministry is centered in godly affection for people and for the whole of creation, especially in its intercession for the weak and the poor and in efforts to bring about righteousness and peace among humans. Equally far removed from a utopianism that leaps over the reality of the here and now and from a resignation that is only concerned with what is at hand, this ministry calls people into fellowship with God and to the life that is lived out according to his creative and rectifying will. Insofar as it seeks to live this life, it becomes the alternative to both utopianism and fatalism. Despite the fact that it is certainly not yet a perfect fellowship, it nevertheless remains a real community that lives for people in defiance of the "rules of this world"[214] and seeks to serve them. It is not a question of what strategy is to be used to extend Christianity within this world. Instead, it is first and foremost a matter of the Christian community standing as a fellowship of believers and disciples who remain at the disposal of God's actions that are occurring in the world.

In this connection, a twofold observation needs to occupy our attention. On the one hand, we sometimes have the impression that the theme of God's reign indicates a reality which rarely shapes and transforms the concrete form of the church on earth or its actual deeds. On the other hand, we notice that a small but increasing number of persons are ever more urgently seeking honest answers to the urgent questions of life as well as meaningful goals for the orientation of their lives. We live in a society in which the question about meaningful living is being increasingly asked. Many in our day are not living simply from hand to mouth. They are not satisfied with the preformulated answers and the ideological baggage, which can easily be exchanged at the earliest opportunity. Can Christians and can churches offer a helpful suggestion at this point? Can they at least formulate the right questions and make clear what the connections are between these questions and the message of the gospel?

Religious expectations are increasing. However, many no longer are expecting to receive meaningful answers from the churches. Perhaps this mistrust is ultimately based on the widespread perception that the churches are not really concerned with people but concerned more with their own self-preservation or the advancement of their own existence. The church at times has identified itself with the kingdom of God, and by this self-understanding, it has been led astray by the quest for power and domination within society, which can hardly or only with difficulty be reconciled with the New Testament criteria for a Christian congregation.[215] An understanding of the theme of the kingdom of God, which shows its contrast with churches as they actually exist and which also promotes serious reflection on the meaning of the church, has almost totally disappeared from theology.[216] At times, the theme of the kingdom of God was made to refer to the other world or to the inner realm of human life.[217] Luther related the second petition of the Lord's Prayer primarily to the spiritual existence of Christians (repentance and justification): God's kingdom draws near in the Word and in faith, and with the return of Christ.[218] In the kingdom of Christ, understood as the present, hidden kingdom of God, there may be no worldly ruler but rather the rule of Christ through Word and sacrament within his congregation. God's kingdom may become evident only in the future when all are allowed to see that which is now hidden. In the Reformed tradition, God's reign is also seen above all in the fact that God is working through his Spirit and is ruling among those who belong to him.

In the theology of the twentieth century as well, a very close connection, and even an identification, has been maintained between the kingdom of God and the Christian congregation. Taking its cue from the tradition that traces back to Origen, in which Jesus Christ is himself viewed as the kingdom of God, Karl Barth has written, "We cannot avoid a statement which Protestantism has far too hastily and heedlessly contested—that the kingdom of God is the community." From this basis, Barth declares that "the kingdom of God is the Lordship of God established in the world in Jesus Christ. It is the rule of God as it takes place in Him." He acknowledges that the congregation may not be the kingdom of God in its perfected form: "We refer to it in the guise of the new and obedient humanity, as in the historical time which moves towards this end it is provisionally and very imperfectly but genuinely actualized where . . . there is an awareness of its incursion."[219] A direct identification of the kingdom of God with certain historical movements is found in the representatives of a theology of revolution or of liberation, as it was earlier among some religious socialists or among exponents of the social gospel.[220]

To avoid the tendency of the church of overestimating itself and so divesting the concept of the reign of God of any power, we should hold fast to the nonidentity of the church and the kingdom of God. It is not a matter of there being a relationship of identity between these two realities, but rather there is a relationship of analogy. This analogy must be recognized above all in two signs. First, it is known by the fact that Christ is recognized as the Head of the congregation, even in this present time, and, second, in the fact that it makes room for a place in which persons can be invited into a living encounter with Christ. Under earthly conditions, this analogy certainly has only a preliminary, imperfect, fragmentary and blemished form; nevertheless it is authentic because it emerges from the acts of God. God's reign is found precisely there—under the circumstances of its earthly existence—because and insofar as persons are set free through God's Spirit to believe the gospel of Jesus Christ and to live in this world according to his standards. They experience a foretaste of the coming reign of God in worship, praise, hearing the message of the gospel, and in the celebration of holy communion. It is a reign that not accidentally is described in the New Testament as table fellowship.

Hence, the church is also the place and the realm of the reign of God, because those who share in the life of the church are there making their appearance at the *basileia,* or the place of God's royal reign (Colossians 4:11). God has positioned the church in the kingdom of his Son, so that it proclaims his Lordship and serves him in faith, hope, and love, so that God's kingdom repeatedly becomes a present reality.[221] Hence, the church could be what the bishops of The United Methodist Church have called a mark of the Christian congregation: the "alternative community to an alienated and fractured world," which is a fellowship of persons who also reach out to their "enemies."[222]

4.4.1 *The World as the Place of God's Reign*

The concept of "world" has a twofold meaning in the New Testament: on the one hand, it designates the "world that is gathered by the God who created it" (hence, the place in which the church also lives), or the totality of all persons (hence, those who belong to the church); and, on the other hand—especially in the Johannine writings, but also with Paul—it is the world that is alienated from God, and is even opposed to the divine, and which stands in hostility against the church.[223]

In the New Testament, Christians are called "holy,"[224] not because they may have been that in a perfect sense, but because they belong to Christ. Because Christ, their Head, is holy, all members of his body are also holy.[225] They are now able to begin to live in a manner that conforms to the holiness that is given to them, and increasingly become defined by love. In that is found their holiness. In that also resides the great treasure and the great task of the congregation as the body of Christ, that God's love comes to dwell within it and is passed on, so that persons belong to it who want to let themselves be formed by God's Spirit into the image of God. They do so in order to become free from their egoistic preoccupation with themselves, and begin to live to the honor of God and for the service of their fellow human beings. The fact that personal holiness also must comprehend the realm of social life is not a supplemental demand but is inextricably bound together with the essence of this transformation.[226]

God's winsome grace places believers in a new relationship to their world. Thus, the kingdom of God remains, which is "in the midst of us" and not only "within us." The objection that the understanding of the kingdom of God as we find it in Wesley leads to a pious individualism does not address Wesley's theology at all. Sanctification and the reign of God go hand in hand,[227] and the reign of God directs persons beyond the borders of their personal lives.

The finitude of the created world, in contrast to the eternality of the reign of God, in no way renders it worthless and therefore does not permit us to devalue things of this world. By contrast, the love of God's creatures is to become a spring from which social change can flow into the world.[228] The call to service and to stewardship entrusts to Christians the care of all those persons with whom their lives come in contact.

In Wesley's doctrine of sanctification, there are two perspectives that point beyond individuals in their private lives. One is the perspective of the coming reign of God, which is only partially and fragmentarily present in the lives of Christians and within their congregations, and another is the perspective of the society, the nation, and the world, which cannot be thought of apart from the responsibility of social holiness. "As those who are made holy in love, having a foretaste of glory, they bring Christ's kingdom into the ways of the earthly community."[229] This bringing in of the power and criteria of God's rule serves to effect changes within society, such as the overcoming of enmity through reconciliation, of wrath through peace, and of repression through righteousness. Any attempt to stay at the individual or the inward level of life is excluded. "Love leaps over the boundaries of personal piety. . . . That which was born in the inward part of the individual quickly proceeds to be expressed on a corporate level, and even on the level of society as a whole. It expresses itself concretely through missionary activity and good works directed to all persons. Here we see how, for Wesley, the divine Spirit's work of sanctification excludes every narrow pietistic interpretation, because it is understood as a sanctification that progresses as a mission within the world, expressed through word and deed."[230]

Sanctification is therefore always achieved as worship within the context of the daily life of the world, and as a witness to the approaching kingdom of God. This activity is accompanied and directed by prayer, in which persons petition for the coming of the kingdom and commend their destiny, along with that of their fellow humans and fellow creatures, to God's faithfulness. Faith and political responsibility, hope in the coming of God's kingdom, and actions taken in response to this hope therefore belong together in a United Methodist understanding of sanctification.

The fact that expectations often overpower existing circumstances is a sign of the tension between a reality that can be experienced and one that is yet to be expected. This tension repeatedly leads us away from the danger of overvaluing our own actions and into a confident waiting upon God's action. In the provisional actions of Christians, which are enabled and directed by God's Spirit, the kingdom of God becomes a reality that can be experienced in the present. Even nature and history receive their sense of direction through the acts of God that are revealed in Christ, whereby he will finally bring his glory into fruition, which in its core is love.[231]

The unmistakable accent upon the acts of God that are being actualized in the present, through the accomplishment of his will, is an emphasis that we have found within the writings of Wesley, with regard to his understanding of the reign of God. Above all, by accepting Paul's words "For the kingdom of God is not food and drink but righteousness and peace and joy in the Holy Spirit" (Romans 14:17), he can give emphasis to the presence of God: "*For the kingdom of God*—That is, true religion, does not consist in external observances. *But in righteousness*—The image of God stamped on the heart; the love of God and man, accompanied with the peace that passeth all understanding, and joy in the Holy Ghost."[232]

But this emphasis upon the presence of God's kingdom belongs within a larger context in which Wesley's references to the glory or the kingdom of God have a twofold meaning. These concepts indicate "not barely a future happy state, in heaven, but a state to be enjoyed on earth: the proper disposition for the glory of heaven, rather than the possession of it."[233] He addresses this theme quite similarly, yet in a way more clearly contoured and integrated, in sermon 26, where he states that "the kingdom of God [has] begun below, set up in the believer's heart." This "kingdom of grace" is the victory of God through Jesus Christ within the soul of a person, which has become manifest so that God "is King of kings and Lord of lords." The fulfillment of the kingdom of grace is completed with the coming of the kingdom of glory, when "all mankind receiving him for their king, truly believing in his name, may be filled with righteousness and peace and joy, with holiness and happiness, till they are removed hence into his heavenly kingdom, there to reign with him for ever and ever." Although this end-time perspective is seldom missing, Wesley refrains from giving a more precise description of that state, in order to direct his thinking to the theme of God's rule within the present and to the tasks which result from that fact. He is mainly concerned with the reign of God producing a renewal of humanity and of the world as a whole, with petitioning the coming of the eternal kingdom and with the will of God being accomplished. This necessarily and immediately happens "wherever the kingdom of God is come; wherever God dwells in the soul by faith, and Christ reigns in the heart by love."[234]

It is noteworthy that Wesley in no way lapsed into accepting that persons might be able to accelerate or bring about the coming of God's reign through their own actions. Rather, in his depiction of this motif, he is attempting to emphasize again and again that God is the One who gathers persons into a new fellowship through the gospel, awakens their faith and love, and engages them as coworkers in the building of his kingdom. The way that Christians are to live is also to be the way into the kingdom of God.[235] It begins with repentance, by which we "can receive the kingdom of God, and it proceeds further, whenever the love of God is first shed abroad in our hearts and his kingdom is erected within us." In its present aspect, the kingdom of God is therefore the reign of God within us, which is "true religion."

While this personal experience of salvation can be described as a "realized eschatology," this does not mean that Wesley abandoned any expectation of a future kingdom within history or had made a purely inward and individualistic affair out of the reign of God. In connection with the Pauline-Reformation understanding of justification by grace through faith, this future perspective keeps Wesley from speaking in an erroneous way about the "work of the kingdom of God," in which the chief function is attributed to human beings. Wesley certainly saw the greater danger in the Methodists possibly becoming superficial and shallow in their piety. In a letter of 1771, he complains that they were "continually forgetting that the kingdom of God is *within us,* and that our fundamental principle is, We are saved *by faith,* producing all *inward* holiness."[236]

As a logical consequence, Wesley made use of this conception of the kingdom of God in his evangelistic preaching, as his sermon that is entitled "The Way into the Kingdom of God" makes abundantly clear. After he has described the kingdom of God to his hearers as "the nature of true religion," which does not consist in outer forms or actions, not in right belief or right intentions, but in righteousness (love for God and neighbor), peace (with God and the certainty of salvation), as well as joy in the Holy Spirit (holiness and happiness), he shows them that the kingdom of God is present today even as it was with Christ. "Wheresoever therefore the gospel of Christ is preached, this his 'kingdom is nigh at hand.' It is not far from every one of you. Ye may this hour enter thereinto, if so be ye hearken to his voice, 'Repent ye, and believe the gospel.' "[237]

Yet the acts of turning about and believing, which establish the Christian's new position, also have their consequences for the conduct of life. As a result, Wesley concludes this sermon as follows: "Dost thou now

375

believe? Then 'the love of God is' now 'shed abroad in thy heart.' Thou lovest him, because he first loved us. And because thou lovest God, thou lovest thy brother also. And, being filled with 'love, peace, joy,' thou art also filled with 'long-suffering, gentleness, fidelity, goodness, meekness, temperance,' and all other fruits of the same Spirit."[238] The decisive emphasis in John Wesley's theology of the twofold understanding of the kingdom of God resides in the fact that the content and the essential form is the love of God. Having established this, the church and its members are shown their place in the world, which, because the world is God's creation, even if it is also an estranged world that has turned away from God or that has even become his complete adversary, nonetheless likewise belongs to God and stands under his grace.[239]

4.4.2 *The Diaconal Task of the Church*

The basis for the task of engaging in diaconal work is also derived from the experience of the saving presence of God and the conviction that God's reign has decisive significance for our lives in the here and now. Therefore, for us to share in God's glory and to do God's will entails the promotion of righteousness and love among people within the whole of society. The diaconal work of Theodore Fliedner, the social activities of Johann Henrich Wilchern, or the social impact of the holiness revival and the social gospel movement within the United States have all shaped the work of United Methodist congregations in the past century and have led to their own forms of ministry. Admittedly, the church has not often been profoundly concerned with the condition of the poor and the deprived. Accordingly, it has been from the experience of God's benefits in their own lives that persons have often been led to demonstrate a concern for the needy in society and have either brought them into their own living conditions or have made particular arrangements to provide them with the necessary aid. They have thereby weakened, at least in part, the accusation which critics of the church like Karl Marx have raised. Through their service it has become clear that the Christian faith is not to be likened to some resplendent halo which shines over the slough of despond in which people live, thereby misleading them concerning their actual condition.[240]

In the New Testament, diaconal work is the sign both of the mission of Jesus and that of his congregation. "I am among you as one who serves," said Jesus to his disciples (Luke 22:27). However, his ministry was not only intended for his disciples and for the church, "for the Son of Man came not to be served but to serve, and to give his life a ransom for many"

(Mark 10:45). Through his ministry of love, which was perfected in his submission to the cross, Jesus received persons into the fellowship of the reign of God. There is no other door into the kingdom of God save that of submitting to Jesus' ministry of love.

Hence, it is not at all a case of earning one's way into the kingdom of God through ministry to other persons. This kind of thinking is unequivocally rejected by Jesus (Mark 10:35-45). It is much more the reverse: the motivation for ministry to others arises from the experience of the love of God and from one's certainty of belonging to his kingdom. This is the mode of living and acting that corresponds to God's love as the most inward essence of Christian existence. The source of all Christian diaconal or social work is the love of Jesus, who himself became the deacon of others and thereby brought near the reign of God. This means that the ministry of Christians is also an event in which the kingdom of God becomes reality in a symbolical and fragmentary manner. At the same time, we can assume that God's glory is disseminated and extended not only through the overt activity of Christian witness but also through every act of ministry which takes place out of love for humanity and for creation.

It is not by accident that a form of the ministry of love that frequently appears is seen in Jesus' table fellowship, to which Jesus invites other persons and which is celebrated in the congregation as a remembrance of the surrender of their Lord. All believers are bound together in this fellowship, those who give and those who receive, the rich and the poor, the healthy and the disabled, the influential and those who live at the edge of society.

The worthiness of those who receive help belongs to the essential aspects of Christian diaconal work. John Wesley repeatedly pressed this point and reminded us to give one's fellow human beings, even the poorest and the most rejected among them, the esteem and regard due them as recipients of the love of God in the same way as one's own people, a love to which no one can contest their right on pain of becoming guilty before God.[241] The solidarity of the sinners who are beloved of God prohibits every condescending form of "caritas." If we discover God's creation in the one who suffers the most, then we will also find the correct attitude in relating ourselves to that person.

This solidarity with the poorest and the most rejected, which has its basis in the unconditional love of God, was and is the mark of genuine diaconal work, which not only gives what it has received but also receives while it gives. It is not only the gift of grace but also the means of grace that certainly makes one conscious of the power and the greatness of God's love ever anew. Through this attitude and the conduct that is marked by it, Wesley and his Methodist societies succeeded in communicating a sense of self-worth to the poor without which those persons could not have found the way out of their social misery. The ministry of love transforms both the giver and the receiver. What is at stake in our perception of the diaconal task of the congregation—whether it is achieved through individuals, small groups, or institutions—is not a matter for trivial debate; it is the very identity and the credibility of the existence of the church of Jesus Christ. It is a matter of something that is profoundly simple and yet often so difficult: being a congregation of disciples of Jesus in this world, and letting this become visible to others in our conduct, so that they may find healing and salvation.

4.4.2.1 THE DIACONAL EXISTENCE OF CHRISTIANS

Diaconal work is the presence of the congregation within the context of its social network. Within its diaconal presence, congregations transcend the boundaries of their communities. For the world in which they live, Christians have "found a new understanding, namely, that God so loves them that he gave His Son for them. Therefore, the congregation evangelizes and does missionary work in word and in deed. Social and diaconal acts are expressions of this new relationship, and sharing of God's mercy."[242] It is this same love of God, by which Christians live, that also lets them live in service to other persons. They are convinced that this love gives each person a sense of integral dignity, which must not be violated. From this sense of the value of all persons, something of the nature of an "ethic of reciprocity" can arise.[243] This reciprocity does not arise from the fact that Christians give other persons their due, in terms of what they have experienced from them in discrimination, insults, or injuries. Instead, it is an ethic of reciprocity that has its basis in the golden rule of Jesus, "In everything do to others as you would have them do to you" (Matthew 7:12). Thus, a new point of departure for corporate human existence is created, which becomes the basis for mutuality arising from living love.[244] Because of their connection to God, both individuals and the Christian congregation are recipients of God's love, but they are also its mediators. Christians are the beloved enemies who can learn to love their enemies. They are accepted sinners who are concerned not with claiming their rights, but rather with actualizing the new, boundless fellowship of the children of God. They know that they are wholly dependent upon God, but at the same time they are employed and empowered by God to be conveyors of the good news for all persons, and especially for the poor (Luke 6:20).

It is often not easy to proceed along this course. It takes power, it often brings disappointment and ingratitude, it imposes burdens that often render life more difficult. Persons who have set out in this direction also speak of a deep experience of the nearness of God and of their significant encounters with other persons. The congregation serves as the practice arena for this kind of Christian living. It also offers the possibility for forming a binding covenant among its members.[245] The "Ministry and Mission of the Church" is defined in the *Book of Discipline* in the following terms:

> God's self-revelation in the life, death, and resurrection of Jesus Christ summons the church to ministry in the world through witness by word and deed in light of the church's mission. The visible church of Christ as a faithful community of persons affirms the worth of all humanity and the value of interrelationship in all of God's creation.
>
> In the midst of a sinful world, through the grace of God, we are brought to repentance and faith in Jesus Christ. We become aware of the presence and life-giving power of God's Holy Spirit. We live in confident expectation of the ultimate fulfillment of God's purpose.
>
> We are called together for worship and fellowship and for the upbuilding of the Christian community. We advocate and work for the unity of the Christian church. We call persons into discipleship.
>
> As servants of Christ we are sent into the world to engage in the struggle for justice and reconciliation. We seek to reveal the love of God for men, women, and children of all ethnic, racial, cultural, and national backgrounds and to demonstrate the healing power of the gospel with those who suffer.[246]

Persons who give honest assent to this statement are ready to bind themselves to God, out of gratitude for the goodness and love he has shown them. Experience shows that such an obligation, in which persons can "bind" themselves to one another out of trust in God, can also be a source of power for their servanthood existence within the world.[247]

The first social creed of the former Methodist Episcopal Church (1908) was also written in the form of a covenant to be ratified. United Methodist women in particular have bound themselves to this personal commitment to the church. They have been especially familiar with the problems of people who are victims of social deprivations, which are also a reflection of the inequities of societies as a whole. They have seen these people suffer while the church at large has long overlooked them. With their social engagement, they have motivated others to take action to begin to remove these areas of social evil that prevail in their day.

Hence, servanthood existence begins by drawing near to humanity. This is how the "Methodist Covenant for Social Service" originated. The concern of the authors of this covenant was not the radical change of the social order of their land. Rather they had grasped that no particular social order can guarantee the rule of justice. Many individual families, indeed entire groups and classes, were found to be in deep misery that could not be overlooked by Christians. As a result, Methodist women's groups, and soon also other groups and movements, used the sense of connection within their churches as a point of departure for choosing to connect themselves to the people in their society and set about finding those people who lacked the essentials of life. Their intent has been to find ways to speak with prophetic truth to those who are most flagrantly responsible for unjust and inequitable conditions.

4.4.2.2 THE MINISTRY TO THE WEAK

This ministry has never been disputed as a needed task of the church, although the prevailing practice has often varied. Hence, we read in the *Book of Discipline* of The United Methodist Church that the ministry of the church, particularly through the office of deacons, is that of "love, justice, and service; of connecting the church with the most needy, neglected, and marginalized among the children of God. This ministry grows out of the Wesleyan passion for social holiness and ministry among the poor."[248] Perhaps Christians are never nearer to their Lord than when they are engaged in this kind of ministry to the weak. United Methodists are pledged to a valuable heritage, which is Wesley's involvement with the poorest members of society. The servanthood that finds its first expression in the good deeds of individual believers also led John Wesley to the founding of schools, the erection of apothecaries for the poor, and involvement in the reform of the penal institutions and the abolition of slavery. Today the ministry to the weak has other target groups and other forms of expression, but in its essence it is still the same as in the time of the first Christian congregations, as well as the hospitals of the Middle Ages and the poor aid of early Methodism.

The proclamation of the glad tidings of the gospel to the poor and the deeds of mercy that accompany it are related to one another and are integrated in the actual execution of that ministry on behalf of the needy. Just as the word of the cross is the unmistakable content of Christian proclamation, so is it also the mark and the motif of unselfish, serving love. The congregation becomes a credible witness to Christ in its linking word and deed, witness and service. As it lives out of its surrender to its Lord, who gave his life as the ransom for many, even so service thrives through the persons who are ready to surrender themselves in obedience to Jesus. The receiving and giving and the participating and sharing that are characteristic of the community of believers make the congregation become the basis for all deeds of diaconal service.

The Christian ministry of servanthood holds in view that the whole person is formed in the image of God. The fact that it takes pains to view persons in that light also has the consequence that all human categorizing becomes relativized, one's attachment to a particular nation, race, social class, or religious group, which can never become the basis for either positively or negatively predetermining who is preferred or qualified for being the recipient of Christian ministry. The mark of Christian diaconal service is mercy, which does not categorize but is directed to one's neighbor because it recognizes in him or her the image of God.

In addition, the love for which one is freed by faith in Christ makes no preferential selection based upon which ones are worthy of love, but rather turns precisely to the weak and the needy. This distinguishing mark of the ministry of Christian servanthood is based upon God's love for us, and this is so in a twofold manner: (1) We ourselves have been recipients of this love without having had to prove our worthiness for receiving it. We are not distinguished from other persons by special qualities or achievements, as though we had been unconditionally predestined for fellowship with God. Each Christian must submit to the question, whose answer is already self-evident: "What do you have that you did not receive?" (1 Corinthians 4:7). Every kind of presumption or condescension is thereby forbidden with regard to Christian service. We are only passing on what we have already received—precisely for this purpose. (2) God's love makes the beloved worthy of love.[249] In his eyes, there is therefore no person who would not be worthy of our love. Christian service is the willingness and capacity to see persons with the eyes of God and to draw near to them, just as Jesus was and is near to them.

The ministry to the especially needy and disabled is the one Christians have recognized as theirs and which even secularized civil governments are often glad to hand over to their care. Hence, this servanthood ministry also becomes a partisan label for those who are rejected, by which they now are not avoided but are deemed as significant in God's eyes. Such persons who conceal their need for love under the sway of wealth, power, or success also need the love of God. Through gracious acceptance, persons experience esteem and healing, freedom from an incapacitating sense of low self-esteem or a hardened overestimation of themselves. They experience afresh what it means to be loved by God, and they can now gratefully discover their gifts.

Even if it is primarily a question of the well-being of people, the ministry of servanthood would deny its task if it limited itself mainly to addressing the need for earthly prosperity. A person cannot receive salvation without attaining a new relationship with God. This inward and final goal of servanthood ministry, as well as its origin, cannot disappear from the orbit of the serving ministry. Since this ministry has its spiritual and historical origin in the ministry of Jesus, to the poor, the sick, and the imprisoned, Christians no longer see in them only those to whom they may give things, but also see persons who help them to live as disciples of Jesus. The gift comes for the benefit of the needy, but the needy are also a blessing to those who give. Love becomes efficacious in this mutuality of giving for others and for one another, and Christ is acknowledged in the least of these sisters and brothers.

4.4.2.3 MINISTRY IN SOCIETY

The motto that has guided Methodism since its earliest times has been described as being "to save souls and to spread scriptural holiness over the land."[250] Despite some objections which could be marshaled against such a brief formulation, this is a task which directs us toward the widest breadth of ministry. Here we do not have in mind the small, world-denying and inwardly focused groups of the pious. It is much more evident that Wesley's statement about the world being his parish is very much speaking to this task.[251] The fact that "the earth is the Lord's . . . and those who live in it" is also a biblical conviction.[252] God's glory, his all-embracing kingdom, includes the whole of created reality.

Within this broad scope we must now consider how divine and human actions belong together, a joining which may be regarded as the task of Christians and of the church within society. By doing so, we are rebutting every kind of flight into a personally selected world of pious fantasy or of warm subjectivity, which cannot free us from caring for those who are entrusted to us. Hence, Dietrich Bonhoeffer rightly wrote that "only those who love the earth and God in one love can believe in the kingdom of God." In this context, prayer and deeds of love would be regarded not as two different kinds of activity but as two related modes of conduct of the Christian. "The hour in which the church prays for the kingdom today forces it to become part and parcel of the earth's flourishing and decay— and of its children, and it swears its faithfulness to the earth, to the poor, to the hungry, and to the dying."[253] The central basis for the social responsibility of Christians lies in their belief in God and in his deeds. Since God is the Creator and Jesus is the brother of all human beings, those who believe in him are responsible for treating their fellow humans as sisters and brothers of one human family.

Like the destiny of the recipients, so also is the essence of the ministry of Christians to be found within the prototype of the ministry of Jesus. As the Redeemer, whose reconciling love works for the return of persons to their true destiny, he calls persons to change their attitudes as well as their modes of relating to others into a reconciling mode.[254] God's protecting and reconciling deeds are valid for all humans in the universality of his kingdom, for the righteous as well as for the unrighteous (Matthew 5:45). Accordingly, Jesus intercedes for the benefit of all persons, and above all for the rejected, so that all might participate in the kingdom of God. Hence, even those who are enemies are included in his love, and so this love of enemies is made real in the forgiveness of debts. Jesus Christ is peace for humanity; he has "broken down the dividing wall, that is, the hostility between us" (Ephesians 2:14). He is the glory of God and its central realization within the context of history. He represents the moment in history that signifies the activity of God for the salvation of the world, which is the *kairos*.[255] As such, he summons Christians to become messengers of a new order of love and righteousness. In relation to him, they understand that it is a matter not only of words and decisions but also of reliance upon God's presence and upon those actions that flow from this trust, that it depends on alertness which recognizes, discerns, and identifies God's actions, and that it entails being set on fire by him to reflect his love in their own deeds. The church has to bear witness to the world that "reality in all of its multiplicity is nevertheless one, namely in the incarnate God Jesus Christ." The world has been standing in relationship to this Christ since its creation.[256]

In light of God's acts, we also comprehend how he enables us to take part in his battle as God's co-workers against the destructive forces of this world, which threaten human life and wound God's creation. In this participation in God's redemptive deeds, a twofold purpose is achieved. First, the "old Adam" is crucified through God's Word, and the new person grows through God's accepting love. "So it is no way only a matter of an event between God and the individual, but a matter of the glory of God in association with humanity."[257] As with Luther, so also for Wesley it was not at all simply a matter of fulfilling God's will only at the individual or congregational level. Rather, each in his own way also had in view the prospect of the transformation of social relationships for the particular society in which he lived. It is astounding to see how they busied themselves in similar ways with the matters of establishing schools, righteously ordering the economic sphere, and perceiving the issues of social responsibility. Both men were certainly aware that human deeds cannot bring about the rule of God. However, that in no way allowed them to doubt the social tasks of the Christian faith.

The church lives as an alternative society within the society that surrounds it, and its members belong to both societies. They live as a fellowship of those who are declared as righteous and reconciled to God, those who can now live in peace with God. They have experienced God's love through other humans, and their actions are marked by that experience. However, this love safeguards their power in relation to strangers and to those who think and live differently. Therefore, an ethic of love connects the actions of Christians in the areas of righteousness, peace, and reconciliation. An ethic of love reckons with human sinfulness and their proneness to wrongdoing. It proceeds from the experience of forgiveness, and it opens the freedom to confess one's own guilt, to be open to self-criticism, and to have forbearance with the weaknesses of others. However, it also recognizes the sins of others and is ready to share the weight of their consequences, wherever that is possible and appropriate.

Such a comprehensively understood ministry also has its political dimensions. This is so because in every society there are persons who forfeit their benefits and lose their privileges through their acts of reconciliation, justice, and tolerance. Whoever raises her or his voice about the existence of prejudice and the difficulties that attend this soon becomes aware of the presence of hostility. Whoever identifies with the oppressed is often made to share their fate. Such a horrific outcome was not only the destiny of Jesus; it has also been the experience of many of his disciples to the present time. For the sake of their social and political activity, the Christian ministry of servanthood must carefully examine its integrity. It must neither hitch itself to other causes nor lobby for goals other than the well-being of human beings. Of course, this also means this ministry can make use of all ethical means of pursuing that end, within the context of a democratic society, in order to practice ministry as effectively as possible. In cases of necessity, it may be necessary for this ministry to be carried forward in opposition to the decisions of governments and authorities. Christians cannot be the salt of the earth if they simply accommodate themselves to all forms of opposition as soon as those forces bring discomfort and pressure upon them. While such opposition to authority certainly cannot be their intention, it can under some circumstances become a viable mode of ministry in such a society.

Finally, we can also learn from Wesley[258] how society is constituted and how the people Christians intend to serve, actually live. To achieve that understanding in our day, congregations need to have areas of contact with those beyond their own communities. Using figurative speech, we may say that two walls of a church building should be missing, so that on the one hand the congregation may offer protection and on the other hand can keep in view the people round about them and enable encounters with them. In a certain respect, our hospitals, social institutions, and homes offer such areas of contact, but the connection between the congregations and these "outer stations" is often still quite weak. Correctly understood, congregations are also the "supports" and "bases" for all the ecclesial and nonecclesial activities that are part of the action of ministry. Entering into the congregation and exiting into the larger society forms a twofold movement in which diaconal ministry becomes able to live and to operate. Hence, Christians with their ministry penetrate society and bring the benefits of God's love to bear upon the lives of individuals as well as society as a whole. By this activity, they help the church to remain true to its task of being the light to the world (Matthew 5:14).

4.4.3 *The Ethical Task of the Church*

"The church should continually exert a strong ethical influence upon the state, supporting policies and programs deemed to be just and opposing policies and programs that are unjust."[259]

In a day in which political boundaries are losing their significance and totalitarian systems are losing their grip, the need for orientation for ethical behavior has not lessened. The capacity to make a free decision or to commit an act with civil freedom does not in itself constitute something which is good. Either good or evil can flow out of such liberty, and moving with the times ordinarily does not include adequate goals. Hence, we must give fresh consideration to establishing proper goals and strategies for extending the witness of the church into the sphere of right ethical conduct. The church certainly should not give the appearance of being inherently superior to other institutions of society, for that would not only be a sign of its own arrogance; it would also be inappropriate given its own proneness to error and fallibility. For the same reason, we are to bear in mind that we have no right to declare that our ethical principles are absolute and final in their truth. In our effort to let our actions be guided by God's will, we must always first be critical of ourselves, and we always need to ask where the church has failed to come to terms with upholding the truth with courage, or with fulfilling its call to be peacemakers on earth, and to prepare the next generation for its responsibilities. This honest self-appraisal is needed by our church in all lands of the world where it is serving. These are issues to which our German sisters and brothers have been seriously responding, in light of their recent history, as they grapple with the "question of guilt concerning the past, . . . and guilt which can still be committed afresh today."[260] (Translator's observation: For Americans, a comparable issue would likely be our continuing need to come to terms with the legacy of American slavery and the lingering effects of racism.) In prior times, as well as today, the measure for this assessment is the will of God for every social structure—it is righteousness as the vehicle of love,[261] together with the entire social meaning of the decalogue. Guilt arises where personal responsibility for the restoration and the protection of righteousness was not taken seriously. Churches and Christians bear responsibility for the authentic implementation of the gospel, as we have tried to indicate in this chapter.[262]

The identification and explication of guilt, confession, and conversion are only possible where there is also a way to forgiveness and the possibility of living with guilt that is forgiven though not forgotten. This possibility is given "through the gracious will of God as actually revealed in the destiny of Jesus Christ," and it can be certified as the living experience of faith. It concerns not only "the feeling of guilt of the individual conscience in private concerns. No, the invitation of God's grace certainly always has to do with the consciences of individuals, but not just with their private guilt, but also their guilt with regard to the past events of history."[263]

As we have already indicated, the source from which the church derives its standard, which it is obligated to uphold, is found in its connection to the will of God, as he has disclosed this in the Bible and above all in the love commandment, with its various manifestations. From this source the church is to develop and specify the direction of his will for each actual situation that is encountered. Unlike people living in the time of the New Testament, Christians living in nations with democratic constitutions share responsibility for the political, economic, and social structures of their respective lands. They cannot then regard themselves as persons disengaged from this responsibility, persons who limit their primary responsibilities to matters of family, vocational, and congregational life. Due to the democratic political constitutions under which they live, they are to see themselves as part of the "principalities and powers," of whom Paul always spoke only in the third person.[264]

United Methodists see the ethical duty of the church above all as being applicable to all activities and structures of the church itself, which stand in reciprocal relationship to the world around it and concern persons who are outside as well as those inside the church. What is true for the political realm is also applicable to the spheres of economic activities, education, and culture. Our task of being the light of the world and the salt of the earth has already been comprehensively understood in the origins of Methodism. Hence, United Methodists, like other Christians, have understood themselves as advocates of those who are victims of injustice in society, not everywhere, but everywhere the destructive and degrading use of power becomes evident. Furthermore, they attempt to stand by those who have been injured through their direct help and their public intercession on behalf of those persons.[265]

The Social Principles have paraphrased this broad understanding in a series of themes in an exemplary way, without developing them with explicit detail. The public support for minorities—from Methodist preachers accompanying those condemned to death on the way to the scaffold to the work of the deprived communities in Latin America and the theological joining of sanctification and liberation[266]—was and is characteristic of the original Methodism. Those who have pursued this ministry of love and justice have seldom been given recognition. Moreover, this kind of emphasis has certainly not been without controversy within the established churches. This affinity for the weak and the theological-ethical critique of every kind of misuse of power, which stimulate and lead to the development of alternative proposals for ordering social life, cannot be suppressed, because they are connected with the understanding of the gospel and because Methodism always depends on the practice of love and a pragmatic theology.[267]

The official position of the church, which is set forth and accounted for by the Social Principles of The United Methodist Church, is intended to inform the ethical orientation of its own actions as well as those of others. Annual conferences or ecumenical boards in which The United Methodist Church participates approve other texts that provide information and help to formulate policy. In addition, the messages of the bishops and the articles in the church publications are supposed to assist church members in forming a basic concept of ethical themes that are crucial for living. In recent years, M. D. Meeks has discussed the area of economics in a number of publications under the heading of the "question of the preservation of life," which is important for contemporary society on both the national and the international levels.[268] It also provides a model for the social and ethical task of the church, which contributes to the development of a new direction to be taken by government and economics as they seek to address these concerns. By appealing to the biblical concept of the *oikonomia tou theou,*[269] the "economy of God" can be more precisely delineated: it consists of deeds whereby "all of God's creatures can find abundant life, and God's economy in Israel and Jesus Christ is to begin with the poor and the oppressed, those who are most threatened by death, evil, and sin, in order to build a new household for all of God's creatures."[270] For its part, the church should "live the economy of God" but it should also try to convince the world of the fact that "there is another logic" than that which is given by the market, one that aims at the creation of other kinds of economic communities.[271] The churches thereby have a twofold responsibility in addressing the ethics of economics: one side is to formulate a model of economic activity that provides for the protection of life, a model that also can be connected to other forms of communities,[272] and the other is to describe and disseminate visions of alternative forms of economics.

The addressees who receive such proposals as the official position of the church are therefore not only the congregations and individual Christians but also the public authorities in government and economics, research and education, medicine and culture, whose decisions affect the lives and rights of many persons. To inform oneself and to examine one's own thoughts and actions, to take seriously one's responsibility and to do what is needed and also possible to address these issues—these are the steps for which the church can and intends to provide guidance in its statements on ethical themes. "We ask"—so it says at the conclusion of such a memorandum—"our congregational members, constituents and friends, to participate actively in the formation of the public will in our democratic state and in the social groups to which they belong, in order to facilitate a hearing of ethical points of view, and a sense of their importance."[273]

4.4.3.1 THE UNITED METHODIST CHURCH AS A "FREE CHURCH"

[Introductory statement from the translator: Whereas United Methodism in the United States has developed under the auspices of the constitutional separation of church and state, in continental Europe, like the Wesleyan Church in Great Britain, it has attained the status of a free church, over against the established state church system. As the numerical influence and theological cohesiveness of the Methodist Church in the United States has lessened in recent decades, a pattern that is shared by other "mainstream" Protestant denominations, United Methodism no longer functions within a social context that can be identified as a broad-based, evangelical ethos, such as that which undergirded American civil religion in the nineteenth and early twentieth centuries. Accordingly, our situation increasingly approximates many of the features of the European free-church status of United Methodism, which understands its witness in terms of a voluntary, connectional community of faith that seeks to interface with and impact the larger secular order with the witness of the gospel, as expressed in a many-faceted ministry of word and deed. Hence, an examination of the free-church pattern of contemporary European United Methodism may serve to amplify our awareness of how such a vital witness to the social order might be shaped.]

The expression "free church" can be understood in different ways.

(a.) Most persons understand this "in contrast to the state or national church" *(Volkskirche)*.[274] This contrast has seldom or never played any essential role in the developments of United Methodism in Europe. Unlike other free churches, such as the Mennonite and Baptist churches, The United Methodist Church did not arise as a response to doctrinal controversies or through flight from persecution of believers. Hence, as an evangelical free church, it is not a church that was instituted on the basis of a polemic being made over against the state.[275] It esteems and values the order of the state, in which the individual, and above all the weak, are safeguarded, so that they may live and pursue their work in peace. Because of the freedom of our ministry from every civil and political influence, United Methodists prefer the constitution of a free church, in which only its members make decisions regarding the form and ministry of the church. The rise of our church in Germany and the history of free churches in the decades after its rise was often characterized by repression and persecution through political boards which worked in tandem with the state church and which carried out policies that were instigated by the state churches.[276] This situation has changed considerably in recent decades, and now a positive working relationship on ecumenical terms has developed with the established churches. Nevertheless, United Methodists retain in their collective memory the experiences of the past, in which the close connection of church and state tended to forestall peace and the protection of human rights. For the existence of Christians in their state, it can and must be valid that they are to be the salt of the earth and the light of the world. That means that their capacity to contribute to the well-being of the political community lies in their being and their conduct, with which they bear witness to God's presence in the world and to his will for the world. They can also credibly address important themes that would demonstrate the gospel and would speak blessing to humanity. Such a word can take the character of a protest, whenever human life and creation are endangered or are injured and ruined. However, this word is also to be an encouragement and a strengthening for those who take seriously their responsibility within society and the state, so that these structures may be made to conform to the will of God, whether the persons who do this act consciously as Christians or whether they act out of other convictions.[277] The goal of our engagement in society is in the final analysis not the perpetuation of the interests of the church and the promotion of its own existence, nor primarily the well-being of the state, but rather it is the serving of those who need our attention.

(b.) "Free churches" can also be understood in the sense of a voluntary agreement of persons with a specific Christian conviction. To the present day, believers have repeatedly come together to be able to live out their kind of piety and Christian faith. Not infrequently, this has occurred within the context of national or *Volk* churches, in conscious demarcation from the mode of existence that is expressed by the major denominations, without this aspect having to be the decisive one. What allowed the model of a "free church" to be understood as conforming more closely to the gospel model was also the perception of the opposition between church membership advanced through the tradition of national churches (which says membership occurs apart from any personal decision on the part of the member) and the freedom of faith (which insists on a personal decision for life with Christ). The freedom of self-determination, which was sought by those who had found a living faith, was not consistent with the understanding of a national church, whereby all infants were regarded as baptized members of the church, and the question whether they intended to belong to it was never asked. Under such circumstances, the freedom of decision was (and is) exercised mostly by those who separate themselves from such a church rather than by those who intend to remain within the church out of their personal faith.

It can certainly be objected that one can, on the basis of one's own decision, affirm the church wherein one is found apart from one's own doing. This objection will be considered more closely. Only two issues should be addressed in response: (1) Within the context of the national church *(Volkskirche)*, the impression is that someone could be an adult member of the church without having to affirm her or his own "yes" to the Christian faith.[278] In the church[279] all can remain together who were once baptized as infants (or later), and that is without recourse to their convictions and conduct of life. That is the impression which is left by the structure of a national church *(Volkskirche)*, an impression which is not without support in its actual form.[280] (2) In the context of an actual national church *(Volkskirche)*, a free decision concerning church membership usually coincides with the freedom to exit, which rejects the effort to bring a person into conformity with the Christian faith. Consequently, faith remains without any structural possibility for making a decision about church membership, a position a person already finds himself or herself to be in. Such a structure contradicts the core of Christian faith, which includes the free response of a person to God's call and the empowerment of that response.[281]

On the other hand, we want to prevent a misunderstanding of the free-church position that would assume that a congregation may arise as a result of a voluntary coming together of a group of people. If that were the case, then the church would merely be the result of human decisions and actions. Instead, the congregation of the church of Jesus Christ only arises and exists through the working of the Holy Spirit, who calls the church to life, forms it into the body of Christ, and proceeds to lead the people of God toward the purpose of fulfilling God's promises to them.[282] In this regard, humans are only tools of the Holy Spirit and cannot fully disregard the fact that the church of Jesus Christ is one church and so it is not a matter of human preference to establish "new" congregations or to split those that already exist. Here we must be careful to distinguish Jesus' task of calling persons into faith and gathering them into communities from those often very human decisions concerning the actual building of structures for the church. All too frequently in the history of the church, including the history of United Methodism, tensions have resulted from trivial causes, which in retrospect were not justified and were often overcome through subsequent church unions.[283] The Protestant principle of freedom of personal faith has not always been able to guard the church from falsehood and the misuse of that principle.

(c.) The United Methodist understanding of a free church is oriented neither toward opposition to the state nor toward a critique of the structures of a national church *("Volkskirche"),*[284] but rather toward our understanding of the church. The church arose and continues to go forth by the action of God, in which God turns himself graciously toward human beings, lets them experience his love, and thereby enables the response of trusting faith.[285] Call and response, love and reciprocated love, pardon and trust, all make possible the interfacing of the prevenient and creative actions of God and the process of allowing God to do God's work on us and also for us to respond to that action. Despite the different impressions that are found in the life history of believers, the structure of this event is always identical. It is always God's prevenient, creative action of love that enables the new relationship with God, and it is always the free, trusting response of humans to that action that enjoys God's gift and its acceptance. This structure of a spiritual process that encounters the being of a person in its entirety finds its correlation in the self-understanding of The United Methodist Church: there is God's prevenient love as a consolation of pardon and a pledge of our acceptance into adoption as his children through the proclamation of the Word and baptism, and there is the free response of faith as a personal confession and as acceptance into church membership. This process is connected with a change in living for Christians, who have a "before" and an "after" history that can run its course and be recognized in very different ways but always marks the beginning of an "unending history" of God with the persons who have placed their trust in him. The free and personal response of faith pertains not only to the affirmation of God's saving acts that are spoken in the word of confession, but it also includes one's voluntary participation in the work of the congregation, spreading the gospel and ministering through deeds of love. In this sense, the church can only exist as a free church, as a community of persons who know their own need and God's self-giving love, and who, in this knowledge, intend to exist for others.

Thus, it becomes clear that The United Methodist Church cannot understand itself as an elite, "pure congregation."[286] In contrast, it is a typical, "unsectarian" church, which is averse to every special doctrine and is concerned about all persons. Hence, it is not easy to make its identity clearly recognizable in the "ensemble" of churches. To fret about this would certainly be as uncharacteristic of United Methodists as would complaining about the universality of God's love. So long as United Methodists place themselves at the disposal of his grace as instruments they need not be concerned either for their existence or for preserving their identity.

4.4.3.2 CHURCH AND STATE

It is of course not possible to describe in this section the full historical development of political ordinances in their various stages, nor even to discuss the most important theories concerning their rise. In spite of the extensive ambiguity that surrounds the meaning of political community, we can occupy ourselves in relation to this work only with the theological perspective upon political activity.

When, after the recognition of American independence from Great Britain (1783), Wesley acknowledged that the Methodist societies in America had become an independent church, he gave them his so-called Sunday service,[287] a liturgy, along with the "Articles of Religion," a primer for Methodist doctrine. Since the founding conference of the Methodist Episcopal Church in 1784, these articles have continued in The United Methodist Church as one of its basic doctrinal standards, alongside the Confession of Faith of the Evangelical United Brethren Church.[288] With only one exception, the twenty-five Articles of Religion represented a revision and abbreviation of the Thirty-nine Articles of the Church of England. The single exception was Article XXIII, "Concerning Authority," which was newly inserted into his doctrinal list. It affirmed that "since there is no authority apart from God, it is the duty of all Christians, for the sake of conscience, to give obedience to the authority and the laws of the land in which they dwell, and to show themselves to be peace-loving citizens."[289] Wesley clearly relied on the assertions of the apostle Paul in Romans 13, and, as one who was committed to the tradition of a constitutional monarchy, it was not easy for him to accept the revolutionary changes that had occurred in the British colonies of North America, in relation to the Methodists within the new United States, who now were prepared to declare their obedience to their newly autonomous authorities.

Like Paul and Luther before him, Wesley was of the conviction that the existence of a political order not only serves the well-being of the citizens but also conforms to the will of God. Even if one were not to agree with the conception of Thomas Hobbes that the natural condition of human society is one of "war of all against all" *(bellum omnium contra omnes)*, of war and mutual antagonism,[290] a realistic evaluation of human community under the conditions of sin nevertheless needs to be made, so that an ordering of the state can be achieved that will provide for a sharing of power in government.

The conviction that such an ordered community originates in the will of God also certainly includes the tenet that its concrete expression must be set forth in terms of clearly explicated goals, which conform in their content to the divine will. While he described different alternative ways for the interaction of "subjects" and authorities, the apostle Paul set an ethical goal for political power by which both must let themselves be measured: "For rulers are not a terror to good conduct, but to bad. Do you wish to have no fear of the authority? Then do what is good and you will receive its approval; for it is God's servant for your good. But if you do what is wrong, you should be afraid, for the authority does not bear the sword in vain. It is the servant of God to execute wrath on the wrongdoer" (Romans 13:3-4.). In these statements, there lurks the explosive which in the history of the Christian church has often led to protest and opposition against those authorities that happen to contradict God's standards.

The well-known objection of Peter (the "Petrine clause")[291] brings to expression the fact that the conscience of Christians stands on the side of obedience, and this means that one is bound to the law and its ordinances, but it can also lead to opposition against those political ordinances and to the refusal of obedience. According to the United Methodist tradition, the protection of the rights of all citizens, and above all the weak, has precedence over the maintenance of power by the elected or appointed officeholders. The limit of obedience to political standards of justice is reached whenever the conscience that is bound to the known will of God is wounded by that authority. "After having exhausted all legal recourse" in the effort to rectify that situation, then "we recognize the right of individuals . . . to resist or disobey laws that they deem to be unjust." A Christian is then to disclaim all kinds of violence and "to accept the costs of disobedience."[292] Christians are to obey laws and ordinances that are legitimate and valid, so long as they conform to the ethical standards of justice, for a political commonwealth cannot fulfill the tasks assigned to it by God, to promote justice, freedom, and peace, without the inner agreement and the active support of its citizens. "God intends to rule upon earth.

However, He does not intend for the world to be ruled by dictators and police states. God intends to have a state that praises work that is good and thereby distinguishes itself from work that is bad. The state can only do this in a credible way if it also lets its own actions be measured by this distinction."[293]

The prophetic task of reminding authorities of their duties therefore belongs to the important tasks of the church. According to John Wesley's conviction, the bearers of political power are "accountable to God" in their decisions, "who permitted no ruler to rob his subjects of their civil or religious liberty. Legitimacy and responsibility are inseparably derived from God. Therefore Wesley stood against any misuse of power."[294] We must certainly see that such thinking is not explicitly discussed in the works of John Wesley. For him, political authority is first of all set in place by God independent of the actual form taken by that state. His often repeated warning that his preachers were to refrain from making political statements was not based only on the fact that he regarded the constitutional monarchy in England, with its civil rights, as being one of the freest political orders in the world, but also on the fact that the revolution in France and efforts to demolish the monarchy and to introduce democracy were linked with the struggle against Christianity and the church. On the other hand, he also emphasized that the political authority may demand loyalty from its citizens only so long as it does not coerce them to act disobediently toward God.

The text of our Social Principles takes up this latter reservation when it maintains that "While our allegiance to God takes precedence over our allegiance to any state, we acknowledge the vital function of government as a principal vehicle for the ordering of society. Because we know ourselves to be responsible to God for social and political life, we declare the following relative to governments. . . . "[295] A pragmatic reason is then added to his ethical one: "The strength of a political system depends upon the full and willing participation of its citizens."[296] In saying this, the text acknowledges the fact that as Christians we live, along with other citizens, in a democracy, which we endorse as a form of government because it comes closer than other familiar forms of government to the Christian understanding of persons. Today we are precisely both: we are not only the governed but also those who govern. Hence, we need to consider how the statements of the apostle Paul appear to a congregation in a democratic state.[297] The political existence of Christians today pertains to their "worship in the daily life of the world," which consists in an interweaving of loyalty and nonaccommodation which we need to explore in more detail (Romans 12–13). In being joined to God, we recognize the important function of the state as the bearer of the social order and we know ourselves to be called to involvement in that order. However, the exercise of political power must conform to its task of protecting and guarding the dignity of persons and of doing that which is necessary and possible to promote a peaceful and just common life for all citizens. The misuse of power must be prevented so far as possible. Whenever it nonetheless appears, it provides the moral basis for dismissal from office. Christians must remind others about this. Christians and churches are in need of maintaining an open attitude whenever it is no longer a question of political judgment, but also whenever God's command is violated in the political realm, particularly where this does not occur just occasionally and perhaps by chance but in a programmatic and conscious manner. This obligation to publicly take a position is in regard not only to the political arena in the narrower sense but also to the parties and the political movements that exercise or strive for power within our countries.

United Methodists can also say, along with Luther's distinction between the two kinds of kingdoms of God,[298] that God rules the world on one hand through restraining sin and its consequences and, on the other, through forgiving guilt and the overcoming of the power of sin. The overcoming of sin and its power happens through the operation of the gospel, which through the Holy Spirit brings forth renewal within the hearts of persons. The restraining of sin and its consequences takes place through persons who make use of their power under divine mandate. This distinction between the two kinds of ways in which God orders the world has repeatedly led, in the structure of the so-called two-kingdom doctrine, to removing the area of worldly concerns from the demands of the Word of God and to limiting these demands to the realm of the church. Conversely, the lack of such a distinction has led to an unacceptable mixing of church and society, by which either the worldly rulers also have become heads of the church (Caesaropapism) or bishops have become and are the *de facto* rulers of the world. So it is a matter of making a distinction between the two kinds of divine rule over the world and yet not separating them from one another. This has been concisely and clearly summarized by the fifth thesis of the Barmen Declaration, when it declares that "We discard the false doctrine that the state should and could make its task that of becoming the only and the total order for human life, and hence that it would also fulfill the vocation of the church. We reject the false doctrine that the church should and could make its task that of appropriating a political form, a political mandate and political dignity, and hence become itself an organ of the state."[299]

In conclusion it can be said that God acts in the world in a twofold manner, as Creator and Redeemer. As Creator, who has created as good this earth and everything that lives upon it, God intends to preserve it despite human sin. God therefore gives to his creatures everything necessary for their lives. The worldly authorities are supposed to serve this preserving work of God. Its task lies in protecting the living environment of persons and of other forms of life. To that end, the right to the exercise of power is also given to the state, or to the "governing authorities" (Romans 13:1). Paul, as well as Luther and Wesley, was only too well aware that political power can be misused. In spite of this, it was their conviction that it was God's will that there might be a political authority to act as an instrument of the preserving activity of God.

God also acts in the world as Reconciler and Redeemer. In Christ, he has reconciled the guilt-ridden world with himself and offers to all persons forgiveness and peace through the proclamation of the gospel. The instrument of God's reconciling activity is the community of believers. Here the law does not prevail, which coerces one into a particular mode of behavior and forbids and punishes another, but rather it is the gospel, which acquits and sets a person free for a new life. In the congregation, the customary social rules are in part turned upside down; it is not the most powerful who are the most important ones, but rather "Whoever wishes to be first among you must be slave of all" (Mark 10:44). What prevails there is not command and obedience but the acting out of spontaneous love. Because everything is not always being so ordered within a congregation, in spite of the example and the words of Jesus, it regularly needs self-critical scrutiny and an openness to the operation of the Spirit that is ever new. Then this imperfect congregation is also an instrument in the hand of God, who wants to reach all persons with his saving love.

Christians will repeatedly attempt to open themselves to the will of God, as Jesus has proclaimed to us and embodied it in his own life, in order to transfer it into acts that are politically significant. Hence, they will not simply rest content with an available privilege, but will also inquire whether it really serves people or is only being exercised for their own purposes (see Mark 2:27). They will attempt to bring the love commandment of Jesus into public ordinances and political decisions as extensively and concretely as they are able, and they will seek to orient the implementation of these ordinances and decisions by this command. Police officers who are Christians will therefore continue to carry out their service and exercise power, but they will also be mindful of the fact that they are ministering a temporal and not an eternal ordinance, and they remain bound to the will of God and to the command of neighbor love in their execution of this service. This remains true even if that love is being fulfilled in terms of the framework of their office, which is different from the way it would be fulfilled in the context of their personal lives. That principle applies for all who are called to make decisions that pertain to others, whether this be in the setting of a school or industry, in a court of judgment or of civil administration. All stand under God's will and are accountable to him. As Christians, they are also witnesses to the eternal kingdom of God, circumscribes all human ordinances and kingdoms and which finally will abolish them.

A further distinction in this regard should be made, which is that between individual Christians and the church as a whole. In distinction to individual Christian citizens of a nation, who depending on their personal insights and convictions can accordingly get involved as individuals, in its public pronouncements the church must devote itself to a twofold reservation. (1.) A church—if possible together with other churches—must hand over the deliberation of issues to a careful process of consensus-building through the clear votes of its authorized spokespersons or boards, a process that certainly leaves open a limited sphere for decision making to those individuals and bodies. However, being free of conflict within itself, their decisions are to be discernibly bound to the biblical message,[300] and they ought to provide clear assistance for the making of decisions. The Social Principles of The United Methodist Church and its Social Creed provide us with basic points of view and norms that aid us in this process.[301] (2.) It must also concentrate on the ethical aspects of political and economic activity. "We believe that the state should not attempt to control the church, nor should the church seek to dominate the state."[302] As the church must be allowed to regulate its concerns without political intervention, it must conversely claim no political authority for itself. However, its authority in ethical questions not only remains untouched because of this, rather it receives an even higher measure of credibility because it is not joined to the special interests of the institutional church.

The standard of ecclesial expressions can be more precisely described as the responsibility for attending to human worth and protecting those rights which are closely bound with this sense of human self-worth. This responsibility involves the tasks of promoting free and adequate elections, with secret balloting, the freedom of speech and the exercise of religion, as well as the freedom to assemble and to receive information, the protection of the personal areas of life, and the right to living conditions that are fit for humans. Respect for humanity and the right that flows from that respect comes to all persons alike, regardless of their origin, skin color, culture, or religion. Congregations and churches are of course encouraged to intercede for those persons who are taken advantage of or defrauded of human rights. As citizens and as participants in the process of social formation, United Methodists should first and foremost do their part to see that such rights are realized for all persons in all areas of life without exception.[303] The readiness to give uncritical obedience to authorities has as little place in a Christian social ethic as does the egoism of individuals or groups that seek their advantage at the expense of others.

In special situations it can be the task of the church not only to speak openly but also to restrain political injustice through individual actions.[304] The church does not sanction the use of power in making this effort either, and it is only to be carried out through the uncoerced intercession for persons who are threatened or who suffer. Furthermore, the appropriate boards need to take responsibility for such decisions. This often necessitates a difficult process of consensus-building. However, wherever God's will is sought as a basis for action and wherever this occurs as a response to hearing the Word of God and through prayer, the church will receive clarity and courage for the perception of its ethical responsibility in the state and in society.[305]

In each case, what counts is that the church realizes this task indirectly and regularly through intercession on behalf of those who bear responsibility and through the open preaching of the gospel. The church also attempts to grant clarity, credibility, and effectiveness to its ethical pronouncements through its members who are inspired and molded by God's love.

4.4.3.3   A CHURCH FOR THE PEOPLE

Since its beginnings, Methodism has viewed itself as leaven and as a light in this world which lightens the path for others. Wesley remarked that "the very design of God in giving you this light was, that it might shine."[306] The General Rules of 1739 have given this objective a very concrete description. The congregation, which is bestowed with the experience of God's love in worship, in the use of the means of grace, and in fellowship with other Christians, is not a ghetto in the midst of the world, but rather it seeks to live and to act according to the standards of the kingdom of God within the world. It allows itself to be newly entrusted with the task God gives it to serve in the midst of the daily life of the world, whenever it gathers together for worship on Sundays. The congregation understands that kind of life, within the perspective of God's rule, as a congregation of coworkers who allow themselves to be put to God's work. Their faith, their awareness, and their experience lead them to a life that conforms to God's will and which causes them to be responsible for those who are entrusted to them. This is their grateful response to God's faithfulness to them.

In the Social Creed of The United Methodist Church, which was enlarged to be part of the Social Principles in 1972, the matter of one's personal commitment to this ministry in the world is expressed in the following terms:

> We commit ourselves to the rights of men, women, children, youth, young adults, the aging, and people with disabilities; to improvement of the quality of life; and to the rights and dignity of racial, ethnic, and religious minorities.
>
> We believe in the right and duty of persons to work for the glory of God and the good of themselves and others and in the protection of their welfare in so doing; in the rights to property as a trust from God, collective bargaining, and responsible consumption; and in the elimination of economic and social distress.
>
> We dedicate ourselves to peace throughout the world, to the rule of justice and law among nations, and to individual freedom for all people of the world.
>
> We believe in the present and final triumph of God's Word in human affairs and gladly accept our commission to manifest the life of the gospel in the world.[307]

These should not be empty words or inconsequential resolutions. All who affirm this confession with sincerity of conviction are ready to let themselves be put to service by God, out of gratitude for the benefits they have received from him, and out of love for others.

4.4.3.4 THE GLOBAL COMMUNITY AND THE WHOLE OF CREATION

The peace that Christ has brought includes the peace between God and humans and the peace among humans. Peace with God is genuine whenever persons allow themselves to be consoled by the promise of pardon for their guilt and by their acceptance as children of God, and also whenever they begin to live out of this peace. Christ, who is our peace (Ephesians 2:14), calls the author of peace "blessed." The community of his disciples develops a significant objective out of this: "In the power and unity of the Holy Spirit, the church of Jesus Christ is called to serve as an alternative community to an alienated and fractured world: a loving and peaceable international company of disciples transcending all governments, races and ideologies, reaching out to all 'enemies,' and ministering to all victims of poverty and oppression."[308]

Such an ethic of love is fundamentally universal, because the love commandment knows no limitations.[309] All political, racial, economic, cultural, gender, religious, or other kinds of separating boundaries are overcome through God's love. These things can no longer claim to separate us from God nor can they legitimize any differentiated valuation of human beings. An ethic of love will also direct us to action that conforms to the will of the Creator on behalf of all nonhuman aspects of God's creation, for God has handed over this responsibility to humans, who are created in God's own image.[310] As an ethic of ecological stewardship, this ethic of love will also need to keep in mind that the misfortune that has already arisen diminishes the possibility that what is arising and already widely threatening will be avoided and prevented.

(a.) The peace of God among humanity does not fall like manna from heaven. It grows as the fruit of God's Spirit, who renews human beings. The peace of God comes upon earth through that which has been promised in Scripture: "The Spirit of the Lord is upon me, because he has anointed me to bring good news to the poor. He has sent me to proclaim release to the captives and recovery of sight to the blind, to let the oppressed go free, to proclaim the year of the Lord's favor" (Luke 4:18-19). And the peace of God comes upon earth through persons of whom it is said, "The Spirit of God is resting on you" (1 Peter 4:14), in whom the fruit of the Spirit grows: love, joy, peace, patience, friendliness, goodness, faithfulness, gentleness, and self-control (Galatians 5:22).

Hence, the alternative that is available to us is not between God and humanity; this would mean that either God gives peace, or people create it; either Christ brings righteousness, or humans extend it; either God heals the fallen creation, or people safeguard it. It is much more correct to say that because God gives peace, it can grow in and through humans. Those who are justified by Christ can ensure righteousness. God's acts do not make our acts unnecessary or impossible, but rather make them possible and significant. Because God creates righteousness and peace, Christians can enter into righteousness and peace with other persons.

Not infrequently have national interests forced into the background the obligation of Christian churches to promote the international work of peace. The capacity to envision what conforms to the will of God and serves peace has often been clouded through emotions or through a slick propaganda policy directed by prevailing governmental regimes. Yet, we find at the beginning of Methodism that there were clear and basic convictions and activities that were opposed to this usual tendency.[311] John Wesley did not experience the trauma of war in his native land, and he participated in no fighting,[312] but he was informed about the results of war for the combatants as well as for the general population, through reports he received from arenas of battle in Europe and later in America. Consequently, he wrote in 1757 that "there is a still more horrid reproach to the Christian name, yea, to the name of man, to all reason and humanity. There is war in the world! war between men! war between Christians!"[313] However, Wesley did not let the matter rest with that kind of complaint, caused by the Seven Years' War (The French and Indian War in America). Instead, he pointed out that the responsibility for war and its consequences always lay with people. And even if the comprehensive reconciliation of the world with God might lead to the expectation of a cessation of warfare, it may yet be conceivable that those responsible for it "might be moved to an active commitment to ending the current war and preventing any further armed struggles from beginning."[314]

The general conferences of our church have repeatedly not only pointed to the dire consequences of war but have also at various intervals pled for them to be outlawed and abolished. Especially significant is the understanding of the corresponding section in the Social Creed, which was passed by the General Conference of the former Methodist Church in 1944, after the United States had entered into the war with Nazi Germany:

Christianity cannot be nationalistic; it must be universal in its outlook and appeal. War makes its appeal to force and hate, Christianity to reason and love. The influence of the church must, therefore, always be on the side of every effort seeking to remove animosities and prejudices which are contrary to the spirit and teaching of Christ. It does not satisfy the Christian conscience to be told that war is inevitable. It staggers the imagination to contemplate another war with its unspeakable horrors, in which modern science will make possible the destruction of whole populations. The methods of Jesus and the methods of war belong to different worlds. War is a crude and primitive force. It arouses passions which in the beginning may be unselfish and generous, but in the end war betrays those who trust in it. It offers no security that its decisions will be just and righteous. It leaves arrogance in the heart of the victor and resentment in the heart of the vanquished. . . . The time is at hand when the Church must rise in its might and demand an international organization which will make another war impossible.[315]

The development of nuclear weapons and the bombing of Hiroshima and Nagasaki only too quickly confirmed the fears of the General Conference. The founding of the United Nations, which held its first gathering in the Methodist Central Hall in London in 1946, was the first step to meet the challenges of the General Conference.

In the age of the Old and even the New Testament, war was an inevitable event in the life of all people. Nowhere does the Bible explicitly repudiate it within the context of this temporal world. Nevertheless, Christians can certainly endorse it as little as any other activities which do not conform to the will of God. In the Social Principles, it is stated quite concisely that "we believe war is incompatible with the teachings and example of Christ. We therefore reject war as an instrument of national foreign policy."[316] What specific consequences are to be drawn from this assertion is certainly the subject of disagreement even with our church. Yet, The United Methodist Church, being an internationally organized church body, has to attend to and improve the relationship of human beings in ways that go beyond national borders, so that prejudices and caricatures of enemies may be demolished or so that they may not even arise.

The doctrine of a just war, which arose in the course of church history,[317] and does not justify war but intends to place it within defined limits of acceptability, must lead to the conclusion that such a just war is no longer a viable possibility, given the nature of modern mass warfare. So far as the insertion of military power is necessary, perhaps for the purpose of carrying out an embargo, it should serve to avoid war and be subject to particular rules that can be agreed to on an international scale. What is urgently needed is an adaptation of the armaments of all national military forces, as far as possible, into purely defensive forces. Institutions need to be established and strengthened, on both the national and international levels, that could serve the preservation and maintenance of peace and provide for a nonviolent resolution of conflicts. Christians and churches within democratic nations must not shirk their responsibilities to work toward a political process that is ethically responsible with regard to these concerns, nor can they justify their abstinence from these political issues on theological grounds. Anyone who does nothing, when something can be done, becomes guilty. Rather, all Christians need to inquire into the will of God and also always include those who are considered "enemies" within the scope of their reflections and prayers, even if the conduct of those enemies is to be condemned.

(b.) The reconciliation of peoples upon this earth is to include the poor, the hungry, those imprisoned unjustly, and the persecuted. Neither the Old Testament prophets nor Jesus himself leave any doubt that it contradicts God's will when we abandon those who are hungry and ignore the afflicted and the imprisoned.[318] This sharing with one another and concern for one another is a self-evident consequence of the love commandment.[319] This is true not only of the area of one's personal life, but also of the relations between peoples and between areas of the earth. Peace cannot arise apart from righteousness, and unrighteousness and prejudice will always be a source of unrest. Moreover, the neglect and suppression of persons also signifies injury to their worth, which God has conferred upon them. Hence, Christian churches have acted properly in coming together to deliberate in the so-called conciliar process for justice, peace, and the integrity of the creation. With its diverse institutions, publications, and services of worship, this process has contributed to a change of consciousness among many persons both within and without the church.[320] Yet, more remains to be done than has been accomplished to this point, and most people have not yet learned to really share, which sometimes hurts.

An ecumenical disposition, to which our church has committed itself, must also have in view those persons who are suffering under the current systems of economics and under the inequitable distribution of economic and political power of the world. The information which we receive through our sister churches in the countries of the so-called Third World, and which is accessible to all, speaks clearly. The knowledge of suffering in the world can certainly lead to resignation and can unleash feelings of excessive demand and being confounded. This is why the combined work of Christians of diverse churches is needed among all who are of goodwill and who seek to concentrate upon those particular tasks that appear with the greatest urgency. Possibilities of political influence and personal support are open to us, as well as the possibility of relaying the most authentic information possible and striving for a new attitude toward people in the poorer nations of this world.

This new outlook really will not come to pass without our own thoughtful reflection and our repentance, especially when we consider that our present-day prosperity in the nations of the Western and Northern hemispheres rests upon a twofold unrighteousness. "Raw materials and agrarian products are purchased far below their actual value from the nations of the third world, and the ecology in those lands is destroyed by the debris of harmful substances that, according to the principle of the user being responsible, should be being cleaned up by the ones using the resources."[321] Hence, what is being proposed is not retrogression in industrialization nor an implementation of illusory utopias, but rather the assumption of the full costs of our progress. Without justice there is no way to peace, and only in a peaceful interchange of persons and ideas are we able to provide for greater measures of justice. Geoffrey Wainwright has drawn attention to the following: "True peace, shalom, includes justice. However, temporary tranquility is often purchased at the price of injustice. Failure in justice and peace is a major cause of grief."[322]

(c.) For Christians, faith in God as the Creator and Preserver of the world as well as its Redeemer and Perfecter is the self-evident basis of their attitude toward nature and the environment. This conviction is thoroughly compatible with the discoveries of the newer natural sciences, which certainly do not teach "what things are, why and to what purpose they exist, but only, how they exist."[323] The Christian faith in God, the Creator of heaven and earth, expresses itself first of all in thankfulness and worship.[324] Everything created is imbued by the Spirit of God and is thereby sanctified. Hence, the world exists not only for human beings, as has tacitly been assumed for untold centuries of human history. The rest of creation has its own right to existence, for God enjoys the praise of God's creatures.[325] All creation reflects the brightness that proceeds from God, which also pervades humans, who are their fellow creatures. They are part of this creation and are oriented toward God, as are all of God's creatures. God has given humans the special task of being concerned for the rest of creation as well as for the condition and the preservation of the earth. Yet, they are also permitted to enjoy what God has granted to them, and they rejoice in the beauty of that which he has created.

The experience of nature, in its splendid and glorious aspects, relaxes and rests us, grants recovery and a sense of perspective from our daily lives, and it broadens the soul and gladdens all the senses. However, nature also has another, unfathomable side, which are the catastrophes of nature and the law of survival, whereby life is attained and extended at the expense of other lives, where nature appears as alien and even hostile toward life, including human life. Hence, we experience the surrounding creation in a rather ambivalent way, as being both sensible and senseless, as beautiful and also frightening, as bestowing life and threatening it, and since we are part of this created order, we belong inextricably to it. Even the research of the natural scientists has contributed to our discovery not only of the beauty and the fascinating order of nature, but also of its power and vastness. The limitation of our discussion of the fitness of the created order for humans has led to a principle of action that reflects a godless anthropocentrism, for which the nonhuman creation is nothing other than the "stage upon which the drama of human life is played out" (Charles Birch) or the commodity depot from which we are permitted to fetch for ourselves whatever we may want. For this reason, it is the task of theology to discover the fundamental unity of human and extrahuman life as well as the life inherent within all aspects of creation.

The fact that human beings are able to and must do this indicates that although they stand in continuity with all the rest of creation, they certainly have a special place within the created order. They can transcend the limits of the environment that has been given to them, and they must consider what they do in terms of what will likely be the results of their actions. Because alternative modes of acting are available to them, and because they do not simply do that which nature bids, it is necessary for people to be conscious of how they see, accept, and order their lives.

Many have attempted to justify our often inconsiderate exploitation of creation by appealing to the so-called charge to take dominion (Genesis 1:28). However, the original intention of this account is quite different. To be master does not mean to destroy; rather, to be master means to have concern for creation and to strive for its well-being and protection. It also means the power to marshal good and to restrain all forms of destructive forces.[326] Also, the charge to cultivate and preserve the created order (Genesis 2:15) in no way signifies that our first priority is to be productive and exploit others in order to maximize our profits. The garden exists not only for humans; humans also exist for the garden. Man *(adam)* and soil *(adamah)* are related to one another, as is even evident by their linguistic relationship, and humans and animals are created out of the same *adamah* (Genesis 2:7, 19).

It is interesting to see how these old accounts of the origin of life upon earth are also being verified through modern genetic research, which shows most emphatically that the genotype of every living thing, from bacteria to human beings, is composed of the same four basic building blocks. Animals are related to humans and are capable of fellowship with them (Genesis 2:18-19). Like humans, they perceive lust and pain, fear and pleasure. An animal can threaten a human, and humans often regard animals with both fear and fascination. As house pets, animals are friends of humans and live in community with them. Both the Old and the New Testaments are filled with witnesses of God's concern for all creatures and of the concern of human beings for the animals who live with them and those that are useful to them.[327]

Here we are not attempting to provide a detailed accounting of the long history of that mode of thinking in which the creation has progressively been made into an instrument for the gratification of human desires. There have also been statements of Christian theology that have inappropriately pushed this kind of thought. The acceptance of the doctrine of the immortality of the human soul has placed humans incredibly far over the animal world. Assessments that have been provided by thinkers as diverse as Augustine and Descartes have led to a vast devaluation of extrahuman aspects of creation, in contrast with humanity itself. We speak of the distinction between the outer and the inner worlds with the conviction that the actual world leads to the inner world (Augustine), and the distinction which the French philosopher René Descartes has proposed, that everything which exists can be divided into two distinct groups, the *res extensae* and the *res cogitans* (extended objects and thinking objects). Other developments, which no longer have anything to do with Christian theology, have served to strengthen this tendency, including the industrialization of agriculture and animal breeding, which have contributed to the desensitization of modern people to the suffering of their fellow creatures in ways that are too extensive to be noted. We may also cite the millionfold and often unjustified destruction of animal life for research purposes, as well as for other causes, that has made it especially urgent in our day to arrive at a new appreciation of creation and a new awareness of our need to become sensitized in our involvement with extrahuman forms of life.

Hence, this conversion is necessary not only due to our guilt in presumptuously misusing nature, but also because nature itself is now increasingly striking back. The consequences of our misuse have long since been enumerated, including acid rain, air pollution, breaches in the ozone, the death of forests, the destruction of rain forests, inconsiderate exploitation of mineral wealth, and other issues. These issues already constitute a disaster, issues that have resulted from a documentable human exploitation of nature that has vastly accelerated in recent decades. This is a tragedy whose extent is not yet ascertainable and whose removal—even if it becomes possible—will entail sacrifice on every part. A well-known zoologist has written as follows on this theme, which has heretofore not been widely discussed: "Everything speaks to the fact that we will have to bring forth all our future knowledge and ability to come to terms with this counter-evolution. For the transformation of our environment that has been brought about by human activity operates retroactively as a colossal, manifold, and yet scarcely noticeable pressure of selection that comes to bear upon numerous other forms of life."[328]

This example has been brought up to point out that "time is hastening"[329] even in such situations about which the average citizen is scarcely aware. In light of this development, what Christians must newly acquire for themselves and for others is an ethical awareness that will bring human actions "into harmony with the ecosystem of the earth."[330] This applies not only to agriculture and to economics, nor just to a new relationship with animals and with such basic elements of life as water, earth, and atmosphere, but to all areas of life, since they all stand in a reciprocal and symbiotic relationship with one another. However, the path from talking to acting is long and a new way of living with the old earth needs to be learned quickly.[331] We know so much more than we practice (Albert Schweitzer).

What is required is nothing less than a voluntary asceticism.[332] It is necessary to respect limits, without being forced to do so. Limits are to be set to our actions, because a boundless exploitation of all possibilities threatens the foundations of life. Boundlessness is not freedom. It is chaos. It is not scientific or economic or technical progress as such which threatens creation, even if the question is raised whether every kind of progress serves to bring about overall improvement in the long term. No, it is much more a problem of human attitudes, which are continually probing more deeply into the issues of life and creation, without taking into account the need for responsibility for the possible and the actual consequences of their actions.[333] If we were to do this now, it could protect us from crossing over an invisible barrier, on the other side of which we will find ourselves locked with no return possible. Then such a regression would no longer be a possibility. This barrier is especially difficult to recognize in those areas where the good and the dangerous are close together, such as in the field of genetic technology. Such technology can help us arrest life-threatening diseases, but it can also have life-threatening consequences. If we do not begin to learn and to practice voluntary asceticism, in order to safeguard life, the very foundations of our lives may well be destroyed in the not-too-distant future. Human beings, God's image, will have finally failed the entire creation. Even if there are no easy answers at hand, the following at least seems to be clear: we need to obtain reliable information about these life-threatening processes, so that we can come to an informed decision, and we will need to inquire what conduct best conforms to the love of our fellow human beings, particularly the weak and those with disabilities, as well as to a sense of reverence for all creatures. At this point, Christians might also form an alternative kind of community in which these insights are learned and practiced. Even if it does not become immediately apparent, such action would help to achieve freedom and also serve to enhance life itself.

4.4.4 *Penultimate Actions and the Hope of Fulfillment*

In the best of cases, it is correct that we only attain that which is penultimate. Whenever we celebrate the Lord's Supper with one another, we then recognize a sign of the large-scale justice with which God invites to God's table those who are hungry and thirsty (Isaiah 55:1; Luke 6:21). As a creaturely model of the celebration that God is preparing for all peoples, it awakens and nourishes the hope of the victory of life over all the powers of death (Isaiah 25:6-9). Whenever Christians earnestly pray, "Thy kingdom come, thy will be done, on earth as it is in heaven," they are then making themselves available for involvement in the issues of justice in the midst of this world.[334] A church that stands in obedience to Christ is summoned by the charge of its Lord to enter into solidarity with the poor. Hence, it must become an advocate for the weak. This is true of developing a sense of solidarity with the poor within one's own nation, as well as with persons within the poor nations of the world.

Finally, it is not least confidence in the renewing power of the Holy Spirit and hope for the dawning and coming of God's kingdom that help Christians and churches not to come to terms with unjust conditions of power but rather to take steps toward effecting change that serves suffering humanity itself as well as peace upon the whole earth. This eschatological perspective in which believers come to terms with the world and the development that lies before it is critical for their existence within the world because they live from their encounter with God, from which they recognize "the eternal purpose of all God's ways," which is "the manifestation, the appearance, that illumination of the truth of the gospel and the entering by faith into this light."[335]

4.4.4.1 PROVISIONAL ACTS OF SIGNIFICANCE

In the prayer that embraces the world, we say with all Christians, "Thy kingdom come," and "Thine is the kingdom." The Christian community awaits the reign of God. We are not those who bring about God's kingdom; rather, it is God himself who will consummate his kingdom. "The kingdom of God" is also a metaphor for the Christian hope for God's new world. After the disappointment of so many expectations of having a better world through human actions, we have good reason to direct our expectations again upon the living God himself. Our actions remain acts that precede the consummation of God's kingdom. As Dietrich Bonhoeffer has said, what we do remains a penultimate and not an ultimate act.[336]

God's beginning comes before our beginning; God's future reaches further than our goals. God stands at both ends of life. In the creation of the world, God has provided the basis of life for all. In his liberating deeds he has opened new possibilities of action—in reconciliation our guilt is forgiven and we are accepted as his children. In being vivified through his Spirit, an inner renewal takes place which reaches into all areas of our lives. All of this constitutes God's fundamental action, apart from which neither humanity nor membership in the family of God could be possible. This action of God gives us courage and power for the ministry of reconciliation and healing, to which he has called his children. And at the same time, our sight is directed toward the goal which renders our acts significant, because that goal fits the fragmentary nature of our individual actions together into a meaningful whole.

The knowledge of what we may term these penultimate actions has a twofold significance: on the one hand, it puts us to the task, because God has called us to it. On the other hand, it exonerates us from the exorbitant demand of intending to create that which is final and perfect. Because God has overcome sin, our struggle against sin and its consequences is not meaningless. However, because the evil in the world is not yet conclusively stripped of its power, we await and hope for the victory of the love of God. Because with Christ a new life has entered into this world, and a new community of love has been initiated among human beings, it makes sense to enter into this community and to invite others to do so. Nevertheless, because estrangement, evil, and disruption remain, we await and hope for the victory of God's love. Because God has already initiated the salvation of humanity and of the world as a whole with his redemptive deeds in Christ, we can reckon with salvation and healing wherever we encounter human suffering and wherever human beings are injured and want to be made whole. Yet, because sickness and death persist, we await and hope for the victory of life that can no longer be destroyed by death. Faith makes experiences with the reign of God that give the courage for life as well as strength to follow Christ. And at the same time, there remain questions, uncertainties, and cares, and in the midst of these things we join together in the prayer to God that he may give sustenance to our hope and our patience until he perfects his kingdom.

In Wesley's theology, this future aspect of the reign of God plays a subordinate role, and it has seldom received a prominent place in the tradition of United Methodism. Yet, we find in Wesley's exposition of the Lord's Prayer a noteworthy interpretation of this future aspect of the kingdom of God. In the sixth sermon on his exposition of our Lord's Sermon on the Mount, Wesley asserts that "it is meet for all those who 'love his appearing' to pray that he would hasten the time; that this his kingdom, the kingdom of grace, may come quickly, and swallow up all the kingdoms of the earth. . . . For this also we pray in those words, 'Thy kingdom come.' We pray for the coming of his everlasting kingdom, the kingdom of glory in heaven, which is the continuation and perfection of the kingdom of grace on earth."[337]

It is not so much the condition of oppression through a situation that burdens or endangers a person in the present that evokes the petition for a hastened arrival of the perfected reign of God, but rather the longing for his kingdom, for the fulfillment of that which has already begun "set up in the believer's heart." Likewise, the following prayer is offered at the funeral of the deceased: "Beseeching thee, that it may please thee, of thy gracious goodness, shortly to accomplish the number of thine elect, and to hasten thy kingdom; that we, with all those that are departed in the true faith of thy holy name, may have our perfect consummation and bliss, both in body and soul, in thy everlasting glory."[338] However, Wesley prefers to emphasize the responsibility of persons to do the will of God and to live in conformity with it.

People search for the goal, for fluctuating and provisional goals, often vacillating between doubt and certainty about their meaning and their attainability. God's Spirit directs us toward a goal, which is our participating in his kingdom. That does not mean that we do not need any further short-term and long-term goals that we set for ourselves; without these, significant actions are scarcely possible. However, all of our goals have a common means of orientation, if God's Spirit leads and directs us. In spite of all the unclarities which persist in the realms of personal, church, and social life, we can still count on God's Spirit bringing us to our goal. He leads us through the times, through the events, and also through our errors and our guilt toward perfection.

This certainly does not arise from illusory, wishful thinking, but is based in the cross and the resurrection of Christ, in whom God's new world has already begun. It awaits "the future of the One who has already come" (W. Kreck). Following the One who has come and who is yet to come, we try to live in conformity with his will. However, this begins in changing our thinking, in the new orientation of our volition and our actions toward him. Neither of these things is easy. Often we intend that which is good. We want to be just and to act justly. Yet, in view of the complex relationships that constitute our world, we hardly know what is really the good. There have been times when we really grasped quite well what something was about and what we should do but our courage and our energy failed to allow us the insight to lead to a new mode of conduct.

Christians are undoubtedly familiar with these difficulties. Sometimes "the spirit is willing but the flesh is weak." Sometimes Christians set out and then discover that they lack a clear sense of direction. Faith also does not easily come to terms with forms of resistance that obstruct actions that are in accordance with God's will. It relies upon God's presence in the world. Christians stand under God's promise that he allows the upright to succeed (Proverbs 2:7-8), whenever they gather for the corporate hearing of the Word of God, in their common efforts to understand the divine will, in their acts of corporate prayer, and as they begin to carry out "the deeds of the righteous" (D. Bonhoeffer).

The totality of what we are expressing here is embedded in the anticipation of the kingdom of God. We do not place our primary hope in the fact that we are to be redeemed out of this world and "go to heaven." There is scarcely any biblical foundation for such an assertion.[339] The hope for God's kingdom is also much more an act of faithfulness to the earth and to its Creator. It is a hope "which denies the authorities and powers that rule within this world, and it is a hope which repeatedly provokes Christians to disobedience and to non-accommodation with those powers."[340] Being oriented toward the reign of God is therefore a training of our actions in all the dimensions of our lives, and at the same time encouragement to active hope, to patient waiting, and to trusting prayer through which we entrust ourselves, along with the entire creation, to the preserving, redeeming, and perfecting action of God.

In the preceding observations, it has already become clear that if, from our expectation that God himself carries through his glory, we desired to draw the conclusion that we may have been exempted from our obligation, then we would have totally misunderstood the relationship between divine and human actions. Our very petition for the coming of the kingdom of God does not absolve us from the responsibility in which faith places all Christians in relation to this reign of God.

4.4.4.2 The Overcoming of Evil

The Christian faith does not include "faith" in the devil, although such a notion may be heard upon occasion. We rely solely upon the one God, the Father, Son, and Holy Spirit, to whom there is no comparable counterpower in any form whatsoever. On the other hand, the Christian faith includes the conviction that there is a power of evil within the world, a power opposed to the will of God in many ways.[341] Our hope in the fulfillment of the kingdom of God includes also the hope of the overcoming of this power. That which is opposed to God and all that is transitory will have no place in the coming reign of God.[342] Any injustice that has taken place in a hidden or open way will come to light. What is decisive is that Christ will be the Victor over all evil in the world, and there will be no more place for evil in his kingdom.[343]

4.4.4.3 The Consummation of Creation

The positive side of this overcoming of evil that has been described is the perfection of all that which has God created. The kingdom of God is a new creation in an unsurpassable fellowship with God that is no longer tarnished by anything. This perfection is not the restoration of an earlier condition that had been ruined through sin. It is the new creation, in which that which is created by God is certainly fashioned into a renewed form.[344] In this kingdom, suffering and tears will be no more (Revelation 21:3-4), but the remembrance of them continues, which means this is not to be an unconscious state of paradise. On the contrary, this kingdom will be marked by a new level of compassion in humans' relations with one another. The expectation of the perfection certainly bursts open the concepts we have in space and time. Jesus spoke openly of the reign of God in quite concrete images, and he thereby made clear that we should imagine it as being something "totally other" than what we are able to ascribe to either the present or the future.

The suspicion of illusionary thinking is also certainly not to be excluded wherever we speak about the future of the reign of God in its consummation. Yet the vision of hope is not the byproduct of our experience of the deficiencies within the present order of reality. It is based in the encounter with Christ, with his words and deeds and with his death and life. For those who believe in him, trust and hope in God remain, who perfects his kingdom despite all earthly impediments. Wherever Christian hope enters into the fire baptism of suffering, God knows his own and guards them in faith.

In his sermon "Biblical Christianity,"[345] John Wesley depicts the extension of Christianity and the course of evangelism as it traverses the world. Opposing powers countered Christianity, the messengers of the gospel were persecuted and mortified, and yet, within its own ranks, the message of the gospel grew like "wheat amid tares." After this portrayal of the negative aspects of the mission of the gospel, Wesley did not continue with a lament or a resigned estimation of the future of the Christian faith. Instead he develops a "great vision of the approaching kingdom of God."[346] The message about which he was concerned is that of the kingdom of faith and of righteousness, which began with Christ and will in the future encompass the entire earth. Life in the future kingdom will wholly transform this created order and also perfect our earthly lives.

The fact that not only persons but also the entire creation is included in this consummation of creation is part of this hope (Romans 8:18-24). Because God will perfect his kingdom, faith, hope, and love have an eternal, imperishable, and durable basis.

In Lieu of a Summary

W hat can I believe? What must I do? Upon what am I permitted to hope? By slightly varying an expression of Immanual Kant, we have formulated the questions to which theology needs to respond in our day.

What can I believe? Upon what am I permitted to rely? The answer that is given to this question by a United Methodist theology declares that I can with all my heart trust that God calls all persons into his saving fellowship and that he therefore also summons me, whenever I allow myself to be moved to respond to his call. Whoever I am, I can rely on this.

What must I do? Whenever it is a question of human salvation, the answer of classical Protestant theology to this question is plain: you must and you can do nothing at all; God has done everything for you in Jesus Christ. However, it is noteworthy that the New Testament does not refuse a response to the one who asks, "What must I do to be saved?" According to Acts 16:31, Paul responds to the similar question asked by the prison keeper of Philippi with, "Believe on the Lord Jesus, and you will be saved, you and your household."

Jesus himself led the one who asked him, "Teacher, what must I do to inherit eternal life?" to the response, "You shall love the Lord your God with all your heart, and all your soul, and with all your strength, and with all your mind; and your neighbor as yourself" (Luke 10:25-28). In a certain sense, the theology of John Wesley is the large-scale attempt to see both of these answers as *one* and to maintain at the same time with Paul and the Reformers that people can do nothing by themselves for their salvation. Hence, what the Johannine Christ says in response to the analogous question posed by Nicodemus—which is not explicitly stated but is silently implied—is also applicable here: "Very truly, I tell you, no one can see the kingdom of God without being born from above" (John 3:3).

God's salvation is wholly a gift, and it is nothing other than grace. However, because God created humanity as his personal object, his grace also includes their action in his work of salvation. The message of the gospel intends to provoke persons to faith. Justification and sanctification are the deeds of God for and in us, from which the new being and a conduct defined by love increasingly develop. In the new birth, God creates in us the new person, who is formed after his own image and who lives and acts with the disposition of Christ. God's love kindles within our hearts love for God and for other persons. This love becomes the decisive foundation and the basic norm for life that is conducted from faith.

"The decisive meaning of the human in the realm of God's saving acts" is undoubtedly one of the essential characteristics of Methodist theology.[1] The fact that this takes place on the basis of a consequential theology of grace gives a special ring to this assessment. God's grace always precedes our response. It is *prevenient* grace not only in the specialized sense that it already affects the beginning of the order of salvation, but also quite basically in its operation as justifying and santifying grace. However, this grace involves us in its activity. That is, grace that is experienced should be living grace—lived in the certainty of our acceptance through God and in our gracious turning toward our neighbors. Grace creates in and through us the "work of faith," the "labor of love" and the "steadfastness of hope" (1 Thessalonians 1:3)!

And so we ask once again, "What must I do?" The answer: nothing other than accept and take into my life God's "Yes" and allow myself to be infected by his love as my very own.

What am I permitted to hope? I can hope that God forms and completes my life through his love. I can hope that through the implementation of his reign he leads this world unto a salvific end, at which he who is God will wipe away all tears, and the God who is love will be all in all.

Ethics and eschatology belong closely together in United Methodist theology. Love, with which the perfected fellowship of the redeemed with God is described, is the power for concrete deeds toward the needs of our world, and the Holy Spirit, whom he pours out into our hearts, is precisely the pledge and the deposit of that coming consummation. However problematic Wesley's doctrine of Christian perfection is in its specialized elaboration, its biblical basis is the expectation that God's grace creates an actual transformation in the lives of persons and in their fellowship. An ethic in the perspective of the kingdom of God is based upon this and also in the full power of love, which God's Spirit grants.

And yet, not everything that is to be said at the end of a United Methodist theology has been said with this summation. The United Methodist theologian Ted A. Campbell has asked why the renaissance of scholarly research into Wesleyan history and theology has had so little impact for a renewal or even a rebirth of United Methodist churches.[2]

The answer lies close at hand. Wesley's theology and that of his early successors was a "practical theology." Only where it is taught and practiced this way can its activity unfold. This is also true of our attempt to sketch "An Outline of United Methodist Theology."

"The universality of grace" is not aimed at the incorporation of the world with a defining stroke of the pen. It challenges us as messengers of the universal love of God to follow Christ, who is always involving us in the overcoming of boundaries and in moving us toward reconciling encounters with persons throughout the entire world.

"Personal faith" is not one theological expression among others. Personal faith is the door to the experience of the reality of grace. In faith, existentially experienced grace becomes lived grace, and it will also fill the old, difficult-to-grasp concepts of justification and sanctification with life, with the new life that God grants to us and creates within us.

"Christianity with integrity" is no stylish catchword in the trend of wholeness, but rather it is the description of the reality of love, which defines and fills our personal lives as well as our common life within the congregation and our engagement in society and the world. The difference between our description of this reality and the reality that we ourselves shape *ipso facto* will never be fully abolished. However, a theology of grace must never accept the contention that this difference is becoming an abyss that cannot be overcome.

Wesley expressed his concern that this could still happen in a pointed warning to his people. "I am not afraid that the people called Methodists should ever cease to exist either in Europe or America. But I am afraid lest they should only exist as a dead sect, having the form of religion without the power. And this undoubtedly will be the case unless they hold fast both the doctrine, spirit, and discipline with which they first set out."[3]

Appendix

Foundations for the Doctrine and the Theological Task of The United Methodist Church

In the year 1972 the General Conference of The United Methodist Church accepted the report of a "Study Commission for Doctrine and Doctrinal Norms" which bore the signature of Methodist theologian Albert C. Outler. In 1984, the General Conference authorized a Study Commission consisting of twenty-five theologians and lay persons to undertake a revision of this theological document from 1972. This commission was the first to include members from the conferences outside the United States. The draft of this commission was revised by a committee of the General Conference of 1988, and then it was accepted by the plenary conference with an overwhelming majority.

In the 1996 *Book of Discipline,* the document contains four sections:

Section One—Our Doctrinal Heritage (¶ 60)
Section Two—Our Doctrinal History (¶ 61)
Section Three—Our Doctrinal Standards and General Rules (¶ 62)
Section Four—Our Theological Task (¶ 63)

Sections Three and Four and reprinted in this Appendix. We also recommend study of the new edition of the Social Principles of the United Methodist Church, which is contained in Part III of the 1996 *Book of Discipline.*

¶ 62. Section 3—Our Doctrinal Standards and General Rules

THE ARTICLES OF RELIGION OF THE METHODIST CHURCH

[Bibliographical Note: The Articles of Religion are here reprinted from the *Discipline* of 1808 (when the first Restrictive Rule took effect), collated against Wesley's original text in *The Sunday Service of the Methodists* (1784). To these are added two Articles: "Of Sanctification" and "Of the Duty of Christians to the Civil Authority," which are legislative enactments and not integral parts of the document as protected by the Constitution (*see* Judicial Council Decisions 41, 176).]

ARTICLE I—Of Faith in the Holy Trinity

There is but one living and true God, everlasting, without body or parts, of infinite power, wisdom, and goodness; the maker and preserver of all things, both visible and invisible. And in unity of this Godhead there are three persons, of one substance, power, and eternity—the Father, the Son, and the Holy Ghost.

ARTICLE II—Of the Word, or Son of God, Who Was Made Very Man

The Son, who is the Word of the Father, the very and eternal God, of one substance with the Father, took man's nature in the womb of the blessed Virgin; so that two whole and perfect natures, that is to say, the Godhead and Manhood, were joined together in one person, never to be divided; whereof is one Christ, very God and very Man, who truly suffered, was crucified, dead, and buried, to reconcile his Father to us, and to be a sacrifice, not only for original guilt, but also for actual sins of men.

ARTICLE III—Of the Resurrection of Christ

Christ did truly rise again from the dead, and took again his body, with all things appertaining to the perfection of man's nature, wherewith he ascended into heaven, and there sitteth until he return to judge all men at the last day.

ARTICLE IV—Of the Holy Ghost

The Holy Ghost, proceeding from the Father and the Son, is of one substance, majesty, and glory with the Father and the Son, very and eternal God.

ARTICLE V—Of the Sufficiency of the Holy Scriptures for Salvation

The Holy Scripture containeth all things necessary to salvation; so that whatsoever is not read therein, nor may be proved thereby, is not to be required of any man that it should be believed as an article of faith, or be thought requisite or necessary to salvation. In the name of the Holy Scripture we do understand those canonical books of the Old and New Testament of whose authority was never any doubt in the church. The names of the canonical books are:

Genesis, Exodus, Leviticus, Numbers, Deuteronomy, Joshua, Judges, Ruth, The First Book of Samuel, The Second Book of Samuel, The First Book of Kings, The Second Book of Kings, The First Book of Chronicles, The Second Book of Chronicles, The Book of Ezra, The Book of Nehemiah, The Book of Esther, The Book of Job, The Psalms, The Proverbs, Ecclesiastes or the Preacher, Cantica or Songs of Solomon, Four Prophets the Greater, Twelve Prophets the Less.

All the books of the New Testament, as they are commonly received, we do receive and account canonical.

ARTICLE VI—Of the Old Testament

The Old Testament is not contrary to the New; for both in the Old and New Testament everlasting life is offered to mankind by Christ, who is the only Mediator between God and man, being both God and Man. Wherefore they are not to be heard who feign that the old fathers did look only for transitory promises. Although the law given from God by Moses as touching ceremonies and rites doth not bind Christians, nor ought the civil precepts thereof of necessity be received in any commonwealth; yet notwithstanding, no Christian whatsoever is free from the obedience of the commandments which are called moral.

ARTICLE VII—Of Original or Birth Sin

Original sin standeth not in the following of Adam (as the Pelagians do vainly talk), but it is the corruption of the nature of every man, that naturally is engendered of the offspring of Adam, whereby man is very far gone from original righteousness, and of his own nature inclined to evil, and that continually.

ARTICLE VIII—Of Free Will

The condition of man after the fall of Adam is such that he cannot turn and prepare himself, by his own natural strength and works, to faith, and calling upon God; wherefore we have no power to do good works, pleasant and acceptable to God, without the grace of God by Christ preventing us, that we may have a good will, and working with us, when we have that good will.

ARTICLE IX—Of the Justification of Man

We are accounted righteous before God only for the merit of our Lord and Saviour Jesus Christ, by faith, and not for our own works or deservings. Wherefore, that we are justified by faith, only, is a most wholesome doctrine, and very full of comfort.

ARTICLE X—Of Good Works

Although good works, which are the fruits of faith, and follow after justification, cannot put away our sins, and endure the severity of God's judgment; yet are they pleasing and acceptable to God in Christ, and spring out of a true and lively faith, insomuch that by them a lively faith may be as evidently known as a tree is discerned by its fruit.

ARTICLE XI—Of Works of Supererogation

Voluntary works—besides, over and above God's commandments—which they call works of supererogation, cannot be taught without arrogancy and impiety. For by them men do declare that they do not only render unto God as much as they are bound to do, but that they do more for his sake than of bounden duty is required; whereas Christ saith plainly: When you have done all that is commanded you, say, We are unprofitable servants.

ARTICLE XII—Of Sin After Justification

Not every sin willingly committed after justification is the sin against the Holy Ghost, and unpardonable. Wherefore, the grant of repentance is not to be denied to such as fall into sin after justification. After we have received the Holy Ghost, we may depart from grace given, and fall into sin, and, by the grace of God, rise again and amend our lives. And therefore they are to be condemned who say they can no more sin as long as they live here; or deny the place of forgiveness to such as truly repent.

ARTICLE XIII—Of the Church

The visible church of Christ is a congregation of faithful men in which the pure Word of God is preached, and the Sacraments duly administered according to Christ's ordinance, in all those things that of necessity are requisite to the same.

ARTICLE XIV—Of Purgatory

The Romish doctrine concerning purgatory, pardon, worshiping, and adoration, as well of images as of relics, and also invocation of saints, is a fond thing, vainly invented, and grounded upon no warrant of Scripture, but repugnant to the Word of God.

ARTICLE XV—Of Speaking in the Congregation in Such a Tongue as the People Understand

It is a thing plainly repugnant to the Word of God, and the custom of the primitive church, to have public prayer in the church, or to minister the Sacraments, in a tongue not understood by the people.

ARTICLE XVI—Of the Sacraments

Sacraments ordained of Christ are not only badges or tokens of Christian men's profession, but rather they are certain signs of grace, and God's good will toward us, by which he doth work invisibly in us, and doth not only quicken, but also strengthen and confirm, our faith in him.

There are two Sacraments ordained of Christ our Lord in the Gospel; that is to say, Baptism and the Supper of the Lord.

Those five commonly called sacraments, that is to say, confirmation, penance, orders, matrimony, and extreme unction, are not to be counted for Sacraments of the Gospel; being such as have partly grown out of the *corrupt* following of the apostles, and partly are states of life allowed in the Scriptures, but yet have not the like nature of Baptism and the Lord's Supper, because they have not any visible sign or ceremony ordained of God.

The Sacraments were not ordained of Christ to be gazed upon, or to be carried about; but that we should duly use them. And in such only as worthily receive the same, they have a wholesome effect or operation; but they that receive them unworthily, purchase to themselves condemnation, as St. Paul saith.

ARTICLE XVII—Of Baptism

Baptism is not only a sign of profession and mark of difference whereby Christians are distinguished from others that are not baptized; but it is also a sign of regeneration or the new birth. The Baptism of young children is to be retained in the Church.

ARTICLE XVIII—Of the Lord's Supper

The Supper of the Lord is not only a sign of the love that Christians ought to have among themselves one to another, but rather is a sacrament of our redemption by Christ's death; insomuch that, to such as rightly, worthily, and with faith receive the same, the bread which we break is a partaking of the body of Christ; and likewise the cup of blessing is a partaking of the blood of Christ.

Transubstantiation, or the change of the substance of bread and wine in the Supper of our Lord, cannot be proved by Holy Writ, but is repugnant to the plain words of Scripture, overthroweth the nature of a sacrament, and hath given occasion to many superstitions.

The body of Christ is given, taken, and eaten in the Supper, only after a heavenly and spiritual manner. And the mean whereby the body of Christ is received and eaten in the Supper is faith.

The Sacrament of the Lord's Supper was not by Christ's ordinance reserved, carried about, lifted up, or worshiped.

ARTICLE XIX—Of Both Kinds

The cup of the Lord is not to be denied to the lay people; for both the parts of the Lord's Supper, by Christ's ordinance and commandment, ought to be administered to all Christians alike.

ARTICLE XX—Of the One Oblation of Christ, Finished upon the Cross

The offering of Christ, once made, is that perfect redemption, propitiation, and satisfaction for all the sins of the whole world, both original and actual; and there is none other satisfaction for sin but that alone. Wherefore the sacrifice of masses, in the which it is commonly said that the priest doth offer Christ for the quick and the dead, to have remission of pain or guilt, is a blasphemous fable and dangerous deceit.

ARTICLE XXI— Of the Marriage of Ministers

The ministers of Christ are not commanded by God's law either to vow the estate of single life, or to abstain from marriage; therefore it is lawful for them, as for all other Christians, to marry at their own discretion, as they shall judge the same to serve best to godliness.

ARTICLE XXII—Of the Rites and Ceremonies of Churches

It is not necessary that rites and ceremonies should in all places be the same, or exactly alike; for they have been always different, and may be changed according to the diversity of countries, times, and men's manners, so that nothing be ordained against God's Word. Whosoever, through his private judgment, willingly and purposely doth openly break the rites and ceremonies of the church to which he belongs, which are not repugnant to the Word of God, and are ordained and approved by common authority, ought to be rebuked openly, that others may fear to do the like, as one that offendeth against the common order of the church, and woundeth the consciences of weak brethren.

Every particular church may ordain, change, or abolish rites and ceremonies, so that all things may be done to edification.

ARTICLE XXIII—Of the Rulers of the United States of America

The President, the Congress, the general assemblies, the governors, and the councils of state, *as the delegates of the people,* are the rulers of the United States of America, according to the division of power made to them by the Constitution of the United States and by the constitutions of their respective states. And the said states are a sovereign and independent nation, and ought not to be subject to any foreign jurisdiction.

ARTICLE XXIV—Of Christian Men's Goods

The riches and goods of Christians are not common as touching the right, title, and possession of the same, as some do falsely boast. Notwithstanding, every man ought, of such things as he possesseth, liberally to give alms to the poor, according to his ability.

ARTICLE XXV—Of a Christian Man's Oath

As we confess that vain and rash swearing is forbidden Christian men by our Lord Jesus Christ and James his apostle, so we judge that the Christian religion doth not prohibit, but that a man may swear when the magistrate requireth, in a cause of faith and charity, so it be done according to the prophet's teaching, in justice, judgment, and truth.

[The following Article from the Methodist Protestant *Discipline* is placed here by the Uniting Conference (1939). It was not one of the Articles of Religion voted upon by the three churches.]

OF SANCTIFICATION

Sanctification is that renewal of our fallen nature by the Holy Ghost, received through faith in Jesus Christ, whose blood of atonement cleanseth from all sin; whereby we are not only delivered from the guilt of sin, but are washed from its pollution, saved from its power, and are enabled, through grace, to love God with all our hearts and to walk in his holy commandments blameless.

[The following provision was adopted by the Uniting Conference (1939). This statement seeks to interpret to our churches in foreign lands Article XXIII of the Articles of Religion. It is a legislative enactment, but is not a part of the Constitution. (*See* Judicial Council Decisions 41, 176, and Decision 6, Interim Judicial Council.)]

OF THE DUTY OF CHRISTIANS TO THE CIVIL AUTHORITY

It is the duty of all Christians, and especially of all Christian ministers, to observe and obey the laws and commands of the governing or supreme authority of the country of which they are citizens or subjects or in which they reside, and to use all laudable means to encourage and enjoin obedience to the powers that be.

The Confession of Faith
of the Evangelical United Brethren Church

[Bibliographical Note: The text of the Confession of Faith is identical with that of its original in *The Discipline of The Evangelical United Brethren Church* (1963).]

ARTICLE I—God

We believe in the one true, holy and living God, Eternal Spirit, who is Creator, Sovereign, and Preserver of all things visible and invisible. He is infinite in power, wisdom, justice, goodness and love, and rules with gracious regard for the well-being and salvation of men, to the glory of his name. We believe the one God reveals himself as the Trinity: Father, Son and Holy Spirit, distinct but inseparable, eternally one in essence and power.

ARTICLE II—Jesus Christ

We believe in Jesus Christ, truly God and truly man, in whom the divine and human natures are perfectly and inseparably united. He is the eternal Word made flesh, the only begotten Son of the Father, born of the Virgin Mary by the power of the Holy Spirit. As ministering Servant he lived, suffered, and died on the cross. He was buried, rose from the dead, and ascended into heaven to be with the Father, from whence he shall return. He is eternal Savior and Mediator, who intercedes for us, and by him all men will be judged.

ARTICLE III—The Holy Spirit

We believe in the Holy Spirit who proceeds from and is one in being with the Father and the Son. He convinces the world of sin, of righteousness, and of judgment. He leads men through faithful response to the gospel into the fellowship of the Church. He comforts, sustains, and empowers the faithful and guides them into all truth.

ARTICLE IV—The Holy Bible

We believe the Holy Bible, Old and New Testaments, reveals the Word of God so far as it is necessary for our salvation. It is to be received through the Holy Spirit as the true rule and guide for faith and practice. Whatever is not revealed in or established by the Holy Scriptures is not to be made an article of faith nor is it to be taught as essential to salvation.

ARTICLE V—The Church

We believe the Christian Church is the community of all true believers under the Lordship of Christ. We believe it is one, holy, apostolic, and catholic. It is the redemptive fellowship in which the Word of God is preached by men divinely called, and the sacraments are duly administered according to Christ's own appointment. Under the discipline of the Holy Spirit the Church exists for the maintenance of worship, the edification of believers and the redemption of the world.

ARTICLE VI—The Sacraments

We believe the Sacraments, ordained by Christ, are symbols and pledges of the Christian's profession and of God's love toward us. They are means of grace by which God works invisibly in us, quickening, strengthening, and confirming our faith in him. Two Sacraments are ordained by Christ our Lord, namely Baptism and the Lord's Supper.

We believe Baptism signifies entrance into the household of faith, and is a symbol of repentance and inner cleansing from sin, a representation of the new birth in Christ Jesus and a mark of Christian discipleship.

We believe children are under the atonement of Christ and as heirs of the Kingdom of God are acceptable subjects for Christian Baptism. Children of believing parents through Baptism become the special responsibility of the Church. They should be nurtured and led to personal acceptance of Christ, and by profession of faith confirm their Baptism.

We believe the Lord's Supper is a representation of our redemption, a memorial of the sufferings and death of Christ, and a token of love and union which Christians have with Christ and with one another. Those who rightly, worthily, and in faith eat the broken bread and drink the blessed cup partake of the body and blood of Christ in a spiritual manner until he comes.

ARTICLE VII—Sin and Free Will

We believe man is fallen from righteousness and, apart from the grace of our Lord Jesus Christ, is destitute of holiness and inclined to evil. Except a man be born again, he cannot see the Kingdom of God. In his own strength, without divine grace, man cannot do good works pleasing and acceptable to God. We believe, however, man influenced and empowered by the Holy Spirit is responsible in freedom to exercise his will for good.

ARTICLE VIII—Reconciliation Through Christ

We believe God was in Christ reconciling the world to himself. The offering Christ freely made on the cross is the perfect and sufficient sacrifice for the sins of the whole world, redeeming man from all sin, so that no other satisfaction is required.

ARTICLE IX—Justification and Regeneration

We believe we are never accounted righteous before God through our works or merit, but that penitent sinners are justified or accounted righteous before God only by faith in our Lord Jesus Christ.

We believe regeneration is the renewal of man in righteousness through Jesus Christ, by the power of the Holy Spirit, whereby we are made partakers of the divine nature and experience newness of life. By this new birth the believer becomes reconciled to God and is enabled to serve him with the will and the affections.

We believe, although we have experienced regeneration, it is possible to depart from grace and fall into sin; and we may even then, by the grace of God, be renewed in righteousness.

ARTICLE X—Good Works

We believe good works are the necessary fruits of faith and follow regeneration, but they do not have the virtue to remove our sins or to avert divine judgment. We believe good works, pleasing and acceptable to God in Christ, spring from a true and living faith, for through and by them faith is made evident.

ARTICLE XI—Sanctification and Christian Perfection

We believe sanctification is the work of God's grace through the Word and the Spirit, by which those who have been born again are cleansed from sin in their thoughts, words, and acts, and are enabled to live in accordance with God's will, and to strive for holiness without which no one will see the Lord.

Entire sanctification is a state of perfect love, righteousness, and true holiness which every regenerate believer may obtain by being delivered from the power of sin, by loving God with all the heart, soul, mind, and strength, and by loving one's neighbor as one's self. Through faith in Jesus Christ this gracious gift may be received in this life both gradually and instantaneously, and should be sought earnestly by every child of God.

We believe this experience does not deliver us from the infirmities, ignorance, and mistakes common to man, nor from the possibilities of further sin. The Christian must continue on guard against spiritual pride and seek to gain victory over every temptation to sin. He must respond wholly to the will of God so that sin will lose its power over him; and the world, the flesh, and the devil are put under his feet. Thus he rules over these enemies with watchfulness through the power of the Holy Spirit.

ARTICLE XII—The Judgment and the Future State

We believe all men stand under the righteous judgment of Jesus Christ, both now and in the last day. We believe in the resurrection of the dead; the righteous to life eternal and the wicked to endless condemnation.

ARTICLE XIII—Public Worship

We believe divine worship is the duty and privilege of man who, in the presence of God, bows in adoration, humility, and dedication. We believe divine worship is essential to the life of the Church, and that the assembling of the people of God for such worship is necessary to Christian fellowship and spiritual growth.

We believe the order of public worship need not be the same in all places but may be modified by the church according to circumstances and the needs of men. It should be in a language and form understood by the people, consistent with the Holy Scriptures to the edification of all, and in accordance with the order and *Discipline* of the Church.

ARTICLE XIV—The Lord's Day

We believe the Lord's Day is divinely ordained for private and public worship, for rest from unnecessary work, and should be devoted to spiritual improvement, Christian fellowship and service. It is commemorative of our Lord's resurrection and is an emblem of our eternal rest. It is essential to the permanence and growth of the Christian church, and important to the welfare of the civil community.

ARTICLE XV—The Christian and Property

We believe God is the owner of all things and that the individual holding of property is lawful and is a sacred trust under God. Private property is to be used for the manifestation of Christian love and liberality, and to support the Church's mission in the world. All forms of property, whether private, corporate or public, are to be held in solemn trust and used responsibly for human good under the sovereignty of God.

ARTICLE XVI—Civil Government

We believe civil government derives its just powers from the sovereign God. As Christians we recognize the governments under whose protection we reside and believe such governments should be based on, and be responsible for, the recognition of human rights under God. We believe war and bloodshed are contrary to the gospel and spirit of Christ. We believe it is the duty of Christian citizens to give moral strength and purpose to their respective governments through sober, righteous, and godly living.

THE STANDARD SERMONS OF WESLEY

[Bibliographical Note: The Wesleyan "standards" have been reprinted frequently. The critical edition of Wesley's *Sermons* is included in *The Works of John Wesley,* vols. 1-4 (Nashville: Abingdon Press, 1984–87).]

THE EXPLANATORY NOTES UPON THE NEW TESTAMENT

[Bibliographical Note: *The Explanatory Notes Upon the New Testament* (1755) is currently in print (Ward's 1976 edition) and is forthcoming as vols. 5–6 of *The Works of John Wesley.*]

THE GENERAL RULES OF THE METHODIST CHURCH

[Bibliographical Note: The General Rules are printed here in the text of 1808 (when the fifth Restrictive Rule took effect), as subsequently amended by constitutional actions in 1848 and 1868.]

**THE NATURE, DESIGN, AND GENERAL RULES OF
OUR UNITED SOCIETIES**

In the latter end of the year 1739 eight or ten persons came to Mr. Wesley, in London, who appeared to be deeply convinced of sin, and earnestly groaning for redemption. They desired, as did two or three more the next day, that he would spend some time with them in prayer, and advise them how to flee from the wrath to come, which they saw continually hanging over their heads. That he might have more time for this great work, he appointed a day when they might all come together, which from thenceforward they did every week, namely, on Thursday in the evening. To these, and as many more as desired to join with them (for their number increased daily), he gave those advices from time to time which he judged most needful for them, and they always concluded their meeting with prayer suited to their several necessities.

This was the rise of the **United Society,** first in Europe, and then in America. Such a society is no other than "a company of men having the *form* and seeking the *power* of godliness, united in order to pray together, to receive the word of exhortation, and to watch over one another in love, that they may help each other to work out their salvation."

That it may the more easily be discerned whether they are indeed working out their own salvation, each society is divided into smaller companies, called **classes,** according to their respective places of abode. There are about twelve persons in a class, one of whom is styled the **leader.** It is his duty:

1. To see each person in his class once a week at least, in order: (1) to inquire how their souls prosper; (2) to advise, reprove, comfort, or exhort, as occasion may require; (3) to receive what they are willing to give toward the relief of the preachers, church, and poor.

2. To meet the ministers and the stewards of the society once a week, in order: (1) to inform the minister of any that are sick, or of any that walk disorderly and will not be reproved; (2) to pay the stewards what they have received of their several classes in the week preceding.

There is only one condition previously required of those who desire admission into these societies: "a desire to flee from the wrath to come, and to be saved from their sins." But wherever this is really fixed in the soul it will be shown by its fruits.

It is therefore expected of all who continue therein that they should continue to evidence their desire of salvation,

First: By doing no harm, by avoiding evil of every kind, especially that which is most generally practiced, such as:

The taking of the name of God in vain.

The profaning the day of the Lord, either by doing ordinary work therein or by buying or selling.

Drunkenness: buying or selling spirituous liquors, or drinking them, unless in cases of extreme necessity.

Slaveholding; buying or selling slaves.

Fighting, quarreling, brawling, brother going to law with brother; returning evil for evil, or railing for railing; the using many words in buying or selling.

The buying or selling goods that have not paid the duty.

The giving or taking things on usury—i.e., unlawful interest.

Uncharitable or unprofitable conversation; particularly speaking evil of magistrates or of ministers.

Doing to others as we would not they should do unto us.

Doing what we know is not for the glory of God, as:

The putting on of gold and costly apparel.

The taking such diversions as cannot be used in the name of the Lord Jesus.

The singing those songs, or reading those books, which do not tend to the knowledge or love of God.

Softness and needless self-indulgence.

Laying up treasure upon earth.

Borrowing without a probability of paying; or taking up goods without a probability of paying for them.

It is expected of all who continue in these societies that they should continue to evidence their desire of salvation,

Secondly: By doing good; by being in every kind merciful after their power; as they have opportunity, doing good of every possible sort, and, as far as possible, to all men:

To their bodies, of the ability which God giveth, by giving food to the hungry, by clothing the naked, by visiting or helping them that are sick or in prison.

To their souls, by instructing, reproving, or exhorting all we have any intercourse with; trampling under foot that enthusiastic doctrine that "we are not to do good unless *our hearts be free to it.*"

By doing good, especially to them that are of the household of faith or groaning so to be; employing them preferably to others; buying one of another, helping each other in business, and so much the more because the world will love its own and them only.

By all possible diligence and frugality, that the gospel be not blamed.

By running with patience the race which is set before them, denying themselves, and taking up their cross daily; submitting to bear the reproach of Christ, to be as the filth and offscouring of the world; and looking that men should say all manner of evil of them *falsely,* for the Lord's sake.

It is expected of all who desire to continue in these societies that they should continue to evidence their desire of salvation,

Thirdly: By attending upon all the ordinances of God; such are:

The public worship of God.

The ministry of the Word, either read or expounded.

The Supper of the Lord.

Family and private prayer.

Searching the Scriptures.

Fasting or abstinence.

These are the General Rules of our societies; all of which we are taught of God to observe, even in his written Word, which is the only rule, and the sufficient rule, both of our faith and practice. And all these we know his Spirit writes on truly awakened hearts. If there be any among us who observe them not, who habitually break any of them, let it be known unto them who watch over that soul as they who must give an account. We will admonish him of the error of his ways. We will bear with him for a season. But then, if he repent not, he hath no more place among us. We have delivered our own souls.

¶ 63. Section 4—Our Theological Task

Theology is our effort to reflect upon God's gracious action in our lives. In response to the love of Christ, we desire to be drawn into a deeper relationship with the "author and perfecter of our faith." Our theological explorations seek to give expression to the mysterious reality of God's presence, peace, and power in the world. By so doing, we attempt to articulate more clearly our understanding of the divine-human encounter and are thereby more fully prepared to participate in God's work in the world.

The theological task, though related to the Church's doctrinal expressions, serves a different function. Our doctrinal affirmations assist us in the discernment of Christian truth in ever-changing contexts. Our theological task includes the testing, renewal, elaboration, and application of our doctrinal perspective in carrying out our calling "to spread scriptural holiness over these lands."

While the Church considers its doctrinal affirmations a central feature of its identity and restricts official changes to a constitutional process, the Church encourages serious reflection across the theological spectrum.

As United Methodists, we are called to identify the needs both of individuals and of society and to address those needs out of the resources of Christian faith in a way that is clear, convincing, and effective. Theology serves the Church by interpreting the world's needs and challenges to the Church and by interpreting the gospel to the world.

THE NATURE OF OUR THEOLOGICAL TASK

Our theological task is both critical and constructive. It is *critical* in that we test various expressions of faith by asking: Are they true? Appropriate? Clear? Cogent? Credible? Are they based on love? Do they provide the Church and its members with a witness that is faithful to the gospel as reflected in our living heritage and that is authentic and convincing in the light of human experience and the present state of human knowledge?

Our theological task is *constructive* in that every generation must appropriate creatively the wisdom of the past and seek God in their midst in order to think afresh about God, revelation, sin, redemption, worship, the Church, freedom, justice, moral responsibility, and other significant theological concerns. Our summons is to understand and receive the gospel promises in our troubled and uncertain times.

Our theological task is both individual and communal. It is a feature in the ministry of *individual* Christians. It requires the participation of all who are in our Church, lay and ordained, because the mission of the Church is to be carried out by everyone who is called to discipleship. To be persons of faith is to hunger to understand the truth given to us in Jesus Christ.

Theological inquiry is by no means a casual undertaking. It requires sustained disciplines of study, reflection, and prayer.

Yet the discernment of "plain truth for plain people" is not limited to theological specialists. Scholars have their role to play in assisting the people of God to fulfill this calling, but all Christians are called to theological reflection.

Our theological task is *communal*. It unfolds in conversations open to the experiences, insights, and traditions of all constituencies that make up United Methodism.

This dialogue belongs to the life of every congregation. It is fostered by laity and clergy, by the bishops, by the boards, agencies, and theological schools of the Church.

Conferences speak and act for United Methodists in their official decisions at appropriate levels. Our conciliar and representative forms of decision-making do not release United Methodists as individuals from the responsibility to develop sound theological judgment.

Our theological task is contextual and incarnational. It is grounded upon God's supreme mode of self-revelation—the incarnation in Jesus Christ. God's eternal Word comes to us in flesh and blood in a given time and place, and in full identification with humanity. Therefore, theological reflection is energized by our incarnational involvement in the daily life of the Church and the world, as we participate in God's liberating and saving action.

Our theological task is essentially practical. It informs the individual's daily decisions and serves the Church's life and work. While highly theoretical constructions of Christian thought make important contributions to theological understanding, we finally measure the truth of such statements in relation to their practical significance. Our interest is to incorporate the promises and demands of the gospel into our daily lives.

Theological inquiry can clarify our thinking about what we are to say and do. It presses us to pay attention to the world around us.

Realities of intense human suffering, threats to the survival of life, and challenges to human dignity confront us afresh with fundamental theological issues: the nature and purposes of God, the relations of human beings to one another, the nature of human freedom and responsibility, and the care and proper use of all creation.

THEOLOGICAL GUIDELINES: SOURCES AND CRITERIA

As United Methodists, we have an obligation to bear a faithful Christian witness to Jesus Christ, the living reality at the center of the Church's life and witness. To fulfill this obligation, we reflect critically on our biblical and theological inheritance, striving to express faithfully the witness we make in our own time.

Two considerations are central to this endeavor: the sources from which we derive our theological affirmations and the criteria by which we assess the adequacy of our understanding and witness.

Wesley believed that the living core of the Christian faith was revealed in Scripture, illumined by tradition, vivified in personal experience, and confirmed by reason.

Scripture is primary, revealing the Word of God "so far as it is necessary for our salvation." Therefore, our theological task, in both its critical and constructive aspects, focuses on disciplined study of the Bible.

To aid his study of the Bible and deepen his understanding of faith, Wesley drew on Christian tradition, in particular the Patristic writings, the ecumenical creeds, the teachings of the Reformers, and the literature of contemporary spirituality.

Thus, tradition provides both a source and a measure of authentic

Christian witness, though its authority derives from its faithfulness to the biblical message.

The Christian witness, even when grounded in Scripture and mediated by tradition, is ineffectual unless understood and appropriated by the individual. To become our witness, it must make sense in terms of our own reason and experience.

For Wesley, a cogent account of the Christian faith required the use of reason, both to understand Scripture and to relate the biblical message to wider fields of knowledge. He looked for confirmations of the biblical witness in human experience, especially the experiences of regeneration and sanctification, but also in the "common sense" knowledge of everyday experience.

The interaction of these sources and criteria in Wesley's own theology furnishes a guide for our continuing theological task as United Methodists. In that task Scripture, as the constitutive witness to the wellsprings of our faith, occupies a place of primary authority among these theological sources.

In practice, theological reflection may also find its point of departure in tradition, experience, or rational analysis. What matters most is that all four guidelines be brought to bear in faithful, serious, theological consideration. Insights arising from serious study of the Scriptures and tradition enrich contemporary experience. Imaginative and critical thought enables us to understand better the Bible and our common Christian history.

SCRIPTURE

United Methodists share with other Christians the conviction that Scripture is the primary source and criterion for Christian doctrine. Through Scripture the living Christ meets us in the experience of redeeming grace. We are convinced that Jesus Christ is the living Word of God in our midst whom we trust in life and death.

The biblical authors, illumined by the Holy Spirit, bear witness that in Christ the world is reconciled to God. The Bible bears authentic testimony to God's self-disclosure in the life, death, and resurrection of Jesus Christ as well as in God's work of creation, in the pilgrimage of Israel, and in the Holy Spirit's ongoing activity in human history.

As we open our minds and hearts to the Word of God through the words of human beings inspired by the Holy Spirit, faith is born and nourished, our understanding is deepened, and the possibilities for transforming the world become apparent to us.

The Bible is sacred canon for Christian people, formally acknowledged as such by historic ecumenical councils of the Church. Our doctrinal standards identify as canonical thirty-nine books of the Old Testament and the twenty-seven books of the New Testament.

Our standards affirm the Bible as the source of all that is "necessary" and "sufficient" unto salvation (Articles of Religion) and "is to be received through the Holy Spirit as the true rule and guide for faith and practice" (Confession of Faith).

We properly read Scripture within the believing community, informed by the tradition of that community. We interpret individual texts in light of their place in the Bible as a whole.

We are aided by scholarly inquiry and personal insight, under the guidance of the Holy Spirit. As we work with each text, we take into account what we have been able to learn about the original context and intention of that text. In this understanding we draw upon the careful historical, literary, and textual studies of recent years, which have enriched our understanding of the Bible.

Through this faithful reading of Scripture, we may come to know the truth of the biblical message in its bearing on our own lives and the life of the world. Thus the Bible serves both as a source of our faith and as the basic criterion by which the truth and fidelity of any interpretation of faith is measured.

While we acknowledge the primacy of Scripture in theological reflection, our attempts to grasp its meaning always involve tradition, experience, and reason. Like Scripture, these may become creative vehicles of the Holy Spirit as they function within the Church. They quicken our faith, open our eyes to the wonder of God's love, and clarify our understanding.

The Wesleyan heritage, reflecting its origins in the catholic and reformed ethos of English Christianity, directs us to a self-conscious use of these three sources in interpreting Scripture and in formulating faith statements based on the biblical witness. These sources are, along with Scripture, indispensable to our theological task.

The close relationship of tradition, experience, and reason appears in the Bible itself. Scripture witnesses to a variety of diverse traditions, some of which reflect tensions in interpretation within the early Judeo-Christian heritage. However, these traditions are woven together in the Bible in a manner that expresses the fundamental unity of God's revelation as received and experienced by people in the diversity of their own lives.

The developing communities of faith judged them, therefore, to be an authoritative witness to that revelation. In recognizing the interrelationship and inseparability of the four basic resources for theological understanding, we are following a model that is present in the biblical text itself.

TRADITION

The theological task does not start anew in each age or each person. Christianity does not leap from New Testament times to the present as though nothing were to be learned from that great cloud of witnesses in between. For centuries Christians have sought to interpret the truth of the gospel for their time.

In these attempts, tradition, understood both in terms of process and form, has played an important role. The passing on and receiving of the gospel among persons, regions, and generations constitutes a dynamic element of Christian history. The formulations and practices that grew out of specific circumstances constitute the legacy of the corporate experience of earlier Christian communities.

These traditions are found in many cultures around the globe. But the history of Christianity includes a mixture of ignorance, misguided zeal, and sin. Scripture remains the norm by which all traditions are judged.

The story of the church reflects the most basic sense of tradition, the continuing activity of God's Spirit transforming human life. Tradition is the history of that continuing environment of grace in and by which all Christians live, God's self-giving love in Jesus Christ. As such, tradition transcends the story of particular traditions.

In this deeper sense of tradition, all Christians share a common history. Within that history, Christian tradition precedes Scripture, and yet Scripture comes to be the focal expression of the tradition. As United Methodists, we pursue our theological task in openness to the richness of both the form and power of tradition.

The multiplicity of traditions furnishes a richly varied source for theological reflection and construction. For United Methodists, certain strands of tradition have special importance as the historic foundation of our doctrinal heritage and the distinctive expressions of our communal existence.

We are now challenged by traditions from around the world that accent dimensions of Christian understanding that grow out of the sufferings and victories of the downtrodden. These traditions help us rediscover the biblical witness to God's special commitment to the poor, the disabled, the imprisoned, the oppressed, the outcast. In these persons we encounter the living presence of Jesus Christ.

These traditions underscore the equality of all persons in Jesus Christ. They display the capacity of the gospel to free us to embrace the diversity of human cultures and appreciate their values. They reinforce our traditional understanding of the inseparability of personal salvation and social justice. They deepen our commitment to global peace.

A critical appreciation of these traditions can compel us to think about God in new ways, enlarge our vision of shalom, and enhance our confidence in God's provident love.

Tradition acts as a measure of validity and propriety for a community's faith insofar as it represents a consensus of faith. The various traditions that presently make claims upon us may contain conflicting images and insights of truth and validity. We examine such conflicts in light of Scripture, reflecting critically upon the doctrinal stance of our Church.

It is by the discerning use of our standards and in openness to emerging forms of Christian identity that we attempt to maintain fidelity to the apostolic faith.

At the same time, we continue to draw on the broader Christian tradition as an expression of the history of divine grace within which Christians are able to recognize and welcome one another in love.

EXPERIENCE

In our theological task, we follow Wesley's practice of examining experience, both individual and corporate, for confirmations of the realities of God's grace attested in Scripture.

Our experience interacts with Scripture. We read Scripture in light of the conditions and events that help shape who we are, and we interpret our experience in terms of Scripture.

All religious experience affects all human experience; all human experience affects our understanding of religious experience.

On the personal level, experience is to the individual as tradition is to the church: It is the personal appropriation of God's forgiving and empowering grace. Experience authenticates in our own lives the truths revealed in Scripture and illumined in tradition, enabling us to claim the Christian witness as our own.

Wesley described faith and its assurance as "a sure trust and confidence" in the mercy of God through our Lord Jesus Christ, and a steadfast hope of all good things to be received at God's hand. Such assurance is God's gracious gift through the witness of the Holy Spirit.

This "new life in Christ" is what we as United Methodists mean when we speak of "Christian experience." Christian experience gives us new eyes to see the living truth in Scripture. It confirms the biblical message for our present. It illumines our understanding of God and creation and motivates us to make sensitive moral judgments.

Although profoundly personal, Christian experience is also corporate; our theological task is informed by the experience of the church and by the common experiences of all humanity. In our attempts to understand the biblical message, we recognize that God's gift of liberating love embraces the whole of creation.

Some facets of human experience tax our theological understanding. Many of God's people live in terror, hunger, loneliness, and degradation. Everyday experiences of birth and death, of growth and life in the created world, and an awareness of wider social relations also belong to serious theological reflection.

A new awareness of such experiences can inform our appropriation of scriptural truths and sharpen our appreciation of the good news of the kingdom of God.

As a source for theological reflection, experience, like tradition, is richly varied, challenging our efforts to put into words the totality of the promises of the gospel. We interpret experience in the light of scriptural norms, just as our experience informs our reading of the biblical message. In this respect, Scripture remains central in our efforts to be faithful in making our Christian witness.

REASON

Although we recognize that God's revelation and our experiences of God's grace continually surpass the scope of human language and reason, we also believe that any disciplined theological work calls for the careful use of reason.

By reason we read and interpret Scripture.

By reason we determine whether our Christian witness is clear.

By reason we ask questions of faith and seek to understand God's action and will.

By reason we organize the understandings that compose our witness and render them internally coherent.

By reason we test the congruence of our witness to the biblical testimony and to the traditions that mediate that testimony to us.

By reason we relate our witness to the full range of human knowledge, experience, and service.

Since all truth is from God, efforts to discern the connections between revelation and reason, faith and science, grace and nature, are useful endeavors in developing credible and communicable doctrine. We seek nothing less than a total view of reality that is decisively informed by the promises and imperatives of the Christian gospel, though we know well that such an attempt will always be marred by the limits and distortions characteristic of human knowledge.

Nevertheless, by our quest for reasoned understandings of Christian faith we seek to grasp, express, and live out the gospel in a way that will commend itself to thoughtful persons who are seeking to know and follow God's ways.

In theological reflection, the resources of tradition, experience, and reason are integral to our study of Scripture without displacing Scripture's primacy for faith and practice. These four sources—each making distinctive contributions, yet all finally working together—guide our quest as United Methodists for a vital and appropriate Christian witness.

THE PRESENT CHALLENGE TO THEOLOGY IN THE CHURCH

In addition to historic tensions and conflicts that still require resolution, new issues continually arise that summon us to fresh theological inquiry. Daily we are presented with an array of concerns that challenge our proclamation of God's reign over all of human existence.

Of crucial importance are concerns generated by great human struggles for dignity, liberation, and fulfillment—aspirations that are inherent elements in God's design for creation. These concerns are borne by theologies that express the heart cries of the downtrodden and the aroused indignation of the compassionate.

The perils of nuclear destruction, terrorism, war, poverty, violence, and injustice confront us. Injustices linked to race, gender, class, and age are widespread in our times. Misuse of natural resources and disregard for the fragile balances in our environment contradict our calling to care for God's creation. Secularism pervades high-technology civilizations, hindering human awareness of the spiritual depths of existence.

We seek an authentic Christian response to these realities that the healing and redeeming work of God might be present in our words and deeds.

Too often, theology is used to support practices that are unjust. We look for answers that are in harmony with the gospel and do not claim exemption from critical assessment.

A rich quality of our Church, especially as it has developed in the last century, is its global character. We are a Church with a distinctive theological heritage, but that heritage is lived out in a global community, resulting in understandings of our faith enriched by indigenous experiences and manners of expression.

We affirm the contributions that United Methodists of varying ethnic, language, cultural, and national groups make to one another and to our Church as a whole. We celebrate our shared commitment to clear theological understanding and vital missional expression.

United Methodists as a diverse people continue to strive for consensus in understanding the gospel. In our diversity, we are held together by a shared inheritance and a common desire to participate in the creative and redemptive activity of God.

Our task is to articulate our vision in a way that will draw us together as a people in mission.

In the name of Jesus Christ we are called to work within our diversity while exercising patience and forbearance with one another. Such patience stems neither from indifference toward truth nor from an indulgent tolerance of error but from an awareness that we know only in part and that none of us is able to search the mysteries of God except by the Spirit of God. We proceed with our theological task, trusting that the Spirit will grant us wisdom to continue our journey with the whole people of God.

ECUMENICAL COMMITMENT

Christian unity is founded on the theological understanding that through faith in Jesus Christ we are made members-in-common of the one body of Christ. Christian unity is not an option; it is a gift to be received and expressed.

United Methodists respond to the theological, biblical, and practical mandates for Christian unity by firmly committing ourselves to the cause of Christian unity at local, national, and world levels. We invest ourselves in many ways by which mutual recognition of churches, of members, and of ministries may lead us to sharing in Holy Communion with all of God's people.

Knowing that denominational loyalty is always subsumed in our life in the church of Jesus Christ, we welcome and celebrate the rich experience of United Methodist leadership in church councils and consultations, in multilateral and bilateral dialogues, as well as in other forms of ecumenical convergence that have led to the healing of churches and nations.

We see the Holy Spirit at work in making the unity among us more visible.

Concurrently, we have entered into serious interfaith encounters and explorations between Christians and adherents of other living faiths of the world. Scripture calls us to be both neighbors and witnesses to all peoples. Such encounters require us to reflect anew on our faith and seek guidance for our witness among neighbors of other faiths. We then rediscover that the God who has acted in Jesus Christ for the salvation of the whole world is also the Creator of all humankind, the One who is "above all and through all and in all" (Ephesians 4:6).

As people bound together on one planet, we see the need for a self-critical view of our own tradition and accurate appreciation of other traditions. In these encounters, our aim is not to reduce doctrinal differences to some lowest common denominator of religious agreement but to raise all such relationships to the highest possible level of human fellowship and understanding.

We labor together with the help of God toward the salvation, health, and peace of all people. In respectful conversations and in practical cooperation, we confess our Christian faith and strive to display the manner in which Jesus Christ is the life and hope of the world.

CONCLUSION

Doctrine arises out of the life of the church—its faith, its worship, its discipline, its conflicts, its challenges from the world it would serve.

Evangelism, nurture, and mission require a constant effort to integrate authentic experience, rational thought, and purposeful action with theological integrity.

A convincing witness to our Lord and Savior Jesus Christ can contribute to the renewal of our faith, bring persons to that faith, and strengthen the Church as an agent of healing and reconciliation.

This witness, however, cannot fully describe or encompass the mystery of God. Though we experience the wonder of God's grace at work with us and among us, and though we know the joy of the present signs of God's kingdom, each new step makes us more aware of the ultimate mystery of God, from which arises a heart of wonder and an attitude of humility. Yet we trust that we can know more fully what is essential for our participation in God's saving work in the world, and we are confident in the ultimate unfolding of God's justice and mercy.

In this spirit we take up our theological task. We endeavor through the power of the Holy Spirit to understand the love of God given in Jesus Christ. We seek to spread this love abroad. As we see more clearly who we have been, as we understand more fully the needs of the world, as we draw more effectively upon our theological heritage, we will become better equipped to fulfill our calling as the people of God.

> Now to God
> who by the power at work within us
> is able to do far more abundantly
> than all that we ask or think,
> to God be glory in the church
> and in Christ Jesus to all generations,
> for ever and ever. Amen.
> —Ephesians 3:20-21 (based on RSV)

Notes

The original German edition of this book makes use of many sources written in languages other than English. Whenever possible, official English translations of these sources have been used for quotations in the text. Some quotations, however, have been made from materials not available in English versions and have been translated by Steven O'Malley. These are indicated by the abbreviation "tr. trans." (translator's translation) in parentheses following publication information.

The major abbreviations used in the notes are listed on page 509ff.

1. Responsible Proclamation, or Fundamentals for a Theology of The United Methodist Church

1. Letter to Carl Friedrich Städlin of May 4, 1793 (*Gesammelte Schriften*, II, 2nd ed., 1922), 429.
2. Cf. Jürgen Moltmann, *The Crucified God* (New York: Harper and Row, 1973), 7-24.
3. Meyers, *Grosses Taschenlexikon*, 4th ed. (1992), 22:75; see also "Theology," in *A Handbook of Theological Terms*, ed. Van A. Harvey (New York: Macmillan, 1964), 239-41.
4. Emil Brunner, "The Other Task of Theology," and Karl Barth, "No! Answer to Emil Brunner" in Emil Brunner and Karl Barth, *Natural Theology* (London: Centenary, 1946; reprinted by University Microfilms International, Ann Arbor, Mich. and London, 1979).
5. E. Jüngel, *Der Gott entsprechende Mensch,* in *Entsprechungen: Gott-Wahrheit-Mensch* (1980), 290-317, here 290; for the account set aside in relation to every person as "a necessary function of dogmatics," compare Karl Barth, *CD*, IV/3, 109.
6. On the effects of John Wesley, see M. Schmidt, *John Wesley,* 1 (London: Epworth, 1962), 1953; 2, 1966 (new ed. in 3 vols. under the title, *John Wesley: Life and Work*, 1987). On the history of The United Methodist Church in Europe, see *Die Geschichte der Evangelisch-methodistischen Kirche,* ed. K. Steckel and C. E. Sommer (1982); G. Wainwright, (art.) "Methodism," and J. Hale, (art.) "Methodist Church," EKL, 3rd. ed., III (1982), 391-402; J. S. O'Malley, (art.) "Methodists," in *New Twentieth-Century Encyclopedia of Religious Knowledge,* ed. J. D. Douglas, 2nd ed. (Grand Rapids: Baker, 1991), 555-59.
7. A comparable course of development occurred in other European nations, such as Norway, Sweden, Finland, Denmark, and the former Yugoslavia.

8. For this, see the recent series by R. E. Richey, D. M. Campbell, and W. B. Lawrence, eds., *United Methodism and American Culture* (Nashville: Abingdon, 1997–1999), four vols. published, two forthcoming.

9. Sermon 112, "On Laying the Foundation of the New Chapel," II, 1; WJW 3:585.

10. In *Der Streit der Fakultäten, 1798.* Kant says with respect to this, and with a certain undertone of irony, "Cobbler, stick to your trade!" Then he continues, "To say that God himself has spoken through the Bible, cannot be demonstrated as such, because it is a historical matter; for that question properly is the domain of the philosophical faculty" (from *Kant's Works*, ed. W. Weischedel, 9:285; tr. trans.). This essay is cited in Clement C. J. Webb, *Kant's Philosophy of Religion* (Oxford: Clarendon, 1926), 169 and 171.

11. This narrow understanding is the problem of the older description of the biblical evidence: e.g., Hannelies Schulte, *Der Begriff der Offenbarung im Neuen Testament,* BEvTh 13 (1949); Dieter Lührmann, *Das Offenbarungsverständnis bei Paulus und in paulinischen Gemeinden,* WMANT 16 (1965); see also "Revelation" in *A Handbook of Theological Terms,* ed. V. A. Harvey, 207-10. Compare the comprehensive presentation of the biblical concept of revelation by Hans Hübner, *Biblische Theologie des Neuen Testaments,* 1:990, 101-239; and "The Multiplicity of Biblical Ideas of Revelation" in Wolfhart Pannenberg, *Systematic Theology* (Grand Rapids: Eerdmans, 1991), 1:198-214.

12. Cf. Hübner, *Biblische Theologie, 135* f.; see also C. F. D. Moule, "Revelation," in *The Interpreter's Dictionary of the Bible* (Nashville: Abingdon, 1962), 4:54-58.

13. Walter Bauer, *Wörterbuch zum Neuen Testament,* 6: the fully revised edition edited by Kurt Aland and Barbara Aland (Berlin, 1988), 615; see also K. Lake, "Epiphany," in *Hastings Encyclopedia of Religion and Ethics* (New York: Scribner's, 1928), 5:330-32.

14. On the philosophical questions concerning the conditions of the divine work of revelation within the realm of temporal circumstances, see the detailed treatment of the Methodist theologian William J. Abraham in his work *Divine Revelation and the Limits of Historical Reason* (Oxford, 1982), which gives special attention to the Anglo-American discussion of this theme.

15. Cf. Gerhard Ebeling's volumes of essays entitled *Wort und Glaube* (1, 1967, 3rd ed.; 2, 1969; 3, 1975). In the foreword to the first volume, Ebeling quotes Luther: "For God does not deal, nor has he ever dealt, with man otherwise than through a word of promise. . . . We in turn cannot deal with God otherwise than through faith in the Word of his promise."—from the "Babylonian Captivity of the Church" (1520), in WA 6:516, as translated in *Luther's Works*, ed. H. T. Lehmann (Philadelphia: Muhlenburg, 1959), 36:42. From the exegetical perspective, Hans Hübner has emphatically declared that "the polarity of revelation given and revelation received" is fundamental for the biblical idea of revelation (*Biblische Theologie,* 1985, 165): "Revelation and faith are a totality, which in its mutuality is to be regarded as indissoluble. Faith is the response to revelation. Received revelation is faith. Faith is the revelation that has reached its goal" (tr. trans.). For a related discussion, see D. Guthrie, *New Testament Theology* (Downer's Grove, Ill.: InterVarsity, 1981), 116-20.

16. For this, cf. 3.1.4 below.

17. Cf. the relationship that was extensively elaborated by D. Bonhoeffer: "Only he who believes is obedient and only he who is obedient believes." *The Cost of Discipleship* (London: SCM, 1959, 2nd ed.), 40.

18. Hübner, *Biblische Theologie,* 136, gives the idea that is translated mostly as "kindness" or "goodness" or, in a looser paraphrase, as "affection" (tr. trans.). On the entire matter, see H. J. Stroebe, "Häsäd/Goodness," THAT, I, 600-621; also, C. L. Mitton, "Grace," in *The Interpreter's Dictionary of the Bible,* 2:463-68.

19. John 1:17 describes no contrast, but the Torah of Moses and the revelation of Christ are described "in the relationship of allusion and reality" (H. Gese, "Der Johannesprolog," in *Zur Biblischen Theologie,* 3rd ed. [1989], 152-201; here: 190).

20. W. Joest, *Dogmatik,* I (1984), 17.

21. Article II of the Confession of Faith of the Evangelical United Brethren Church; cf. Article II of the Articles of Religion of the Methodist Church, which were made unalterable from the time of the General Conference (Methodist Episcopal) of 1808. Both forms retain their validity for the United Church; see the Appendix for the full text.

22. Article VI of the Articles of Religion of the Methodist Church.

23. In addition, see G. Gerleman, "Dabar/Word," THAT I, 437f.; and J. N. Sanders, "Word, the," in *The Interpreter's Dictionary of the Bible,* 4:868-72.

24. Cf. the profound symbolism of the encounter of Elijah at Horeb (1 Kings 19:11-13)!

25. Cf. A. Debrunner, H. Kleinknecht, O. Procksch, G. Kittel, "Lego," ThWNT 4, 69-147; also, "Lego" in W. F. Arndt, F. W. Gingrich, *A Greek-English Lexicon of the New Testament* (Chicago/Cambridge, 1957), 469-71.

26. Also, O. Hofius, *Wort Gottes und Glaube bei Paulus,* in "Paulusstudien," WUNT 51 (1989), 148-74, here: 148-54; also, A. C. Purdy, the sections "The Word of the Cross" and "To Everyone Who Has Faith" under the article "Paul" in *The Interpreter's Dictionary of the Bible,* 3:695-97.

27. Karl Barth, CD I/I, 98-140.

28. Cf. CD I/I, 132-33.

29. Doctrinal Standards, Sect. 4: Our Theological Task (Board of Discipleship, 1996) para 63. p. 72.; see also M. B. Stokes, *The Bible in the Wesleyan Heritage* (Jackson, Miss., 1979), 48-51, 61-89; see Appendix, esp. Section 3, "The Scripture."

30. Article IV of The Confession of Faith of the Evangelical United Brethren Church, in *The Book of Discipline of The United Methodist Church* (Nashville: The United Methodist Publishing House, 1996), ¶ 62; see Appendix.

31. See Article V of the Methodist Articles of Religion, and Article IV of the Confession of Faith (EUB), in *The Book of Discipline* (UMC, 1996), ¶ 62; see Appendix.

32. See "Our Theological Task," *The Book of Discipline* (UMC, 1996), ¶ 63, p. 75; see Appendix.

33. Cf. G. Rupp, "Word and Spirit in the First Years of the Reformation," ARG 49 (1958), 13-26; see "Spirit/Holy Spirit" in *A Handbook of Theological Terms,* ed. V. A. Harvey, 228-29.

34. This is especially apparent in the hymns of Charles Wesley: "Spirit of faith, come down, / Reveal the things of God, / And make to us the Godhead known, / And witness with the blood: / 'Tis thine the blood to apply." Hymn 83, 1 = UMH 322, 1; see also (Hymn 83, 1; 93, 5 [372 in UMH]; 194, 4; 244, 3).

35. Cf. W. Rebell, *Erfüllung und Erwartung: Erfahrungen mit dem Geist im Urchristentum* (1991), 69: "The typing of the Spirit back to Jesus distinguishes the Johannine theology from every form of Gnosis, including every form of present-day Gnosis" (tr. trans.). See also commentary on John 14:26 and 16:13-15 by C. K. Barrett, *The Gospel According to St. John* (London: SPCK, 1962), 391, 403-9.

36. See H. Ray Dunning, *Grace, Faith, and Holiness: A Wesleyan Systematic Theology* (1988), 161-70.

37. John Wesley, "A Survey of the Wisdom of God in the Creation: or a Compendium of Natural Philosophy," 1775, 1777, 3rd ed., cited in *John Wesley's Theology: A Collection from His Works,* ed. R. Burtner and R. Chiles (1954; reprint, Nashville: Abingdon, 1982), 36.

38. "Unterwegs mit Christus. Glaubensbuch der Evangelisch-methodistischen Kirche," *EmK Heute* 72 (1991), 36. See also "Basic Christian Affirmations" in *The Book of Discipline* (UMC, 1996), ¶ 60.

39. Cf. J. Eccles, *The Human Mystery* (Berlin/Heidelberg/New York: Springer International, 1979); Paul Davies, *God and the New Physics* (New York: Simon and Schuster, 1983); C. Bresch, S. M. Daecke, and H. Riedinger, "Kann man Gott aus der Natur erkennen? Evolution als Offenbarung," QD 125, 2nd ed. (1992). A classic study of the relation of religion to issues of natural science and reason is George Santayana, *Reason in Religion* (New York: Collier, 1962).

40. See esp. P. Davies, *Gott und die moderne Physik,* 286 (*God and the New Physics* and C. Bresch, "Kann man Gott aus der Natur erkennen?" 169; also, for a classic study of the relation of science to religious theism, see C. S. Lewis, *Mere Christianity* (New York: Macmillan, 1943), Part I.

41. Isaiah 40:6-8; Proverbs 1:2; Romans 8:19-22; etc.

42. Theophil Spörri, "Der Mensch und die frohe Botschaft," *Christliche Glaubenslehre,* Part 2 (1952), 69 (tr. trans.).

43. For the more recent theological and philosophical discussions of the matter of conscience, see J. G. Blühdorn, M. Wolter, F. Krüger, A. Weyer, and H. G. Heimbrock, "Gewissen" I-V, TRE 13 (1984); also, "Conscience" in *A Handbook of Theological Terms,* ed. V. A. Harvey, 56-58.

44. For this, see below, 2.1.2.3 and 3.1.2.

45. This is based on Kant's self-styled "moral argument for the existence of God" as a "postulate of practical reason" in his critique of the practical reason (*Works,* in 10 vols., ed. W. Weischedel, 6:254-63).; see also Clement C. J. Webb, *Kant's Philosophy of Religion* (Oxford: Clarendon, 1926); and I. Kant, *Lectures on Ethics,* trans. L. Infield (New York: Harper, 1963), 186ff.

46. Theophil Spörri, *Der Mensch und die frohe Botschaft,* 2:59.

47. Cf. R. Otto, *The Idea of the Holy,* trans. J. W. Harvey (New York: Oxford, 1923).
48. J. Schempp, *Dogmatik* (Reutlingen, 1925), 24.
49. Cf. H. Wildberger, "der Monotheismus Deuterojesjas," in *Jahweh und sein Volk,* ThB 66 (1979), 249-73. On the so-called monotheism debate in the Old Testament, see *Monotheismus im alten Israel und seiner Umwelt,* ed. O. Keel (Bibe, 1980); *Der einzige Gott. Die Geburt des biblischen Monotheismus,* ed. B. Lang (1981); *Gott, der einzige. Zur Entstehung des Monotheismus in Israel,* ed. E. Haag, QD 104 (1985); also, C. F. D. Moule, "God, NT," *The Interpreter's Dictionary of the Bible,* 2:430-36.
50. U. Wilckens, in his commentary on Romans 3:29, has rightly stressed the meaning of this position for the "interreligious dialog" (Brief an die Römer, Evangelische-katholischer Kommentar zum Neuen Testament VI/I, 2nd ed. [1987], 251). This is to be directed against "all tendencies in the church to delineate itself over against the non-Christian 'world.' " However, he does not indicate just what he means in saying that the "faith in Christ" is that which is "not only for all *Christians* . . . but is basically for all *persons* as justificati impii, *Juden wie Heiden.*" That indicates something quite different from the recognition of a pluralistic truth in religion. See also the discussion of "The God of the Gentiles" in C. K. Barrett, *The Epistle to the Romans* (New York: Harper, 1957), 80-84.
51. On Acts 17:22-31, cf. W. Klaiber, *Call and Response: Biblical Foundations of a Theology of Evangelism,* trans. H. Perry-Trauthig and J. A. Dwyer (Nashville: Abingdon, 1997), 83-86, and the literature therein cited.
52. On this, see the study of the *Verein der Evangelisch-Lutherischen Kirche Deutschlands: Religionen, Religiosität, und Christlicher Glaube. Eine Studie* (1991); also, P. Tillich, *Dynamics of Faith* (New York: Harper, 1957).
53. Cf. Q. Huonder, *Die Gottesbeweise. Geschichte und Schicksal,* Urban Bücher, 106, (1968); R. Swinburne, *The Existence of God* (1979), and the rejoinder, J. L. Mackie, *The Wonder of Theism: Arguments for and Against the Existence of God* (1985); J. Clayton, "Gottesbeweise," II/III, TRE, 13 (1984), 724-84.
54. J. Neuner, and H. Roos, *The Teaching of the Catholic Church.* (New York: Alba House, 1967), p. 38. (=Denzinger-Hünermann, Enchiridion Symbolorum 3026).
55. Augustine, *Confessions,* trans. by Henry Chadwick (Oxford: Oxford University Press, 1997), 1/1, 13f.
56. W. Joest, *Fundamentaltheologie,* 3rd ed. (1988), 76 (cf. Thomas Aquinas, *Summa Theologica* 1, q. 2, a. 1).
57. *Summa Theologica* I, q. 2, a. 3.
58. Anselm of Canterbury, *Proslogion,* in *Opera Omnia* I (1938), 89-139.
59. E.g., Karl Barth, *Fides quaerens intellectum. Anselms Beweis der Existenz Gottes im Zusammenhang eines Theologischen Programms,* Grundrisse zum Alten Testament, Abt. II 13 (1931; 2nd ed., 1986), and through H. G. Hubbeling, *Einführung in die Religionsphilosophie* (Göttingen, 1981), 78-87. Hubbeling comes to the following conclusion from his discussion: "We can say that the ontological argument for the existence of God is certainly largely plausible, but it does not possess any convincing power of persuasion."
60. Cf. Luther's observation: "The entire creation is the most beautiful book or bible, in which God has described and depicted Himself." (WA 48; 201, 2-5; following Kurt Aland [ed.] *Lutherlexikon,* 4th ed. [1989], 286); note also his critical comment, "The entire creation is the face and mask of God. But wisdom is needed to discern God in His mask. The world does not have this wisdom, thus it cannot distinguish God from His masks" (Luthers Galaterbrief-Auslegung from 1531), ed. H. Kleinknecht (1980), 70 = WA 40, i, 174, 13-15. See also P. Althaus, *The Theology of Martin Luther,* trans. R. C. Schultz (Philadelphia: Fortress, 1966), 15-24.
61. Sermon 44, "Original Sin," WJW 2:170-85.
62. "To renounce reason is to renounce religion," he writes in a letter to Dr. Rutherford (*Letters,* ed. Telford, 5:364), and he adds that "religion and reason go hand in hand, and that all irrational religion is false religion."
63. Sermon 44, II, 3; WJW 2:177.
64. Th. Spörri, *Der Mensch und die Frohe Botschaft,* 2:60.
65. Jonathan Edwards, *Treatise Concerning Religious Affections* (New Haven: Yale University Press, 1959), 100f.
66. Edwards's most far-reaching discussion of his reformulation of the grounds of theological discourse is found in his *Freedom of the Will* (New Haven: Yale University Press, 1957).

67. From Horace Bushnell, *God in Christ* (Hartford: Brown and Parsons, 1849), cited in *Theology in America: The Major Protestant Voices from Puritanism to Neo-Orthodoxy,* ed. S. E. Ahlstrom (Indianapolis: Bobbs-Merrill, 1967), 328.

68. Ibid. 355-58.

69. Ibid., 366.

70. William James, *The Varieties of Religious Experience* (London: Longmans and Green, 1902), cited in Ahlstrom, *Theology in America,* 503.

71. Ibid., 510.

72. J. Schempp, in his *Dogmatik* (38), was even able to speak of a "religious tendency" that humans innately possess, and thus he could formulate: "In the religious tendency of humans we possess the demonstration of the fact of an inner relationship, which joins God and human beings. Religion is inherently the revelation of God's essence, but it is also an essential part of the spiritual life of humanity." The hypothesis of a "religious tendency" is quite controversial today and is infrequently maintained. See "Image of God," in *A Handbook of Theological Terms,* ed. V. A. Harvey, 125-27.

73. On the "pluralism" debate, see P. F. Knitter, *No other Name? A Critical Survey of Christian Attitudes Toward the World Religions,* (New York: Maryknoll 1985). R. Bernhardt, *Der Absolutheitsanspruch des Christentums. Von der Aufklärung bis zur pluralistischen Religiontheologie* (1990); see also "Dialog der Religionen? *Evangelische Theologie* 49 (1989), (Heft 6, 491ff.); on the dialogical debate in the WCC, see S. J. Samartha, *Courage for Dialogue: Ecumenical Issues in Inter-Religious Relationships* (Maryknoll, N.Y.: Orbis, 1982); on Wesley's position, see Sermon 67, WJW 2:534-50; Sermon 16, WJW 1:376-97; Sermon 91, WJW 3:290-307; Sermon 1, WJW 1:109-30; Sermon 3, WJW 1:142-58. See also R. Bernhardt, *Christianity Without Absolutes* (London: SCM, 1994).

74. See Acts 17:28.

75. This is also the intent of the official expression of the World Council of Churches to the theme of dialogue; cf. *Commission on Faith and Order, World Council of Churches. Series V: 1980–89* (Glendale, Ariz.: Ecumenism Research Agency, 1989: includes reports from San Antonio); and *Let the Spirit Speak to the Churches: A Guide for the Study of the Theme and the Issues: World Council of Churches, Seventh Assembly, 1991 (Canberra),* (Geneva: World Council of Churches Publications, 1990–).

76. Cf. the parallel warnings in Romans 11:17-34 to the Gentile Christians in the face of arrogance toward the Jews.

77. For this, see below, section 2.2.4; also, Sermon 63, WJW 2:485-99, and Sermon 22, WJW 1:488-509, where Wesley expresses the hope that the greatest hindrance against the mission would be removed, namely, that the behavior of Christians does not come up to the standard that is written within the hearts of the heathen (Sermon 63, 22, WJW 2:496).

78. Cf. also H. Leipold and H-R. Müller-Schwefe, "Anknüpfung," I/II, TRE, 2 (1978), 743-52; Th. Wettach, "Missionskonferenzen," EKL, 3rd ed., III (1992), 456-62. For a discussion of these issues within the larger context of "natural theology" see "Natural Theology," in *A Handbook of Theological Terms,* ed. V. A. Harvey, 158-62. See also the treatment of this theme in the *New Twentieth-Century Encyclopedia of Religious Knowledge,* 712-13.

79. T. Aquinas, *Summa Theologica* I, 9.1, a8, ad2. (Garden City, N.Y.: Image, 1969), 43 "gratia non tollit naturam, sed perficit."

80. Cf. K. H. Miskotte, "Natürliche Religion und Philosophie," *Religion in Geschichte und Gregenwart,* 3rd. ed., IV (1960), 1322-26; C. Link, "Natürliche Theologie," EKL, 3rd ed., III (1992), 631-34. See also the articles on P. Althaus and E. Brunner in *The New Twentieth-Century Encyclopedia of Religious Knowledge,* 13, 126.

81. Cf. his sermon on original sin, Sermon 44, WJW 2:170-85; Sermon 1, WJW 1:109-30; Sermon 3, WJW 1:142-58.

82. Sermon 85, 1-3, WJW 3:199-201; Sermon 69, WJW 2:567-586.

83. Sermon 17, I, 6, and II, 1ff., WJW 1:404-5, 409ff.

84. Sermon 79, 7, WJW 3:118; see also Sermon 7, WJW 1:217-32; Sermon 44, I, 3, WJW 2:175.

85. Cf. R. Watson, *Theological Institutes,* vol. 1 (1985), 13-35; W. B. Pope, *A Compendium of Christian Theology,* vol. 1, 2nd ed. (1880), 49-61; J. J. Escher, *Christliche Theologie,* vol. 1 (1899), 2f.; also, Th. Spörri, *Leitfaden für den Katechismusunterricht,* 46th. ed. (1965), Questions 6-8.

86. Cf. Ch. Link, "Die Welt als Gleichnis. Studien zum Problem der natürlichen Theologie,"

BEvTh 73 (1976), 249; also E. L. Allen, *Creation and Grace: A Guide to the Thought of Emil Brunner* (New York: Philosophical Library, 1951), see esp. 7-14. See also *The Christian Theology Reader,* ed. A. E. McGrath (London: Blackwell, 1993), 55-57.

87. Cf. the interesting theological concurrence between E. Jüngel and W. Pannenberg in this matter. E. Jüngel's essay is entitled "Das Dilemma der natürlichen Theologie und die Wahrheit ihres Problems. Überlegungen für ein Gespräch mit Wolfhart Pannenberg" (in *Entsprechungen,* BEvTh 88 (1980), 158-77); he designated the universal demand of the Word of God as the problem that natural theology fails to take into consideration (*Entsprechungen,* 174f.). On his side, W. Pannenberg seized upon the critique of natural theology in his *Systematic Theology,* trans. G. W. Bromiley (Grand Rapids: Eerdmans, 1994), 1:107-87. He posed the question of the theological meaning of the "natural" knowledge of God and of a religious relationship in its facticity and ambiguity, which for many persons conformed to the conception that is represented here.

88. For this, see also E. Jüngel, *Gott als Geheimnis der Welt,* 5th ed. (1986), in particular, 430 ff., 505 ff.; J. Moltmann, *The Trinity and the Kingdom,* trans. Margaret Kohl (San Francisco: Harper and Row, 1981), 71ff.

89. *Grace upon Grace: A Mission Statement of The United Methodist Church* (Nashville: Graded Press, 1990), p. 5. "The triune God himself is grace."

90. For an emphatic portrayal of this theme, see Charles Wesley's hymn "Wrestling Jacob" (Hymn 136 = UMH 387); in support of Genesis 32:29, he asks the unknown adversary: "And tell me if thy name is love." The answer breaks forth, "Tis love! Tis love! Thou diedst for me; / I hear thy whisper in my heart. / The morning breaks, the shadows flee, / Pure, Universal Love thou art: / To me, to all, thy bowels move— / Thy nature, and thy name, is Love." (Stanza 7; this and the following five stanzas end with the same last line!).

91. Article I of the Articles of Religion of the Methodist Church and Article I of the Confession of Faith of the Evangelical United Brethren Church; Sermon 55, WJW 2:373-86.

92. *Hymns on the Trinity* (1767; reprint 1998) (cf. Hymns 244-55; WJW 7:386-91).

93. Hymn 83, 1; 93, 4; 85, 4; 141, 3: "God only knows the love of God."

94. Hymn 83, 1; 93, 5; 127, 1; 194, 4.

95. Hymn 244, 1-4: "Jesus, my Lord, my God! / The God supreme thou art, / The Lord of hosts, whose precious blood / Is sprinkled on my heart. // Jehovah is thy name; / And, through thy blood applied, / Convinced and certified I am / There is no God beside. // Soon as thy Spirit shows / That precious blood of thine, / The happy, pardoned sinner knows / It is the blood divine. // But only he who feels / 'My Saviour died for me,' / Is sure that all the Godhead dwells / Eternally in thee."

96. Cf. the striking stanzas of Hymn 9, 2, and 3: "Ready the Father is to own / And kiss his late-returning son; / Ready your loving Saviour stands, / And spreads for you his bleeding hands. // Ready the Spirit of his love / Just now the stony to remove; / T'apply, and witness with the blood, / And wash, and seal the sons of God."

97. On 1.2.1–1.2.4 see F. W. Beare, "Bible," in *The Interpreter's Dictionary of the Bible,* 1:407; for general introductions, see B. W. Anderson, *Understanding the Old Testament* (Englewood Cliffs, N.J.: Prentice-Hall, 1966); and H. C. Kee, F. W. Young, and K. Froehlich, *Understanding the New Testament* (Englewood Cliffs, N.J.: Prentice-Hall, 1973).

98. In spite of the danger that the designation "Old Testament" can cause discrimination toward the Jews, we consider it difficult to replace it with the phrase "Hebrew Bible." For the greater part of ancient Judaism and early Christianity, this was the "Scripture" in its Greek version. The corresponding designation "Greek Bible" also came to comprise not only the New Testament, but also the Septuagint. Thus, we shall abide by the designation "Old Testament," without associating it with a negative connotation. These writings were finally the Bible of Jesus, of Paul, and of all of early Christendom.

99. Cf. Article VI of the "Thirty-nine Articles" with Article V of the "Articles of Religion of the Methodist Church" (see below, Section 1.2.3.4). For the Apocrypha, see C. T. Fritsch, "Apocrypha," in *The Interpreter's Dictionary of the Bible,* 1:161-66.

100. See Margaret Baxter, *The Formation of the Christian Scriptures* (Philadelphia: Westminster, 1988); also, R. M. Grant, *A Short History of the Interpretation of the Bible* (New York: Macmillan, 1966); cf. H. Frh. von Campenhausen, The Formation of the Christian Bible (Philadelphia: Fortress, 1972), 147-268; and from the conservative perspective, *Der Kanon der Bibel,* ed. G. Maier (1990).

101. Some of the apocrypha and the so-called Apostolic Fathers, among which were included the letters of Ignatius and of Polycarp, writings of Clement and Barnabas, and the "Shepherd of Hermas."

102. Preface to the Sermons, 5, WJW 1:104-6.

103. July 24, 1776, Journal (ed. Curnock) 6:117.

104. On this, cf. Philip S. Watson, "Die Autorität der Bibel bei Luther and Wesley," BGEmK 14 (1983); J. T. Clemons, "John Wesley, Biblical Literalist?" *Religion in Life*, 46 (1977), 332-42; R. L. Shelton, "John Wesley's Approach to Scripture in Historical Perspective," WThJ 16 (1981), 25-50; W. Abraham, "The Concept of Inspiration in the Classical Wesleyan Tradition," in *A Celebration of Ministry*, ed. K. C. Kinghorn (1982), 33-47; K. Steckel, *"Die Bibel im deutschsprachigen Methodismus,"* BGEmK 25 (1987).

105. Watson, "Die Autorität der Bibel," 17.

106. W. Nast (1807–1893) had studied in the Evangelisches Stift in Tübingen, and he migrated to America because of a crisis in faith. There he came to saving faith under the influence of Methodist preaching; he affiliated with the Methodist Church and founded and led its German-speaking work in the USA. Cf. K. H. Voigt, "Der deutschsprachige Zweig der Methodistenkirche in den Vereinigten Staaten von Amerika," in *Geschichte der EmK*, ed. K. Steckel and C. E. Sommer, 41ff.; see also Carl Wittke, *William Nast* (Detroit: Wayne State University Press, 1959).

107. On this, see K. Steckel, "Die Bibel," 19-28, and Abraham, "The Concept of Inspiration"; Esher, in his *Christliche Theologie*, had earlier clarified the historical "authenticity" question in light of particular writings and their theological value.

108. It is not by accident that there are two Methodist authors who have in recent times attempted to develop an understanding of the inspiration of the Bible within the context of the American neo-evangelical literature; cf. I. H. Marshall, *Biblical Inspiration* (Grand Rapids: Eerdmans, 1983); W. Abraham, *The Divine Inspiration of the Holy Scripture* (1981).

109. H. J. Kraus, *Geschichte der historisch-kiritischen Erforschung des Alten Testaments*, 2nd ed. (1969); W. G. Kümmel, *Das Neue Testament. Geschichte der Erforschung seiner Probleme*, 2nd ed. (1970); W. G. Kümmel, *Das Neue Testament im 20. Jahrhundert. Ein Forschungsbericht*, SBS 50 (1970).

110. E. Troeltsch, "Über historische und dogmatische Methode in der Theologie," in *Gesammelte Schriften*, 2 (1913), 729-53; republished in "Theologie als Wissenschaft," ed. Sauter, ThB 43 (1971), 105-27. Cf. P. D. L. Avis, *The Methods of Modern Theology* (Basingstoke: Marshall Pickering, 1986).

111. As an example, cf. the accomplishments of P. Stuhlmacher, *Vom Verstehen des Neuen Testaments. Eine Hermeneutik*, 2nd ed. (1986), 222-57; cf. P. Stuhlmacher, *How to Do Biblical Theology* (Allison Park, Pa.: Pickwick, 1995).

112. For "alternative" methods of expositing the Bible, see H. K. Berg, *Ein Wort wie Feuer. Wege lebendiger Bibelauslegung* (1991); and for the development of critical work, see *Das Buch Gottes. Elf Zugänge zur Bibel. Ein Votum des Theologischen Ausschusses der Arnoldshainer Konferenz* (1992); cf. W. Wink, *The Bible in Human Transformation: Toward a New Paradigm for Biblical Studies* (Philadelphia: Fortress, 1973).

113. For the clearest and most intelligible explanation of the inerrancy discussion with regard to the Bible, see N. L. Geissler, *Inerrancy*, 493ff. A "fundamentalist" and a "biblicist" understanding of the Bible are to be distinguished; the latter shares a basic conviction regarding the full authority of Scripture, but it is not connected with a full-blown theory of inspiration.

114. Charles Hodge, *Systematic Theology* (New York: Charles Scribner's Sons, 1878), vol. 1, cited in Ahlstrom, *Theology in America*, 258.

115. Donald W. Dayton, *Theological Roots of Pentecostalism* (Grand Rapids: Zondervan, 1987), 25.

116. See the discussion of dispensationalism in Ahlstrom, *Theology in America*, 811.

117. Ammzi C. Dixon, Louis Meyer, and Reuben A. Torrey served successively as the editors of *The Fundamentals*, and three million copies were distributed. See Ahlstrom, *Theology in America*, 815-16.

118. See E. Troeltsch, Über historische und dogmatische Methode, 104.

119. Walter Rauschenbusch, *Christianity and the Social Crisis* (New York: Macmillan, 1907), 7; cited in S. E. Ahlstrom, *A Religious History of the American People* (New Haven: Yale University Press, 1972), 781.

120. This included the so-called Progressive Orthodoxy, which was a term chosen by the faculty of Andover Seminary (Massachusetts) as its manifesto in 1884, and would include W. A. Brown, W. A. Rauschenbusch, and others. See Ahlstrom, *Religious History of the American People*, 782.

121. This option would include the transcendentalist-Unitarian position of Ralph W. Emerson (a

prototype), and the later Chicago school of S. Mathews, S. J. Case, and others. See Ahlstrom, *Religious History of the American People,* 782f.

122. For a treatment of these figures from United Methodist traditions, see William Naumann, *Theology and German-American Evangelicalism: The Role of Theology in the Church of the United Brethren in Christ and the Evangelical Association* (unpub. Ph.D. diss., Yale University, 1966), 381-96; and Robert E. Chiles, *Theological Transition in American Methodism, 1790–1935* (Lanham, Md.: University Press of America, 1983), 64, 65, 68.

123. On this, see on the one hand the work of E. Käsemann, "Zum gegenwärtigen Streit um die Schriftauslegung," in *Exegetische Versuche und Besinnungen,* 2, 3rd ed. (1970), 268-90; on the other side, there is the conservative treatment by his student, P. Stuhlmacher, *How to Do Biblical Theology* (Allison Park, Pa.: Pickwick, 1995).

124. See A. Schlatter, *Das Christliche Dogma,* 2nd ed. (1923; 3rd ed., 1977), 364-80; as well as his "Atheistische Methoden in der Theologie," in *Zur Theologie des Neuen Testaments und zur Dogmatik* (1969), 134-50. From recent Pietism, see G. Maier, *Biblische Hermeneutik* (1990); from Methodism, see I. H. Marshall, *Biblical Inspiration* (Grand Rapids: Eerdmans, 1983); cf. J. Barr, *The Semantics of Biblical Language* (London: SCM, 1961).

125. On Karl Barth, see the text by C. Green, *Karl Barth: Theologian of Freedom* (London: Collins, 1989), 114-40; esp. the texts from K. Barth, *The Epistle to the Romans,* trans. C. Hoskyns (London: Oxford, 1933). On R. Bultmann, see "New Testament and Mythology" in *Kerygma and Myth,* ed. H. W. Bartsch, vol. 1 (London: SPCK, 1961), 1-44; and "Ist voraussetzungslose Exegese möglich?" in *Glauben und Verstehen,* III, 3rd ed. (1965), 142-50.

126. See *Unterwegs mit Christus,* 341 cf.; W. Klaiber, *Der Bibel kann ich trauen, Orientierung* 4, 2nd ed. (1991); cf. M. Stokes, *The Bible in the Wesleyan Heritage* (Nashville: Abingdon, 1981).

127. Also J. Wesley, *Explanatory Notes on the N.T.,* on 2 Tim. 3:16; further: "Unser Verhältnis zu den Evangelikalen," *EMK heute,* 23 (1976), 3:1 and 4:1.

128. *Notes on NT,* 2 Tim. 3:16; also, in the expressive hymns of Charles Wesley on the inspiration of the Bible, see Hymn 247, "Spirit of truth, essential God, / Who didst thy ancient saints inspire, / Shed in their hearts thy love abroad, / And touch their hallowed lips with fire; // . . . / Still we believe, almighty Lord, // . . . // Come then, divine Interpreter, / The Scriptures to our hearts apply; / And taught by thee we God revere, / Him in Three Persons magnify; / . . ."; 85, 1-2: "Come, Holy *Ghost,* our hearts inspire / . . . // Unlock the truth, thyself the key, / Unseal the sacred book." On the inspiration of the commentator, see also M. Welker, *God the Spirit* (1994), 277ff., which refers to parallel interpretations of Calvin.

129. Martin Luther, "Preface to the Old Testament," in *Luther's Works,* vol. 35, ed. E. J. Bachman (Philadelphia: Muhlenburg, 1960), 236.

130. Preface to Sermons, 5, WJW 1:104-6.

131. See the introduction to the exposition of the Bible in John Wesley's *Notes on the NT,* i (1765), IX, and the citation in note 128 above.

132. Doctrinal Standards, see Appendix, section 4. The configuration of the four key terms under the concept "quadrilateral" is not Wesleyan, but was given its systematic expression by Albert Outler and the General Conference study commission which prepared the document, "The Foundations of Doctrine and the Theological Responsibility of the United Methodist Church" (1972). See also Albert C. Outler, "The Wesleyan Quadrilateral—In John Wesley," in *Doctrine and Theology in The United Methodist Church,* ed. Thomas A. Langford (Nashville: Kingswood, 1991), 75-88; Ted A. Campbell, "The Wesleyan Quadrilateral: The Story of a Modern Methodist Myth," in Langford, Doctrine and Theology, 154-61; P. Borgen, "Biblical Authority and the Authenticity of the Church in Relationship to Auxiliary Keys such as Reason, Experience, and Social Contexts," *Epworth Review* 8 (1981), 71-81; W. J. Abraham, "The Wesleyan Quadrilateral," in *Wesleyan Theology Today: A Bicentennial Theological Consultation,* ed. T. Runyon (Nashville: Kingswood, 1985), 119-26; W. Klaiber, "Gibt es eine methodistische Exegese?" TfP 14 (1988), 1-13.

133. See the Reformation principle *sacra scriptura sui ipsius interpres* ("the Holy Scripture is its own interpreter"), as also M. Luther, "Lectures on Deuteronomy (Vorlesungen über das Deuteronium)," 1523/4, WA 14, 556, 26-29; also, P. Althaus, *The Theology of Martin Luther,* trans. R. C. Schultz (Philadelphia: Fortress, 1966), 72-86.

134. Romans 12:6; Wesley: "according to the analogy of faith," Sermon 64, 2, WJW 2:501.

135. See T. Campbell, "The Wesleyan Quadrilateral," 160, n.132; and T. A. Campbell, *John Wesley and Christian Antiquity: Religious Vision and Cultural Change* (Nashville: Kingswood, 1991).

136. For example, the depth psychological exposition of the category of experience can be associated with this, which however needs to be measured by the hermeneutical precedence of the historical message of the text; see section 1.2.3.6 above.

137. Minutes, June 25, 1744, Works, 3rd ed. 8:275.

138. Compare R. E. Richey, D. M. Campbell, and W. B. Lawrence (eds.), *United Methodism and American Culture,* vol. 1: *Connectionalism* (Nashville: Abingdon, 1997).

139. For this, see also section 4.2.2.4 below.

140. See F. Schäfer, *Bekenntnis und Freiheit in der Kirche,* MiD 13 (1978), 23; cf. L. F. Church, *The Early Methodist People* (London: Epworth, 1948).

141. On this, see Thomas A. Langford, *Practical Divinity: Theology in the Wesleyan Tradition,* rev. ed., 2 vols. (Nashville: Abingdon, 1998–1999), a short synopsis of Methodist theological history. The emphasis is placed on an observation by John Wesley in the foreword of "A Collection of Hymns for the Use of the People Called Methodists" from 1779, which he refers to as "a little body of experimental and practical divinity" and thereby recognized this collection as an illustration of the most important truths of the Christian religion, to be demonstrated through the reason as well as the experience of actual Christians. On this, see also Robert E. Cushman, *John Wesley's Experimental Divinity: Studies in Methodist Doctrinal Standards* (Nashville: Kingswood, 1989).

142. On the history of Methodist theology see Thomas A. Langford, *Practical Divinity.*

143. For a discussion see *Doctrine and Theology in The United Methodist Church,* ed. Thomas A. Langford (Nashville: Kingswood, 1991).

144. Moreover, Wesley is concerned less with the pedagogical consensus in the basic questions of Christian dogmatics (in Sermon 39, "Catholic Spirit," WJW 3:2, 79-95) and is primarily concerned with finding agreement in the basic attitudes toward God and humans. For further discussion, see "The Character of a Methodist," 1, WJW 9:31-46: "But as to all opinions which do not strike at the root of Christianity, we 'think and let think' " (WJW 9:34). Under the category of "opinions," Wesley included the questions of church order, the baptism of children or adults through sprinkling or immersion, or questions concerning the ordering of worship (see Sermon 39, II, 2; WJW 2:89-90), but also the question of the doctrine of predestination (Letter to John Newton from May 14, 1765; *Letters,* ed. Telford, 4:297-300)!

145. Letter to George Downing from April 6, 1761 (*Letters,* ed. Telford, 4:146) and to "Various Clergymen" of April 19, 1764 (Telford, 4:237); see A. C. Outler, "The Theological Thought of John Wesley," ThStBeitr 4 (1991), 28. In "The Character of a Methodist," Wesley describes the inspiration of the Bible, its sole authority in questions of faith and life, and the eternal and true divinity of Christ as the basic and decisive signs, which however only provides for an outer delineation (1, WJW 9:34). On this, see G. Wainwright, "Lehre und Meinungen," in *Grundkonsens—Grunddifferenz,* ed. A. Birmele (1992), 155-68; cf. G. Wainwright, *Doxology: A Systematic Theology* (New York: Oxford, 1980).

146. *Sermons on Several Occasions,* vols. 1-4, 1777 (I.A. 1-3, 1746); 5-8, 1788. See also M. Weyer, "Die Bedeutung von Wesleys Lehrpredigten für die Methodisten," BGEmK 26 (1987); cf. T. C. Oden, *John Wesley's Scriptural Christianity: A Plain Exposition of His Teaching on Christian Doctrine* (Grand Rapids: Zondervan, 1994).

147. Large Minutes (Works, 3rd ed., 8:331). The "Notes upon the New Testament" appeared in 1754; vols. 1-4 of the Sermons were called standard sermons. Since the content of the individual editions differs, the editions of the "Standard Sermons" vary between 44, 52, or 53 sermons; see A. Outler in his preface to the Sermons, in WJW 1:38-45.

148. See Appendix, section 3a. See also Thomas C. Oden, *Doctrinal Standards in the Wesleyan Tradition* (Grand Rapids: Francis Asbury, 1988), which describes the process of receiving these doctrinal documents in the larger Wesleyan tradition; further, see R. E. Cushman, *Experimental Divinity;* and *Doctrine and Theology,* ed. Thomas A. Langford. An influential document in this tradition is the "Sunday Service for North America," which Wesley prepared as a reworked and shortened form of the Anglican Book of Common Prayer, and which also provided the theological basis for the twofold understanding of ordination, based on deacons and elders, as well as the office of superintendent. See J. S. O'Malley, "Methodists," in *The New Twentieth-Century Encyclopedia of Religious Knowledge,* 555-59.

149. See K. H. Voigt, "Ökumenische Wirkungen der Wittenberger Reformation in den angelsächsischen Ländern," MSGEmK 10 (1981/2), 4-34. A synopsis of the Thirty-nine Articles of Religion and their revision by Wesley is found in Oden, Doctrinal Standards, 112-26, and "Articles of Religion,"

in the *Encyclopedia of World Methodism* (Nashville: United Methodist Publishing House, 1974), 1:146-58.

150. See Appendix, Section 3b. An article "On the Last Things" was added; on the history of further revisions, see Oden, Doctrinal Standards, 168ff.; and J. Steven O'Malley, "A Distinctive German-American Credo: The United Brethren Confession of Faith," *Asbury Theological Journal* (spring 1987), 51-64.

151. On this so-called first restrictive rule (Section III, ¶ 16, Article 1 of the Constitution of the UMC), see Oden, Doctrinal Standards, 53f.

152. See Robert E. Chiles, *Theological Transition in American Methodism (1790–1935)* (Lanham, Md.: University Press of America, 1983), Chiles denotes four transitional theologians to indicate major shifts in American Methodist theology during this era: John Wesley, Richard Watson (Wesleyan systematician), John Miley (liberal evangelical), and Albert Knudson (personalism), and assesses their positions on revelation, anthropology, and grace/free will to develop a barometer for evaluating the direction of Methodist theology in its historical development. The major evaluation of historical developments in EUB theology is provided by William Naumann, *Theology and German-American Evangelicalism; The Role of Theology in the Church of the United Brethren in Christ and the Evangelical Association* (unpublished Ph.D. diss., Yale University, 1966).

153. According to N. Burwash (ed.), *Wesley's Doctrinal Standards* (1881), p. XI (cited by Oden, Doctrinal Standards, 23).

154. See K. Steckel, "Bekenntnis' in der EmK," MSGEmK 2 (1981/2), 17-30; cf. R. L. Maddox, *Responsible Grace: John Wesley's Practical Theology* (Nashville: Kingswood, 1994).

155. In the first draft of the Fundamentals of Doctrine and Our Theological Task from 1972, these documents were designated as "landmark documents," or writings that provide us with doctrinal orientation and thus assist us in arriving at appropriate biblical perspectives for the present day. In 1984 this terminology was revised with the appearance of the term "Foundation Documents."

156. See Appendix section 3c; also H. Nausner, "The Meaning of Wesley's General Rules: An Interpretation," trans. J. Steven O'Malley, *Asbury Theological Journal* (fall 1989), 43-60.

157. See *The Book of Discipline* (UMC, 1996), Part III, Social Principles, ¶¶ 64-70.

158. The Theological Task of The United Methodist Church (the 1972 edition of *The Book of Discipline;* it was reformulated in 1988 by deleting this passage).

159. J. J. Escher, *Christliche Theologie. Eine Darstellung biblischer Lehre vom Standpunkt der Evangelischen Gemeinschaft,* I-III (1899–1901); A Sulzberger, *Christliche Glaubenslehre,* 3rd ed. (1898); Th. Spörri, *Der Mensch und die frohe Botschaft. Christliche Glaubenslehre, I-III* (Fragment) (1939–1956).

160. "Doctrinal Standards and Our Theological Task," *The Book of Discipline* (UMC, 1996), ¶ 60, pp. 39-40.

161. This geographical focus is necessary for our readers; although Methodism worldwide has relied upon the doctrinal standards that include Wesley's doctrinal sermons, his Notes on the New Testament, and the General Rules, their exposition and usage is reflected in differing ways according to the structure, the proclamation, and the ministry that is being expressed.

162. M. Schmidt, *John Wesley,* vol. 2: *John Wesley's Life Mission,* trans. Denis Inman (Nashville: Abingdon, 1973), 102. The author explicitly describes the undertaking of the Christian library of Wesley (101-8).

163. "Doctrinal Standards and Our Theological Task," in *The Book of Discipline* (UMC, 1996), ¶ 60, p. 41.

164. This can also be found in A. C. Outler, "Theologische Akzente," in *Der Methodismus,* ed. C. E. Sommer, K W 6 (1968); 84-101; further, *Geschichte der EmK,* 262-76; cf. A. Outler, *Theology in the Wesleyan Spirit* (Nashville: Discipleship Resources, 1996).

165. Foreword to *Hymns and Sacred Poems. Published by John Wesley . . . and Charles Wesley . . .* (1739), in *Works,* 3rd ed., 14:321.

2. Universal Salvation, or God's Love for God's World

1. Sermon 1, 3; WJW 1:118.

2. *Grace upon Grace: The Mission Statement of The United Methodist Church* (Nashville: Graded Press, 1990), 97.

3. "Doctrinal Standards and Our Theological Task," *The Book of Discipline of The United Methodist Church* (Nashville: United Methodist Publishing House, 1996), ¶ 60, pp. 44-45.

4. These aspects of the theology of creation, which keep in mind the characteristic value of that portion of creation that is exclusive of humanity, have been strongly brought into the foreground in the last decades of the twentieth century; see C. Link, "Schöpfung," vol. 2 (HSTh 7/2) (1991), 358ff.; see the related discussion in W. Pannenberg, *Systematic Theology,* 1:401f., 416ff.

5. "Erklärung von Stuttgart" (1988), section 4, 1.

6. New attempts at a doctrine of creation are provided by: C. Link, "Schöpfung"; J. Moltmann, *"Gott in der Schöpfung: Ökologische Schöpfung als Anrede,* 2nd ed. (1990); A. Ganoczy, *Schöpfung. Zu den Fundamentalsätzen der christlichen Schöpfungslehre heute,* Theologische Existenz Heute 212 (1981); see also J. Moltmann, *The Trinity and the Kingdom* (San Francisco: Harper and Row, 1981), 99-114.

7. The Darwinist Ernst Haeckel (1834–1919) did not refrain from mocking God as "a gaseous vertebrate."

8. C. Westermann, *Schöpfung* 1971, 14f. (tr. trans.).

9. Westermann, *Schöpfung,* 22. See also C. Westermann, *Genesis I-II* (Minneapolis: Fortress, 1994), 22f.

10. It is noteworthy that the created world in Genesis is described in a way that has no exact precedents in the mythic accounts of the ancient world. "It is exactly the sobriety of Genesis 1, the frank description of a world structured from water, land, and heavenly bodies, plants, animals and humans, which recalls the work and discourse of science." (H. and W. Hemminger, *Jenseits der Weltbilder* (Stuttgart, 1991), 78f. (tr. trans.).

11. Genesis 1 and 2; Psalm 104; Job 38; etc.

12. Romans 8:19-23; 1 Peter 2:11-12.; Matthew 22:15-22; etc.

13. Martin Luther, "Sermons on the Catechism," reprinted in *Martin Luther: Selections from His Writings,* ed. J. Dillenberger (Garden City, N.Y.: Doubleday, 1961), 208.

14. The discoveries of the heliocentric theory of the universe, the rotation of the earth on its own axis, and the fact that distant stars actually were suns with their own systems of planets were especially shocking and revolutionary.

15. *Der Wille zur Macht,* Edition Schlechta (1977), 882 (tr. trans.).

16. *Evolution und Gottesglaube,* ed. W. Boehme (1988); A. M. K. Müller and others, *Schöpfungsglaube heute* (1985); cf. "The Conflict Between Science and Theology: Biblical Criticism and Darwinism" in J. C. Livingston, *Modern Christian Thought: From the Enlightenment to Vatican II* (New York: Macmillan, 1971), 209-44.

17. "Schöpfung und Weltentstehung," in *Die Tragweite der Wissenschaft,* vol. 1 (1964), 28 (tr. trans.).

18. "Glaube konkret," No. 16 (tr. trans.).

19. D. von Oppen, *Moral* (1973), 29 (tr. trans.).

20. See C. Westermann, "Schöpfung und Evolution," in *Evolution und Glaube,* ed. W. Boehme, 240-50, and J. Ebach, "Schöpfung in der hebräischen Bibel," in *Ökologische Theologie,* ed. G. Altner (1989), 98-120; see also Livingston, *Modern Christian Thought,* 222-41.

21. On the doctrine of creation out of nothing (creation ex nihilo) see E. Wölfel, "Welt als Schöpfung," 20-35; cf. B. W. Anderson, "Creation ex Nihilo," in *The Interpreter's Dictionary of the Bible* (Nashville: Abingdon, 1962), 1:728.

22. H. Hemminger and W. Hemminger, Jenseits der Weltbilder, 27 (tr. trans.).

23. From an address, printed in *Dienste im Übersee* 15 (1979), No. 3, 14 (tr. trans.).

24. C. Schwöbel, "Theologie der Schöpfung im Dialog zwischen Naturwissenschaft und Dogmatik," in *Unsere Welt-Gottes Schöpfung,* ed. W. Härle, et al. (1992), 199-221 (219) (tr. trans.); cf. Livingston, *Modern Christian Thought,* 209-16.

25. See the newspaper, Deutsches Allgemeines Sonntagsblatt of Aug 5, 1979.

26. On the topic of Sin and its consequences, see section 2.2.1.

27. T. Spörri, "Der Mensch und die frohe Botschaft," I, 36-46.

28. *Letters and Papers from Prison,* enlarged ed., trans. Eberhard Bethge (New York: Macmillan, 1971), 347-48.

29. E. Biser, "Der Mensch im Spannungsfeld von Grösse und Ohnmacht," in *Wer ist das eigentlich—der Mensch?* ed. E. Stammler (München, 1973), 127f. (tr. trans.).

30. P. Tillich, *Systematic Theology* (Chicago: University of Chicago Press, 1957), 2:13.

31. Tillich, *Systematic Theology,* 2:31-36; see also the brief work "Der Mensch in den Veränderungsprozessen unserer Zeit. Zur Frage nach dem Menschen" (Zürich, 1986), which was prepared by the Theological Study Commission of The United Methodist Church (EmK) in Europe.

32. Konrad Lorenz, a research authority in the field of modern human behavior, has referred to this as "being a specialist on not being a specialist."

33. See section 2.2.2 (God's Covenant Faithfulness) and 3.1.1 (The Abiding Love of God).

34. K. Marti, *Der Vorsprung Leben* (1989), 89.

35. Genesis 1:27; 9:6; 1 Corinthians 11:7 (for the male); James 3:9.

36. See Genesis 2; Psalm 8, etc.

37. Sermon 45, "The New Birth"; WJW 2:186-201.

38. Ibid., I, 4; 2:190.

39. Ibid., 2:189-95.

40. See Sermon 2, WJW 1:131-41, and Sermon 9, WJW 1:248-66.

41. E. Lohse, "Imago Dei bei Paulus," in *Libertas Christiana, Festschrift für F. Delekat,* BEvTh 26 (München, 1957), 123f.; W. Härle, "Die Rechtfertigungslehre als Grundlage der Anthropologie," in W. Härle and E. Herms, *Rechtfertigung: Das Wirklichkeitsverständnis des christlichen Glaubens* (Göttingen, 1979), 91f.; J. Jervell, H. Crousel, J. Maier, A. Peters, "Bild Gottes," I-IV, TRE 6 (1980), 491-515.

42. J. Jervell, "Bild Gottes," I, TRE 6, 497; cf. "Image of God," in *A Handbook of Theological Terms,* ed. V. A. Harvey, 125-27.

43. *Der Mensch als Bild Gottes,* ed. L. Scheffcyzk (1969); A. Peters, *Der Mensch* (1979); G. Ebeling, *Dogmatik des Christlichen Glaubens,* I (1979), 404-14.

44. W. Härle, "Die Rechtfertigungslehre als Grundlage," 97 (tr. trans.).

45. Ebeling, *Dogmatik des Christlichen Glaubens,* I, 414.

46. On this, see section 2.3 for details.

47. See also M. Marquardt, "Imago Christi als Leitbild der Heiligung," in *Unsere Welt—Gottes Schöpfung; Festschrift E. Wölfel,* ed. W. Härle, et al. (Marburg, 1992), 235-50 (printed in ThFPr 18, 1992); see also W. Pannenberg, *Systematic Theology* (Grand Rapids: Eerdmans, 1991), 2:205ff.

48. I. Kant, *The Metaphysical Foundations of Morals,* Section I, trans. C. J. Friedrich, in *Foundations of Western Thought: Six Major Philosophers,* ed. J. G. Clapp, M. Philipson, and H. M. Rosenthal (New York: Knopf, 1962), 789.

49. Above all, what is to be noted here is the emphasis on the will of God and the respectability of humanity; but also note the concept of their creation in the image of God as the key to understanding human existence before and after the fall and in the renewal through God (see section 2.1.2.2).

50. See section 3.2 below, "The Renewal to Life in God."

51. K. Barth, CD III/2, 395.

52. See sections 3.2.3 and 4.1.

53. Sermon 105, WJW 3:480. "On Conscience" (WJW 3:479-90) is on 2 Corinthians 1:12; however, the sermon text plays a subordinate role in the rather thematic treatment.

54. Sermon 105, I, 1, 3; WJW 3:481.

55. Pertinent information is to be found in C. E. Nelson, *Conscience: Theological and Psychological Perspectives* (New York: Newman, 1973); and W. E. Conn, *Conscience: Development and Self-Transcendence* (Birmingham, Ala.: Religious Education Press, 1981).

56. This refers to the fully unconscious operation of the so-called biological conscience, to which belong the simplest "mechanisms for restraint" (see Walter Furrer, *Psychoanalyse und Seelsorge,* 2nd ed., 1972).

57. The basic requirements of ethics and human behavior are indicated in numerous statements concerning the New Testament command of the love of neighbor, expressed through particular concrete commands (see Matthew 22:37-40; John 13:34-35; 15:9-17; Romans 13:8-10; etc.).

58. On the problem of the identity see the novel by Max Frisch *I'm Not Stiller* (Harcourt, Brace, and Co., 1994); and see below, 3.2.2.5.

59. In his sermon on conscience, John Wesley also speaks of the possibility of a "good conscience" based on the conviction that actions have conformed to the command (Sermon 105, I, 12; WJW 3:485); this agreement is not possible without the influence of the Holy Spirit, who teaches us to recognize God's will in our actions and who enables us to do the appropriate deeds (Sermon 105, I, 13f.; WJW 3:486). Wesley does not entertain the possibility of a positive judgment of conscience apart from the relationship to God.

60. On this theme, see section 2.2.2, "God's Covenant Faithfulness."

61. On the doctrine of providence, see G. Harkness, *The Providence of God* (Nashville: Abingdon, 1960); and F. Cloud, *God's Hand in Our Lives: A Study of Providence* (Nashville: Tidings, 1964).

62. "On Divine Providence," Sermon 67, WJW 2:535-50. Wesley's arguments and the content of his sermon commend nothing on this subject that is not previously found in the classical statements of this catholic Christian doctrine; Wesley warmly embraces this theme because he sees it as being applicable not only for personal, pastoral work but also for his social, medical, and diaconal work.

63. Sermon 67, 13; WJW 2:539: It is impossible that God in heaven does not observe the "poor inhabitants of earth." "He hath made us, not we ourselves; and he cannot despise the work of his own hands. We are his children." Wesley does not appear to be overly concerned by the question that is occasionally discussed concerning how this manner of kinship to God is related to the one who is received through faith in Christ (see section 3.2.2.4). It is unquestionable, both from a biblical and a dogmatic perspective, that these are to be distinguished, and one may infer this from Wesley's doctrinal sermons (see Sermon 1, "The Salvation by Faith," II, 7, WJW 1:124-25; Sermon 5, "Justification by Faith," IV, 9; WJW 1:198-99) and elsewhere.

64. Sermon 67, "On Divine Providence," 21; WJW 2:545-46.

65. Also Wesley, Sermon 67, 26, WJW 2:548; and Augustine, *Confessions*, ed. J. J. O'Donnell (New York: Oxford, 1992), 3:11.

66. Sermon 67, 27-29; WJW 2:548-50.

67. It remains important with all of these considerations to keep in mind the differences between the perspectives of theology and natural science: "It is an illusory game for us to think that scientists have excluded God from the world whenever they reply to the 'how' questions without making reference to God. We tend to think that there is less room for God whenever we understand better how the world functions. This 'forces' God into the ever smaller gaps of our knowledge" (Robert J. Berry, *God and Evolution*, London, 1988), 20.

68. W. Trillhaas, *Dogmatik* (Walter De Gruyter, 1972), 169 (tr. trans.).

69. An introduction to this problem is given by N. Pike, *God and Evil* (Englewood Cliffs, N.J.: Prentice-Hall, 1964); *The Problem of Evil*, ed. M. M. and R. M. Adams (New York: Oxford, 1990); The Problem of Evil, ed. M. L. Peterson (Notre Dame, 1992).

70. For an in-depth discussion of this difficult theme, see A. W. Harper, *The Theodicy of Suffering* (Lewiston, Me.: Mellen, 1990); *The Mystery of Suffering and Death*, ed. M. J. Taylor (Staten Island, N.Y.: Alba House, 1973); and J. Moltmann, *History and the Triune God: Contributions to Trinitarian Theology*, trans. J. Bowden (New York: Crossroad, 1991).

71. See for example, G. G. Büchner, *Danton's Death*, trans. V. Prie (New York: Oxford, 1988), or Albert Camus, *The Plague*, trans. S. Gilbe (New York: Knopf, 1948).

72. See E. Brunner, *Dogmatics II: The Christian Doctrine of Creation and Redemption*, trans. O. Wyon (Philadelphia: Westminster, 1952), 76.

73. H. Hemminger and W. Hemminger, *Jenseits der Weltbilder*, 266; cf. J. B. Metz, "Suffering from God: Theology as Theodicy," *Pacifica* 5 (1992), 274-87.

74. Cf. K. H. zur Mühlen, "Gotteslehre und Schriftverständnis in Luthers Schrift 'De servo arbitrio,'" *Jahrbuch für biblische Theologie* 2 (1987), 210-25; also, P. Alhaus, *The Theology of Martin Luther*, 15-34.

75. Namely that God neither deplores nor abolishes the death of a sinner *(neque deplorat neque tollit)*, but wills it according to that impenetrable will *(vult autem illam voluntate illa imperscrutabili)*. Luther, De servo arbitrio, WA 18, 685.

76. Suffering as punishment or as means of education.

77. The example of suffering of Christians leads others to faith.

78. Cf. also D. Bonhoeffer's poem "Christians and Pagans," in *Letters and Papers from Prison*, 348-49.

79. "Without eschatology there is no theodicy" (W. Härle, *Leiden als Fels des Atheismus?* 143); cf. A. W. Harper, *The Theodicy of Suffering* (Lewiston, Me.: Mellen, 1992); and B. Hebblethwaite, *Evil, Suffering and Religion* (New York: Hawthorn, 1976).

80. C. Link, *Schöpfung*, 2:582 (tr. trans.).

81. K. Wendler, "Kann ich Gott noch vertrauen? Annäherungen an die Theodizeefrage im seelsorgerlichen Dienst an Krebskranken," PTh 78 (1989), 173-84; cf. J. L. Maes, *Suffering: A Caregiver's Guide* (Nashville: Abingdon, 1990).

82. This is already indicated in the Old Testament in Genesis 4:7.

83. Latin: *peccatum originale*. W. Joest (*Dogmatik*, 2:405) speaks of the "basic sin ['Grundsünde'] of humanity"; cf. A. Vanneste, *The Dogma of Original Sin*, trans. E. P. Callens (Brussels: Nauwelaerts, 1975).

84. See the evidence in A. Outler, "Das theologische Denken John Wesley," ThStBeitr 4 (1991), 83 (A. 25 f.); further: J. Wesley, Sermon 44, "Original Sin," WJW 2:170-85.

85. Sermon 44, III, 2; WJW 2:182-83.

86. Søren Kierkegaard, *Fear and Trembling/ The Sickness unto Death*, trans. W. Lowrie (Garden City, N.Y.: Doubleday, 1954), 247-49.

87. See W. Pannenberg, *Systematic Theology*, 2:241ff.

88. The ideas of *Pelagian* and *semi-Pelagian* are derived from a monk named Pelagius (died after 418), who opposed the doctrine of the later Augustine concerning original sin; he replaced it with his emphasis upon the voluntary sinful habits and slavish imitation of Adam, which continue among his progeny. By nature, humans are endowed with the ability to fulfil God's law, and here the laws of the Old and the New Testaments are distinguished through the content of the commands (see R. Lorenz, "Pelagius und Pelagianismus," Religion in Geschichte und Gegenwart, 3rd ed., V, 206f,). Although Wesley was not in agreement with the doctrine of Pelagius, he occasionally defended it because he presumed that Pelagius had been judged improperly in the shadow of the great Augustine (see Sermon 68, WJW 2:555-56 with notes). For an evaluation of Pelagianism in Methodism, see Articles. VII-VIII of the Articles of Religion of the Methodist Church and Article VII of the Confession of Faith (Evangelical United Brethren), in section 3 of the Appendix.

89. See Conrad Cherry, *God's New Israel* (Englewood Cliffs, N.J.: Prentice Hall, 1971).

90. See the architects of the New Divinity as discussed in Ahlstrom, *Theology in America*, 406-7.

91. Robert Chiles, *Theological Transition in American Methodism, 1790–1835,* 115-43.

92. For Paul's use of terms, see Galatians 3:19, Romans 5:13-17, 20f. and P. Fiedler, "*Hamartia*" in *Exegetical Dictionary of the New Testament* ed. H. Balz and G. Schneider (Grand Rapids: Eerdmans, 1990), 1:65-69; and M. Wolter, "Paraptoma" in *Exegetical Dictionary of the New Testament,* 3:33f.

93. W. Zimmerli, *Old Testament Theology in Outline* (Atlanta: John Knox, 1978); further H.-J. Kraus, *Systematische Theologie* (1983), 241f.

94. See Wesley, *Notes NT* on Romans 5:12, 14, 19; see also H. Lindstrom, *Wesley and Sanctification* (London: Epworth, 1946), 21-23.

95. On the figures of the serpent, see C. Westermann, *Genesis 1–11*, 237-42; its description as a creation of God requires no dualistic explanation for the origin of evil.

96. Gerhard von Rad notes that to know what is good and evil probably means, in biblical language, knowing all things. ("Genesis". A Commentary, trans. by J. H. Marks, 1961, 86f.)

97. See Wesley, Sermon 45, "The New Birth," I, 2; WJW 2:189-90; and Sermon 57, "On the Fall of Man," I, 1f.; WJW 2:401ff.

98. O. H. Steck, "Die Paradieserzählung," Biblische Studien 60 (1970), 105; similarly, J. Barr, *The Garden of Eden and the Hope of Immortality* (Minneapolis: Fortress, 1993); see also Wesley, Sermon 45, I, 2; WJW 2:188-89.

99. So some Gnostic systems; see K. Rudolph, *Gnosis: The Nature and History of Gnosticism,* trans. R. M. Wilson (San Francisco: Harper and Row, 1984), 99; E. Pagels, *Adam, Eve and the Serpent* (New York: Random House, 1988). For a dialectical description of the necessary relationship between knowledge and guilt, see: G. W. F. Hegel, *Lectures on the Philosophy of Religion* (London: Routledge & Paul, 1962), 263ff.; and E. Fromm, *You Shall Be as Gods: A Radical Interpretation of the Old Testament and Its Tradition* (New York: Holt, Rinehart and Winston, 1966). On the theological side, Paul Tillich has above all emphasized the ambivalent character of the "fall into sin," in that he describes "the tragic element in the transition from essential to existential being" (*Systematic Theology*, 2:36ff.).

100. See Wesley, Sermon 57, "On the Fall of Man," II, 2; WJW 2:403-4. For the relationship between shame and guilt, and between self-knowledge and the relationship with God, according to depth psychology, see L. Arnold-Carey, *Und sie erkannten daß sie nackt waren. Geschlechtswahrnehmung und kindliche Entwicklung* (1972); cf. M. Oraison, et al., *Sin*, trans. B. Murchland and R. Meyerpeter (New York: Macmillan, 1962).

101. See Sermon 45, "The New Birth," I, 2; WJW 2:189-90; Sermon 57, "On the Fall of Man," II, 6; WJW 2:409-10; Sermon 59, "God's Love to Fallen Man," 1; WJW 2:423; Sermon 62, I, 1, 10;

WJW 2:473-74, 477; and on this, see H. R. Dunning, *Reflecting the Divine Image: A Wesleyan View of Christian Ethics* (Downer's Grove, Ill.: InterVarsity, 1998); and J. Weissbach, *Der neue Mensch im theologischen Denken John Wesleys,* BGEmK 2 (1970), 4ff., 30ff. For a present-day treatment of this theme, see above, section 2.1.2.2. Wesley's concern is taken up, in which the image of God is conceived as a function and not as a possession. Thus, W. Joest has correctly said that "in the perverting of its performance" the image of God is "missed totally." But concerning the destiny of humanity and the faithfulness of God to humans, it can be said that "for those who are created according to God's image, that image remains inextinguishable" (*Dogmatik,* 2:419).

102. Wesley, Sermon 44, "Original Sin," II, 3ff.; WJW 2:177-82; Sermon 45, I, 2; WJW 2:189-90. Ch. Gestrich, *The Return of Splendor in the World: The Christian Doctrine of Sin and Forgiveness,* trans. D. W. Bloesch (Grand Rapids: Eerdmans, 1997), speaks of humans' "lack of God" and wanting "to be like God" as the "mystery of sin" (203f.); cf. A. Vanneste, *The Dogma of Original Sin,* trans. E. P. Callens (Brussels: Nauwelaerts, 1975).

103. Kraus, *Systematische Theologie,* 238; Wesley, Sermon 44, "Original Sin," II, 7; WJW 2:178-79: "Atheism itself does not screen us from idolatry."

104. Sermon 44, II, 7-11; WJW 2:178-82; Wesley here represents essentially the same viewpoint as Luther in his exposition of the first commandment in his Larger Catechism: "That upon which you hang and leave your heart, that is actually your God" (BSLK 560).

105. W. Pannenberg, *Systematic Theology* 2:243f.

106. "Lecture on the Epistle to the Romans," WA 56, 365f.

107. See Romans 5:10; 8:7. W. Pannenberg, *Systematic Theology,* 2:250f.

108. See Genesis 8:21; Job 14:1-4; 15:14; 25:4; Psalm 143:2.

109. See Sermons 34-36; WJW 2:1-43; see section 2.2.1.3 below. This also corresponds to the Reformation doctrine of the *usus theologicus* of the law; see "Law," in *A Handbook of Theological Terms,* ed. V. A. Harvey, 143. See O. Weber, *Foundations of Dogmatics,* trans. D. J. Gruder (Grand Rapids: Eerdmans, 1981), I, 587f.

110. Sermon 44, II, 2; WJW 2:176-77. O. Weber, *Gundlagen,* 591 "It is first in forgiveness that sin is first 'recognized' as sin" (see also Barth, *Church Dogmatics,* II/2, 768ff.; IV/I, 359-413.

111. Pannenberg, *Systematic Theology,* 2:236. See also U. Eibach, "Schulderleben-Schuldgefühle-Sündenerkenntnis" in *Seelische Krankheit und Christlicher Glaube. Theologie in Seelsorge, Beratung und Diakonie,* Band 3 (1992), 142: That the knowledge of sin occurs "first in faith" does not "exclude that there is already the beginning of an awareness of this in humans' knowledge of themselves, so that humans are guilty before God."

112. Sermon 44, II, 2; WJW 2:176-77 (on Genesis 6:5).

113. See H. Ottmann and H. G. Ulrich, "Entfremdung," I/II, TRE 9 (1982), 657-80; P. Tillich, *Systematic Theology,* 2:29-78; W. Pannenberg, *Systematic Theology,* 2:179-181. The biblical basis for the concept lies in Eph. 2:12, 19; 4:18.

114. Horst Eberhard Richter, *All Mighty: A Study of the God Complex in Western Man,* trans. Jan van Heurck (San Bernandino, Calif.: Borgo, 1986).

115. Herein lies also the positive principle of the first works of Drewermann, in which he set the psychological category of anxiety and the theological dimension of guilt and sin in connection with one another (*Strukturen des Bösen* III); for further elaboration of his treatment of this problem, see Drewermann, *Tiefenpsychologie und Exegese* II, 6th ed. (1990); see also *Counseling and the Human Predicament: A Study of Sin, Guilt and Forgiveness,* ed. L. Aden and D. G. Benner (Grand Rapids: Baker, 1980); and D. Capps, *The Depleted Self* (Minneapolis: Fortress, 1992).

116. Sermon 44, II; WJW 2:176-82.

117. Ibid., III, 3, WJW 2:184.

118. Sermon 45, I, 2; WJW 2:189-90; Sermon 76, II, 9, WJW 3:79-80; similarly, Sermon 57, I, 1, WJW 2:401-3.

119. W. H. Schmidt and G. Delling, *Wörterbuch zur Bibel* (1971), 542 (tr. trans.). See also Schmidt, *The Faith of the Old Testament* (Philadelphia: Westminster, 1983), 37.

120. See R. Knierim, *Die Hauptbegriffe für Sünde im Alten Testament,* 2nd ed. (1967).

121. See above, note 92.

122. Genesis 39:9; 2 Samuel 12:13; Psalm 51:4.

123. E. Lohmeyer, *Our Father,* trans. John Bowden (New York: Harper & Row, 1965), 160-84.

124. Literature: K. Koch, "Gibt es ein Vergeltungsdogma im Alten Testament?" in *Spuren des hebräischen Denkens. Beiträge zur alttestamentlichen Theologie.* Grundrisse zum Alten Testament,

vol. 1 (1991), 5-103; Koch, "Der Spruch, Sein Blut bleibe auf seinem Haupt und die israelitische Auffassung vom vergossenen Blut," *Spuren,* 128-45; K. Koch, "Sühne und Sündenvergebung um die Wende von der exilischen zur nachexilischen Zeit," *Spuren,* 184-205; H. Gese, *Essays on Biblical Theology,* trans. Keith Crim (Minneapolis: Augsburg, 1981), 93-116. On the two aspects of the Hebrew *asam* (responsibility for guilt) see R. Knierim, THAT I, 251-57; on the meaning of *awon* (perversity) in the total realm of Hebrew thought see R. Knierim, *Hauptbegriffe,* 251; see THAT II, 245; cf. S. J. De Vries, "Sin/Sinners," in *Interpreter's Dictionary of the Bible,* 4:361-76; and J. A. Wharton, "Perverse," in *Interpreter's Dictionary of the Bible,* 3:748.

125. In this connection, the issue of homosexuality for Paul is not a voluntary sin, as the basis for punishment, but rather it is the result of what happens when God surrenders humanity to its narcissistic tendencies. The imprisonment of humans to love of their own gender is for Paul a symptom for the basic sin of all humanity, of worshiping the creature rather than the Creator, and that is finally expressed as self-love. From this standpoint a responsible position on the question of homosexuality can be formulated for our day which does not place homosexuality on the same level as heterosexuality but also does not declare it to be the personal guilt of the individual (see *Book of Discipline* ([UMC, 1996)], Social Principles, (¶ 65, II, G).

126. See W. Schrage, *The Ethics of the New Testament,* trans. David Green (Philadelphia: Fortress, 1988).

127. On this, see the valuation of sin as deed by U. Eibach, *Seelische Krankheit* 70, 136, 222f. See *The Westminster Dictionary of Christian Theology,* ed. A. Richardson and J. Bowden (Philadelphia: SCM, 1983), 539-40.

128. Letter "from ND," April 15, 1749: and "To N.D." May 27, 1749 in WJW 26:349-51, 358-60.

129. Sermon 44, II, 9; WJW 2:181.

130. See section 4.1.3.

131. On this, see M. Marquardt, *John Wesley's Social Ethics: Praxis and Principles,* trans. J. E. Steely and W. Stephen Gunter (Nashville: Abingdon, 1992), which also demonstrated the problem of the ongoing renunciation of structural change of society by Wesley. For further study, see J. Moltmann, *The Spirit of Life, a Universal Affirmation* (Minneapolis: Fortress, 1992), 153ff.

132. The meaning of the law for Paul is one of the most controversial areas in current New Testament exegesis. The most important publications on this are: H. Hübner, *Law in Paul's Thought* (Edinburgh: T. and T. Clark, 1984), 69-82; U. Wilckens, *Zur Entwicklung des paulinischen Gesetzesverständnisses,* NTS 28 (1982), 154-90; E. P. Sanders, *Paul, the Law, and the Jewish People* (Philadelphia: Fortress, 1985); H. Räisänen, "Paul and the Law," WUNT 29 (1983); G. Klein, "Gesetz," III, TRE 13 (1984), 58-75; P. v. d. Osten-Sacken, *Die Heiligkeit der Thora: Studien zum Gesetz des Paulus* (1989); J. D. G. Dunn, *Jesus, Paul, and the Law* (1990).

133. The law as paidagogos (taskmaster) does not have the function of relating to Christ pedagogically, but functions instead to watch as an overseer. See *Exegetical Dictionary of the New Testament,* ed. H. Balz and G. Schneider (Grand Rapids: Eerdmans, 1992), 2-3.

134. Sermon 34, IV, 2; WJW 2:16.

135. Sermon 35, "The Law Established Through Faith I," I, 3; WJW 2:22; see Wesley's letter, "To an Evangelical Layman," of December 20, 1751, WJW 26:482-85.

136. See E. Wolf, "Gesetz" V, *Religion in Geschichte und Gegenwart,* 3rd ed., II, 1523f.: "Evangelium facit ex lege paedagogum in Christum" ("The gospel makes the law an educator to Christ," WA 39/1, 446). See also B. Metzger and M. Coogan, *The Oxford Companion to the Bible* (New York: Oxford University Press), 421-27.

137. See below, 2.2.2.3.

138. On this terminology, see the evidence cited in W. Klaiber, *Call and Response: Biblical Foundations of a Theology of Evangelism,* trans. H. Perry-Trauthig and J. A. Dwyer (Nashville: Abingdon, 1997), 225, n. 108.

139. This was important biographically for Luther as well as for Wesley, and it was evaluated theologically by both. In place of the pride of those who suppose that they have fulfilled the law, there enters the doubt whether they are able to fulfill God's will.

140. See Romans 2:17; 4:2; 11:18; 1 Cor. 1:18-31; 4:7. See also R. Bultmann, *Theology of the New Testament,* trans. K. Grobel (New York: Scribner's, 1951), 239-46.

141. The reverse side of this position is the repeated flare-up of anxiety concerning one's own salvation, which, from the concern about being guilty, avoids the hazard of every hard decision. Herzog-Dürck speaks in this connection about guilt, as "not to be able to be guilty." A person "avoids life and

feels the lovelessness which is his actual guilt" (*Probleme menschlicher Reifung,* 1969, 38f.). See also T. Butler, "Guilt," in *Holman Bible Dictionary* (Nashville: Holman Bible Publishers, 1991), 586-87.

142. The American theologian Judith Plaskow has written that the "sin" that is produced by the role of women in modern society and which is encouraged among women, is not an illegitimate ego reference but rather the failure to relate oneself to the ego and the failure to accept responsibility for one's own life (*Sex, Sin, and Grace* [New Haven: Yale, 1980], 92).

143. See below, 2.2.2.3.

144. Concerning this translation, see U. Wilckens, *Der Brief an die Römer,* Evangelisch-katholischer Kommentar zum Neuen Testament VI/1, 78. See also Wilckens, *God's Revelation,* trans. W. Glen-Doepel (Philadelphia: Westminster, 1967), 35-70.

145. See E. Käsemann, *Commentary on Romans* (Grand Rapids: Eerdmans, 1980), 36-52, and the citation from Luther, note 133 above: The gospel makes the law an educator pointing toward Christ. Similarly, he states in his lectures on Romans that "Thus God converts whom he converts through the view of His goodness. And that is the only way to be converted in truth, that is, through love and goodness. For whoever is converted through threats and intimidation is never converted in truth" (WA 56, 474, 10ff.). Wesley's position is not unequivocal. On the one hand he emphasizes that "the ordinary method of God is to convict sinners by the law, and that only. The gospel is not the means which God hath ordained, or which our Lord himself used, for this end" (Sermon 35, I, 3; WJW 2:22-23). But this is precisely the work of the Holy Spirit (Sermon 34, IV and I; WJW 2:15-19, 6-8); only where God opens to persons the eyes of their hearts do they recognize that they are sinners and are without God (Sermon 44, II, 2; WJW 2:176-77). Thus, in the conference discussion of August 2, 1745, Wesley can ask: "Do not some of our assistants preach too much of the wrath, and too little of the love, of God?" And the answer resounds, "We fear they have leaned to that extreme; and hence some of their hearers may have lost the joy of faith" (Q. 17, Works, 3rd ed., 8:284). See also the conference proceedings of 1746 in Williams, *Theology,* 174: "Question: Why is it unsuitable to speak much of God's wrath and little of love? - Answer: In general, this only hardens those who do not believe, and discourages those who do believe." With Wesley and the Pietists' proclamation of the gospel there lies the danger of viewing the interplay of gospel and law in preaching, as being under psychological categories (on Spener and Francke, see F. W. Graf, "Gesetz," VI, TRE 13 (1984), 100f; and H. M. Barth, *Gesetz und Evangelium* I, TRE 13, 128); cf. D. Brown, *Understanding Pietism* (Grand Rapids: Eerdmans, 1978).

146. D. Bonhoeffer, *The Cost of Discipleship* (London: SCM, 2nd ed., 1959), chapter 1, "Costly Grace."

147. According to J. Herzog-Dürck, *Probleme menschlicher Reifung* (1969), 19. See D. Noel, "Sin," in *The Anchor Bible Dictionary* (New York: Doubleday, 1992), 6:31-46.

148. D. Bonhoeffer, *Letters and Papers From Prison* (New York: Macmillan, 1971), 343-47.

149. For this, see below, 2.2.2.3.

150. G. von Rad, *Genesis,* 98.

151. See above, n.125, where the perversion of sexuality is mentioned. But it is also important to see that the perverting power of sin works itself out in all human relationships, according to Paul!— see Käsemann, *Romans,* 33-85.

152. See also James 2:1-13; 5:1-6 (see above, n. 131).

153. K. Seybold and U. Müller, *Sickness and Healing,* trans. D. W. Stott (Nashville: Abingdon, 1981), 90.

154. Psalm 107:17; Job 33:21; Isaiah 38:10ff.; see Seybold and Müller, *Sickness and Healing,* 43f.; also, section 2.2.1.5.

155. Mark 2:1-12 says nothing about the sickness of the lame man having been caused by his sin and that the forgiveness of sins was the precondition of his healing. Yet the relation of sin and sickness, forgiveness and healing is more fundamental. See Seybold and Müller, *Sickness and Healing.* 126ff.

156. 2 Corinthians 12:7-10 is the witness to Paul's existential grappling with this question. 2 Corinthians 11–12 shows that for Paul suffering and weakness are not only expressions of an eschatological reservation but a necessary form of the apostolic service that is rooted in the cross of Christ. In 1 Corinthians 11:30, the illness of some people are symptoms of the problems of the entire congregation.

157. On this, see Sermon 57, II, 8; WJW 2:410-11.

Notes to Pages 145-150

158. See Journal entry for May 10, 1741 (WJW 19:194); March 17, 1746 (WJW 20:116); May 18, 1772 (WJW 22:324); December 21, 1782 (WJW 23:261).

159. See Sermon 62, III, 3; WJW 2:482, where it is expressly denied that corporeal and mental weaknesses are to be overcome as the result of the victory of Jesus over the sin already existing in temporal life.

160. This topic pertains to those biblical statements that were first rediscovered in recent times on the basis of a transformed situation: see E. Käsemann, *Perspectives on Paul,* trans. M. Kohl (Philadelphia: Fortress, 1971), 60-78; W. Bindemann, "Die Hoffnung der Schöpfung. Römer 8-18-27 und die Frage einer Theologie der Befreiung von Mensch und Natur," *Neukirchener Studienbücher* 14 (1983).

161. Sermon 60, I, 2-5; WJW 2:439-41; see W. Cannon, *The Theology of John Wesley,* 196.

162. Yet, note the quite different manner in which W. Pannenberg brings into conversation these aspects of the understanding of natural science in the present day with Pauline statements, in *Systematic Theology* 2:96f.; 108f.; 172-4; 274.

163. On the human "task of creation" compare besides the commentaries on Gen. 1:26, K. Koch, "Gestaltet die Erde, doch heget das Leben! Einige Klarstellungen zum 'Dominium terrae' in Genesis 1." in *Wenn nicht jetzt, wann dann? Festschrift für H. J. Kraus* (1983), 23-26; U. Krolzik, "Die Wirkungsgeschichte von Genesis 1:28," in *ökologische Theologie. Perspektiven zur Orientierung,* ed. G. Altner (1989), 149-63; D. N. Freedman, ed., *The Anchor Bible Dictionary,* 6:31-46.

164. See the O.T. motif of the poor = the oppressed, who stand up for righteousness (R. Martin-Achard, "'*nhj,*'" II, THAT, 341-50). Also, the theology of suffering in Paul and in the first letter of Peter is aware of this aspect: whoever lives for Christ and the gospel will have to suffer the opposition of the world. See Matthew 5:10, 1 Peter 3:14, and on this, N. Brox, "Situation und Sprache der Minderheit im I. Petrusbrief," *Kairos* 19 (1977), 1-13.

165. The same presupposition apparently stands behind Romans 8:19-23.

166. On the complicated prehistory of the account of the two trees in the garden of Eden, see C. Westermann, *Genesis: An Introduction,* trans. J. L. Scullion (Minneapolis: Fortress, 1992), 47-55.

167. See E. Jüngel, *Death: The Riddle and the Mystery,* trans. L. and U. Nichol (Philadelphia: Westminster, 1974), 115-36, differently W. Pannenberg, *Systematic Theology,* 2:271ff. He refers to Wisdom 1:13: "God has not created death."

168. So Westermann, *Genesis* 1 to 3:22: God is "not concerned for His being as God but for men, who must be prevented from overstepping their limits" (372).

169. See C. Westermann, *Genesis* I, 327 (on 3:4f.); 362 (on 3:19).

170. Sermon 45, I, 2; WJW 2:189-90.

171. M. Heidegger, *On Time and Being,* trans. J. Stambaugh (New York: Harper & Row, 1972).

172. W. Pannenberg, *Systematic Theology.* 2:273.

173. Ibid., 274.

174. O. Weber, *Foundations of Dogmatics,* trans. D. Guder (Grand Rapids: Eerdmans, 1981), I, 624. Weber continues, "Our death is nothing other than the final revelation of the fatal fallen state in which it always had been lived. The moment of death is the moment in which the meaning of life is revealed as the meaning which we did not grasp" (624).

175. Compare the numerous eyewitness reports of dying among Methodist Christians that Wesley published in the Arminian Magazine: see H. Ertle, "Dignity in Simplicity, Studien zur Prosaliteratur des englischen Methodismus im 18. Jahrhundert" (1988), 147.

176. The problem in John 8:44 is that here the identification of Judaism and being children of the devil is firmly asserted; see G. Baumbach, "Die Funktion des Bösen in neutestamentlichen Schriften," EvTh 52 (1992), 23-42, 40.

177. H. Haag, *Teufelsglaube,* 2nd ed. (1980); for discussion, see W. Kasper and K. Lehmann (ed.), *Teufel-Dämonen-Besessenheit. Zur Wirklichkeit des Bösen* (1978), and the thematic issue entitled "Wohin mit dem Teufel?" EvTh 52 (1992), Issue 1; this has also been a concern of clergy who deal with the confusion between demonic possession and mental illness: see *A Mental Illnesses Awareness Guide for the Clergy* (Washington, D.C.: The American Psychiatric Association Division of Public Affairs, 1996).

178. See 2 Samuel 19:23; Psalm 109:6. On this, see T. H. Gaster, "Satan," in *The Interpreter's Dictionary of the Bible,* 4:224-28.

179. See W. H. Schmidt, *The Faith of the Old Testament,* 35-37.

180. The curse in Genesis 3:14-15 falls upon the serpent!

181. Compare Deuteronomy 13:3 and Matthew 6:13 with James 1:13!

182. See W. Foerster, "*Satanas*," ThWNT VII, 151ff. Also see *The Oxford Companion to the Bible*, 696.

183. G. Baumbach, *Die Funktion des Bösen*, 30. See *The Westminster Dictionary of Christian Theology*, ed. A. Richardson and J. Bowden (Philadelphia: Westminster, 1983), 521-22.

184. G. Ebeling, *Dogmatik*, 3:487. See L. Urban, *A Short History of Christian Thought* (New York: Oxford University Press, 1995), 102-8.

185. See Ebeling, *Dogmatik*, 448; in his own way, C. G. Jung has also pled for this in *Answer to Job*, trans. R. F. C. Hull (London: Routledge and Paul, 1954).

186. This does not take in a broad scope, but it is explicitly developed in Sermon 62; WJW 2:471-84, where the text is from 1 John 3:8*b*: "The Son of God was revealed for this purpose, to destroy the works of the devil." This point of view is also found in Luther; see his lecture on 1 John in WA 20:658, 35-40.

187. G. Baumbach, *Das Funktion des Bösen*, 30; see also *Dictionary of the Later New Testament and Its Development*, ed. R. P. Martin and P. H. Davids (Downers Grove, Ill.: InterVarsity, 1997), 1077-81.

188. Contrary to K. Barth, CD III/3, 289-302, and H. Haag, "Teufelsglaube," with J. Moltmann, "Zwölf Bemerkungen zum Symbolik des Bösen," EvTh 52 (1992), 2-6. This may be compared with the concept of an evil principle, a "radical evil," with Kant, which brought him the rebuke of Goethe, who asserted that Kant might have his "philosophical mantle . . . besmirched with the stain of radical evil" (see K. Barth, *Protestant Theology in the Nineteenth Century* [Valley Forge, Pa.: Judson, 1973], 294); also, *Dictionary of Jesus and the Gospels*, ed. J. B. Green, S. McKnight, and I. H. Marshall (Downers Grove, Ill.: 1992), 163-71.

189. While in Matthew 6:13 the neuter rendering is probably the original form (see U. Luz, *Das Evangelium nach Matthäus* [Matthew 1–7], Evangelisch-katholischer Kommentar zum Neuen Testament 1/1, 2nd ed. [1989], 349), the "refusal formula" hints of the masculine gender (see E. Kutsch, "Abrenuntiatio Diaboli," *Religion in Geschichte und Gegenwart*, I, 3rd ed. [1957], 73). See also Luz, *Matthew: A Commentary*, trans. W. C. Linss (Minneapolis: Augsburg, 1989).

190. Eibach, *Seelische Krankheit*, 86.

191. Moltmann, *Zwölf Bemerkungen*, 6; also, P. L. Hammer, "Devil," in *The Interpreter's Dictionary of the Bible*, 1:838.

192. See Sermon 67, "On Divine Providence," 15, WJW 2:540-41; also, Sermon 60, I, 5; WJW 2:441.

193. Sermon 59, I, 6, WJW 2:428; also see Sermon 57, II, 10 WJW 2:411-12; see Sermon 59, 3-4 and I, 1 WJW 2:424-25.

194. See Wesley, Sermon 34, I, 3; WJW 2:7.

195. For Wesley's treatment of this circle of questions, see above all Sermon 67, "On Divine Providence," and the discussion in 2.1.3.2.

196. Westermann, *Genesis*, I, 424.

197. The "Noahite command" in Genesis 9:3-7 corresponds to this, as a definition for the protection of life (see Westermann, *Genesis*, I, 618-28).

198. See Zimmerli, *Old Testament Theology in Outline* (Atlanta: John Knox, 1978) 55-7; also, "Covenant," in *The International Standard Bible Encyclopedia*, ed. J. Orr (Peabody, Mass.: Hendricksons, 1996), 2:727-32.

199. For this aspect of the biblical concept of the "righteousness of God" see H. H. Schmid, "Gerechtigkeit als Weltordnung," Beiträge zur historischen Theologie 40 (1968); and Schmid, "Schöpfung, Gerechtigkeit, und Heil. 'Schöpfungstheologie' als Gesamthorizont biblischer Theologie," ZThK 70 (1973), 1-19. See O. Weber, *Foundations of Dogmatics*, vol. 1, trans. D. L. Guder (Grand Rapids: Eerdmans, 1981), 428-37.

200. See for example, Sermon 69, "The Imperfection of Human Knowledge," WJW 2:567-86.

201. L. Perlitt, "Bund," EKL, 3rd ed., I (1986), 567. A basic treatment is E. Kutsch, *Neues Testament—neuer Bund? Eine Fehlübersetzung wird korrigiert* (1978); Kutsch, "Bund," I-III, TRE 7 (1981), 397-410; cf. W. H. Schmidt, *The Faith of the Old Testament* (Philadelphia: Westminster, 1983), 53-84.

202. On this, see H. Wildberger, "*Bhr/Erwählen*," THAT I, 275-300; H. Seebaß, "G. J. Botterweck und H. Ringgren (eds.) *Theologisches Wörterbuch zum Alten Testament* I, 603ff.; cf. L. Urban, *A*

Short History of Christian Thought (New York: Oxford University Press, 1995), 12-15; and G. E. Mendenhall, "Election," in *The Interpreter's Dictionary of the Bible,* 2:76-82.

203. Genesis 12:1-3; 15:1-21 (first covenant ratification, 15:18; the relationship to the sources is difficult to determine—see Zimmerli, *Outline* 51f.); 17:1-27 (covenant ratification according to the priestly tradition); also, Urban, *A Short History of Christian Thought,* 13-19.

204. Exodus 19:5-6; 24:7; Deuteronomy 5:2-3. (26:16-19). On the complicated traditional historical relationships, see W. Zimmerli, *Outline,* 50-57; also, G. E. Mendenhall, "Covenant," in *The Interpreter's Dictionary of the Bible,* 1:714-23.

205. Sermon 6, 1, WJW 1:202-34; see Sermon 34, I, WJW 2:6-8, and further discussion in 2.2.2.3.

206. "A Farther Appeal to Men of Reason and Religion," Part 2, I, 3-19; WJW 11:204-13.

207. Introduction, WJW 11:123ff.

208. "A Farther Appeal," Part 2, III, 14, WJW 11:262-63. The entire passage is a noticeable piece of an unpolemical, ecumenical sermon on repentance that includes not only the Jews but also all who acknowledge neither Jewish nor Christian revelation.

209. See E. F. Ströter, "Die Judenfrage und ihre göttliche Lösung nach Römer Kap. 11" (Bremen, n.d.) (cf. K. Barth, CD II/2, 267); cf. J. Bright, *A History of Israel,* 3rd ed. (Philadelphia: Westminster, 1981), 107-269.

210. "Deism" is a religious-philosophical movement that was widely disseminated in seventeenth- and eighteenth-century England. It knew God as a Creator and adhered to a general "natural" religion, but it rejected every special revelation and also the necessity of a supernatural redemption. See T. Penelhum, "Deism," in *The New Twentieth-Century Encyclopedia of Religious Knowledge,* 255f.

211. Notes NT on Romans 11:12.

212. Wesley: "moral law"; see Sermon 34, I/II, WJW 2:6-10.

213. In addition to Sermon 34; WJW 2:4-19, see Sermon 25; I; WJW 1:551-53 (the 10 commandments); "Letter to an Evangelical Layman," 20.12.1751, WJW 26:482 (the commands of Christ, as formulated in the Sermon on the Mount); Sermon 30, 21-27; WJW 1:660-63 (Golden Rule); on the love command as a summary of the law, see the discussion in note 232.

214. Sermon 34, I, 1-3; WJW 2:6-7. Enoch and Noah are examples for Wesley of the fact that the law was known from the beginning.

215. Sermon 34, II, 6; WJW 2:10.

216. Sermon 34, I, 5; WJW 2:7-8 (The revelation of the law to the fathers and to Moses is therefore an expression of the goodness of God!)

217. H. Heppe and E. Bizer, *Dogmatik der evangelisch-reformierten Kirche* (1958), 224: "The covenant for which God had originally created man was a covenant of works." Wesley explicitly developed this thought in Sermon 6, 1; WJW 1:202-3: "But it is the covenant of *grace* which God through Christ hath established with men in all ages (as well before, and under the Jewish dispensation, as since God was manifest in the flesh), which St. Paul here opposes to the covenant of *works,* made with Adam while in paradise, but commonly supposed to be the only covenant which God had made with man."

218. Sermon 6, I, 1; WJW 1:204.

219. Sermon 6, I, 11-12, WJW 1:208.

220. See the exposition of Romans 10:5ff. in Sermon 6, WJW 1:200-216.

221. Sermon 36, 2; WJW 2:33-34. In this sense, Wesley can also occasionally say that Christ is the end of the law, Romans 10:4 (see Sermon 29 par. 21, WJW 1:632-49. Moreover, Wesley gives a double meaning to the Greek word *telos:* in light of the justification of humanity, Christ is the end of the law (Sermon 1, III, 8; WJW 1:128-29; Sermon 6, 3; WJW 1:203-4; Sermon 29, 21; WJW 1:643-44; Sermon 34, IV, 3; WJW 2:16-17); in view of the definition given to the law, which is to aid humans in forming their lives with God, Christ is its end and its fulfillment (see Notes NT on Romans 10:4; Sermon 34, IV, 3-4; WJW 2:16-17).

222. That is the basic structure of both Sermons 35 and 36, WJW 2:20-43: "The Law Established through Faith, I-II"; see the brief summation of Wesley's position as given in the short summary of this concern of Wesley's in Notes NT on Romans 3:31.

223. There are few descriptions in the Christian context of the positive aspect of the piety of the law according to the Old and New Testaments. See the quite loveless description of this aspect in the articles "Gesetz I und III" in TRE, 13 (1984), 40-52 (K. Koch), 58-75 (G. Klein). The Old Testament motif of joy in the Law (see Psalm 19:11) is found in Sermon 34, III, 11; WJW 2:14; cf. W. D. Davies, "Law," in *The Interpreter's Dictionary of the Bible,* 3:77-102.

224. Sermon 34, IV, 1ff., WJW 2:16-19.

225. In particular, weighty distinctions certainly endure. With Luther, the first function of the law is that of the *usus civilis* or politicus, its application in restraining transgressions within civil life. The second function is the *usus theologicus, elenchticus* or *päedagogicus*. This conforms to Wesley's first function. Wesley's second function of the law conforms to what Luther says about the general operation of the law and the gospel: "Evangelium fecit ex lege paedagogum in Christum" (WA 39/I, 446). The *tertius usus legis*, which corresponds to Wesley's third function, is found in Reformation theology since Melanchthon and Calvin, but it was contested; see the compromise formulation in the Formula of Concord (BSLK 962). See R. Mau, "Gesetz," V, TRE 13 (1984), 82-90; E. Wolf, "Gesetz," V. RGG, 3rd ed., 1519-1526; W. Joest, "Gesetz und Freiheit. Das Problem des tertius usus legis bei Luther und die neutestamentliches Parainese," 3rd ed. (1961). The main sources are found in E. Hirsch, *Hilfsbuch zum Studium der Dogmatik,* 3rd ed. (1958), 77ff., 104, 116f. See also Marquardt, *John Wesley's Social Ethics,* 103-16.

226. Sermon 34, IV, 1-2; WJW 2:15-16.

227. Ibid., IV, 3; WJW 2:16.

228. Ibid., IV, 4; WJW 2:17.

229. Ibid., IV, 7; WJW 2:18.

230. See 2.2.1.3.

231. On this, see the autobiographical work of Tilmann Moser, *Gottesvergiftung,* 3rd ed. (1977), which describes the permanent cycle of becoming guilty and depending upon grace (93f.); cf. W. Elert, *The Christian Ethos* (Philadelphia: Muhlenberg, 1957), 143-330.

232. In the New Testament, the statement is recorded of Jesus (see Mark 12:28-34), Paul (cf. Romans 13:8-10; Galatians 5:14), James (James 2:8) and in a certain sense, also in John 13:34f.; 1 John 2:7-11; 3:11; 4:7-12. See W. Schrage, *The Ethics of the New Testament* (Philadelphia: Fortress, 1982), 40-56. On the background of the history of traditions, see A. Nissen, "Gott und der Nächste im antiken Judantum," WUNT 15 (1974), and on the remaining meaning of the law for Paul under the sign of the command of love, P. v.d. Osten-Sacken, *Heiligkeit,* 40-46; cf. J. Muilenburg, "Holiness," in *The Interpreter's Dictionary of the Bible,* 2:616-25. Wesley deals with these and related statements in Sermon 16, I, 2, WJW 1:378; Sermon 17, I, 11 and II, 10, WJW 1:407, 413-14; Sermon 24, III, 2, WJW 1:542; Sermon 76, I, 3-4, WJW 3:73-74; Sermon 83, 10, WJW 3:174-76.

233. Sermon 25, II, 2; WJW 1:554. This is the basic direction of Wesley's interpretation of the Sermon on the Mount, especially his exposition of its "Beatitudes" as command and promise. Wesley deals in Sermons 22 and 23, WJW 1:488-530, with the so-called antitheses of the Sermon on the Mount (Matthew 5:21-48) in the context of the exposition of the "blessing statements." It is instructive to heed the parallel yet characteristically different conception of Luther in this matter (as cited by W. Joest): "In each moment in which Christians encounter the command of God, a person is being confronted who is a sinner and yet who is called to Christ. The command encounters that one, the sinner as a deadly law: You should but you cannot do it. The one who is called to Christ and who believes this call is hid as a believer in Christ. Hence, that person comes to terms with the commands as an evangelical exhortation: Christ can—you will. The turning point for both of these types of occurrences is the 'now however' of the gospel and the source of faith" (W. Joest, *Gesetz und Freiheit,* 133).

234. Karl Barth, *Evangelium und Gesetz,* TEH 32=TEH.NF 50, 3rd ed. (1961), 13 (reprinted in *Gesetz und Evangelium. Beiträge zur gegenwärtigen theologischen Diskussion,* ed. E. Kinder and K. Haendler WdF, 142 [1968], 1-29, 9). See also Elert, *The Christian Ethos,* 23-171.

235. Karl Barth, Evangelium 31.

236. See Sermon 36 (esp. II, 1ff.); WJW 2:33-43 and the comments by W. Klaiber, "Aus Glauben, damit aus Gnaden. Der Grundsatz paulinischer Soteriologie und die Gnadenlehre John Wesleys," ZThK 88 (1991), 313-38, here, 330f. See also Notes NT on Romans 3:31: We establish the law "by defending that which the law attests, by pointing out Christ, the end of it, and by showing how it may be fulfilled in its purity." See also P. Stuhlmacher, *Der Brief an die Römer,* Das Neuen Testament Deutsch, 6 (1989), 64: Paul establishes the law as God's "obligatory demand of justice (see Romans 2:12-16), which Christ has vicariously fulfilled (5:18), as the witness to justification (3:21; 5:13), and as the instruction for the believers, who enter upon the way of righteousness in the Spirit of Christ (8:3ff.)." See also P. Lapide and P. Stuhlmacher, *Paul, Rabbi and Apostle* (Minneapolis: Augsburg, 1984), 36-47.

237. "By faith, taken in its more particular meaning for a confidence in a pardoning God, we establish his law in our own hearts in a still more effectual manner. For there is no motive which so

powerfully inclines us to love God as the sense of the love of God in Christ. Nothing enables us like a piercing conviction of this to give our hearts to him who was given for us. And from this principle of grateful love to God arises love to our brother also. Neither can we avoid loving our neighbour, if we truly believe the love wherewith God has loved us" (Sermon 36, III, 3; WJW 2:41-42). Galatians 5:6 is one of the most important texts for Wesley, helping him interface the basis of *sola fide* with his desire for a holy life. See the summary of the evidence given by A. Outler in WJW 1:139-40, n. 58. Exegetically it is important that the participial complement *di agapen energumenen* is understood to be an essential description of faith and not a supplemental condition that must be added to faith. See J. Rohde, *Der Brief des Paulus an die Galater, Theologischer Handkommentar zum Testament* 9 (1989), 219 (more explicitly and clearly given in the older work by A. Oepke, 3rd ed. [1973], 158f.). Against this is the view of the Catholic exegete F. Mußner, *Der Galaterbrief, Herders Theologischer Kommentar zum Neuen Testament* IX, 5th ed. (1988), 352-54: he speaks of the "basic definition [quality] that justifying faith *must* occupy" (335, our emphasis), and he thereby links the basic description of justifying faith to the designation of a limiting condition! Cf. F. D. Alexander, *From Paradise to the Promised Land* (Great Britain: Paternoster), 48-94.

238. W. Elert, *Der christliche Glaube. Grundlinien der lutherischen Dogmatik* (1960), 138-43 (also in *Gesetz und Evangelium,* ed. Kinder and Heaendler, 159-65, [here: 162]); cf. W. Elert, *The Christian Ethos,* esp. chapter 1.

239. The statements concerning the wisdom as preexisting mediator of creation are related to the Torah in early Judaism and, by contrast, in early Christianity they are related to Jesus as the Son of God; see Proverbs 8:22-31; Wisdom 7:25 with Sirach 24 and Colossians 1:15-16; Hebrews 1:2; John 1:1ff. See discussion in M. Hengel, *Son of God* (Philadelphia: Fortress, 1976), 57-77.

240. Sermon 34, II, 3; WJW 2:9; similarly III, 11 on Colossians 2:3.

241. That is, harmonious in essential characteristics, but not simply identical!

242. Since Christian theology basically or *de facto* confines the theological meaning of the Mosaic law to the Ten Commandments (with distinctive exceptions, above all with regard to the law of sexual practice), it has scarcely undertaken the effort to produce a detailed demonstration of it so that the entire law may be included in the twofold love commandment. That would at least be a worthwhile undertaking for segments of the Mosaic law, as possibly the law of holiness (Leviticus 17–26).

243. See Marquardt, *John Wesley's Social Ethics: Praxis and Principles.* 67-118.

244. See below sections 3.1.3.2 and 4.2.2.2.

245. R. Minor, "Der Bundesschluss als Weg zu verpflichteter Gemeinschaft der Kirchen—eine Einladung aus Vancouver und ihre Umsetzung in Kirchen und Geimeinden, I. Ein Gesprächsbeitrag aus der Evangelisch-methodishschen Kirche," ÖR 36 (1987), 477-79, here: 477; also, on the covenantal thought that influenced P. W. Otterbein, see J. S. O'Malley, *Pilgrimage of Faith: The Legacy of the Otterbeins* (Metuchen, N.J.: Scarecrow, 1973), 2-92; on Wesley, see Robert Monk, *John Wesley: His Puritan Heritage,* rev. ed. (Lanham, Md.: Scarecrow, 1999).

246. J. Steven O'Malley, *Early German-American Evangelicalism: Pietist Sources on Discipleship and Sanctification* (Lanham, Md.: UPA/Scarecrow Press, 1995), Parts 3 and 6.

247. Reformed Westminster Confession, in *The Creeds of Christendom,* ed. Philip Schaff (New York: Harper, 1977), 600-673.

248. Cited by R. Minor, "Der Bundesschluss," 477. The fact that one could arrive at different conclusions from the same Reformed basis is illustrated by Karl Barth in his doctrine of baptism (Karl Barth, *The Christian Life* [Lexington, Ky.: American Theological Library Association, 1962]).

249. See J. Steven O'Malley, *Pilgrimage of Faith: The Legacy of the Otterbeins,* 94-164; and A. W. Drury, *Doctrines and Disciplines of the United Brethren in Christ, 1814–1841* (Dayton: Otterbein Press, 1895).

250. This contrasts with the dialectical hermeneutic of Luther, which was based upon the imputational theory of "simul iustus et peccator." See J. S. O'Malley, *Early German-American Evangelicalism,* 233-45.

251. Philip William Otterbein, "Letter Concerning the Millennium," Arthur Core, *Philip William Otterbein: Pastor, Ecumenist* (Dayton: Board of Publication of the Evangelical United Brethren Church, 1968), 102-3.

252. Traces of this Reformed Pietist schema are evident at several points in the 1814 edition of the Confession of Faith: First, that document addresses salvation within the context of God's active, Providential governance of creation (Article 1). Second, Jesus Christ is presented as the "Saviour and Reconciler of the whole world," although the doctrine of the fall has not yet been mentioned. Third,

the nature of this redemptive work is embellished by the statement that "all men may become blessed through Him, if they will," in anticipation of His final return "to judge the living and the dead" (Article 2). The meaning of "becoming blessed" is explicated in Article 3, concerning the Holy Spirit. Here, the Spirit's ministry is comprehended under the statement that "we must be made holy through Him." The purpose of salvation is that "we may attain that faith which purifies us from all blemishes of the flesh and the spirit." Hence, the work of the Spirit is to enable us to reach sanctifying faith, marked by empirical, life-transforming effects. Further, this personal transformation is comprehended under, and perhaps even correlated with, God's overarching, grace-transforming reordering of history in its entirety (the "Heilsgeschichte"), for God "continually conveys, rules, protects and upholds all things" that have been created (Article 1). See A. W. Drury, *Disciplines of the United Brethren in Christ* (Dayton: United Brethren Pub. House, 1895), Part I, 3.

253. It states that "The Bible contains the true way to the salvation and blessedness of our souls," in that each actual believer (as opposed to nominal or "unawakened" church members) must lay hold of this as her or his sole guide ("Richtschnur"), together with the influences of the Spirit of God (Drury, Disciplines of the United Brethren, Part I, 3).

254. Drury, Disciplines of the United Brethren, Part I, 3.

255. See also J. Steven O'Malley, "The Understanding of Sanctification in the Evangelical United Brethren Tradition" (unpublished lecture delivered at Garrett-Evangelical Theological Seminary, Evanston, Ill., March, 1996).

256. H. Barth, ÖR 36 (1987), 488. See also M. R. Hotle, *A Layman's Guide to Wesleyan Terminology* (Salem, Ohio: Schmul Publishing, 1995), 15-16.

257. H. Hübner, "Bund," 2, EKL, 3rd ed., I, 569. See also *New Bible Commentary,* edited by G. J. Wenham, J. A. Motyer, D. A. Carson, and R. France (Downers Grove: InterVarsity, 1994), 246.

258. Sermon 6, WJW 1:200-216; see above, 2.2.2.3.

259. C. W. Williams, *John Wesley's Theology Today* (Nashville: Abingdon, 1960), 87.

260. J. Wiebering, *Partnerschaftlich leben. Christliches Ethos im Alltag* (1985), 28, also, "Covenant/Covenantal Theology," in *A Handbook of Theological Terms,* ed. V. A. Harvey, 60-62.

261. Translated from the *Liturgie der EmK* (Zürich, 1981), 21. See also the *Book of Worship* (Nashville: The United Methodist Publishing House, 1992), 288.

262. For an introduction to his service of covenant renewal, Wesley appended to his text a statement from the Puritan theologian Richard Alleine.

263. Wesley's "Covenant Service" appeared in print in 1780, and it has remained in print and is still in use to this day with alterations in British Methodism, and it is also being reinstituted in other parts of the world Methodist family of churches.

264. See Wesley's Journal entries for December 25, 1747 (WJW 20:203); August 6, 1755 (WJW 21:23); August 11, 1755 (WJW 21:23); January 3, 1770 (WJW 22:213), etc.

265. "An Order of Worship for Such as Would Enter into or Renew Their Covenant with God," in *The Book of Worship for Church and Home* (Nashville: Methodist Publishing House, 1965), 387, (in different form in the 1992 revised United Methodist *Book of Worship,* 291-94).

266. G. Wainwright points toward this in his study *On Wesley and Calvin* (Melbourne: 1987), 36f.

267. Minor, Bundesschluss, ÖR 36 (1982), 478.

268. Sermon 55, "On the Trinity," 14; WJW 2:383-84.

269. J. Deschner, *Wesley's Christology: An Interpretation* (Dallas: SMU, 1960), 37f. and XIV.

270. Deschner, *Wesley's Christology,* 15ff., 191; J. Weißbach, *Der neue Mensch,* 103-9. Yet, see the emphasis upon the humanity of Jesus in Sermon 85, 4; WJW 3:201: "a common man, without any peculiar beauty or excellency" (cf. Philippians 2:6ff.). Methodist theologians in the nineteenth century somewhat deepened the emphasis upon the divinity of Christ; see Deschner 5, on Pope and Watson.

271. For the concept of the threefold office of Christ, see K. H. zur Mühlen, "Jesus Christus," IV, TRE, 16, 764ff.; O. Weber, *Foundations* 2: 165-77. Deschner cites the evidence for Wesley's use of this motif (*Christology,* 73ff.; 203-10). The principal texts he cites are: the "Letter to a Roman Catholic" (from July 18, 1749) 7 (Works, 3rd ed.,10:81); also Sermons 36, I, 6; WJW 2:37-38; Sermon 43, II, 2; WJW 2:161. The meaning of this concept for the practical proclamation of the gospel shows the "spiritual order for preachers" of the Evangelical Association (1809–1946) and of the Evangelical United Brethren Church (1846–1968), which until 1967 required the following to be read at each annual conference: "Our fathers intended that the most effective preaching of Christ is to preach Him in all of His offices: in His prophetic office as Teacher and Preacher, in His high priestly

office as Reconciler and Redeemer, and in His kingly office as Lord of His congregation and the perfector of the Kingdom of God" (Agende der Ev. Gemeinschaft, 1963, 183).

272. The most important citations are found in Gal. 4:4; Rom. 8:3; John 3:17. On the history of
this circle of traditions, see U. B. Müller, *Die Menschwerdung des Gottessohnes. Frühchristliche
Inkarnationsvorstellungen und die Anfänge des Doketismus,* Stuttgarter Bibelstudien 140 (1990).

273. See also Romans 8:29 and the extraordinary summary of the theological meaning of the Son
in the statements of the New Testament in Hengel, *Son of God,* 143f.

274. The mode of expression is rooted in the history of the offering of Isaac (Genesis 22:2, 12, and
16); the Hebraic word used there for "only" *(jahid)* is transmitted differently into the Greek *(idios;
agapetos; monogenes).* "The expression designates Jesus' particular personality, His relationship to
the Father, and His mission," J. A. Fitzmeyer, EWNT II, 1081-83 (tr. trans.).

275. See also John 1:1, where the likeness of the *Logos* is indicated, but it is also made clear that
in the identity of the Son with God there is also a difference: he was *with* God and is nevertheless
God. The mystery that is sketched here is that of God going forth from himself and yet he being able
to remain God! See H. Schlier, "Im Anfang war das Wort. Zum Prolog des Johannesevangeliums," in
Die Zeit der Kirche, 4th ed. (1966), 274-87. This is one of the New Testament signs of the later doctrine of the Trinity. See also H. Küng, *On Being a Christian,* trans. E. Quinn (New York: Doubleday
and Company, 1968), 145-65.

276. See Pannenberg, *Systematic Theology* 2:367-72; W. Joest, *Dogmatik,* I, 241f.

277. See H. Küng, *On Being a Christian,* 145-65. Concerning the Chalcedonian Formula, see
L. R. Wickham, "Chalkedon," TRE 7 (1981), 668-75, as well as the pertinent descriptions of the
Christology of the early church; cf. "The Road to Chalcedon" in W. C. Placher, *A History of Christian
Theology* (Philadelphia: Westminster, 1983), 80-87; see also Charles Wesley's explanation of Phil.
2:7: "His glory is no longer seen, but God with God is man with men" (Hymn 30).

278. Wesley not only held to the New Testament statements about the generation of Jesus through
the Spirit, but also to the Catholic conception of the perpetual virginity of Mary (see Notes on the N.T.
Matthew 1:25; "Letter to a Roman Catholic," 7 (Works, 3rd ed., 10:81); Deschner, *Christology,* 30).
Present-day proclamation is committed to the task of confirming the message of the New Testament
statements, without making a legal requirement of having to believe in particular biological circumstances. On this, see W. Klaiber, "Eine lukanische Fassung des sola gratia. Beobachtungen zu Lk. 1:5-
56," in: *Rechtfertigung; Festschrift für Käsemann* (1976), 211-28; W. Joest, *Dogmatik,* I, 240f.: "The
question whether it is really the fact of an actual sign intended by God to clarify the mystery of Jesus'
origin, or whether it is a *symbolic* evidence developed in the course of the faithful reflection of the
early faith community, should remain an open question. Even if it is only regarded as a symbolic evidence, it is to be held the faith as the expression of truth, that Jesus, as the 'only begotten' Son, has
not come to be from a human possibility, but rather, he has come to us from the will and the deed of
God."

279. It is disputed whether by this heading, Mark 1:1-13, or the entire Gospel is described as the
beginning of the gospel of Jesus Christ. With Gnilka, "Das Evangelium nach Markus (Markus 1-
8:26)," EKK II/1, 2nd ed. (1986). With Gnilka we prefer the first option, but in any case it is sure that
the concept of the gospel, that came into use in missionary proclamation, is now used to designate the
larger purpose of an account of the history and the destiny of Jesus. For further details in this discussion, see P. Stuhlmacher (ed.), "Das Evangelium und die Evangelien," WUNT 28 (1983); further,
H. Frankemölle, "Begriff und Gattung. Ein Forschungsbericht," Stuttgarter biblische Beiträge 15
(1988).

280. The Gospel of John in a certain way links (a) and (b) of our description for a comprehensive
conception; see W. Klaiber, "Die Aufgabe einer theologischen Interpretation des 4. Evangeliums,"
ZThK 82 (1985), 300-324. See also Klaiber, *Call and Response,* 61f., 156.

281. The newest description of the "message and history" of Jesus correctly confirms that "The
thrust of the research in the trustworthiness of the Jesus traditions has become apparent in opposition
to the position that prevailed in the previous era dominated by Bultmann."—J. Gnilka, *Jesus of
Nazareth,* trans. S. S. Schatzmann (Peabody, Mass.: 1997), 2-25.

282. On this, see H. Merklein, *Jesu Botschaft von der Gottesherrschaft,* 3rd ed. (1989); also, G. B.
Caird and L. D. Hurst, *New Testament Theology* (Oxford: Clarendon, 1994), 345-408.

283. This is seen most clearly in the story of the healing of the possessed ranter (Mark 5:1-15).

284. A pathbreaking understanding of this motif is provided in J. Jeremias, *The Parables of Jesus*
(New York: Charles Scribner's Sons, 1972), 146-60.

285. The different conceptions of the beatitudes in Luke and in Matthew are to be interpreted in a reciprocal manner. With Luke, Jesus speaks directly to the poor, without additional qualifications. He means persons who really live in poverty, but his word to them is no neutral statement about the consequences of an economic condition of poverty, but a personal care for persons who stand in need of help and hope. Matthew formulates the beatitudes in the third person, but limits the general statements through the addition of "in the Spirit." Thus, he describes the poor as persons "whose outer condition forces them so that they must expect all things from God alone, and whose inner condition is such that they really expect everything from God alone" (J. Schniewind, *Das Evangelium nach Mathäus,* Das Neue Testament Deutsch 2, 9th ed., 1960, 41). See also H. Gese, *Essays on Biblical Theology* (Minneapolis: Augsburg, 1981), 141-66.

286. J. Jeremias, *The Parables of Jesus,* 128ff.; Klaiber, *Call and Response,* 30-39. *132f.*

287. See Matthew 5:31-32 (in the original wording according to Luke 16:18) and Matthew 19:18; on this, see Schrage, *The Ethics of the New Testament,* 40-52.

288. On the so-called antithesis of Jesus (Matthew 5:21-48), see Schrage, *Ethics,* 35ff.; Gnilka, *Jesus,* 199-247; Weder, *Rede der Reden,* 2nd ed. (1987), 98-155.

289. See Sermon 22, WJW 1:488-509 on Matthew 5:5-7 (and 5:21-26) and Sermon 23, WJW 1:510-30 on Matthew 5:8-12 (and 5:27-30, 31-32, 33-37 and 38-48). On Wesley's exposition of the Sermon on the Mount, see T. Lessmann, "Die Auslegung der Bergpredigt bei John Wesley," MSGEmK, NF6/2 (1985), 5-29; T. Meistad, *To Be a Christian in the World: Martin Luther's and John Wesley's Interpretation of the Sermon on the Mount* (MA Dissertation—Trondheim; Oslo, 1989). The fact that Matthew does not distinguish between indicative and imperative in the Sermon on the Mount in the same way as Paul (G. Strecker, *The Sermon on the Mount: An Exegetical Commentary,* trans. O. C. Dean Jr. (Nashville: Abingdon, 1988) does not mean that he describes the new being of man only in the imperative mood (cf. H. Weder, *Die Rede,* 32f.). The interrelationship of the indicative and the imperative by Matthew corresponds to the relationships of the law and the gospel in Wesley: in each command of God there lies a promise and in each promise a demand; see Sermon 25, II, 2; WJW 1:554 (on Matthew 5:17-20).

290. Beside the classic call of the disciples in Mark 1:16-20 (paralleled in Luke 9:57-62 and in Mark 10:17-22), where the example of transitory callings is paradigmatic for the meaning of discipleship. On this see M. Hengel, *The Charismatic Leader and His Followers* (Scotland: T. & T. Clark, 1996), 61.

291. In the history of the church, the radical call of Jesus into discipleship was intended to be understood with reference to Matthew 19:21 ("If you wish to be perfect") in the framework of a two-step ethic as an introduction to "perfection" (see Weder, *Die Rede,* 18-21; G. Barthart. "Bergpredigt," TRE 5 [1980], 621f.). Against this, see the influential presentation of the relationship of pre- and post-Easter obedience to Christ, under the caption "the congregation as a society of contrast" by G. Lohfink, *Wie hat Jesus Gemeinde gewollt?* 8th ed. (1989). For Wesley, there was of course no doubt that Jesus' demand for "perfection" applied to every person (see below 3.2.4). See also G. Bornkamm, G. Barth, and H. J. Held, *Tradition and Interpretation in Matthew* (London: SCM Ltd., 1960), 105-21.

292. See J. Gnilka, *Jesus of Nazareth,* 161-88, and the literature of the so-called Jesus Seminar.

293. In this connection, the "implicit Christology" of Jesus is spoken of in New Testament research (Gnilka, *Jesus of Nazareth,* 257). Also, W. Pannenberg, *Systematic Theology* 2:397-449.334ff.

294. This is the content and the goal of the Johannine Christology; see W. Klaiber, *Aufgabe,* 314. See also Urban, *A Short History of Christian Thought,* 34-40.

295. E. Jüngel, *God as the Mystery of the World* (Edinburgh: T. & T. Clark, 1983), 359f.

296. On the Christological concepts of Mark, see E. Schweizer, "Die theologische Leistung des Markus," in *Beiträge zur Theologie des NT* (1970), 21-42, esp. 40. The other Gospels have not continued to report this concept with the same emphasis and they abandon it in favor of the statement that Jesus has already revealed himself as God's Son during his earthly activities. (See for e.g., Mark 6:52, cf. with Matthew 14:33).

297. On the newer research regarding the causes for the death of Jesus, see X. Leon-Dafour, *Life and Death in the New Testament: The Teachings of Jesus and Paul* (San Francisco: Harper and Row, 1986); and P. Stuhlmacher, "Warum mußte Jesus sterben? in *Jesus von Nazareth—Der Christus des Glaubens* (1988), 47-64.

298. Among the literature on the saving meaning of Jesus' death, the following cannot be overlooked: G. Bornkamm, *Jesus of Nazareth,* trans. I. and F. McLuskey (New York: Harper and Row,

1960), esp. 153-68; G. Delling, *Der Kreuzestod Jesu in der urchristlichen Verkündigung* (1972); H. Conzelmann, E. Flesseman-van Leer, E. Haenchen, E. Käsemann, E. Lohse, *Zur Bedeutung des Todes Jesu. Exegetische Beiträge* (1967); E. Bizer, E. Fürst, J. F. G. Goeters, W. Kreck, W. Schrage, *Das Kreuz Jesu als Grund des Heils,* 3rd ed. (1969); H. Kessler, *Die theologische Bedeutung des Todes Jesu,* 2nd ed. (1971); K. Kertelge (ed.), "Der Tod Jesu. Deutungen im Neuen Testament," QD 74, 2nd ed. (1982); G. Friedrich, "Die Verkündigung des Todes Jesu im Neuen Testament," BthSt 6 (1982); H. Merklein, "Die Bedeutung des Kreuzestodes Christi für die paulinische Gerechtigkeits-und Gesetzesthematik," in *Studien zu Jesus und Paulus,* WUNT 43 (1987), 1-106; G. Barth, *Der Tod Jesu Christi im Verständnis des Neuen Testamentes* (1992) (a distinguished treatment!); W. Pannenberg, *Systematic Theology,* 2:416ff.

299. D. E. Nineham, *St. Mark* (Baltimore: Penguin, 1963), esp. 259-86 and 373-453; L. Morris, *The Apostolic Preaching of the Cross* (Grand Rapids: Eerdmans, 1965); P. Stuhlmacher, "Existenzstellvertretung für die vielen: Mark 10:45 (Matthew 20:28)," in *Versöhnung, Gesetz und Gerechtigkeit. Aufsätze zur biblischen Theologie* 1981, 27-42, H. W. Wolff, *Jesaja 53 im Urchristentum,* 3rd ed. (1952); E. Lohse, *Märtyrer und Gottesknecht. Untersuchungen zur urchristlichen Verkündigung vom Sühnetod Jesu Christi,* 2nd ed. (1963).

300. See Leviticus 4–8; Romans 3:25f.; on this, see H. Gese, *Die Sühne;* B. Janowski, *Sühne als Heilsgeschehen* (1982); also "Atonement," in *A Handbook of Theological Terms,* ed. V. A. Harvey, 33-35.

301. See John 11:50; 15:13 (cf. 10:11-18); Romans 5:7; on this, see M. Hengel, *The Atonement, A Study of the Origins of the Doctrine in the New Testament* (Philadelphia: Fortress, 1981) 6-27; W. Klaiber, "Rechtfertigung und Kreuzesgeschehen," in *Das Wort vom Kreuz,* ed. E. Lubahn and O. Rodenberg, 2nd ed. (1988), 93-126.

302. See for example R. Bultmann, "New Testament and Mythology" in *Kerygma and Myth,* ed. H. W. Bartsch, trans. R. H. Fuller (London: SPCK, 1972), 1-44; also, H. Wöller, *Zum Glauben ver-führen,* EKK.NT, 12 (1979), 220-22, 221; similarly, H. Wolff, *Neuer Wein Alte Schläuche. Das Identitätsproblem des Christentums im Lichte der Tiefenpsychologie* (1981), 79ff.; L. Schottroff, "Die Crux mit dem Kreuz; Feministische Kritik und Re-vision der Kreuzestheologie," *EKK.NT* 25 (1992), 216-18.

303. See K. Koch, *Vergeltungsdogma,* 91; also G. Schrader, "Crimes and Punishments," in *Hastings Encyclopedia of Religion and Ethics,* 4:248-304.

304. See for ex. Psalm 32:1; 51:3f.; 85:3; 103:12; compare K. Koch, *Sühne und Sündenvergebung;* and "sin/guilt" in *A Theological Wordbook of the Bible,* ed. A. Richardson, 226-29.

305. See J. Herzog-Dürck, *Probleme menschlicher Reifung* 32ff.; G. Condreau, *Angst und Schuld;* R. Girard, *Das Ende der Gewalt* (1983); R. Schwager, *Brauchen wir einen Sündenbock? Gewalt und Erlösung in den biblischen Schriften* (1978); U. Eibach, *Seelische Krankheit,* 49-102. For a discussion of earlier psychoanalysis, see *The Writings of Martin Buber,* ed. W. Herberg (Cleveland: Meridian, 1956), esp. 89-96 and 123-31.

306. See E. Jüngel, " . . . für uns zur Sünde gemacht . . . " (2. Kor 5, 20-21), in *Worte zum Kreuz heute gesagt,* ed. H. Nitschke (1973), 140-45; also F. V. Filson, exegesis of 2 Corinthians 5:20-21 in *The Interpreter's Bible* (Nashville: Abingdon, 1952–1957), 10:342-44 and his introduction to 2 Corinthians, 265-76.

307. For this, in addition to the commentaries of von Wilckens and Käsemann, see above all W. G. Kümmel, *paresis* and *endeixis,* "Zum Verständnis der paulinischen Rechtfertigungslehre," in *Heilsgeschehen und Geschichte,* MThSt 3 (1965), 260-70; W. Schrage, "Römer 3:21-26 und die Bedeutung des Todes Christi bei Paulus" in *Das Kreuz Jesu, Theologische Überlegungen,* ed. P. Rieger, Forum H 12 (1969), 65-88; E. Käsemann, *Zum Verständnis von Römer 3:24-26,* in *Exegetische Versuche und Besinnungen,* I, 6th ed. (1970), 96-100; O. Hofius, "Sühne und Versühnung. Zum paulinischen Verständnis des Kreuzestodes Jesu," in *Paulusstudien,* 33-49; W. Klaiber, *Rechtfertigung und Kreuzesgeschehen,* 103ff. It is not astonishing that here Wesley represented the traditional interpretation along with Protestant Orthodoxy, which proceeds from the concept of the punitive justice of God; see Notes on the NT on Romans 3:25; but compare Wesley's comments on Romans 1:17, "both justice and mercy," in his *Notes* on the New Testament; see also R. Seeberg, *Textbook of the History of Doctrines,* trans. C. H. Hay (Grand Rapids: Baker, 1964), 2:332-89 (on The Augsburg Confession and the Formula of Concord).

308. See H. B. Workman, "Anselm of Canterbury" in *Hastings Encyclopedia of Religion and Ethics,* 1:557-59; also, H. Thurston, "Expiation and Atonement," in *Hastings Encyclopedia of*

Religion and Ethics, 5:635-73. On this, see P. Tillich, *Systematic Theology,* 2:172-73; W. Pannenberg, *Systematic Theology,* 2:405ff.

309. Anselm, *Cur deus homo* I c. 21.

310. From the Christmas hymn "Den die Hirten lobeten sehre"; similarly, in some hymns by Charles Wesley: Hymns 123, 8; 194, 4-5. John Wesley represented this exposition: Jesus' atoning death occurred "to appease an offended God" (Notes on the NT, Romans 3:25), and the Articles of Religion of the Methodist Church say: "to reconcile his Father to us." (Article II; a contrast is seen in Article VIII in the Confession of Faith of the EUB Church, reflecting 2 Corinthians 5:18-19).

311. God's "wrath" is not his affect, but rather the inevitiable consequence of the wounded fellowship with God (see below 2.3.3.1).

312. See above, 2.1.3.3.

313. See the following strophe from Charles Wesley: "Jehovah in thy person show, / Jehovah crucified; / And then the pard'ning God I know, / And feel the blood applied" (Hymn 124, 7; for the formula of "the blood applied," see T. Berger, *Theology in Hymns?* (Nashville: Kingswood Books, 1995) 120-25; see also Hymns 26, 2; 27, 1-4; 133, 3; 193, 1; 206, 4; and others. In the Lutheran sphere, see the strophe of J. Rist: "O Große Not! Gott selbst liegt tot. / Am Kreuz ist er gestorben / hat dadurch das Himmelreich / uns aus Lieb erworben" (1941); E. Jüngel, "Gott als Geheimnis der Werk," 63-104, traces the pre- and post-history of this statement (especially with Hegel and Nietzsche). Also, G. Ebeling, *Dogmatik,* 2:202ff. and J. Moltmann, *The Crucified God* (New York: Harper and Row, 1973), 187ff.; as well as Moltmann, *The Way of Jesus Christ: Christology in Messianic Dimensions* (San Francisco: HarperCollins, 1990), 196ff.

314. Klaiber, *Rechtfertigung und Gemeinde,* 74ff.; W. Schrage, "Der erste Brief an die Korinther (1 Cor 1:1-6, 11)" Evangelische-katholischer Kommentar zum Neuen Testament VII/1 (1991), 190ff. Here is where the main emphasis of Bultmann's interpretation of the cross is to be located; see R. Bultmann, *Theology of the New Testament,* 1, 298-305; see also G. Ebeling, *Dogmatik,* 2:211ff.

315. See above all Romans 6:3-11; on the terminology and the matter at stake, see W. Joest, *Dogmatik,* 1:258-60; W. Pannenberg, *Systematic Theology,* vol. 2: 426f; 429-37.

316. Like any comparison, this one is also imperfect: the reality of Christ's complete appropriation of our guilt is not sufficiently clear by the example.

317. On this, see Romans 1:4; Philippians 2:9-11; Ephesians 1:20-22; Colossians 1:18; Hebrews 1:3-4; also in Matthew 28:18, the Resurrected Lord already speaks with the full power of the Ascended Lord. The descriptions of Jesus' ascension make these two aspects especially clear, see J. M. Robinson, "Ascension," in *The Interpreter's Dictionary of the Bible,* 1:245-47.

318. See Romans 10:9*b;* 1 Thessalonians 1:10*b;* Romans 1:4; 4:24; 8:11; Galatians 1:1; and then 1 Corinthians 15:3-5; on this, see Richard R. Niebuhr, *Resurrection and Historical Reason: A Study in Theological Method* (New York: Scribner's, 1957); "Resurrection," in *A Theological Wordbook of the Bible,* ed. A. Richardson, 193-95; J. A. T. Robinson, "Resurrection in the New Testament," in *The Interpreter's Dictionary of the Bible,* 4:43-53; and Hans W. Frei, et al. "Theological Reflections on the Gospel Accounts of Jesus' Death and Resurrection," in *The Christian Scholar* (winter 1996), 259-315.

319. See H. Conzelmann, *The Theology of St. Luke* (New York: Harper and Row, 1961), esp. 187-206; O. Cullmann, *The Christology of the New Testament* (Philadelphia: Westminster, 1963); C. H. Dodd, *The Apostolic Preaching and Its Developments* (London: Hodder and Stoughton, 1936); and the historical reconstruction provided by Hans von Campenhausen remains decisive; Hans von Campenhausen, "The Events of Easter and the Empty Tomb," *Tradition and Life in the Church,* trans. A. V. Littledale (London: Collins, 1968), 42-89; also H. Graß, *Ostergeschehen und Osterberichte,* 2nd ed. (1962); U. Wilckens, *Auferstehung. Das biblische Auferstehungszeugnis historisch untersucht und erklärt,* 4th ed. (1988). For the older discussion, see W. Marxsen, U. Wilckens, G. Delling, H. G. Geyer, *Die Bedeutung der Auferstehungsbotschaft für den Glauben an Jesus Christus,* 6th ed. (1968); *Diskussion um Kreuz und Auferstehung,* ed. B. Klappert, 2nd ed. (1967), a more recent and comprehensive discussion is H. Kessler, *Sucht den Lebenden nicht bei den Toten. Die Auferstehung Jesu in biblischer, fundamentaltheologischer und systematischer Sicht* (1995).

320. Exegetically fundamental is E. Käsemann, "Kritische Analyse von Phil. 2:5-11," in *Exeget. Versuche und Besinnungen* I, 51-95; cf. Fred Craddock, *Philippians* (Atlanta: John Knox, 1985); nevertheless, see the views of Wesley in Sermon 85, WJW 3:199-209, and Sermon 4, WJW 1:159-80, where he appeals to the exemplary character of the life of Jesus, as did the entire older exegetical tradition, but the section that gives his comment on Philippians 2:12-13 understands at the same time

that we can work for our salvation precisely because God has acted in Christ and through him God is working in us as well!

321. See D. R. Hare, *Matthew.* Interpretation: A Bible Commentary for Teaching and Preaching. Louisville: Westminster/John Knox, 1993; D. E. Garland, *Reading Matthew: A Literary and Theological Commentary on the First Gospel* (New York: Crossroad, 1993); G. Bornkamm, "Der Auferstandene und der Irdische, Mt. 28:16-20," in G. Bornkamm-G. Barth-J. J. Held, *Überlieferung und Auslegung im Matthäusevangelium,* WMANT I, 5th ed. (1968), 289-310; F. Hahn, "Der Sendungsauftrag des Auferstandenen. Matthäus 28:16-20," in *Fides promusundi vita, Festschrift H. W. Gensichen* (1980), 28-34.

322. 1 Corinthians 15:8-11; Galatians 1:15; on this, see Ch. Dietzfelbinger, "Die Berufung des Paulus als Ursprung seiner Theologie," WMANT 58, 2nd ed. (1989); also, C. K. Barrett, *Paul: An Introduction to His Thought* (Louisville: Westminster/John Knox, 1994).

323. In the Christian tradition, the motif of the descent of Christ into hell (see 1 Peter 3:19-20; 4:6) offers a possibility of also extending the preaching of salvation in Christ to those who died before his earthly ministry began (see F. W. Beare, *The First Epistle of Peter: The Greek Text with Introduction and Notes,* 3rd ed. (Oxford: Basil Blackwell, 1970). Wesley has stricken the reference to this motif from his Twenty-five Articles of Religion, American conference removed the corresponding passage from the Apostles' Creed, as it had been found in the Sunday Service liturgy of Wesley (see J. Deschner, *Wesley's Christology,* 50f., 63). The basis for this decision above all seems to have been of an exegetical nature, yet theological reflection may also have played a role, since for Wesley the eternal destiny of a man is decided at the moment of his death (see Notes NT on Hebrews 9:27).

324. See especially G. Bornkamm, "Taufe und neues Leben (Röm. 6)," in *Das Ende des Gesetzes, Paulus studien,* 3rd ed. (Grundrisse zum Alten Testament I, BEvTh 16 [1961]), 34-50; also, the exposition of Romans 6 in C. K. Barrett, *The Epistle to the Romans,* 48-54. Strange to say, Romans 6 appears not to have played any great role in Wesley's doctrine of holiness (see W. E. Sangster, *The Path to Perfection* [1943], 44).

325. Cf. Colossians 2:12-13 with 3:1ff. and Ephesians 2:5f. with 4:17ff.; on this, see Markus Barth, and Helmut Blanke, *Colossians,* Anchor Bible (New York: Doubleday, 1994); and R. Schnackenburg, *The Epistle to the Ephesians: A Commentary* (Edinburgh: T. & T. Clark, 1991).

326. See the evidence given in Deschner, *Wesley's Christology,* 116ff.

327. See the following: C. F. Evans, *Resurrection and the New Testament* (London: SCM, 1970); W. Marxsen, *The Significance of the Message of the Resurrection for Faith in Jesus Christ,* ed. C. F. D. Moule (London: SCM, 1968); O. O'Donovan, *Resurrection and Moral Order* (Grand Rapids: Eerdmans, 1986); and P. Selby, *Look for the Living: The Corporate Nature of Resurrection Faith* (Philadelphia: Fortress, 1976).

328. See the exposition of E. Best, *Second Corinthians,* Interpretation: A Bible Commentary for Teaching and Preaching (Atlanta: John Knox, 1987); W. Klaiber, *Call and Response,* 53-56.

329. Jüngel, "Die Autorität des bittenden Christus," in "Unterwegs zur Sache," BEvTh 61 (1972), 179-88.

330. See 2 Corinthians 4:7-18; 6:1-10; 1 Peter 2:21ff.; see also D. Soelle, *Suffering* (Philadelphia: Fortress, 1975).

331. See Galatians 2; Acts 15. Accounts such as that reported in Acts 10–11 convey the basic truth of the direction to the heathen mission through the operation of the Spirit rather than the detailed process. Matthew 28:16-20 summarizes that the mission to all peoples and the duty to proclaim Christ to the end of the world arises from the meeting of the disciples with the resurrected Lord; see above, note 200.

332. See the Large Minutes, Q. 8; Works, 3rd ed., 8:300.

333. Ephesians 2:6-7; 3:10; 4:11-16; see E. Schweizer, "The Church as the Missionary Body of Christ," In *Neotestamentica,* Essays 1951–1963, 1963, 317-29.

334. On Wesley's description of the Methodist movement in "heilsgeschichtlichen" terms, see sermons 61, 63, 89, 99, and 102.

335. W. Klaiber, "Rechenschaft über den Glauben. Der Römerbrief, Bibelauslegung für die Praxis 21," 1989, 106; see also P. J. Achtemeier, *Romans.* Interpretation: A Bible Commentary for Teaching and Preaching (Atlanta: John Knox, 1985).

336. Charles Wesley, Hymn 30, 1: "His thoughts, and words, and actions prove— / His life and death—that God is love!"

337. For the development of the history of dogma, see J. Pelikan, *The Christian Tradition I: The*

Emergence of the Catholic Tradition (100–600) (Chicago: University of Chicago Press, 1971), esp. 211-18; for current reflection on the doctrines of pneumatology and the trinity, see J. Moltmann, *The Trinity and the Kingdom* (1986), 137ff.; 185f., 184ff.; and by the same author, *The Spirit of Life: A Universal Affirmation* trans. M. Kohl (Minneapolis: Fortress, 1993), 73-82; 306ff.; W. Pannenberg, *Systematic Theology* 1:308ff.; 370ff. On the corresponding discussion in John Wesley, see L. M. Starkey, Jr. *The Work of the Holy Spirit: A Study in Wesleyan Theology* (1962), 26-33.

338. See L. M. Starkey, *The Work of the Holy Spirit,* in which he writes that Wesley "relates these doctrines immediately to man's redemption" (37); see also M.B. Stokes, *The Holy Spirit in the Wesleyan Heritage* (Nashville: Graded Press, 1985); Thomas Lessmann, "Rolle und Bedeutung des Heiligen Geistes in der Theologie John Wesleys," BGEmK 30 (1987). In Sermon 117 (On the Discoveries of Faith), 7; WJW 4:31-32, where Wesley formulates a kind of trinitarian confession of faith, he says concerning the third article, "By faith I know that the Holy Spirit is the giver of all spiritual life; of righteousness, peace, and joy in the Holy Ghost; of holiness and happiness, by the restoration of that image of God wherein we are created."

339. See above, 2.1.3.

340. See the basic statement of the Augustinian doctrine of the Trinity: "Opera trinitatis ad extra sunt indivisa" (The external works of the Trinity are undivided works of the Trinity as such"), cited by G. Ebeling, *Dogmatik* 3:538f.; see further: J. Moltmann, *The Trinity and the Kingdom,* 114-29; W. Pannenberg, *Systematic Theology,* 1:319ff., 442ff. On the creative and continuing efficacy of the Spirit for Wesley; see Sermon 120, "The Unity of the Divine Being," 21; WJW 4:69-70, and further evidence cited by Starkey, *Work of the Holy Spirit,* 39f.

341. On the difficult meaning of Genesis 1:2, see C. Westermann, *Genesis.* Text and Interpretation: A Practical Commentary (Grand Rapids: Eerdmans, 1987), chapter 1.

342. On the relation of concrete, historical redemption and eschatological recreation in Isaiah ("deutero-Isaiah"), see C. Westermann, *Isaiah 40–66,* Old Testament Library (Philadelphia: Augsburg, 1991); cf. J. D. W. Watts, *Isaiah 34–66* (Waco, Tex.: Word, 1987).

343. See Zimmerli, *Outline,* 211-13. For a discussion of the picture of history in apocalyptic; see M. Hengel, *Judentum und Hellenismus,* 3rd ed. (1988), 330-57; also, J. Ellul, *Apocalypse: The Book of Revelation* (New York: Seabury, 1977); M. Rist, "Apocalypticism," in *The Interpreter's Dictionary of the Bible,* 1:157-61; and M. R. Mulholland, *Revelation: Holy Living in an Unholy World* (Grand Rapids: Zondervan, 1990).

344. See Zechariah 6:8 (note C. L. and E. M. Meyers, *Haggai, Zechariah 1–8* New York: Doubleday, 1987).

345. See Judges 3:10; 6:34; 11:29; 13:25; 14:6, 19; 15:14; 1 Samuel 10:6; 11:6.

346. H. Wildberger, *Isaiah,* II, 1281. See G. W. H. Lampe, "Holy Spirit (Old Testament)," in *The Interpreter's Dictionary of the Bible,* 2:625-30.

347. See also Isaiah 31:1-3: " 'The Egyptians are men and not God, their steeds are flesh and not spirit,' signifies the *total demythologization of the historical powers* and at the same time the radical *deification of God,*" H. Wildberger, *Isaiah,* II, 1235.

348. This was so strongly set forth in the preliminary documents for the seventh plenary assembly of the World Council of Churches in Canberra (see the official document, *Let the Spirit Speak to the Churches: A Guide for the Study of the Theme and the Issues: WCC Seventh Assembly, Canberra 1991;* Geneva: WCC publications); see also the address for the defense of the unity of world history and salvation history in Latin American liberation theology, as presented by J. Moltmann, *The Spirit of Life,* 109-14.

349. On Luther's concept of the *deus absconditus,* see "de servo arbitrio," 1525, WA 18, 683-91, and P. Althaus, *The Theology of Martin Luther,* 15-34.

350. Sermon 67; WJW 2:534-50; see also above, 2.1.3.2.

351. See Minutes for August 2, 1745, Q.8 Works, 3rd ed., 8:283; Sermon 99, I, 4; WJW 3:403-4 (note 1); yet see also the partial agreement in "Predestination Calmly Considered," 32 (Works, 3rd ed., 10:222), and Sermon 5, III, 5; WJW 1:192-93.

352. Minutes for August 2, 1745, Q. 7, Works, 3rd ed., 8:283; on the meaning of the story of Cornelius in current missiological discussion, see W. Hollenweger, *Evangelism Today* (Belfast: Christian Journals Ltd., 1976), 102-6; W. Klaiber, *Call and Response,* 82f.

353. The operation of the Spirit is not identified with the religiosity of the heathen as such; see Starkey, *Work of the Holy Spirit,* 40f.; however, Wesley can speak occasionally of the "faith of the

heathen" (Sermon 106, I, 3; WJW 3:494). On the knowledge of God in the religions of the world, see above, 1.1.3.2.

354. M. Welker, *God the Spirit,* 332f. rightly points the way to the relationship of the Abba-cry with the maternal aspects in the image of God as found within Scripture; see also S. V. McCastland, "Abba, Father," *JBL* 72 (1953), 79ff.

355. This concern is often missing where the addition of the *filoque* is rejected. See "Filoque," in *A Handbook of Theological Terms,* ed. V. A. Harvey, 99f.; and J. Gonzalez, *A History of Christian Thought,* rev. ed., vol. 2 (Nashville: Abingdon, 1987), 127-30.

356. *The Book of Discipline* (UMC, 1996), ¶ 62, Confession of Faith (EUB), Article III.

357. For further pneumatological aspects see the *Book of Discipline,* Articles IV, V, IX, and XI.

358. On this, see G. V. Rad, *Old Testament Theology,* trans. D. M. G. Stalker (Edinburgh: Oliver and Boyd, 1965), II, 212ff.

359. According to H. W. Wolff, "Dodekapropheton 2, Joel und Amos," BK XIV/2, 78-84, Joel is not so much thinking of a capacity for prophetic proclamation as the basis for a new relationship with God (79).

360. See E. Schweizer, *The Holy Spirit* (Philadelphia: Fortress, 1980); G. T. Montague, *The Holy Spirit: Growth of a Biblical Tradition* (New York: Paulist, 1976); and W. Rebell, *Erfüllung und Erwartung; Erfahrungen mit dem Geist im Urchristentum* (1991).

361. Montanism, named for its founder in second-century Christianity (Montanus), represented the view that Montanus embodied the Paraclete promised by Jesus, and preached the imminent end of the world with prophetic certainty (see H. J. Lawler, "Montanism," *Hastings Encyclopedia of Religion and Ethics,* 8:828-30). Wesley upon occasion expressed himself very positively concerning Montanus, whom he regarded as having renewed the prophetic preaching of repentance in the early church (see Wesley, "The Real Character of Montanus," *Works,* 3rd ed., 11:485-86; also Sermons 61, 24, WJW 2:461; Sermon 68, 9, WJW 2:555-56), and Rupert Davies goes so far as to say that the Montanist movement was the "earliest clear example of Methodism" (*Methodism* [1963], 13ff.).

362. On this, see L. Spitz, *The Protestant Reformation* (New York: Harper and Row, 1984), 96-107; R. Bainton, *The Reformation of the Eighteenth Century* (Boston: Beacon, 1952), 63-67; and K. Holl, "Luther und die Schwärmer," *GA zur Kirchengeschichte,* I, 5th ed. (1948), 420-67.

363. See W. S. Gunter, *The Limits of 'Love Divine': John Wesley's Response to Antinomianism and Enthusiasm* (Nashville: Kingswood, 1989); W. Klaiber, *Aus Glauben,* 326f.; see further, H. D. Rack, *Reasonable Enthusiast: John Wesley and the Rise of Methodism,* 2nd ed. (Nashville: Abingdon, 1993); R. A. Knox, *Enthusiasm,* Oxford, 1950.

364. Letter to John Smith, December 30, 1745, 17 (WJW 26:175-83).

365. See also the hymns of Charles Wesley, who described the gift of the Spirit as "to witness with the blood" and "to apply the blood," Hymns 9, 3; 83, 1; 244, 2; see J. E. Rattenbury, *The Evangelical Doctrines of Charles Wesley's Hymns* (London: Epworth, 1941).

366. Mark 1:8, Matthew 3:11; Luke 3:16; John 1:33; see also D. E. Nineham, *St. Mark* (Baltimore: Penguin, 1963), 55-64.

367. God's Spirit is received (Acts 1:8; 2:38; 8:17; Galatians 3:2) or poured out (Acts 2:18, 33; Romans 5:5); he falls upon some (Acts 8:16; 10:44; 11:15) or he comes upon them (Acts 19:6), and persons are filled with the Spirit (Acts 9:17; Ephesians 5:18).

368. On this, see Donald W. Dayton, *The Theological Roots of Pentecostalism* (Grand Rapids: Zondervan, 1987).

369. See Laurence W. Wood, "Purity and Power: The Pentecostal Experience According to John Wesley and John Fletcher" (Paper presented at Fourth Plenary Session of the 27th Annual Meeting of the Society for Pentecostal Studies/Wesleyan Theological Society, Cleveland, Tenn., March 13, 1998).

370. See the discussion of these issues in Norman Laurence Kellett, "John Wesley and the Restoration of the Doctrine of the Holy Spirit to the Church of England in the Eighteenth Century" (unpublished Ph.D. dissertation, Brandeis University, 1975)."

371. James D. G. Dunn, *Baptism in the Holy Spirit* (Philadelphia: Westminster Press, 1970). See especially Articles III, IV, V, IX, and XI of the Confession of Faith (EUB) in the 1996 *Book of Discipline* (UMC, 1996), ¶ 68.

372. John Wesley, "The Character of a Methodist," WJW 9:31-41.

373. See the evidence from Wesley, as cited by Leßmann, *Rolle und Bedeutung,* 24f, 39f.; also, K. J. Collins, *Wesley on Salvation* (Grand Rapids: Zondervan, 1989).

374. See note 365 above.

375. The reference to "making room" for inward renewal of the person by God's grace has a strong precedent in the writings of the Pietist Gerhard Tersteegen (1697–1769), whose writings were influential upon the founders of the Evangelical Association, the United Brethren in Christ, and even upon John Wesley himself. Tersteegen spoke of "making room" ("Raum geben") as the precondition for one's inward transformation by grace (called the "Grundneigung"). For a discussion of these connections see J. Steven O'Malley, "The Distinctive Witness of the Evangelical United Brethren Confession of Faith in Comparison with the Methodist Articles of Religion" (unpublished address presented at the Duke Divinity School Conference on "United Methodist in American Culture," held at St. Simons, Ga., July, 1995. See also J. Steven O'Malley "Pietist Influence on John Wesley: Wesley and Gerhard Tersteegen," *Wesleyan Theological Journal* (fall 1996), 48-70. For an extensive examination of this concept in Tersteegen, see Hansgunter Ludewig, *Gebet und Gotteserfahrung bei Gerhard Tersteegen* (Göttingen: Vandenhoeck und Ruprecht, 1986).

376. See the sermon on Romans 8:15, "The Spirit of Bondage and of Adoption" (Sermon 9, WJW 1:248-66) and on Romans 8:16, "The Witness of the Spirit I and II" (Sermons 10 and 11, WJW 1:267-98), the songs of Charles Wesley, "Spirit of Faith" (Hymn 83 = UMH 332) and "How can we sinners know" (Hymn 93 = UMH 372). Further, see Starkey, *Work of the Holy Spirit,* 63ff.; Leßmann, *Rolle,* 47ff.

377. However, a recent inquiry into Pauline pneumatology begins its concise description of the work of the Spirit with the following two points: "Representatio—The Spirit brings to mind the love of God" (Romans 5:5) and "Testificatio—The Spirit attests to the position of Sonship" (Romans 8:16), F. W. Horn, "Das Angeld des Geistes. Studien zur paulinischen Pneumatologie," FRLANT 154 (1992), 406ff.; see the related discussion of Pauline pneumatology in G. W. H. Lampe, "Holy Spirit in Pauline Theology," in *The Interpreter's Dictionary of the Bible,* 2:636-38.

378. One may observe the exegetical linking of Romans 5:1-11 and Romans 8: the consequences of the event of Christ and the event of justification are described at times through the confirming operation of the Spirit. Both verses, which are central for Wesley (5:5 and 8:16) are also cornerstones of Paul's argument.

379. See for example Sermon 34, IV; WJW2, 15-19. Also with Wesley, the law as such cannot lead to the knowledge of sin (see above 2.2.1.3 and note 145).

380. In regard to the summons in Romans 8:16, Wesley speaks of a double witness of the Spirit, the direct and the indirect witness. The latter refers to the witness of our spirit on the basis of the experience which the Holy Spirit confers. See Sermon 10, I, 11; WJW 1:275-76; Sermon 11, III, 7f.; WJW 1:291-93; Starkey, *Work of the Holy Spirit,* 63ff. Stokes, *The Holy Spirit,* 49f.; Leßmann, *Rolle,* 47ff. Also, J. Moltmann displays his pneumatology in relation to the phenomenon of "experience," in Moltmann, *The Spirit of Life,* 31-38.

381. See Charles Wesley: "Inspire the living faith / . . . / The faith that conquers all" (Hymn 83, 4 = UMH 332, 4) and the evidence cited by Leßmann, 30.

382. Sermon 45, "The New Birth," 1; WJW 1:187.

383. On the relationship of the Spirit and the means of grace, see Starkey, Work of the Holy Spirit, 79ff; Leßmann, *Rolle,* 81ff.

384. See Sermon 16 "The Means of Grace," II; WJW 1:381-84; see below 3.1.2 and 4.2.2.2.

385. See W. Schrage, also R. Bring, *Commentary on Galatians,* trans. E. Wahlstrom (Philadelphia: Muhlenburg, 1961) 247-69. F. F. Bruce, *The Epistle to the Galatians: A Commentary on the Greek Text* (Grand Rapids: Eerdmans, 1982).

386. Sermon 11, V, 2-3; WJW 1:297-98 describes the circle between the witness of the Spirit in the common life of humanity and the assurance that comes from this experience (see Stokes, *Holy Spirit,* 50, 74).

387. On these concepts, see P. Tillich, *Systematic Theology,* 1:83-86.

388. The extraordinary historical description of the particular gifts with well-disposed critical comments of their present significance is found in Rebel, *Erfüllung,* 77-106.

389. Klaiber, *Rechtfertigung und Gemeinde,* 215ff. On the meaning of love as the summation of all the gifts, see also Colossians 3:14.

390. See Stokes, *Holy Spirit,* 38; K. H. Voigt, "The charismatische Grundstruktur der EmK"; *EMK heute* 28 (1979); also, L. F. Church, *The Early Methodist People* (London: Epworth, 1949), esp. 95-183.

391. On this, see Stokes, *Holy Spirit,* 64-73.

392. See W. Klaiber, *Call and Response,* 59-60.

393. See the discussion of Wesley's early use of lay preachers in *A History of the Methodist Church in Great Britain,* ed. R. Davies and G. Rupp (London: Epworth, 1965), I, 73-79, and 190-208.

394. See Charles Wesley, "We by his Spirit prove / And know the things of God; / The things which freely of his love / He hath on us bestowed" (Hymn 93, 4 = UMH 372, 4); see above 1.1.4.

395. See Wesley's response to Luther's critical statements on reason in his great commentary on Galatians, *Journal,* June 15, 1741 (WJW 19:200-201) and above, 1.1.3.3.

396. See above 1.3.1.

397. For this, see Horn, *Das Angeld des Geistes* (esp. 389ff.); see also the examination of "Life in the Spirit" (Romans 8:1-11) in C. K. Barrett, *The Epistle to the Romans,* 153-60.

398. We find all three aspects of the Christian hope in Charles Wesley's hymn, "Love divine, all loves excelling" (Hymn 374 = UMH 384); see especially the third stanza: "Finish then thy new creation, / Pure and spotless let us be; / Let us see thy great salvation / Perfectly restored in thee; / Changed from glory into glory, / Till in heaven we take our place, / Till we cast our crowns before thee, / Lost in wonder, love, and praise."

399. On this, see W. H. Schmidt and J. Becker, *Zukunft und Hoffnung, Biblische Konfrontationen* 1014 (1981), 70ff.

400. See Psalms 6:5; 30:9; 88:5, 10-12; 115:17; Isaiah 38:18-19.

401. See Psalms 16:10; 73:26.

402. For historical context on this, see James P. Martin, *The Last Judgment* (Grand Rapids: Eerdmans, 1963), esp. chaps. 1 and 2; see also Isaiah 26:19.

403. See Mark 12:18-27.

404. On the resurrection in the New Testament, see beside W. H. Schmidt and J. Becker, *Zukunft und Hoffnung,* P. Hoffman, "Auferstehung," I/3, TRE 4 (1979), 450-67; also, Richard R. Niebuhr, *Resurrection and Historical Reason* (New York: Scribner's, 1957), esp. chap. 1: "The Resurrection of Jesus Christ and the Modern Historical Mind," 1-31; see above 2.2.3.3d.

405. For this, see the foundational study by G. Sellin, *Der Streit um die Auferstehung der Toten. Eine religionsgeschichtliche und exegetische Untersuchung von I. Korinther 15,* 1986; also, C. T. Craig, "Exegesis of First Corinthians 15" in *The Interpreter's Bible,* 10:214-54.

406. Compare Romans 4:5, 17, 24 with 8:11 and 1 Corinthians 15:45.

407. 2 Corinthians 5:10 literally states, "For we must all appear before the judgment seat of Christ, that each one may receive what is due him for the things done *through* the body, whether good or bad" (NRSV states, " . . . done in the body . . .") (tr. Elberfeld version).

408. See G. Greshake, in G. Greshake, J. Kremer (see note 359 above) 165ff.; P. Althaus, "The Sleep of Death and the Resurrection" in *The Theology of Martin Luther,* 410-18. On the very pronounced concept of Wesley's on the continuing existence of the soul, see Sermon 51, II; WJW 2:286-92.

409. See Philippians 1:21ff; Luke 23:34; however, on the other side, see also 2 Corinthians 5:1-5 and further, 1 Peter 3:19f; 4:6.

410. It is certainly not "being taken up with God," the ground of our being, as the pantheistic mystics described it. It retains the character of an encounter and because of that, it is the character of love!

411. *The Book of Discipline* (UMC, 1996), ¶ 62, Confession of Faith (EUB), Articles XII and VI.

412. See above 2.2.2.2.

413. See also Romans 15:14-21.

414. For the classification of the Methodist movement from the standpoint of salvation history, see Sermon 61, WJW 2:451-70; Sermon 63, 27, WJW 2:499: "All unprejudiced persons may see with their eyes that he is already renewing the face of the earth. And we have strong reason to hope that the work he hath begun he will carry on unto the day of his Lord Jesus; that he will never intermit this blessed work of his Spirit until he has fulfilled all his promises; until he hath put a period to sin, and misery, and infirmity, and death, and re-established universal holiness and happiness, and caused all the inhabitants of the earth to sing together, 'Hallelujah! The Lord God omnipotent reigneth!' " See also Sermon 68, WJW 2:551-66; Sermon 99, I, WJW 3:402-5. For the expectation of a Christian world as the first goal of God's redemptive deeds see Sermon 4, 3; Sermon 26, III, 8, WJW 1:581-2. This hope is traditionally bound to the concept of the thousand-year kingdom (Revelation 20:4-6). Through an interesting, but rather artificial interpretation Wesley speaks of a twofold thousand-year kingdom, in order to separate positive aspect as a rule of peace for the Christian church from the negative one as a time of dangerous persecution (Notes NT, Rev. 20:4-6).

415. See the intensive joining of American Methodism with the concept of the "social gospel" in R. M. Miller, *Bishop G. Bromley Oxnam: Paladin of Liberal Protestantism* (Nashville: Abingdon, 1990), 65; on the important relationship between nineteenth-century American holiness evangelists and social reform, see Donald W. Dayton, *Discovering an Evangelical Heritage* (New York: Harper and Row, 1976).

416. See above, note 398 and the section "Describing Heaven" in *A Collection of Hymns for the Use of the People called Methodists* (WJW 7:161-76).

417. See Isaiah 65:17; 2 Peter 3:13; Revelation 21:1f. Wesley occasionally treated these accounts quite thoroughly; Sermon 61, 36, WJW 2:469-70; Sermon 64 (The New Creation); WJW 2:500-510.

418. Isaiah 65:25 (cf. Ezekiel 47:1-12); Romans 8:21-23; Revelation 22:1f.

419. Revelation 21:3-4; cf. 7:17; Isaiah 25:8.

420. *The Book of Discipline* (UMC, 1996), ¶ 62, Confession of Faith (EUB).

421. See "Judge/Judgment," in *A Theological Wordbook of the Bible*, ed. A. Richardson, 117-18; W. Klaiber, *Call and Response*, 113-23.

422. K. Seybold, 401.

423. See Amos 7:1-9; 8:1-3; 9:1-4; Hosea 1:2-9; Isaiah 5:1-7; 6:8-12. On this, see the discussion of judgment and divine wrath in A. Heschel, *The Prophets* (New York: Harper and Row, 1955), 275-98; and H. W. Wolff, "Das Thema 'Umkehr' in der alttestamentlichen Prophetie, Gesammelte Studien zum," AT, 2nd ed. (1973), 130-50.

424. H. W. Wolff, "Die eigentliche Botschaft der klassischen Propheten," in *Beiträge zur alttestamentlichen Prophetie. Festschrift W. Zimmerli* (1977), 547-57, and Heschel's treatment of Amos in *The Prophets*, 27-38.

425. Seybold, 462; in the New Testament this phrase is a synonym for the judgment of God. See also the discussion of *hemah* in Heschel, *The Prophets*, 115f.

426. On this concept, see W. Klaiber, *Call and Response*, 141f.; for John the Baptist's judgment preaching, see W. R. Farmer, "John the Baptist," in *The Interpreter's Dictionary of the Bible*, 2:955-62.

427. See Matthew 11:20-24 and 23:37-39; for discussion, see J. C. Fenton, *St. Matthew* (Baltimore: Penguin, 1963), 182-85 and 377f.

428. A uniting of the two lines is seen in Matthew 22:1-14, through the summary of the parable of the wedding banquet with the motif of the "wedding garments." For Wesley this union was very important (see Sermon 127 "On the Wedding Garment"; WJW 4:139-48).

429. This meaning is supported by its close relationship to Luke 10:25-37, the parable of the merciful Samaritan. It speaks against all attempts to limit Matthew 25:31-46 to the relationship of heathens toward Christians. This is a falsification of the message of Jesus. For the exegetical problems of the account see J. Friedrich, *Gott im Bruder?* CMT 7 (1977); U. Wilckens, "Gottes geringste Brüder—Zu Matthäus 25:31-46," in *Jesus und Paulus, Festschrift W. G. Kümmel* (1975), 363-83; and J. C. Fenton, "Blessed and Cursed" (Matt. 25:31-46), in *St. Matthew*, 400-403.

430. See L. Mattern, "Das Verständnis des Gerichts bei Paulus," Abhandlungen zur Theologie des Alten und Neuen Testaments 47 (1966); E. Synofzik, *Die Gerichts-und Vergeltungsansagen bei Paulus*, Göttinger Theologische Arbeiten 8 (1977), also B. C. Witherington III, *Jesus, Paul, and the End of the World* (Downers Grove: InterVarsity, 1992).

431. So, according to K. Heim, *Jesus der Weltvollender. Der Glaube an die Versöhnung und Weltverwandlung. Der evangelische Glaube und das Denken der Gegenwart*, vol. 3 (1937), 40ff.; see also F. C. Grant, "Jesus Christ: The Coming Parousia and Judgment," in *The Interpreter's Dictionary of the Bible*, 2:884f.

432. The statements of the Mishna in Sanhedrin X, 1 are to be recalled: "All Israel has a part in the coming world. . . . Those who follow have no part. . . . "

433. See the analysis in Klaiber, *Call and Response*, 111-12 and 237, n.145.

434. Deschner, *Christology*. 126ff. On the difficulties in this thought, see O. Weber, Foundations. J. Roloff, *Offenbarung des Johannes*, Zürcher Bibelkommentar Neuen Testament 18 (1984), 187f., 2:678f.; also, F. C. Grant, "Jesus Christ: The Message of the Kingdom of God," in *The Interpreter's Dictionary of the Bible*, 2:882-84.

435. See the overview by Klaiber, *Call and Response*, 171-73.

436. I. Kant, *Religion Within the Limits of Reason Alone*, trans. T. H. Greene and H. H. Hudson (LaSalle, Ill.: Open Court Publishing Co., 1960), 54-57.

437. Sermon 73, "Of Hell"; WJW 3:30-44.

438. Sermon 91, I, 3, WJW 3:295-96; see 106, I, 4, WJW 3:494-5, and above all 130, 14-15, WJW 4:174-75, and "A Farther Appeal," Part 2, III, 13-15, WJW 11:261-64; further, G. Wainwright, *Doxology, The Praise of God in Worship, Doctrine and Life. A Systematic Theology* (1980), 68f.

439. Wesley intended that God asks about the "goodness of the heart rather than the clearness of the head" (Sermon 130, 15; WJW 4:175), a thought which influenced his pastoral work but is also dangerous if it serves as an argument against clear theological formulations. See also Wesley's corresponding assertions about the doctrine of justification in the Journal entry of December 1, 1767, WJW 22:114.

440. Hence, E. Jüngel says "that God's grace even in hell forestalls our self-chosen disaster"; in *Gericht und Gnade, epd-dokumentation 28* (1989), 35-62, 61; cf. Luther's understanding of God's wrath as the "other" side of his grace: see WA 17/11, 66; and P. Althaus, *The Theology of Martin Luther*, 168-78.

3. Personal Faith, or the Personal Experience of Salvation

1. This development is foreshadowed in Ezekiel 18 and 33 (see below 3.1.3.1); but the Mishna still affirms in Sanhedrin X, 1: "All of Israel has part in the coming kingdom," which certainly calls for a series of exceptions. Paul cites the same principle in Romans 11:26; within the dialectical dynamic of Romans 9–11, he stands under the sign of Romans 1:16, where it is declared that the gospel is the power of God that saves all who believe in him, the Jews first and also the Greeks; on this, see W. Klaiber, *Rechtfertigung und Gemeinde*, 174-90; also K. Barth, T*he Epistle to the Romans* (London: Oxford, 1933), 330-423.

2. On this, see Romans 14:7-10 and the beginning of Luther's Invocavit sermons: "We are altogether required to die and no one can die for another. . . ." (BOA VII, 363).

3. See sermon 24; WJW 1:531-49; see also *Grace upon Grace: A Mission Statement of The United Methodist Church* (Nashville: Graded Press, 1990), 5 (Introduction).

4. See M. Marquardt, *John Wesley's Social Ethics: Praxis and Principles* (Nashville: Abingdon, 1992), 136-37.

5. See C. K. Barrett, *The Epistle to the Romans*, 174-230; also, C. Müller, *Gottes Gerechtigkeit und Gottes Volk. Eine Untersuchung zu Römer 9–11*, FRLANT 86 (1984). U. Luz, *Das Geschichtsverständnis der Paulus*, BEvTh 49 (1968).

6. See E. Dinkler, "Prädestination," II, in NT, *RGG*[3] v. 481f. See W. Klaiber, *Die Aufgabe einer Theologischen Interpretation*, 318f., on the theme of predestination in John's Gospel.

7. On the doctrine of predestination see E. Köhler/W. Pannenberg, "Prädestination," III/IV. RGG[3] V. 483-488; O. Weber, *Foundations* 2:411ff.

8. Sol. Decl. II, 24 (BSLK 822); but also see II, 89 (BSLK, 909f.).

9. Köhler, RGG V, 486; vgl. Sol. Decl. II. 57-60 (BSLK, 894f.).

10. See the correspondence with his mother in the summer of 1725 (for example, the letter of July 29, 1725, WJW 25:175-76).

11. See W. R. Cannon, *The Theology of John Wesley* (Nashville: Abingdon, 1946), 90-106; and W. Klaiber, *Aus Glauben, damit aus Gnaden*, 331ff., and the literature cited there.

12. Sermon 110 (Free Grace), 2; WJW 3:544.

13. Notes on the NT on 1 Peter 1:2, further, Sermon 110; WJW 3:542-63.

14. A Letter to the Rev. Mr. John Wesley (24.12.1740) (in: The Works of the Rev. George Whitefield, M.A., London 1771, 4:53-73, 71).

15. *The Book of Discipline of The United Methodist Church* (Nashville: United Methodist Publishing House, 1996), ¶ 62, Article VIII of the Articles of Religion of the Methodist Church (On Free Will): " . . . wherefore we have no power to do good works, pleasant and acceptable to God, without the grace of God by Christ preventing us, that we may have that good will."

16. See Sermon 85, III, 4; WJW 3:207.

17. "The Question, 'What is an Arminian?' Answered. By a Lover of Free Grace," Works, 3rd ed., 10:358-61; see also J. S. O'Malley, "Arminianism," in *Dictionary of Christianity in America*, ed. D. G. Reid, 77-79.

18. From G. J. Hoenderdaal, "Arminius/Arminianism," TRE 4 (1979), 65 (tr. trans.).

19. Hoenderdaal, 65 (tr. trans.).

20. Minutes, 2.8.1745, Works, 3rd ed., 8:285; see C. Williams, *John Wesley's Theology Today* (Nashville: Abingdon, 1960), 44.

21. Sermon 110, 2; WJW 3:544.

22. Ibid., 3; WJW 3:545.

23. Sermon 63, 11; WJW 2:489.

24. Sermon 85, III, 7; WJW 3:208-9; the easily changed citation is derived from Augustine, Sermon 169 on Philippians 3:3-16, XI (13) J. Migne, *Patrologia latina* 38.923; see WJW 2:490, n. 33.

25. This is most clearly summarized in Sermon 85, WJW 3:199-209 on Philippians 2:12-13, "On Working Out Our Own Salvation": "First, God worketh in you; therefore you can work—otherwise it would be impossible. . . . Secondly, God worketh in you; therefore you *must* work: you must be 'workers together with him' (they are the very words of the apostle); otherwise he will cease working" (Sermon 85, III, 3 and 7; WJW 3:206, 208). On Wesley's synergism, see W. R. Cannon, *The Theology of John Wesley,* 103-18, and M. Marquardt, *John Wesleys "Synergismus,"* MSGEmK 1980, 4-13.

26. See Notes NT, Romans 2:14 ("By Nature" means "by preventing grace"!); Sermon 12, para. 5, WJW 1:302; Sermon 85, WJW 3:199-209; Sermon 105, I, 3-5, WJW 3:481-82; Sermon 129, I, 1, WJW 4:163. It is the enlightenment through the logos, according to John 1:9, which gives people at least a slight notion of good and evil. (Notes on the NT) see also above, 2.1.2.3.

27. Sermon 85, II, 1; WJW 3:203-4.

28. See above I, 1.1.

29. A. Outler, "Theologische Akzente," in *Der Methodismus. Die Kirchen der Welt,* ed. C. E. Sommer, VI (1968), 84-102, here 97 (tr. trans.); see a related discussion in *John Wesley,* ed. A. Outler (New York: Oxford University Press, 1964), 3-33.

30. The unity within the Trinity corresponds to the unity within grace; see *Grace upon Grace* 5; also, J. Pelikan, *The Christian Tradition; I: The Emergence of the Catholic Tradition (100–600)* (Chicago: University of Chicago Press, 1971), 172-225.

31. Sermon 85, III, 4; WJW 3:207.

32. Sermon 16, V, I; WJW 1:393-94.

33. Sermon 16, V, 4; WJW 1:395-96.

34. A comparable discussion is to be found in James F. White, "The Order of Worship: The Ordinary Parts" and "The Proper Parts," in *Companion to the Book of Worship,* ed. W. F. Dunkle Jr. and J. D. Quillian Jr. (Nashville: Abingdon, 1970), 11-43.

35. Williams, *John Wesley's Theology Today,* 42.

36. See the answer to the question about what is the best procedural method in a sermon: "(1.) To invite. (2.) To convince. (3.) To offer Christ. (4.) To build up; and to do this in some measure in every sermon" (Large Minutes, Q. 36, Works, 3rd ed., 8:317).

37. Notes NT on Matthew 3:8.

38. A basic work is A. Heschel, *The Prophets* (New York: Harper Bros., 1955), esp. 35-36 and 104-5; also, H. W. Wolff, "Das Thema Umkehr in der alttestamentlichen Prophetie" in Wolff, *Gesammelte Studien zum AT, 1,* 2nd ed. (1973), 130-50. Walter P. Welten, L. Jacobs, and J. Becker, "Buße," II-IV, TRE 7 (1981), 432-51. For the entire section, see W. Klaiber, *Call and Response,* 155-81.

39. See John Wesley's report about a sermon on Ezekiel 18:31 (Journal, July 10, 1743, WJW 19:328): Charles Wesley's Hymns 6-8, which appeal to Ezekiel 18:31, or hymn 30, on Ezekiel 33:11. For an exegetical analysis see H. G. May, "Ezekiel 18:1-32," in *The Interpreter's Bible* (Nashville: Abingdon, 1952–1957), 6:157-63; and A. Heschel, *The Prophets,* 390-346.

40. For this, see above 2.3.3.4 (note 411).

41. See Mark 1:14-15; Matthew 4:17; Luke 5:32.

42. See Matthew 11:20-24/Luke 10:12-15; Matthew 12:41/Luke 11:32.

43. See Acts 16:14-15.

44. See Luke 19:1-10; Mark 10:17-26.

45. In spite of the emphatic denial in Hebrews 6:4-6; 10:26-29; see W. A. Quanbeck, "Repentance," in *The Interpreter's Dictionary of the Bible,* 4:33-34.

46. See S. McComb, "Repentance in Christianity," in *Hastings Encyclopedia of Religion and Ethics,* 10:732-35.

47. "Disputatio pro declaratione virtuis indulgentiarum 1517," reprinted in *Martin Luther: Selections from His Writings,* ed. J. Dillenberger (Garden City, N.Y.: Doubleday, 1961), 490.

48. See Sermon 7, II, 1-7, WJW 1:225-29; Sermon 85, II, WJW 3:203-6.
49. Sermon 34, IV, 1, WJW 2:15; Sermon 35, WJW 2:20-32; Sermon 44, WJW 2:170-85; Sermon 2, WJW 1:131-41; further, see above 2.2.1.3, note 142; 2.3.2.
50. See Sermon 9, II, 5-8; WJW 1:257-58 (on this, see Williams, *John Wesley's Theology Today,* 57-59); Journal, August 31, 1739, WJW 19:92-93.
51. "Principles of a Methodist Farther Explained" VI, 4-9; WJW 9:226-33; and on this, see Williams, *John Wesley's Theology Today,* 39-40.
52. See above, 2.3.2.2, and below, 3.1.4.3. For the coordination of the "penitential faith" of the slave with the "justifying faith" of the son, see Williams, *John Wesley's Theology Today,* 64-66.
53. For the discussion with the Moravians, see W. Klaiber, *Aus Glauben, damit aus Gnaden,* 328ff. and the literature cited there; also, see "The Rift with the Moravians," in *John Wesley,* ed. A. Outler, 345-76.
54. "The Nature, Design, and General Rule of the United Societies" (1743), WJW 9:69-73.
55. See Sermon 2, "The Almost Christian," I, 4, WJW 1:132-33; Sermon 3, 1, 5-6, WJW 1:142, 144; Sermon 9, I, 8–II, 2, WJW 1:254-56.
56. Sermon 7, II, 1; WJW 1:225-26.
57. See Williams, *John Wesley's Theology Today,* 60ff. On Wesley's discussion concerning Luther's solafideism, see Journal, April 4, 1739, WJW 19:46-47; and Letters (ed. Telford, 1931), 4:175 ("We are justified by faith alone and yet by such a faith as is not alone."). On this, see the citation from Luther in 3.1.4.2 below!
58. An example of the first is the thief in Luke 23:39-43 (see Notes NT), for the second, see the example of Zacchaeus in Luke 19:1-10.
59. See Sermon 43, "The Scriptural Way of Salvation," esp. III, 2; WJW 2:162-63. See also Williams, *John Wesley's Theology Today,* 98-140, esp. 126-30.
60. However, see the monograph on Thomas Aquinas by O. H. Pesch and A. Peters, *Einführung in die Lehre von Gnade und Rechtfertigung* (1982), 90ff.; cf. *Aquinas on Nature and Grace.* ed. A. M. Fairweather, The Library of Christian Classics (Louisville: Westminster/John Knox, 1980), Introduction.
61. Sermon 5, III; WJW 1:190-93. The quotation alludes to Goethe, Faust II.
62. Sermon 7, II, 1, WJW 1:225-26; Sermon 21, WJW 1:446-87; Sermon 1, WJW 1:109-30.
63. See Sermon 14, "The Repentance of Believers," WJW 1:335-52; further, Sermon 43, III, 6-8; WJW 2:164-66, in connection with the repentance of the one who does not yet believe. See also Williams, *John Wesley's Theology Today,* 126-30.
64. See A. Sulzberger, *Christliche Gaubenslehre,* 548ff.; J. Schempp, *Christenlehre,* Question 81; for a comparable discussion, see F. Norwood, *The Story of American Methodism* (Nashville: Abingdon, 1973), esp. chap. 14, "Revivalism and Camp Meetings," 156-63.
65. EUB Catechism, Question 82; similarly, Spörri, *Leitfaden,* Question 73; cf. *The Book of Discipline* (UMC, 1996), ¶ 62., Article IX of the EUB Confession of Faith, entitled "Justification and Regeneration," which relates penitence and justification by faith.
66. J. Schniewind, *Die Freude der Buße,* KVR 32 (1956).
67. See above, 2.2.1.3 (esp. note 142).
68. Williams quite poignantly characterizes the "fruit of repentance" as "the sign of our readiness to allow God to continue his work within us" (*John Wesley's Theology Today,* 66). So, to answer to the work of God, is "a sign of our readiness to receive his further gifts."
69. Among the recent works that appeared in 1988 in relation to the 250th anniversary of Wesley's Aldersgate experience are: M. Weyer, "Die Bedeutung von 'Aldersgate' in Wesley's Leben und Denken" (in M. Weyer, W. Klaiber, M. Marquardt, and D. Sackmann, *Im Glauben gewiß. Die bleibende Bedeutung der Aldersgate-Erfahrung John Wesleys,* BGEmK 32 (1988), 7-33, 56-72; K. H. Voigt, "Hat John Wesley sich am 24. Mai 1738 'bekehrt' " EmK heute 57 (1988); R. P. Heitzenrater, "Great Expectations: Aldersgate and the Evidence of Genuine Christianity," in *Mirror and Memory, Reflections on Early Methodism,* ed. Heitzenrater (1989), 106-49, 241-55. R. Maddox (ed.), *Aldersgate Reconsidered* (Nashville: Abingdon, 1990). Further, H. D. Rack, *Reasonable Enthusiast,* 137-57.
70. Articles on the term *faith* are foundational: R. Bultmann and A. Weiser, ThWNT V, 193-230, O. Michel, ThBLNT I, 560-75; H. Wildberger, THAT I, 177-209; G. Barth, EWNT III, 216-31; K. Haacker, TRE 13 (1984), 277-304; see the related discussion in V. Harvey, "Faith," in *A Handbook of Theological Terms,* 95-99.

71. See also 2 Chronicles 20:20.

72. Mark 2:5 and 5:36, and Matthew 8:10 and 9:29; the formula used in this connection is "Your faith has made you well" (Mark 5:34 and 10:52; Luke 7:50; 8:48); see also Mark 6:5 and the rejection of the demand for signs (Matthew 12:38-39; Mark 8:11-12).

73. G. Barth, EWNT III, 223 on Mark 9:23f; Matthew 17:20 and Matthew 21:21; see also C. H. Dodd, *The Epistle of Paul to the Romans* (London: Collins, 1959), 41-45, 79-80, 177-78; for a form-critical viewpoint, see R. Bultmann, *Jesus and the Word* (New York: Charles Scribner's, 1958), 133-219.

74. John 3:18; 11:27; 12:46; 1 John 3:23; 5:1-5; similar formulations are found in John 5:24, 38; 6:29; 12:44; 14:10-11; 16:27, 30; 17:8, 21.

75. G. Barth, EWNT III, 227; compare John 3:16, 1 John 4:8, 16.

76. See Romans 1:16; 3:22; 4:11; 10:4.

77. Romans 3:27; 4:16ff.; 1 Corinthians 5:7.

78. See "The Faith of Abraham (Romans 4:1-25)," in C. H. Dodd, *The Epistle of Paul to the Romans,* 2nd ed. (1972), 140-77.

79. See P. Althaus, *The Theology of Martin Luther* (Philadelphia: Fortress, 1966), 43-63; also, R. Slenczka, "Glaube," VI, TRE, 13 (1984), 320ff.

80. R. Slenczka, "Glaube," 321ff. (tr. trans.). cf. also the next quotation.

81. Slenczka, "Glaube," 325ff. (tr. trans.). See Question 21 of the Heidelberg Catechism: "What is true faith?—It is not only a certain knowledge by which I accept as true all that God has revealed to us in his Word, but also a wholehearted trust which the Holy Spirit creates in me through the gospel, that, not only to others, but to me also God has given the forgiveness of sins, everlasting righteousness and salvation, out of sheer grace solely for the sake of Christ's saving work."

82. Sermon 18, I, 3, (WJW, 1, 418); Journal, February 1, 1738 (WJW 18:215f.); Sermon 18, I, 3 (WJW 1:418-19); "An Earnest Appeal to Men of Reason and Religion," 59 (WJW 11:68-69). On the origins of Welsey's theology in this matter see also W. R. Cannon, *The Theology of John Wesley,* 65-81; and W. Klaiber, *Aus Glauben* 320, n. 26.

83. Sermon 18, I, 2; WJW 1:418; see Thomas Aquinas, *Summa theologiae* III.ii, Q.1.

84. Sermon 5, IV, 2; WJW 1:194; cf. Sermon 43, II, 1, WJW 2:160-61.

85. On the qualification for the faith of a "son" see Journal, February 1, 1738 (WJW 18:215); Sermon 106, I, 10-12; WJW 3:497-98; see above, no. 52.

86. Sermon 7, II, 12; WJW 1:231; Sermon 44, III, 3; WJW 184; Sermon 91, I, 2; WJW 3:294-95.

87. Sermon 46, III, 3, WJW 2:215; Sermon 43, III, 1 and 3, WJW 2:162, 163-64.

88. "The Principles of a Methodist Farther Explained" (1746) IV, 5-6; WJW 9:228-29.

89. Sermon 18, I, 1; WJW 1:417-18; Sermon 42, I, 8; WJW 2:143-44; Sermon 91, I, 23; WJW 3:294-95.

90. Sermon 14, II, 5; WJW 1:349.

91. Sermon 14, III, 4; WJW 1:352.

92. Sermon 5, IV, 3 and 5; WJW 1:195, 196.

93. "The Principles of a Methodist" (1742), 7; WJW 9:52; compare Sermon 20, II, 13, WJW 1:459.

94. "An Earnest Appeal," 9-11 (WJW 11:47-49); see Sermon 5, IV, 5; WJW 1:195. The justification of believers is also for Wesley never the justification of the godly but of the godless (Sermon 5, IV, 2 and 5, WJW 1:194, 195; Sermon 9, WJW 1:248-66; Sermon 6, I, 14, WJW 1:209). In his hymns, Charles Wesley described quite impressively the teachableness of the person who genuinely seeks salvation in God's saving works. Hymn 114 begins, "Author of faith, to thee I cry" and continues in verse 3, "I know the work is only thine—/ The gift of faith is all divine"; 142, 3: "Command the light of faith to shine, / To shine in my dark, drooping heart, / And fill me with the life divine; / Now bid the new creation be! / O God, let there be faith in me!"; 152, 1: "I have neither will nor power"; verse 4: "Force me to be saved by grace!"; 98, 1: "Stone to flesh, O God convert, / Cast a look and break my heart!" (Ezekiel 11:19 is the biblical citation which is being played out in these verses.)

95. "An Earnest Appeal," 7 (WJW 11:46f.)

96. Sermon 6, III, 1-6; WJW 1:214-16; cf. Sermon 5, IV, 3; WJW 1:195.

97. Cf. O. Weber, *Foundations* 2:274ff.; W. Joest, *Dogmatik* 2:467f.

98. EKD-Studie: "Christsein gestalten. Eine Studie zum Weg der Kirche," 1986, 45; for a related discussion, see W. A. Whitehouse, "Faith," in *A Theological Wordbook of the Bible,* ed. A. Richardson (New York: Macmillan, 1962), 75-76.

99. Karl Barth, *CD* IV/I, 744.

100. Ibid., 745.
101. Ibid., 747.
102. Ibid., 748.
103. W. Vorländer, *Christus erkennen* (1986), 63ff. (tr. trans.).
104. W. Vorländer, 71. Yet more bluntly, I. U. Dalferth declares that "In the event of faith, a person is such a perplexed beneficiary that he can say that in no way has he participated in this event, neither actively nor passively." *Existenz Gottes und christlicher Glaube*, BEvTh 93 (1984), 243 (tr. trans.); Ql of the Heidelberg Catechism evokes this understanding of faith for commentator Andrew Pere, who wrote, "Anyone who wishes to be comforted must begin by acknowledging, that is to say, by admitting through faith, that through *faith* he no longer belongs to himself; he has been taken into custody by the protection of the one who will free him from the curse of mortal egoism."—*The Heidelberg Catechism with Commentary*, 18f.
105. F. Neugebauer, *In Christus* (1961), 165. Note also the tenor of the work by H. Binder, *Der Glaube bei Paulus* (1968); and see also C. H. Dodd, *The Epistle of Paul to the Romans*, 37-45, on 1:16-17.
106. G. Friedrich, "Glaube und Verkündigung bei Paulus," in, *Glauben im NT*, ed. F. Hahn and H. Klein, BThSt 7 (1988), 93-113, here:109.
107. Ibid., 112. O. Hofius sees already in the confession that a person can reject grace, an actual surrender of the correct insight that faith is the gift of God (*Wort Gottes und Glaube*, 157, n. 70) (tr. trans.).
108. W. Klaiber, *Call and Response*, 178f.; 204ff.
109. P. Tillich, "Rechtfertigung und Zweifel," *Werke* 8, 85-100, esp. 96ff.; see also P. Tillich, *Systematic Theology*, 3:227: "How is the faith through which justification comes to us related to the situation of radical doubt? Radical doubt is existential doubt concerning the meaning of life itself."
110. Tillich, "Rechtfertigung und Zweifel," 99 (tr. trans.).
111. P. Tillich, *The Courage to Be* (1952; New Haven: Yale University Press, 35th printing, 1971), 170.
112. Ibid., 172.
113. R. Bultmann, "The Case for Demythologizing," in *Kerygma and Myth*, vol. 2, ed. H. W. Bartsch, trans. R. H. Fuller (London: SPCK, 1972), 181-94.
114. R. Bultmann, "New Testament and Mythology," in *Kerygma and Myth*, vol. 1, ed. H. W. Bartsch, 1-44.
115. R. Bultmann, "Faith," trans. G. W. Bromiley, in *Theological Dictionary of the New Testament* (Grand Rapids: Eerdmans, 1968), 6:220.
116. Ibid., 6:220: "Faith as a movement of the will is the negation of the will itself." Cf. also his basic definition of faith as "an act of obedience" (R. Bultmann, *Theology of the New Testament*, 314-17).
117. Bultmann, "Faith," in *Theological Dictionary of the New Testament*, 6:221.
118. E. Drewermann, *Tiefpsychologie und Exegese*, I, 8th ed. (1990), 349f., see also W. Daim, *Depth Psychology and Salvation* (New York: Ungar, 1963).
119. See R. Bultmann, "Welchen Sinn hat es, von Gott zu reden?" GuV1:, 26-37, 37: "Hence, would faith be the archimedial point, from which the world would be taken off its hinges?" (tr. trans.). Bultmann's "yes" to this question is only warranted if faith remains full with regard to its contents. Cf. W. Lohff, "Rechtfertigung und Anthropologie," in *Rechtfertigung im neuzeitlichen Lebenszusammenhang, Studien zur Interpretation der Rechfertigungslehre* (1974), 126-45, 139; for a survey of critiques of Bultmann's position, see W. Hordern, *A Layman's Guide to Protestant Theology* (New York: Macmillan, 1955), 191-209.
120. I. W. E. Sommer has reduced this to the formula: "As certain as it may be that the faithful person is receptive in faith, yet he is certainly not passive." ("Die christliche Erfahrung im Methodismus," 1949, 13); on this see also E. Brunner, *Dogmatics III: The Christian Doctrine of the Church, Faith, and the Consummation* (Philadelphia: Westminster, 1962), 12f.; and M. Luther, Lecture on Romans 10:3-9, in *Luther: Lectures on Romans*, ed. W. Pauch, Library of Christian Classics (Philadelphia: Westminster, 1961), 288-93.
121. H. Weder, "Die Entdeckung des Glaubens im Neuen Testament," in *Glaube heute. Christ werden—Christ bleiben* (1988), 52-63; 58f. Cf. the "General Introduction" to *Luther: Lectures on Romans*, by W. Pauck, ed., xvii-lxvi; and W. Härle, "Der Glaube als Gottes-und/oder Menschenwerk in der Theologie Martin Luthers," in W. Härle and R. Preul, "Glaube," *Marburger Jahrbuch*

Theologie, IV, 1993, 37-77, esp. 75f.; and the reflections by F. Schleiermacher, *The Christian Faith* (from German 2nd ed.; New York: Harper and Bros., 1963), II, par. 108.6 (492-96).

122. Cf. also: *Unterwegs mit Christus,* 50f., and V. Harvey, "fides qua/quae creditur," in *A Handbook of Theological Terms* (Macmillan: Collier, 1964).

123. Sermon 106, I, 10-12; WJW 3:497-98. On the theme of the certainty of salvation, see 3.2.2.4 below.

124. O. Pesch sees this as a total misunderstanding of the opposing views (in Pesch and Peters, *Einführung,* 195ff.), while V. Subilia, *Die Rechtfertigung aus Glauben* (1981), 84ff., already sees in this the decisive indication that Trent does not speak of the righteousness of faith; for a comparable discussion, see Jean Delumeau, *Catholicism Between Luther and Voltaire* (Philadelphia: Westminster, 1977), 1-43, and now The Joint Declaration on the Doctrine of Justification (1999), 34-36.

125. See "Assurance," in V. A. Harvey, *A Handbook of Theological Terms* (New York: Macmillan, 1964), 32; also, O. Hänisch, *Biblische Heilsgewißheit* (1934) (2nd ed.,1988), (BGEmK 33).

126. When Wesley uses the term "salvation," he means to include both the initial phases of redemption as well as its goal, the salvation of humanity.

127. See the programmatic statements Wesley makes in Sermon 43, I, 1; WJW 2:156, in reference to Ephesians 2:8, "You have been saved through faith." "The salvation which is here spoken of might be extended to the entire work of God, from the first dawning of grace in the soul, till it is consummated in glory" (I, 1, WJW 2:156).

128. Wesley makes use of this formula for the description of the "original position" of humanity (Sermon 5, I, 4, WJW 1:184-85; Sermon 6, I, 11, WJW 1:208-9), as well as for the present fellowship with God (Sermon 17, I, 12 and II, 5, WJW 1:408, 411; Sermon 18, I, 7, WJW 1:421-22; Sermon 23, IV, WJW 1:530; Sermon 24, IV, 1, WJW 1:547-48; Sermon 28, 4-5, WJW 1:614-15; Sermon 29, 5, WJW 1:635; Sermon 45, III, 3, WJW 2:195-96; Sermon 59, WJW 2:422-35; Sermon 61, 2, WJW 2:452; Sermon 63, 8 and 10, WJW 2:488, 489; Sermon 77, II, 5 and III, WJW 3:96, 97-102; Sermon 90, I and II, 11, WJW 3:282-84, 289) and also for our eschatological position with God (Sermon 64, 18, WJW 2:509-10).

129. Wesley refers to these as "branches" (Sermon 85, II, 1; WJW 3:203-4).

130. Sermon 5, II, 1; WJW 1:187.

131. Sermon 85, II, 1, WJW 3:203-4; cf. Sermon 43, I, 3-4, WJW 2:157-58.

132. Sermon 1, "Salvation by Faith," II, 2; WJW 1:122.

133. Sermon 127, "The Wedding Garment," 18; WJW 4:148.

134. Sermon 45, 1; WJW 2:187.

135. Sermon 45, IV, 3; WJW 2:198.

136. See Sermon 58, 9 (on Romans 8:30), WJW 2:418; Sermon 83, 9-10 WJW 3:174-76.

137. Sermon 5, II, 1; WJW 1:187.

138a. In this regard, see J. Moltmann's description of "life in the Spirit," which is developed in *The Spirit of Life: A Universal Affirmation* (Minneapolis: Fortress, 1992); see "Liberation for Life" in 114-22. For a discussion of Wesley's *ordo salutis* with reference to life development, see William R. Cannon, *The Theology of John Wesley* (Nashville: Abingdon, 1946), chapter 10: "The Moral Life and Christian Perfection," 221-43.

138b. F. Käsemann, "The Righteousness of God" in Paul, New Testament Questions of Today (Philadelphia: Fortress) 1969, 168-82; P. Stuhlmacher, Gerechtigkeit Gottes bei Paulus, FRLANT 87, 2nd ed., 1966; K. Kertelge, "Rechtfertigung bei Paulus," New Testament Abstracts NF 3, 2nd ed., 1972; J. Reumann, *Righteousness in the New Testament* (Philadelphia/New York, 1982); J. D. G. Dunn, "The Justice of God," JThSt NS43, 1992, 1-22; W. Klaiber, "Gerecht vor Gott. Rechtfertigung in der Bibel und heute." BTSP 20, 2000.

139. See Proverbs 24:24; 1 Samuel 24:17; Genesis 38:26.

140. A. Ritschl, *The Christian Doctrine of Justification and Reconciliation* (New York: Scribners, 1900), 3rd. ed., 3:140, has coined the terms "analytic" or "synthetic" judgment of righteousness, with reference to the terminology of Kant. Yet, W. Härle has shown that this abstraction is misleading ("Analytische und synthetische Urteile in der Rechtfertigungslehre," Neuen Zeitschrift für systematische Theologie 16, 1974, 16-34).

141. This hope lives further in the apocalyptic writings and the community of Qumran (see I. Her 91, 14; IQH 14, 16; CD 20, 16-21; IQ27, I, 6).

142. On the pre-Pauline message of justification, see 1 Corinthians 1:30; 6:9-11; Romans 3:25-26; 4:25; as background, see Isaiah 53:11. See also P. Stuhlmacher, "Jesus' Resurrection and the View of

Righteousness in the Pre-Pauline Mission Congregations," in *Reconciliation, Law, and Righteousness: Essays in Biblical Theology* (Philadelphia: Fortress, 1986), 50-67.

143. See John Knox, *Chapters in a Life of Paul* (Nashville: Abingdon, 1950), and esp. 114-27 for the meaning of Paul's conversion.

144. Based upon the present-day exposition of "righteousness" as "faithfulness to community, faithfulness to salvation," the genitive in "righteousness of God" needs to be understood as a subjective genitive (that is, God's own faithfulness to salvation), whereas Luther needed to search for a paraphrase (see below). On this, see the literature now cited in note 138b.

145. The doctrine of justification was described in such a manner in the history of exposition as the *Nebenkrater* ("nearby crater") of the Pauline doctrine of redemption, see A. Schweitzer, *Die Mystik des Apostels Paulus* (1930), 220; today this position has been represented by K. Stendahl, "The Apostle Paul's View of Righteousness," in *Reconciliation, Law, and Righteousness,* 68-93.

146. See W. Klaiber, *Rechtfertigung und Gemeinde,* 149ff.; E. P. Sanders, *Paul and Palestinian Judaism* (London, 1972); *Paul, the Law, and the Jewish People* (Philadelphia, 1983).

147. See the parallel explanation above in 3.1.4.1 (faith).

148. The relation of justification and reconciliation in Paul is also treated in J. Knox, *Chapters in a Life of Paul,* 146-55. In addition, see E. C. Blackman, "Reconciliation," in *Interpreter's Dictionary of the Bible,* 4:16-17.

149. For Paul, redemption is basically yet to be realized: 1 Thessalonians 1:10; 1 Corinthians 1:18-21; 3:15; 5:5; Romans 5:9-10; 10:9, 13; see also Galatians 5:5; and yet justification and reconciliation through the work of the Spirit is already salvation present—even if it is present in faith (2 Corinthians 5:5) and in hope (Romans 8:24).

150. Preface to vol. 1 of the Opera Latina, Wittenburg, 1545, WA 54, 185; see also *Martin Luther,* ed. J. Dillenberger (Garden City, N.Y.: Doubleday, 1961), 10-11.

151. For a discussion of "Jesus Christ as Reconciler and Redeemer" in relation to the "Righteousness in Faith," see P. Althaus, *The Theology of Martin Luther* (Philadelphia: Fortress, 1966), 201-50.

152. E. Kinder, "Rechtfertigung," II, RGG, 3rd ed. 440 (tr. trans.).

153. W. Joest, *Dogmatik* 2:440; see also Athaus, *The Theology of Martin Luther,* 35-63.

154. Joest, *Dogmatik* 2:440f. (tr. trans.).

155. See Luther's lectures on Romans: "Has he now been made fully righteous? No, but he is simultaneously a sinner and a righteous man *(simul iustus et peccator),* a sinner in reality, but righteous from the certain imputation and promise of God, who intends to make him free from sin, until he is fully healed" (WA 56, 272, 14ff.; tr. trans.); see John Tonkin, *The Church and the Secular Order in Reformation Thought* (New York: Columbia, 1971), "The Pattern of Dialectic," 40-72.

156. Fifth disputation concerning Romans 3:28, on 1.6.1537, WA 39/I, 202ff. (tr. trans.). See also WA 39, I, 96, 6: "Opera sunt necessaria ut testentur nos esse iustos."

157. CR 21, 421.

158. W. Joest, *Dogmatik,* 2:443 (tr. trans.); see also *Melanchthon and Bucer,* ed. Wilhelm Pauck, *Library of Christian Classics,* vol. 19 (Philadelphia: Westminster, 1969), Introduction, 3-17.

159. *John Calvin: Institutes of the Christian Religion* (1559), ed. J. T. McNeill, *Library of Christian Classics,* vol. 20 (Philadelphia: Westminster, 1960), III, 16, 1.

160. Ibid.

161. See the positive evaluation of the Council in H. Outram Evennett, *The Spirit of the Counter-Reformation* (London: Cambridge, 1968); for a critical study that seeks to advance ecumenical discussion, see A. D. Wright, *The Counter-Reformation: Catholic Europe and the Non-Christian World* (London: Weidenfeld and Nicolson, 1982); a fair, but not harmonious presentation that takes into account the ecumenical discussion, is found in W. Pannenberg, "Die Rechtfertigungslehre im ökumenischen Gespräch," ZThK 88 (1991), 237-46.

162. For the canons of Trent on justification, see *Canons and Decrees of the Council of Trent* (St. Louis: Herder, 1941), canons 1-19, 33-36.

163. It is clear that, for Trent, there is no justification *sola fide*—also not as a beginning; such a view is rejected (canons 9, 11f., 14, *Canons and Decrees,* 35-36); faith belongs to the *praeparatio,* and a person is justified through the infused love (canons 7-9, *Canons and Decrees,* 34-35).

164. See below, 3.2.2.4; on Trent, see Subilia, *Die Rechtfertigung aus Glauben,* 87f.; Pesch and Peters, *Einführung,* 195ff.

165. See W. R. Cannon, *The Theology of John Wesley* (Nashville: Abingdon, 1946); Williams, *John Wesley's Theology Today*, 57-73.

166. Sermon 43, I, 3; WJW 2:157-58.

167. Sermon 5, II, 3; WJW 1:188.

168. See Notes on NT, Romans 1:17: "God's . . . righteousness . . . includes both justice and mercy, and is . . . shown in condemning sin, and yet justifying the sinner."

169. Sermon 43, I, 3; WJW 2:157-58, with reference to Romans 5:1-2.

170. In the original, the term is relative.

171. See especially Sermon 1, II, 7, WJW 1:124-25; Sermon 5, WJW 1:181-99; Sermon 6, WJW 1:200-216; Sermon 20, WJW 1:444-65; Sermon 42, WJW 2:138-51.

172. For a discussion of this issue, see W. Klaiber, *Aus Glauben*, 320ff. and the sources cited therein. See also the background discussion in Rupert Davies, "The People Called Methodists—I. 'Our Doctrines,' " in *A History of the Methodist Church in Great Britain* ed. R. Davies and G. Rupp (London: Epworth, 1965), I, 145-80.

173. On this, see W. S. Gunter, *The Limits of "Love Divine." John Wesley's Response to Antinomianism and Enthusiasm* (Nashville: Kingswood, 1989).

174. Therefore, Wesley distinguished between the value of good works done *before* and *after* justification (see above, 3.2.1.2, on Luther's concept, and see also *John Wesley*, ed. A. Outler (New York: Oxford University Press, 1964), "Faith at Work," 221f.), M. Marquardt, *John Wesleys "Synergismus."*

175. Sermon 12, 20, WJW 1:313.

176. See the conference proceedings from 1770 (Large Minutes, Q.77, Works, 3rd ed., 8:377; on this, see P. Streiff, *Reluctant Saint: A Theological Biography of Fletcher of Madeley* (London: Epworth Press, 2001; Gunter, *Limits*, 251-66).

177. Sermon 20, II, 12-13, WJW 1:458-59; see further Sermon 29, WJW 1:632-49; Sermon 21, WJW 1:466-87; Notes NT on 2 Corinthians 5:21.

178. Journal, December 13, 1739, WJW 19:128.

179. Notes NT James 2:21. More recently, see the discussion of J. Jeremias, *Paul and James,* ET 66 (1954/55), 368-71.

180. Sermon 127, 18 (see above 3.2); WJW 4:147-48.

181. On this see L. Mattern, *Das Verständnis des Gerichts bei Paulus,* Abhandlungen zur Theologie des Alten und Neuen Testaments 47 (1966); relevant discussion is to be found in Hans Hübner, *The Law in Paul's Thought. Studies of the New Testament and Its World* (Edinburgh: T & T Clark, 1984), and in B. Witherington III, *Jesus, Paul, and the End of the World: A Comparative Study in New Testament Eschatology* (Downers Grove, Ill.: InterVarsity, 1992); (see also above, 2.3.3.4).

182. Sermon 5, IV, 9; WJW 1:198-99.

183. Cited by W. Mostert, *Ist die Frage nach der Existenz Gottes wirklich radikaler als die Frage nach dem gnädigen Gott?* ZThK 74 (1977), 86 (tr. trans.). See also William Hordern, *A Layman's Guide to Protestant Theology* (New York: Macmillan, 1968), on the "death of God" discussion, 237-44.

184. Klaiber, *Gerecht vor Gott*; also, Hendrikus Boers, *The Justification of the Gentiles: Paul's Letters to the Romans and Galatians* (Peabody, M.: Boers, 1994).

185. In this connection, see the "ontological" interpretation of the doctrine of justification by W. Härle and E. Herms, *Rechtfertigung. Das Wirklichkeitsverständnis des christlichen Glaubens*, Uni-Taschenbücher 1016 (1980), 53ff.; and the presentation of the doctrine of justification in J. Moltmann, *The Spirit of Life,* 123-43.

186. This statement is to be understood in the context of Wesley's Anglican tradition; there were, of course, numerous precedents for the exposition of the doctrine of regeneration in the English Puritans and in the German Pietists (see Robert Monk, *John Wesley: His Puritan Heritage*, rev. ed. (Lanham, Md.: Scarecrow, 1999); and F. Ernest Stoeffler, *Continental Pietism and Early American Christianity* (Eerdmans, 1976), esp. 184ff.

187. See "Regeneration" by J. M. Robinson, in *The Interpreter's Dictionary of the Bible,* 4:24-29.

188. In the history of traditions, Jesus' words of Matthew 18:3 probably stand behind John 3:3, whose Aramaic is to be possibly translated with "if you do not become once again like children" (J. Jeremias, *The Parables of Jesus,* 190f.). The new existence before God is being expressed here in parabolic terms, as with children. See below 3.2.2.4.

189. Goppelt, *Religion in Geschichte und Gegenwart,* 3rd ed., IV, 1968; see also C. K. Barrett, *The Gospel According to St. John,* 176-82.

190. See C. K. Barrett, *The Gospel According to St. John,* 174-75.

191. Sermon 19, "The Great Privilege of Those That Are Born of God," 1-2; WJW 1:431-32; cf. 45, 1 (WJW 2:187). On this, see W. Joest, "Wiedergeburt," III, *Religion in Geschichte und Gegenwart,* 3rd ed., VI, 1699f.; Regeneration "means the whole of salvation under the point of view of its essence as the creation of a new life" (for a comparable discussion, see J. T. Marshall, "Regeneration," in *Hasting's Encyclopedia of Religion and Ethics,* 9:939-646); further, the description of the different relations between justification and regeneration in J. Moltmann, *The Spirit of Life,* 123ff. The unity of justification and regeneration is emphasized in *Unterwegs mit Christus,* 54.

192. Sermon 45, "The New Birth," I, WJW 2:188-90.

193. Ibid., II; WJW 2:190-94.

194. Ibid., II, 4; WJW 2:192-93.

195. Ibid., II, 5; WJW 2:193-94.

196. Sermon 18, "The Marks of the New Birth," WJW 1:415-30.

197. Sermon 45, III, 1-2; WJW 2:194-95.

198. Sermon 45, III, 3; WJW 2:196.

199. Sermon 45, IV, 4, WJW 199-201; Sermon 18, WJW 1:415-30.

200. *The Book of Discipline* (UMC, 1996), ¶ 62, Article IXb. The order in which regeneration is presented in the Confession of Faith locates this doctrine within the sequence of the ordo salutis of justification—regeneration—sanctification—Christian perfection (Articles IX and XI) that closely mirrors the ordo salutis of Otterbein and the Reformed Pietists; see J. S. O'Malley, *Pilgrimage of Faith,* Part II.

201. See Williams, *John Wesley's Theology Today,* 115-22; R. Cushman, "Baptism and the Family of God" in *The Doctrine of the Church,* ed. D. Kirkpatrick (1964), 79-102; O. Borgen, *John Wesley and the Sacraments;* 972; see below, 4.2.1.3.

202. Sermon 18, 1; WJW 1:417.

203. "A Treatise on Baptism," Works, 3rd ed., 10:188-201.

204. Sermon 18, IV, 5; WJW 1:430.

205. Sermon 45, IV, 1f.; WJW 2:196-201. Wesley is here referring to the formulas of the catechisms of the Church of England.

206. See G. Maier, "Gottes Heilstat und die Bekehrung des Sünders im Pietismus und im Zeugnis der Schrift," in *Taufe, Wiedergeburt, und Bekehrung in evangelischer Perspektive,* ed. G. Maier and G. Rost (1980), 37-57, 47. For a comparable discussion, see F. E. Stoeffler, "German Reformed Pietism and Prominent Neo-Pietists" in *German Pietism in the Eighteenth Century* (Leiden: Brill, 1973), 219-65; as well as E. G. Rupp, *Methodism in Relation to Protestant Tradition* (London, 1954); and P. H. Eller, *History of Evangelical Missions* (Cleveland, 1942), 137-70.

207. See Acts 8:14-24; 10:44-48. These reports do not permit a basic separation between water baptism and receiving the Spirit. Their narrative power of expression certainly lives by a basic correlation of both aspects.

208. See J. Schempp, *Christenlehre,* Q. 86, "What is holy baptism?—Baptism is that means of grace through which the forgiveness of sins and the renewal of adoption by God is promised to us through the application of water." Compare Article VI of the Confession of Faith (*Book of Discipline* [UMC, 1996], ¶ 62): "Children of believing parents . . . should be nurtured and led to personal acceptance of Christ, and by profession of faith confirm their Baptism." The document, "By Water and the Spirit: A United Methodist Understanding of Baptism" (Discipleship Resources, Nashville, Tenn., 1996) comes much closer to the sacramental understanding of the Catholic and Lutheran tradition. For a critical assessment see Maja Friedrich-Buser, "Taufe und Kirchengliedschaft in evangelisch—methodistischer Perspektive," Emk-Forum 8, 1997.

209. The new birth and receiving the Holy Spirit therefore belong together (see above, 2.3.2).

210. Schleiermacher argues by use of this analogy, that as birth is for the new born, so also the new birth is "something unconscious" (*The Christian Faith* [New York: Harper, 1963], 2:486).

211. On the address of God with "Abba," see J. Jeremias, "Abba. Studien zur neutestamentlichen Theologie und Zeitgeschichte," 1969, 15-67; op cit. *Neutestamentliche Theologie,* I, 67-73; see also Karl Barth, *The Epistle to the Romans* (London: Oxford, 1975), 296-98.

212. See James D. G. Dunn, *The Theology of Paul's Letter to the Galatians* (Cambridge: Cambridge University Press, 1993).

213. See J. Jeremias, *The Parables of Jesus,* 128-32.

214. See T. J. Tasker, "Certainty," in *Hastings Encyclopedia of Religion and Ethics,* 3:320-31.

215. On Paul, see 1 Corinthians 10:1-13 and 1 Corinthians 1:8-9; Philippians 1:6 (on this, see also W. Klaiber, *Rechtfertigung und Gemeinde*, 125ff.). Wesley occasionally distinguished between a present assurance of faith, which consists in the witness of the Spirit that we are justified through faith in Christ, and the future assurance of salvation or "assurance of hope," which he did not teach, since the word for this does not appear in the Bible and since the danger of a retrogression or loss of faith can not be excluded (Letter of September 28, 1738 to Rev. A. Bedford, WJW 25:562-66); a similar account is found in his open letter to the Bishop of Exeter, Dr. Lavington, WJW 11:379-429). However, this includes the confidence that God's faithfulness will accept us to the end (see WJW 25:563-64; Sermon 110, 14-16, WJW 3:549-50). It is the danger of false "assurance of salvation," which leads to this restriction, not the conception of a double justification. See Williams, *John Wesley's Theology Today*, 98-105, 114ff.; also, M. Marquardt, "Gewißheit und Anfechtung bei Martin Luther und John Wesley," TfP 14 (1988), 14-28; and John Lawson, *Introduction to Christian Doctrine* (Printice-Hall, 1967), 217-19.

216. See Helmut Thielicke, *Our Heavenly Father* (New York: Harper, 1960), on prayer as a route to faith, based upon meditations on the Lord's Supper.

217. See Cannon, *The Theology of John Wesley*, 120-34.

218. See on this Adolf Deissmann, "The Christ Mystic," in *The Writings of St. Paul*, ed. W. A. Meeks (New York: Norton, 1972), 374-87; W. Klaiber, *Call and Response*, 190-91; and Klaiber, *Wo Leben wieder Leben ist*. 21ff.

219. On the significance of Galatians 2:19-20 in this connection, see D. Stollberg/D. Lührmann, "Tiefenpsychologische oder historich-kritische Exegese? Identität und der Tod des Ichs" (Gal. 2:19-20), in *Doppeldeutig. Tiefendimensionen biblischer Texte*, ed. Y. Spiegel (1978), 215-36. See also C. K. Barrett, *Freedom and Obligation: A Study of the Epistle to the Galatians* (Philadelphia: Westminster, 1985).

220. See Wesley's Sermon 63, 11; WJW 2:489, where he demonstrates, in connection with Galatians 2:20, that God does not destroy our impulses of feeling, but rather lays claim to them for himself.

221. Colossians 3:10; 2 Corinthians 3:18; see M. Marquardt, "Sanctification as Formation in the Image of Christ," in: *Serving God with Heart and Mind: A Festschrift in Honor of R. Ireson*, ed. by H. R. Pieterse, Nashville: General Board of Higher Education and Ministry, 2001.

222. Large Minutes, Q.3, Works, 3rd ed., 8:299. In like fashion, the early United Brethren and Evangelicals were intent not upon founding new sects but upon fashioning a spiritual fellowship of persons in Christ who would leaven existing church structures. See chapters 1 and 2 of B. Behney and P. Eller, *History of the Evangelical United Brethren Church* (Nashville: Abingdon, 1979).

223. For a discussion of their relationship, see W. R. Cannon, *The Theology of John Wesley*, 119-50; John Lawson, *Introduction to Christian Doctrine*, 204-35; and J. Moltmann, *The Spirit of Life*, 123ff.

224. See J. L. Neve, *A History of Christian Thought* (Philadelphia: Muhlenberg, 1946), 256-63.

225. K. Barth, CD IV/2, 499.

226. Yet, the conjecture of Outler that Wesley was influenced by the Orthodox doctrine of "theosis" (deification of humans through grace) has not been confirmed; see T. Campbell, *John Wesley and Christian Antiquity*, X, 66f.

227. Sermon 5, II, 1; WJW 1:187; Sermon 85, II, 1, WJW 3:203-4; in addition, Sermon 58, WJW 2:413-21.

228. On the relation of indicative and imperative in sanctification, see Cannon, *The Theology of John Wesley*, 221-54; also, K. Barth emphasizes that God is the "acting Subject" in justification as well as in sanctification (CD IV/2, 56).

229. J. Muhlenburg, "Holiness," *Interpreter's Dictionary of the Bible*, 2:617-25; E. C. Blackman, "Sanctification," *Interpreter's Dictionary of the Bible*, 4:210-13; Van A. Harvey, "sanctification," in *A Handbook of Theological Terms* (New York: Macmillan, 1964), 214-15.

230. See Exodus 15:11; 1 Samuel 2:2; Psalms 22:4; 33:21; 71:22; 99:4ff.; Isaiah 31:1.

231. See John H. Hayes, "Leviticus: The Holiness of Life," in *Harper's Bible Commentary*, 171-73.

232. On this, see F. Crüsemann, "Der Exodus als Heiligung. Zur rechtsgeschichtlichen Bedeutung des Heiligkeitsgesetzes," in *Die hebräische Bibel. Festschrift R. Rendtorff* (1990), 117-29; also, Bernhard W. Anderson, "Revelation and Response," in *Understanding the Old Testament* (Prentice-Hall, 1966), 43-65.

233. See John Bright, "The Faith of Early Israel," in *A History of Israel* (Philadelphia: Westminster, 1959), 128-41.

234. On Mark 7:15, see James M. Robinson, *The Problem of History in Mark* (London: SCM, 1957), 43-46; and E. Käsemann, *Exegetische Versuche und Besinnungen* I, 6th ed. (1970), 117 and 219.

235. See J. Muilenburg, "Holiness," in *Interpreter's Dictionary of the Bible*, 2:616-25. This includes a discussion of holiness in relation to the church as the "holy temple in the Lord" (Eph. 2:21-22).

236. Further, Colossians 1:22; Ephesians 5:25-27f.; Hebrews 13:12; 1 Peter 1:18-19.

237. E. Käsemann, *An die Römer*, Handbuch zum Neuen Testament 8as, 3rd ed. (1974), 175; see the related discussion in John Knox, "Leading Ideas in Paul's Preaching," in *The Interpreter's Bible*, 9:368-71.

238. See Karl Barth, "The New Man" (on Paul's understanding of the new creation in Christ), in *The Writings of St. Paul*, ed. W. A. Meeks, 268-76; also, W. Schrage, "Heiligung als Prozess bei Paulus," in *Jesu Rede von Gott und ihre Nachgeschichte im frühen Christentum, Festschrift Willi Marxsen* (1988), 222-34, 226.

239. See Philip S. Watson, *The Message of the Wesleys* (New York: Macmillan, 1964), 195-220; H. Lindström, *Wesley and Sanctification* (London: Epworth, 1946); Martin Schmidt, *John Wesley: A Theological Biography* (Nashville: Abingdon, 1962), 91-123; W. R. Cannon, *The Theology of John Wesley*, 221-43; K. C. Kinghorn, *The Gospel of Grace; The Way of Salvation in the Wesleyan Tradition* (Nashville: Abingdon, 1992), 101-20; Melvin Dieter, et al., *Five Views on Sanctification* (Grand Rapids: Academie for Zondervan, 1987); Stephen Neill, *Christian Holiness* (New York: Harper, 1960), R. Newton Flew, *The Idea of Perfection in Christian Theology* (London: Oxford, 1934); *John Wesley*, ed. Albert Outler (New York: Oxford University Press, 1964), 251-305; John R. Tyson, *Charles Wesley on Sanctification* (Grand Rapids: Francis Asbury, 1986); and W. Klaiber and M. Marquardt, "Heiligung aus biblischer und evangelisch-methodischer Sicht," BGEmK, 27 (1987).

240. See Sermon 45, III, 1; WJW 2:194-95.

241. See Sermon 36, III, 3; WJW 2:41-42 and further discussion above, 2.2.2.3 note 237.

242. Sermon 43, III, 3; WJW 2:163-64.

243. See the preface to the 1739 "Hymns and Sacred Poems," 5 (Works, 3rd ed., 14:321-22): "The gospel of Christ knows of no religion, but social; no holiness but social holiness." Similarly, see Sermon 24, I, 1; WJW 1:533-34. On this see also "Faith at Work," in *John Wesley*, ed. Albert Outler, 221-50; and V. Schneeberger, *Theologische Wurzeln des sozialen Akzents bei John Wesley* (1974), 143ff. and above, section 1.3.4.

244. See Sermon 1, II, 1ff., WJW 1:121-25; Sermon 43, I, 1, WJW 2:156; etc.

245. See Notes on the NT on John 3:36.

246. "A Plain Account of Christian Perfection," 25, Q33 (Works, 3rd ed., 11:430): "The heaven of heavens is love"! See the last stanza of "O for a thousand tongues to sing": "With me, your chief, ye then shall know, / Shall feel your sin forgiven; / Anticipate your heaven below, / And own that love is heaven" (Hymn 1, 9). On the formulation "heaven below," see also hymn 19, 3 ("To us it is given In Jesus to know / A kingdom of heaven, A heaven below"); 77, 2; 93, 3; 197, 2; 198, 4.

247. See the report of the provocative conversation of Wesley with Zinzendorf on September 3, 1741 (WJW 19:211-15).

248. Wesley translated and incorporated Zinzendorf's hymn "Christi Blut und Gerechtigkeit" in his collection of hymns, although some verses almost appear as an anti-Wesleyan battle song! See Hymn 183 (WJW 7:309-11).

249. Sermon 45, II, 3-4; WJW 2:191-93.

250. See H. E. Raser, "Holiness Movement," *Dictionary of Christianity in America* 543-47; also, Melvin Dieter, *The Holiness Revival of the Nineteenth Century* (Metuchen, N.J.: Scarecrow, 1980).

251. See Donald L. Alexander, *Christian Spirituality* (Downers Grove: InterVarsity, 1988); G. C. Berkouwer, *Faith and Sanctification* (Grand Rapids: Eerdmans, 1952); W. Klaiber, *Wo Leben wieder Leben ist*, 47ff.; *Unterwegs mit Christus*, 58f.; J. Moltmann, *The Spirit of Life*, 144ff.

252. In this connection, we note the necessity emphasized by E. Jüngel of distinguishing between faith and love (see E. Jüngel, *Gott als Geheimnis der Welt*, 453-69); this distinction is also perceived by Wesley in his making faith prior to love, on the side of the human response to the love of God. See also A. Outler, "Faith at Work," in *John Wesley*, 211-50.

253. See the strict rejection of a "hermit Christianity" in the citation found in note 244 above.

254. On this often misused word of Augustine, see A. Schindler, "Augustine/Augustinianism," I, TRE, 4, 668. On the New Testament basis for the development of the love commandment in concrete individual commandments, see C. H. Dodd, "The Law of Christ," in *Gospel and Law: The Relation of Faith and Ethics in Early Christianity* (New York: Columbia, 1960), 64-83; and W. Schrage, *Ethik des Neuen Testaments* II (passim). See also below pp. 313-19.

255. See James W. Fowler, *Stages of Faith in Religious Development* (New York: Crossroads, 1991); and J. Fowler, "John Wesley's Development in Faith," in *The Future of the Methodist Theological Traditions,* ed. M. D. Meeks (1985), 172-92.

256. It belongs to the most important results of the newer exegesis, that the human body is seen as the field for sanctification and by this it is incorporated into the service for God's righteousness. A basic study of this theme is E. Käsemann, *Gottesdienst im Alltag der Welt, Zu Röm. 12, Exegetische Versuche* II, 198-204; for a related discussion, see Wayne Meeks, "The Christian Proteus," in *The Writings of St. Paul,* ed. W. A. Meeks, 435-44.

257. See above, note 243.

258. See BSLK 24; J. Hainz, "Koinonia," Biblische Untersuchungen 16 (1982), 207ff.; On Wesley, see Williams, *John Wesley's Theology Today*, 128.

259. On the inner conflict which resulted for Wesley, see Williams, *John Wesley's Theology Today,* 232, note 21.

260. BSLK, 671f. (tr. trans.).

261. See Wesley, Sermon 7, I, 12, WJW 1:224; Sermon 26, II, 8-9, WJW 1:581-84.

262. Large Minutes, Q.3, Works 3rd ed., 8:299.

263. According to Williams, *John Wesley's Theology Today,* 166 (and see above, Section 2.3.3.).

264. Ibid., 157ff.

265. See *Sanctification and Liberation,* ed. Th. Runyon (1981); Th. Kemper, "Methodistisches Erbe und Theologie der Befreiung," *EmK heute* 66 (1989); Th. W. Jennings Jr., *Good News to the Poor: John Wesley's Evangelical Economics* (Nashville: Kingswood, 1990); J. Moltmann, *The Spirit of Life,* 144ff.

266. See Sermon 40, "Christian Perfection," WJW 2:97-124; Sermon 76, "On Perfection," WJW 3:70-87; "A Plain Account of Christian Perfection," (Works, 3rd ed., 11:366-446); also, Williams, *John Wesley's Theology Today,* 147-67; Lindstrom, *Wesley and Sanctification,* 85ff.; R. N. Flew, *The Idea of Perfection in Christian Theology* (1934); W. E. Sangster, *The Path to Perfection: An Examination and Restatement of John Wesley's Doctrine of Christian Perfection* (1943) (1984); M. B. Wynkoop, *A Theology of Love: The Dynamic of Wesleyanism* (1972). On the history of the doctrine, see J. L. Peters, *Christian Perfection and American Methodism* (1956; 2nd ed., 1985).

267. Williams, *John Wesley's Theology Today,* 147f.

268. "A Plain Account of Christian Perfection" (Works, 3rd ed., 11:374).

269. Ibid., 384.

270. A conspicuous example is seen in Sermon 40, "Christian Perfection," WJW 2:97-124, in which the text from Phil. 3:12 is not mentioned, but the actual text used is 1 John 3:9.

271. Sermon 83, 9-10; WJW 3:174-76.

272. So M. B. Wynkoop, *A Theology of Love,* 301. Wynkoop belongs to the Church of the Nazarene, which has maintained the doctrine of Christian perfection to the present day.

273. For the exegetical background, see E. Kutsch, "Das *posse non peccare* und verwandte Formulierungen als Aussagen biblischer Theologie," ZThK 84 (1987), 267-78, which maintains that the position of *non posse non peccare* fails to provide for the possibility of the redemption of humanity: "yet for the one who is reconciled by faith in God and who anticipates the endtime salvation, the possibility is given that he *does not* sin, and therefore *posse non peccare*" (277). For a related discussion, see N. P. Williams, *The Ideas of the Fall and of Original Sin* (London, 1927); also, E. Portalie, *A Guide to the Thought of St. Augustine* (Chicago, 1960).

274. It is also not exegetically tenable, at least not in the form *"totus-totus"* (wholly sinner and wholly righteous), especially if—as is generally recognized today—Romans 7:7f. is not applied to Christians. W. Joest, Paulus und das lutherische Simul Iustus et Peccator, KuD 1, 1955, 269-320. See on this Paul Althaus, "Paulus und Luther über den Menschen," SLA 14, 3rd ed. (1958); Joest, contrary to Paul, voted for Luther, because he finds in this a clearer understanding of sin that is more suitable for today's understanding of sin. There is also an implicit problem being addressed here that impinges upon the exposition of Wesley, but no effort has here been made to translate the New Testament "optimism of grace" into contemporary thinking.

275. This aspect is also found in Luther, for example, in WA 39, I, 542, 5ff. (see Joest, *Gesetz und Freiheit*, 3rd ed. [1961], 65-70) and still more plainly in the lecture on 1 John 3:9: "Non stant simul peccare et nasci ex deo" WA 20, 707.

276. Sermon 14, III, 4, WJW 1:352; also Sermon 21, II, 3-5, WJW 1:483-86; Sermon 25, IV, 13, WJW 1:570-71; Sermon 74, WJW 3:45-57; Sermon 21, WJW 1:469-87.

277. "Plain Account of Christian Perfection," 25, Works, 3rd. ed. 11:417; also see Sermon 76, I, 3; WJW 3:73-74.

278. On this, see Eibach, *Seelische Krankheit*, 70; also the perceptive discussion in P. Tournier, "This Contradictory Being," in *The Meaning of Persons* (London: SCM, 1965), 46-63.

279. See Donald W. Dayton, *Discovering an Evangelical Heritage* (New York: Harper and Row, 1976); the holiness movement also was instrumental in promoting women's causes and in addressing poverty—see Dayton, 85-120; and Timothy Smith, *Revivalism and Social Reform* (Baltimore: John Hopkins University Press, 1980). For its social impact in England, see the chronicles of the Salvation Army, that was launched by the Booths under the influence of American holiness advocates (especially Phoebe Palmer, who has been called the most influential woman theologian of Protestantism of her time); see *Phoebe Palmer*, ed. Thomas Oden (New York: Paulist, 1988), 14.

280. See Carl Bangs, "The Idea of Perfection in a Future Christian Theology," in *Wesleyan Theology Today: A Bicentennial Theological Consultation*, ed. T. Runyon (Nashville: Kingswood, 1985), 88-94, 91.

281. *Poetical Works of John and Charles Wesley*, ed. G. Osborn (London: Wesleyan-Methodist Conference Office, 1868–1872), 9:353; see F. Hildebrandt, *Christianity According to the Wesleys* (1956), 62f.

282. On this, see Charles Wesley, *Poetical Works*, 13:222: "Happy the man, who poor and low / Less goodness in himself conceives / Than Christ doth of His servant know; / Who saved from self-reflection lives, / Unconscious of the grace bestow'd / Simply resign'd, and lost in God. // Himself he cannot perfect call, / Or to the meanest saint prefer, / Meanest himself, and least of all: / And when the glorious character / His spotless soul with Christ receives, / His state—to that great day he leaves."

283. From this perspective, the United Methodist Central Conference for Middle and Southern Europe has reformulated the ordinational questions for ministerial candidates, "Do you expect to be made perfect in this life?" (*Book of Discipline*, 425, 3; see Large Minutes, Q.51, *Works*, 3rd ed., 8:325-26) as follows: "Do you expect that perfect love will ever more define your being and living?" (*Kirchenordnung der EmK, Zentralkonferenz für Mittel-und Südeuropa* [Zürich, 1974], 332, 3). The United Methodist Church in Germany no longer asks these historical questions, although they are retained within the Church in the United States.

284. Hymn 136, 11-12 (WJW 7:252; UMH 387).

285. G. Ebeling, *Dogmatik*, 3:47.

286. Ibid., 49.

287. Hymn 207, 9; see also Hymn 381, 4: "Now let me gain perfection's height; / Now let me into nothing fall, / As less than nothing in thy sight, / And feel that Christ is all in all!"

4. Christian Existence in Its Wholeness, or the Reality of Love

1. Sermon 112, "On Laying the Foundation of the New Chapel," WJW 3:577-92. On the Meaning of the City Road Chapel, see John Telford, *Wesley's Chapel and Wesley's House* (1926).

2. "An Earnest Appeal to Men of Reason and Religion" (1743), WJW 11:45-94.

3. Sermon 112, II, 1, WJW 3:585, and "An Earnest Appeal," 2-3, WJW 11:45-46.

4. A clear approval of Galatians 5:22; see also section 4.2.1.2.

5. Sermon 112, II, 1; WJW 3:585, quoting "An Earnest Appeal" (cf. WJW 11:46).

6. Journal (ed. Curnock), 8:143 (from "Elizabeth Ritchie's Account of Wesley's Last Days," Journal, 131-44).

7. Genesis 3:8-10; Isaiah 6:1-7, Luke 5:8.

8. Psalm 97:8; John 20:20.

9. 1 Samuel 3:1-21; Isaiah 6:8-13; Matthew 28:1-10; John 20:11-18.

10. Matthew 27:54; Mark 15:39.

11. This already applies to Jahweh's holy zeal, as it is described in the Old Testament (Exodus

20:5; 34:14; Deuteronomy 6:14); in union with Jahweh's covenant ratification with his people, the will of salvation that stands behind the prohibition of worshiping strange gods is understandable: it is finally the love which wants to keep his people far from the worship of idols (see Hosea 11:1-11). Also, Jesus' zeal for the Temple (John 2:13-17) could not be understood apart from care for the preservation of the true worship of God and for the salvation of pilgrims who enter it for worship.

12. Ezekiel 33:11; Matthew 9:13; Romans 11:32. On the problem of the relationship of the judgment/wrath of God and God's love, see "Wrath," by H. Kleinknecht, J. Fichtner, and G. Stählin, reprinted from Kittel's *Theologisches Wörterbuch* (London: Adam & Charles Blac, 1964); and K. Stock, "Gott der Richter, Der Gerichtsgedanke als Horizont der Rechtfertigungslehre." EvTh 40 (1980), 240-257; W. Härle, "Die Rede von der Liebe und vom Zorn Gottes," ZThK (Beiheft, 1990), 50-69.

13. "It was not because you were more numerous than any other people that the LORD set his heart on you and chose you—for you were the fewest of all peoples. It was because the LORD loved you and kept the oath that he swore to your ancestors. . . ." (Deuteronomy 7:7-8).

14. The 28th Heidelberg Thesis of 1518: "Amor Dei non invenit sed creat suum diligibile, Amor hominis fit a suo diligibili" (WA I, 354; BoA, 379; as cited in "Theses for the Heidelberg Disputation" in *Martin Luther: Selections from His Writings,* ed. John Dillenberger [Garden City, N.Y.: Doubleday, 1961], 503).

15. On this, see the discussion above, section 2.1.2.

16. On this see section 1.1.4 above, and J. Moltmann, *The Crucified God,* 5th ed. (New York: Harper & Row, 1987); E. Schlink, *Ökumenische Dogmatik,* 2nd ed. (1985); 775-77, 790; and Andrew Pere, "The Holy Trinity," in *The Heidelberg Catechism with Commentary* (Philadelphia: United Church Press, 1963), 49-51.

17. H. Balz, *"Der erste Johannesbrief* (NTD 10)" (1986), 195 (tr. trans.).

18. Sermon 10 (1746); WJW 1:267-84.

19. At this point, Wesley warned of the danger of a false self-assurance, which can easily fall into doubt; therefore it matters to observe the witness of the Spirit and the test of conscience in self-critical sobriety, and to rejoice in the ways in which the Spirit of God actually produces fruit in one's life. The fact that Wesley submitted himself to self-examination, based upon this challenge, led him to ground that was not without its dangers; however, he arrived at the point of recognizing the actual which also means the recognizable operation of the Spirit of God.

20. See Sermon 7, "The Way into the Kingdom of God," II, 9-12; WJW 1:230-31.

21. S. Kierkegaard, *Der Liebe Tun,* ed. by E. Hirsch and H. Gerdes, 1:241 (tr. trans.); see a parallel essay in English translation, "Love Conquers All," in *Kierkegaard: Edifying Discourses,* ed. P. Holmer (New York: Harper, 1958), 177-208.

22. See James 2:14-17. In Luther's Preface to the Epistle to the Romans, in which he describes saving faith, he declared, "O, it is a living, active, busy, powerful thing about faith, so that it is impossible that it should not work that which is good unceasingly." The Holy Spirit works so that "a person is willing and ready to do good to every person without coercion, to suffer all things, and to love and to praise God, who has granted to him such grace. . . ." (Martin Luther's Prefaces to the Bible, ed. H. Bornkamm [1967], 148; tr. trans.).

23. Sermon 39, "Catholic Spirit," I, 14, WJW 2:88; Sermon 2, "The Almost Christian," II, 6, WJW 1:139.

24. Sermon 8, "The First Fruits of the Spirit," III, 3, WJW 1:244-45, and Sermon 30, "Upon Our Lord's Sermon on the Mount X," 27, WJW 1:662-63.

25. The fact that in this relationship there is no explicit discussion of love for God is related to the methodological considerations that chapter 4 delineates. The love of believers for God is the theme of section 3.2.3.

26. The epistemological and the ontological relationship of our discussion of God's love and of human love is thereby characterized by two counter movements: If we say that God is love, we thus make use of our experience of love and transfer it to God, whereby it is clear to us that this transfer transforms and purifies the presentation of love. Our mode of understanding thus proceeds from the human to the divine love. Conversely, the movement from which every human love arises proceeds from the gift of divine love, and it retains its source in this. At the beginning, this ontological relationship makes meaningful and possible the use of the same concept for both of these different and yet inseparable realities.

27. See section 1.1.4, "The Triune God and the Missionary Dimension of Revelation."

28. See M. Marquardt, *John Wesley's Social Ethics: Praxis and Principles,* 103-118, "Standards for Social Ethics."

29. See Paul's arguments concerning the role of Jewish influences within the early Christian community.

30. "Dilige, et quod vis fac!" (In primum epistulam Johannis, *MPL,* 35, 2533).

31. J. Fletcher, *Situation Ethics* (Philadelphia: Westminster, 1966); J. A. T. Robinson, *Christian Morals Today* (Philadelphia: Westminster, 1964).

32. R. Ginters, *Typen ethischer Argumentation. Zur Begründung sittlicher Normen* (1976), 63 (tr. trans.).

33. Fletcher, *Situation Ethics,* 62. For Fletcher, love exists substantively only in God, and among humans it is a predicate, or formal principle. Only with God is it an attribute, for God is love, but mortal humans only do love, that is, they attempt to be like God in obedience to the divine commandment of love.

34. As an example of this, perhaps the problem of indirect euthanasia can be mentioned, by which the mitigation of pain and the protection of life stand in competition with one another.

35. See *The Book of Discipline of the United Methodist Church* (Nashville: United Methodist Publishing House, 1996), Part III, "Social Principles," ¶¶ 64-70. See also "Denominations, Gender, and Sexuality," by Thomas Edward Frank, in his *Polity, Practice and Mission of the United Methodist Church* (Nashville: Abingdon, 1997), 87-91.

36. In Sermon 34, Wesley makes clear that even when the law functions as a "severe schoolmaster," it is nevertheless true that "love is the spring of it all" (34, IV, 2; WJW 2:16).

37. He perceived this danger above all in the example of some Calvinistic Methodists and in the Moravian preachers, and he reproached them with the term "antinomianism." The fact that John Wesley approached the border of a theology of works righteousness is indicated by the record of the conference protocol from 1770 and 1772; for this, see C. W. Williams, *John Wesley's Theology Today,* 61-72; for a detailed treatment, see Alan Coppedge, *John Wesley in Theological Debate* (1987), Part III: The Minute Controversy, 1770–1778 (191-264).

38. This is how Bonhoeffer referred to an inconsequential proclamation of the gospel: D. Bonhoeffer, *The Cost of Discipleship,* 2nd ed. (London: SCM, 1959), chapter 1, "Costly Grace."

39. In Reformation theology, the law finds its meaning in the fact that it leads persons to their sins *(usus elenchticus)* and that it directs them to corporate life in the greater fellowship *(polis) (the usus politicus).* See G. W. Forell, "law and gospel," in *The Protestant Faith* (Englewood Cliffs: Prentice Hall, 1960), 90-101; also, G. Ebeling, *Dogmatik,* 3:251-95. A distinct doctrine of *usus politicus legis* does not appear to have been developed by Wesley. The love commandment and reasonable reflection upon it are for him the criteria for the formation of a modern society. See above, section 2.2.2.3: "The Covenant of Law and the Covenant of Grace."

40. Sermon 34, IV, 4, WJW 2:17.

41. See also his treatment of that which is perfect (1 Corinthians 13:10f.) in Sermon 34, II, 5; WJW 2:10.

42. For example, see the conflict of Jesus with those who were pious according to the law, with regard to the Sabbath or the adherence to the commands for purification.

43. Sermon 36, II, 1, "The Law Established through Faith"; WJW 2:38. A developed discussion of the meaning of love as the basic norm in the New Testament is found in W. Schrage, *Ethik des Neuen Testaments,* 5th ed. (1989), 73-90, 218-24, 301-24; for a comparable discussion, see V. P. Furnish, *The Love Commandment in the New Testament* (Nashville: Abingdon, 1972).

44. See below, section 4.2.1: The Community as the Body of Christ.

45. Mark 1:15 and par.; see also Matthew 28:16ff.; Romans 11:11-18; Acts 1:6-8; 15:6-12; 1 Peter 2:9f., etc.

46. Acts 2:22-36; Philippians 2:9-11; Ephesians 1:18-23; 2:14-22.

47. On the problem of the visibility and the hiddenness of the church, see W. Härle, "Kirche," VII. Dogmatisch, TRE 18, 286-89; also, the commentary on Questions 54 and 55 of the Heidelberg Catechism by Andrew Pere, in *The Heidelberg Catechism with Commentary,* 97-100.

48. See below Section 4.2.1.3.

49. See Wesley's "Character of a Methodist" (WJW 9:31-46), in which he regards himself and his followers as not yet being complete Christians, in light of the Pauline motto, "Not that I have already obtained this or have already reached the goal" (Philippians 3:12). Wesley writes this to counteract any misunderstandings of the Methodist movement.

50. "An Invitation for Christians in the Methodist Tradition to Claim and Reaffirm the Essential Apostolic and Universal Teachings of the Historic Christian Faith," accepted by the Fifteenth Methodist World Conference in 1986 in Nairobi, *Proceedings,* 303, 9f.

51. In its etymology, the term is derived from *ek-kaleo* = to be called out, and this became the concept that seemed best to represent the "totality of those who have been called out." However, in its New Testament usage, this derivation has receded wholly into the background. In its profane meaning, it signifies the gathering of those free persons who have been selected (see also Acts 19:32), and it is rendered in most New Testament citations within the context of "the gathering of a community" or "congregation" (J. Roloff, "ekklesia," EWNT 1, 999f.).

52. Fellowship, participation (Latin: *communio)*, is used within the New Testament above all by Paul and those authors influenced by him. See J. Hainz, *Koinonia,* "Kirche" *als Gemeinschaft bei Paulus* (1982).

53. Note the concept "holy communion," used for participation in the Lord's Supper or for the Lord's Supper as a whole.

54. Greek, *"laos tou theou,"* which also leads to the concept of "laity," which originally designated all of the people of God, but which later came to be distinguished from the *"kleros,"* or those who carried the office of representative ministry.

55. Israel is also regarded in the New Testament as the chosen people of God (see Romans 11:1-4; 15:7-10; Matthew 2:6; Luke 2:32; Acts 13:17, etc). On the other side, God elects in Christ a new people out of all peoples; their election is no longer traced from the lineage of Abraham, nor by other external marks, but through the salvation that is received by faith (Romans 9:24-26; 2 Corinthians 6:16; 1 Peter 2:9-10). On this theme, see J. Roloff, "Die Bedeutung des Gottesvolk-Gedankens für die neutestamentliche Ekklesiologie," Glaube und Lernen, 2 (1987), 33-46; cf. G. D. Mendenhall, "Covenant," in *The Interpreter's Dictionary of the Bible,* 1:713-23.

56. Romans 12:4-8; 1 Corinthians 10:17; 12:12-30; Ephesians 2:14-18; 3:5-6; 4:4, 11-16; Colossians 3:15. On this theme see John A. T. Robinson, *The Body: A Study in Pauline Theology* (London: SCM, 1963); and the still important study by E. Käsemann, *Leib und Leib Christi* (1933) (Beiträge zur historischen Theologie 9).

57. "Lastly: the true members of the church of Christ 'endeavor,' with all possible diligence, with all care and pains, with unwearied patience (and all will be little enough), 'to keep the unity of the Spirit in the bond of peace'; to preserve inviolate the same spirit of lowliness and meekness, of long-suffering, mutual forebearance and love; and all these cemented and knit together by that sacred tie, the peace of God filling the heart. Thus only can we be and continue living members of that church which is the body of Christ."—(Wesley, Sermon 74, "Of the Church," 27, WJW 3:55).

58. L. Schieck in an unpublished manuscript, "New Testament Aspects on the Theme of Love," 1992 (tr. trans.).

59. Sermon 107, "On God's Vineyard": God "hath made all nations of men to dwell on all the face of the earth, that they might seek the Lord, if haply they may feel after him, and find him." WJW 3:503.

60. Luke 15:1-7; John 10:1-29; 1 Peter 2:25.

61. *The Book of Discipline* (UMC, 1996), ¶ 60, p. 44.

62. See also section 3.1.1, "The Abiding Love of God—Prevenient Grace."

63. Both of the following sections will speak in depth about this.

64. If she or he was baptized in The United Methodist Church.

65. Upon request, if the baptism was carried out in another church.

66. "I look upon all the world as my parish" (WJW 25:616; from a letter of Wesley's, whose recipient is no longer known; it was apparently written on March 28, 1739; for the problem of the dating and the addressee, see WJW 25:614, n. 1).

67. On this see, "Berufen—Beschenkt—Beauftragt," *EmK heute,* 68, 1991, 22f. For a discussion of apostolic precedents, see Gregory Dix, *The Shape of the Liturgy* (London: Adam and Clarke, 1978), see esp. the role of the "synaxis," or the "liturgy of the Spirit," in the ordering of the apostolic community of faith (36-47).

68. See Frederick A. Norwood, *The Story of American Methodism* (Nashville: Abingdon, 1973), 257.

69. For a discussion of the African Methodist Episcopal (AME), and AME Zion, and the CME (Christian Methodist Episcopal) Churches in their historical development, see Norwood, *Story of*

American Methodism, Ch. 24; merger discussions are currently under way among these denominations, also including The United Methodist Church.

70. K. H. Voigt, "Verbindlicher Glaube—Verbindliche Gemeinde—Verbindliche Lehre. Kennzeichen der Methodisten in Europa," *EmK heute,* 41 (1984), 11 (tr. trans.).

71. For example, see Romans 6:11; 8:1; 12:5; 16:3; 1 Corinthians 1:30; 4:10; 15:18, 22; 2 Corinthians 5:17; Galatians 3:28; Philippians 1:1; Colossians 1:27; 1 Thessalonians 2:14; also Romans 8:10; 2 Corinthians 13:5; Galatians 2:20; 4:19; Ephesians 3:17.

72. G. Bornkamm, *Paulus,* 6th ed. (1987), 163: "Thus, membership in the church mentioned is not infrequently mentioned." See also Hans Freiherr von Soden, "Sacrament and Ethics in Paul," in *The Writings of St. Paul,* ed. W. A. Meeks, 257-67.

73. G. Ebeling, "Das Sein in Christus als Sein im Geist," *Dogmatik,* 3:62-75; see also Adolf Deissmann, "The Christ Mystic," in Meeks, *The Writings of St. Paul,* 395-408.

74. E. Käsemann, *Paulinische Perspektiven,* 2nd ed. (1972), 207f. (tr. trans.).

75. Williams, *John Wesley's Theology Today,* 194. The related theme of sanctification has been given explicit treatment in Section 3.2.3. A comparable discussion is found in the commentary on Part III of the Heidelberg Catechism (under the heading of the "Life of Gratitude"), in *The Heidelberg Catechism with Commentary,* 147-222.

76. J. Wesley, Sermon 74, "Of the Church," 27, WJW 3:55.

77. *The Book of Discipline* (UMC, 1996), ¶¶ 221 and 229.

78. In the United Methodist tradition, exclusion from the Lord's Supper is not now among the provisions for church discipline, although it was practiced by Philip William Otterbein in the German Reformed congregations which he served in Lancaster, Pa., and Baltimore, Md., in accordance with his adherence to the provisions of the Heidelberg Catechism. See J. S. O'Malley, *Pilgrimage of Faith: The Legacy of the Otterbeins* (Metuchen, N.J.; Scarecrow, 1973), Part III.

79. Mark 7:21; Matthew 5:8; 12:34f., and others.

80. This can best be seen in the number of statements from Wesley that recognize the poor and slaves, as in his "Thoughts upon Slavery," *Works* 3rd ed., 11:59-79.

81. On this, see Section 3.2, "The Renewal of Life from God."

82. Concerning the relationship of God's love to the formation and structuring of human relationships, see Bruce C. Birch, *To Love as We Are Loved: The Bible and Relationships* (1992).

83. E. Wölfel, *Welt als Schöpfung,* 46 (tr. trans.).

84. W. Klaiber, "Die eine Taufe," *EmK heute* 53 (1987), 17. See *The Book of Discipline* (UMC, 1996), ¶ 62, Article VI (Confession of Faith): "We believe Baptism signifies entrance into the household of faith, and is a symbol of repentance and inner cleansing from sin, a representation of the new birth in Christ Jesus and a mark of Christian discipleship."

85. "Treatise on Baptism," 1756; this tract is largely an abstract from the work of his father (*Works,* 3rd ed., 10:188-201).

86. The renewal of the covenant with God is referred to in the introduction to this service as "founded exclusively upon God's covenant with us. Therefore, in this ceremony we gratefully remember that we were baptized into this covenant with Christ and we through this we acknowledge our acceptance into church membership." See Wesley's "An Order of Worship for Such as Would Enter into or Renew Their Covenant with God," in the *Book of Worship* (Nashville: Methodist Publishing House, 1965), 382-88.

87. See Section 2.2.2.4.

88. See the comment of the United Methodist Church in Europe (EmK) on the convergence of the explanations of the Commission on Faith and the Church Order concerning "Taufe, Eucharistie und Amt" ("Baptism, Eucharist, and Ministry"), *EmK heute,* 48 (1986), 8.

89. This second baptismal action is unsatisfactory because it obscures the objective character of baptism based upon the death of Christ, that took place once for all (Romans 6:8-11; Hebrews 10:10).

90. *The United Methodist Book of Worship* (Nashville: Abingdon, 1992), "Baptismal Covenant III: Reaffirmation of Faith," 106-8.

91. W. Klaiber, "Die eine Taufe," 7. See also W. Willimon, *Remembering Who You Are* (Nashville: Upper Room, 1980).

92. F. Herzog, *God-Walk* (1988), 148. The author also points to the inevitable danger of the baptism of children.

93. *Gesprächsgrundlage für Taufverständnis und Taufpraxis,* 1991, 12. See Willimon,

Remembering Who You Are, and G. W. Bromiley, *Children of Promise: The Case for Baptizing Infants* (Grand Rapids: Eerdmans, 1979).

94. "We believe children are under the atonement of Christ and as heirs of the Kingdom of God are acceptable subjects for Christian Baptism. Children of believing parents through Baptism become the special responsibility of the Church. They should be nurtured and led to personal acceptance of Christ, and by profession of faith confirm their Baptism."—*The Book of Discipline* (UMC, 1996), The Confession of Faith, Article VI, ¶ 62.

95. G. Wainwright, "Proceedings of the 15th World Methodist Conference, Nairobi," 1986, 235.

96. Note also, "Whatever further steps in faith and life the baptized may take, baptism is not administered to any person more than once, for while our baptismal vows are less than reliable, God's promise to us in the sacrament is steadfast. Once baptized, we have been initiated into Christ's body the Church and are members of Christ's family. . . . After confirmation, or after baptism when candidates take the vows for themselves, Christians are encouraged to reaffirm the Baptismal Covenant at significant moments. . . . Such a reaffirmation is not, however, to be understood as baptism." "Since the love of God made known in the gospel through Jesus Christ is valid for all persons, the church baptizes. It baptizes children and adults. Baptism is unrepeatable."—*The United Methodist Book of Worship* (1992), 83-84. At the 1996 United Methodist General Conference, the category of "Preparatory Members" (the role of the baptized) was eliminated, in preference for maintaining that baptized person are already members of the church, although not yet professing members. This interpretation has recently been called into question and awaits further clarification.

97. *The United Methodist Book of Worship* (1992), 83. This statement is to be held in balance with the affirmation of the Confession, as cited in note 94 above.

98. "When persons unite with a local United Methodist church, they . . . make known their desire to live their daily lives as disciples of Jesus Christ."—*The Book of Discipline* (UMC, 1996), ¶ 217.

99. At their acceptance before the congregation, in the context of their corporate confession of the Apostles' Creed, candidates for church membership who have just professed their faith through baptism or confirmation (which includes their affirmation of the Apostles' Creed), as well as those who are transferring their membership into the United Methodist Church, are addressed as follows: "Will you be loyal to The United Methodist Church, and . . . participate in its ministries by your prayers, your presence, your gifts, and your service?" The baptismal covenant that precedes this affirmation also includes pledges to renounce evil, the confession of Christ, and the profession of the Christian faith as contained in the Scriptures of the Old and New Testament; these affirmations are not repeated by those entering by transfer of membership.—*The United Methodist Church Book of Worship* (1992), 86-93.

100. *The United Methodist Book of Worship* (1992), 94; and *Agende* (1991), 77.

101. *Agende* (1991), 60.

102. It is instructive to observe that European United Methodists make more clear the distinction that whoever has completed confirmation study is not thereby also received into the church. In the Central Conference of Northern Europe, young persons are received into church membership at the same time that they are recognized for their completion of confirmation studies—which is also the typical practice in the United Methodist Church of North America—if they have opted for this and if they have met the appropriate requirements (baptism and personal confession of faith); in this context, the church is also authorized to speak of "confirmation" as the fulfillment of the baptismal covenant. In the remaining European Central Conferences, it is not customary for there to be a connection between the completion of church instruction and acceptance into church membership.

103. *Agende* (1991), 65: "You thus assume the task of instructing *NN* through word and example by faith in Jesus Christ, to pray for her or him and to lead her or him into the way of faith. If you promise to do this, so far as it is in your power, to do so, answer 'yes, with God's help.' " (tr. trans.).

104. "Confirmation," in the tradition of the Lutheran Churches of Europe, is inseparably connected with acceptance into church membership, where personal faith is attested by the taking of a solemn vow. The United Methodist Church in Europe is of the conviction that this confession is not to be fixed at a particular point in time and thus cannot be structured according to an age group (*Agende* [1991], 177)—an understanding that surely heightens the meaning of church membership, though also serving to inhibit the rapid numerical expansion of congregations! (Note: European UM congregations are typically smaller than those in the United States, although their percentage of active members is undoubtedly higher. Would American United Methodists not be well advised to heed the practice of their European colleagues? *Translator's question.*)

105. *The Book of Discipline* (UMC, 1996), ¶ 62, Article XVII (Methodist Articles of Religion).

106. See G. Wainwright, *Doxology* (1980), and G. C. Felton, *This Gift of Water: The Practice and Theology of Baptism Among Methodists in America* (Nashville: Abingdon, 1992), as examples of only two of the numerous contemporary positions to be cited. While Wainwright advocates a postponement of baptism (141), we find in his colleague Felton a position that decisively advocates the baptism of children, which is explicated from a Wesleyan point of view. Her view represents a process understanding of baptism and to that extent, she moderates Wesley's position on baptismal regeneration. The most comprehensive and plainest understanding of baptism and the Lord's Supper in Wesley's theology and in the Wesleyan tradition is given by R. L. Staples, *Outward Sign and Inward Grace: The Place of Sacraments in Wesleyan Spirituality* (1991); always worthy of reading is O. E. Borgen, *John Wesley on the Sacraments* (1973).

107. G. C. Felton, *This Gift of Water*, 173.

108. Sermon 45, "The New Birth," IV, 1; WJW 2:196-97.

109. He also held firmly to this position in his sermon on the New Birth (Sermon 45, IV; WJW 2:196-201), but he emphasized the character of baptism as an outward sign. The similarity of the concept of "baptismal regeneration" cannot be allowed to lead to the misunderstanding that Wesley had understood baptism in the sense of an *opus operatum*. On this theme, see section 3.2.2.3.

110. The clearest doctrinal affirmation of this perspective in the American United Methodist *Book of Discipline* is found in Article VI of the Confession of Faith (¶ 62); also, K. Steckel, "Zum Taufverständnis der EmK," *EmK heute*, 17 (1975), 16f.

111. See "The Ministry of all Christians," in *The Book of Discipline* (UMC, 1996), ¶¶ 101-20; and also the text produced by the theological commission and published by the European Council of the United Methodist Church (EmK), entitled "Dienstauftrag der Kirche. Amt. Allgemeines Priestertum." ("The Task of Ministry of the Church.—Office.—The General Priesthood"), BGEmK 9 (1981).

112. For a further discussion of the understanding of the office of ministry within the United Methodist Church in Europe, see the previously cited work, "Dienstauftrag, etc.," above, all 27-40. In ministry in the church within North America is treated in R. F. Kohler, et al., *The Christian as Minister* (General Board of Higher Education and Ministry, 1997).

113. Pastors are church members who have received ordination as elders and have been admitted into the membership of an annual conference (¶¶ 301-27 of *Book of Discipline*, UMC, 1996). They know that they have been called by the Lord to this ministry and are authorized by the church. District superintendents and superintendents are pastors who are selected by the bishop to a position of leadership in a district within an annual conference, for a limited period of time. For the office of bishop, a Jurisdictional or Central Conference elects persons from among the elders, who are to have oversight of the annual conferences that fall within their episcopal areas. In the United States, the temporary order of deacon and the lay order of diaconal minister has been superseded in 1996 by the permanent office of deacon, so that there are now two options for full-time ordained or representative ministry: deacon and elder. Whereas elders are ordained to service, word, sacrament, and order, deacons are ordained to Word and Service (¶¶ 319-20, *Book of Discipline*, UMC, 1996).

114. J. Wesley, Sermon 107, "On God's Vineyard" II, 5; WJW 3:510.

115. W. Klaiber, *Rechtfertigung und Gemeinde*, 266.

116. The fact that there are contrary observations should not be used as a counter argument, but as an incentive to correction.

117. See *The Book of Discipline* (UMC, 1996), ¶¶ 217-21, on the opportunities and responsibilities of local church membership. Also note the reflections on this theme that are found in H. Schäfer, "Der Gottesdienst in der EmK. Unmaßgebliche Überlegungen eines Teilhabers," *EmK heute* 58 (1988). According to his view, the congregations of a free church like the United Methodist Church (churches separated from the state in Europe are called free churches) are to be challenged to shape their worship services together.

118. See W. Willimon and R. Wilson, *Rekindling the Flame* (Nashville: Abingdon, 1988).

119. Whoever experiences Methodist services of worship in other lands as a rule has come to know the meaning of the phrase "singing Methodists"; even the "cool British" radiate a new warmth when they are singing the hymns of Charles Wesley (or others)!

120. J. Wesley's sermon on the "means of grace" is very worthy of reading (Sermon 16, V; WJW 1:393-97), where he highlights the fact that the misuse of the means of grace through a formal Christianity is in no way to lessen or suspend its importance and operation among earnest Christians.

121. Rules of the Band Societies, III (On the use of the means of grace; WJW 9:79). For worship,

see also Section 4.2.2.1 above; and for baptism, which does not appear as one of the means of grace in Wesley, see Section 4.2.1.3.

122. "I also advise the elders to administer the Lord's Supper on every Lord's Day," wrote Wesley in 1784 to his "brothers in America" (*Letters,* ed. Telford, 7:239).

123. See also "Vom Dialog zur Kanzel-und Abendmahlsgemeinschaft," 1987 ("From Dialog to Fellowship of the Pulpit and the Lord's Supper"), 17. In view of the many aspects of the understanding of the Lord's Supper and the numerous, intensive discussions in and between the churches we sense the difficulty of responding to the pressure to offer a concise explanation of these issues; here only the most important aspects of the United Methodist understanding of sacramental theology will be set forth.

124. A. Niebergall, "Abendmahlsfeier," III, TRE, 1, 302, 35f.

125. In the former EUB Church in Europe ("Die Evangelische Gemeinschaft") it was necessary for the pastor to give a personal notification for nonmembers prior to the service of the Lord's Supper, so that they might be suitably prepared for this service. This practice may be traced back to the early EUB in America, when P. W. Otterbein required that those coming to the service of the Lord's Supper in his congregation in Lancaster be interviewed by the pastor prior to the service to ascertain their readiness to commune. Also, United Brethren and Evangelical typically concluded their "Große Versammlungen" (big meetings) with "sacramental services," so that the celebration of the Lord's Supper became here the testimony of the newly awakened converts to their faith in Christ's saving work and as thanksgiving to God for that fact. See A. Core, *Philip William Otterbein: Pastor, Ecumenist* (Nashville: Board of Publication, 1972), 109; and J. S. O'Malley, *Pilgrimage of Faith: The Legacy of the Otterbeins* (Metuchen, N.J.: Scarecrow, 1973), 176f. Also, from the beginning of the Methodist Church in Germany there are witnesses to this usage. Above all, the class meetings were viewed as a place for preparation for the service of the Lord's Supper.

126. Note the availability of supplemental worship resources, intended to strengthen Eucharistic observance, such as *Word and Table: A Basic Pattern of Sunday Worship for United Methodists* (Nashville: Abingdon, 1980).

127. With regard to those who might be endangered by drinking alcohol, unfermented grape juice is being offered.

128. Citation from the *Agende* (1991), 90.

129. J. Wesley, Sermon 101, "The Duty of Constant Communion"; WJW 3:427-39, which he advocated by reference to the practice of the first Christians and the command of Christ. "In an age in which the Lord's Supper was typically celebrated four times per year," Wesley communicated on the average every day, and he admonished his followers to "constant communion." See J. Wesley, "The Duty of Constant Communion" (Sermon 101), reprinted in *John Wesley,* ed. A. Outler (New York: Oxford University Press, 1964), 332-44.

130. *Journal* entry for June 28, 1740 (WJW 19:159).

131. Nelson, "Eucharist, Ecumenism, Methodism" in *Wesleyan Theology Today: A Bicentennial Theological Consultation,* ed. T. Runyon (Nashville: Kingswood, 1985), 134; The United Methodist Hymnal today contains more than thirty hymns for use in the Lord's Supper.

132. See Articles XVI-XIX of the Methodist Articles of Religion and Articles V-VI of the EUB Confession of Faith.

133. It is always noteworthy that Wesley reckoned the use of the "means of grace" by those who might be designated as the "formally religious," and as a sign of the "almost Christian" (Sermon 2, "The Almost Christian," I, 13; WJW 1:136-37). Also, in contrast to the "quietism" of the Moravians, he commended their use by those who had not yet given testimony of justifying grace, but who had "a desire to flee from the wrath to come, to be saved from their sins," although they had not yet found the way to Christ ("Nature, Design, and General Rules of the United Societies" of 1739, see below, Appendix, section B).

134. See the discussion in *Word and Table,* 12-23.

135. G. Wainwright, "Methodismus," EKL, 3rd ed., III, 391. See also, S. Harper and R. Wilson, *Faith and Form* (Grand Rapids: Zondervan, 1988).

136. D. Sackmann has maintained this in his treatise entitled "Wesleys Klassen: ein Modell für verbindliche Gemeinschaft vom Evangelium her" (ThFPr 16 [1990], 10-25); according to K. Zehrer, this model is no longer worth reviving (ThFPr 15 [1989], 16-27). The best informed authority on Wesley's classes is D. Watson, *The Early Methodist Class Meeting,* 2nd ed. (1987).

137. General Rules (see below, Appendix, Section B).

138. G. Wainwright, "Methodismus," 391; see also D. Watson, T*he Early Methodist Class Meeting,* chap. 1.

139. E.g., youth bands, congregational choirs, women's circles, etc. (see *Book of Discipline,* UMC, 1996, 255-62).

140. See D. L. Watson, *Accountable Discipleship* (Nashville: Abingdon, 1990).

141. On the charge conference, see the next section, 4.2.2.4.

142. On this, see Section 5.2 ("The Connection of Christians") in "Berufen—Beschenkt—Beauftragt," *EmK heute,* 68 (1991), 31-35, and Theo Schaad, "Wer glaubt, gehört zusammen," *EmK heute,* 73 (1992).

143. See "The Journey of a Connectional People" in *The Book of Discipline* (UMC, 1996), ¶ 109.

144. The term "connection" is a derivative from the Latin "connexio."

145. *Letters* (ed. Telford), 5:143-45; 6:376.

146. Frank Baker in *A History of the Methodist Church in Great Britain,* vol. 1 (1965), 230.

147. Bishop C. E. Sommer in a conference address, Wuppertal, 1971, Manuscript, 9.

148. *The Book of Discipline* (UMC, 1996), ¶ 109.

149. This General Conference of the United Methodist Church is not identical with the worldwide council of Methodist Churches, The World Methodist Council, to which other Methodist bodies who share the Wesleyan tradition also belong.

150. M. Hammer, "Konsensbildung in der Evangelisch-methodistischen Kirche," BGEmK 31 (1988), 9.

151. Thomas E. Frank, *Polity, Practice, and the Mission of the United Methodist Church* (Nashville: Abingdon, 1997), 120. Frank offers a detailed exposition of major changes effected by the *1996 Book of Discipline.*

152. *Grace Upon Grace,* 4; for further elaboration, see *The Book of Discipline* (UMC, 1996), ¶¶ 1301-1326, for an explanation of the Church in mission; see also above 1.1.4.

153. Distorted accounts of Christian missions have appeared in the past, as a project of the "Enlightenment" (Aufklärung), which can only with effort conceal their spite or their perversity, but they neither can nor should hinder us from attempting to examine critically this era of church history. Of course, it must be recognized that not everything which occurred "in the name of Christianity" had something to do with real Christianity. In contrast, this name was often appropriated on the basis of expediency.

154. *Grace Upon Grace,* 7 (par. 2). A similar emphasis is found in the "Requirements for Admission to Full Connection and Ordination as Elder" in *The Book of Discipline* (UMC, 1996), ¶ 326a.6.

155. *Book of Discipline* (UMC, 1996) (Preamble to the Social Principles, p. 85).

156. Klaiber understands mission to be the controlling concept for the overall sending out of the church, through which it truly directs itself to the Lord's charge to go into the world. (See his discussion in *Call and Response,* 29ff.).

157. "Doctrinal Standards and Our Theological Task," *The Book of Discipline* (UMC, 1996), ¶ 60, p. 45; see also the discussion of "Servant Leadership" in ¶ 115.

158. M. Schmidt, *Der junge Wesley als Heidenmissionar und Missionstheologe* (1955), 26f.; also, R. Davies and G. Rupp, *A History of the Methodist Church in Great Britain,* 1:1-34.

159. G. Seebaß, "May Your kingdom come to this world and thereafter into eternity." — "Von Gottes und des Menschen Zukunft in der Kirchengeschichte." *Jahrbuch des Ev. Bundes,* 29 (1986), 32-48 (39).

160. José Míguez Bonino, *Doing Theology in a Revolutionary Situation* (1975); see also T. Kemper, "Methodistisches Erbe und Theologie der Befreiung," *EmK heute* 66 (1989), and E. Castro, *Freed to Be Sent: Mission and Unity in Light of the Kingdom of God* (1986).

161. This statement is more valid for European United Methodists than for the North American church, where this transition occurred at an earlier date. In Europe, the terms used for "church treasurer" were "treasurer of missions" ("Missionskasse"), and the field of labor for a congregation was referred to as a "mission field" ("Missionsfeld").

162. This is taken from the declaration of mission that was adopted by the 1996 General Conference of The United Methodist Church. *The Book of Discipline* (UMC, 1996), ¶ 104.

163. Leslie Davison, *Sender and Sent: A Study in Mission* (London, 1969), 214.

164. "The Nature, Design, and General Rules of the United Societies," WJW 9: 67-75.

165. *Book of Discipline* (UMC, 1996), ¶ 62, p. 71.

166. "Berufen—Beschenkt—Beauftragt," *EmK heute* 68, 36 (tr. trans.); see the related discussion under "Servant Ministry and Servant Leadership" in *The Book of Discipline* (UMC, 1988), ¶ 110.

167. "The Character of a Methodist," 4, WJW 9:35.

168. See K. Stock, who explains this using the example of Albert Schweitzer; in "Pneumatologie und ethische Theorie," *Neuen Zeitschrift für systematische Theologie* 30 (1988), 163-78; United Methodists, along with all Christians, "are to live in active expectancy: faithful in service of God and their neighbor; faithful in waiting for the fulfillment of God's universal love, justice, and peace on earth as in heaven." *The Book of Discipline* (UMC, 1996), ¶ 110.

169. *Charisma und Erneuerung der Kirche,* 17.

170. "Pro-existence" means "existing for others."

171. "Your deeds are crying out so loudly that I can no longer hear your words"—that is the response of someone to the Christian who is inviting him to faith in Christ.

172. Matthew 5:16; see 1 Peter 2:12; John 15:8; Ephesians 5:8f.

173. Relative to Wesley's sermons, we may here cite: Sermon 50, "The Use of Money," WJW 2:263-80; Sermon 51, "The Good Steward," WJW 2:281-98; Sermon 87, "The Danger of Riches," WJW 3:227-46; Sermon 89, "The More Excellent Way," WJW 3:262-77 on Wesley, see H. Carter, *The Methodist Heritage* (London: Epworth, 1951), 111-29; L. D. Hulley, *To Be and To Do. Exploring Wesley's Thought on Ethical Behavior* (1988).

174. The participants in the course for preaching assistants and lay preachers, or participation in such programs as lay schools and seminars in local churches and seminaries can provide preparation.

175. W. Abraham, *The Logic of Evangelism* (1989); K. H. Voigt "Die Predigt durch Laien in der EmK damals und heute," *EmK heute* 51 (1987); A. C. Outler, *We Intend to Be His Witnesses: Evangelization in the Spirit of Wesley* (1971).

176. 1 Corinthians 12:28-31; Ephesians 4:11-16; Mark 1:16-20; John 20:19-23; 21:15-23, etc.

177. See *Book of Discipline* (UMC, 1996), ¶¶ 301-4.

178. *Vom Dialog zur Kanzel- und Abendmahlsgemeinschaft* (1987), 18 (Section 7.2) (tr. trans.).

179. *Dienstauftrag,* 28.

180. See below, 4.3.3.

181. See *Book of Discipline* (UMC, 1996), ¶ 305, for Wesley's historic questions to preaching candidates.

182. Candidates for elder must complete the M. Div. degree or its equivalent (*Book of Discipline,* UMC, 1996, ¶ 326). Experience as a local pastor may in some cases now lead to acceptance as a probationary member and then to the office of ordained elder with the completion of a specified program of theological education in a seminary approved by the University Senate. See Thomas E. Frank, *Policy, Practice, and Mission of The United Methodist Church,* 187.

183. See *Book of Discipline* (UMC, 1996), ¶ 326, and D. M. Campbell, *The Yoke of Obedience: The Meaning of Ordination in Methodism* (1988).

184. See above, 4.2.2.4.

185. Richard Bondi, *Leading God's People: Ethics for the Practice of Ministry* (1989).

186. John 13:34-35; 1 Corinthians 12:12-27; Ephesians 2:11-22; J. Wesley, Sermon 74, "Of the Church," 7-14, WJW 3:48-50; W. Klaiber, *Rechtfertigung und Gemeinde,* 70-74.

187. This statement is not made by a representative of medieval atonement theory, but by the social psychologist Horst Eberhard Richter, in "Eine Welt oder keine. Wege in die Vernunft," *Friedensforum vom 1.* September 1989, 28.

188. W. Popkes, *Gemeinde—Raum des Vertrauens* (1984), 126ff.; see also the redemptive ways to handle complaints against clergy or laypersons within the Church, as described in *The Book of Discipline* (UMC, 1996), ¶ 358.

189. G. Lohfink, *Wie hat Jesus Gemeinde gewollt? Zur gesellschaftlichen Dimension des christlichen Glaubens* (1989), 69f.; see also the discussion of the economic issues of consumption and poverty in relation to the witness of the Church, in "The Social Principles," *The Book of Discipline* (UMC, 1996), ¶ 67.

190. Christine Lienemann-Perrin, *Taufe und Kirchenzugehörigkeit* (1983), 17f.; it is recommended that local congregations make frequent use of "Our Social Creed," where these priorities are uplifted. See *The Book of Discipline* (UMC, 1996), ¶ 70.

191. The fact that John Wesley himself nurtured a style of confrontation which was "inspired by the gospel," in instances in which he was challenged by opposition, was convincingly described by H. Renders in his scholarly study, "John Wesley als Apologet" (=BGEmK 39 [1990]); see also

Wesley's demeanor amid instances of persecution, as reported in the Journal, January 4, 1742, WJW 19:244; April 19, 1742, WJW 19:259; and June 6, 1742, WJW 19:273.

192. "Wesen und Struktur christlicher Gemeinde," supplement to the official publication ("Amtsblatt") III/79 of the EmK in the DDR (German Democratic Republic), published also as *EmK heute,* vol. 31 (1980); the sentence cited here is found on page 9.

193. See the above introduction to Section 4.3, "The Church as the Mission of God."

194. *The United Methodist Book of Worship* (1992), 674-75.

195. Matthew 28:16-20; John 20:19-23; Acts 1:6-8; 6:1-7; 10:17-20; 13:1-3, etc.

196. In this regard, see the work by Donald E. Messer (ed.), *Send Me? The Itineracy in Crisis* (Nashville: Abingdon, 1991). He assembled and evaluated the views of numerous American UM pastors and found that they are clearly critical of the "inhuman" side of a rigorously handled principle of appointment, as represented by the image of the early traveling preachers. They come to the conclusion that only a new, flexible system of consultation will address the needs of pastoral service in our time. Similar pressures on the itineracy are being felt in European United Methodism; some changes have already been made, although a theologically consistent conception has yet to be accomplished.

197. *Dienstauftrag—Amt—Allgemeines Priestertum,* 8.

198. "Soup and salvation" is the terse way in which this is expressed by the Salvation Army, which had its origins in the Wesleyan holiness movement of the nineteenth century.

199. These include open-air preaching, tent mission, cell-group evangelization, radio and television ministries, etc.

200. H. Hauzenberger, *Einheit auf evangelischer Grundlage. Vom Werden und Wesen der Evangelischen Allianz* (1986), 175; see also Arnold H. Rowdon, "Evangelical Alliance," in *New Twentieth-Century Encyclopedia of Religious Knowledge,* 308f.

201. Hauzenberger, *Einheit auf evangelischer Grundlage,* 176.

202. On this theme, see also K. H. Voigt, *Die Evangelische Allianz als ökumenische Bewegung;* 1990, and Erich Beyreuther, *Der Weg der Evangelischen Allianz in Deutschland* (1969), and for the context of evangelicalism in North America, see Mark Ellingsen, *The Evangelical Movement: Growth, Impact, Controversy, Dialog* (1988), and Fritz Laubach, *Aufbruch der Evangelikalen* (1972).

203. A. Erhard in "Neulandmission in der EmK. Eine Handreichung für unsere Gemeinden," *EmK heute* 69 (1991), 7.

204. From the UM Book of Discipline for the German Central Conference (LVO, ¶ 531, 2); see also the discussion of mission strategies for local congregations, including various options for "cooperative parishes," in *The Book of Discipline* (UMC, 1996), ¶¶ 201-6; and K. H. Voigt, "Die missionarische Existenz der Gemeinde," *EmK heute* 40 (1983).

205. One of the most important theological works that has appeared in this field is the work by W. J. Abraham, *The Logic of Evangelism* (1989). See also W. Klaiber, *Call and Response: Biblical Foundations of a Theology of Evangelism* (Nashville: Abingdon, 1997).

206. "Methodism," EKL III, 392 (tr. trans.).

207. See above, Section 1.1.3.2. "The Knowledge of God in Other Religions."

208. This is taken from the *Book of Discipline* for the German Central Conference (EmK); compare with ¶ 1302 of the *Book of Discipline* (UMC, 1996).

209. Article 5 of Division One of the Constitution of The United Methodist Church: "As part of the church universal, The United Methodist Church believes that the Lord of the church is calling Christians everywhere to strive toward unity; and therefore it will seek, and work for, unity at all levels of church life." See also, *From Dialog to Pulpit and Table Fellowship* (1987).

210. John Wesley, Sermon 39, "Catholic Spirit"; WJW 2:79-95, and H. Carter, *The Methodist Heritage* (1951).

211. *Grace upon Grace,* 36 (par. 52).

212. *Methodists Linking Two Continents* is the title of a book by the former German Methodist bishop Friedrich Wunderlich, and also of a biography which K. H. Voigt has written about this leader. On this theme, see the discussion of "Ecumenical Shared Ministries" in *The Book of Discipline* (UMC, 1996), ¶¶ 207-11.

213. John 15:19; 17:13-16; 1 John 4:1-6. On the concept of "world," see below, 4.4.1.

214. Avarice, revenge, violence, etc., see Romans 12:14-21.

215. See above, Section 4.2.

216. See the historical treatment of the theme "Kingdom of God" in relation to the church in W. S. Barker, "Kingdom of God," in *The Dictionary of Christianity in America,* 616-17.

217. See Luther's translation of Luke 17:21, "The kingdom of God is within you."

218. See W. A. 39 I, 348, 535, 351. This theme is contained in Luther's treatment of the Lord's Prayer in the Larger Catechism; see *The Book of Concord* ed. T. G. Tappert (Philadelphia: Fortress, 1959), 363f.; see also P. Althaus, *The Theology of Martin Luther,* 261.

219. K. Barth, *CD* IV/2, 655-56. In agreement with Barth, H. J. Kraus can also maintain that "The kingdom of God is the congregation. . . . But this congregation is not the kingdom of God. . . . It anticipates the goal for humanity and in this preliminary condition it is the announcement of the coming kingdom of God in its cosmic dimension" (*Reich Gottes: Reich der Freiheit, Grundriß Systematischer Theologie* [1975], 370). See also K. Barth, "The Christian Community and the Civil Community," in *Karl Barth: Theologian of Freedom,* ed. Clifford Green (London: Collins, 1989), 265-95.

220. A comprehensive overview is provided by H. A. Snyder, in *Models of the Kingdom* (1991).

221. See W. Pannenberg, *Grundzüge der Christologie* (Gütersloher Verlagshaus: Gerd Mohn, 1966), 392.

222. *In Defense of Creation,* 1986, 20. In this regard, see also the "Preamble" to the Social Principles in *The Book of Discipline* (UMC, 1996), p. 85.

223. See C. R. North, "World," in *The Interpreter's Dictionary of the Bible,* 4:873-78.

224. For example, Romans 1:7; 1 Corinthians 1:2; 3:17; Colossians 3:12; 1 Peter 2:9 etc.

225. See also John Wesley in his Sermon 74, "Of the Church," 28, WJW 3:55-56.

226. On the dynamic relationship of personal and social holiness, see Theressa Hoover, "The Road Ahead for United Methodists," in *Methodism's Destiny in an Ecumenical Age,* ed. Paul Minus (Nashville: Abingdon, 1969), 176-208, esp. 200-202; on the theme of the model of Christ, see M. Marquardt, Sanctification as Formation, in the image of Christ, in: *Serving God with Heart and Mind: A Festschrift in Honor of Roger W. Ireson,* ed. by H. R. Pieterse, Nashville, The General Board of Higher Education and Ministry, 2001.

227. Thus he speaks as follows in his ninth sermon of the Sermon on the Mount: " 'Seek the kingdom of God and his righteousness.' Righteousness is the fruit of God's reigning in the heart. And what is righteousness but love? The love of God and of all mankind, flowing from faith in Jesus Christ, and producing humbleness of mind, meekness, gentleness, long-suffering, patience, deadness to the world; and every right disposition of heart toward God and toward man. And by these it produces all holy actions, whatsoever are lovely or of good report; whatsoever works of faith and labour of love are acceptable to God and profitable to man" (Sermon 29, 20; WJW 1:642-43).

228. That perspective also becomes apparent in the Methodist movement; on the other hand, the church repeatedly falls short of fulfilling its social obligations, as Wesley also complained of Methodists who would become "rich," although for him wealth was not evil per se (on this theme, see especially T. W. Jennings, *Good News to the Poor: John Wesley's Evangelical Economics,* and Wesley's sermon, "The Use of Money," Sermon 50, WJW 2:263-80).

229. L. O. Hynson, *To Reform the Nation: Theological Foundations of Wesley's Ethics* (Grand Rapids: 1984), 135.

230. M. Weyer, Introduction to German edition of Wesley's Sermon No. 4.

231. Romans 8:18-39; 11:25-36; Revelation 21–22.

232. *Notes on the New Testament,* on Romans 14:17. See also Sermon 26, WJW 1:572-91 and Sermon 29, WJW 1:632-49.

233. So Wesley writes in his notes on Matthew 3:2.

234. Sermon 26, "Upon Our Lord's Sermon on the Mount VI," III, 8-9; WJW 1:581-83.

235. Sermon 7, "The Way into the Kingdom of God," II, 1-13 (WJW 1:230-32).

236. Letter of November 12, 1771, Letters (ed. Telford), 5:289.

237. Sermon 7, "The Way into the Kingdom," I, 1-13; WJW 1:218-25.

238. Sermon 7, II, 12; WJW 1:231.

239. It is noteworthy that dualistic conceptions play virtually no role in Wesley's cosmology, which is probably a function of his understanding of the universal grace of God.

240. K. Marx, on the critique of the Hegelian philosophy of law, MEW, vol. 1 (Berlin, 1973), 373f. "Religion is the sigh of the oppressed creature, the sentiment of a heartless world, and the soul of soulless conditions. It is the opium of the people."—from Karl Marx, "Contribution to the Critique of Hegel's Philosophy of Right, Introduction," in *Early Writings,* trans. and ed. T. B. Bottomore (New York: McGraw-Hill, 1964), 43; see the analysis of Marx in Henry Grosshans, *The Search for Modern Europe* (New York: Houghton-Mifflin, 1970), 174-82. The removal of religion as the illusionary happiness of the people is the request for their real happiness. The request to give up the illusion about

their state is the request to give up a state which needs illusions. The critique of religion is, in its core, the critique of the vale of tears whose gloriole is religion.

241. Sermon 100, "On Pleasing All Men," II, 5 (WJW 3:425); see M. Marquardt, *John Wesley's Social Ethics*. 32-33.

242. T. Schaad, *Wer glaubt, gehört zusammen,* 17.

243. This is the term used by the United Methodist bishops in their letter "On the Protection of the Environment."

244. Joachim Wiebering has referred to this ethic of mutuality under the title *"Partnerschaftlich Leben."* His book by the same name appeared in 1985 in East Berlin.

245. See also Section 2.2.2.4 above: "Covenant and Covenant Ratification in the Methodist Tradition."

246. *The Book of Discipline* (UMC, 1996), ¶ 103.

247. See above, Section 2.2.2.4.

248. See the *Book of Discipline* (UMC, 1996), ¶ 319.

249. M. Luther, "Heidelberg Thesis No. 28," found in *Martin Luther: Selections from His Writings,* ed. J. Dillenberger (Garden City, N.Y.: Doubleday, 1961), 503.

250. This quote is not drawn directly from Wesley, even if its content can certainly be derived from his writings and from his missionary and social work.

251. See above, 4.2.1.1: "The Community of Seekers and Believers."

252. Psalm 24:1; 1 Corinthians 10:26.

253. D. Bonhoeffer, *Dein Reich Komme,* in *Gesammelte Schriften* 3:270-85 (tr. trans.). This is as valid today as in 1932, when it was first written.

254. S. Paul Schilling, *Methodism and Society in Theological Perspective* (Nashville: Abingdon, 1960), describes the social responsibilities in the Methodist tradition in this manner (see above all 131f.).

255. See P. Tillich, *Systematic Theology,* 3:369-70.

256. D. Bonhoeffer, *Ethics* (London: SCM Press 1955), p. 77; see "Christ, Reality, and Good," in *Dietrich Bonhoeffer: Witness to Jesus Christ,* ed. John de Gruchy (Minneapolis: Fortress, 1991), 233-41.

257. G. Seebaß, "Es komm dein Reich zu dieser Zeit und dort hernach in Ewigkeit," JbEB 29 (1986), 34 (ed. trans.).

258. "Wesley's lively gift of observation and that were nurtured by his extensive preaching trips among all classes of the English population allowed him to develop an insight into the multiplicity and the severity of social problems, which he otherwise could hardly have received in the day in which he lived" (M. Marquardt, *John Wesley's Social Ethics,* 137).

259. *The Book of Discipline* (UMC, 1996), "Social Principles," ¶ 68B.

260. Eilert Herms "Schuld in der Geschichte. Zum Historikerstreit," ZThK 85 (1988), 349-70 (363).

261. Exodus 23:6; Isaiah 9:6; Amos 5:24; Proverbs 14:34; 31:9; Hebrews 1:9, etc.

262. See above, section 4.3.

263. Eilert Herms, 370. See also Joachim Mehlhausen, "Die Identifikation von Sünde in der jüngeren deutschen Geschichte," ThFPr 19 (1993), 3ff. For a penetrating analysis of these issues in English, see Gordon A. Craig, *The Germans* (New York: Meridian, 1983), esp. 289-309 ("Democracy and Nationalism").

264. See Romans 13:1-7. Reference is also to be made to the preamble of the Constitution of the United States of America.

265. John Wesley described the extent of this ethical duty with these well-known words: "Q.3. What may we reasonably believe to be God's design in raising up the Preachers called Methodists? A. Not to form any new sect; but to reform the nation, particularly the Church; and to spread scriptural holiness over the land." (Large Minutes, *Works,* 3rd ed., 8:299). See also L. O. Hynson, *To Reform the Nation* (1984); T. W. Jennings, *Good News to the Poor* (1990).

266. *Sanctification and Liberation,* ed. T. Runyon (Nashville: Abingdon, 1981).

267. The fact that this overcoming duty has not become completely untrue is indicated by different texts, such as the episcopal letter "In Defense of Creation: The Nuclear Crisis and a Just Peace" and the important book by the Methodist theologian M. D. Meeks, *God the Economist: The Doctrine of God and Political Economy* (Minneapolis: Fortress, 1989), see 15-28.

268. Meeks, *God the Economist,* 37; also the recent discussion of the Social Principles in T. E. Frank, *Polity, Practice, and the Mission of the United Methodist Church,* 89-90, 137-38.

269. Colossians 1:25; 1 Corinthians 9:17; Ephesians 1:9-10; 1 Timothy 1:4, etc.

270. *God the Economist,* 24.

271. Ibid., 37ff.

272. Because many questions cannot be resolved on a local basis, Meeks argues that communities need to organize a common strategy whereby "all might have access to life," for the "household of God" is to exist "for the sake of God's liberation of the polis and the kosmos through God's liberation of the poor, the oppressed, the sinners, and the dying." (Ibid., 36).

273. "Stellungnahme der Emk zu Fragen der Künstlichen Befruchtung und der Gentechnologie." *EmK heute* 54, 8 (tr. trans.).

274. For an extensive discussion of modern European forms of the church, see K. S. Latourette, *Christianity in a Revolutionary Age,* vol. 2: *The Nineteenth Century in Europe* (Grand Rapids: Zondervan, 1969), esp. 89-100.

275. For the historical context of this problem in England, see M. Edwards, "The Place of Methodism in the Free Churches: A Short Historical Survey," in *This Methodism: Eight Studies* (London, 1939), 115-28.

276. In addition to the discussion in Latourette, vol. 2, as cited in n. 274, earlier phases of development are ably surveyed in K. Aland, *A History of Christianity* (Philadelphia: Fortress, 1982), 2:221-330. E. Geldbach, "Freikirche," EKL 3:359-62.

277. A new outline for the participation of the churches in the restoration of political openness has been set forth by the American United Methodist theologian and social scientist, W. J. Everett, in *God's Federal Republic* (1991).

278. This is in no way to maintain that a great part of the members of a "Volkskirche" (national church) have never made such a personal affirmation; to maintain this is not an empirically verifiable task. However, if one takes seriously the statements made in response to inquiries, it shows that the central content of the Christian faith is denied by many persons who belong to a church.

279. A reference to the church is not to be drawn from the parable of the tares among the wheat (Matthew 13:24-30, 36-43), that often is given as an "argument" against making a separation between believers and known unbelievers. It is therefore inappropriate to use this as a basis for making a decision in this ecclesiastical matter.

280. See "The Union of the Churches and the Development of the Constitution of the Church in Germany," in K. Aland, *A History of Christianity,* 2:331-38.

281. Hence, it should not be argued but be explicitly recognized that there is also room in the national church "for the confession of faith (in word and deed) that responds to the Word of God." See W. Härle, "Kirche," TRE 18, 308, 10f.; and the discussion in Aland, "The Loss of Christian Substance and the Opposing Forces: The Awakening and Confessionalism," *A History of Christianity,* 2:338-45.

282. For a closer examination of this matter, see *Berufen—Beschenkt—Beauftragt,* 22f.; also, see the powerful expression of this concern in Syo Ladigbolu, "Let the Redeemed of the Lord Say So," in *The World Forever Our Parish,* 56-67 (Ladigbolu has been Bishop of the United Methodist Church in Nigeria).

283. This is evident in the case of the secession of the United Evangelical Church from the Evangelical Association in 1891–1894, a separation that later was healed in the reunion of 1922, producing the Evangelical Church.

284. Nevertheless, we would maintain with good reason the mutual independence of church and state, and separation from national church structures *("Volkskirchen"),* as has been indicated.

285. See W. Klaiber, "Volkskirche und Freikirche—eine fruchtbare Spannung im Protestantismus," in *Der Glaube hat Zukunft. Perspektiven für eine evangelische Kirche von Morgen,* ed. U. Hahn (1991), 158-66; also see the discussion of "What makes Methodists different from other churches?" in *Gathered Into One: The World Methodist Conference Speaks,* ed. Scott Jones (Nashville: Discipleship Resources, 1982), 97-110.

286. The expression "the fellowship of the saints" (D. F. Durnbaugh, "Kirche," 3.6, *Freikirchliche Ekklesiologie,* EKL, 3rd ed., 2:1084) does not clearly convey the specific difference that stands in question, since this New Testament expression is being narrowed in an unacceptable manner. The community of saints is the community of Jesus not on the basis of its moral qualifications or resemblances, but on the basis of the holiness ascribed to it by Christ and by the change of life that is

effected through this (see *Berufen—Beschenkt—Beauftragt,* 36ff.). It remains to be said that United Methodist ecclesiology in the article cited is seen as being quite limited, and this also applies to the article "Freikirche" in vol. 11 of TRE (550-63), which contains a series of incorrect statements about the free churches in Germany and their history. Durnbaugh's work can also be examined in his *The Believer's Church The History and Character of Radical Protestantism* (New York: Macmillan, 1968).

287. "The Sunday Service of the Methodists in North America, with Other Occasional Services," which was basically derived from the Anglican *Book of Common Prayer.* For a closer examination of this theme, see N. B. Harmon, "Sunday Service," *Encyclopedia of World Methodism,* 2:2281-83, and F. Baker, *John Wesley and the Church of England* (1970).

288. See the texts of these two doctrinal standards in the Appendix.

289. In the original text, the term used was not "citizens" but "subjects." However, Wesley's text was soon changed to suit the new political climate in America, with the addition of a declaration of obedience to the authority of the United States of America (see Article XXIII below, and compare with Article XVI of the EUB Confession of Faith).

290. See T. Hobbes, *Leviathan,* chapter 13.

291. "We must obey God rather than any human authority" (Acts 5:29).

292. See "The Social Principles," *The Book of Discipline* (UMC, 1996), ¶ 68, V. E. "Civil Obedience and Civil Disobedience," as well as Article XXIII of the Articles of Religion.

293. E. Jüngel, "Each person must be subject to the authority . . ." A Bible Study on Romans 13:1-7 in E. Jüngel, R. Herzog, and H. Simon, *Evangelische Christen in unserer Demokratie* (1986), 29.

294. M. Marquardt, *John Wesley's Social Ethics,* 124. This ethical task of the church is also found in the fifth thesis of the "Theological Declaration of Barmen," where it states that the church "draws attention to God's kingdom, God's command, and God's righteousness, and hence it places emphasis upon the responsibility of rulers and those who are ruled."

295. *The Book of Discipline* (UMC, 1996), "Social Principles," ¶ 68.

296. Ibid.

297. The fact that the word of Paul to the governed does not parallel any comparable word to those who govern has been misused in history for the disciplining of the governed. Our best response to this objection is to consider the context of the epistle to the Romans itself: God gives his righteousness; it is his grace, which overcomes sin; sinners are those who are accepted; his love fulfills the law; God's saving actions are completed for the Jews as well as for non-Jews. God therefore does not stand on the side of the holders of power, in order to keep the weak in their situation of powerlessness.

298. See above all Luther's work "Von weltlicher Obrigkeit" ("Concerning Worldly Authority") and the exposition of the Sermon on the Mount. See also G. W. Forell, *Faith Active in Love: An Investigation of the Principles Underlying Luther's Social Ethics* (New York: American, 1954); and also W. Härle, "Luthers Regimentenlehre als Lehre vom Handeln Gottes" (MJTh I [1987], 12-32).

299. Among the many editions of this text, the translation recommended is in Clifford Green, *Karl Barth: Theologian of Freedom,* 148-51; the fifth thesis is found on page 150 of this work.

300. This does not signify that criteria for action must be directly drawn from particular texts of the Bible or that all statements must be adorned with biblical citations. On the basis of the love commandment and the basic conception of actual problems at hand, Scripture should rather serve as a point of orientation for congregations and their members, and also for those who hold responsibility in the state and in society to promote ethically sound and correct actions.

301. The Social Creed was formulated in 1908 by the Methodist Episcopal Church (USA) and was first passed by its General Conference as the official text reflecting its deliberations. In the course of the following decades, other churches followed its example. Since 1972 a more complete statement of Social Principles became the official text, which was required to be approved by the General Conference.

302. *The Book of Discipline* (UMC, 1996), "Social Principles," ¶ 68B.

303. "Social Principles," ¶ 66: Section III: The Social Community, and ¶ 68: Section V: The Political Community.

304. As in the case of Germany's "Third Reich," this can come to pass through legal means. Whenever it contradicts fundamental human rights, there is a failure of legitimate norms of justice, the ethical basis for all political activity, and the perception of the duty of caring for persons within its area of administration.

305. On the subject of prayer "as a perception of political responsibility" as a whole, see W. Härle,

"Die politische Verantwortung der Kirche—aus evangelischer Sicht, in *Glaube—Bekenntnis—Kirchenrecht*, in H. Ph. Meyer 1989, 141-51; also, see Karl Barth's exposition of the role of prayer in the struggle for righteousness within humanity, in CD III/3, 264-71.

306. Notes on the NT, on Matthew 5:15.

307. "Our Social Creed," *Book of Discipline* (UMC, 1996), ¶ 70.

308. From the Council of Bishops of The United Methodist Church, "In Defense of Creation" 1986, p. 82.

309. It also corresponds to Wesley's ethics (see above, Section 4.4.2), even if he does not yet have the global perspective that is available to us today.

310. Genesis 1:26-28; Proverbs 12:10.

311. In addition to the literature that informs the Methodist contributions to the international work of peace, K. H. Voigt has demonstrated the relationship between the German branch of the United Methodist Church and the ecumenical movement in "Der kontinentaleuropäische Methodismus zwischen den beiden Weltkriegen," ed. M. Weyer, BGEmK 36 (1990), 155-88. See also, Paul M. Minus Jr., *Methodism's Destiny in an Ecumenical Age* (Nashville: Abingdon, 1969).

312. In earlier years he had offered his own contribution for the defense of the country against the pretender to the throne of the house of Stuart, although that proposal was never accepted.

313. "The Doctrine of Original Sin," Part 1, II, 10, *Works*, 3rd ed., 9:221.

314. M. Marquardt, *John Wesley's Social Ethics*, 129. Wesley's attitude toward the war is depicted in detail on pages 128-30. See also E. W. Gerdes, *John Wesley's Attitude Toward War* (1960), and B. K. Turley, "John Wesley and War," *Methodist History*, 29 (1991), 96-111.

315. Journal of the 1944 General Conference of the Methodist Church (Kansas City, Mo.: The Methodist Publishing House, 1944), 180f.; also, for a comprehensive treatment, see the dissertation by Martin Kupsch, *Krieg und Frieden. Die Stellungnahmen der methodistischen Kirchen in den Vereinigten Staaten, Großbritannien und Kontinentaleuropa* (1992) (=EHS 23, vol. 455), 2 Parts, LXIV, 905 pages.

316. *The Book of Discipline* (UMC, 1996), "Social Principles," ¶ 69, C.

317. For an incisive discussion of the just-war theory in the context of the "justitia originalis," see Reinhold Niebuhr, *The Nature and Destiny of Man* (New York: Scribner's, 1964), 2:280-95; also A. Hertz, "Die Lehre vom 'gerechten Krieg' als ethischer Kompromiß," in *Handbuch Christlicher Ethik*, III (1982), 425-48. A comprehensive study is *Friede und Gerechtigkeit*, ed. G. Planer-Friedrich (1989); W. Joest, *Der Friede Gottes und der Friede auf Erden*, 1990.

318. Those who enter into the Kingdom of God are those to whom the Son of Man will say, "Come, you that are blessed by my Father, inherit the kingdom prepared for you from the foundation of the world; for I was hungry, and you gave me food, I was thirsty and you gave me something to drink, I was a stranger and you welcomed me, I was naked and you gave me clothing, I was sick and you took care of me; I was in prison and you visited me. . . . Truly I tell you, just as you did it to one of the least of these who are members of my family, you did it to me" (Matthew 25:34-36, 40).

319. See above Section 4.4.3.

320. Of the many publications on this theme, the following may be cited: José Míguez-Bonino, "Methodism: A World Movement," in *Methodism's Destiny in an Ecumenical Age*, ed. P. M. Minus Jr. 90-107; also, H. Vorster, "Konziliarität, Bundesschluß und Uberlebenskrise," ZThK 88 (1991), 526ff.; *Okologische Theologie*, ed. G. Altner (1989); *Okumenisches Forum Graz* (1989); W. Joest, *Der Friede Gottes.*

321. C. Oeyen, *Plädoyer für eine Reform des Christentums*, 121 (tr. trans.).

322. Wainwright, *Doxology*, 425.

323. E. Süßmann, "Naturwissenschaft und Christentum," RGG, 3rd ed., IV, column 1378; also R. Eucken, "Natural Law," in *Hastings Encyclopedia of Religion and Ethics*, 7:805-7.

324. "O LORD, how manifold are your works! / In wisdom you have made them all; / the earth is full of your creatures" (Psalm 104:24).

325. Psalm 19:1-2; 104, etc.

326. K. Koch, "Gestaltet die Erde, doch heget das Leben! Einige Klarstellungen zum 'dominium terrae' in Genesis 1," in *Wenn nicht jetzt, wann dann?* FS H-J Kraus (1983), 23-26.

327. *The Book of Discipline* (UMC, 1996), "Social Principles," ¶ 64, C.

328. Hubert Markl, "Die Natur schlägt zurück" (*Die Zeit* from April 12, 1987, 82). The billions of persons, the world harvest of grains, fruits, and vegetables, the billions of cows, sheep, swine, and chickens that are bred for meat production constitute an "almost inexhaustible opportunity for nour-

ishment for every parasite, fungus, and worm, which is known to exist. . . . The few species of our useful plants are cultivated under the most uniform conditions possible on gigantic plains and this dictates that even the pests that prey on them are being provided for. The ensuing struggle with these pests involves millions of tons of herbicides, fungicides, insecticides, and bacterial and viral poisons, which are used over a period of several years and thereby enable the pests to develop resistance to them. . . . We are in need of finding ever new ways of counteracting pests. And yet, the results of this struggle are highly disillusioning: of the total harvest in the United States over the past forty years, perhaps only 7% of all insects have become victims of pesticides" (Markl, 82). By the same author, see *Evolution, Genetik, und menschliches Verhalten* (1985); on the relation of biology and religion, see also H. P. Santmire, "Pierre Teilhard de Chardin: The Christianization of Evolution," in *Critical Issues in Modern Religion,* ed. R. A. Johnson, et al. (Englewood Cliffs: Prentice-Hall 1973), 114-40.

329. C. F. von Weizsäcker, *Die Zeit drängt* (1986).

330. G. Altner, *Schöpfung am Abgund,* 2nd ed. (1977), 155.

331. The consequences of our actions are far from the mark. Despite the cost of tens of thousands of lives annually in traffic accidents, our population is scarcely prepared to accept lower speed limits or other limitations on their driving habits. The high price that is paid for massive consumption of meat is the need of maintaining great masses of livestock, that are made to live in ways that are not conducive to their well-being and that must endure endless suffering. Europeans and North Americans profit from the monocultures of the third world, whose yields not only leave behind despoiled earth and ruined economies among those people who are dependent upon the earth, but which also throws them into the world market with prices that are kept arbitrarily low.

332. The importance of voluntary asceticism has certainly not become evident only in our day; it already lay near at hand for the early Christian congregations (see 1 Timothy 6:6-10), but it is more vigorously exposed in view of the possibilities for high living standards in our present day.

333. See Ian G. Barbour, *Issues in Silence and Religion* (Englewood Cliffs: Prentice Hall, 1966); and G. Altner, *Naturvergessenheit; Grundlagen einer umfassenden Bioethik* (1991).

334. See G. Wainwright, *Doxology,* 427f.

335. E. Herms, "Die eschatologische Existenz des neuen Menschen," in E. Herms, *Offenbarung und Glaube* (1992), 316.

336. *Ethics,* (1955), 79-100.

337. John Wesley, Sermon 26, III, 8; WJW 1:582.

338. Sermon 26, III, 8; WJW 1:581-82.

339. See also 1 Thessalonians 4:17 and 2 Corinthians 5:1-2, which do not speak of this. The New Testament statement "enter the kingdom of heaven" (Matthew 5:20; 18:3; 19:23-24; Mark 10:15) signifies much more an "entry into the reign of God," which is brought near by the works of Jesus.

340. K. Haacker, "Das kommende Reich Gottes als Ansatz sachgemäßer und zeitgemäßer evangelischer Predigt," TheolBeitr 13 (1982), 244-56; also, J. Moltmann, *The Trinity and the Kingdom* (San Francisco: Harper and Row, 1981), 191-222.

341. See above, Section 2.2.1.6.

342. See above, Section 2.3.3.: The Perfection of the World.

343. Revelation 22:1-5; Philippians 2:9-11; 1 Corinthians 15:54-57.

344. 2 Corinthians 5:1-5.

345. Sermon 4; WJW 1:159-80.

346. This is taken from M. Weyer's introduction to the German edition of this sermon.

In Lieu of a Summary

1. A. Outler, in *Der Methodismus. Die Kirchen der Welt,* ed. C. E. Sommer, VI (1968), 90 (tr. trans.); see also, A. Outler, *Theology in the Wesleyan Spirit* (Nashville: Discipleship Resources, 1996).

2. Ted A. Campbell, "Is It Just Nostalgia? The Renewal of Wesleyan Studies," in *The Christian Century* (April 4, 1990), 396-98.

3. "Thoughts upon Methodism," WJW 9:527.

Selected Literature for Further Reading

In the following bibliography, sources and works are compiled that are important for the study of United Methodist theology.

Abbreviations

ARG Archiv für Reformationsgeschichte, Berlin 1903ff.

BEvTh Beiträge zur evangelischen Theologie, München 1940ff.

BGEmK Beiträge zur Geschichte der Evangelisch-methodistischen Kirche. Hg. v. der Studiengemeinschaft für Geschichte der EmK, Stuttgart 1974ff. (formerly: Beiträge zur Geschichte des Methodismus).

BK Biblischer Kommentar, Neukirchen 1955ff.

BKL Beiträge zur kirchlichen Literatur.

BSLK Bekenntnisschriften der evangelisch-Lutherischen Kirche, Göttingen 10, 1986.

CD Karl Barth. Church Dogmatics. 13 vols. Translated by G. W. Bromiley. Edinburgh: T & T Clark, 1956–1969.

EKL H. Brunotte and O. Weber (eds.), Evangelisches Kirchenlexikon (4 vols., 1956–62); 3rd edition: E. Fahlbusch et al. (eds.), 5 vols., 1986–97.

EmK heute EmK heute. Material für die Gemeindearbeit in der Evangelisch-methodistischen Kirche, Stuttgart, 1975ff. (formerly: Beiheft zu "Der Mitarbeiter," Stuttgart 1969ff.).

ET Expository Times, Edinburgh 1889f.

EvTh Evangelische Theologie, München 1934ff.

EWNT H. Balz and G. Schneider (eds.), Exegetisches Wörterbuch zum Neuen Testament (3 vols., 1980–83).

FRLANT Forschungen zur Religion und Literatur des Alten und Neuen Testaments.

Hymn Hymns of Charles and John Wesley are cited from *A Collection of Hymns for the Use of The People Called Methodists,* 1780 (WJW 7, 1983) with hymn and verse numbers.

Journal (ed. Curnock) Journal of John Wesley, edited by Nehemiah Curnock (1938), cited with date of entry. Entries through May 1765 are cited from WJW 18-21, 1988ff.; thereafter citations are from Curnock's edition.

Large Minutes Minutes of Several Conversations between the Rev. Mr. Wesley and others, from the year 1744 to the year 1789. Works, ed. Thomas Jackson, 3rd ed. 8:299-338.

Letters (ed. Telford) Letters of John Wesley, cited by recipient and date from the edition of J. Telford, 1931. Letters to 1755 are cited from WJW 25-26, 1980, 1982; thereafter they are cited from Telford's edition.

MSGEmK Mitteilungen der Studiengemeinschaft für Geschichte der EmK, Reutlingen 1962–67; NF 1980ff.

MThA Münsteraner Theologische Abhandlungen, Altenberge 1988ff.

MThSt Marburger Theologische Studien.

Notes NT John Wesley, *Explanatory Notes Upon the New Testament.* 1754 (reprint, London 1976; cited by the indicated point of reference).

Or Orientalia (Rome).

Sermon The Sermons of John Wesley, cited according to their enumeration with the original sections in WJW 1-4, 1984ff.

TEH.NF Theologische Existenz heute. Neue Folge 1946ff. München 1933–41.

ThFPr Theologie für die Praxis. Reutlingen 1975ff.

THAT Theologisches Handwörterbuch zum Alten Testament, München 1984.

ThB Theologische Beiträge, Wuppertal 1970ff.

ThR Theologische Rundschau, Tübingen (1897-1917), 1929ff.

ThStBeitr Theologische Studienbeiträge, Stuttgart 1988ff.

ThWNT G. J. Botterweck and H. Ringgren (eds.). Theologisches Wörterbuch zum Neuen Testament

TRE G. Krause and G. Müller (eds.), Theologische Realenzyklopädie. Berlin 1976.

UMH *The United Methodist Hymnal.* Nashville: United Methodist Publishing House, 1989.

WA Martin Luther, Werke, Kritische Gesamtausgabe (= "Weimar" edition).

WJW *The Works of John Wesley* (ed. Frank Baker et al.), The Oxford/Bicentennial Edition, 1975ff.

WMANT Wissenschaftliche Monographien zum Alten und Neuen Testament, Neukirchen 1960ff.

Works 3rd. ed *The Works of the Rev. John Wesley.* 3rd ed. 14 vols. London 1928–31. Ed. Thomas Jackson (many reprints).

WThJ Westminster Theological Journal, Philadelphia 1938ff.

WUNT Wissenschaftliche Untersuchungen zum Neuen Testament, Tübingen 1950ff.

ZThK Zeitschrift für Theologie und Kirche, Tübingen, 1891ff.

Bibliography, Sources, and Works

1. Reference Works and Official Theological Documents

The Book of Discipline of The United Methodist Church. Nashville: United Methodist Publishing House, 1996.

The Book of Resolutions of The United Methodist Church. Nashville: United Methodist Publishing House, 1996.

Davies, Rupert E. *Methodism.* Penguin Books, 1963.

Harmon, Nolan B., ed. *Encyclopedia of World Methodism.* 2 vols. Nashville, 1974.

The United Methodist Hymnal. Nashville: United Methodist Publishing House, 1989.

The United Methodist Book of Worship. Nashville: United Methodist Publishing House, 1992.

2. Works of John and Charles Wesley

The Works of John Wesley. Editor in Chief Frank Baker (WJW). They first appeared in 1975 through Clarendon Press of Oxford University, London, as the Oxford Edition of the Works of John Wesley; the series continued in 1984 as the Bicentennial Edition through Abingdon Press, Nashville (General Editor, Richard P. Heitzenrater. Textual Editor, Frank Baker).

WORKS PUBLISHED TO DATE

A Collection of Hymns for the Use of the People Called Methodists. Ed. Franz Hildebrandt and Oliver A. Beckerlegge. WJW, 7, 1983.

John Wesley. *Works of John Wesley: Bicentennial Edition.* Frank Baker (ed.) Oxford, 1979–83; Nashville: Abingdon, 1984.

———. *Works of the Rev. John Wesley.* Thomas Jackson (ed.). 14 vols. London: Wesleyan Conference Office, 1872.

———. *Letters of the Rev. John Wesley.* John Telford (ed.). London: Epworth, 1931.

———. *Minutes of Several Conversations between John and Charles Wesley and others, From the Year 1744 to the Year 1780.* London: J. Paramore, 1780.

———. *Sermons on Several Occasions.*

———. *The Sunday Service.* London, 1784.

The Appeals to Men of Reason and Religion and Certain Related Open Letters. Ed. Gerald R. Cragg. WJW 11, 1975.

Journals and Diaries I-V (1735–1776). Ed. W. Reginald Ward and Richard P. Heitzenrater, WJW 18-22, 1988–1993.

Letters I-II (1721–1755). Ed. Frank Baker. WJW 25-26, 1980, 1982.
The Methodist Societies. Ed. Rupert E. Davies. WJW 9, 1989.
Sermons I-IV. Ed. Albert C. Outler. WJW 1-4, 1984–1987.

FOR WORKS OF WESLEY THAT HAVE NOT BEEN PUBLISHED

The Works of the Rev. John Wesley. 3rd ed. Ed. Thomas Jackson. 14 vols. London: Wesleyan Conference Office, 1829–1831; reprint, 1872.
The Journal of the Rev. John Wesley. Ed. Nehemiah Curnock. 8 vols. London, 1938.
The Letters of the Rev. John Wesley. Ed. John Telford. 8 vols. London, 1931.
Explanatory Notes upon the New Testament. London, 1755 (reprint: London, 1976).
Explanatory Notes upon the Old Testament. Vol. 1, 1765; vol. 2, 1767.
A Survey of the Wisdom of God in the Creation: or a Compendium of Natural Philosophy. 3rd ed. enlarged. 5 vols. London, 1777.

ANTHOLOGIES

Charles Wesley's Earliest Evangelical Sermons, transcribed by Thomas R. Albin and Oliver A. Beckerlegge, Oxford, 1987.
Charles Wesley: Short Hymns on Select Passages of the Holy Scripture. 2 vols. Bristol, 1762.
Early German-American Evangelicalism (EUB sources) ed. J. Steven O'Malley. Metuchen, N.J., 1995.
John and Charles Wesley. Ed. F. Whaling. London, 1981.
John Wesley. Ed. Albert C. Outler. New York: Oxford University Press, 1964.
John Wesley's Theology: A Collection from His Works. Ed. Robert W. Burtner and Robert E. Chiles. 1954; reprint, Nashville, 1984.
The Journal of The Rev. Charles Wesley, M.A. Ed. Thomas Jackson, 2 vols. London, 1849.
The Poetical Works of John and Charles Wesley. Ed. George Osborne, 13 vols. London 1868–72.
Representative Verse of Charles Wesley. Ed. Frank Baker. Nashville, 1962.
The Unpublished Poetry of Charles Wesley. Ed. S. T. Kimbrough, Jr., and Oliver A. Beckerlegge. Vols I-III. Nashville: Kingswood, 1988–1992.

3. Documents and Works on the Rise of the United Methodist Traditions and the History of The United Methodist Church

Albright, R. W. *A History of the Evangelical Church.* Harrisburg, Pa., 1956.
The Arminian Magazine 1 (1789). Philadelphia: Princard and Hall, 1789.
Asbury, Francis. *Journals and Letters.* Ed. E. T. Clark. 3 vols. Nashville: Abingdon, 1958.

Selected Literature for Further Reading

Baker, Frank. *From Wesley to Asbury.* Durham: Duke University Press, 1979.

Bangs, Nathan. *History of the M.E. Church.* 4 vols. New York: Mason and Lane, 1840.

Behney, B. and Eller P. *The History of the Evangelical United Brethren Church.* Nashville, 1979.

Borgen, Ole E. *John Wesley on the Sacraments.* Francis Asbury Press, 1972.

Buckley, James Monroe. *History of Methodism in the United States.* 2 vols. New York: Christian Literature, 1896.

Campbell, Ted. *The Apostolate of United Methodism.* Nashville: Discipleship Resources, 1979.

Cannon, William R. *The Theology of John Wesley.* Abingdon Press, 1946.

Chiles, Robert E. *Theological Transition in American Methodism: 1790–1935.* University Press of America, 1983.

Clapper, Gregory S. *John Wesley on Religious Affections.* Pietist and Wesley Studies no. 1. The Scarecrow Press, 1989.

Curtiss, George L. *A Study of the Constitution of the Methodist Episcopal Church.* New York: Hunt and Eaton, 1889.

The Discipline of the Evangelical United Brethren Church. Harrisburg, Pa.: United Evangelical Press, 1894.

Drury, A. W. *History of the Discipline of the Methodist Episcopal Church.* New York: Lane and Sanford, 1844, 1945, 1951, 1956.

"First Discipline of the Methodist Episcopal Church Compared with Large Minutes." In *History of the Discipline.* Emory, Robert. New York: Lane and Sanford, 1844, 26-79.

Harris, William L. *The Constitutional Powers of the General Conference.* Cincinnati, 1860.

Howard, Ivan C. "Controversies in Methodism over Methods of Education of Ministers up to 1856." Ph.D. diss. State University of Iowa, 1965.

Journal of the General Conference of 1792. Ed. Thomas B. Neely. New York: Methodist Book Concern, 1899.

Journals of the General Conference, 1796–1836. New York: Carlton and Phillips, 1855.

Kimbrough, S T, Jr., ed. *Charles Wesley, Poet and Theologian.* Nashville, 1992.

Knight, Henry H. *The Presence of God in the Christian Life: John Wesley and the Means of Grace.* Pietist and Wesleyan Studies no. 3. The Scarecrow Press, 1992.

Lee, Jesse. *History of the Methodists.* Baltimore: Magill and Clime, 1810.

Lindström, Harald. *Wesley and Sanctification.* London: Epworth Press, 1946.

McTyeire, Holland N. *A History of Methodism.* Nashville: Southern Methodist Publishing House, 1884.

———. *Manual of the Discipline.* 1st ed. Nashville: Southern Methodist Publishing House, 1870. 20th ed., 1931.

Maddox, Randy L., ed. *Aldersgate Reconsidered.* Nashville, 1990.

513

Minutes of the Annual Conference of the Methodist Episcopal Church for the Years 1773–1828, vol. 1. New York: T. Mason and G. Lane, 1840.

The Minutes of the Methodist Conference Annually Held in America, from 1771 to 1794. Philadelphia: Henry Tuckness, 1795.

Minutes of Several Conversations Between the Rev. Thomas Coke, the Rev. Francis Asbury and Others, at a Conference Begun in Baltimore, December 27th, 1784, Composing a Form of Discipline. Philadelphia: C. Cist, 1785. Full text reprinted in J. Tigert, CH, 532-602. Disc., 1784.

Norwood, F. A. *The Story of American Methodism.* Nashville/New York, 1974.

Peck, Jesse T. "Methodism: Its Method and Mission." *Methodist Quarterly Review* 51 (April, 1869).

Phoebus, William. *Memoirs of Bishop Whatcoat.* New York, 1828.

Pullman, Joseph. "Methodism and Heresy." *Methodist Quarterly Review* (April 1879): 334-57.

Rack, Henry D. *Reasonable Enthusiast: John Wesley and the Rise of Methodism.* London, 1989.

Rupp, E. Gordon, and Rupert E. Davies, eds. *A History of the Methodist Church in Great Britain.* Vols. I-IV. London, 1965/73/83/88.

Schmidt, Martin. John Wesley, Band 1, Die Zeit vom 17. Juni 1703 bis 24. Mai 1738, Zürich/Frankfurt a.M. 1953; 2, Das Lebenswerk John Wesleys, 1966; New edition under the title *John Wesley—Leben und Werk, Band 1: Aufbruch zur Veränderung; Band 2: Ruf in die Auseinandersetzung; Band 3: Christsein als Ganzes,* 2. A. Zurich, 1988.

Sherman, David. *History of the Revisions of the Discipline of the Methodist Episcopal Church.* New York: Nelson and Phillips, 1874.

Stacey, John, ed. *John Wesley: A Contemporary Perspective.* London, 1988.

Steckel, K., and C. E. Sommer, Hg. *Die Geschichte der Evangelisch-methodistischen Kirche.* 1982.

Stevens, Abel. *Centenary Reflections on the Providential Character of Methodism.* New York, 1840.

———. *History of the M. E. Church.* New York: Carlton and Porter, 1859.

———. *The Life and Times of Nathan Bangs.* New York: Carlton and Porter, 1865.

Streiff, Patrick P., *Jean Guillaume de la Fléchère,* John William Fletcher 1729–1785, BBSHST 51, 1984.

Tigert, John J. *A Constitutional History of American Episcopal Methodism.* 1st ed. Nashville: Smith and Lamar, 1894. 2nd ed., 1901.

———. *The Doctrines of the Methodist Episcopal Church in America, as Contained in the Disciplines of Said Church from 1788 to 1808.* 2 vols. New York: Eaton and Mains, 1902.

Tuttle, Robert G., Jr. *John Wesley: His Life and Theology.* Zondervan Publishing, 1978.

———. *Mysticism in the Wesleyan Tradition.* Francis Asbury Press, 1989.

Weyer, Michel, Hg. *Der kontinentaleuropäische Methodismus zwischen den bei-den Weltkriegen.* BGEmK 36 (1990).

Whatcoat, Richard. Memoirs, 1806, in J. Telford, *Wesley's Veterans.* Salem, Ohio: Schmul, n.d. 2:219-28.

Yeakel, Reuben. *History of the Evangelical Association.* Vols. 1-2. Cleveland, Ohio, 1895.

4. Works on the Theology of Wesley

Borgen, Ole. *John Wesley on the Sacraments.* Nashville/New York, 1972.

Campbell, Ted A. *John Wesley and Christian Antiquity.* Religious Version and Cultural Change, Nashville, 1991.

———. The "Wesleyan Quadrilateral": The Story of a Modern Methodist Myth. In *Doctrine and Theology in the United Methodist Church,* ed. Thomas A. Langford, 154-61. Nashville, 1991.

Cannon, William Ragsdale. *The Theology of John Wesley. With special reference to the Doctrine of Justification.* Nashville, 1974.

Carter, Henry. *Das Erbe John Wesleys und die Oekumene.* Frankfurt/Main-Zürich, 1951.

Cell, George Croft. *The Rediscovery of John Wesley.* New York, 1935.

Clemons, J. T. "John Wesley—Biblical Literalist?" *Religion in Life* 46 (1977), 332-42.

Coppedge, Allen. *John Wesley in Theological Debate.* 1987.

Deschner, John. *Wesley's Christology: An Interpretation.* Dallas, 1960 (repr. 1985).

Heitzenrater, Richard P. *Mirror and Memory: Reflections on Early Methodism.* Nashville: Abingdon Press, 1989.

Hildebrandt, Franz. *Christianity According to the Wesleys.* London, 1956.

———. *From Luther to Wesley.* London, 1951.

Hynson, Leon O. *To Reform the Nation: Theological Foundations of Wesley's Ethics.*

Jennings, Theodore W., Jr. *Good News to the Poor: John Wesley's Evangelical Economics.* Nashville, 1990.

Kimbrough, ST, Jr. Lost in Wonder. *Charles Wesley: The Meaning of His Hymns Today.* Nashville, 1987.

Klaiber, Walter. Aus Glauben, damit aus Gnaden. Der Grundsatz paulinischer Soteriologie und die Gnadenlehre John Wesleys. ZThK 88 (1991), 313-38.

Langford, Thomas A. *Practical Divinity: Theology in the Wesleyan Tradition.* Rev. ed. 2 vols. Nashville: Abingdon, 1998–1999.

Marquardt, Manfred. *Praxis und Prinzipien der Sozialethik John Wesleys.* Göttingen, 1986. *John Wesley's Social Ethics. Praxis and Principles,* Nashville: Abingdon, 1991.

Marquardt, Manfred. John Wesley's "Synergismus," in: Die Einheit der Kirche, Festschrift P. Reinhold, Mainz, 1977, 96-102, = MSGEmK 1980, 4-13.

Meistad, Tore. *To Be a Christian in the World: Martin Luther's and John Wesley's Interpretation of the Sermon on the Mount.* Oslo, 1989 (M.A.—Dissertation Trondheim).

Nausner, Helmut. "The Meaning of John Wesley's General Rules." *Asbury Theological Journal* (fall 1989), 43-60.

Outler, A. *John Wesley.* New York: Oxford University Press, 1964.

———. "The Wesleyan Quadrilateral—In John Wesley." In *Doctrine and Theology in The United Methodist Church,* ed. Thomas A. Langford. Nashville: Kingswood, 1991.

Rattenbury, J. Ernest. *The Evangelical Doctrines of Charles Wesley's Hymns.* London, 1941.

Rupp, Gordon E. John Wesley und Martin Luther—ein Beitrag zum lutherisch-methodistischen Dialog. BGEmK 16 (1983).

Sangster, W. E. *The Path to Perfection: An Examination and Restatement of John Wesleys Doctrine of Christian Perfection.* London, 1943 (1984).

Starkey, Lycurgus M., Jr. *The Work of the Holy Spirit: A Study in Wesleyan Theology.* 1962.

Stoeffler, F. Ernest. "Tradition and Renewal in the Ecclesiology of John Wesley." In *Traditio Krisis—Renovatio aus theologischer Sicht.* FS W. Zeller, 298-316. Marburg, 1976.

Wainwright, Geoffrey. *On Wesley and Calvin.* Melbourne, 1987.

5. Methodist Theology Between 1800 and 1950

Abraham, William J. "The Concept of Inspiration in the Classical Wesleyan Tradition." In *A Celebration of Ministry,* ed. K. C. Kinghorn, 33-47. 1982.

———. The Wesleyan Quadrilateral. In *Wesleyan Theology Today,* ed. Th. Runyon, 119-26. 1985.

Burwash, Nathaniel, ed. *Wesley's Doctrinal Standards.* Toronto: William Briggs, 1881.

Chiles, Robert E. *Theological Transition in American Methodism.* Nashville/New York, 1965.

Clarke, Adam. *Christian Theology.* London, 1835.

Cushman, Robert E. *John Wesley's Experimental Divinity: Studies in Methodist Doctrinal Standards.* Nashville, 1989.

Dubose, Horace Mellard. *The Symbol of Methodism.* Nashville: Methodist Episcopal Church, South, 1907.

Flew, R. N. *The Idea of Perfection in Christian Theology.* 1934.

Langford, Thomas A. *Practical Divinity: Theology in the Wesleyan Tradition.* Rev. ed. 2 vols. Nashville: Abingdon, 1998–1999.

————. *Wesleyan Theology: A Source Book.* Durham, N.C., 1984.

Oden, Thomas C. *Doctrinal Standards in the Wesleyan Tradition.* Grand Rapids, Mich.: Zondervan, 1988.

Outler, Albert C., ed. "The Theological Study Commission Doctrine and Doctrinal Standards: A Report to the General Conference." April 1972.

Peters, John L. *Christian Perfection and American Methodism.* Nashville, 1956 (2nd ed., 1985).

Pope, William Burt. *A Compendium of Christian Theology.* Vol. 1-3. New York, 1875–1876 (1880 2).

Ralston, Thomas. *Elements of Divinity.* Louisville: Morton and Griswold, 1847.

Schempp, Johannes (d.J.). *Christenlehre für die Jugend der Evangelischen Gemeinschaft nach dem Katechismus von J. J. Escher unter Verwendung des Kleinen Katechismus von Dr. Martin Luther.* Stuttgart, 1938.

————. *Dogmatik.* Reutlingen, 1925.

Tillet, Wilbur F. *A Statement of the Faith of World-Wide Methodism.* Nashville: Methodist Publishing House, 1907.

Watson, Richard. *Theological Institutes.* Vol. 1, 1855; vol 2, 1855.

Wheatly, Richard. "Methodist Doctrinal Standards." *Methodist Quarterly Review* 65 (1883), 26-51.

Wheeler, Henry. *History and Exposition of the Twenty-five Articles of Religion of the Methodist Episcopal Church.* New York: Eaton and Mains, 1908.

6. Works on Contemporary United Methodist Theology

Blankenship, Paul F. "The Significance of John Wesley's Abridgment of the Thirty-nine Articles as Seen from his Deletions." *Methodist History* (April 1964), 35ff.

Campbell, Dennis M. *The Yoke of Obedience: The Meaning of Ordination in Methodism.* Nashville, 1988.

Chilcote, Thomas E. *United Methodist Doctrine.* Nashville, 1989.

Cushman, Robert E. "Doctrinal Standards and the Ecumenical Task Today." *Religion and Life* 45 (winter 1975). Reprinted in amended form in *Faith Seeking Understanding,* 317-27. Durham: Duke University, 1981.

Davies, Rupert E. *What Methodists Believe.* London, 1976 (1988 2).

"The Development of Wesleyan Theological Method," series of articles in *The Wesleyan Theological Journal* 20 (spring 1985).

Dunning, H. Ray. *Grace, Faith and Holiness: A Wesleyan Systematic Theology.* 1988.

Felton, G. C. *This Gift of Water.* Nashville: Abingdon, 1992.

Hammer, Martin. *Konsensbildung in der Evangelisch-methodistichen Kirche.* BGEmK 31. 1988.

Heitzenrater, Richard P. "At Full Liberty: Doctrinal Standards in Early American Methodism." *Quarterly Review* 5 (fall 1985).

Jones, Ivor H., and Kennth B.Wilson. *Freedom and Grace*. London, 1988.

Kemper, Thomas. *Methodistisches Erbe und Theologie der Beifreiung*. EmK heute 66. 1989.

Kirkpatrick, Dow, ed. *The Doctrine of the Church*. Nashville/New York, 1964.

Klaiber, Walter. *Der Auftrag der Evangelische-methodischen Kirche. Ziele unserer Arbeit in den neunziger Jahren*. EmK heute 70. 1991.

―――. *Biblische Perspektiven einer heutigen Lehre von der Heiligung*. ThBeitr 16 (1985), 26-39.

―――. *Dienen und sich dienen lassen-vom Gebrauch der Gnadenmittel*. EmK heute 42. 1986.

―――. Die *eine* Taufe. Taufverständnis und Taufpraxis in der Evangelisch-methodischen Kirche. EmK heute 53. 1987.

―――. *Gibt es eine methodische Exegese?* TfP 14 (1988), 1-13.

―――. *Ruf und Antwort. Biblische Grundlagen einer Theologie der Evangelisation*. Stuttgart 1990.

―――. *Zwischen Schwärmerei und Erstarrung. Vom Wirken des Heiligen Geistes in unserer Kirche*. EmK heute 21. 1976.

Langford, Thomas A., ed. *Doctrine and Theology in The United Methodist Church*. Nashville, 1991.

―――. *God Made Known*. Nashville, 1992.

―――. *Practical Divinity: Theology in the Wesleyan Tradition*. Rev. ed. 2 vols. Nashville: Abingdon, 1998–1999.

Marquardt, Manfred. Imago Christi als Leitbild der Heiligung. In W. Härle, M. Marquardt, W. Nethöfel (Hg.), *Unsere Welt—Gottes Schöpfung,* FSE. Wölfel, 235-50. 1992 (=TfP 18, 1992, 17-35).

―――. "Die Vorstellung des "ordo salutis" in ihrer Funktion für die Lebensführung der Glaubenden. In: W. Härle and Reiner Preul (Hg.), Lebenserfahrung, Marburger Jahrbuch Theologie 111 (1990), 29-53.

Marquardt, Manfred and Walter Klaiber. *Heiligung aus biblischer und evangelisch-methodistischer Sicht*. BGEmK 27. 1987.

Marquardt, Manfred Dieter Sackmann, and David Tripp. *Theologie des Gotteslobs*. BGEmK 39. 1991.

Meeks, M. Douglas, ed. *The Future of the Methodist Theological Traditions*. Nashville, 1985.

―――, ed. *What Should Methodists Teach? Wesley Tradition and Modern Diversity*. Nashville, 1990.

Messer, Donald E., ed. *Send Me? The Itineracy in Crisis*. Nashville, 1991.

Oden, Thomas C. *The Living God. Systematic Theology*. Vol. 1. San Francisco 1987; The Word of Life. Syst. Theolog. Vol. 11, 1989.

Ogden, Schubert M. "Doctrinal Standards in the United Methodist Church," *Perkins Journal* (Fall 1974): 20-25.

Outler, Albert C., ed. "The Methodist Standards of Doctrine." In *A Handbook of Selected Creeds and Confessions,* Dallas: Perkins School of Theology, 1958.

————, ed. "The Theological Study Commission on Doctrine and Doctrinal Standards: Interim Report to the General Conference," 1970.

Runyon, Theodore, ed. *Sanctification and Liberation*. Nashville, 1981.

————. *Wesleyan Theology Today: A Bicentennial Theological Consultation.* Nashville, 1985.

Schilling, S. Paul. *Methodism and Society in Theological Perspective*. New York/Nashville, 1960.

Staples, R. L. *Outward Sign and Inward Grace: The Place of Sacraments in Wesleyan Spirituality.* Kansas City, 1991.

Steckel, Karl, "Bekenntinis" in der Evangelisch-methodistischen Kirche, MSGEmK 2 (1981), Heft 2, 17-30.

Stokes, Mack B. *The Bible in the Wesleyan Heritage*. Nashville, 1979.

————. *The Holy Spirit in the Wesleyan Heritage*. Nashville, 1985.

Wainwright, Geoffrey. "The Assurance of Faith: A Methodist Approach to the Question Raised by the Roman Catholic Doctrine of Infallibility." OiC 22 (1986), 44-61.

————. *Doxology: The Praise of God in Worship, Doctrine and Life. A Systematic Theology.* London/New York, 1980.

Walls, Jerry L. *The Problem of Pluralism: Recovering United Methodist Identity.* Wilmore, Ky.: Good News, 1986.

Watson, David Lowes. *God Does Not Foreclose: The Universal Promise of Salvation.* Nashville, 1990.

Wynkoop, M. B. *A Theology of Love: The Dynamic of Wesleyanism.* 1972.

English Language Works Cited by Section

God's Revelation as an Expression of God's Love (Section 1.1ff.)

Barclay, John M. G., and John Sweet P.M., eds. *Early Christian Thought in Its Jewish Context.* New York: Cambridge University Press, 1996.

Bloesch, Donald G. "Holy Scriptures: Revelation, Inspiration, and Interpretation." *Restoration Quarterly* 38 no. 4:244 (1996).

Carpenter, David. "Revelation, History, and the Dialogue of Religions: A Study of Bhartrhar and Bonaventure." Maryknoll: Orbis Books, 1995.

Coburn, Robert C. "God, Revelation, and Religious Truth: Some Themes and Problems in the Theology of Paul Tillich." *Faith and Philosophy* 13:3-33 (Ja. 1996).

D'Costa, Gavin. "Revelation and Revelations: Discerning God in Other Religions." *Modern Theology* 10:165-83 (Ap. 1994).

Fries, Henreich. *Fundamental Theology.* Trans. Robert J. Daly. Washington, D.C.: Catholic University of America Press, 1996.

Fulljames, Peter. *God and Creation in Intercultural Perspective: Dialogue*

Between the Theologies of Barth, Dickson, Pobee, Nyamiti, and Pannenberg. Frankfurt am Main; New York: P. Lang, 1996.

Green, Garrett. *Imaging God: Theology and the Religious Imagination.* Grand Rapids: Eerdmans, 1998.

Gunton, Colin E. *A Brief Theology of Religion: The 1993 Warfield Lectures.* Edinburgh: T & T Clark, 1995.

Hart, Trevor A. "The Word, the Words and the Witness: Proclamation as Divine and Human Reality in the Theology of Karl Barth." *Tyndale Bulletin* 46:81-102 (May 1995).

Jensen, Robert W. *Systematic Theology (or Triune God).* New York: Oxford University Press, 1997-.

Julian of Norwich. "A Revelation of Divine Love." Trans. John Skinner. *Epworth Review* 24:118-19 (Ap. 1997).

Kangas, Ron. "Knowing the Triune God as Revealed in the Word of God." *Affirmation & Critique* 1:12- (Ja. 1996).

Knight, Christopher, "Psychology, Revelation, and Interfaith Dialogue." *International Journal for Psychology of Religion* 40:147-58 (Dec. 1996).

Matt, Daniel Chanan. *God and the Big Bang: Discovering Harmony Between Science and Spirituality.* Woodstock: Jewish Lights Publishing, 1996.

McCutcheon, Lillie S. *God's Magnificent Masterpiece.* Springfield: Reformation Publishing, 1996.

Mwakabana, Hance A. O., ed. "Theological Perspectives on Other Faiths: Toward a Christian Theology of Religions." LWF Documentation no. 41:1-292, 1997.

Neusner, Jacob, and Bruce D. Chilton. *Revelation: The Torah and the Bible.* Valley Forge: Trinity Press International, 1995.

O'Collins, Gerald. *Retrieving Fundamental Theology: The Three Styles of Contemporary Theology.* New York: Paulist Press, 1993.

Padgett, Alan G., ed. *Reason and the Christian Religion.* Oxford: Clarendon Press, 1994.

Placher, William C. "The Acts of God: What Do We Mean by Revelation?" *Christian Century* 113:337-42 (March 20-27 1996).

"Revelation and Truth: Unity and Plurality in Contemporary Theology." *Journal of Religion* 75:137-38 (Ja 1995).

Stackhouse, Max L. "Tradition and Revelation: Changing to Preserve the Truth." *Christian Century* 113:1061-1602 (Nov. 6 1996).

Torrance, Thomas F. "The Uniqueness of Divine Revelation and the Authority of the Scriptures: the Creed Association's Statement." *Scottish Bulletin of Evangelical Theology* 13:97-101 (autumn 1995).

The Holy Scripture as the Foundation for Theology (Section 1.2ff.)

Barton, John. *Holy Writings, Sacred Text: The Canon in Early Christianity (The Spirit and the Letter).* Louisville: Westminster/John Knox: 1998.

Brenneman, James E. *Canons in Conflict: Negotiating in True and False Prophecy.* New York: Oxford University Press, 1997.

Clements, R. E. *Old Testament Prophecy: From Oracles to Canon.* Louisville: Westminster John Knox Press, 1996.

McDonald, Lee Martin. *The Formation of the Christian Biblical Canon.* Peabody: Hendrickson Publishing, 1995.

Muller, Richard A. "Biblical Interpretation in the Era of the Reformation: The View from the Middle Ages." In *Biblical Interpretation in the Era of the Reformation,* ed. Muller et al., 3-22. 1996.

Nicholls, Bruce J., ed. "Scripture and Tradition." *Evangelical Review of Theology* 19:99-200 (Ap. 1995).

Pelikan, Jaroslav Jan, Valerie R. Hotchkiss, and David Price. "The Reformation of the Bible/The Bible of the Reformation." *Christian Century* 114:58-59 (Ja. 15 1997).

Trueman, Carl R. "Pathway to Reformation: William Tyndale and the Importance of the Scriptures." In *A Pathway into the Holy Scripture,* ed. P. Satterthwaite et al., 11-29. 1994.

Witherington, Ben. "Praeparato Evangelii: The Theological Roots of Wesley's View of Evangelism." In *Theology and Evangelism in the Wesleyan Heritage,* ed. J. Logan, 51-80. 1994.

Methodist Doctrine as a Theology for Praxis (Section 1.3ff.)

Abraham, William J. "The Revitalization of United Methodist Doctrine and the Renewal of Evangelism." In *Theology and Evangelism in the Wesleyan Heritage.* Nashville: Abingdon Press, 1994.

Beck, Brian E. "A Theology of Restructuring" *Epworth Review* 23:6-8 (May 1996).

Clapper, Gregory S. "John Wesley's 'Heart Religion' and the Righteousness of Christ." *Methodist History* 35:148-56 (Ap. 1997).

Logan, James C., ed. *Christ for the World: United Methodist Bishops Speak on Evangelism.* Nashville: Abingdon Press, 1996.

―――. *Theology and Evangelism in the Wesleyan Heritage.* Nashville: Abingdon Press, 1994.

Maddox, Randy L. "Reading Wesley as a Theologian." *Wesleyan Theological Journal* 30:7-54 (spring 1995).

Miller, Kenneth H. "The Church and Its Discipline in the Thought of John Wesley." *Evangelical Journal* 13:63-73 (fall 1995).

Reed, W. Kirk. *Reclaiming a Theological Heritage: John Wesley's Theology and Covenant Discipleship Groups in the United Methodist Church.* Northern Baptist Theological Seminary, 1996.

Wainwright, Geoffrey. "Tradition and the Spirit of Faith in a Methodist Perspective." *New Perspectives on Historical Theology,* ed. B. Nassif, 45-69. 1996.

God's Care in God's Creative Activity (Section 2.1ff.)

Anderson, Bernhard W. "The Presence of Chaos in God's Creation." *Bible Review* 12:19, 44 (fall 1996).

Bouma-Prediger, Steven. "Creation as the Home of God: The Doctrine of Creation in the Theology of Jürgen Moltmann." *Calvin Theological Journal* 32:72-90 (Ap. 1997).

"God in Creation: Towards an Ecumenical and Scientific Consensus." *Bangalore Theological Forum* 27:17-26 (Mr-Je 1995).

Kaiser, Christopher B. "The Integrity of Creation and the Social Nature of God." *Scottish Journal of Theology* 49 no. 3:261-90 (1996).

Nicholls, Bruce J. "God as Creator and Redeemer: In Response to the Ecological Crisis." *Stimulus* 1:2-9 (May 1993).

"The Vision of God for All Creation: The Old Creation Is Still with Us and Life Has Not Escaped the Shadow of Decay." *Church and Society* 84:26-32 (Sept.-Oct. 1993).

Wacome, Donald H. "Evolution, Foreknowledge, and Creation." *Christian Scholar's Review* 26 no. 3:306-21 (1997).

Welker, Michael. "Creation: Big Bang or the Work of Seven Days?" *Theology Today* 52:173-87 (July 1995).

Wilkinson, Loren. "The New Story of Creation: A Trinitarian Perspective." *ARC* 23:137-52 (1995).

Zank, Michael. "The God of Sinai, the God of Creation, and the God of Abraham: Three Recent Books in Jewish Philosophy." *Modern Judaism* 16:291-316 (Oct. 1996).

God's Care in God's Reconciling Acts (Section 2.2ff.)

Arbogast, Marianne. "How Sin Works: The Views of Ted Peters" *Witness* 78:31-53 (Mr. 1995).

Borg, Marcus J. "How Did Jesus Die for Our Sins?" *Bible Review* 11:18, 46 (Ap. 1995).

Farley, Wendy. "Beyond Sociology: Studies of Tragedy, Sin and Symbols of Evil." *Religious Studies Review* 22:124-28 (Ap. 1996).

Golubou, Alexander. "The Rays of Mortality: Original Sin and Human Nature." *Sourozh* no 64:23-32 (May 1996).

Greer, Rowan A. "Sinned We All in Adam's Fall?" The Social World of the First Christians, 382-94. 1995.

Hart, Trevor A. and Daniel Thimell eds. "Christ in Our Place: The Humanity of God in Christ for the Reconciliation of the World." *Scottish Bulletin of Evangelical Theology* 14:78-79 (spring 1996).

Hoffman, Mark A. "The Bondage of Humanity to Sin." *Lutheran Forum* 29:23-25 (Nov. 1995).

Jones, L. Gregory. "Finding the Will to Embrace the Enemy: What It Means to Follow the Crucified Christ in the Midst of Ethnic and Racial Conflict." *Christianity Today* 41:29-31 (Ap. 28 1997).

L'Engle, Madeleine. "Our Sin and God's Mercy." *Witness* 78:22-23 (Mr. 1995).

Moloney, Brian. "Thoughts on Original Sin." *Faith and Freedom* 49:34-40 (spr.-sum. 1996).

Sugden, Christopher. "Christ as Savior from Sin and Death and as Liberator from Socio-Economic and Political Oppression." *Evangelical Review of Theology* 18:128-36 (Ap. 1994).

Van Houten, Christina. "Heirs to the Covenant." *Perspectives* 11:24 (F 1996).

God's Care in God's Renewing Actions (Section 2.3ff.)

Brouwer, Wayne. "The Spirit Is Among Us: A Service of Expectation, Renewal, and Encouragement." *Reformed Worship* 35:42-43 (Mr. 1995).

Eder, Jochen, et al. "Affirming Our Eschatological Hope in Christ's Kingly Return to Reign, the Final Judgment, and the Creation in Righteousness of a New Earth and a New Heaven." *Evangelical Review of Theology* 21:31-33 (Ja. 1997).

Harrop, Kent. "Renewing the Mainline Church." *American Baptist Quarterly* 15:280-347 (Dec. 1996).

Hinton, Jenane. "Walking in the Same Direction: A New Way of Being Church." *Rick* no 67:1-106 (1995).

Kimbrough, ST, Jr., ed. *Methodism in Russia and the Baltic States: History and Renewal.* Nashville: Abingdon Press, 1995.

Linn, Gerhard, ed. *Hear What the Spirit Says to the Churches: Towards Missionary Congregations in Europe.* Geneva: WCC Pub., 1994.

Schonborn, Christoph. "The Hope of Heaven, the Hope of Earth." Trans. Brain McNeil. *First Things* 52:32-38 (Ap. 1995).

Tiwari, Ravi. "Mission, Unity, and Renewal." *Indian Journal of Theology* 35:67-74 (Mr. 1994).

Wilson, Mark W., ed. *Spirit and Renewal: Essays in Honor of J. Rodman Williams.* Sheffield: Sheffield Academic Press, 1994.

Liberation for Hearing and Conversion (Section 3.1ff.)

Beeke, Joel R. "Assurance of Faith: Calvin, English Puritanism, and the Dutch Second Reformation." *Scottish Bulletin of Evangelical Theology* 13:164-65 (autumn 1995).

Ferguson, Sinclair B. "Repentance, Recovery and Confession." *Here We Stand!* 131-52, 202-3 (1996).

Harakas, Stanley S. "Provoked to Repentance." *Christian Century* 114:217 (Feb. 26 1997).

Johnson, Susan B. W. "Remorse and Hope" *Christian Century* 114:95 (Ja. 29 1997).

Kolb, Robert. "God's Gift of Martyrdom: The Early Reformation Understanding of Dying for the Faith." *Church History* 64:339-411 (spr. 1995).

Meilaender, Gilbert. "Veritatis Splendor: Reopening Some Questions of the Reformation." *Journal of Religious Ethics* 23:225-38 (Fall 1995).

Mogabgab, John S., ed. "Put a New and Right Spirit Within Me." *Weavings* 10:2-40 (Mr.-Ap. 1995).

Moore, Mary Elizabeth Mullino. "Poverty, Human Depravity, and Prevenient Grace." *Quarterly Review* 16:343-60 (winter 1996).

Palau, Luis. "Whatever Happened to Evangelism? Palau Wants to Rekindle Our Passion for the Lost." *Christianity Today* 40:38-39 (Ap. 8 1996).

Whaling, Frank. "John Wesley's Premonitions of Inter-faith Discourse." *Pure, Universal Love* (1995), 15-31.

The Renewal to Life in God (Section 3.2ff.)

Christensen, Michael J. "Theosis and Sanctification: John Wesley's Reformulation of a Patristic Doctrine." *Wesleyan Theological Journal* 31:71-94 (fall 1996).

Collins, Kenneth J. "John Wesley's Doctrine of the New Birth." *Wesleyan Theological Journal* 32:53-68 (spr. 1997).

Cranfield, Charles E. B. "Paul's Teaching on Sanctification." *Reformed Review* 48:217-29 (spr. 1995).

Das, A. Andrew. "Oneness in Christ: The Nexus Individulsus Between Justification and Sanctification in Paul's Letter to the Galatians." *Concordia Journal* 21:173-86 (Apr. 1995).

Dunn, James D. G. "A Protestant Response." *Pentecostal Movements as an Ecumenical Challenge,* 109-15. 1996.

Hewitt, Glenn A. "Nevin on Regeneration." *Reformed Confessionalism in Nineteenth-Century America,* 153-67. 1995.

Kisker, Scott. "Justified but Unregenerate? The Relationship of Assurance to Justification and Regeneration in the Thought of John Wesley." *Wesleyan Theological Journal* 28:44-58 (spr.-fall 1993).

Raabe, Paul R. "The Law and Christian Sanctification: A Look at Romans." *Concordia Journal* 22:178-85 (Ap. 1996).

Runyon, Theodore. "The New Creation: The Wesleyan Distinctive." *Wesleyan Theological Journal* 31:5-19 (fall 1996).

Thompson, William M. "The Saints' Justification and Sanctification: An Ecumenical Thought Experiment." *Pro Ecclesia* 4:16-36 (winter 1995).

Truesdale, Albert. "Reification of the Experience of Entire Sanctification in the American Holiness Movement." *Wesleyan Theological Journal* 31:95-119 (fall 1996).

God's Renewing Presence in the World (Section 4.1ff.)

Gillingham, Susan. "The Ethics of Love: Doing the Right Thing in the Christian Tradition." *Expository Times* 106:231-34 (May 1995).

Grenz, Stanley J. "The Holy Spirit: Divine Love Guiding Us Home." *Ex Auditu* 12:1-13 (1996).

Gunton, Colin E., ed. *God and Freedom: Essays in Historical and Systematic Theology.* Edinburg: T. & T. Clark, 1995.

Kapp, Robert. "God Is Love, but He Hates . . ." *Preaching* 12:44-46 (May-June 1997).

Kownack, Mary Lou. "Torrent of Love: May the Gifts Flow On." *Other Side* 29:28-29 (Sept.-Oct. 1993).

Macquiban, Tim Ed. *Pure, Universal Love: Reflections on the Wesley's and Interfaith Dialogue.* Oxford: Applied Theology Press, 1995.

Pinnock, Clark H. "Flame of Love: A Theology of the Holy Spirit." *Christianity Today* 40:52-54 (Nov. 11 1996).

The Community as the Creation of the Love of God (Section 4.2ff.)

Byun, Paul S. *Church Renewal Through Discipleship Group.* McCormick Theological Seminary, 1994.

Chapman, James Day. *Building a Sense of Belonging in the Community of Faith: A Telephone Ministry.* Hartford Seminary, 1996.

Chu, Dong H. *Congregational Love of the Local Churches for Newcomers.* McCormick Theological Seminary, 1993.

Hunter, Richard A. *Making Disciples in a Rapidly Growing Church.* McCormick Theological Seminary, 1994.

Justice, John R. *A Program Using Lay Church Members in a One-on-One Discipleship Experience with New Christians for the Grant Avenue Baptist Church.* Midwestern Baptist Theological Seminary, 1996.

Kim, Bo J. *The Living Well United Methodist Church: Towards a Cross-Cultural Model in Ministry.* Wesley Theological Seminary, 1994.

Mogabgab, John S., ed. "Woven Together in Love" *Weavings* 8:2-43 (May-June 1993).

Scates, Ronald W. "Why They Come, Why They Stay: What Draws Visitors and Keeps Them Coming Back?" *Reformed Worship* 39:11-13 (Mr. 1996).

The Church as the Mission of God (Section 4.3ff.)

Bouman, Stephen P. "Evangelism, Church Growth, and the Swinging Door." *Lutheran Forum* 29:50-52 (Fall 1995).

Chung, Rosa, "Hecheng New Village: Bearing Witness to Christ Through Love," and Peter Barry, tr. *Tripod* 74:47-49 (Mr.-Ap. 1993).

Hunsberger, George R., and Craig Van Gelder, eds. "The Church Between Gospel and Culture: The Emerging Mission in North America." Grand Rapids: Eerdmans, 1996.

Logan, James C., ed. *Christ for the World: United Methodist Bishops Speak on Evangelism.* Nashville: Abingdon Press, 1996.

Mhogolo, G. Mdimi. "The Bible Is Our Tool for Evangelism and Church Planting: The Diocese of Central Tangoyika." The Anglican Communion and Scripture, 1996.

Okorocha, Cyril C. "Scripture, Mission and Evangelism." The Anglican Communion and Scripture, 1996.

Smithies, Ruth. "Evangelism and Deep Mission." *Stimulus* 4:12-17 (fall 1996).

Wind, LaDonna. "Small Church Evangelism and Education." *Anglican Theological Review* 78:628-34 (fall 1996).

The Church in the World (Section 4.4ff.)

Bodie, Darryl A. *Equipping the Spiritual Warfare.* Trinity Evangelical Theological Seminary, 1994.

Colson, William, and Rose A Royce., eds. "The Teaching Ministry of the Church." *Southwestern Journal of Theology* 38:4-39 (spr 1996).

Dayton, Donald W. "From 'Christian Perfection' to the 'Baptism of the Holy Ghost.' " *In Perspectives on American Methodism.* Nashville: Kingswood Books, 1993.

Green, Clifford J., ed. *Churches, Cities, and Human Community: Urban Ministry in the United States, 1945–1985.* Grand Rapids: Eerdmans, 1996.

Grenz, Stanley J. "Anticipating God's New Community: Theological Foundations for Women in Ministry." *Journal of the Evangelical Theological Society* 38:595-611 (Dec. 1995).

Holcamb, Wayne C. "A Full Ministry with People with Mental Illness." *Church and Society* 85:76-781 (May-Jume 1995).

Kearns, Curtis A. Jr. "The City a Place for People: Cities Are for People, and Here the Church Finds Its Rationale for Ministry in the Cities." *Church and Society* 86:20-23 (Nov-Dec 1995).

Moessner, Jeanne Stevenson, ed. *Through the Eyes of Women: Insights for Pastoral Care.* Fortress Press, 1996.

Robertson, Paul E., ed. "Ministering to the Aging." *Theological Education* no. 53:31-89 (spring 1996).

Stuart, Charles H. Ed. "Mission in Changing Times: Asia and Europe." *American Baptist Quarterly* 15:90-186 (June 1996).

Vandiver, Michael L. *Urban Ministry: Enabling the Church to Hear God's Call.* Wesley Theological Seminary, 1994.

Wood, Laurence W. "The Attainment of Christian Perfection as a Wesleyan/Holiness Re-Interpretation of the Anglican Rite of Confirmation." *Asbury Theological Journal* 50-51: 173-95 (fall-spr. 1995–1996).

Index of Biblical Citations

Subject Index

Index of Names

Bibliographic data on the works of cited authors are found at the initial citation of that work. If additional works of an author are cited the dates of these works are found at the location of the corresponding key term. The names of John and Charles Wesley do not appear in this register since they are cited throughout the work.